Programming Massively Parallel Processors

A Hands-on Approach

Programming Massively Parallel Processors
A Hands-on Approach

Fourth Edition

Wen-mei W. Hwu

University of Illinois at Urbana-Champaign and NVIDIA, Champaign, IL, United States

David B. Kirk

Formerly NVIDIA, United States

Izzat El Hajj

American University of Beirut, Beirut, Lebanon

ISBN: 978-0-323-91231-0

For Information on all Morgan Kaufmann publications
visit our website at https://www.elsevier.com/books-and-journals

Publisher: Katey Birtcher
Acquisitions Editor: Stephen R. Merken
Editorial Project Manager: Naomi Robertson
Production Project Manager: Kiruthika Govindaraju
Cover Designer: Bridget Hoette

Printed in China by 1010 Printing International Ltd
Last digit is the print number: 9 8 7 6 5 4

To Sabrina, Amanda, Bryan, and Carissa
To Caroline, Rose, and Leo
To Mona, Amal, and Ali

for enduring our absence while working on the course
and the book—once again!

Contents

Foreword xv

Preface xvii

Acknowledgments xxvii

CHAPTER 1   Introduction 1
    1.1   Heterogeneous parallel computing 3
    1.2   Why more speed or parallelism? 7
    1.3   Speeding up real applications 9
    1.4   Challenges in parallel programming 11
    1.5   Related parallel programming interfaces 13
    1.6   Overarching goals 14
    1.7   Organization of the book 15
           References 19

Part I Fundamental Concepts

CHAPTER 2   Heterogeneous data parallel computing 23
    With special contribution from David Luebke
    2.1   Data parallelism 23
    2.2   CUDA C program structure 27
    2.3   A vector addition kernel 28
    2.4   Device global memory and data transfer 31
    2.5   Kernel functions and threading 35
    2.6   Calling kernel functions 40
    2.7   Compilation 42
    2.8   Summary 43
           Exercises 44
           References 46

CHAPTER 3   Multidimensional grids and data 47
    3.1   Multidimensional grid organization 47
    3.2   Mapping threads to multidimensional data 51
    3.3   Image blur: a more complex kernel 58
    3.4   Matrix multiplication 62
    3.5   Summary 66
           Exercises 67

CHAPTER 4   Compute architecture and scheduling **69**
    4.1 Architecture of a modern GPU 70
    4.2 Block scheduling 70
    4.3 Synchronization and transparent scalability 71
    4.4 Warps and SIMD hardware 74
    4.5 Control divergence 79
    4.6 Warp scheduling and latency tolerance 83
    4.7 Resource partitioning and occupancy 85
    4.8 Querying device properties 87
    4.9 Summary 90
          Exercises 90
          References 92

CHAPTER 5   Memory architecture and data locality **93**
    5.1 Importance of memory access efficiency 94
    5.2 CUDA memory types 96
    5.3 Tiling for reduced memory traffic 103
    5.4 A tiled matrix multiplication kernel 107
    5.5 Boundary checks 112
    5.6 Impact of memory usage on occupancy 115
    5.7 Summary 118
          Exercises 119

CHAPTER 6   Performance considerations **123**
    6.1 Memory coalescing 124
    6.2 Hiding memory latency 133
    6.3 Thread coarsening 138
    6.4 A checklist of optimizations 141
    6.5 Knowing your computation's bottleneck 145
    6.6 Summary 146
          Exercises 146
          References 147

Part II Parallel Patterns

CHAPTER 7   Convolution
          An introduction to constant memory and caching 151
    7.1 Background 152
    7.2 Parallel convolution: a basic algorithm 156
    7.3 Constant memory and caching 159

7.4	Tiled convolution with halo cells	163
7.5	Tiled convolution using caches for halo cells	168
7.6	Summary	170
	Exercises	171

CHAPTER 8   Stencil 173

8.1	Background	174
8.2	Parallel stencil: a basic algorithm	178
8.3	Shared memory tiling for stencil sweep	179
8.4	Thread coarsening	183
8.5	Register tiling	186
8.6	Summary	188
	Exercises	188

CHAPTER 9   Parallel histogram 191

9.1	Background	192
9.2	Atomic operations and a basic histogram kernel	194
9.3	Latency and throughput of atomic operations	198
9.4	Privatization	200
9.5	Coarsening	203
9.6	Aggregation	206
9.7	Summary	208
	Exercises	209
	References	210

CHAPTER 10 Reduction

	And minimizing divergence	211
10.1	Background	211
10.2	Reduction trees	213
10.3	A simple reduction kernel	217
10.4	Minimizing control divergence	219
10.5	Minimizing memory divergence	223
10.6	Minimizing global memory accesses	225
10.7	Hierarchical reduction for arbitrary input length	226
10.8	Thread coarsening for reduced overhead	228
10.9	Summary	231
	Exercises	232

CHAPTER 11 Prefix sum (scan)
An introduction to work efficiency in
parallel algorithms 235
With special contributions from Li-Wen Chang,
Juan Gómez-Luna and John Owens
11.1 Background..236
11.2 Parallel scan with the Kogge-Stone algorithm.........238
11.3 Speed and work efficiency consideration.............244
11.4 Parallel scan with the Brent-Kung algorithm.........246
11.5 Coarsening for even more work efficiency............251
11.6 Segmented parallel scan for arbitrary-length inputs.....253
11.7 Single-pass scan for memory access efficiency.......256
11.8 Summary..259
Exercises..260
References..261

CHAPTER 12 Merge
An introduction to dynamic input data identification..........263
With special contributions from Li-Wen Chang and
Jie Lv
12.1 Background..263
12.2 A sequential merge algorithm.............................265
12.3 A parallelization approach 266
12.4 Co-rank function implementation 268
12.5 A basic parallel merge kernel 273
12.6 A tiled merge kernel to improve coalescing 275
12.7 A circular buffer merge kernel 282
12.8 Thread coarsening for merge 288
12.9 Summary..288
Exercises..289
References..289

Part III Advanced Patterns and Applications
CHAPTER 13 Sorting **293**
With special contributions from Michael Garland
13.1 Background..294
13.2 Radix sort 295

13.3 Parallel radix sort 296

13.4 Optimizing for memory coalescing 300

13.5 Choice of radix value..302

13.6 Thread coarsening to improve coalescing 305

13.7 Parallel merge sort 306

13.8 Other parallel sort methods....................................308

13.9 Summary...309

Exercises 310

References..310

CHAPTER 14 Sparse matrix computation.....................................**311**

14.1 Background...312

14.2 A simple SpMV kernel with the COO format 314

14.3 Grouping row nonzeros with the CSR format............317

14.4 Improving memory coalescing with the ELL format.............320

14.5 Regulating padding with the hybrid ELL-COO format 324

14.6 Reducing control divergence with the JDS format 325

14.7 Summary...328

Exercises 329

References..329

CHAPTER 15 Graph traversal...**331**

*With special contributions from John Owens and
Juan Gómez-Luna*

15.1 Background...332

15.2 Breadth-first search 335

15.3 Vertex-centric parallelization of breadth-first search.............338

15.4 Edge-centric parallelization of breadth-first search 343

15.5 Improving efficiency with frontiers.........................345

15.6 Reducing contention with privatization....................348

15.7 Other optimizations 350

15.8 Summary...352

Exercises 353

References..354

CHAPTER 16 Deep learning...**355**

*With special contributions from Carl Pearson and
Boris Ginsburg*

16.1 Background...356

16.2 Convolutional neural networks 366

16.3 Convolutional layer: a CUDA inference kernel 376
16.4 Formulating a convolutional layer as GEMM 379
16.5 CUDNN library 385
16.6 Summary..387
     Exercises 388
     References.. 388

**CHAPTER 17 Iterative magnetic resonance imaging
reconstruction** **391**
17.1 Background..391
17.2 Iterative reconstruction...394
17.3 Computing $F^H D$...396
17.4 Summary..412
     Exercises 413
     References.. 414

CHAPTER 18 Electrostatic potential map **415**
With special contributions from John Stone
18.1 Background..415
18.2 Scatter versus gather in kernel design 417
18.3 Thread coarsening 422
18.4 Memory coalescing 424
18.5 Cutoff binning for data size scalability 425
18.6 Summary..430
     Exercises 431
     References.. 431

**CHAPTER 19 Parallel programming and computational
thinking** **433**
19.1 Goals of parallel computing..433
19.2 Algorithm selection..436
19.3 Problem decomposition..440
19.4 Computational thinking...444
19.5 Summary..446
     References.. 446

Part IV Advanced Practices

CHAPTER 20 Programming a heterogeneous computing cluster

An introduction to CUDA streams 449

*With special contributions from Isaac Gelado and
Javier Cabezas*

20.1 Background..449
20.2 A running example..450
20.3 Message passing interface basics....................................452
20.4 Message passing interface point-to-point communication.......455
20.5 Overlapping computation and communication.....................462
20.6 Message passing interface collective communication.............470
20.7 CUDA aware message passing interface.............................471
20.8 Summary...472
Exercises 472
References...473

CHAPTER 21 CUDA dynamic parallelism **475**

With special contributions from Juan Gómez-Luna

21.1 Background..476
21.2 Dynamic parallelism overview 478
21.3 An example: Bezier curves 481
21.4 A recursive example: quadtrees......................................484
21.5 Important considerations 490
21.6 Summary...492
Exercises 493
A21.1 Support code for quadtree example 495
References...497

CHAPTER 22 Advanced practices and future evolution **499**

*With special contributions from Isaac Gelado and
Mark Harris*

22.1 Model of host/device interaction 500
22.2 Kernel execution control..505
22.3 Memory bandwidth and compute throughput 508
22.4 Programming environment..510
22.5 Future outlook 513
References...513

CHAPTER 23 Conclusion and outlook **515**

    23.1 Goals revisited 515

    23.2 Future outlook 516

Appendix A: Numerical considerations 519

Index 537

Foreword

Written by two exceptional computer scientists and pioneers of GPU computing, Wen-mei and David's *Programming Massively Parallel Processors*, Fourth Edition, by Wen-mei W. Hwu, David B. Kirk, and Izzat El Hajj continues to make an invaluable contribution to the creation of a new computing model.

GPU computing has become an essential instrument of modern science. This book will teach you how to use this instrument and give you a superpower tool to solve the most challenging problems. GPU computing will become a time machine that lets you see the future, a spaceship that takes you to new worlds that are now within reach.

Computing performance is needed to solve many of the world's most impactful problems. From the beginning of the history of computers, architects sought parallel computing techniques to boost performance. A hundredfold increase is equivalent to a decade of CPU advancements that relied on sequential processing. Despite the great benefits of parallel computing, creating a new computing model with a virtuous cycle of users, developers, vendors, and distributors has been a daunting chicken-and-egg problem.

After nearly three decades, NVIDIA GPU computing is pervasive, and millions of developers have learned parallel programming, many from earlier editions of this book.

GPU computing is affecting every field of science and industry, even computer science itself. The processing speed of GPUs has enabled deep learning models to learn from data and to perform intelligent tasks, starting a wave of invention from autonomous vehicles and robotics to synthetic biology. The era of AI is underway.

AI is even learning physics and opening the possibility of simulating the Earth's climate a millionfold faster than has ever been possible. NVIDIA is building a GPU supercomputer called Earth-2, a digital twin of the Earth, and partnering with the world's scientific community to predict the impact of today's actions on our climate decades from now.

A life science researcher once said to me, "Because of your GPU, I can do my life's work in my lifetime." So whether you are advancing AI or doing groundbreaking science, I hope that GPU computing will help you do your life's work.

Jensen Huang
NVIDIA, Santa Clara, CA, United States

Preface

We are proud to introduce to you the fourth edition of *Programming Massively Parallel Processors: A Hands-on Approach.*

Mass market computing systems that combine multicore CPUs and many-thread GPUs have brought terascale computing to laptops and exascale computing to clusters. Armed with such computing power, we are at the dawn of the widespread use of computational experiments in the science, engineering, medical, and business disciplines. We are also witnessing the wide adoption of GPU computing in key industry vertical markets, such as finance, e-commerce, oil and gas, and manufacturing. Breakthroughs in these disciplines will be achieved by using computational experiments that are of unprecedented levels of scale, accuracy, safety, controllability, and observability. This book provides a critical ingredient for this vision: teaching parallel programming to millions of graduate and undergraduate students so that computational thinking and parallel programming skills will become as pervasive as calculus skills.

The primary target audience of this book consists of graduate and undergraduate students in all science and engineering disciplines in which computational thinking and parallel programming skills are needed to achieve breakthroughs. The book has also been used successfully by industry professional developers who need to refresh their parallel computing skills and keep up to date with ever-increasing speed of technology evolution. These professional developers work in fields such as machine learning, network security, autonomous vehicles, computational financing, data analytics, cognitive computing, mechanical engineering, civil engineering, electrical engineering, bioengineering, physics, chemistry, astronomy, and geography, and they use computation to advance their fields. Thus these developers are both experts in their domains and programmers. The book takes the approach of teaching parallel programming by building up an intuitive understanding of the techniques. We assume that the reader has at least some basic C programming experience. We use CUDA C, a parallel programming environment that is supported on NVIDIA GPUs. There are more than 1 billion of these processors in the hands of consumers and professionals, and more than 400,000 programmers are actively using CUDA. The applications that you will develop as part of your learning experience will be runnable by a very large user community.

Since the third edition came out in 2016, we have received numerous comments from our readers and instructors. Many of them told us about the existing features they value. Others gave us ideas about how we should expand the book's contents to make it even more valuable. Furthermore, the hardware and software for heterogeneous parallel computing have advanced tremendously since 2016. In the hardware arena, three more generations of GPU computing architectures, namely, Volta, Turing, and Ampere, have been introduced since the third edition.

In the software domain, CUDA 9 through CUDA 11 have allowed programmers to access new hardware and system features. New algorithms have also been developed. Accordingly, we added four new chapters and rewrote a substantial number of the existing chapters.

The four newly added chapters include one new foundational chapter, namely, Chapter 4 (Compute Architecture and Scheduling), and three new parallel patterns and applications chapters: Chapter 8 (Stencil), Chapter 10 (Reduction and Minimizing Divergence), and Chapter 13 (Sorting). Our motivation for adding these chapters is as follows:

- Chapter 4 (Compute Architecture and Scheduling): In the previous edition the discussions on architecture and scheduling considerations were scattered across multiple chapters. In this edition, Chapter 4 consolidates these discussions into one focused chapter that serves as a centralized reference for readers who are particularly interested in this topic.
- Chapter 8 (Stencil): In the previous edition the stencil pattern was briefly mentioned in the convolution chapter in light of the similarities between the two patterns. In this edition, Chapter 8 provides a more thorough treatment of the stencil pattern, emphasizing the mathematical background behind the computation and aspects that make it different from convolution, thereby enabling additional optimizations. The chapter also provides an example of handling three-dimensional grids and data.
- Chapter 10 (Reduction and Minimizing Divergence): In the previous edition the reduction pattern was briefly presented in the performance considerations chapter. In this edition, Chapter 10 provides a more complete presentation of the reduction pattern with an incremental approach to applying the optimizations and a more thorough analysis of the associated performance tradeoffs.
- Chapter 13 (Sorting): In the previous edition, merge sort was briefly alluded to in the chapter on the merge pattern. In this edition, Chapter 13 presents radix sort as a noncomparison sort algorithm that is highly amenable to GPU parallelization and follows an incremental approach to optimizing it and analyzing the performance tradeoffs. Merge sort is also discussed in this chapter.

In addition to the newly added chapters, all chapters have been revised, and some chapters have been substantially rewritten. These chapters include the following:

- Chapter 6 (Performance Considerations): Some architecture considerations that were previously in this chapter were moved to the new Chapter 4, and the reduction example was moved to the new Chapter 10. In their place, this chapter was rewritten to provide a more thorough handling of thread granularity considerations and, more notably, to provide a checklist of common performance optimization strategies and the performance bottlenecks that each strategy tackles. This checklist is referred to throughout the rest of the textbook as we optimize the code for implementing various parallel patterns and applications. The goal is to reinforce a systematic and incremental methodology for optimizing the performance of parallel programs.

- Chapter 7 (Convolution): In the previous edition the chapter on the convolution pattern used a one-dimensional convolution as a running example, with a brief handling of two-dimensional convolutions toward the end. In this edition this chapter was rewritten to focus more on two-dimensional convolution from the start. This change allows us to address the complexity and intricacies of higher-dimensional tiling and equip the readers with a better background for learning convolutional neural networks in Chapter 16.

- Chapter 9 (Parallel Histogram): In the previous edition the chapter on the histogram pattern applied the thread coarsening optimization from the start and combined the privatization optimization with the use of shared memory. In this edition this chapter was rewritten to follow a more incremental approach to performance optimization. The initial implementation that is now presented does not apply thread coarsening. Privatization and the use of shared memory for the private bins are distinguished as two separate optimizations, the former aimed at reducing contention of atomics and the latter aimed at reducing access latency. Thread coarsening is applied after privatization, since one major benefit of coarsening is to reduce the number of private copies committed to the public copy. The new organization of the chapter is more consistent with the systematic and incremental approach to performance optimization that is followed throughout the book. We also moved the chapter to precede the chapters on the reduction and scan patterns in order to introduce atomic operations sooner, since they are used in multiblock reduction and single-pass scan kernels.

- Chapter 14 (Sparse Matrix Computation): In this edition this chapter was rewritten to follow a more systematic approach for analyzing the tradeoffs between different sparse matrix storage formats. The beginning of the chapter introduces a list of considerations that go into the design of different sparse matrix storage formats. This list of design considerations is then used throughout the chapter to systematically analyze the tradeoffs between the different formats.

- Chapter 15 (Graph Traversal): In the previous edition the chapter on graph traversal focused on a particular BFS parallelization strategy. In this edition this chapter was significantly expanded to cover a more comprehensive set of alternative parallelization strategies and to analyze the tradeoffs between them. These strategies include vertex-centric push-based, vertex-centric pull-based, edge-centric, and linear algebraic implementations in addition to the original implementation, which was the vertex-centric push-based frontier-based implementation. The classification of these alternatives is not unique to BFS but applies to parallelizing graph algorithms in general.

- Chapter 16 (Deep Learning): In this edition this chapter was rewritten to provide a comprehensive yet intuitive theoretical background for understanding modern neural networks. The background makes it easier for the reader to fully understand the computational components of neural networks, such as fully connected layers, activation, and convolutional layers. It also removes some of the common barriers to understanding the kernel functions for training a convolutional neural network.
- Chapter 19 (Parallel Programming and Computational Thinking): In the previous edition this chapter discussed algorithm selection and problem decomposition while drawing examples from the chapters on iterative MRI reconstruction and electrostatic potential map. In this edition the chapter was revised to draw examples from many more chapters, serving as a concluding chapter for Parts I and II. The discussion of problem decomposition was particularly expanded to introduce the generalizations of output-centric decomposition and input-centric decomposition and to discuss the tradeoffs between them, using many examples.
- Chapter 21 (CUDA Dynamic Parallelism): In the previous edition this chapter went into many programming details relating to the semantics of different programming constructs and API calls in the context of dynamic parallelism. In this edition the focus of the chapter has shifted more toward the application examples, with the other programming details discussed more briefly while referring interested readers to the CUDA programming guide.

While making all these improvements, we tried to preserve the features that seem to contribute most to the book's popularity. First, we keep our explanations as intuitive as possible. While it is tempting to formalize some of the concepts, especially when we cover the basic parallel algorithms, we have striven to keep all our explanations intuitive and practical. Second, we keep the book as concise as possible. Although it is tempting to keep adding new material, we wanted to minimize the number of pages a reader needs to go through to learn all the key concepts. We accomplished this by moving the previous chapter on numerical considerations to the appendix. While numerical considerations are an extremely important aspect of parallel computing, we found that a substantial amount of the content in the chapter was already familiar to many of our readers who come from a computer science or computational science background. For this reason we preferred to dedicate more space to covering additional parallel patterns.

In addition to adding new chapters and substantially rewriting others since the previous edition, we have also organized the book into four major parts. This organization is illustrated in Fig. P.1. The first part introduces the fundamental concepts behind parallel programming, the GPU architecture, and performance analysis and optimization. The second part applies these concepts by covering six common computation patterns and showing how they can be parallelized and optimized. Each parallel pattern also introduces a new programming feature or technique. The third part introduces additional advanced patterns and applications

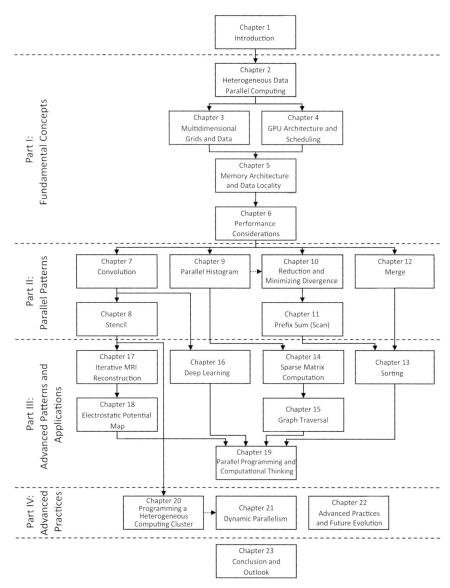

FIGURE P.1

Organization of the book.

and continues to apply the optimizations that are practiced in the second part. However, it puts more emphasis on exploring alternative forms of problem decomposition to parallelize a computation and analyzes the tradeoffs between different decompositions and their associated data structures. Finally, the fourth part exposes the reader to advanced practices and programming features.

How to use the book

We would like to offer some of our experience in teaching courses with this book. Since 2006 we have taught multiple types of courses: in one-semester format and in one-week intensive format. The original ECE498AL course has become a permanent course known as ECE408 or CS483 at the University of Illinois at Urbana-Champaign. We started to write up some of the early chapters of this book when we offered ECE498AL the second time. The first four chapters were also tested in an MIT class taught by Nicolas Pinto in the spring of 2009. Since then, we have used the book for numerous offerings of ECE408 as well as the Coursera Heterogeneous Parallel Programming course and the VSCSE and PUMPS summer schools.

A two-phased approach

Most of the chapters in the book are designed to be covered in approximately a single 75-minute lecture each. The chapters that may need two 75-minute lectures to be fully covered are Chapter 11 (Prefix Sum (Scan)), Chapter 14 (Sparse Matrix Computation), and Chapter 15 (Graph Traversal). In ECE408 the lectures, programming assignments, and final project are paced with each other and are organized into two phases.

In the first phase, which consists of Parts I and II of this book, students learn about fundamentals and basic patterns, and they practice the skills that they learn via guided programming assignments. This phase consists of 12 chapters and typically takes around seven weeks. Each week, students work on a programming assignment corresponding to that week's lectures. For example, in the first week, a lecture based on Chapter 2 is dedicated to teaching the basic CUDA memory/ threading model, the CUDA extensions to the C language, and the basic programming tools. After that lecture, students can write a simple vector addition code in a couple of hours.

The following 2 weeks include a series of four lectures based on Chapters 3 through 6 that give students the conceptual understanding of the CUDA memory model, the CUDA thread execution model, GPU hardware performance features, and modern computer system architecture. During these two weeks, students work on different implementations of matrix-matrix multiplication in which they see how the performance of their implementations increases dramatically throughout this period. In the remaining four weeks, the lectures cover common data-parallel programming patterns that are needed to develop a high-performance parallel application based on Chapters 7 through 12. Throughout these weeks, students complete assignments on convolution, histogram, reduction, and prefix sum. By the end of the first phase, students should be quite comfortable with parallel programming and should be ready to implement more advanced code with less handholding.

In the second phase, which consists of Parts III and IV, students learn about advanced patterns and applications while they work on a final project that involves accelerating an advanced pattern or application. They also learn about advanced practices that they may find useful when finalizing their projects. Although we do not usually assign weekly programming assignments during this phase, the project typically has a weekly milestone to help the students pace themselves. Depending on the duration and format of the course, instructors may not be able to cover all the chapters in this phase and may need to skip some. Instructors might also choose to replace some lectures with guest lectures, paper discussion sessions, or lectures that support the final project. For this reason, Fig. P.1 uses arrows to indicate the dependences between chapters to assist instructors in selecting what chapters they can skip or reorder to customize the course for their particular context.

Tying it all together: the final project

While the lectures, labs, and chapters of this book help to lay the intellectual foundation for the students, what brings the learning experience together is the final project. The final project is so important to the full-semester course that it is prominently positioned in the course and commands nearly two months' worth of focus. It incorporates five innovative aspects: mentoring, workshop, clinic, final report, and symposium. While much of the information about the final project is available in the Illinois-NVIDIA GPU Teaching Kit, we would like to offer the reasoning behind the design of these aspects.

Students are encouraged to base their final projects on problems that represent current challenges in the research community. To seed the process, the instructors should recruit several computational science research groups to propose problems and serve as mentors. The mentors are asked to contribute a one- to two-page project specification sheet that briefly describes the significance of the application, what the mentor would like to accomplish with the student teams on the application, the technical skills (particular types of math, physics, and chemistry courses) that are required to understand and work on the application, and a list of web and traditional resources on which students can draw for technical background, general information, and building blocks, along with specific URLs or FTP paths to particular implementations and coding examples. These project specification sheets also provide students with learning experiences in defining their own research projects later in their careers. Several examples are available in the Illinois-NVIDIA GPU Teaching Kit.

The design document

Once the students have decided on a project and formed a team, they are required to submit a design document for the project. This helps them to think through the project steps before they jump into it. The ability to do such planning will be important to their later career success. The design document should discuss the background and motivation for the project, the application-level objectives and potential impact, the main features of the end application, an overview of their design, an implementation plan, their performance goals, a verification plan and acceptance test, and a project schedule.

The project report and symposium

Students are required to submit a project report on their team's key findings. We also recommend a whole-day class symposium. During the symposium, students use presentation slots proportional to the size of the teams. During the presentation the students highlight the best parts of their project report for the benefit of the whole class. The presentation accounts for a significant part of the students' grades. Each student must answer questions that are directed to the student individually, so different grades can be assigned to individuals in the same team. The symposium is an opportunity for students to learn to produce a concise presentation that motivates their peers to read a full paper.

Class competition

In 2016 the enrollment level of ECE408 far exceeded the level that could be accommodated by the final project process. As a result, we moved from the final project to a class competition. At the midpoint of the semester we announce a competition challenge problem. We use one lecture to explain the competition challenge problem and the rules that will be used for ranking the teams. All student submissions are auto-graded and ranked. The final ranking of each team is determined by the execution time, correctness, and clarity of their parallel code. The students do a demo of their solution at the end of the semester and submit a final report. This compromise preserves some of the benefits of final projects when the class size makes final projects infeasible.

Course resources

The Illinois-NVIDIA GPU Teaching Kit is a publicly available resource that contains lecture slides and recordings, lab assignments, final project guidelines, and sample project specifications for instructors who use this book for their classes. In addition, we are in the process of making the courses of the Illinois undergraduate-level and graduate-level offerings based on this book publicly available. While this book provides the intellectual contents for these classes, the additional material will be crucial in achieving the overall education goals.

Finally, we encourage you to submit your feedback. We would like to hear from you if you have any ideas for improving this book. We would like to know how we can improve the supplementary online material. Of course, we also like to know what you liked about the book. We look forward to hearing from you.

Wen-mei W. Hwu
David B. Kirk
Izzat El Hajj

Acknowledgments

There are so many people who have made special contributions to this fourth edition. We would like first to thank the contributing chapter coauthors. Their names are listed in the chapters to which they made special contributions. Their expertise made a tremendous difference in the technical contents of this new edition. Without the expertise and contribution of these individuals, we would not have been able to cover the topics with the level of insight that we wanted to provide to our readers.

We would like to especially acknowledge Ian Buck, the father of CUDA, and John Nickolls, the lead architect of Tesla GPU Computing Architecture. Their teams built excellent infrastructure for this course. Many engineers and researchers at NVIDIA have also contributed to the rapid advancement of CUDA, which supports the efficient implementation of advanced parallel patterns. John passed away while we were working on the second edition. We miss him dearly.

Our external reviewers have spent numerous hours of their precious time to give us insightful feedback since the third edition: Sonia Lopez Alarcon (Rochester Institute of Technology), Bedrich Benes (Purdue University), Bryan Chin (UCSD), Samuel Cho (Wake Forest University), Kevin Farrell (Institute of Technology, Blanchardstown, Dublin, Ireland), Lahouari Ghouti (King Fahd University of Petroleum and Minerals, Saudi Arabia), Marisa Gil (Universitat Politecnica de Catalunya, Barcelona, Spain), Karen L. Karavanic (Portland State University), Steve Lumetta (University of Illinois at Urbana-Champaign), Dejan Milojici (Hewlett-Packard Labs), Pinar Muyan-Ozcelik (California State University, Sacramento), Greg Peterson (University of Tennessee—Knoxville), José L. Sánchez (University of Castilla—La Mancha), Janche Sang (Cleveland State University), and Jan Verschelde (University of Illinois at Chicago). Their comments helped us to significantly improve the content and readability of the book.

Steve Merken, Kiruthika Govindaraju, Naomi Robertson, and their staff at Elsevier worked tirelessly on this project.

We would like to especially thank Jensen Huang for providing a great amount of financial and human resources for developing the course that laid the foundation for this book.

We would like to acknowledge Dick Blahut, who challenged us to embark on the project. Beth Katsinas arranged a meeting between Dick Blahut and NVIDIA Vice President Dan Vivoli. Through that gathering, Blahut was introduced to David and challenged David to come to Illinois and create the original ECE498AL course with Wen-mei.

We would like to especially thank our colleagues Kurt Akeley, Al Aho, Arvind, Dick Blahut, Randy Bryant, Bob Colwell, Bill Dally, Ed Davidson, Mike Flynn, Michael Garland, John Hennessy, Pat Hanrahan, Nick Holonyak, Dick Karp, Kurt Keutzer, Chris Lamb, Dave Liu, David Luebke, Dave Kuck, Nacho

Navarro, Sanjay Patel, Yale Patt, David Patterson, Bob Rao, Burton Smith, Jim Smith, and Mateo Valero, who have taken the time to share their insight with us over the years.

We are humbled by the generosity and enthusiasm of all the great people who contributed to the course and the book.

Introduction

1

Chapter Outline

1.1 Heterogeneous parallel computing 3
1.2 Why more speed or parallelism? 7
1.3 Speeding up real applications 9
1.4 Challenges in parallel programming 11
1.5 Related parallel programming interfaces 13
1.6 Overarching goals 14
1.7 Organization of the book 15
References 19

Ever since the beginning of computing, many high-valued applications have demanded more execution speed and resources than the computing devices can offer. Early applications rely on the advancement of processor speed, memory speed, and memory capacity to enhance application-level capabilities such as the timeliness of weather forecasts, the accuracy of engineering structural analyses, the realism of computer-generated graphics, the number of airline reservations processed per second, and the number of fund transfers processed per second. More recently, new applications such as deep learning have demanded even more execution speed and resources than the best computing devices can offer. These application demands have fueled fast advancement in computing device capabilities in the past five decades and will continue to do so in the foreseeable future.

Microprocessors based on a single central processing unit (CPU) that appear to execute instructions in sequential steps, such as those in the $\times 86$ processors from Intel and AMD, armed with fast increasing clock frequency and hardware resources, drove rapid performance increases and cost reductions in computer applications in the 1980s and 1990s. During the two decades of growth, these single-CPU microprocessors brought GFLOPS, or giga (10^9) floating-point operations per second, to the desktop and TFLOPS, or tera (10^{12}) floating-point operations per second, to data centers. This relentless drive for performance improvement has allowed application software to provide more functionality, have better user interfaces, and generate more useful results. The users, in turn, demand even more improvements once they become accustomed to these improvements, creating a positive (virtuous) cycle for the computer industry.

Programming Massively Parallel Processors. DOI: https://doi.org/10.1016/B978-0-323-91231-0.00006-9

However, this drive has slowed down since 2003, owing to energy consumption and heat dissipation issues. These issues limit the increase of the clock frequency and the productive activities that can be performed in each clock period within a single CPU while maintaining the appearance of executing instructions in sequential steps. Since then, virtually all microprocessor vendors have switched to a model in which multiple physical CPUs, referred to as processor cores, are used in each chip to increase the processing power. A traditional CPU can be viewed as a single-core CPU in this model. To benefit from the multiple processor cores, users must have multiple instruction sequences, whether from the same application or different applications, that can simultaneously execute on these processor cores. For a particular application to benefit from multiple processor cores, its work must be divided into multiple instruction sequences that can simultaneously execute on these processor cores. This switch from a single CPU executing instructions in sequential steps to multiple cores executing multiple instruction sequences in parallel has exerted a tremendous impact on the software developer community.

Traditionally, the vast majority of software applications are written as sequential programs that are executed by processors whose design was envisioned by von Neumann in his seminal report in 1945 (von Neumann et al., 1972). The execution of these programs can be understood by a human as sequentially stepping through the code based on the concept of a program counter, also known as an instruction pointer in the literature. The program counter contains the memory address of the next instruction that will be executed by the processor. The sequence of instruction execution activities resulting from this sequential, stepwise execution of an application is referred to as a thread of execution, or simply *thread*, in the literature. The concept of threads is so important that it will be more formally defined and used extensively in the rest of this book.

Historically, most software developers relied on the advances in hardware, such as increased clock speed and executing multiple instructions under the hood, to increase the speed of their sequential applications; the same software simply runs faster as each new processor generation is introduced. Computer users also grew to expect that these programs run faster with each new generation of microprocessors. This expectation has not been valid for over a decade. A sequential program will run on only one of the processor cores, which will not become significantly faster from generation to generation. Without performance improvement, application developers will no longer be able to introduce new features and capabilities into their software as new microprocessors are introduced; this reduces the growth opportunities of the entire computer industry.

Rather, the application software that will continue to enjoy significant performance improvement with each new generation of microprocessors will be *parallel programs*, in which multiple threads of execution cooperate to complete the work faster. This new, dramatically escalated advantage of parallel programs over sequential programs has been referred to as the concurrency revolution (Sutter and Larus, 2005). The practice of parallel programming is by no means new. The high-performance computing (HPC) community has been developing parallel programs for decades. These parallel programs typically ran on expensive large-scale computers. Only a few elite applications could justify the use of these computers, thus limiting the practice of parallel programming to a small number of application developers. Now that all new microprocessors are parallel computers, the number of applications that need to be developed as parallel programs has increased dramatically. There is now a great need for software developers to learn about parallel programming, which is the focus of this book.

1.1 **Heterogeneous parallel computing**

Since 2003 the semiconductor industry has settled on two main trajectories for designing microprocessors (Hwu et al., 2008). The *multicore* trajectory seeks to maintain the execution speed of sequential programs while moving into multiple cores. The multicores began with two-core processors, and the number of cores has increased with each semiconductor process generation. A recent example is a recent Intel multicore server microprocessor with up to 24 processor cores, each of which is an out-of-order, multiple instruction issue processor implementing the full $\times 86$ instruction set, supporting hyperthreading with two hardware threads, designed to maximize the execution speed of sequential programs. Another example is a recent ARM Ampere multicore server processor with 128 processor cores.

In contrast, the *many-thread* trajectory focuses more on the execution throughput of parallel applications. The many-thread trajectory began with a large number of threads, and once again, the number of threads increases with each generation. A recent exemplar is the NVIDIA Tesla A100 graphics processing unit (GPU) with tens of thousands of threads, executing in a large number of simple, in-order pipelines. Many-thread processors, especially GPUs, have led the race of floating-point performance since 2003. As of 2021, the peak floating-point throughput of the A100 GPU is 9.7 TFLOPS for 64-bit double-precision, 156 TFLOPS for 32-bit single-precision, and 312 TFLOPS for 16-bit half-precision. In comparison, the peak floating-point throughput of the recent Intel 24-core processor is 0.33 TLOPS for double-precision and 0.66 TFLOPS for single-precision. The ratio of peak floating-point calculation throughput between many-thread GPUs and multicore CPUs has been increasing for the past several years. These are not necessarily application speeds; they are merely the raw speeds that the execution resources can potentially support in these chips.

Such a large gap in peak performance between multicores and many-threads has amounted to a significant "electrical potential" buildup, and at some point, something will have to give. We have reached that point. To date, this large peak performance gap has already motivated many applications developers to move the computationally intensive parts of their software to GPUs for execution. Perhaps even more important, the drastically elevated performance of parallel execution has enabled revolutionary new applications such as deep learning that are intrinsically composed of computationally intensive parts. Not surprisingly, these computationally intensive parts are also the prime target of parallel programming: When there is more work to do, there is more opportunity to divide the work among cooperating parallel workers, that is, threads.

One might ask why there is such a large peak performance gap between many-threaded GPUs and multicore CPUs. The answer lies in the differences in the fundamental design philosophies between the two types of processors, as illustrated in Fig. 1.1. The design of a CPU, as shown in Fig. 1.1A, is optimized for sequential code performance. The arithmetic units and operand data delivery logic are designed to minimize the effective latency of arithmetic operations at the cost of increased use of chip area and power per unit. Large last-level on-chip caches are designed to capture frequently accessed data and convert some of the long-latency memory accesses into short-latency cache accesses. Sophisticated branch prediction logic and execution control logic are used to mitigate the latency of conditional branch instructions. By reducing the latency of operations, the CPU hardware reduces the execution latency of each individual thread. However, the low-latency arithmetic units, sophisticated operand delivery logic, large cache memory, and control logic consume chip area and power that could otherwise be used to provide more arithmetic execution units and memory access channels. This design approach is commonly referred to as latency-oriented design.

The design philosophy of the GPUs, on the other hand, has been shaped by the fast-growing video game industry, which exerts tremendous economic pressure for the ability to perform a massive number of floating-point calculations and memory accesses per video frame in advanced games. This demand motivates GPU vendors to look for ways to maximize the chip area and power budget dedicated to floating-point calculations and memory access throughput.

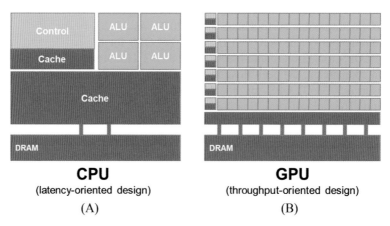

CPU
(latency-oriented design)
(A)

GPU
(throughput-oriented design)
(B)

FIGURE 1.1

CPUs and GPUs have fundamentally different design philosophies: (A) CPU design is latency oriented; (B) GPU design is throughput-oriented.

The need for performing a massive number of floating-point calculations per second in graphics applications for tasks such as viewpoint transformations and object rendering is quite intuitive. Additionally, the need for performing a massive number of memory accesses per second is just as important and perhaps even more important. The speed of many graphics applications is limited by the rate at which data can be delivered from the memory system into the processors and vice versa. A GPU must be capable of moving extremely large amounts of data into and out of graphics frame buffers in its DRAM (dynamic random-access memory) because such movement is what makes video displays rich and satisfying to gamers. The relaxed memory model (the way in which various system software, applications, and I/O devices expect their memory accesses to work) that is commonly accepted by game applications also makes it easier for the GPUs to support massive parallelism in accessing memory.

In contrast, general-purpose processors must satisfy requirements from legacy operating systems, applications, and I/O devices that present more challenges to supporting parallel memory accesses and thus make it more difficult to increase the throughput of memory accesses, commonly referred to as *memory bandwidth*. As a result, graphics chips have been operating at approximately 10 times the memory bandwidth of contemporaneously available CPU chips, and we expect that GPUs will continue to be at an advantage in terms of memory bandwidth for some time.

An important observation is that reducing latency is much more expensive than increasing throughput in terms of power and chip area. For example, one can double the arithmetic throughput by doubling the number of arithmetic units at the cost of doubling the chip area and power consumption. However, reducing the arithmetic latency by half may require doubling the current at the cost of more than doubling the chip area used and quadrupling the power consumption. Therefore the prevailing solution in GPUs is to optimize for the execution throughput of massive numbers of threads rather than reducing the latency of individual threads. This design approach saves chip area and power by allowing pipelined memory channels and arithmetic operations to have long latency. The reduction in area and power of the memory access hardware and arithmetic units allows the GPU designers to have more of them on a chip and thus increase the total execution throughput. Fig. 1.1 visually illustrates the difference in the design approaches by showing a smaller number of larger arithmetic units and a smaller number of memory channels in the CPU design in Fig. 1.1A, in contrast to the larger number of smaller arithmetic units and a larger number of memory channels in Fig. 1.1B.

The application software for these GPUs is expected to be written with a large number of parallel threads. The hardware takes advantage of the large number of threads to find work to do when some of them are waiting for long-latency memory accesses or arithmetic operations. Small cache memories in Fig. 1.1B are provided to help control the bandwidth requirements of these applications so that multiple threads that access the same memory data do not all need to go to the

DRAM. This design style is commonly referred to as throughput-oriented design, as it strives to maximize the total execution throughput of a large number of threads while allowing individual threads to take a potentially much longer time to execute.

It should be clear that GPUs are designed as parallel, throughput-oriented computing engines, and they will not perform well on some tasks on which CPUs are designed to perform well. For programs that have one or very few threads, CPUs with lower operation latencies can achieve much higher performance than GPUs. When a program has a large number of threads, GPUs with higher execution throughput can achieve much higher performance than CPUs. Therefore one should expect that many applications use both CPUs and GPUs, executing the sequential parts on the CPU and the numerically intensive parts on the GPUs. This is why the Compute Unified Device Architecture (CUDA) programming model, introduced by NVIDIA in 2007, is designed to support joint CPU-GPU execution of an application.

It is also important to note that speed is not the only decision factor when application developers choose the processors for running their applications. Several other factors can be even more important. First and foremost, the processors of choice must have a very large presence in the marketplace, referred to as the *installed base* of the processor. The reason is very simple. The cost of software development is best justified by a very large customer population. Applications that run on a processor with a small market presence will not have a large customer base. This has been a major problem with traditional parallel computing systems that have negligible market presence compared to general-purpose microprocessors. Only a few elite applications that are funded by the government and large corporations have been successfully developed on these traditional parallel computing systems. This has changed with many-thread GPUs. Because of their popularity in the PC market, GPUs have been sold by the hundreds of millions. Virtually all desktop PCs and high-end laptops have GPUs in them. There are more than 1 billion CUDA-enabled GPUs in use to date. Such a large market presence has made these GPUs economically attractive targets for application developers.

Another important decision factor is practical form factors and easy accessibility. Until 2006, parallel software applications ran on data center servers or departmental clusters. But such execution environments tend to limit the use of these applications. For example, in an application such as medical imaging, it is fine to publish a paper based on a 64-node cluster machine. But actual clinical applications on Magnetic Resonance Imaging (MRI) machines have been based on some combination of a PC and special hardware accelerators. The simple reason is that manufacturers such as GE and Siemens cannot sell MRIs that require racks of computer server boxes in clinical settings, while this is common in academic departmental settings. In fact, the National Institutes of Health (NIH) refused to fund parallel programming projects for some time; they believed that the impact of parallel software would be limited because huge cluster-based machines would not work in the clinical setting. Today, many companies ship MRI products with GPUs, and the NIH funds research using GPU computing.

Until 2006, graphics chips were very difficult to use because programmers had to use the equivalent of graphics API (application programming interface) functions to access the processing units, meaning that OpenGL or Direct3D techniques were needed to program these chips. Stated more simply, a computation must be expressed as a function that paints a pixel in some way in order to execute on these early GPUs. This technique was called GPGPU, for general purpose programming using a GPU. Even with a higher-level programming environment, the underlying code still needs to fit into the APIs that are designed to paint pixels. These APIs limit the kinds of applications that one can actually write for early GPUs. Consequently, GPGPU did not become a widespread programming phenomenon. Nonetheless, this technology was sufficiently exciting to inspire some heroic efforts and excellent research results.

Everything changed in 2007 with the release of CUDA (NVIDIA, 2007). CUDA did not represent software changes alone; additional hardware was added to the chip. NVIDIA actually devoted silicon area to facilitate the ease of parallel programming. In the G80 and its successor chips for parallel computing, GPGPU programs no longer go through the graphics interface at all. Instead, a new general-purpose parallel programming interface on the silicon chip serves the requests of CUDA programs. The general-purpose programming interface greatly expands the types of applications that one can easily develop for GPUs. All the other software layers were redone as well so that the programmers can use the familiar C/C++ programming tools.

While GPUs are an important class of computing devices in heterogeneous parallel computing, there are other important types of computing devices that are used as accelerators in heterogeneous computing systems. For example, field-programmable gate arrays have been widely used to accelerate networking applications. The techniques covered in this book using GPUs as the learning vehicle also apply to the programming tasks for these accelerators.

1.2 Why more speed or parallelism?

As we stated in Section 1.1, the main motivation for massively parallel programming is for applications to enjoy continued speed increases in future hardware generations. As we will discuss in the chapters on parallel patterns, advanced patterns, and applications (Parts II and III, Chapters 7 through 19), when an application is suitable for parallel execution, a good implementation on a GPU can achieve a speed up of more than 100 times over sequential execution on a single CPU core. If the application includes what we call "data parallelism," it is often possible to achieve a $10\times$ speedup with just a few hours of work.

One might ask why applications will continue to demand increased speed. Many applications that we have today seem to be running quite fast enough. Despite the myriad of computing applications in today's world, many exciting mass market applications of the future are what we previously considered supercomputing applications, or superapplications. For example, the biology research community is moving more and more into the molecular level. Microscopes, arguably the most important instrument in molecular biology, used to rely on optics or electronic instrumentation. However, there are limitations to the molecular-level observations that we can make with these instruments. These limitations can be effectively addressed by incorporating a computational model to simulate the underlying molecular activities with boundary conditions set by traditional instrumentation. With simulation we can measure even more details and test more hypotheses than can ever be imagined with traditional instrumentation alone. These simulations will continue to benefit from increasing computing speeds in the foreseeable future in terms of the size of the biological system that can be modeled and the length of reaction time that can be simulated within a tolerable response time. These enhancements will have tremendous implications for science and medicine.

For applications such as video and audio coding and manipulation, consider our satisfaction with digital high-definition (HD) TV in comparison to older NTSC TV. Once we experience the level of details in the picture on an HDTV, it is very hard to go back to older technology. But consider all the processing that is needed for that HDTV. It is a highly parallel process, as are three-dimensional (3D) imaging and visualization. In the future, new functionalities such as view synthesis and high-resolution display of low-resolution videos will demand more computing power in the TV. At the consumer level, we will begin to see an increasing number of video and image-processing applications that improve the focus, lighting, and other key aspects of the pictures and videos.

Among the benefits that are offered by more computing speed are much better user interfaces. Smartphone users now enjoy a much more natural interface with high-resolution touch screens that rival a large-screen TV. Undoubtedly, future versions of these devices will incorporate sensors and displays with 3D perspectives, applications that combine virtual and physical space information for enhanced usability, and voice and computer vision−based interfaces, requiring even more computing speed.

Similar developments are underway in consumer electronic gaming. In the past, driving a car in a game was simply a prearranged set of scenes. If your car bumped into an obstacle, the course of your vehicle did not change; only the game score changed. Your wheels were not bent or damaged, and it was no more difficult to drive, even if you lost a wheel. With increased computing speed, the games can be based on dynamic simulation rather than prearranged scenes. We can expect to experience more of these realistic effects in the future. Accidents will damage your wheels, and your online driving experience will be much more realistic. The ability to accurately model physical phenomena has already inspired the concept of *digital twins*, in which physical objects have accurate models in the simulated space so that stress testing and deterioration prediction can be thoroughly conducted at much lower cost. Realistic modeling and simulation of physics effects are known to demand very large amounts of computing power.

An important example of new applications that have been enabled by drastically increased computing throughput is deep learning based on artificial neural networks. While neural networks have been actively researched since the 1970s, they have been ineffective in practical applications because it takes too much labeled data and too much computation to train these networks. The rise of the Internet offered a tremendous number of labeled pictures, and the rise of GPUs offered a surge of computing throughput. As a result, there has been a fast adoption of neural network—based applications in computer vision and natural language processing since 2012. This adoption has revolutionized computer vision and natural language processing applications and triggered fast development of self-driving cars and home assistant devices.

All the new applications that we mentioned involve simulating and/or representing a physical and concurrent world in different ways and at different levels, with tremendous amounts of data being processed. With this huge quantity of data, much of the computation can be done on different parts of the data in parallel, although they will have to be reconciled at some point. In most cases, effective management of data delivery can have a major impact on the achievable speed of a parallel application. While techniques for doing so are often well known to a few experts who work with such applications on a daily basis, the vast majority of application developers can benefit from a more intuitive understanding and practical working knowledge of these techniques.

We aim to present the data management techniques in an intuitive way to application developers whose formal education may not be in computer science or computer engineering. We also aim to provide many practical code examples and hands-on exercises that help the reader to acquire working knowledge, which requires a practical programming model that facilitates parallel implementation and supports proper management of data delivery. CUDA offers such a programming model and has been well tested by a large developer community.

1.3 Speeding up real applications

How much speedup can we expect from parallelizing an application? The definition of *speedup* for an application by computing system A over computing system B is the ratio of the time used to execute the application in system B over the time used to execute the same application in system A. For example, if an application takes 10 seconds to execute in system A but takes 200 seconds to execute in System B, the speedup for the execution by system A over system B would be 200/10=20, which is referred to as a 20× (20 times) speedup.

The speedup that is achievable by a parallel computing system over a serial computing system depends on the portion of the application that can be parallelized. For example, if the percentage of time spent in the part that can be parallelized is 30%, a $100\times$ speedup of the parallel portion will reduce the total execution time of the application by no more than 29.7%. That is, the speedup for the entire application will be only about $1/(1 - 0.297)=1.42\times$. In fact, even infinite amount of speedup in the parallel portion can only slash 30% off the execution time, achieving no more than $1.43\times$ speedup. The fact that the level of speedup that one can achieve through parallel execution can be severely limited by the parallelizable portion of the application is referred to as Amdahl's Law (Amdahl, 2013). On the other hand, if 99% of the execution time is in the parallel portion, a $100\times$ speedup of the parallel portion will reduce the application execution to 1.99% of the original time. This gives the entire application a $50\times$ speedup. Therefore it is very important that an application has the vast majority of its execution in the parallel portion for a massively parallel processor to effectively speed up its execution.

Researchers have achieved speedups of more than $100\times$ for some applications. However, this is typically achieved only after extensive optimization and tuning after the algorithms have been enhanced so that more than 99.9% of the application work is in the parallel portion.

Another important factor for the achievable level of speedup for applications is how fast data can be accessed from and written to the memory. In practice, straightforward parallelization of applications often saturates the memory (DRAM) bandwidth, resulting in only about a $10\times$ speedup. The trick is to figure out how to get around memory bandwidth limitations, which involves doing one of many transformations to utilize specialized GPU on-chip memories to drastically reduce the number of accesses to the DRAM. However, one must further optimize the code to get around limitations such as limited on-chip memory capacity. An important goal of this book is to help the reader to fully understand these optimizations and become skilled in using them.

Keep in mind that the level of speedup that is achieved over single-core CPU execution can also reflect the suitability of the CPU to the application. In some applications, CPUs perform very well, making it harder to speed up performance using a GPU. Most applications have portions that can be much better executed by the CPU. One must give the CPU a fair chance to perform and make sure that the code is written so that GPUs *complement* CPU execution, thus properly exploiting the heterogeneous parallel computing capabilities of the combined CPU/GPU system. As of today, mass market computing systems that combine multicore CPUs and many-core GPUs have brought terascale computing to laptops and exascale computing to clusters.

Fig. 1.2 illustrates the main parts of a typical application. Much of a real application's code tends to be sequential. These sequential parts are illustrated as the "pit" area of the peach; trying to apply parallel computing techniques to these portions is like biting into the peach pit—not a good feeling! These portions are very hard to parallelize. CPUs tend to do a very good job on these portions. The good news is that although these portions can take up a large portion of the code, they tend to account for only a small portion of the execution time of superapplications.

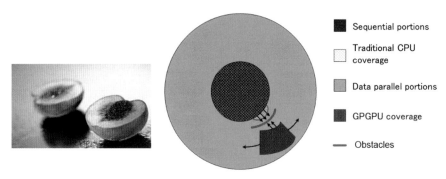

FIGURE 1.2

Coverage of sequential and parallel application portions. The sequential portions and the traditional (single-core) CPU coverage portions overlap with each other. The previous GPGPU technique offers very limited coverage of the data parallel portions, since it is limited to computations that can be formulated into painting pixels. The obstacles refer to the power constraints that make it hard to extend single-core CPUs to cover more of the data parallel portions.

Then come what we call the "peach flesh" portions. These portions are easy to parallelize, as are some early graphics applications. Parallel programming in heterogeneous computing systems can drastically improve the speed of these applications. As illustrated in Fig. 1.2, early GPGPU programming interfaces cover only a small portion of the peach flesh section, which is analogous to a small portion of the most exciting applications. As we will see, the CUDA programming interface is designed to cover a much larger section of the peach flesh of exciting applications. Parallel programming models and their underlying hardware are still evolving at a fast pace to enable efficient parallelization of even larger sections of applications.

1.4 Challenges in parallel programming

What makes parallel programming hard? Someone once said that if you do not care about performance, parallel programming is very easy. You can literally write a parallel program in an hour. But then why bother to write a parallel program if you do not care about performance?

This book addresses several challenges in achieving high performance in parallel programming. First and foremost, it can be challenging to design parallel algorithms with the same level of algorithmic (computational) complexity as that of sequential algorithms. Many parallel algorithms perform the same amount of work as their sequential counterparts. However, some parallel algorithms do more work than their sequential counterparts. In fact, sometimes they may do so much more work that they ended up running slower for large input datasets. This is especially a problem because fast processing of large input datasets is an important motivation for parallel programming.

For example, many real-world problems are most naturally described with mathematical recurrences. Parallelizing these problems often requires nonintuitive ways of thinking about the problem and may require redundant work during execution. There are important algorithm primitives, such as prefix sum, that can facilitate the conversion of sequential, recursive formulation of the problems into more parallel forms. We will more formally introduce the concept of *work efficiency* and will illustrate the methods and tradeoffs that are involved in designing parallel algorithms that achieve the same level of computational complexity as their sequential counterparts, using important parallel patterns such as prefix sum in Chapter 11, Prefix Sum (Scan).

Second, the execution speed of many applications is limited by memory access latency and/or throughput. We refer to these applications as memory bound; by contrast, compute bound applications are limited by the number of instructions performed per byte of data. Achieving high-performance parallel execution in memory-bound applications often requires methods for improving memory access speed. We will introduce optimization techniques for memory accesses in Chapter 5, Memory Architecture and Data Locality and Chapter 6, Performance Considerations, and will apply these techniques in several chapters on parallel patterns and applications.

Third, the execution speed of parallel programs is often more sensitive to the input data characteristics than is the case for their sequential counterparts. Many real-world applications need to deal with inputs with widely varying characteristics, such as erratic or unpredictable data sizes and uneven data distributions. These variations in sizes and distributions can cause uneven amount of work to be assigned to the parallel threads and can significantly reduce the effectiveness of parallel execution. The performance of parallel programs can sometimes vary dramatically with these characteristics. We will introduce techniques for regularizing data distributions and/or dynamically refining the number of threads to address these challenges in the chapters that introduce parallel patterns and applications.

Fourth, some applications can be parallelized while requiring little collaboration across different threads. These applications are often referred to as *embarrassingly parallel*. Other applications require threads to collaborate with each other, which requires using *synchronization operations* such as barriers or atomic operations. These synchronization operations impose overhead on the application because threads will often find themselves waiting for other threads instead of performing useful work. We will discuss various strategies for reducing this synchronization overhead throughout this book.

Fortunately, most of these challenges have been addressed by researchers. There are also common patterns across application domains that allow us to apply solutions that were derived in one domain to challenges in other domains. This is the primary reason why we will be presenting key techniques for addressing these challenges in the context of important parallel computation patterns and applications.

1.5 **Related parallel programming interfaces**

Many parallel programming languages and models have been proposed in the past several decades (Mattson et al., 2004). The ones that are the most widely used are OpenMP (Open, 2005) for shared memory multiprocessor systems and Message Passing Interface (MPI) (MPI, 2009) for scalable cluster computing. Both have become standardized programming interfaces supported by major computer vendors.

An OpenMP implementation consists of a compiler and a runtime. A programmer specifies directives (commands) and pragmas (hints) about a loop to the OpenMP compiler. With these directives and pragmas, OpenMP compilers generate parallel code. The runtime system supports the execution of the parallel code by managing parallel threads and resources. OpenMP was originally designed for CPU execution and has been extended to support GPU execution. The major advantage of OpenMP is that it provides compiler automation and runtime support for abstracting away many parallel programming details from programmers. Such automation and abstraction can help to make the application code more portable across systems produced by different vendors as well as different generations of systems from the same vendor. We refer to this property as *performance portability*. However, effective programming in OpenMP still requires the programmer to understand all the detailed parallel programming concepts that are involved. Because CUDA gives programmers explicit control of these parallel programming details, it is an excellent learning vehicle even for someone who would like to use OpenMP as their primary programming interface. Furthermore, from our experience, OpenMP compilers are still evolving and improving. Many programmers will likely need to use CUDA-style interfaces for parts in which OpenMP compilers fall short.

On the other hand, MPI is a programming interface in which computing nodes in a cluster do not share memory (MPI, 2009). All data sharing and interaction must be done through explicit message passing. MPI has been widely used in HPC. Applications written in MPI have run successfully on cluster computing systems with more than 100,000 nodes. Today, many HPC clusters employ heterogeneous CPU/GPU nodes. The amount of effort that is needed to port an application into MPI can be quite high, owing to the lack of shared memory across computing nodes. The programmer needs to perform domain decomposition to partition the input and output data across individual nodes. On the basis of the domain decomposition, the programmer also needs to call message sending and receiving functions to manage the data exchange between nodes. CUDA, by contrast, provides shared memory for parallel execution in the GPU to address this difficulty. While CUDA is an effective interface with each node, most application developers need to use MPI to program at the cluster level. Furthermore, there has been increasing support for multi-GPU programming in CUDA via APIs such as the NVIDIA Collective Communications Library (NCCL). It is therefore important that a parallel programmer in HPC understands how to do joint MPI/CUDA programming in modern computing clusters employing multi-GPU nodes, a topic that is presented in Chapter 20, Programming a Heterogeneous Computing Cluster.

In 2009, several major industry players, including Apple, Intel, AMD/ATI, and NVIDIA, jointly developed a standardized programming model called Open Compute Language (OpenCL) (The Khronos Group, 2009). Similar to CUDA, the OpenCL programming model defines language extensions and runtime APIs to allow programmers to manage parallelism and data delivery in massively parallel processors. In comparison to CUDA, OpenCL relies more on APIs and less on language extensions. This allows vendors to quickly adapt their existing compilers and tools to handle OpenCL programs. OpenCL is a standardized programming model in that applications that are developed in OpenCL can run correctly without modification on all processors that support the OpenCL language extensions and API. However, one will likely need to modify the applications to achieve high performance for a new processor.

Those who are familiar with both OpenCL and CUDA know that there is a remarkable similarity between the key concepts and features of OpenCL and those of CUDA. That is, a CUDA programmer can learn OpenCL programming with minimal effort. More important, virtually all techniques that are learned in using CUDA can be easily applied to OpenCL programming.

1.6 Overarching goals

Our primary goal is to teach you, the reader, how to program massively parallel processors to achieve high performance. Therefore much of the book is dedicated to the techniques for developing high-performance parallel code. Our approach will not require a great deal of hardware expertise. Nevertheless, you will need to have a good conceptual understanding of the parallel hardware architectures to be able to reason about the performance behavior of your code. Therefore we are going to dedicate some pages to the intuitive understanding of essential hardware architecture features and many pages to techniques for developing high-performance parallel programs. In particular, we will focus on computational thinking (Wing, 2006) techniques that will enable you to think about problems in ways that are amenable to high-performance execution on massively parallel processors.

High-performance parallel programming on most processors requires some knowledge of how the hardware works. It will probably take many years to build tools and machines that will enable programmers to develop high-performance code without this knowledge. Even if we have such tools, we suspect that programmers who have knowledge of the hardware will be able to use the tools much more effectively than those who do not. For this reason we dedicate Chapter 4, Compute Architecture and Scheduling, to introduce the fundamentals of the GPU architecture. We also discuss more specialized architecture concepts as part of our discussions of high-performance parallel programming techniques.

Our second goal is to teach parallel programming for correct functionality and reliability, which constitutes a subtle issue in parallel computing. Programmers who have worked on parallel systems in the past know that achieving initial performance is not enough. The challenge is to achieve it in such a way that you can debug the code and support users. The CUDA programming model encourages the use of simple forms of barrier synchronization, memory consistency, and atomicity for managing parallelism. In addition, it provides an array of powerful tools that allow one to debug not only the functional aspects, but also the performance bottlenecks. We will show that by focusing on data parallelism, one can achieve both high performance and high reliability in one's applications.

Our third goal is scalability across future hardware generations by exploring approaches to parallel programming such that future machines, which will be more and more parallel, can run your code faster than today's machines. We want to help you to master parallel programming so that your programs can scale up to the level of performance of new generations of machines. The key to such scalability is to regularize and localize memory data accesses to minimize consumption of critical resources and conflicts in updating data structures. Therefore the techniques for developing high-performance parallel code are also important for ensuring future scalability of applications.

Much technical knowledge will be required to achieve these goals, so we will cover quite a few principles and patterns (Mattson et al., 2004) of parallel programming in this book. We will not be teaching these principles and patterns on their own. We will teach them in the context of parallelizing useful applications. We cannot cover all of them, however, so we have selected the most useful and well-proven techniques to cover in detail. In fact, the current edition has a significantly expanded number of chapters on parallel patterns. We are now ready to give you a quick overview of the rest of the book.

1.7 **Organization of the book**

This book is organized into four parts. Part I covers fundamental concepts in parallel programming, data parallelism, GPUs, and performance optimization. These foundational chapters equip the reader with the basic knowledge and skills that are necessary for becoming a GPU programmer. Part II covers primitive parallel patterns, and Part III covers more advanced parallel patterns and applications. These two parts apply the knowledge and skills that were learned in the first part and introduce other GPU architecture features and optimization techniques as the need for them arises. The final part, Part IV, introduces advanced practices to complete the knowledge of readers who would like to become expert GPU programmers.

Part I on fundamental concepts consists of Chapters 2–6. Chapter 2, Heterogeneous Data Parallel Computing, introduces data parallelism and CUDA C programming. The chapter relies on the fact that the reader has had previous experience with C programming. It first introduces CUDA C as a simple, small extension to C that supports heterogeneous CPU/GPU computing and the widely used single-program, multiple-data parallel programming model. It then covers the thought processes that are involved in (1) identifying the part of application programs to be parallelized, (2) isolating the data to be used by the parallelized code, using an API function to allocate memory on the parallel computing device, (3) using an API function to transfer data to the parallel computing device, (4) developing the parallel part into a kernel function that will be executed by parallel threads, (5) launching a kernel function for execution by parallel threads, and (6) eventually transferring the data back to the host processor with an API function call. We use a running example of vector addition to illustrate these concepts. While the objective of Chapter is to teach enough concepts of the CUDA C programming model so that the reader can write a simple parallel CUDA C program, it covers several basic skills that are needed to develop a parallel application based on any parallel programming interface.

Chapter 3, Multidimensional Grids and Data, presents more details of the parallel execution model of CUDA, particularly as it relates to handling multidimensional data using multidimensional organizations of threads. It gives enough insight into the creation, organization, resource binding, and data binding of threads to enable the reader to implement sophisticated computation using CUDA C.

Chapter 4, Compute Architecture and Scheduling, introduces the GPU architecture, with a focus on how the computational cores are organized and how threads are scheduled to execute on these cores. Various architecture considerations are discussed, with their implications on the performance of code that is executed on the GPU architecture. These include concepts such as transparent scalability, SIMD execution and control divergence, multithreading and latency tolerance, and occupancy, all of which are defined and discussed in the chapter.

Chapter 5, Memory Architecture and Data Locality, extends Chapter 4, Compute Architecture and Scheduling, by discussing the memory architecture of a GPU. It also discusses the special memories that can be used to hold CUDA variables for managing data delivery and improving program execution speed. We introduce the CUDA language features that allocate and use these memories. Appropriate use of these memories can drastically improve the data access throughput and help to alleviate the traffic congestion in the memory system.

Chapter 6, Performance Considerations, presents several important performance considerations in current CUDA hardware. In particular, it gives more details about desirable patterns of thread execution and memory accesses. These details form the conceptual basis for programmers to reason about the consequences of their decisions on organizing their computation and data. The chapter concludes with a checklist of common optimization strategies that GPU programmers often use to optimize any computation pattern. This checklist will be used throughout the next two parts of the book to optimize various parallel patterns and applications.

Part II on primitive parallel patterns consists of Chapters 7–12. Chapter 7, Convolution, presents convolution, a frequently used parallel computing pattern that is rooted in digital signal processing and computer vision and requires careful management of data access locality. We also use this pattern to introduce constant memory and caching in modern GPUs. Chapter 8, Stencil, presents stencil, a pattern that is similar to convolution but is rooted in solving differential equations and has specific features that present unique opportunities for further optimization of data access locality. We also use this pattern to introduce 3D organizations of threads and data and to showcase an optimization introduced in Chapter 6, Performance Considerations, that targets thread granularity.

Chapter 9, Parallel Histogram, covers histogram, a pattern that is widely used in statistical data analysis as well as pattern recognition in large datasets. We also use this pattern to introduce atomic operations as a means for coordinating concurrent updates to shared data and the privatization optimization, which reduces the overhead of these operations. Chapter 10, Reduction and Minimizing Divergence, introduces the reduction tree pattern, which is used to summarize a collection of input data. We also use this pattern to demonstrate the impact of control divergence on performance and show techniques for how this impact can be mitigated. Chapter 11, Prefix Sum (Scan), presents prefix sum, or scan, an important parallel computing pattern that coverts inherently sequential computation into parallel computation. We also use this pattern to introduce the concept of work efficiency in parallel algorithms. Finally, Chapter 12, Merge, covers parallel merge, a widely used pattern in divide-and-concur work-partitioning strategies. We also use this chapter to introduce dynamic input data identification and organization.

Part III on advanced parallel patterns and applications is similar in spirit to Part II, but the patterns that are covered are more elaborate and often include more application context. Thus these chapters are less focused on introducing new techniques or features and more focused on application-specific considerations. For each application we start by identifying alternative ways of formulating the basic structure of the parallel execution and follow up with reasoning about the advantages and disadvantages of each alternative. We then go through the steps of code transformation that are needed to achieve high performance. These chapters help the readers to put all the materials from the previous chapters together and support them as they take on their own application development projects.

Part III consists of Chapters 13–19. Chapter 13, Sorting, presents two forms of parallel sorting: radix sort and merge sort. This advanced pattern leverages more primitive patterns that were covered in previous chapters, particularly prefix sum and parallel merge. Chapter 14, Sparse Matrix Computation, presents sparse matrix computation, which is widely used for processing very large datasets.

The chapter introduces the reader to the concepts of rearranging data for more efficient parallel access: data compression, padding, sorting, transposition, and regularization. Chapter 15, Graph Traversal, introduces graph algorithms and how graph search can be efficiently implemented in GPU programming. Many different strategies are presented for parallelizing graph algorithms, and the impact of the graph structure on the choice of best algorithm is discussed. These strategies build on the more primitive patterns, such as histogram and merge.

Chapter 16, Deep Learning, covers deep learning, which is becoming an extremely important area for GPU computing. We introduce the efficient implementation of convolutional neural networks and leave more in-depth discussion to other sources. The efficient implementation of the convolution neural networks leverages techniques such as tiling and patterns such as convolution. Chapter 17, Iterative Magnetic Resonance Imaging Reconstruction, covers non-Cartesian MRI reconstruction and how to leverage techniques such as loop fusion and scatter-to-gather transformations to enhance parallelism and reduce synchronization overhead. Chapter 18, Electrostatic Potential Map, covers molecular visualization and analysis, which benefit from techniques to handle irregular data by applying lessons learned from sparse matrix computation.

Chapter 19, Parallel Programming and Computational Thinking, introduces computational thinking, the art of formulating and solving computational problems in ways that are more amenable to HPC. It does so by covering the concept of organizing the computation tasks of a program so that they can be done in parallel. We start by discussing the translational process of organizing abstract scientific, problem-specific concepts into computational tasks, which is an important first step in producing high-quality application software, serial or parallel. The chapter then discusses parallel algorithm structures and their effects on application performance, which is grounded in the performance tuning experience with CUDA. Although we do not go into the implementation details of these alternative parallel programming styles, we expect that the readers will be able to learn to program in any of them with the foundation that they gain in this book. We also present a high-level case study to show the opportunities that can be seen through creative computational thinking.

Part IV on advanced practices consists of Chapters 20−22. Chapter 20, Programming a Heterogeneous Computing Cluster, covers CUDA programming on heterogeneous clusters, in which each compute node consists of both CPUs and GPUs. We discuss the use of MPI alongside CUDA to integrate both internode computing and intranode computing and the resulting communication issues and practices. Chapter 21, CUDA Dynamic Parallelism, covers dynamic parallelism, which is the ability of the GPU to dynamically create work for itself based on the data or program structure rather than always waiting for the CPU to do so. Chapter 22, Advanced Practices and Future Evolution, goes through a list of miscellaneous advanced features and practices that are important for CUDA programmers to be aware of. These include topics such as zero-copy memory, unified virtual memory, simultaneous execution of multiple kernels, function calls, exception handling, debugging, profiling, double-precision support, configurable cache/scratchpad sizes, and others. For example, early versions of CUDA provided limited shared memory capability between the CPU and the GPU. The programmers needed to explicitly manage the data transfer between CPU and GPU. However, current versions of CUDA support features such as unified virtual memory and zero-copy memory that enable seamless sharing of data between CPUs and GPUs. With such support, a CUDA programmer can declare variables and data structures as shared between CPU and GPU. The runtime hardware and software maintain coherence and automatically perform optimized data transfer operations on behalf of the programmer on a need basis. Such support significantly reduces the programming complexity that is involved in overlapping data transfer with computation and I/O activities. In the introductory part of the textbook, we use the APIs for explicit data transfer so that reader gets a better understanding of what happens under the hood. We later introduce unified virtual memory and zero-copy memory in Chapter 22, Advanced Practices and Future Evolution.

Although the chapters throughout this book are based on CUDA, they help the readers to build up the foundation for parallel programming in general. We believe that humans understand best when we learn from concrete examples. That is, we must first learn the concepts in the context of a particular programming model, which provides us with solid footing when we generalize our knowledge to other programming models. As we do so, we can draw on our concrete experience from the CUDA examples. In-depth experience with CUDA also enables us to gain maturity, which will help us to learn concepts that may not even be pertinent to the CUDA model.

Chapter 23, Conclusion and Outlook, offers concluding remarks and an outlook for the future of massively parallel programming. We first revisit our goals and summarize how the chapters fit together to help achieve the goals. We then conclude with a prediction that these fast advances in massively parallel computing will make it one of the most exciting areas in the coming decade.

References

Amdahl, G.M., 2013. Computer architecture and amdahl's law. Computer 46 (12), 38–46.

Hwu, W.W., Keutzer, K., Mattson, T., 2008. The concurrency challenge. IEEE Design and Test of Computers 312–320.

Mattson, T.G., Sanders, B.A., Massingill, B.L., 2004. Patterns of Parallel Programming, Addison-Wesley Professional.

Message Passing Interface Forum, 2009. MPI – A Message Passing Interface Standard Version 2.2. http://www.mpi-forum.org/docs/mpi-2.2/mpi22-report.pdf, September 4.

NVIDIA Corporation, 2007. CUDA Programming Guide, February.

OpenMP Architecture Review Board, 2005. OpenMP application program interface.

Sutter, H., Larus, J., 2005. Software and the concurrency revolution, in. ACM Queue 3 (7), 54–62.

The Khronos Group, 2009. The OpenCL Specification version 1.0. http://www.khronos. org/registry/cl/specs/opencl-1.0.29.pdf.

von Neumann, J., 1972. First draft of a report on the EDVAC. In: Goldstine, H.H. (Ed.), The Computer: From Pascal to von Neumann. Princeton University Press, Princeton, NJ, ISBN 0–691-02367-0.

Wing, J., 2006. Computational thinking. Communications of the ACM 49 (3).

PART

I

Fundamental Concepts

Heterogeneous data parallel computing

2

With special contribution from David Luebke

Chapter Outline

2.1 Data parallelism 23
2.2 CUDA C program structure 27
2.3 A vector addition kernel 28
2.4 Device global memory and data transfer 31
2.5 Kernel functions and threading 35
2.6 Calling kernel functions 40
2.7 Compilation 42
2.8 Summary 43
Exercises 44
References 46

Data parallelism refers to the phenomenon in which the computation work to be performed on different parts of the dataset can be done independently of each other and thus can be done in parallel with each other. Many applications exhibit a rich amount of data parallelism that makes them amenable to scalable parallel execution. It is therefore important for parallel programmers to be familiar with the concept of data parallelism and the parallel programming language constructs for writing code that exploit data parallelism. In this chapter we will use the CUDA C language constructs to develop a simple data parallel program.

2.1 Data parallelism

When modern software applications run slowly, the problem is usually data—too much data to process. Image-processing applications manipulate images or videos with millions to trillions of pixels. Scientific applications model fluid dynamics using billions of grid points. Molecular dynamics applications must simulate interactions between thousands to billions of atoms. Airline scheduling deals with thousands of flights, crews, and airport gates. Most of these pixels, particles, grid points, interactions, flights, and so on can usually be dealt with largely independently. For example, in image processing, converting a color pixel to grayscale requires only the data of that pixel. Blurring an image averages each pixel's color with the colors of nearby pixels, requiring only the data of that small neighborhood of pixels. Even a seemingly global operation, such as finding the average brightness of all pixels in an image, can be broken down into many smaller computations that can be executed independently. Such independent evaluation of different pieces of data is the basis of *data parallelism*. Writing data parallel code entails (re)organizing the computation around the data such that we can execute the resulting independent computations in parallel to complete the overall job faster—often much faster.

Let us illustrate the concept of data parallelism with a color-to-grayscale conversion example. Fig. 2.1 shows a color image (left side) consisting of many pixels, each containing a red, green, and blue fractional value (r, g, b) varying from 0 (black) to 1 (full intensity).

To convert the color image (left side of Fig. 2.1) to a grayscale image (right side), we compute the luminance value L for each pixel by applying the following weighted sum formula:

$$L = r^*0.21 + g^*0.72 + b^*0.07$$

FIGURE 2.1

Conversion of a color image to a grayscale image.

RGB Color Image Representation

In an RGB representation, each pixel in an image is stored as a tuple of (r, g, b) values. The format of an image's row is (r g b) (r g b) ... (r g b), as illustrated in the following conceptual picture. Each tuple specifies a mixture of red (R), green (G) and blue (B). That is, for each pixel, the r, g, and b values represent the intensity (0 being dark and 1 being full intensity) of the red, green, and blue light sources when the pixel is rendered.

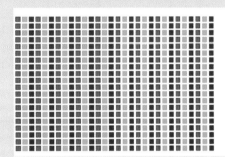 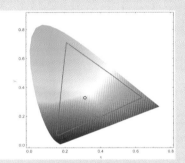

The actual allowable mixtures of these three colors vary across industry-specified color spaces. Here, the valid combinations of the three colors in the AdbobeRGB™ color space are shown as the interior of the triangle. The vertical coordinate (y value) and horizontal coordinate (x value) of each mixture show the fraction of the pixel intensity that should be G and R. The remaining fraction (1-y−x) of the pixel intensity should be assigned to B. To render an image, the r, g, b values of each pixel are used to calculate both the total intensity (luminance) of the pixel as well as the mixture coefficients (x, y, 1-y-x).

If we consider the input to be an image organized as an array I of RGB values and the output to be a corresponding array O of luminance values, we get the simple computation structure shown in Fig. 2.2. For example, $O[0]$ is generated by calculating the weighted sum of the RGB values in $I[0]$ according to the formula above; $O[1]$ is generated by calculating the weighted sum of the RGB values in $I[1]$; $O[2]$ is generated by calculating the weighted sum of the RGB values in $I[2]$; and so on. None of these per-pixel computations depend on each other. All of them can be performed independently. Clearly, color-to-grayscale conversion exhibits a rich amount of data parallelism. Of course, data parallelism in complete applications can be more complex, and much of this book is devoted to teaching the parallel thinking necessary to find and exploit data parallelism.

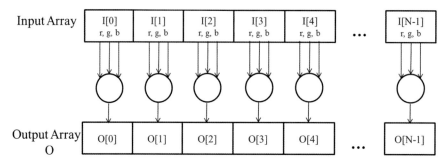

FIGURE 2.2

Data parallelism in image-to-grayscale conversion. Pixels can be calculated independently of each other.

Task Parallelism vs. Data Parallelism

Data parallelism is not the only type of parallelism used in parallel programming. Task parallelism has also been used extensively in parallel programming. Task parallelism is typically exposed through task decomposition of applications. For example, a simple application may need to do a vector addition and a matrix-vector multiplication. Each of these would be a task. Task parallelism exists if the two tasks can be done independently. I/O and data transfers are also common sources of tasks.

In large applications, there are usually a larger number of independent tasks and therefore larger amount of task parallelism. For example, in a molecular dynamics simulator, the list of natural tasks includes vibrational forces, rotational forces, neighbor identification for non-bonding forces, non-bonding forces, velocity and position, and other physical properties based on velocity and position.

In general, data parallelism is the main source of scalability for parallel programs. With large datasets, one can often find abundant data parallelism to be able to utilize massively parallel processors and allow application performance to grow with each generation of hardware that has more execution resources. Nevertheless, task parallelism can also play an important role in achieving performance goals. We will be covering task parallelism later when we introduce streams.

2.2 **CUDA C program structure**

We are now ready to learn how to write a CUDA C program to exploit data parallelism for faster execution. CUDA C[1] extends the popular ANSI C programming language with minimal new syntax and library functions to let programmers target heterogeneous computing systems containing both CPU cores and massively parallel GPUs. As the name implies, CUDA C is built on NVIDIA's CUDA platform. CUDA is currently the most mature framework for massively parallel computing. It is broadly used in the high-performance computing industry, with essential tools such as compilers, debuggers, and profilers available on the most common operating systems.

The structure of a CUDA C program reflects the coexistence of a *host* (CPU) and one or more *devices* (GPUs) in the computer. Each CUDA C source file can have a mixture of host code and device code. By default, any traditional C program is a CUDA program that contains only host code. One can add device code into any source file. The device code is clearly marked with special CUDA C keywords. The device code includes functions, or *kernels*, whose code is executed in a data-parallel manner.

The execution of a CUDA program is illustrated in Fig. 2.3. The execution starts with host code (CPU serial code). When a kernel function is called, a large number of threads are *launched* on a device to execute the kernel. All the threads that are launched by a kernel call are collectively called a *grid*. These threads are the primary vehicle of parallel execution in a CUDA platform. Fig. 2.3 shows the execution of two grids of threads. We will discuss how these grids are organized soon. When all threads of a grid have completed their execution, the grid terminates, and the execution continues on the host until another grid is launched.

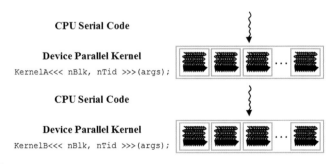

CPU Serial Code

Device Parallel Kernel
KernelA<<< nBlk, nTid >>>(args);

CPU Serial Code

Device Parallel Kernel
KernelB<<< nBlk, nTid >>>(args);

FIGURE 2.3

Execution of a CUDA program.

---

[1] There has been a steady movement for CUDA C to adopt C++ features. We will be using some of these C++ features in our programming examples.

Note that Fig. 2.3 shows a simplified model in which the CPU execution and the GPU execution do not overlap. Many heterogeneous computing applications manage overlapped CPU and GPU execution to take advantage of both CPUs and GPUs.

Launching a grid typically generates many threads to exploit data parallelism. In the color-to-grayscale conversion example, each thread could be used to compute one pixel of the output array O. In this case, the number of threads that ought to be generated by the grid launch is equal to the number of pixels in the image. For large images, a large number of threads will be generated. CUDA programmers can assume that these threads take very few clock cycles to generate and schedule, owing to efficient hardware support. This assumption contrasts with traditional CPU threads, which typically take thousands of clock cycles to generate and schedule. In the next chapter we will show how to implement color-to-grayscale conversion and image blur kernels. In the rest of this chapter we will use vector addition as a running example for simplicity.

Threads

A thread is a simplified view of how a processor executes a sequential program in modern computers. A thread consists of the code of the program, the point in the code that is being executed, and the values of its variables and data structures. The execution of a thread is sequential as far as a user is concerned. One can use a source-level debugger to monitor the progress of a thread by executing one statement at a time, looking at the statement that will be executed next and checking the values of the variables and data structures as the execution progresses.

Threads have been used in programming for many years. If a programmer wants to start parallel execution in an application, he/she creates and manages multiple threads using thread libraries or special languages. In CUDA, the execution of each thread is sequential as well. A CUDA program initiates parallel execution by calling kernel functions, which causes the underlying runtime mechanisms to launch a grid of threads that process different parts of the data in parallel.

2.3 A vector addition kernel

We use vector addition to demonstrate the CUDA C program structure. Vector addition is arguably the simplest possible data parallel computation—the parallel equivalent of "Hello World" from sequential programming. Before we show the kernel code for vector addition, it is helpful to first review how a conventional vector addition (host code) function works. Fig. 2.4 shows a simple traditional

```
01   // Compute vector sum C_h = A_h + B_h
02   void vecAdd(float* A_h, float* B_h, float* C_h, int n) {
03       for (int i = 0; i < n; ++i) {
04           C_h[i] = A_h[i] + B_h[i];
05       }
06   }
07   int main() {
08       // Memory allocation for arrays A, B, and C
09       // I/O to read A and B, N elements each
10       ...
11       vecAdd(A, B, C, N);
12   }
```

FIGURE 2.4

A simple traditional vector addition C code example.

C program that consists of a main function and a vector addition function. In all our examples, whenever there is a need to distinguish between host and device data, we will suffix the names of variables that are used by the host with "_h" and those of variables that are used by a device with "_d" to remind ourselves of the intended usage of these variables. Since we have only host code in Fig. 2.4, we see only variables suffixed with "_h".

Pointers in the C Language

The function arguments A, B, and C in Fig. 2.4 *are pointers. In the C language, a pointer can be used to access variables and data structures. While a floating-point variable V can be declared with:*

   float V;

a pointer variable P can be declared with:

   float *P;

By assigning the address of V to P with the statement P = &V, we make P "point to" V. *P becomes a synonym for V. For example, U = *P assigns the value of V to U. For another example, *P = 3 changes the value of V to 3.

An array in a C program can be accessed through a pointer that points to its 0th element. For example, the statement P = &(A[0]) makes P point to the 0th element of array A. P[i] becomes a synonym for A[i]. In fact, the array name A is in itself a pointer to its 0th element.

In Fig. 2.4, *passing an array name A as the first argument to function call to vecAdd makes the function's first parameter A_h point to the 0th element of A. As a result, A_h[i] in the function body can be used to access A[i] for the array A in the main function.*

See Patt & Patel (Patt & Patel, 2020) *for an easy-to-follow explanation of the detailed usage of pointers in C.*

Assume that the vectors to be added are stored in arrays A and B that are allocated and initialized in the main program. The output vector is in array C, which is also allocated in the main program. For brevity we do not show the details of how A, B, and C are allocated or initialized in the main function. The pointers to these arrays are passed to the vecAdd function, along with the variable N that contains the length of the vectors. Note that the parameters of the vecAdd function are suffixed with "_h" to emphasize that they are used by the host. This naming convention will be helpful when we introduce device code in the next few steps.

The vecAdd function in Fig. 2.4 uses a `for-loop` to iterate through the vector elements. In the ith iteration, output element C_h[i] receives the sum of A_h[i] and B_h[i]. The vector length parameter n is used to control the loop so that the number of iterations matches the length of the vectors. The function reads the elements of A and B and writes the elements of C through the pointers A_h, B_h, and C_h, respectively. When the vecAdd function returns, the subsequent statements in the main function can access the new contents of C.

A straightforward way to execute vector addition in parallel is to modify the vecAdd function and move its calculations to a device. The structure of such a modified vecAdd function is shown in Fig. 2.5. Part 1 of the function allocates space in the device (GPU) memory to hold copies of the A, B, and C vectors and copies the A and B vectors from the host memory to the device memory. Part 2

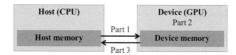

```
01      void vecAdd(float* A, float* B, float* C, int n) {
02          int  size = n* sizeof(float);
03          float  *d_A *d_B, *d_C;
04
05          // Part 1: Allocate device memory for A, B, and C
06          // Copy A and B to device memory
07          ...
08
09          // Part 2: Call kernel - to launch a grid of threads
10          // to perform the actual vector addition
11          ...
12
13          // Part 3: Copy C from the device memory
14          // Free device vectors
15          ...
16      }
```

FIGURE 2.5

Outline of a revised vecAdd function that moves the work to a device.

calls the actual vector addition kernel to launch a grid of threads on the device. Part 3 copies the sum vector C from the device memory to the host memory and deallocates the three arrays from the device memory.

Note that the revised vecAdd function is essentially an outsourcing agent that ships input data to a device, activates the calculation on the device, and collects the results from the device. The agent does so in such a way that the main program does not need to even be aware that the vector addition is now actually done on a device. In practice, such a "transparent" outsourcing model can be very inefficient because of all the copying of data back and forth. One would often keep large and important data structures on the device and simply invoke device functions on them from the host code. For now, however, we will use the simplified transparent model to introduce the basic CUDA C program structure. The details of the revised function, as well as the way to compose the kernel function, will be the topic of the rest of this chapter.

2.4 Device global memory and data transfer

In current CUDA systems, devices are often hardware cards that come with their own dynamic random-access memory called device *global* memory, or simply global memory. For example, the NVIDIA Volta V100 comes with 16GB or 32GB of global memory. Calling it "global" memory distinguishes it from other types of device memory that are also accessible to programmers. Details about the CUDA memory model and the different types of device memory are discussed in Chapter 5, Memory Architecture and Data Locality.

For the vector addition kernel, before calling the kernel, the programmer needs to allocate space in the device global memory and transfer data from the host memory to the allocated space in the device global memory. This corresponds to Part 1 of Fig. 2.5. Similarly, after device execution the programmer needs to transfer result data from the device global memory back to the host memory and free up the allocated space in the device global memory that is no longer needed. This corresponds to Part 3 of Fig. 2.5. The CUDA runtime system (typically running on the host) provides applications programming interface (API) functions to perform these activities on behalf of the programmer. From this point on, we will simply say that data is transferred from host to device as shorthand for saying that the data is copied from the host memory to the device global memory. The same holds for the opposite direction.

In Fig. 2.5, Part 1 and Part 3 of the vecAdd function need to use the CUDA API functions to allocate device global memory for A, B, and C; transfer A and B from host to device; transfer C from device to host after the vector addition; and free the device global memory for A, B, and C. We will explain the memory allocation and free functions first.

Fig. 2.6 shows two API functions for allocating and freeing device global memory. The cudaMalloc function can be called from the host code to allocate a piece

cudaMalloc()
- Allocates object in the device global memory
- Two parameters
  - o   **Address of a pointer** to the allocated object
  - o   **Size** of allocated object in terms of bytes

cudaFree()
- Frees object from device global memory
  - o   **Pointer** to freed object

FIGURE 2.6

CUDA API functions for managing device global memory.

of device global memory for an object. The reader should notice the striking similarity between `cudaMalloc` and the standard `C` runtime library malloc function. This is intentional; CUDA C is C with minimal extensions. CUDA C uses the standard C runtime library malloc function to manage the host memory[2] and adds `cudaMalloc` as an extension to the C runtime library. By keeping the interface as close to the original C runtime libraries as possible, CUDA C minimizes the time that a C programmer spends relearning the use of these extensions.

The first parameter to the `cudaMalloc` function is the **address** of a pointer variable that will be set to point to the allocated object. The address of the pointer variable should be cast to (void **) because the function expects a generic pointer; the memory allocation function is a generic function that is not restricted to any particular type of objects.[3] This parameter allows the `cudaMalloc` function to write the address of the allocated memory into the provided pointer variable regardless of its type.[4] The host code that calls kernels passes this pointer value to the kernels that need to access the allocated memory object. The second parameter to the `cudaMalloc` function gives the size of the data to be allocated, in number of bytes. The usage of this second parameter is consistent with the size parameter to the C malloc function.

We now use the following simple code example to illustrate the use of `cudaMalloc` and `cudaFree`:

```
float *A_d
int size=n*sizeof(float);
cudaMalloc((void**)&A_d, size);
...
cudaFree(A_d);
```

[2] CUDA C also has more advanced library functions for allocating space in the host memory. We will discuss them in Chapter 20, Programming a Heterogeneous Computing Cluster.

[3] The fact that `cudaMalloc` returns a generic object makes the use of dynamically allocated multidimensional arrays more complex. We will address this issue in Section 3.2.

[4] Note that `cudaMalloc` has a different format from the C malloc function. The C malloc function returns a pointer to the allocated object. It takes only one parameter that specifies the size of the allocated object. The `cudaMalloc` function writes to the pointer variable whose address is given as the first parameter. As a result, the `cudaMalloc` function takes two parameters. The two-parameter format of `cudaMalloc` allows it to use the return value to report any errors in the same way as other CUDA API functions.

This is a continuation of the example in Fig. 2.5. For clarity we suffix a pointer variable with "_d" to indicate that it points to an object in the device global memory. The first argument passed to `cudaMalloc` is the **address** of pointer A_d (i.e., &A_d) casted to a void pointer. When `cudaMalloc`, returns, A_d will point to the device global memory region allocated for the A vector. The second argument passed to `cudaMalloc` is the size of the region to be allocated. Since size is in number of bytes, the programmer needs to translate from the number of elements in an array to the number of bytes when determining the value of size. For example, in allocating space for an array of n single-precision floating-point elements, the value of size would be n times the size of a single-precision floating number, which is 4 bytes in computers today. Therefore the value of size would be $n*4$. After the computation, cudaFree is called with pointer A_d as an argument to free the storage space for the A vector from the device global memory. Note that cudaFree does not need to change the value of A_d; it only needs to use the value of A_d to return the allocated memory back to the available pool. Thus only the value and not the address of A_d is passed as an argument.

The addresses in A_d, B_d, and C_d point to locations in the device global memory. These addresses should not be dereferenced in the host code. They should be used in calling API functions and kernel functions. Dereferencing a device global memory pointer in host code can cause exceptions or other types of runtime errors.

The reader should complete Part 1 of the `vecAdd` example in Fig. 2.5 with similar declarations of B_d and C_d pointer variables as well as their corresponding `cudaMalloc` calls. Furthermore, Part 3 in Fig. 2.5 can be completed with the `cudaFree` calls for B_d and C_d.

Once the host code has allocated space in the device global memory for the data objects, it can request that data be transferred from host to device. This is accomplished by calling one of the CUDA API functions. Fig. 2.7 shows such an API function, `cudaMemcpy`. The `cudaMemcpy` function takes four parameters. The first parameter is a pointer to the destination location for the data object to be copied. The second parameter points to the source location. The third parameter specifies the number of bytes to be copied. The fourth parameter indicates the types of memory involved in the copy: from host to host, from host to device, from device to host, and from device to device. For example, the memory copy function can be used to copy data from one location in the device global memory to another location in the device global memory.

cudaMemcpy()
- memory data transfer
- Requires four parameters
  - Pointer to destination
  - Pointer to source
  - Number of bytes copied
  - Type/Direction of transfer

FIGURE 2.7

CUDA API function for data transfer between host and device.

The vecAdd function calls the cudaMemcpy function to copy the A_h and B_h vectors from the host memory to A_d and B_d in the device memory before adding them and to copy the C_d vector from the device memory to C_h in the host memory after the addition has been done. Assuming that the values of A_h, B_h, A_d, B_d, and size have already been set as we discussed before, the three cudaMemcpy calls are shown below. The two symbolic constants, cudaMemcpyHostToDevice and cudaMemcpyDeviceToHost, are recognized, predefined constants of the CUDA programming environment. Note that the same function can be used to transfer data in both directions by properly ordering the source and destination pointers and using the appropriate constant for the transfer type.

```
cudaMemcpy(A_d, A_h, size, cudaMemcpyHostToDevice);
cudaMemcpy(B_d, B_h, size, cudaMemcpyHostToDevice);
...
cudaMemcpy(C_h, C_d, size, cudaMemcpyDeviceToHost);
```

To summarize, the main program in Fig. 2.4 calls vecAdd, which is also executed on the host. The vecAdd function, outlined in Fig. 2.5, allocates space in device global memory, requests data transfers, and calls the kernel that performs the actual vector addition. We refer to this type of host code as a *stub* for calling a kernel. We show a more complete version of the vecAdd function in Fig. 2.8.

```
01    void vecAdd(float* A_h, float* B_h, float* C_h, int n) {
02        int size = n * sizeof(float);
03        float *A_d, *B_d, *C_d;
04
05        cudaMalloc((void **) &A_d, size);
06        cudaMalloc((void **) &B_d, size);
07        cudaMalloc((void **) &C_d, size);
08
09        cudaMemcpy(A_d, A_h, size, cudaMemcpyHostToDevice);
10        cudaMemcpy(B_d, B_h, size, cudaMemcpyHostToDevice);
11
12        // Kernel invocation code - to be shown later
13        ...
14
15        cudaMemcpy(C_h, C_d, size, cudaMemcpyDeviceToHost);
16
17        cudaFree(A_d);
18        cudaFree(B_d);
19        cudaFree(C_d);
20    }
```

FIGURE 2.8

A more complete version of vecAdd().

Compared to Fig. 2.5, the `vecAdd` function in Fig. 2.8 is complete for Part 1 and Part 3. Part 1 allocates device global memory for `A_d`, `B_d`, and `C_d` and transfers `A_h` to `A_d` and `B_h` to `B_d`. This is done by calling the `cudaMalloc` and `cudaMemcpy` functions. The readers are encouraged to write their own function calls with the appropriate parameter values and compare their code with that shown in Fig. 2.8. Part 2 calls the kernel and will be described in the following subsection. Part 3 copies the vector sum data from the device to the host so that the values will be available in the main function. This is accomplished with a call to the `cudaMemcpy` function. It then frees the memory for `A_d`, `B_d`, and `C_d` from the device global memory, which is done by calls to the `cudaFree` function (Fig. 2.9).

Error Checking and Handling in CUDA

In general, it is important for a program to check and handle errors. CUDA API functions return flags that indicate whether an error has occurred when they served the request. Most errors are due to inappropriate argument values used in the call.

For brevity, we will not show error checking code in our examples. For example, Fig. 2.9 shows a call to cudaMalloc:

cudaMalloc((void**) &A_d, size);

In practice, we should surround the call with code that test for error condition and print out error messages so that the user can be aware of the fact that an error has occurred. A simple version of such checking code is as follows:

```
cudaError_t    err = cudaMalloc((void**) &A_d, size);
if (error! = cudaSuccess)    {
    printf("%s in %s at line %d\n",     cudaGetErrorString(err),
    __FILE__, __LINE__);
    exit(EXIT_FAILURE);
}
```

This way, if the system is out of device memory, the user will be informed about the situation. This can save many hours of debugging time.

One could define a C macro to make the checking code more concise in the source.

2.5 Kernel functions and threading

We are now ready to discuss more about the CUDA C kernel functions and the effect of calling these kernel functions. In CUDA C, a kernel function specifies the code to be executed by all threads during a parallel phase. Since all these threads execute the same code, CUDA C programming is an instance of the well-known single-program multiple-data (SPMD) (Atallah, 1998) parallel programming style, a popular programming style for parallel computing systems.[5]

When a program's host code calls a kernel, the CUDA runtime system launches a grid of threads that are organized into a two-level hierarchy. Each grid is organized as an array of *thread blocks*, which we will refer to as blocks for brevity. All blocks of a grid are of the same size; each block can contain up to 1024 threads on current systems.[6] Fig. 2.9 shows an example in which each block consists of 256 threads. Each thread is represented by a curly arrow stemming from a box that is labeled with the thread's index number in the block.

Built-in Variables

Many programming languages have built-in variables. These variables have special meaning and purpose. The values of these variables are often pre-initialized by the runtime system and are typically read-only in the program. The programmers should refrain from redefining these variables for any other purposes.

The total number of threads in each thread block is specified by the host code when a kernel is called. The same kernel can be called with different numbers of threads at different parts of the host code. For a given grid of threads, the number of threads in a block is available in a built-in variable named blockDim. The blockDim variable is a struct with three unsigned integer fields (x, y, and z) that help the programmer to organize the threads into a one-, two-, or three-dimensional array. For a one-dimensional organization, only the x field is used. For a two-dimensional organization, the x and y fields are used. For a three-dimensional structure, all three x, y, and z fields are used. The choice of dimensionality for organizing threads usually reflects the dimensionality of the data. This makes sense because the threads are created to process data in parallel, so it is only natural that the organization of the threads reflects the organization of the data. In Fig. 2.9, each thread block is organized as a one-dimensional array of threads because the data are one-dimensional vectors. The value of the blockDim.x variable indicates the total number of threads in each block, which is 256 in Fig. 2.9. In general, it is recommended that the number of threads in each dimension of a thread block be a multiple of 32 for hardware efficiency reasons. We will revisit this later.

---

[5] Note that SPMD is not the same as SIMD (single instruction multiple data) [Flynn 1972]. In an SPMD system the parallel processing units execute the same program on multiple parts of the data. However, these processing units do not need to be executing the same instruction at the same time. In an SIMD system, all processing units are executing the same instruction at any instant.

[6] Each thread block can have up to 1024 threads in CUDA 3.0 and beyond. Some earlier CUDA versions allow only up to 512 threads in a block.

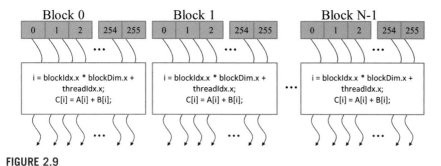

FIGURE 2.9

All threads in a grid execute the same kernel code.

CUDA kernels have access to two more built-in variables (`threadIdx` and `blockIdx`) that allow threads to distinguish themselves from each other and to determine the area of data each thread is to work on. The `threadIdx` variable gives each thread a unique coordinate within a block. In Fig. 2.9, since we are using a one-dimensional thread organization, only `threadIdx.x` is used. The `threadIdx.x` value for each thread is shown in the small shaded box of each thread in Fig. 2.9. The first thread in each block has value 0 in its `threadIdx.x` variable, the second thread has value 1, the third thread has value 2, and so on.

Hierarchical Organizations

Like CUDA threads, many real-world systems are organized hierarchically. The U.S. telephone system is a good example. At the top level, the telephone system consists of "areas" each of which corresponds to a geographical area. All telephone lines within the same area have the same 3-digit "area code". A telephone area is sometimes larger than a city. For example, many counties and cities of central Illinois are within the same telephone area and share the same area code 217. Within an area, each phone line has a seven-digit local phone number, which allows each area to have a maximum of about ten million numbers.

One can think of each phone line as a CUDA thread, with the area code as the value of blockIdx and the seven-digital local number as the value of threadIdx. This hierarchical organization allows the system to have a very large number of phone lines while preserving "locality" for calling the same area. That is, when dialing a phone line in the same area, a caller only needs to dial the local number. As long as we make most of our calls within the local area, we seldom need to dial the area code. If we occasionally need to call a phone line in another area, we dial 1 and the area code, followed by the local number. (This is the reason why no local number in any area should start with a 1.) The hierarchical organization of CUDA threads also offers a form of locality. We will study this locality soon.

The blockIdx variable gives all threads in a block a common block coordinate. In Fig. 2.9, all threads in the first block have value 0 in their blockIdx.x variables, those in the second thread block value 1, and so on. Using an analogy with the telephone system, one can think of threadIdx.x as local phone number and blockIdx.x as area code. The two together gives each telephone line in the whole country a unique phone number. Similarly, each thread can combine its threadIdx and blockIdx values to create a unique global index for itself within the entire grid.

In Fig. 2.9 a unique global index i is calculated as i=blockIdx.x * blockDim.x + threadIdx.x. Recall that blockDim is 256 in our example. The i values of threads in block 0 range from 0 to 255. The i values of threads in block 1 range from 256 to 511. The i values of threads in block 2 range from 512 to 767. That is, the i values of the threads in these three blocks form a continuous coverage of the values from 0 to 767. Since each thread uses i to access A, B, and C, these threads cover the first 768 iterations of the original loop. By launching a grid with a larger number of blocks, one can process larger vectors. By launching a grid with n or more threads, one can process vectors of length n.

Fig. 2.10 shows a kernel function for vector addition. Note that we do not use the "_h" and "_d" convention in kernels, since there is no potential confusion. We will not have any access to the host memory in our examples. The syntax of a kernel is ANSI C with some notable extensions. First, there is a CUDA-C-specific keyword "__global__" in front of the declaration of the vecAddKernel function. This keyword indicates that the function is a kernel and that it can be called to generate a grid of threads on a device.

In general, CUDA C extends the C language with three qualifier keywords that can be used in function declarations. The meaning of these keywords is summarized in Fig. 2.11. The "__global__" keyword indicates that the function being declared is a CUDA C kernel function. Note that there are two underscore characters on each side of the word "global." Such a kernel function is executed on the device and can be called from the host. In CUDA systems that support *dynamic parallelism*, it can also be called from the device, as we will see in Chapter 21,

```
01    // Compute vector sum C = A + B
02    // Each thread performs one pair-wise addition
03    __global__
04    void vecAddKernel(float* A, float* B, float* C, int n) {
05        int i = threadIdx.x + blockDim.x * blockIdx.x;
06        if (i < n) {
07            C[i] = A[i] + B[i];
08        }
09    }
```

FIGURE 2.10

A vector addition kernel function.

Qualifier Keyword	Callable From	Executed On	Executed By
__host__ (default)	Host	Host	Caller host thread
__global__	Host (or Device)	Device	New grid of device threads
__device__	Device	Device	Caller device thread

FIGURE 2.11

CUDA C keywords for function declaration.

CUDA Dynamic Parallelism. The important feature is that calling such a kernel function results in a new grid of threads being launched on the device.

The "__device__" keyword indicates that the function being declared is a CUDA device function. A device function executes on a CUDA device and can be called only from a kernel function or another device function. The device function is executed by the device thread that calls it and does not result in any new device threads being launched.[7]

The "__host__" keyword indicates that the function being declared is a CUDA host function. A host function is simply a traditional C function that executes on the host and can be called only from another host function. By default, all functions in a CUDA program are host functions if they do not have any of the CUDA keywords in their declaration. This makes sense, since many CUDA applications are ported from CPU-only execution environments. The programmer would add kernel functions and device functions during the porting process. The original functions remain as host functions. Having all functions to default into host functions spares the programmer the tedious work of changing all original function declarations.

Note that one can use both "__host__" and "__device__" in a function declaration. This combination tells the compilation system to generate two versions of object code for the same function. One is executed on the host and can be called only from a host function. The other is executed on the device and can be called only from a device or kernel function. This supports a common use case when the same function source code can be recompiled to generate a device version. Many user library functions will likely fall into this category.

The second notable extension to C, in Fig. 2.10, is the built-in variables "threadIdx," "blockIdx," and "blockDim." Recall that all threads execute the same kernel code and there needs to be a way for them to distinguish themselves from each other and direct each thread toward a particular part of the data. These built-in variables are the means for threads to access hardware registers that provide the

---

[7] We will explain the rules for using indirect function calls and recursions in different generations of CUDA later. In general, one should avoid the use of recursion and indirect function calls in their device functions and kernel functions to allow maximal portability.

identifying coordinates to threads. Different threads will see different values in their threadIdx.x, blockIdx.x, and blockDim.x variables. For readability we will sometimes refer to a thread as thread$_{blockIdx.x, threadIdx.x}$ in our discussions.

There is an automatic (local) variable i in Fig. 2.10. In a CUDA kernel function, automatic variables are private to each thread. That is, a version of i will be generated for every thread. If the grid is launched with 10,000 threads, there will be 10,000 versions of i, one for each thread. The value assigned by a thread to its i variable is not visible to other threads. We will discuss these automatic variables in more details in Chapter 5, Memory Architecture and Data Locality.

A quick comparison between Fig. 2.4 and Fig. 2.10 reveals an important insight into CUDA kernels. The kernel function in Fig. 2.10 does not have a loop that corresponds to the one in Fig. 2.4. The reader should ask where the loop went. The answer is that the loop is now replaced with the grid of threads. The entire grid forms the equivalent of the loop. Each thread in the grid corresponds to one iteration of the original loop. This is sometimes referred to as *loop parallelism*, in which iterations of the original sequential code are executed by threads in parallel.

Note that there is an if $(i < n)$ statement in addVecKernel in Fig. 2.10. This is because not all vector lengths can be expressed as multiples of the block size. For example, let's assume that the vector length is 100. The smallest efficient thread block dimension is 32. Assume that we picked 32 as block size. One would need to launch four thread blocks to process all the 100 vector elements. However, the four thread blocks would have 128 threads. We need to disable the last 28 threads in thread block 3 from doing work not expected by the original program. Since all threads are to execute the same code, all will test their i values against n, which is 100. With the if $(i < n)$ statement, the first 100 threads will perform the addition, whereas the last 28 will not. This allows the kernel to be called to process vectors of arbitrary lengths.

2.6 Calling kernel functions

Having implemented the kernel function, the remaining step is to call that function from the host code to launch the grid. This is illustrated in Fig. 2.12. When the host code calls a kernel, it sets the grid and thread block dimensions via *execution*

```
01    int vectAdd(float* A, float* B, float* C, int n) {
02        // A_d, B_d, C_d allocations and copies omitted
03        ...
04        // Launch ceil(n/256) blocks of 256 threads each
05        vecAddKernel<<<ceil(n/256.0), 256>>>(A_d, B_d, C_d, n);
06    }
```

FIGURE 2.12

A vector addition kernel call statement.

```
01   void vecAdd(float* A, float* B, float* C, int n) {
02       float *A_d, *B_d, *C_d;
03       int size = n * sizeof(float);
04
05       cudaMalloc((void **) &A_d, size);
06       cudaMalloc((void **) &B_d, size);
07       cudaMalloc((void **) &C_d, size);
08
09       cudaMemcpy(A_d, A, size, cudaMemcpyHostToDevice);
10       cudaMemcpy(B_d, B, size, cudaMemcpyHostToDevice);
11
12       vecAddKernel<<<ceil(n/256.0), 256>>>(A_d, B_d, C_d, n);
13
14       cudaMemcpy(C, C_d, size, cudaMemcpyDeviceToHost);
15
16       cudaFree(A_d);
17       cudaFree(B_d);
18       cudaFree(C_d);
19   }
```

FIGURE 2.13

A complete version of the host code in the vecAdd function.

configuration parameters. The configuration parameters are given between the " $<<<$ " and " $>>>$ " before the traditional C function arguments. The first configuration parameter gives the number of blocks in the grid. The second specifies the number of threads in each block. In this example there are 256 threads in each block. To ensure that we have enough threads in the grid to cover all the vector elements, we need to set the number of blocks in the grid to the ceiling division (rounding up the quotient to the immediate higher integer value) of the desired number of threads (n in this case) by the thread block size (256 in this case). There are many ways to perform a ceiling division. One way is to apply the C ceiling function to $n/256.0$. Using the floating-point value 256.0 ensures that we generate a floating value for the division so that the ceiling function can round it up correctly. For example, if we want 1000 threads, we would launch ceil(1000/256.0) = 4 thread blocks. As a result, the statement will launch $4 \times 256 = 1024$ threads. With the if ($i < n$) statement in the kernel as shown in Fig. 2.10, the first 1000 threads will perform addition on the 1000 vector elements. The remaining 24 will not.

Fig. 2.13 shows the final host code in the vecAdd function. This source code completes the skeleton in Fig. 2.5. Figs. 2.12 and 2.13 jointly illustrate a simple CUDA program that consists of both host code and a device kernel. The code is hardwired to use thread blocks of 256 threads each.[8] However, the number of thread blocks used depends on the length of the vectors (n). If n is 750, three thread blocks will be used. If n is 4000, 16 thread blocks will be used. If n is 2,000,000, 7813 blocks will be used. Note that all the thread blocks operate on different parts of the vectors. They can be executed in any arbitrary order. The programmer must not make any assumptions regarding execution order. A small GPU with a small amount of execution resources may execute only one or two of these thread blocks in parallel. A larger GPU may execute 64 or 128 blocks in parallel. This gives CUDA kernels scalability in execution speed with hardware. That is, the same code

---

[8] While we use an arbitrary block size 256 in this example, the block size should be determined by a number of factors that will be introduced later.

runs at lower speed on small GPUs and at higher speed on larger GPUs. We will revisit this point in Chapter 4, Compute Architecture and Scheduling.

It is important to point out again that the vector addition example is used for its simplicity. In practice, the overhead of allocating device memory, input data transfer from host to device, output data transfer from device to host, and deallo- cating device memory will likely make the resulting code slower than the original sequential code in Fig. 2.4. This is because the amount of calculation that is done by the kernel is small relative to the amount of data processed or transferred. Only one addition is performed for two floating-point input operands and one floating-point output operand. Real applications typically have kernels in which much more work is needed relative to the amount of data processed, which makes the additional overhead worthwhile. Real applications also tend to keep the data in the device memory across multiple kernel invocations so that the overhead can be amortized. We will present several examples of such applications.

2.7 Compilation

We have seen that implementing CUDA C kernels requires using various exten- sions that are not part of C. Once these extensions have been used in the code, it is no longer acceptable to a traditional C compiler. The code needs to be com- piled by a compiler that recognizes and understands these extensions, such as NVCC (NVIDIA C compiler). As is shown at the top of Fig. 2.14, the NVCC

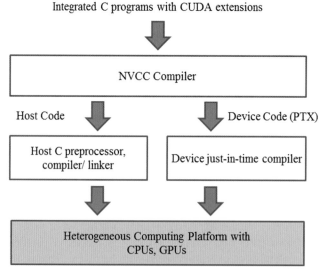

FIGURE 2.14

Overview of the compilation process of a CUDA C program.

compiler processes a CUDA C program, using the CUDA keywords to separate the host code and device code. The host code is straight ANSI C code, which is compiled with the host's standard C/C++ compilers and is run as a traditional CPU process. The device code, which is marked with CUDA keywords that designate CUDA kernels and their associated helper functions and data structures, is compiled by NVCC into virtual binary files called PTX files. These PTX files are further compiled by a runtime component of NVCC into the real object files and executed on a CUDA-capable GPU device.

2.8 Summary

This chapter provided a quick, simplified overview of the CUDA C programming model. CUDA C extends the C language to support parallel computing. We discussed an essential subset of these extensions in this chapter. For your convenience we summarize the extensions that we have discussed in this chapter as follows:

2.8.1 Function declarations

CUDA C extends the C function declaration syntax to support heterogeneous parallel computing. The extensions are summarized in Fig. 2.12. Using one of "__global__," "__device__," or "__host__," a CUDA C programmer can instruct the compiler to generate a kernel function, a device function, or a host function. All function declarations without any of these keywords default to host functions. If both "__host__" and "__device__" are used in a function declaration, the compiler generates two versions of the function, one for the device and one for the host. If a function declaration does not have any CUDA C extension keyword, the function defaults into a host function.

2.8.2 Kernel call and grid launch

CUDA C extends the C function call syntax with kernel execution configuration parameters surrounded by $<<<$ and $>>>$. These execution configuration parameters are only used when calling a kernel function to launch a grid. We discussed the execution configuration parameters that define the dimensions of the grid and the dimensions of each block. The reader should refer to the CUDA Programming Guide (NVIDIA, 2021) for more details of the kernel launch extensions as well as other types of execution configuration parameters.

2.8.3 Built-in (predefined) variables

CUDA kernels can access a set of built-in, predefined read-only variables that allow each thread to distinguish itself from other threads and to determine the area of data to work on. We discussed the `threadIdx`, `blockDim`, and `blockIdx` variables in this chapter. In Chapter 3, Multidimensional Grids and Data, we will discuss more details of using these variables.

2.8.4 Runtime application programming interface

CUDA supports a set of API functions to provide services to CUDA C programs. The services that we discussed in this chapter are `cudaMalloc`, `cudaFree`, and `cudaMemcpy` functions. These functions are called by the host code to allocate device global memory, deallocate device global memory, and transfer data between host and device on behalf of the calling program, respectively. The reader is referred to the CUDA C Programming Guide for other CUDA API functions.

Our goal for this chapter is to introduce the core concepts of CUDA C and the essential CUDA extensions to C for writing a simple CUDA C program. The chapter is by no means a comprehensive account of all CUDA features. Some of these features will be covered in the remainder of the book. However, our emphasis will be on the key parallel computing concepts that are supported by these features. We will introduce only the CUDA C features that are needed in our code examples for parallel programming techniques. In general, we would like to encourage the reader to always consult the CUDA C Programming Guide for more details of the CUDA C features.

Exercises

1. If we want to use each thread in a grid to calculate one output element of a vector addition, what would be the expression for mapping the thread/block indices to the data index (i)?

   (A) `i=threadIdx.x + threadIdx.y;`

   (B) `i=blockIdx.x + threadIdx.x;`

   (C) `i=blockIdx.x*blockDim.x + threadIdx.x;`

   (D) `i=blockIdx.x * threadIdx.x;`

2. Assume that we want to use each thread to calculate two adjacent elements of a vector addition. What would be the expression for mapping the thread/block indices to the data index (i) of the first element to be processed by a thread?

   (A) `i=blockIdx.x*blockDim.x + threadIdx.x +2;`

   (B) `i=blockIdx.x*threadIdx.x*2;`

   (C) `i=(blockIdx.x*blockDim.x + threadIdx.x)*2;`

   (D) `i=blockIdx.x*blockDim.x*2 + threadIdx.x;`

3. We want to use each thread to calculate two elements of a vector addition. Each thread block processes `2*blockDim.x` consecutive elements that form two sections. All threads in each block will process a section first, each processing one element. They will then all move to the next section, each

processing one element. Assume that variable i should be the index for the first element to be processed by a thread. What would be the expression for mapping the thread/block indices to data index of the first element?

(A) i=blockIdx.x*blockDim.x + threadIdx.x +2;

(B) i=blockIdx.x*threadIdx.x*2;

(C) i=(blockIdx.x*blockDim.x + threadIdx.x)*2;

(D) i=blockIdx.x*blockDim.x*2 + threadIdx.x;

4. For a vector addition, assume that the vector length is 8000, each thread calculates one output element, and the thread block size is 1024 threads. The programmer configures the kernel call to have a minimum number of thread blocks to cover all output elements. How many threads will be in the grid?

(A) 8000

(B) 8196

(C) 8192

(D) 8200

5. 5. If we want to allocate an array of v integer elements in the CUDA device global memory, what would be an appropriate expression for the second argument of the cudaMalloc call?

(A) n

(B) v

(C) n * sizeof(int)

(D) v * sizeof(int)

6. If we want to allocate an array of n floating-point elements and have a floating-point pointer variable A_d to point to the allocated memory, what would be an appropriate expression for the first argument of the cudaMalloc () call?

(A) n

(B) (void *) A_d

(C) *A_d

(D) (void **) &A_d

7. If we want to copy 3000 bytes of data from host array A_h (A_h is a pointer to element 0 of the source array) to device array A_d (A_d is a pointer to element 0 of the destination array), what would be an appropriate API call for this data copy in CUDA?

(A) cudaMemcpy(3000, A_h, A_d, cudaMemcpyHostToDevice);

(B) cudaMemcpy(A_h, A_d, 3000, cudaMemcpyDeviceTHost);

(C) cudaMemcpy(A_d, A_h, 3000, cudaMemcpyHostToDevice);

(D) cudaMemcpy(3000, A_d, A_h, cudaMemcpyHostToDevice);

8. How would one declare a variable err that can appropriately receive the returned value of a CUDA API call?

(A) int err;

(B) cudaError err;

(C) cudaError_t err;

(D) cudaSuccess_t err;

9. Consider the following CUDA kernel and the corresponding host function that calls it:

```
01          __global__ void foo_kernel(float* a, float* b, unsigned int N){
02                  unsigned int i=blockIdx.x*blockDim.x + threadIdx.x;
03                      if(i < N) {
04                          b[i]=2.7f*a[i] - 4.3f;
05                      }
06              }
07          void foo(float* a_d, float* b_d) {
08                  unsigned int N=200000;
09                  foo_kernel <<< (N + 128-1)/128, 128 >>>(a_d, b_d, N);
10              }
```

   a. What is the number of threads per block?
   b. What is the number of threads in the grid?
   c. What is the number of blocks in the grid?
   d. What is the number of threads that execute the code on line 02?
   e. What is the number of threads that execute the code on line 04?

10. A new summer intern was frustrated with CUDA. He has been complaining that CUDA is very tedious. He had to declare many functions that he plans to execute on both the host and the device twice, once as a host function and once as a device function. What is your response?

References

Atallah, M.J. (Ed.), 1998. Algorithms and Theory of Computation Handbook. CRC Press.

Flynn, M., 1972. Some computer organizations and their effectiveness. IEEE Trans. Comput. **C-** 21, 948.

NVIDIA Corporation, March 2021. NVIDIA CUDA C Programming Guide.

Patt, Y.N., Patel, S.J., 2020. ISBN-10: 1260565912, 2000, 2004 Introduction to Computing Systems: From Bits and Gates to C and Beyond. McGraw Hill Publisher.

Multidimensional grids and data

3

Chapter Outline

3.1 Multidimensional grid organization 47
3.2 Mapping threads to multidimensional data 51
3.3 Image blur: a more complex kernel 58
3.4 Matrix multiplication 62
3.5 Summary 66
Exercises 67

In Chapter 2, Heterogeneous Data Parallel Computing, we learned to write a simple CUDA C + + program that launches a one-dimensional grid of threads by calling a kernel function to operate on elements of one-dimensional arrays. A kernel specifies the statements that are executed by each individual thread in the grid. In this chapter, we will look more generally at how threads are organized and learn how threads and blocks can be used to process multidimensional arrays. Multiple examples will be used throughout the chapter, including converting a colored image to a grayscale image, blurring an image, and matrix multiplication. These examples also serve to familiarize the reader with reasoning about data parallelism before we proceed to discuss the GPU architecture, memory organization, and performance optimizations in the upcoming chapters.

3.1 Multidimensional grid organization

In CUDA, all threads in a grid execute the same kernel function, and they rely on coordinates, that is, thread indices, to distinguish themselves from each other and to identify the appropriate portion of the data to process. As we saw in Chapter 2, Heterogeneous Data Parallel Computing, these threads are organized into a two-level hierarchy: A grid consists of one or more blocks, and each block consists of one or more threads. All threads in a block share the same block index, which can be accessed via the `blockIdx` (built-in) variable. Each thread also has a thread index, which can be accessed via the `threadIdx` (built-in) variable. When a thread executes a kernel function, references to the `blockIdx` and `threadIdx` variables return the

Programming Massively Parallel Processors. DOI: https://doi.org/10.1016/B978-0-323-91231-0.00004-5

coordinates of the thread. The execution configuration parameters in a kernel call statement specify the dimensions of the grid and the dimensions of each block. These dimensions are available via the `gridDim` and `blockDim` (built-in) variables.

In general, a grid is a three-dimensional (3D) array of blocks, and each block is a 3D array of threads. When calling a kernel, the program needs to specify the size of the grid and the blocks in each dimension. These are specified by using the execution configuration parameters (within $<<<...>>>$) of the kernel call statement. The first execution configuration parameter specifies the dimensions of the grid in number of blocks. The second specifies the dimensions of each block in number of threads. Each such parameter has the type `dim3`, which is an integer vector type of three elements x, y, and z. These three elements specify the sizes of the three dimensions. The programmer can use fewer than three dimensions by setting the size of the unused dimensions to 1.

For example, the following host code can be used to call the `vecAddkernel()` kernel function and generate a 1D grid that consists of 32 blocks, each of which consists of 128 threads. The total number of threads in the grid is $128*32 = 4096$:

```
dim3 dimGrid(32, 1, 1);
dim3 dimBlock(128, 1, 1);
vecAddKernel<<<dimGrid, dimBlock>>>(...);
```

Note that `dimBlock` and `dimGrid` are host code variables that are defined by the programmer. These variables can have any legal C variable name as long as they have the type `dim3`. For example, the following statements accomplish the same result as the statements above:

```
dim3 dog(32, 1, 1);
dim3 cat(128, 1, 1);
vecAddKernel<<<dog, cat>>>(...);
```

The grid and block dimensions can also be calculated from other variables. For example, the kernel call in Fig. 2.12 can be written as follows:

```
dim3 dimGrid(ceil(n/256.0), 1, 1);
dim3 dimBlock(256, 1, 1);
vecAddKernel<<<dimGrid, dimBlock>>>(...);
```

This allows the number of blocks to vary with the size of the vectors so that the grid will have enough threads to cover all vector elements. In this example the programmer chose to fix the block size at 256. The value of variable n at kernel call time will determine dimension of the grid. If n is equal to 1000, the grid will consist of four blocks. If n is equal to 4000, the grid will have 16 blocks. In each case, there will be enough threads to cover all the vector elements. Once the grid has been launched, the grid and block dimensions will remain the same until the entire grid has finished execution.

For convenience, CUDA provides a special shortcut for calling a kernel with one-dimensional (1D) grids and blocks. Instead of using dim3 variables, one can use arithmetic expressions to specify the configuration of 1D grids and blocks. In this case, the CUDA compiler simply takes the arithmetic expression as the x dimensions and assumes that the y and z dimensions are 1. This gives us the kernel call statement shown in Fig. 2.12:

```
vecAddKernel<<<ceil(n/256.0), 256>>>(...);
```

Readers who are familiar with C++ would realize that this "shorthand" convention for 1D configurations takes advantage of how C++ constructors and default parameters work. The default values of the parameters to the `dim3` constructor are 1. When a single value is passed where a `dim3` is expected, that value will be passed to the first parameter of the constructor, while the second and third parameters take the default value of 1. The result is a 1D grid or block in which the size of the x dimension is the value passed and the sizes of the y and z dimensions are 1.

Within the kernel function, the x field of variables `gridDim` and `blockDim` are preinitialized according to the values of the execution configuration parameters. For example, if n is equal to 4000, references to `gridDim.x` and `blockDim.x` in the `vectAddkernel` kernel will result in 16 and 256, respectively. Note that unlike the `dim3` variables in the host code, the names of these variables within the kernel functions are part of the CUDA C specification and cannot be changed. That is, the `gridDim` and `blockDim` are built-in variables in a kernel and always reflect the dimensions of the grid and the blocks, respectively.

In CUDA C the allowed values of `gridDim.x` range from 1 to $2^{31} - 1$,[1] and those of `gridDim.y` and `gridDim.z` range from 1 to $2^{16} - 1$ (65,535). All threads in a block share the same `blockIdx.x`, `blockIdx.y`, and `blockIdx.z` values. Among blocks, the `blockIdx.x` value ranges from 0 to `gridDim.x-1`, the `blockIdx.y` value ranges from 0 to `gridDim.y-1`, and the `blockIdx.z` value ranges from 0 to `gridDim.z-1`.

We now turn our attention to the configuration of blocks. Each block is organized into a 3D array of threads. Two-dimensional (2D) blocks can be created by setting `blockDim.z` to 1. One-dimension blocks can be created by setting both `blockDim.y` and `blockDim.z` to 1, as in the `vectorAddkernel` example. As we mentioned before, all blocks in a grid have the same dimensions and sizes. The number of threads in each dimension of a block is specified by the second execution configuration parameter at the kernel call. Within the kernel this configuration parameter can be accessed as the x, y, and z fields of `blockDim`.

The total size of a block in current CUDA systems is limited to 1024 threads. These threads can be distributed across the three dimensions in any way as long as the total number of threads does not exceed 1024. For example, `blockDim`

---

[1] Devices with a capability of less than 3.0 allow blockIdx.x to range from 1 to $2^{16} - 1$.

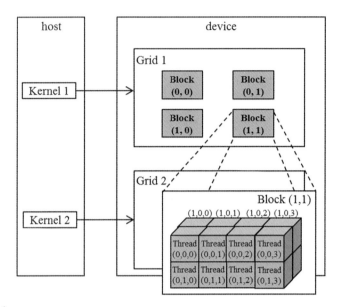

FIGURE 3.1

A multidimensional example of CUDA grid organization.

values of (512, 1, 1), (8, 16, 4), and (32, 16, 2) are all allowed, but (32, 32, 2) is not allowed because the total number of threads would exceed 1024.

A grid and its blocks do not need to have the same dimensionality. A grid can have higher dimensionality than its blocks and vice versa. For example, Fig. 3.1 shows a small toy grid example with a `gridDim` of (2, 2, 1) and a `blockDim` of (4, 2, 2). Such a grid can be created with the following host code:

```
dim3 dimGrid(2, 2, 1);
dim3 dimBlock(4, 2, 2);
KernelFunction<<<dimGrid, dimBlock>>>(...);
```

The grid in Fig. 3.1 consists of four blocks organized into a 2 × 2 array. Each block is labeled with (`blockIdx.y`, `blockIdx.x`). For example, block (1,0) has `blockIdx.y = 1` and `blockIdx.x = 0`. Note that the ordering of the block and thread labels is such that highest dimension comes first. This notation uses an ordering that is the reverse of that used in the C statements for setting configuration parameters, in which the lowest dimension comes first. This reversed ordering for labeling blocks works better when we illustrate the mapping of thread coordinates into data indexes in accessing multidimensional data.

Each `threadIdx` also consists of three fields: the x coordinate `threadId.x`, the y coordinate `threadIdx.y`, and the z coordinate `threadIdx.z`. Fig. 3.1 illustrates the organization of threads within a block. In this example, each block is organized into 4 × 2 × 2 arrays of threads. Since all blocks within a grid have the

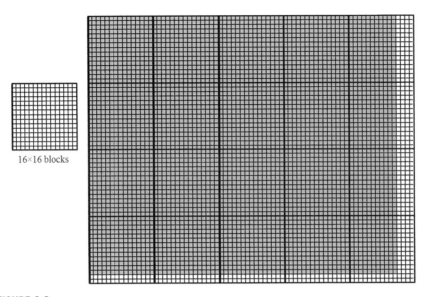

FIGURE 3.2

Using a 2D thread grid to process a 62 × 76 picture P.

same dimensions, we show only one of them. Fig. 3.1 expands block (1,1) to show its 16 threads. For example, thread (1,0,2) has `threadIdx.z = 1`, `threadIdx.y = 0`, and `threadIdx.x = 2`. Note that in this example we have 4 blocks of 16 threads each, with a grand total of 64 threads in the grid. We use these small numbers to keep the illustration simple. Typical CUDA grids contain thousands to millions of threads.

3.2 Mapping threads to multidimensional data

The choice of 1D, 2D, or 3D thread organizations is usually based on the nature of the data. For example, pictures are a 2D array of pixels. Using a 2D grid that consists of 2D blocks is often convenient for processing the pixels in a picture. Fig. 3.2 shows such an arrangement for processing a 62 × 761F1F[2] picture P (62 pixels in the vertical or y direction and 76 pixels in the horizontal or x

---

[2]We will refer to the dimensions of multidimensional data in descending order: the z dimension followed by the y dimension, and so on. For example, for a picture of n pixels in the vertical or y dimension and m pixels in the horizontal or x dimension, we will refer to it as a n × m picture. This follows the C multidimensional array indexing convention. For example, we can refer to P[y][x] as $P_{y,x}$ in text and figures for conciseness. Unfortunately, this ordering is opposite to the order in which data dimensions are ordered in the gridDim and blockDim dimensions. The discrepancy can be especially confusing when we define the dimensions of a thread grid on the basis of a multidimensional array that is to be processed by its threads.

direction). Assume that we decided to use a 16×16 block, with 16 threads in the x direction and 16 threads in the y direction. We will need four blocks in the y direction and five blocks in the x direction, which results in $4 \times 5 = 20$ blocks, as shown in Fig. 3.2. The heavy lines mark the block boundaries. The shaded area depicts the threads that cover pixels. Each thread is assigned to process a pixel whose y and x coordinates are derived from its `blockIdx`, `blockDim`, and `threadIdx` variable values:

$$\text{Vertical (row) row coordinate} = \text{blockIdx.y}^*\text{blockDim.y} + \text{threadIdx.y}$$

$$\text{Horizontal (Column) coordinate} = \text{blockIdx.x}^*\text{blockDim.x} + \text{threadIdx.x}$$

For example, the Pin element to be processed by thread (0,0) of block (1,0) can be identified as follows:

$$\text{Pin}_{\text{blockIdx.y}^*\text{blockDim.y}+\text{threadIdx.y},\text{blockIdx.x}^*\text{blockDim.x}+\text{threadIdx.x}} = \text{Pin}_{1^*16+0,0^*16+0} = \text{Pin}_{16,0}$$

Note that in Fig. 3.2 we have two extra threads in the y direction and four extra threads in the x direction. That is, we will generate 64×80 threads to process 62×76 pixels. This is similar to the situation in which a 1000-element vector is processed by the 1D kernel `vecAddKernel` in Fig. 2.9 using four 256-thread blocks. Recall that an if-statement in Fig. 2.10 is needed to prevent the extra 24 threads from taking effect. Similarly, we should expect that the picture-processing kernel function will have if-statements to test whether the thread's vertical and horizontal indices fall within the valid range of pixels.

We assume that the host code uses an integer variable n to track the number of pixels in the y direction and another integer variable m to track the number of pixels in the x direction. We further assume that the input picture data has been copied to the device global memory and can be accessed through a pointer variable `Pin_d`. The output picture has been allocated in the device memory and can be accessed through a pointer variable `Pout_d`. The following host code can be used to call a 2D kernel `colorToGrayscaleConversion` to process the picture, as follows:

```
dim3 dimGrid(ceil(m/16.0), ceil(n/16.0), 1);
dim3 dimBlock(16, 16, 1);
colorToGrayscaleConversion<<<dimGrid,dimBlock>>>
                          (Pin_d, Pout_d, m, n);
```

In this example we assume for simplicity that the dimensions of the blocks are fixed at 16×16. The dimensions of the grid, on the other hand, depend on the dimensions of the picture. To process a 1500×2000 (3-million-pixel) picture, we would generate 11,750 blocks: 94 in the y direction and 125 in the x direction. Within the kernel function, references to `gridDim.x`, `gridDim.y`, `blockDim.x`, and `blockDim.y` will result in 125, 94, 16, and 16, respectively.

Before we show the kernel code, we first need to understand how C statements access elements of dynamically allocated multidimensional arrays. Ideally, we would like to access `Pin_d` as a 2D array in which an element at row j and column i can be accessed as `Pin_d[j][i]`. However, the ANSI C standard on the basis of which CUDA C was developed requires the number of columns in `Pin` to be known at compile time for `Pin` to be accessed as a 2D array. Unfortunately, this information is not known at compile time for dynamically allocated arrays. In fact, part of the reason why one uses dynamically allocated arrays is to allow the sizes and dimensions of these arrays to vary according to the data size at runtime. Thus the information on the number of columns in a dynamically allocated 2D array is not known at compile time by design. As a result, programmers need to explicitly linearize, or "flatten," a dynamically allocated 2D array into an equivalent 1D array in the current CUDA C.

In reality, all multidimensional arrays in C are linearized. This is due to the use of a "flat" memory space in modern computers (see the "Memory Space" sidebar). In the case of statically allocated arrays, the compilers allow the programmers to use higher-dimensional indexing syntax, such as `Pin_d[j][i]`, to access their elements. Under the hood, the compiler linearizes them into an equivalent 1D array and translates the multidimensional indexing syntax into a 1D offset. In the case of dynamically allocated arrays, the current CUDA C compiler leaves the work of such translation to the programmers, owing to lack of dimensional information at compile time.

Memory Space

A memory space is a simplified view of how a processor accesses its memory in modern computers. A memory space is usually associated with each running application. The data to be processed by an application and instructions executed for the application are stored in locations in its memory space. Each location typically can accommodate a byte and has an address. Variables that require multiple bytes—4 bytes for float and 8 bytes for double—are stored in consecutive byte locations. When accessing a data value from the memory space, the processor gives the starting address (address of the starting byte location) and the number of bytes needed.

Most modern computers have at least 4G byte-sized locations, where each G is 1,073,741,824 (2^{30}). All locations are labeled with an address that ranges from 0 to the largest number used. Since there is only one address for every location, we say that the memory space has a "flat" organization. As a result, all multidimensional arrays are ultimately "flattened" into equivalent one-dimensional arrays. While a C programmer can use multidimensional array syntax to access an element of a multidimensional array, the compiler translates these accesses into a base pointer that points to the beginning element of the array, along with a one-dimensional offset calculated from these multidimensional indices.

There are at least two ways in which a 2D array can be linearized. One is to place all elements of the same row into consecutive locations. The rows are then placed one after another into the memory space. This arrangement, called the *row-major layout*, is illustrated in Fig. 3.3. To improve readability, we use $M_{j,i}$ to denote an element of M at the jth row and the ith column. $M_{j,i}$ is equivalent to the C expression M[j][i] but slightly more readable. Fig. 3.3 shows an example in which a 4×4 matrix M is linearized into a 16-element 1D array, with all elements of row 0 first, followed by the four elements of row 1, and so on. Therefore the 1D equivalent index for an element of M at row j and column i is $j*4 + i$. The $j*4$ term skips over all elements of the rows before row j. The i term then selects the right element within the section for row j. For example, the 1D index for $M_{2,1}$ is $2*4 + 1 = 9$. This is illustrated in Fig. 3.3, in which M_9 is the 1D equivalent to $M_{2,1}$. This is the way in which C compilers linearize 2D arrays.

Another way to linearize a 2D array is to place all elements of the same column in consecutive locations. The columns are then placed one after another into the memory space. This arrangement, called the *column-major layout*, is used by FORTRAN compilers. Note that the column-major layout of a 2D array is equivalent to the row-major layout of its transposed form. We will not spend more time on this except to mention that readers whose primary previous programming experience was with FORTRAN should be aware that CUDA C uses the row-major layout rather than the column-major layout. Also, many C libraries that are

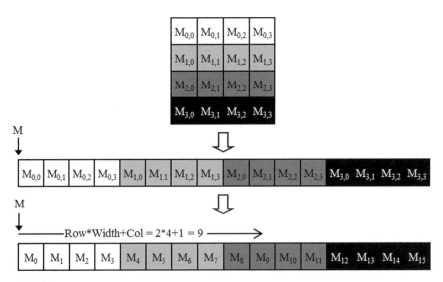

FIGURE 3.3

Row-major layout for a 2D C array. The result is an equivalent 1D array accessed by an index expression j*Width+i for an element that is in the jth row and ith column of an array of Width elements in each row.

```
01  // The input image is encoded as unsigned chars [0, 255]
02  // Each pixel is 3 consecutive chars for the 3 channels (RGB)
03  __global__
04  void colortoGrayscaleConvertion(unsigned char * Pout,
05                    unsigned char * Pin, int width, int height) {
06      int col = blockIdx.x*blockDim.x + threadIdx.x;
07      int row = blockIdx.y*blockDim.y + threadIdx.y;
08      if (col < width && row < height) {
09          // Get 1D offset for the grayscale image
10          int grayOffset = row*width + col;
11          // One can think of the RGB image having CHANNEL
12          // times more columns than the gray scale image
13          int rgbOffset = grayOffset*CHANNELS;
14          unsigned char r = Pin[rgbOffset     ]; // Red value
15          unsigned char g = Pin[rgbOffset + 1]; // Green value
16          unsigned char b = Pin[rgbOffset + 2]; // Blue value
17          // Perform the rescaling and store it
18          // We multiply by floating point constants
19          Pout[grayOffset] = 0.21f*r + 0.71f*g + 0.07f*b;
20      }
21  }
```

FIGURE 3.4

Source code of `colorToGrayscaleConversion` with 2D thread mapping to data.

designed to be used by FORTRAN programs use the column-major layout to match the FORTRAN compiler layout. As a result, the manual pages for these libraries usually tell the users to transpose the input arrays if they call these libraries from C programs.

We are now ready to study the source code of `colorToGrayscaleConversion`, shown in Fig. 3.4. The kernel code uses the following equation to convert each color pixel to its grayscale counterpart:

$$L = 0.21^{*}r + 0.72^{*}g + 0.07^{*}b$$

There are a total of `blockDim.x*gridDim.x` threads in the horizontal direction. Similar to the `vecAddKernel` example, the following expression generates every integer value from 0 to `blockDim.x*gridDim.x−1` (line 06):

```
col = blockIdx.x*blockDim.x + threadIdx.x
```

We know that `gridDim.x*blockDim.x` is greater than or equal to width (m value passed in from the host code). We have at least as many threads as the number of pixels in the horizontal direction. We also know that there are at least as many threads as the number of pixels in the vertical direction. Therefore as long as we test and make sure that only the threads with both row and column values are within range, that is, `(col<width) && (row<height)`, we will be able to cover every pixel in the picture (line 07).

Since there are width pixels in each row, we can generate the 1D index for the pixel at row row and column col as `row*width+col` (line 10). This 1D index grayOffset is the pixel index for Pout since each pixel in the output grayscale image is 1 byte (unsigned char). Using our 62×76 image example, the linearized 1D index of the Pout pixel calculated by thread (0,0) of block (1,0) with the following formula:

$$Pout_{blockIdx.y*blockDim.y+threadIdx.y,blockIdx.x*blockDim.x+threadIdx.x}$$
$$= Pout_{1*16+0,0*16+0} = Pout_{16,0} = Pout[16*76+0] = Pout[1216]$$

As for Pin, we need to multiply the gray pixel index by 3[3] (line 13), since each colored pixel is stored as three elements (r, g, b), each of which is 1 byte. The resulting rgbOffset gives the starting location of the color pixel in the Pin array. We read the r, g, and b value from the three consecutive byte locations of the Pin array (lines 14−16), perform the calculation of the grayscale pixel value, and write that value into the Pout array using grayOffset (line 19). In our 62×76 image example the linearized 1D index of the first component of the Pin pixel that is processed by thread (0,0) of block (1,0) can be calculated with the following formula:

$$Pin_{blockIdx.y*blockDim.y+threadIdx.y,blockIdx.x*blockDim.x+threadIdx.x} = Pin_{1*16+0,0*16+0}$$
$$= Pin_{16,0} = Pin[16*76*3+0] = Pin[3648]$$

The data that is being accessed is the 3 bytes starting at byte offset 3648.

Fig. 3.5 illustrates the execution of colorToGrayscaleConversion in processing our 62×76 example. Assuming 16×16 blocks, calling the colorToGrayscaleConversion kernel generates 64×80 threads. The grid will have $4 \times 5 = 20$ blocks: four in the vertical direction and five in the horizontal direction. The execution behavior of blocks will fall into one of four different cases, shown as four shaded areas in Fig. 3.5.

The first area, marked 1 in Fig. 3.5, consists of the threads that belong to the 12 blocks covering the majority of pixels in the picture. Both col and row values of these threads are within range; all these threads pass the if-statement test and process pixels in the dark-shaded area of the picture. That is all $16 \times 16 = 256$ threads in each block will process pixels.

The second area, marked 2 in Fig. 3.5, contains the threads that belong to the three blocks in the medium-shaded area covering the upper-right pixels of the picture. Although the row values of these threads are always within range, the col values of some of them exceed the m value of 76. This is because the number of threads in the horizontal direction is always a multiple of the blockDim.x value chosen by the programmer (16 in this case). The smallest multiple of 16 needed to cover 76 pixels is 80. As a result, 12 threads in each row will find their col values within range and will process pixels. The remaining four threads in each row will find their col values out of range and thus will fail the if-statement condition. These threads will not process any pixels. Overall, $12 \times 16 = 192$ of the $16 \times 16 = 256$ threads in each of these blocks will process pixels.

---

[3]We assume that CHANNELS is a constant of value 3, and its definition is outside the kernel function.

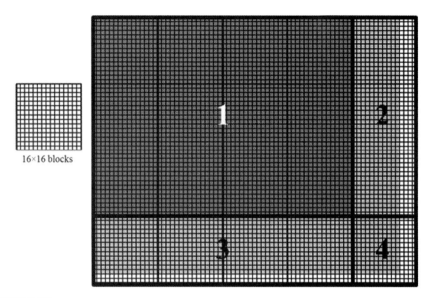

FIGURE 3.5

Covering a 76×62 picture with 16×16 blocks.

The third area, marked 3 in Fig. 3.5, accounts for the four lower-left blocks covering the medium-shaded area of the picture. Although the `col` values of these threads are always within range, the `row` values of some of them exceed the `n` value of 62. This is because the number of threads in the vertical direction is always a multiple of the `blockDim.y` value chosen by the programmer (16 in this case). The smallest multiple of 16 to cover 62 is 64. As a result, 14 threads in each column will find their row values within range and will process pixels. The remaining two threads in each column will not pas the if-statement and will not process any pixels. Overall, $16 \times 14 = 224$ of the 256 threads will process pixels.

The fourth area, marked 4 in Fig. 3.5, contains the threads that cover the lower right, lightly shaded area of the picture. Like Area 2, 4 threads in each of the top 14 rows will find their `col` values out of range. Like Area 3, the entire bottom two rows of this block will find their row values out of range. Overall, only $14 \times 12 = 168$ of the $16 \times 16 = 256$ threads will process pixels.

We can easily extend our discussion of 2D arrays to 3D arrays by including another dimension when we linearize the array. This is done by placing each "plane" of the array one after another into the address space. Assume that the programmer uses variables `m` and `n` to track the number of columns and rows, respectively, in a 3D array. The programmer also needs to determine the values of `blockDim.z` and `gridDim.z` when calling a kernel. In the kernel the array index will involve another global index:

```
int plane = blockIdx.z*blockDim.z + threadIdx.z
```

The linearized access to a 3D array `P` will be in the form of `P[plane*m*n +row*m+col]`. A kernel processing the 3D `P` array needs to check whether all the three global indices, `plane`, `row`, and `col`, fall within the valid range of the array. The use of 3D arrays in CUDA kernels will be further studies for the stencil pattern in Chapter 8, Stencil.

3.3 Image blur: a more complex kernel

We have studied `vecAddkernel` and `colorToGrayscaleConversion`, in which each thread performs only a small number of arithmetic operations on one array element. These kernels serve their purposes well: to illustrate the basic CUDA C program structure and data parallel execution concepts. At this point, the reader should ask the obvious question: Do all threads in CUDA C programs perform only such simple and trivial operations independently of each other? The answer is no. In real CUDA C programs, threads often perform complex operations on their data and need to cooperate with each other. For the next few chapters we are going to work on increasingly complex examples that exhibit these characteristics. We will start with an image-blurring function.

Image blurring smoothes out abrupt variation of pixel values while preserving the edges that are essential for recognizing the key features of the image. Fig. 3.6 illustrates the effect of image blurring. Simply stated, we make the image blurry. To human eyes, a blurred image tends to obscure the fine details and present the "big picture" impression, or the major thematic objects in the picture. In computer image-processing algorithms a common use case of image blurring is to reduce the impact of noise and granular rendering effects in an image by correcting problematic pixel values with the clean surrounding pixel values. In computer vision, image blurring can be used to allow edge detection and object recognition algorithms to focus on thematic objects rather than being bogged down by a massive quantity of fine-grained objects. In displays, image blurring is sometimes used to highlight a particular part of the image by blurring the rest of the image.

Mathematically, an image-blurring function calculates the value of an output image pixel as a weighted sum of a patch of pixels encompassing the pixel in the input image. As we will learn in Chapter 7, Convolution, the computation of such

FIGURE 3.6

An original image (*left*) and a blurred version (*right*).

weighted sums belongs to the *convolution* pattern. We will be using a simplified approach in this chapter by taking a simple average value of the N × N patch of pixels surrounding, and including, our target pixel. To keep the algorithm simple, we will not place a weight on the value of any pixel based on its distance from the target pixel. In practice, placing such weights is quite common in convolution blurring approaches, such as Gaussian blur.

Fig. 3.7 shows an example of image blurring using a 3 × 3 patch. When calculating an output pixel value at (row, col) position, we see that the patch is centered at the input pixel located at the (row, col) position. The 3 × 3 patch spans three rows (row-1, row, row+1) and three columns (col-1, col, col+1). For example, the coordinates of the nine pixels for calculating the output pixel at (25, 50) are (24, 49), (24, 50), (24, 51), (25, 49), (25, 50), (25, 51), (26, 49), (26, 50), and (26, 51).

Fig. 3.8 shows an image blur kernel. Similar to the strategy that was used in `colorToGrayscaleConversion`, we use each thread to calculate an output pixel. That is, the thread-to-output-data mapping remains the same. Thus at the beginning of the kernel we see the familiar calculation of the `col` and `row` indices (lines 03−04). We also see the familiar if-statement that verifies that both `col` and `row` are within the valid range according to the height and width of the image (line 05). Only the threads whose `col` and `row` indices are both within value ranges are allowed to participate in the execution.

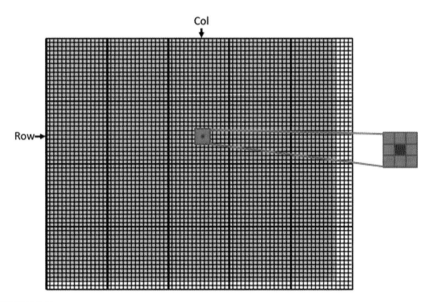

FIGURE 3.7

Each output pixel is the average of a patch of surrounding pixels and itself in the input image.

```
01   __global__
02   void blurKernel(unsigned char *in, unsigned char *out, int w, int h){
03     int col = blockIdx.x*blockDim.x + threadIdx.x;
04     int row = blockIdx.y*blockDim.y + threadIdx.y;
05     if(col < w && row < h) {
06       int pixVal = 0;
07       int pixels = 0;
09           // Get average of the surrounding BLUR_SIZE x BLUR_SIZE box
10       for(int blurRow=-BLUR_SIZE; blurRow<BLUR_SIZE+1; ++blurRow){
11         for(int blurCol=-BLUR_SIZE; blurCol<BLUR_SIZE+1; ++blurCol){
12             int curRow = row + blurRow;
13             int curCol = col + blurCol;
14                 // Verify we have a valid image pixel
15             if(curRow>=0 && curRow<h && curCol>=0 && curCol<w) {
16                 pixVal += in[curRow*w + curCol];
17                 ++pixels; // Keep track of number of pixels in the avg
18             }
19           }
20       }
21       // Write our new pixel value out
22       out[row*w + col] = (unsigned char)(pixVal/pixels);
23     }
24   }
```

FIGURE 3.8

An image blur kernel.

As shown in Fig. 3.7, the `col` and `row` values also give the central pixel location of the patch of input pixels used for calculating the output pixel for the thread. The nested for-loops in Fig. 3.8 (lines 10−11) iterate through all the pixels in the patch. We assume that the program has a defined constant `BLUR_SIZE`. The value of `BLUR_SIZE` is set such that `BLUR_SIZE` gives the number of pixels on each side (radius) of the patch and `2*BLUR_SIZE+1` gives the total number of pixels across one dimension of the patch. For example, for a 3×3 patch, `BLUR_SIZE` is set to 1, whereas for a 7×7 patch, `BLUR_SIZE` is set to 3. The outer loop iterates through the rows of the patch. For each row, the inner loop iterates through the columns of the patch.

In our 3×3 patch example, the `BLUR_SIZE` is 1. For the thread that calculates output pixel (25, 50), during the first iteration of the outer loop, the `curRow` variable is `row-BLUR_SIZE` $= (25 - 1) = 24$. Thus during the first iteration of the outer loop, the inner loop iterates through the patch pixels in row 24. The inner loop iterates from column `col-BLUR_SIZE` $= 50-1 = 49$ to `col+BLUR_SIZE` $= 51$ using the curCol variable. Therefore the pixels that are processed in the first iteration of the outer loop are (24, 49), (24, 50), and (24, 51). The reader should verify that in the second iteration of the outer loop, the inner loop iterates through pixels (25, 49), (25, 50), and (25, 51). Finally, in the third iteration of the outer loop, the inner loop iterates through pixels (26, 49), (26, 50), and (26, 51).

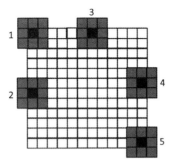

FIGURE 3.9

Handling boundary conditions for pixels near the edges of the image.

Line 16 uses the linearized index of curRow and curCol to access the value of the input pixel visited in the current iteration. It accumulates the pixel value into a running sum variable pixVal. Line 17 records the fact that one more pixel value has been added into the running sum by incrementing the pixels variable. After all the pixels in the patch have been processed, line 22 calculates the average value of the pixels in the patch by dividing the pixVal value by the pixels value. It uses the linearized index of row and col to write the result into its output pixel.

Line 15 contains a conditional statement that guards the execution of lines 16 and 17. For example, in computing output pixels near the edge of the image, the patch may extend beyond the valid range of the input image. This is illustrated in Fig. 3.9 assuming 3×3 patches. In case 1, the pixel at the upper-left corner is being blurred. Five of the nine pixels in the intended patch do not exist in the input image. In this case, the row and col values of the output pixel are 0 and 0, respectively. During the execution of the nested loop, the curRow and curCol values for the nine iterations are $(-1, -1)$, $(-1,0)$, $(-1,1)$, $(0, -1)$, $(0,0)$, $(0,1)$, $(1, -1)$, $(1,0)$, and $(1,1)$. Note that for the five pixels that are outside the image, at least one of the values is less than 0. The curRow<0 and curCol<0 conditions of the if-statement catch these values and skip the execution of lines 16 and 17. As a result, only the values of the four valid pixels are accumulated into the running sum variable. The pixels value is also correctly incremented only four times so that the average can be calculated properly at line 22.

The reader should work through the other cases in Fig. 3.9 and analyze the execution behavior of the nested loop in blurKernel. Note that most of the threads will find all the pixels in their assigned 3×3 patch within the input image. They will accumulate all the nine pixels. However, for the pixels on the four corners, the responsible threads will accumulate only four pixels. For other pixels on the four edges, the responsible threads will accumulate six pixels. These variations are what necessitates keeping track of the actual number of pixels that are accumulated with the variable pixels.

3.4 Matrix multiplication

Matrix-matrix multiplication, or matrix multiplication in short, is an important component of the Basic Linear Algebra Subprograms standard (see the "Linear Algebra Functions" sidebar). It is the basis of many linear algebra solvers, such as LU decomposition. It is also an important computation for deep learning using convolutional neural networks, which will be discussed in detail in Chapter 16, Deep Learning.

Linear Algebra Functions

Linear algebra operations are widely used in science and engineering applications. In the Basic Linear Algebra Subprograms (BLAS), a de facto standard for publishing libraries that perform basic algebra operations, there are three levels of linear algebra functions. As the level increases, the number of operations performed by the function increases. Level 1 functions perform vector operations of the form $y = \alpha x + y$, where x and y are vectors and α is a scalar. Our vector addition example is a special case of a level 1 function with $\alpha = 1$. Level 2 functions perform matrix-vector operations of the form $y = \alpha Ax + \beta y$, where A is a matrix, x and y are vectors, and α and β are scalars. We will be studying a form of level 2 function in sparse linear algebra. Level 3 functions perform matrix-matrix operations in the form of $C = \alpha AB + \beta C$, where A, B, and C are matrices and α and β are scalars. Our matrix-matrix multiplication example is a special case of a level 3 function where $\alpha = 1$ and $\beta = 0$. These BLAS functions are important because they are used as basic building blocks of higher-level algebraic functions, such as linear system solvers and eigenvalue analysis. As we will discuss later, the performance of different implementations of BLAS functions can vary by orders of magnitude in both sequential and parallel computers.

Matrix multiplication between an $I \times j$ (i rows by j columns) matrix M and a $j \times k$ matrix N produces an $I \times k$ matrix P. When a matrix multiplication is performed, each element of the output matrix P is an inner product of a row of M and a column of N. We will continue to use the convention where $P_{row, col}$ is the element at the rowth position in the vertical direction and the colth position in the horizontal direction. As shown in Fig. 3.10, $P_{row,col}$ (the small square in P) is the inner product of the vector formed by the rowth row of M (shown as a horizontal strip in M) and the vector formed by the colth column of N (shown as a vertical strip in N). The inner product, sometimes called the dot product, of two vectors is the sum of products of the individual vector elements. That is,

$$P_{row,col} = \sum M_{row,k} {}^* N_{k,col} \qquad \text{for } k = 0, \ 1, \ldots \text{Width} - 1$$

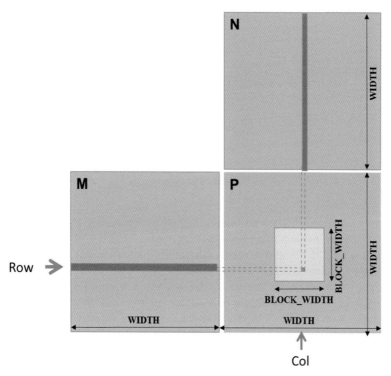

FIGURE 3.10

Matrix multiplication using multiple blocks by tiling P.

For example, in Fig. 3.10, assuming row = 1 and col = 5,

$$P_{1,5} = M_{1,0}{}^*N_{0,5} + M_{1,1}{}^*N_{1,5} + M_{1,2}{}^*N_{2,5} + \dots + M_{1,Width-1}{}^*N_{Width-1,5}$$

To implement matrix multiplication using CUDA, we can map the threads in the grid to the elements of the output matrix P with the same approach that we used for `colorToGrayscaleConversion`. That is, each thread is responsible for calculating one P element. The row and column indices for the P element to be calculated by each thread are the same as before:

```
row = blockIdx.y*blockDim.y + threadIdx.y
```

and

```
col = blockIdx.x*blockDim.x + threadIdx.x
```

With this one-to-one mapping, the `row` and `col` thread indices are also the row and column indices for their output elements. Fig. 3.11 shows the source code of

```
01    __global__ void MatrixMulKernel(float* M, float* N,
02                                    float* P, int Width) {
03        int row = blockIdx.y*blockDim.y+threadIdx.y;
04        int col = blockIdx.x*blockDim.x+threadIdx.x;
05        if ((row < Width) && (col < Width)) {
06            float Pvalue = 0;
07            for (int k = 0; k < Width; ++k) {
08                Pvalue += M[row*Width+k]*N[k*Width+col];
09            }
10            P[row*Width+col] = Pvalue;
11        }
12    }
```

FIGURE 3.11

A matrix multiplication kernel using one thread to compute one P element.

the kernel based on this thread-to-data mapping. The reader should immediately see the familiar pattern of calculating row and col (lines 03−04) and the if-statement testing if row and col are both within range (line 05). These statements are almost identical to their counterparts in colorToGrayscaleConversion. The only significant difference is that we are making a simplifying assumption that matrixMulKernel needs to handle only square matrices, so we replace both width and height with Width. This thread-to-data mapping effectively divides P into tiles, one of which is shown as a light-colored square in Fig. 3.10. Each block is responsible for calculating one of these tiles.

We now turn our attention to the work done by each thread. Recall that $P_{row,col}$ is calculated as the inner product of the rowth row of M and the colth column of N. In Fig. 3.11 we use a for-loop to perform this inner product operation. Before we enter the loop, we initialize a local variable Pvalue to 0 (line 06). Each iteration of the loop accesses an element from the rowth row of M and an element from the colth column of N, multiplies the two elements together, and accumulates the product into Pvalue (line 08).

Let us first focus on accessing the M element within the for-loop. M is linearized into an equivalent 1D array using row-major order. That is, the rows of M are placed one after another in the memory space, starting with the 0th row. Therefore the beginning element of row 1 is M[1*Width] because we need to account for all elements of row 0. In general, the beginning element of the rowth row is M[row*Width]. Since all elements of a row are placed in consecutive locations, the kth element of the rowth row is at M[row*Width+k]. This linearized array offset is what we use in Fig. 3.11 (line 08).

We now turn our attention to accessing N. As is shown in Fig. 3.11, the beginning element of the colth column is the colth element of row 0, which is N[col]. Accessing the next element in the colth column requires skipping over an entire row. This is because the next element of the same column is the same element in the next row. Therefore the kth element of the colth column is N[k*Width+col] (line 08).

After the execution exits the for-loop, all threads have their P element values in the Pvalue variables. Each thread then uses the 1D equivalent index expression `row*Width+col` to write its `P` element (line 10). Again, this index pattern is like that used in the `colorToGrayscaleConversion` kernel.

wWe now use a small example to illustrate the execution of the matrix multiplication kernel. Fig. 3.12 shows a 4×4 P with BLOCK_WIDTH = 2. Although such small matrix and block sizes are not realistic, they allow us to fit the entire example into one picture. The `P` matrix is divided into four tiles, and each block calculates one tile. We do so by creating blocks that are 2×2 arrays of threads, with each thread calculating one `P` element. In the example, thread (0,0) of block (0,0) calculates $P_{0,0}$, whereas thread (0,0) of block (1,0) calculates $P_{2,0}$.

The `row` and `col` indices in `matrixMulKernel` identify the `P` element to be calculated by a thread. The row index also identifies the row of `M`, and the col index identifies the column of `N` as input values for the thread. Fig. 3.13 illustrates the multiplication actions in each thread block. For the small matrix multiplication example, threads in block (0,0) produce four dot products. The `row` and `col` indices of thread (1,0) in block (0,0) are $0*0 + 1 = 1$ and $0*0 + 0 = 0$, respectively. The thread thus maps to $P_{1,0}$ and calculates the dot product of row 1 of `M` and column 0 of `N`.

Let us walk through the execution of the for-loop of Fig. 3.11 for thread (0,0) in block (0,0). During iteration 0 (k = 0), `row*Width + k` = $0*4 + 0 = 0$ and `k*Width + col` = $0*4 + 0 = 0$. Therefore the input elements accessed are `M[0]` and `N[0]`, which are the 1D equivalent of $M_{0,0}$ and $N_{0,0}$. Note that these are indeed the 0th elements of row 0 of `M` and column 0 of `N`. During iteration 1 (k = 1), `row*Width + k` = $0*4 + 1 = 1$ and `k*Width + col` = $1*4 + 0 = 4$. Therefore we are accessing `M[1]` and `N[4]`, which are the 1D equivalent of $M_{0,1}$ and $N_{1,0}$. These are the first elements of row 0 of `M` and column 0 of `N`. During iteration 2 (k = 2), `row*Width + k` = $0*4 + 2 = 2$ and `k*Width + col` = $2*4 + 0 = 8$, which results in `M[2]` and `N[8]`. Therefore the elements accessed are the 1D equivalent of $M_{0,2}$ and $N_{2,0}$. Finally, during iteration 3 (k = 3), `row*Width + k` = $0*4 + 3 = 3$ and `k*Width + col` =

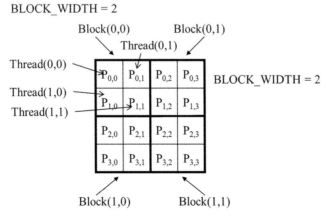

FIGURE 3.12

A small execution example of `matrixMulKernel`.

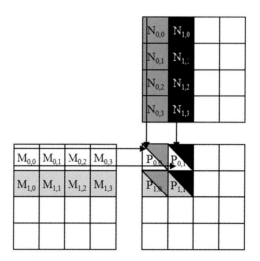

FIGURE 3.13

Matrix multiplication actions of one thread block.

$3*4 + 0 = 12$, which results in M[3] and N[12], the 1D equivalent of $M_{0,3}$ and $N_{3,0}$. We have now verified that the for-loop performs the inner product between the 0th row of M and the 0th column of N for thread (0,0) in block (0,0). After the loop, the thread writes P[row*Width+col], which is P[0]. This is the 1D equivalent of $P_{0,0}$, so thread (0,0) in block (0,0) successfully calculated the inner product between the 0th row of M and the 0th column of N and deposited the result in $P_{0,0}$.

We will leave it as an exercise for the reader to hand-execute and verify the for-loop for other threads in block (0,0) or in other blocks.

Since the size of a grid is limited by the maximum number of blocks per grid and threads per block, the size of the largest output matrix P that can be handled by matrixMulKernel will also be limited by these constraints. In the situation in which output matrices larger than this limit are to be computed, one can divide the output matrix into submatrices whose sizes can be covered by a grid and use the host code to launch a different grid for each submatrix. Alternatively, we can change the kernel code so that each thread calculates more P elements. We will explore both options later in this book.

3.5 Summary

CUDA grids and blocks are multidimensional with up to three dimensions. The multidimensionality of grids and blocks is useful for organizing threads to be mapped to multidimensional data. The kernel execution configuration parameters define the dimensions of a grid and its blocks. Unique coordinates in blockIdx and threadIdx allow threads of a grid to identify themselves and their domains of data. It is the programmer's responsibility to use these variables in kernel functions so that the threads can properly identify the portion of the data to process. When accessing multidimensional data, programmers will often have to linearize multidimensional indices into a 1D offset. The reason is that dynamically allocated multidimensional arrays in C are typically stored as 1D arrays in row-major order. We use examples of increasing complexity to familiarize the reader with the mechanics of processing multidimensional arrays with multidimensional grids. These skills will be foundational for understanding parallel patterns and their associated optimization techniques.

Exercises

1. In this chapter we implemented a matrix multiplication kernel that has each thread produce one output matrix element. In this question, you will implement different matrix-matrix multiplication kernels and compare them.
   a. Write a kernel that has each thread produce one output matrix row. Fill in the execution configuration parameters for the design.
   b. Write a kernel that has each thread produce one output matrix column. Fill in the execution configuration parameters for the design.
   c. Analyze the pros and cons of each of the two kernel designs.
2. A matrix-vector multiplication takes an input matrix B and a vector C and produces one output vector A. Each element of the output vector A is the dot product of one row of the input matrix B and C, that is, $A[i] = \sum^j B[i][j] + C[j]$. For simplicity we will handle only square matrices whose elements are single-precision floating-point numbers. Write a matrix-vector multiplication kernel and the host stub function that can be called with four parameters: pointer to the output matrix, pointer to the input matrix, pointer to the input vector, and the number of elements in each dimension. Use one thread to calculate an output vector element.
3. Consider the following CUDA kernel and the corresponding host function that calls it:

```
01    __global__ void foo_kernel(float* a, float* b, unsigned int M,
      unsigned int N) {
02        unsigned int row = blockIdx.y*blockDim.y + threadIdx.y;
03        unsigned int col = blockIdx.x*blockDim.x + threadIdx.x;
04        if(row < M && col < N) {
05            b[row*N + col] = a[row*N + col]/2.1f + 4.8f;
06        }
07    }
08    void foo(float* a_d, float* b_d) {
09        unsigned int M = 150;
10        unsigned int N = 300;
11        dim3 bd(16, 32);
12        dim3 gd((N - 1)/16 + 1, (M - 1)/32 + 1);
13        foo_kernel <<< gd, bd >>>(a_d, b_d, M, N);
14    }
```

   a. What is the number of threads per block?
   b. What is the number of threads in the grid?

    c. What is the number of blocks in the grid?

    d. What is the number of threads that execute the code on line 05?

4. Consider a 2D matrix with a width of 400 and a height of 500. The matrix is stored as a one-dimensional array. Specify the array index of the matrix element at row 20 and column 10:

    a. If the matrix is stored in row-major order.

    b. If the matrix is stored in column-major order.

5. Consider a 3D tensor with a width of 400, a height of 500, and a depth of 300. The tensor is stored as a one-dimensional array in row-major order. Specify the array index of the tensor element at x = 10, y = 20, and z = 5.

Compute architecture and scheduling

Chapter Outline

4.1 Architecture of a modern GPU 70
4.2 Block scheduling 70
4.3 Synchronization and transparent scalability 71
4.4 Warps and SIMD hardware 74
4.5 Control divergence 79
4.6 Warp scheduling and latency tolerance 83
4.7 Resource partitioning and occupancy 85
4.8 Querying device properties 87
4.9 Summary 90
Exercises 90
References 92

In Chapter 1, Introduction, we saw that CPUs are designed to minimize the latency of instruction execution and that GPUs are designed to maximize the throughput of executing instructions. In Chapters 2, Heterogeneous Data Parallel Computing and 3, Multidimensional Grids and Data, we learned the core features of the CUDA programming interface for creating and calling kernels to launch and execute threads. In the next three chapters we will discuss the architecture of modern GPUs, both the compute architecture and the memory architecture, and the performance optimization techniques stemming from the understanding of this architecture. This chapter presents several aspects of the GPU compute architecture that are essential for CUDA C programmers to understand and reason about the performance behavior of their kernel code. We will start by showing a high-level, simplified view of the compute architecture and explore the concepts of flexible resource assignment, scheduling of blocks, and occupancy. We will then advance into thread scheduling, latency tolerance, control divergence, and synchronization. We will finish the chapter with a description of the API functions that can be used to query the resources that are available in the GPU and the tools to help estimate the occupancy of the GPU when executing a kernel. In the following two chapters, we will present the core concepts and programming considerations of the GPU memory architecture. In particular, Chapter 5, Memory Architecture and Data Locality, focuses on the on-chip memory architecture, and Chapter 6, Performance Considerations, briefly covers the off-chip memory architecture then elaborates on various performance considerations of the GPU architecture as a whole. A CUDA C

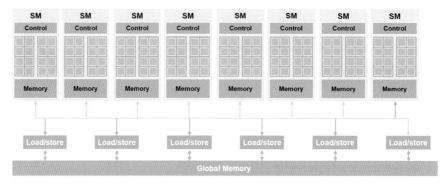

FIGURE 4.1

Architecture of a CUDA-capable GPU.

programmer who masters these concepts is well equipped to write and to understand high-performance parallel kernels.

4.1 Architecture of a modern GPU

Fig. 4.1 shows a high-level, CUDA C programmer's view of the architecture of a typical CUDA-capable GPU. It is organized into an array of highly threaded streaming multiprocessors (SMs). Each SM has several processing units called streaming processors or CUDA cores (hereinafter referred to as just *cores* for brevity), shown as small tiles inside the SMs in Fig. 4.1, that share control logic and memory resources. For example, the Ampere A100 GPU has 108 SMs with 64 cores each, totaling 6912 cores in the entire GPU.

The SMs also come with different on-chip memory structures collectively labeled as "Memory" in Fig. 4.1. These on-chip memory structures will be the topic of Chapter 5, Memory Architecture and Data Locality. GPUs also come with gigabytes of off-chip device memory, referred to as "Global Memory" in Fig. 4.1. While older GPUs used graphics double data rate synchronous DRAM, more recent GPUs starting with NVIDIA's Pascal architecture may use HBM (high-bandwidth memory) or HBM2, which consist of DRAM (dynamic random access memory) modules tightly integrated with the GPU in the same package. For brevity we will broadly refer to all these types of memory as DRAM for the rest of the book. We will discuss the most important concepts involved in accessing GPU DRAMs in Chapter 6, Performance Considerations.

4.2 Block scheduling

When a kernel is called, the CUDA runtime system launches a grid of threads that execute the kernel code. These threads are assigned to SMs on a block-by-block basis. That is, all threads in a block are simultaneously assigned to the same SM.

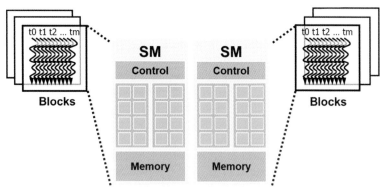

FIGURE 4.2

Thread block assignment to streaming multiprocessors (SMs).

Fig. 4.2 illustrates the assignment of blocks to SMs. Multiple blocks are likely to be simultaneously assigned to the same SM. For example, in Fig. 4.2, three blocks are assigned to each SM. However, blocks need to reserve hardware resources to execute, so only a limited number of blocks can be simultaneously assigned to a given SM. The limit on the number of blocks depends on a variety of factors that are discussed in Section 4.6.

With a limited number of SMs and a limited number of blocks that can be simultaneously assigned to each SM, there is a limit on the total number of blocks that can be simultaneously executing in a CUDA device. Most grids contain many more blocks than this number. To ensure that all blocks in a grid get executed, the runtime system maintains a list of blocks that need to execute and assigns new blocks to SMs when previously assigned blocks complete execution.

The assignment of threads to SMs on a block-by-block basis guarantees that threads in the same block are scheduled simultaneously on the same SM. This guarantee makes it possible for threads in the same block to interact with each other in ways that threads across different blocks cannot.[1] This includes *barrier synchronization*, which is discussed in Section 4.3. It also includes accessing a low-latency *shared memory* that resides on the SM, which is discussed in Chapter 5, Memory Architecture and Data Locality.

4.3 Synchronization and transparent scalability

CUDA allows threads in the same block to coordinate their activities using the barrier synchronization function `__syncthreads()`. Note that "`__`" consists of two

---

[1] Threads in different blocks can perform barrier synchronization through the Cooperative Groups API. However, there are several important restrictions that must be obeyed to ensure that all threads involved are indeed simultaneously executing on the SMs. Interested readers are referred to the CUDA C Programming Guide for proper use of the Cooperative Groups API.

"_" characters. When a thread calls __syncthreads(), it will be held at the program location of the call until every thread in the same block reaches that location. This ensures that all threads in a block have completed a phase of their execution before any of them can move on to the next phase.

Barrier synchronization is a simple and popular method for coordinating parallel activities. In real life, we often use barrier synchronization to coordinate parallel activities of multiple people. For example, assume that four friends go to a shopping mall in a car. They can all go to different stores to shop for their own clothes. This is a parallel activity and is much more efficient than if they all remain as a group and sequentially visit all the stores of interest. However, barrier synchronization is needed before they leave the mall. They must wait until all four friends have returned to the car before they can leave. The ones who finish earlier than the others must wait for those who finish later. Without the barrier synchronization, one or more individuals can be left in the mall when the car leaves, which could seriously damage their friendship!

Fig. 4.3 illustrates the execution of barrier synchronization. There are N threads in the block. Time goes from left to right. Some of the threads reach the barrier synchronization statement early, and some reach it much later. The ones that reach the barrier early will wait for those that arrive late. When the latest one arrives at the barrier, all threads can continue their execution. With barrier synchronization, "no one is left behind."

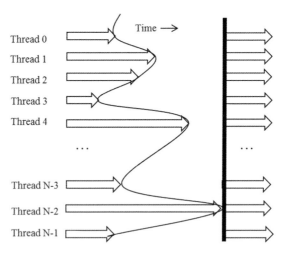

FIGURE 4.3

An example execution of barrier synchronization. The arrows represent execution activities over time. The vertical curve marks the time when each thread executes the __syncthreads statement. The empty space to the right of the vertical curve depicts the time that each thread waits for all threads to complete. The vertical line marks the time when the last thread executes the __syncthreads statement, after which all threads are allowed to proceed to execute the statements after the __syncthreads statement.

```
01    void incorrect_barrier_example(int n) {
02        ...
03        if (threadIdx.x % 2 == 0) {
04            ...
05            __syncthreads{};
06        }
07        else {
08            ...
09            __syncthreads{};
10        }
11    }
```

FIGURE 4.4

An incorrect use of __syncthreads()

In CUDA, if a __syncthreads() statement is present, it must be executed by all threads in a block. When a __syncthreads() statement is placed in an if statement, either all threads in a block execute the path that includes the __syncthreads() or none of them does. For an if-then-else statement, if each path has a __syncthreads() statement, either all threads in a block execute the then-path or all of them execute the else-path. The two __syncthreads() are different barrier synchronization points. For example, in Fig. 4.4, two __syncthreads() are used in the if statement starting in line 04. All threads with even threadIdx.x values execute the then-path while the remaining threads execute the else-path. The __syncthreads() calls at line 06 and line 10 define two different barriers. Since not all threads in a block are guaranteed to execute either of the barriers, the code violates the rules for using __syncthreads() and will result in undefined execution behavior. In general, incorrect usage of barrier synchronization can result in incorrect result, or in threads waiting for each other forever, which is referred to as a *deadlock*. It is the responsibility of the programmer to avoid such inappropriate use of barrier synchronization.

Barrier synchronization imposes execution constraints on threads within a block. These threads should execute in close time proximity with each other to avoid excessively long waiting times. More important, the system needs to make sure that all threads involved in the barrier synchronization have access to the necessary resources to eventually arrive at the barrier. Otherwise, a thread that never arrives at the barrier synchronization point can cause a deadlock. The CUDA runtime system satisfies this constraint by assigning execution resources to all threads in a block as a unit, as we saw in Section 4.2. Not only do all threads in a block have to be assigned to the same SM, but also they need to be assigned to that SM simultaneously. That is, a block can begin execution only when the runtime system has secured all the resources needed by all threads in the block to complete execution. This ensures the time proximity of all threads in a block and prevents an excessive or even indefinite waiting time during barrier synchronization.

This leads us to an important tradeoff in the design of CUDA barrier synchronization. By not allowing threads in different blocks to perform barrier synchronization

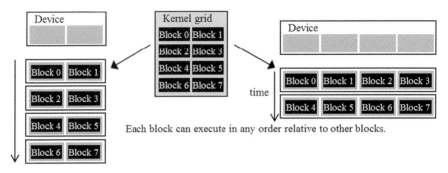

FIGURE 4.5

Lack of synchronization constraints between blocks enables transparent scalability for CUDA programs.

with each other, the CUDA runtime system can execute blocks in any order relative to each other, since none of them need to wait for each other. This flexibility enables scalable implementations, as shown in Fig. 4.5. Time in the figure progresses from top to bottom. In a low-cost system with only a few execution resources, one can execute a small number of blocks at the same time, portrayed as executing two blocks a time on the left-hand side of Fig. 4.5. In a higher-end implementation with more execution resources, one can execute many blocks at the same time, portrayed as executing four blocks at a time on the right-hand side of Fig. 4.5. A high-end GPU today can execute hundreds of blocks simultaneously.

The ability to execute the same application code with a wide range of speeds allows the production of a wide range of implementations according to the cost, power, and performance requirements of different market segments. For example, a mobile processor may execute an application slowly but at extremely low power consumption, and a desktop processor may execute the same application at a higher speed while consuming more power. Both execute the same application program with no change to the code. The ability to execute the same application code on different hardware with different amounts of execution resources is referred to as *transparent scalability*, which reduces the burden on application developers and improves the usability of applications.

4.4 Warps and SIMD hardware

We have seen that blocks can execute in any order relative to each other, which allows for transparent scalability across different devices. However, we did not say much about the execution timing of threads within each block. Conceptually, one should assume that threads in a block can execute in any order with respect to each other. In algorithms with phases, barrier synchronizations should be used whenever we want to ensure that all threads have completed a previous phase of their execution before any of them start the next phase. The correctness of executing a kernel should not depend on any assumption that certain threads will execute in synchrony with each other without the use of barrier synchronizations.

Thread scheduling in CUDA GPUs is a hardware implementation concept and therefore must be discussed in the context of specific hardware implementations. In most implementations to date, once a block has been assigned to an SM, it is further divided into 32-thread units called *warps*. The size of warps is implementation specific and can vary in future generations of GPUs. Knowledge of warps can be helpful in understanding and optimizing the performance of CUDA applications on particular generations of CUDA devices.

A warp is the unit of thread scheduling in SMs. Fig. 4.6 shows the division of blocks into warps in an implementation. In this example there are three blocks—Block 1, Block 2, and Block 3—all assigned to an SM. Each of the three blocks is further divided into warps for scheduling purposes. Each warp consists of 32 threads of consecutive `threadIdx` values: threads 0 through 31 form the first warp, threads 32 through 63 form the second warp, and so on. We can calculate the number of warps that reside in an SM for a given block size and a given number of blocks assigned to each SM. In this example, if each block has 256 threads, we can determine that each block has 256/32 or 8 warps. With three blocks in the SM, we have $8 \times 3 = 24$ warps in the SM.

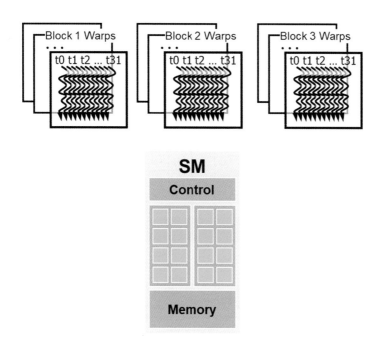

FIGURE 4.6

Blocks are partitioned into warps for thread scheduling.

Blocks are partitioned into warps on the basis of thread indices. If a block is organized into a one-dimensional array, that is, only threadIdx.x is used, the partition is straightforward. The threadIdx.x values within a warp are consecutive and increasing. For a warp size of 32, warp 0 starts with thread 0 and ends with thread 31, warp 1 starts with thread 32 and ends with thread 63, and so on. In general, warp n starts with thread $32 \times n$ and ends with thread $32 \times (n+1) - 1$. For a block whose size is not a multiple of 32, the last warp will be padded with inactive threads to fill up the 32 thread positions. For example, if a block has 48 threads, it will be partitioned into two warps, and the second warp will be padded with 16 inactive threads.

For blocks that consist of multiple dimensions of threads, the dimensions will be projected into a linearized row-major layout before partitioning into warps. The linear layout is determined by placing the rows with larger y and z coordinates after those with lower ones. That is, if a block consists of two dimensions of threads, one will form the linear layout by placing all threads whose threadIdx.y is 1 after those whose threadIdx.y is 0. Threads whose threadIdx.y is 2 will be placed after those whose threadIdx.y is 1, and so on. Threads with the same threadIdx.y value are placed in consecutive positions in increasing threadIdx.x order.

Fig. 4.7 shows an example of placing threads of a two-dimensional block into a linear layout. The upper part shows the two-dimensional view of the block. The reader should recognize the similarity to the row-major layout of two-dimensional arrays. Each thread is shown as $T_{y,x}$, x being threadIdx.x and y being threadIdx.y. The lower part of Fig. 4.7 shows the linearized view of the block. The first four threads are the threads whose threadIdx.y value is 0; they are ordered with increasing threadIdx.x values. The next four threads are the threads whose threadIdx.y value is 1. They are also placed with increasing threadIdx.x values. In this example, all 16 threads form half a warp. The warp will be padded with another 16 threads to complete a 32-thread warp. Imagine a two-dimensional

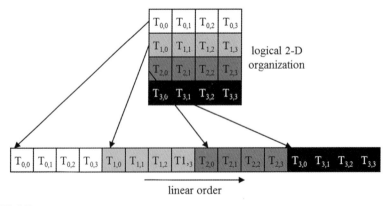

FIGURE 4.7

Placing 2D threads into a linear layout.

block with 8×8 threads. The 64 threads will form two warps. The first warp starts from $T_{0,0}$ and ends with $T_{3,7}$. The second warp starts with $T_{4,0}$ and ends with $T_{7,7}$. It would be useful for the reader to draw out the picture as an exercise.

For a three-dimensional block, we first place all threads whose `threadIdx.z` value is 0 into the linear order. These threads are treated as a two-dimensional block, as shown in Fig. 4.7. All threads whose `threadIdx.z` value is 1 will then be placed into the linear order, and so on. For example, for a three-dimensional $2 \times 8 \times 4$ block (four in the x dimension, eight in the y dimension, and two in the z dimension), the 64 threads will be partitioned into two warps, with $T_{0,0,0}$ through $T_{0,7,3}$ in the first warp and $T_{1,0,0}$ through $T_{1,7,3}$ in the second warp.

An SM is designed to execute all threads in a warp following the single-instruction, multiple-data (SIMD) model. That is, at any instant in time, one instruction is fetched and executed for all threads in the warp (see the "Warps and SIMD Hardware" sidebar). Fig. 4.8 shows how the cores in an SM are grouped into *processing blocks* in which every 8 cores form a processing block and share an instruction fetch/dispatch unit. As a real example, the Ampere A100 SM, which has 64 cores, is organized into four processing blocks with 16 cores each. Threads in the same warp are assigned to the same processing block, which fetches the instruction for the warp and executes it for all threads in the warp at the same time. These threads apply the same instruction to different portions of the data. Because the SIMD hardware effectively restricts all threads in a warp to execute the same instruction at any point in time, the execution behavior of a warp is often referred to as single instruction, multiple-thread.

The advantage of SIMD is that the cost of the control hardware, such as the instruction fetch/dispatch unit, is shared across many execution units. This design choice allows for a smaller percentage of the hardware to be dedicated to control

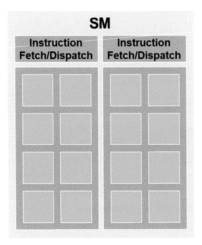

FIGURE 4.8

Streaming multiprocessors are organized into processing blocks for SIMD execution.

and a larger percentage to be dedicated to increasing arithmetic throughput. we expect that in the foreseeable future, warp partitioning will remain a popular implementation technique. However, the size of warp can vary from implementation to implementation. Up to this point in time, all CUDA devices have used similar warp configurations in which each warp consists of 32 threads.

Warps and SIMD Hardware

In his seminal 1945 report, John von Neumann described a model for building electronic computers, which is based on the design of the pioneering EDVAC computer. This model, now commonly referred to as the "von Neumann Model," has been the foundational blueprint for virtually all modern computers.

The von Neumann Model is illustrated in the following figure. The computer has an I/O (input/output) that allows both programs and data to be provided to and generated from the system. To execute a program, the computer first inputs the program and its data into the Memory.

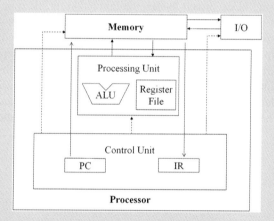

The program consists of a collection of instructions. The Control Unit maintains a Program Counter (PC), which contains the memory address of the next instruction to be executed. In each "instruction cycle," the Control Unit uses the PC to fetch an instruction into the Instruction Register (IR). The instruction bits are then examined to determine the action to be taken by all components of the computer. This is the reason why the model is also called the "stored program" model, which means that a user can change the behavior of a computer by storing a different program into its memory.

The motivation for executing threads as warps is illustrated in the following modified von Neumann model that is adapted to reflect a GPU design. The processor, which corresponds to a processing block in Figure 4.8, has only one control unit that fetches and dispatches instructions. The same control signals (arrows that go from the Control Unit to the Processing Units in Figure 4.8) go to multiple processing units that each correspond to a core in the SM, each of which executes one of the threads in a warp.

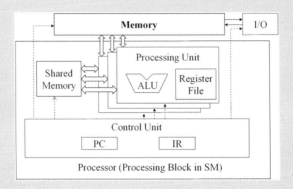

Since all processing units are controlled by the same instruction in the Instruction Register (IR) of the Control Unit, their execution differences are due to the different data operand values in the register files. This is called Single-Instruction-Multiple-Data (SIMD) in processor design. For example, although all processing units (cores) are controlled by an instruction, such as add r1, r2, r3, the contents of r2 and r3 are different in different processing units.

Control units in modern processors are quite complex, including sophisticated logic for fetching instructions and access ports to the instruction cache. Having multiple processing units to share a control unit can result in significant reduction in hardware manufacturing cost and power consumption.

4.5 **Control divergence**

SIMD execution works well when all threads within a warp follow the same execution path, more formally referred to as control flow, when working on their data. For example, for an if-else construct, the execution works well when either all threads in a warp execute the if-path or all execute the else-path. However, when threads within a warp take different control flow paths, the SIMD hardware will take multiple passes through these paths, one pass for each path. For example, for an if-else construct, if some threads in a warp follow the if-path while others follow the else path, the hardware will take two passes. One pass executes the threads that follow the if-path, and the other executes the threads that follow the else-path. During each pass, the threads that follow the other path are not allowed to take effect.

When threads in the same warp follow different execution paths, we say that these threads exhibit *control divergence*, that is, they diverge in their execution. The multipass approach to divergent warp execution extends the SIMD hardware's ability to implement the full semantics of CUDA threads. While the hardware executes the same instruction for all threads in a warp, it selectively lets these threads take effect in only the pass that corresponds to the path that they took, allowing every thread to appear to take its own control flow path. This preserves the independence of threads while taking advantage of the reduced cost of SIMD hardware. The cost of divergence, however, is the extra passes the hardware needs to take to allow different threads in a warp to make their own decisions as well as the execution resources that are consumed by the inactive threads in each pass.

Fig. 4.9 shows an example of how a warp would execute a divergent if-else statement. In this example, when the warp consisting of threads 0–31 arrives at the if-else statement, threads 0–23 take the then-path, while threads 24–31 take the else-path. In this case, the warp will do a pass through the code in which threads 0–23 execute A while threads 24–31 are inactive. The warp will also do another pass through the code in which threads 24–31 execute B while threads 0–23 are inactive. The threads in the warp then reconverge and execute C. In the Pascal architecture and prior architectures, these passes are executed sequentially,

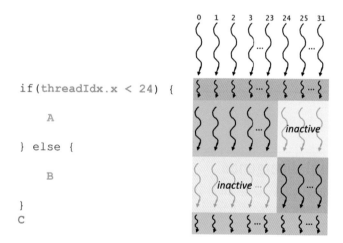

```
if(threadIdx.x < 24) {

    A

} else {

    B

}
    C
```

FIGURE 4.9

Example of a warp diverging at an if-else statement.

meaning that one pass is executed to completion followed by the other pass. From the Volta architecture onwards, the passes may be executed concurrently, meaning that the execution of one pass may be interleaved with the execution of another pass. This feature is referred to as *independent thread scheduling*. Interested readers are referred to the whitepaper on the Volta V100 architecture (NVIDIA, 2017) for details.

Divergence also can arise in other control flow constructs. Fig. 4.10 shows an example of how a warp would execute a divergent for-loop. In this example, each thread executes a different number of loop iterations, which vary between four and eight. For the first four iterations, all threads are active and execute A. For the remaining iterations, some threads execute A, while others are inactive because they have completed their iterations.

One can determine whether a control construct can result in thread divergence by inspecting its decision condition. If the decision condition is based on `threadIdx` values, the control statement can potentially cause thread divergence. For example, the statement `if(threadIdx.x > 2) {...}` causes the threads in the first warp of a block to follow two divergent control flow paths. Threads 0, 1, and 2 follow a different path than that of threads 3, 4, 5, and so on. Similarly, a loop can cause thread divergence if its loop condition is based on thread index values.

A prevalent reason for using a control construct with thread control divergence is handling boundary conditions when mapping threads to data. This is usually because the total number of threads needs to be a multiple of the thread block size, whereas the size of the data can be an arbitrary number. Starting with our vector addition kernel in Chapter 2, Heterogeneous Data Parallel Computing, we had an `if(i<n)` statement in `addVecKernel`. This is because not all vector lengths can be expressed as multiples of the block size. For example, let's assume that the vector length is 1003

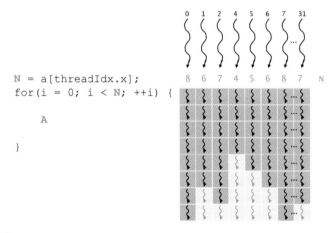

FIGURE 4.10

Example of a warp diverging at a for-loop.

and we picked 64 as the block size. One would need to launch 16 thread blocks to process all the 1003 vector elements. However, the 16 thread blocks would have 1024 threads. We need to disable the last 21 threads in thread block 15 from doing work that is not expected or not allowed by the original program. Keep in mind that these 16 blocks are partitioned into 32 warps. Only the last warp (i.e., the second warp in the last block) will have control divergence.

Note that the performance impact of control divergence decreases as the size of the vectors being processed increases. For a vector length of 100, one of the four warps will have control divergence, which can have significant impact on performance. For a vector size of 1000, only one of the 32 warps will have control divergence. That is, control divergence will affect only about 3% of the execution time. Even if it doubles the execution time of the warp, the net impact on the total execution time will be about 3%. Obviously, if the vector length is 10,000 or more, only one of the 313 warps will have control divergence. The impact of control divergence will be much less than 1%!

For two-dimensional data, such as the color-to-grayscale conversion example in Chapter 3, Multidimensional Grids and Data, if statements are also used to handle the boundary conditions for threads that operate at the edge of the data. In Fig. 3.2, to process the 62×76 image, we used $20 = 4 \times 5$ two-dimensional blocks that consist of 16×16 threads each. Each block will be partitioned into 8 warps; each one consists of two rows of a block. A total 160 warps (8 warps per block) are involved. To analyze the impact of control divergence, refer to Fig. 3.5. None of the warps in the 12 blocks in region 1 will have control divergence. There are $12 \times 8 = 96$ warps in region 1. For region 2, all the 24 warps will have control divergence. For region 3, all the bottom warps are mapped to data that are completely outside the image. As result, none of them will pass the if condition. The reader should verify that these warps would have had control divergence if the picture had an odd number of pixels in the vertical dimension. In region 4, the first 7 warps will have control divergence, but the last warp will not. All in all, 31 out of the 160 warps will have control divergence.

Once again, the performance impact of control divergence decreases as the number of pixels in the horizontal dimension increases. For example, if we process a 200×150 picture with 16×16 blocks, there will be a total of $130 = 13 \times 10$ thread blocks or 1040 warps. The number of warps in regions 1 through 4 will be 864 ($12 \times 9 \times 8$), 72 (9×8), 96 (12×8), and 8 (1×8). Only 80 of these warps will have control divergence. Thus the performance impact of control divergence will be less than 8%. Obviously, if we process a realistic picture with more than 1000 pixels in the horizontal dimension, the performance impact of control divergence will be less than 2%.

An important implication of control divergence is that one cannot assume that all threads in a warp have the same execution timing. Therefore if all threads in a warp must complete a phase of their execution before any of them can move on, one must use a barrier synchronization mechanism such as __syncwarp() to ensure correctness.

4.6 **Warp scheduling and latency tolerance**

When threads are assigned to SMs, there are usually more threads assigned to an SM than there are cores in the SM. That is, each SM has only enough execution units to execute a subset of all the threads assigned to it at any point in time. In earlier GPU designs, each SM can execute only one instruction for a single warp at any given instant. In more recent designs, each SM can execute instructions for a small number of warps at any given point in time. In either case, the hardware can execute instructions only for a subset of all warps in the SM. A legitimate question is why we need to have so many warps assigned to an SM if it can execute only a subset of them at any instant? The answer is that this is how GPUs tolerate long-latency operations such as global memory accesses.

When an instruction to be executed by a warp needs to wait for the result of a previously initiated long-latency operation, the warp is not selected for execution. Instead, another resident warp that is no longer waiting for results of previous instructions will be selected for execution. If more than one warp is ready for execution, a priority mechanism is used to select one for execution. This mechanism of filling the latency time of operations from some threads with work from other threads is often called "latency tolerance" or "latency hiding" (see the "Latency Tolerance" sidebar).

Latency Tolerance

Latency tolerance is needed in many everyday situations. For example, in post offices, each person who is trying to ship a package should ideally have filled out all the forms and labels before going to the service counter. However, as we all have experienced, some people wait for the service desk clerk to tell them which form to fill out and how to fill out the form.

When there is a long line in front of the service desk, it is important to maximize the productivity of the service clerks. Letting a person fill out the form in front of the clerk while everyone waits is not a good approach. The clerk should be helping the next customers who are waiting in line while the person fills out the form. These other customers are "ready to go" and should not be blocked by the customer who needs more time to fill out a form.

This is why a good clerk would politely ask the first customer to step aside to fill out the form while the clerk serves other customers. In most cases, instead of going to the end of the line, the first customer will be served as soon as he or she finishes the form and the clerk finishes serving the current customer.

We can think of these post office customers as warps and the clerk as a hardware execution unit. The customer who needs to fill out the form corresponds to a warp whose continued execution is dependent on a long-latency operation.

Note that warp scheduling is also used for tolerating other types of operation latencies, such as pipelined floating-point arithmetic and branch instructions. With enough warps around, the hardware will likely find a warp to execute at any point in time, thus making full use of the execution hardware while the instructions of some warps wait for the results of these long-latency operations. The selection of warps that are ready for execution does not introduce any idle or wasted time into the execution timeline, which is referred to as *zero-overhead thread scheduling* (see the "Threads, Context-switching, and Zero-overhead Scheduling" sidebar). With warp scheduling, the long waiting time of warp instructions is "hidden" by executing instructions from other warps. This ability to tolerate long operation latencies is the main reason why GPUs do not dedicate nearly as much chip area to cache memories and branch prediction mechanisms as CPUs do. As a result, GPUs can dedicate more chip area to floating-point execution and memory access channel resources.

Threads, Context-switching, and Zero-overhead Scheduling

Based on the von Neumann model, we are ready to more deeply understand how threads are implemented. A thread in modern computers is a program and the state of executing the program on a von Neumann Processor. Recall that a thread consists of the code of a program, the instruction in the code that is being executed, and value of its variables and data structures.

In a computer based on the von Neumann model, the code of the program is stored in the memory. The PC keeps track of the address of the instruction of the program that is being executed. The IR holds the instruction that is being executed. The register and memory hold the values of the variables and data structures.

Modern processors are designed to allow context-switching, where multiple threads can time-share a processor by taking turns to make progress. By carefully saving and restoring the PC value and the contents of registers and memory, we can suspend the execution of a thread and correctly resume the execution of the thread later. However, saving and restoring register contents during context-switching in these processors can incur significant overhead in terms of added execution time.

Zero-overhead scheduling refers to the GPU's ability to put a warp that needs to wait for a long-latency instruction result to sleep and activate a warp that is ready to go without introducing any extra idle cycles in the processing units. Traditional CPUs incur such idle cycles because switching the execution from one thread to another requires saving the execution state (such as register contents of the out-going thread) to memory and loading the execution state of the incoming thread from memory. GPU SMs achieves zero-overhead scheduling by holding all the execution states for the assigned warps in the hardware registers so there is no need to save and restore states when switching from one warp to another.

For latency tolerance to be effective, it is desirable for an SM to have many more threads assigned to it than can be simultaneously supported with its execution resources to maximize the chance of finding a warp that is ready to execute at any point in time. For example, in an Ampere A100 GPU, an SM has 64 cores but can have up to 2048 threads assigned to it at the same time. Thus the SM can have up to 32 times more threads assigned to it than its cores can support at any given clock cycle. This oversubscription of threads to SMs is essential for latency tolerance. It increases the chances of finding another warp to execute when a currently executing warp encounters a long-latency operation.

4.7 Resource partitioning and occupancy

We have seen that it is desirable to assign many warps to an SM in order to tolerate long-latency operations. However, it may not always be possible to assign to the SM the maximum number of warps that the SM supports. The ratio of the number of warps assigned to an SM to the maximum number it supports is referred to as *occupancy*. To understand what may prevent an SM from reaching maximum occupancy, it is important first to understand how SM resources are partitioned.

The execution resources in an SM include registers, shared memory (discussed in Chapter 5, Memory Architecture and Data Locality), thread block slots, and thread slots. These resources are dynamically partitioned across threads to support their execution. For example, an Ampere A100 GPU can support a maximum of 32 blocks per SM, 64 warps (2048 threads) per SM, and 1024 threads per block. If a grid is launched with a block size of 1024 threads (the maximum allowed), the 2048 thread slots in each SM are partitioned and assigned to 2 blocks. In this case, each SM can accommodate up to 2 blocks. Similarly, if a grid is launched with a block size of 512, 256, 128, or 64 threads, the 2048 thread slots are partitioned and assigned to 4, 8, 16, or 32 blocks, respectively.

This ability to dynamically partition thread slots among blocks makes SMs versatile. They can either execute many blocks each having few threads or execute few blocks each having many threads. This dynamic partitioning can be contrasted with a fixed partitioning method in which each block would receive a fixed amount of resources regardless of its real needs. Fixed partitioning results in wasted thread slots when a block requires fewer threads than the fixed partition supports and fails to support blocks that require more thread slots than that.

Dynamic partitioning of resources can lead to subtle interactions between resource limitations, which can cause underutilization of resources. Such interactions can occur between block slots and thread slots. In the example of the Ampere A100, we saw that the block size can be varied from 1024 to 64, resulting in 2−32 blocks per SM, respectively. In all these cases, the total number of threads assigned to the SM is 2048, which maximizes occupancy. Consider, however, the case when each block has 32 threads. In this case, the 2048 thread slots would need to be partitioned and assigned to 64 blocks. However, the Volta SM can support only 32 blocks slots at once. This means that only 1024 of the thread slots will be utilized, that is, 32 blocks with 32 threads each. The occupancy in this case is (1024 assigned threads)/(2048 maximum threads) = 50%. Therefore to fully utilize the thread slots and achieve maximum occupancy, one needs at least 64 threads in each block.

Another situation that could negatively affect occupancy occurs when the maximum number of threads per block is not divisible by the block size. In the example of the Ampere A100, we saw that up to 2048 threads per SM can be supported. However, if a block size of 768 is selected, the SM will be able to accommodate only 2 thread blocks (1536 threads), leaving 512 thread slots unutilized. In this case, neither the maximum threads per SM nor the maximum blocks per SM are reached. The occupancy in this case is (1536 assigned threads)/(2,048 maximum threads) = 75%.

The preceding discussion does not consider the impact of other resource constraints, such as registers and shared memory. We will see in Chapter 5, Memory Architecture and Data Locality, that automatic variables declared in a CUDA kernel are placed into registers. Some kernels may use many automatic variables, and others may use few of them. Therefore one should expect that some kernels require many registers per thread and some require few. By dynamically partitioning registers in an SM across threads, the SM can accommodate many blocks if they require few registers per thread and fewer blocks if they require more registers per thread.

One does, however, need to be aware of potential impact of register resource limitations on occupancy. For example, the Ampere A100 GPU allows a maximum of 65,536 registers per SM. To run at full occupancy, each SM needs enough registers for 2048 threads, which means that each thread should not use more than (65,536 registers)/(2048 threads) = 32 registers per thread. For example, if a kernel uses 64 registers per thread, the maximum number of threads that can be supported with 65,536 registers is 1024 threads. In this case, the kernel cannot run with full occupancy regardless of what the block size is set to be. Instead, the occupancy will be at most 50%. In some cases, the compiler may perform register spilling to reduce the register requirement per thread and thus elevate the level of occupancy. However, this is typically at the cost of increased execution time for the threads to access the spilled register values from memory and may cause the total execution time of the grid to increase. A similar analysis is done for the shared memory resource in Chapter 5, Memory Architecture and Data Locality.

Assume that a programmer implements a kernel that uses 31 registers per thread and configures it with 512 threads per block. In this case, the SM will have (2048 threads)/(512 threads/block) = 4 blocks running simultaneously. These threads will use a total of (2048 threads) × (31 registers/thread) = 63,488 registers, which is less than the 65,536 register limit. Now assume that the programmer declares another two automatic variables in the kernel, bumping the number of registers used by each thread to 33. The number of registers required by 2048 threads is now 67,584 registers, which exceeds the register limit. The CUDA runtime system may deal with this situation by assigning only 3 blocks to each SM instead of 4, thus reducing the number of registers required to 50,688 registers. However, this reduces the number of threads running on an SM from 2048 to 1536; that is, by using two extra automatic variables, the program saw a reduction in occupancy from 100% to 75%. This is sometimes referred to as a "performance cliff," in which a slight increase in resource usage can result in significant reduction in parallelism and performance achieved (Ryoo et al., 2008).

It should be clear to the reader that the constraints of all the dynamically partitioned resources interact with each other in a complex manner. Accurate determination of the number of threads running in each SM can be difficult. The reader is referred to the CUDA Occupancy Calculator (CUDA Occupancy Calculator, Web) which is a downloadable spreadsheet that calculates the actual number of threads running on each SM for a particular device implementation given the usage of resources by a kernel.

4.8 Querying device properties

Our discussion on partitioning of SM resources raises an important question: How do we find out the amount of resources available for a particular device? When a CUDA application executes on a system, how can it find out the number of SMs in a device and the number of blocks and threads that can be assigned to each SM? The same questions apply to other kinds of resources, some of which we have not discussed so far. In general, many modern applications are designed to execute on a wide variety of hardware systems. There is often a need for the application to *query* the available resources and capabilities of the underlying hardware in order to take advantage of the more capable systems while compensating for the less capable systems (see the "Resource and Capability Queries" sidebar).

Resource and Capability Queries

In everyday life, we often query the resources and capabilities in an environment. For example, when we make a hotel reservation, we can check the amenities that come with a hotel room. If the room comes with a hair dryer, we do not need to bring one. Most American hotel rooms come with hair dryers, while many hotels in other regions do not.

Some Asian and European hotels provide toothpaste and even toothbrushes, while most American hotels do not. Many American hotels provide both shampoo and conditioner, while hotels in other continents often provide only shampoo.

If the room comes with a microwave oven and a refrigerator, we can take the leftovers from dinner and expect to eat them the next day. If the hotel has a pool, we can bring swimsuits and take a dip after business meetings. If the hotel does not have a pool but has an exercise room, we can bring running shoes and exercise clothes. Some high-end Asian hotels even provide exercise clothing!

> *These hotel amenities are part of the properties, or resources and capa-*
> *bilities, of the hotels. Veteran travelers check the properties at hotel web-*
> *sites, choose the hotels that best match their needs, and pack more*
> *efficiently and effectively.*

The amount of resources in each CUDA device SM is specified as part of the *compute capability* of the device. In general, the higher the compute capability level, the more resources are available in each SM. The compute capability of GPUs tends to increase from generation to generation. The Ampere A100 GPU has compute capability 8.0.

In CUDA C, there is a built-in mechanism for the host code to query the properties of the devices that are available in the system. The CUDA runtime system (device driver) has an API function `cudaGetDeviceCount` that returns the number of available CUDA devices in the system. The host code can find out the number of available CUDA devices by using the following statements:

```
int devCount;
cudaGetDeviceCount(&devCount);
```

While it may not be obvious, a modern PC system often has two or more CUDA devices. This is because many PC systems come with one or more "integrated" GPUs. These GPUs are the default graphics units and provide rudimentary capabilities and hardware resources to perform minimal graphics functionalities for modern window-based user interfaces. Most CUDA applications will not perform very well on these integrated devices. This would be a reason for the host code to iterate through all the available devices, query their resources and capabilities, and choose the ones that have enough resources to execute the application with satisfactory performance.

The CUDA runtime numbers all the available devices in the system from 0 to `devCount-1`. It provides an API function `cudaGetDeviceProperties` that returns the properties of the device whose number is given as an argument. For example, we can use the following statements in the host code to iterate through the available devices and query their properties:

```
cudaDeviceProp devProp;
for(unsigned int i = 0; i < devCount; i++) {
    cudaGetDeviceProperties(&devProp, i);
    //    Decide    if    device    has    sufficient
resources/capabilities
}
```

The built-in type `cudaDeviceProp` is a C struct type with fields that represent the properties of a CUDA device. The reader is referred to the CUDA C Programming Guide for all the fields of the type. We will discuss a few of these fields that are particularly relevant to the assignment of execution resources to threads. We assume that the properties are returned in the devProp variable whose fields are set by the `cudaGetDeviceProperties` function. If the reader chooses to name the variable differently, the appropriate variable name will obviously need to be substituted in the following discussion.

As the name suggests, the field `devProp.maxThreadsPerBlock` gives the maximum number of threads allowed in a block in the queried device. Some devices allow up to 1024 threads in each block, and other devices may allow fewer. It is possible that future devices may even allow more than 1024 threads per block. Therefore it is a good idea to query the available devices and determine which ones will allow a sufficient number of threads in each block as far as the application is concerned.

The number of SMs in the device is given in `devProp.multiProcessorCount`. If the application requires many SMs to achieve satisfactory performance, it should definitely check this property of the prospective device. Furthermore, the clock frequency of the device is in `devProp.clockRate`. The combination the clock rate and the number of SMs gives a good indication of the maximum hardware execution throughput of the device.

The host code can find the maximum number of threads allowed along each dimension of a block in fields `devProp.maxThreadsDim[0]` (for the x dimension), `devProp.maxThreadsDim[1]` (for the y dimension), and `devProp.maxThreadsDim[2]` (for the z dimension). An example of use of this information is for an automated tuning system to set the range of block dimensions when evaluating the best performing block dimensions for the underlying hardware. Similarly, it can find the maximum number of blocks allowed along each dimension of a grid in `devProp.maxGridSize[0]` (for the x dimension), `devProp.maxGridSize[1]` (for the y dimension), and `devProp.maxGridSize[2]` (for the z dimension). A typical use of this information is to determine whether a grid can have enough threads to handle the entire dataset or some kind of iterative approach is needed.

The field `devProp.regsPerBlock` gives the number of registers that are available in each SM. This field can be useful in determining whether the kernel can achieve maximum occupancy on a particular device or will be limited by its register usage. Note that the name of the field is a little misleading. For most compute capability levels, the maximum number of registers that a block can use is indeed the same as the total number of registers that are available in the SM. However, for some compute capability levels, the maximum number of registers that a block can use is less than the total that are available on the SM.

We have also discussed that the size of warps depends on the hardware. The size of warps can be obtained from the `devProp.warpSize` field.

There are many more fields in the `cudaDeviceProp` type. We will discuss them throughout the book as we introduce the concepts and features that they are designed to reflect.

4.9 Summary

A GPU is organized into SM, which consist of multiple processing blocks of cores that share control logic and memory resources. When a grid is launched, its blocks are assigned to SMs in an arbitrary order, resulting in transparent scalability of CUDA applications. The transparent scalability comes with a limitation: Threads in different blocks cannot synchronize with each other.

Threads are assigned to SMs for execution on a block-by-block basis. Once a block has been assigned to an SM, it is further partitioned into warps. Threads in a warp are executed following the SIMD model. If threads in the same warp diverge by taking different execution paths, the processing block executes these paths in passes in which each thread is active only in the pass corresponding to the path that it takes.

An SM may have many more threads assigned to it than it can execute simultaneously. At any time, the SM executes instructions of only a small subset of its resident warps. This allows the other warps to wait for long-latency operations without slowing down the overall execution throughput of the massive number of processing units. The ratio of the number of threads assigned to the SM to the maximum number of threads it can support is referred to as *occupancy*. The higher the occupancy of an SM, the better it can hide long-latency operations.

Each CUDA device imposes a potentially different limitation on the amount of resources available in each SM. For example, each CUDA device has a limit on the number of blocks, the number of threads, the number of registers, and the amount of other resources that each of its SMs can accommodate. For each kernel, one or more of these resource limitations can become the limiting factor for occupancy. CUDA C provides programmers with the ability to query the resources available in a GPU at runtime.

Exercises

1. Consider the following CUDA kernel and the corresponding host function that calls it:

```
01    __global__ void foo_kernel(int* a, int* b) {
02        unsigned int i = blockIdx.x*blockDim.x + threadIdx.x;
03        if(threadIdx.x < 40 || threadIdx.x >= 104) {
04            b[i] = a[i] + 1;
05        }
06        if(i%2 == 0) {
07            a[i] = b[i]*2;
08        }
09        for(unsigned int j = 0; j < 5 - (i%3); ++j) {
10            b[i] += j;
11        }
12    }
13    void foo(int* a_d, int* b_d) {
14        unsigned int N = 1024;
15        foo_kernel <<< (N + 128 - 1)/128, 128 >>>(a_d, b_d);
16    }
```

a. What is the number of warps per block?
b. What is the number of warps in the grid?
c. For the statement on line 04:
   i. How many warps in the grid are active?
   ii. How many warps in the grid are divergent?
   iii. What is the SIMD efficiency (in %) of warp 0 of block 0?
   iv. What is the SIMD efficiency (in %) of warp 1 of block 0?
   v. What is the SIMD efficiency (in %) of warp 3 of block 0?
d. For the statement on line 07:
   i. How many warps in the grid are active?
   ii. How many warps in the grid are divergent?
   iii. What is the SIMD efficiency (in %) of warp 0 of block 0?
e. For the loop on line 09:
   i. How many iterations have no divergence?
   ii. How many iterations have divergence?

2. For a vector addition, assume that the vector length is 2000, each thread calculates one output element, and the thread block size is 512 threads. How many threads will be in the grid?

3. For the previous question, how many warps do you expect to have divergence due to the boundary check on vector length?

4. Consider a hypothetical block with 8 threads executing a section of code before reaching a barrier. The threads require the following amount of time (in microseconds) to execute the sections: 2.0, 2.3, 3.0, 2.8, 2.4, 1.9, 2.6, and 2.9; they spend the rest of their time waiting for the barrier. What percentage of the threads' total execution time is spent waiting for the barrier?

5. A CUDA programmer says that if they launch a kernel with only 32 threads in each block, they can leave out the __syncthreads() instruction wherever barrier synchronization is needed. Do you think this is a good idea? Explain.

6. If a CUDA device's SM can take up to 1536 threads and up to 4 thread blocks, which of the following block configurations would result in the most number of threads in the SM?
a. 128 threads per block
b. 256 threads per block
c. 512 threads per block
d. 1024 threads per block

7. Assume a device that allows up to 64 blocks per SM and 2048 threads per SM. Indicate which of the following assignments per SM are possible. In the cases in which it is possible, indicate the occupancy level.
a. 8 blocks with 128 threads each
b. 16 blocks with 64 threads each
c. 32 blocks with 32 threads each
d. 64 blocks with 32 threads each
e. 32 blocks with 64 threads each

8. Consider a GPU with the following hardware limits: 2048 threads per SM, 32 blocks per SM, and 64K (65,536) registers per SM. For each of the following kernel characteristics, specify whether the kernel can achieve full occupancy. If not, specify the limiting factor.
   a. The kernel uses 128 threads per block and 30 registers per thread.
   b. The kernel uses 32 threads per block and 29 registers per thread.
   c. The kernel uses 256 threads per block and 34 registers per thread.
9. A student mentions that they were able to multiply two 1024 × 1024 matrices using a matrix multiplication kernel with 32 × 32 thread blocks. The student is using a CUDA device that allows up to 512 threads per block and up to 8 blocks per SM. The student further mentions that each thread in a thread block calculates one element of the result matrix. What would be your reaction and why?

References

CUDA Occupancy Calculator, 2021. https://docs.nvidia.com/cuda/cuda-occupancy-calculator/index.html.

NVIDIA (2017). NVIDIA Tesla V100 GPU Architecture. Version WP-08608-001_v1.1.

Ryoo, S., Rodrigues, C., Stone, S., Baghsorkhi, S., Ueng, S., Stratton, J., et al., Program optimization space pruning for a multithreaded GPU. In: Proceedings of the Sixth ACM/IEEE International Symposium on Code Generation and Optimization, April 6–9, 2008.

Memory architecture and data locality

5

Chapter Outline

5.1 Importance of memory access efficiency 94
5.2 CUDA memory types 96
5.3 Tiling for reduced memory traffic 103
5.4 A tiled matrix multiplication kernel 107
5.5 Boundary checks 112
5.6 Impact of memory usage on occupancy 115
5.7 Summary 118
Exercises 119

So far, we have learned how to write a CUDA kernel function and how to configure and coordinate its execution by a massive number of threads. We have also looked at the compute architecture of current GPU hardware and how threads are scheduled to execute on this hardware. In this chapter we will focus on the on-chip memory architecture of the GPU and begin to study how one can organize and position data for efficient access by a massive number of threads. The CUDA kernels that we have studied so far will likely achieve only a tiny fraction of the potential speed of the underlying hardware. This poor performance is because global memory, which is typically implemented with off-chip DRAM, tends to have long access latency (hundreds of clock cycles) and finite access bandwidth. While having many threads available for execution can theoretically tolerate long memory access latencies, one can easily run into a situation in which traffic congestion in the global memory access paths prevents all but a very few threads from making progress, thus rendering some of the cores in the streaming multiprocessors (SMs) idle. To circumvent such congestion, GPUs provide a number of additional on-chip memory resources for accessing data that can remove the majority of traffic to and from the global memory. In this chapter we will study the use of different memory types to boost the execution performance of CUDA kernels.

Programming Massively Parallel Processors. DOI: https://doi.org/10.1016/B978-0-323-91231-0.00018-5

5.1 Importance of memory access efficiency

We can illustrate the effect of memory access efficiency by calculating the expected performance level of the most executed portion of the matrix multiplication kernel code in Fig. 3.11, which is partially replicated in Fig. 5.1. The most important part of the kernel in terms of execution time is the for-loop that performs the dot product of a row of M with a column of N.

In every iteration of the loop, two global memory accesses are performed for one floating-point multiplication and one floating-point addition. The global memory accesses fetch elements from the M and N arrays. The floating-point multiplication operation multiplies these two elements together, and the floating-point add operation accumulates the product into `Pvalue`. Thus the ratio of floating-point operations (FLOP) to bytes (B) accessed from global memory is 2 FLOP to 8 B, or 0.25 FLOP/B. We will refer to this ratio as the *compute to global memory access ratio*, defined as the number of FLOPs performed for each byte access from the global memory within a region of a program. This ratio is sometimes also referred to as *arithmetic intensity* or *computational intensity* in the literature.

The compute to global memory access ratio has major implications for the performance of a CUDA kernel. For example, the Ampere A100 GPU has a peak global memory bandwidth of 1555 GB/second. Since the matrix multiplication kernel performs 0.25 OP/B, the global memory bandwidth limits the throughput of single-precision FLOPs that can be performed by the kernel to 389 giga FLOPs per second (GFLOPS), obtained by multiplying 1555 GB/second with 0.25 FLOP/B. However, 389 GFLOPS is only 2% of the peak single-precision operation throughput of the A100 GPU, which is 19,500 GFLOPS. The A100 also comes with special purpose units called *tensor cores* that are useful for accelerating matrix multiplication operations. If one considers the A100's tensor-core peak single-precision floating-point throughput of 156,000 GFLOPS, 389 GFLOPS is only 0.25% of the peak. Thus the execution of the matrix multiplication kernel is severely limited by the rate at which the data can be delivered from memory to the GPU cores. We refer to programs whose execution speed is limited by memory bandwidth as *memory-bound* programs.

```
07    for (int k = 0; k < Width; ++k) {
08        Pvalue += M[row*Width+k] * N[k*Width+col];
09    }
```

FIGURE 5.1

The most executed part of the matrix multiplication kernel in Fig. 3.11.

The Roofline Model

The Roofline Model is a visual model for assessing the performance achieved by an application relative to the limits of the hardware it is running on. A basic example of the Roofline model is shown below.

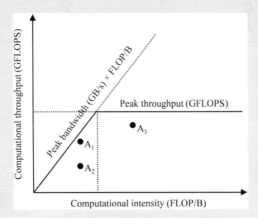

On the x-axis, we have arithmetic or computational intensity measured in FLOP/B. It reflects the amount of work done by an application for every byte of data loaded. On the y-axis, we have computational throughput measured in GFLOPS. The two lines inside of the plot reflect the hardware limits. The horizontal line is determined by the peak computational throughput (GFLOPS) that the hardware can sustain. The line with a positive slope starting from the origin is determined by the peak memory bandwidth that the hardware can sustain. A point in the plot represents an application with its operational intensity on the x-axis and the computational throughput it achieves on the y-axis. Of course, the points will be under the two lines because they cannot achieve higher throughput than the hardware peak.

The position of a point relative to the two lines tells us about an application's efficiency. Points close to the two lines indicate that an application is using memory bandwidth or compute units efficiently, whereas applications far below the lines indicate inefficient use of resources. The point of intersection between these two lines represents the computational intensity value at which applications transition from being memory bound to being compute bound. Applications with lower computational intensity are memory-bound and cannot achieve peak throughput because they are limited by memory bandwidth. Applications with higher computational intensity are compute-bound and are not limited by memory bandwidth.

> *As an example, points A_1 and A_2 both represent memory-bound applications, while A_3 represents a compute-bound application. A_1 uses resources efficiently and operates close to the peak memory bandwidth, whereas A_2 does not. For A_2, there may be room for additional optimizations to improve throughput by improving memory bandwidth utilization. However, for A_1 the only way to improve throughput is to increase the computational intensity of the application.*

To achieve higher performance for this kernel, we need to increase the compute to global memory access ratio of the kernel by reducing the number of global memory accesses it performs. For example, to fully utilize the 19,500 GFLOPS that the A100 GPU provides, a ratio of at least (19,500 GOP/second)/(1555 GB/second)=12.5 OP/B is needed. This ratio means that for every 4-byte floating point value accessed, there must be about 50 floating-point operations performed! The extent to which such a ratio can be achieved depends on the intrinsic data reuse in the computation at hand. We refer the reader to the "The Roofline Model" sidebar for a useful model for analyzing a program's potential performance with respect to its compute intensity.

As we will see, matrix multiplication presents opportunities for reduction of global memory accesses that can be captured with relatively simple techniques. The execution speed of matrix multiplication functions can vary by orders of magnitude, depending on the level of reduction of global memory accesses. Therefore matrix multiplication provides an excellent initial example for such techniques. This chapter introduces a commonly used technique for reducing the number of global memory accesses and demonstrates the technique on matrix multiplication.

5.2 CUDA memory types

A CUDA device contains several types of memory that can help programmers to improve the compute to global memory access ratio. Fig. 5.2 shows these CUDA device memories. At the bottom of the figure, we see global memory and constant memory. Both these types of memory can be written (W) and read (R) by the host. The global memory can also be written and read by the device, whereas the constant memory supports short-latency, high-bandwidth read-only access by the device. We introduced global memory in Chapter 2, Heterogeneous Data Parallel Computing, and we will look at constant memory in detail in Chapter 7, Convolution.

Another type of memory is the local memory, which can also be read and written. The local memory is actually placed in global memory and has similar access latency, but it is not shared across threads. Each thread has its own section of global memory that it uses as its own private local memory where it places data that is private to the thread but cannot be allocated in registers. This data includes statically allocated arrays, spilled registers, and other elements of the thread's call stack.

Registers and shared memory in Fig. 5.2 are on-chip memories. Variables that reside in these types of memory can be accessed at very high speed in a highly parallel manner. Registers are allocated to individual threads; each thread can access only its own registers (see the "CPU versus GPU Register Architecture" sidebar). A kernel function typically uses registers to hold frequently accessed variables that are private to each thread. Shared memory is allocated to thread blocks; all threads in a block can access shared memory variables declared for the block. Shared memory is an efficient means by which threads can cooperate by sharing their input data and intermediate results. By declaring a CUDA variable in one of the CUDA memory types, a CUDA programmer dictates the visibility and access speed of the variable.

CPU vs. GPU Register Architecture

The different design objectives across the CPUs and GPUs result in different register architectures. As we saw in Chapter 4, Compute Architecture and Scheduling, when CPUs context switch between different threads, they save the registers of the outgoing thread to memory and restore the registers of the incoming thread from memory. In contrast, GPUs achieve zero-overhead scheduling by keeping the registers of all the threads that are scheduled on the processing block in the processing block's register file. This way, switching between warps of threads is instantaneous because the registers of the incoming threads are already in the register file. Consequently, GPU register files need to be substantially larger than CPU register files.

We also saw in Chapter 4, Compute Architecture and Scheduling, that GPUs support dynamic resource partitioning where an SM may provision few registers per thread and execute a large number of threads, or it my provision more registers per thread and execute fewer threads. For this reason, GPU register files need to be designed to support such dynamic partitioning of registers. In contrast, the CPU register architecture dedicates a fixed set of registers per thread regardless of the thread's actual demand for registers.

To fully appreciate the difference between registers, shared memory, and global memory, we need to go into a little more detail about how these different memory types are realized and used in modern processors. As we discussed in the "Warps and SIMD Hardware" sidebar in Chapter 4, Compute Architecture and Scheduling, virtually all modern processors find their root in the model proposed by John von Neumann in 1945, which is shown in Fig. 5.3. CUDA devices are no exception. The global memory in a CUDA device maps to the Memory box in Fig. 5.3. The

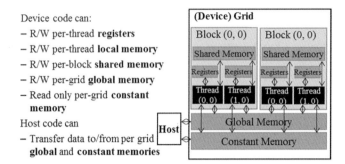

Device code can:
- R/W per-thread **registers**
- R/W per-thread **local memory**
- R/W per-block **shared memory**
- R/W per-grid **global memory**
- Read only per-grid **constant memory**

Host code can
- Transfer data to/from per grid **global** and **constant memories**

(Device) Grid

Block (0, 0)   Block (0, 0)

Shared Memory   Shared Memory

Registers Registers   Registers Registers

Thread (0, 0) Thread (1, 0)   Thread (0, 0) Thread (1, 0)

Host

Global Memory

Constant Memory

FIGURE 5.2

An (incomplete) overview of the CUDA device memory model. An important type of CUDA memory that is not shown in this figure is the texture memory, since its use is not covered in this textbook.

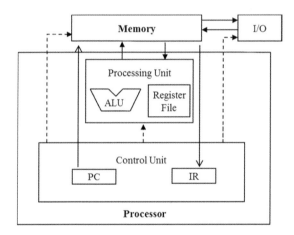

FIGURE 5.3

Memory versus registers in a modern computer based on the von Neumann model.

processor box corresponds to the processor chip boundary that we typically see today. The global memory is off the processor chip and is implemented with DRAM technology, which implies long access latencies and relatively low access bandwidth. The registers correspond to the "Register File" of the von Neumann model. The Register File is on the processor chip, which implies very short access latency and drastically higher access bandwidth when compared to the global memory. In a typical device, the aggregated access bandwidth of all the register files across all the SMs is at least two orders of magnitude higher than that of the global memory. Furthermore, whenever a variable is stored in a register, its accesses no longer consume off-chip global memory bandwidth. This will be reflected as an increased compute to global memory access ratio.

A subtler point is that each access to registers involves fewer instructions than an access to the global memory. Arithmetic instructions in most modern processors have "built-in" register operands. For example, a floating-point addition instruction might be of the following form:

```
fadd r1, r2, r3
```

where r2 and r3 are the register numbers that specify the location in the register file where the input operand values can be found. The location for storing the floating-point addition result value is specified by r1. Therefore when an operand of an arithmetic instruction is in a register, no additional instruction is required to make the operand value available to the arithmetic and logic unit (ALU), where the arithmetic calculation is done.

Meanwhile, if an operand value is in the global memory, the processor needs to perform a memory load operation to make the operand value available to the ALU. For example, if the first operand of a floating-point addition instruction is in the global memory, the instructions that are involved will likely look like the following example:

```
load r2, r4, offset
fadd r1, r2, r3
```

where the load instruction adds an offset value to the contents of r4 to form an address for the operand value. It then accesses the global memory and places the value into register r2. Once the operand value is in r2, the fadd instruction performs the floating-point addition using the values in r2 and r3 and places the result into r1. Since the processor can fetch and execute only a limited number of instructions per clock cycle, the version with an additional load will likely take more time to process than the one without. This is another reason why placing the operands in registers can improve execution speed.

Finally, there is yet another subtle reason why placing an operand value in registers is preferable. In modern computers the energy that is consumed for accessing a value from the register file is at least an order of magnitude lower than for accessing a value from the global memory. Accessing a value from registers has a tremendous advantage in energy efficiency over accessing the value from the global memory. We will look at more details of the speed and energy difference in accessing these two hardware structures in modern computers soon. On the other hand, as we will soon learn, the number of registers that are available to each thread is quite limited in today's GPUs. As we saw in Chapter 4, Compute Architecture and Scheduling, the occupancy that is achieved for an application can be reduced if the register usage in full-occupancy scenarios exceeds the limit. Therefore we also need to avoid oversubscribing to this limited resource whenever possible.

Fig. 5.4 shows the shared memory and registers in a CUDA device. Although both are on-chip memories, they differ significantly in functionality and cost of access. Shared memory is designed as part of the memory space that resides on the processor chip. When the processor accesses data that resides in the shared memory, it needs to perform a memory load operation, just as in accessing data in the global memory. However, because shared memory resides on-chip, it can be accessed with much lower latency and much higher throughput than the global memory. Because of the need to perform a load operation, shared memory has longer latency and lower bandwidth than registers. In computer architecture terminology the shared memory is a form of *scratchpad memory*.

One important difference between the shared memory and registers in CUDA is that variables that reside in the shared memory are accessible by all threads in a block. This contrasts with register data, which is private to a thread. That is, shared memory is designed to support efficient, high-bandwidth sharing of data among threads in a block. As shown in Fig. 5.4, a CUDA device SM typically employs multiple processing units to allow multiple threads to make simultaneous progress (see the "Threads" sidebar) in Chapter 2, Heterogeneous Data Parallel Computing. Threads in a block can be spread across these processing units. Therefore the hardware implementations of the shared memory in these CUDA devices are typically designed to allow multiple processing units to simultaneously access its contents to support efficient data sharing among threads in a block. We will be learning several important types of parallel algorithms that can greatly benefit from such efficient data sharing among threads.

It should be clear by now that registers, local memory, shared memory, and global memory all have different functionalities, latencies, and bandwidth. It is therefore important to understand how to declare a variable so that it will reside in the intended type of memory. Table 5.1 presents the CUDA syntax for declaring program variables into the various memory types. Each such declaration also gives its declared CUDA variable a scope and lifetime. Scope identifies the set of

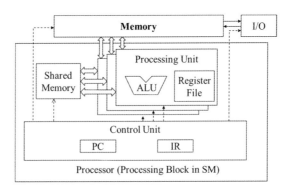

FIGURE 5.4

Shared memory versus registers in a CUDA device SM.

Table 5.1 CUDA variable declaration type qualifiers and the properties of each type.

Variable declaration	Memory	Scope	Lifetime
Automatic variables other than arrays	Register	Thread	Grid
Automatic array variables	Local	Thread	Grid
__device__ __shared__ int SharedVar;	Shared	Block	Grid
__device__ int GlobalVar;	Global	Grid	Application
__device__ __constant__ int ConstVar;	Constant	Grid	Application

threads that can access the variable: a single thread only, all threads of a block, or all threads of all grids. If a variable's scope is a single thread, a private version of the variable will be created for every thread; each thread can access only its private version of the variable. For example, if a kernel declares a variable whose scope is a thread and it is launched with one million threads, one million versions of the variable will be created so that each thread initializes and uses its own version of the variable.

Lifetime tells the portion of the program's execution duration when the variable is available for use: either within a grid's execution or throughout the entire application. If a variable's lifetime is within a grid's execution, it must be declared within the kernel function body and will be available for use only by the kernel's code. If the kernel is invoked several times, the value of the variable is not maintained across these invocations. Each invocation must initialize the variable in order to use it. On the other hand, if a variable's lifetime is throughout the entire application, it must be declared outside of any function body. The contents of these variables are maintained throughout the execution of the application and available to all kernels.

We refer to variables that are not arrays as *scalar* variables. As shown in Table 5.1, all automatic scalar variables that are declared in kernel and device functions are placed into registers. The scopes of these automatic variables are within individual threads. When a kernel function declares an automatic variable, a private copy of that variable is generated for every thread that executes the kernel function. When a thread terminates, all its automatic variables cease to exist. In Fig. 5.1, variables `blurRow`, `blurCol`, `curRow`, `curCol`, `pixels`, and `pixVal` are all automatic variables and fall into this category. Note that accessing these variables is extremely fast and parallel, but one must be careful not to exceed the limited capacity of the register storage in the hardware implementations. Using a large number of registers can negatively affect the occupancy of each SM, as we saw in Chapter 4, Compute Architecture and Scheduling.

Automatic array variables are not stored in registers.[1] Instead, they are stored into the thread's local memory and may incur long access delays and potential

---

[1]There are some exceptions to this rule. The compiler may decide to store an automatic array into registers if all accesses are done with constant index values.

access congestions. The scope of these arrays, like that of automatic scalar variables, is limited to individual threads. That is, a private version of each automatic array is created for and used by every thread. Once a thread terminates its execution, the contents of its automatic array variables cease to exist. From our experience, one seldom needs to use automatic array variables in kernel functions and device functions.

If a variable declaration is preceded by the `__shared__` keyword (each "`_`" consists of two "`_`" characters), it declares a shared variable in CUDA. One can also add an optional `__device__` in front of `__shared__` in the declaration to achieve the same effect. Such a declaration is typically made within a kernel function or a device function. Shared variables reside in the shared memory. The scope of a shared variable is within a thread block; that is, all threads in a block see the same version of a shared variable. A private version of the shared variable is created for and used by each block during kernel execution. The lifetime of a shared variable is within the duration of the kernel execution. When a kernel terminates its grid's execution, the contents of its shared variables cease to exist. As we discussed earlier, shared variables are an efficient means for threads within a block to collaborate with each other. Accessing shared variables from the shared memory is extremely fast and highly parallel. CUDA programmers often use shared variables to hold the portion of global memory data that is frequently used and reused in an execution phase of the kernel. One may need to adjust the algorithms that are used to create execution phases that heavily focus on small portions of the global memory data, as we will demonstrate with matrix multiplication in Section 5.4.

If a variable declaration is preceded by keyword `__constant__`' (each "`_`" consists of two "`_`" characters), it declares a constant variable in CUDA. One can also add an optional `__device__` in front of `__constant__` to achieve the same effect. Declaration of constant variables must be outside any function body. The scope of a constant variable is all grids, meaning that all threads in all grids see the same version of a constant variable. The lifetime of a constant variable is the entire application execution. Constant variables are often used for variables that provide input values to kernel functions. The values of the constant variables cannot be changed by the kernel function code. Constant variables are stored in the global memory but are cached for efficient access. With appropriate access patterns, accessing constant memory is extremely fast and parallel. Currently, the total size of constant variables in an application is limited to 65,536 bytes. One may need to break up the input data volume to fit within this limitation. We will demonstrate the usage of constant memory in Chapter 7, Convolution.

A variable whose declaration is preceded only by the keyword `__device__` (each "`_`" consists of two "`_`" characters) is a global variable and will be placed in the global memory. Accesses to a global variable are slow. Latency and throughput of accessing global variables have been improved with caches in more recent devices. One important advantage of global variables is that they are visible to all threads of all kernels. Their contents also persist through the entire execution. Thus global variables can be used as a means for threads to collaborate across blocks. However, one must be aware that there is currently no easy way to synchronize between threads from different thread blocks or to ensure data consistency across threads in accessing global memory other than using atomic operations or terminating the current kernel execution.[2] Therefore global variables are often used to pass information from one kernel invocation to another kernel invocation.

In CUDA, pointers can be used to point to data objects in the global memory. There are two typical ways in which pointer use arises in kernel and device functions. First, if an object is allocated by a host function, the pointer to the object is initialized by memory allocation API functions such as `cudaMalloc` and can be passed to the kernel function as a parameter, as we saw in Chapter 2, Heterogeneous Data Parallel Computing, and Chapter 3, Multidimensional Grids and Data. The second type of use is to assign the address of a variable that is declared in the global memory to a pointer variable. For example, the statement `{float* ptr=&GlobalVar;}` in a kernel function assigns the address of `GlobalVar` into an automatic pointer variable `ptr`. The reader should refer to the CUDA Programming Guide for using pointers in other memory types.

5.3 **Tiling for reduced memory traffic**

We have an intrinsic tradeoff in the use of device memories in CUDA: The global memory is large but slow, whereas the shared memory is small but fast. A common strategy is to partition the data into subsets called *tiles* so that each tile fits into the shared memory. The term *tile* draws on the analogy that a large wall (i.e., the global memory data) can be covered by small tiles (i.e., subsets that can each fit into the shared memory). An important criterion is that the kernel computation on these tiles can be done independently of each other. Note that not all data structures can be partitioned into tiles, given an arbitrary kernel function.

The concept of tiling can be illustrated with the matrix multiplication example from Chapter 3, Multidimensional Grids and Data. Fig. 3.13 showed a small example of matrix multiplication. It corresponds to the kernel function in Fig. 3.11. We replicate the example in Fig. 5.5 for convenient reference. For brevity we abbreviate P[y*Width+x], M[y*Width+x], and N[y*Width+x] into $P_{y,x}$, $M_{y,x}$, and $N_{y,x}$, respectively. This example assumes that we use four $\times$ 2 blocks to compute the P matrix. The heavy boxes in the P matrix define the P elements that are processed by each block. Fig. 5.5 highlights the computation done by the four threads of block$_{0,0}$. These four threads compute $P_{0,0}$, $P_{0,1}$, $P_{1,0}$, and $P_{1,1}$. The

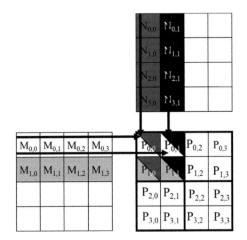

FIGURE 5.5

A small example of matrix multiplication. For brevity we show M[y*Width+x], N[y*Width +x], P[y*Width+x] as $M_{y,x}$, $N_{y,x}$ $P_{y,x}$, respectively.

accesses to the M and N elements by $thread_{0,0}$ and $thread_{0,1}$ of $block_{0,0}$ are highlighted with black arrows. For example, $thread_{0,0}$ reads $M_{0,0}$ and $N_{0,0}$, followed by $M_{0,1}$ and $N_{1,0}$, followed by $M_{0,2}$ and $N_{2,0}$, followed by $M_{0,3}$ and $N_{3,0}$.

Fig. 5.6 shows the global memory accesses done by all threads in $block_{0,0}$. The threads are listed in the vertical direction, with time of access increasing from left to right in the horizontal direction. Note that each thread accesses four elements of M and four elements of N during its execution. Among the four threads highlighted, there is a significant overlap in the M and N elements that they access. For example, $thread_{0,0}$ and $thread_{0,1}$ both access $M_{0,0}$ as well as the rest of row 0 of M. Similarly, $thread_{0,1}$ and $thread_{1,1}$ both access $N_{0,1}$ as well as the rest of column 1 of N.

The kernel in Fig. 3.11 is written so that both $thread_{0,0}$ and $thread_{0,1}$ access row 0 elements of M from the global memory. If we can somehow manage to have $thread_{0,0}$ and $thread_{0,1}$ collaborate so that these M elements are loaded from global memory only once, we can reduce the total number of accesses to the global memory by half. In fact, we can see that every M and N element is accessed exactly twice during the execution of $block_{0,0}$. Therefore if we can have all four threads collaborate in their accesses to global memory, we can reduce the traffic to the global memory by half.

The reader should verify that the potential reduction in global memory traffic in the matrix multiplication example is proportional to the dimension of the blocks that are used. With Width × Width blocks, the potential reduction of global memory traffic would be Width. That is, if we use 16 × 16 blocks, we can potentially reduce the global memory traffic to 1/16 of the original level through collaboration between threads.

Access order

thread$_{0,0}$	$M_{0,0} * N_{0,0}$	$M_{0,1} * N_{1,0}$	$M_{0,2} * N_{2,0}$	$M_{0,3} * N_{3,0}$
thread$_{0,1}$	$M_{0,0} * N_{0,1}$	$M_{0,1} * N_{1,1}$	$M_{0,2} * N_{2,1}$	$M_{0,3} * N_{3,1}$
thread$_{1,0}$	$M_{1,0} * N_{0,0}$	$M_{1,1} * N_{1,0}$	$M_{1,2} * N_{2,0}$	$M_{1,3} * N_{3,0}$
thread$_{1,1}$	$M_{1,0} * N_{0,1}$	$M_{1,1} * N_{1,1}$	$M_{1,2} * N_{2,1}$	$M_{1,3} * N_{3,1}$

FIGURE 5.6

Global memory accesses performed by threads in block$_{0,0}$.

We now present a tiled matrix multiplication algorithm. The basic idea is to have the threads collaboratively load subsets of the M and N elements into the shared memory before they individually use these elements in their dot product calculation. Keep in mind that the size of the shared memory is quite small, and one must be careful not to exceed the capacity of the shared memory when loading these M and N elements into the shared memory. This can be accomplished by dividing the M and N matrices into smaller tiles. The size of these tiles is chosen so that they can fit into the shared memory. In the simplest form, the tile dimensions equal those of the block, as illustrated in Fig. 5.7.

In Fig. 5.7 we divide M and N into 2×2 tiles, as delineated by the thick lines. The dot product calculations that are performed by each thread are now divided into phases. In each phase, all threads in a block collaborate to load a tile of M and a tile of N into the shared memory. This can be done by having every thread in a block load one M element and one N element into the shared memory, as illustrated in Fig. 5.8. Each row of Fig. 5.8 shows the execution activities of a thread. Note that time progresses from left to right. We need to show only the activities of threads in block$_{0,0}$; the other blocks all have the same behavior. The shared memory array for the M elements is called Mds. The shared memory array for the N elements is called Nds. At the beginning of phase 1, the four threads of block$_{0,0}$ collaboratively load a tile of M into shared memory: Thread$_{0,0}$ loads $M_{0,0}$ into Mds$_{0,0}$, thread$_{0,1}$ loads $M_{0,1}$ into Mds$_{0,1}$, thread$_{1,0}$ loads $M_{1,0}$ into Mds$_{1,0}$, and thread$_{1,1}$ loads $M_{1,1}$ into Mds$_{1,1}$. These loads are shown in the second column of Fig. 5.8. A tile of N is also loaded in a similar manner, shown in the third column of Fig. 5.8.

After the two tiles of M and N are loaded into the shared memory, these elements are used in the calculation of the dot product. Note that each value in the shared memory is used twice. For example, the $M_{1,1}$ value, loaded by thread$_{1,1}$ into Mds$_{1,1}$, is used twice, once by thread$_{1,0}$ and once by thread$_{1,1}$. By loading each global memory value into shared memory so that it can be used multiple times, we reduce the number of accesses to the global memory. In this case, we reduce the number of accesses to the global memory by a factor of 2. The reader should verify that the reduction is by a factor of N if the tiles are $N \times N$ elements.

Note that the calculation of each dot product is now performed in two phases, shown as phase 1 and phase 2 in Fig. 5.8. In each phase, each thread accumulates products of two pairs of the input matrix elements into the Pvalue variable. Note

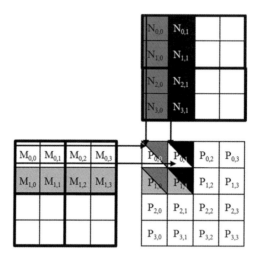

FIGURE 5.7

Tiling M and N to utilize shared memory.

	Phase 0			Phase 1		
$thread_{0,0}$	$M_{0,0}$ ↓ $Mds_{0,0}$	$N_{0,0}$ ↓ $Nds_{0,0}$	$PValue_{0,0}$ += $Mds_{0,0}*Nds_{0,0}$ + $Mds_{0,1}*Nds_{1,0}$	$M_{0,2}$ ↓ $Mds_{0,0}$	$N_{2,0}$ ↓ $Nds_{0,0}$	$PValue_{0,0}$ += $Mds_{0,0}*Nds_{0,0}$ + $Mds_{0,1}*Nds_{1,0}$
$thread_{0,1}$	$M_{0,1}$ ↓ $Mds_{0,1}$	$N_{0,1}$ ↓ $Nds_{0,1}$	$PValue_{0,1}$ += $Mds_{0,0}*Nds_{0,1}$ + $Mds_{0,1}*Nds_{1,1}$	$M_{0,3}$ ↓ $Mds_{0,1}$	$N_{2,1}$ ↓ $Nds_{0,1}$	$PValue_{0,1}$ += $Mds_{0,0}*Nds_{0,1}$ + $Mds_{0,1}*Nds_{1,1}$
$thread_{1,0}$	$M_{1,0}$ ↓ $Mds_{1,0}$	$N_{1,0}$ ↓ $Nds_{1,0}$	$PValue_{1,0}$ += $Mds_{1,0}*Nds_{0,0}$ + $Mds_{1,1}*Nds_{1,0}$	$M_{1,2}$ ↓ $Mds_{1,0}$	$N_{3,0}$ ↓ $Nds_{1,0}$	$PValue_{1,0}$ += $Mds_{1,0}*Nds_{0,0}$ + $Mds_{1,1}*Nds_{1,0}$
$thread_{1,1}$	$M_{1,1}$ ↓ $Mds_{1,1}$	$N_{1,1}$ ↓ $Nds_{1,1}$	$PValue_{1,1}$ += $Mds_{1,0}*Nds_{0,1}$ + $Mds_{1,1}*Nds_{1,1}$	$M_{1,3}$ ↓ $Mds_{1,1}$	$N_{3,1}$ ↓ $Nds_{1,1}$	$PValue_{1,1}$ += $Mds_{1,0}*Nds_{0,1}$ + $Mds_{1,1}*Nds_{1,1}$

time ———————→

FIGURE 5.8

Execution phases of a tiled matrix multiplication.

that Pvalue is an automatic variable, so a private version is generated for each thread. We added subscripts just to clarify that these are different instances of the Pvalue variable created for each thread. The first phase calculation is shown in the fourth column of Fig. 5.8, and the second phase is shown in the seventh column. In general, if an input matrix is of dimension `Width` and the tile size is `TILE_WIDTH`, the dot product would be performed in `Width/TILE_WIDTH` phases.

The creation of these phases is key to the reduction of accesses to the global memory. With each phase focusing on a small subset of the input matrix values, the threads can collaboratively load the subset into the shared memory and use the values in the shared memory to satisfy their overlapping input needs in the phase.

Note also that Mds and Nds are reused across phases. In each phase, the same Mds and Nds are reused to hold the subset of M and N elements used in the phase. This allows a much smaller shared memory to serve most of the accesses to global memory. This is because each phase focuses on a small subset of the input matrix elements. Such focused access behavior is called *locality*. When an algorithm exhibits locality, there is an opportunity to use small, high-speed memories to serve most of the accesses and remove these accesses from the global memory. Locality is as important for achieving high performance in multicore CPUs as in many-thread GPUs We will return to the concept of locality in Chapter 6, Performance Considerations.

5.4 A tiled matrix multiplication kernel

We are now ready to present a tiled matrix multiplication kernel that uses shared memory to reduce traffic to the global memory. The kernel shown in Fig. 5.9 implements the phases illustrated in Fig. 5.8. In Fig. 5.9, lines 04 and 05 declare Mds and Nds, respectively, as shared memory arrays. Recall that the scope of shared memory variables is a block. Thus one version of the Mds and Nds arrays will be created for each block, and all threads of a block have access to the same Mds and Nds version. This is important because all threads in a block must have access to the M and N elements that are loaded into Mds and Nds by their peers so that they can use these values to satisfy their input needs.

Lines 07 and 08 save the threadIdx and blockIdx values into automatic variables with shorter names to make the code more concise. Recall that automatic scalar variables are placed into registers. Their scope is in each individual thread. That is, one private version of tx, ty, bx, and by is created by the runtime system for each thread and will reside in registers that are accessible by the thread. They are initialized with the threadIdx and blockIdx values and used many times during the lifetime of thread. Once the thread ends, the values of these variables cease to exist.

Lines 11 and 12 determine the row index and column index, respectively, of the P element that the thread is to produce. The code assumes that each thread is responsible for calculating one P element. As shown in line 12, the horizontal (x) position, or the column index of the P element to be produced by a thread, can be calculated as bx*TILE_WIDTH+tx. This is because each block covers TILE_WIDTH elements of P in the horizontal dimension. A thread in block bx would have before it bx blocks of threads, or (bx*TILE_WIDTH) threads; they cover

```
01    #define TILE_WIDTH 16
02    __global__ void matrixMulKernel(float* M, float* N, float* P, int Width) {
03
04        __shared__ float Mds[TILE_WIDTH][TILE_WIDTH];
05        __shared__ float Nds[TILE_WIDTH][TILE_WIDTH];
06
07        int bx = blockIdx.x;  int by = blockIdx.y;
08        int tx = threadIdx.x; int ty = threadIdx.y;
09
10        // Identify the row and column of the P element to work on
11        int Row = by * TILE_WIDTH + ty;
12        int Col = bx * TILE_WIDTH + tx;
13
14        // Loop over the M and N tiles required to compute P element
15        float Pvalue = 0;
16        for (int ph = 0; ph < Width/TILE_WIDTH; ++ph) {
17
18            // Collaborative loading of M and N tiles into shared memory
19            Mds[ty][tx] = M[Row*Width + ph*TILE_WIDTH + tx];
20            Nds[ty][tx] = N[(ph*TILE_WIDTH + ty)*Width + Col];
21            __syncthreads();
22
23            for (int k = 0; k < TILE_WIDTH; ++k) {
24                Pvalue += Mds[ty][k] * Nds[k][tx];
25            }
26            __syncthreads();
27
28        }
29        P[Row*Width + Col] = Pvalue;
30
31    }
```

FIGURE 5.9

A tiled matrix multiplication kernel using shared memory.

bx*TILE_WIDTH elements of P. Another tx thread within the same block would cover another tx elements. Thus the thread with bx and tx should be responsible for calculating the P element whose x index is bx*TILE_WIDTH+tx. For the example in Fig. 5.7, the horizontal (x) index of the P element to be calculated by thread$_{0,1}$ of block$_{1,0}$ is $0*2+1=1$. This horizontal index is saved in the variable Col for the thread and is also illustrated in Fig. 5.10.

Similarly, the vertical (y) position, or the row index, of the P element to be processed by a thread is calculated as by*TILE_WIDTH+ty. Going back to the example in Fig. 5.7, the y index of the P element to be calculated by thread$_{0,1}$ of block$_{1,0}$ is $1*2+0=2$. This vertical index is saved in the variable Row for the thread. As shown in Fig. 5.10, each thread calculates the P element at the Colth column and the Rowth row. Thus the P element to be calculated by thread$_{0,1}$ of block$_{1,0}$ is $P_{2,1}$.

Line 16 of Fig. 5.9 marks the beginning of the loop that iterates through all the phases of calculating the P element. Each iteration of the loop corresponds to one phase of the calculation shown in Fig. 5.8. The ph variable indicates the number of phases that have already been done for the dot product. Recall that each phase uses one tile of M and one tile of N elements. Therefore at the beginning

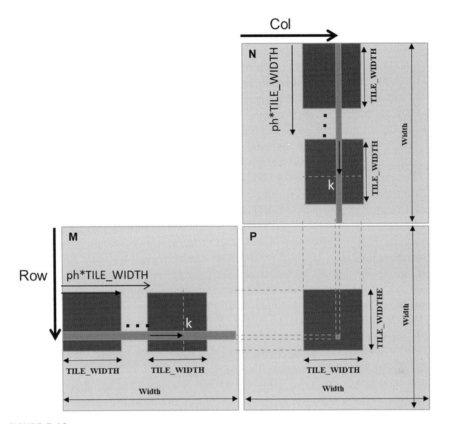

FIGURE 5.10

Calculation of the matrix indices in tiled multiplication.

of each phase, `ph*TILE_WIDTH` pairs of M and N elements have been processed by previous phases.

In each phase, lines 19 and 20 in Fig. 5.9 load the appropriate M and N elements, respectively, into the shared memory. Since we already know the row of M and column of N to be processed by the thread, we now turn our focus to the column index of M and row index of N. As shown in Fig. 5.10, each block has $TILE\_WIDTH^2$ threads that will collaborate to load $TILE\_WIDTH^2$ M elements and $TILE\_WIDTH^2$ N elements into the shared memory. Thus all we need to do is to assign each thread to load one M element and one N element. This is conveniently done by using the `blockIdx` and `threadIdx`. Note that the beginning column index of the section of M elements to be loaded is `ph*TILE_WIDTH`. Therefore an easy approach is to have every thread load an element that is `tx` (the `threadIdx.x` value) positions away from that beginning point. Similarly, the beginning row index of the section of N elements to be loaded is also `ph*TILE_WIDTH`. Therefore every thread loads an element that is `ty` (the `threadIdx.y` value) positions away from that beginning point.

This is precisely what we have in lines 19 and 20. In line 19, each thread loads M[Row*Width + ph*TILE_WIDTH + tx], where the linearized index is formed with the row index Row and column index ph*TILE_WIDTH + tx. Since the value of Row is a linear function of ty, each of the TILE_WIDTH² threads will load a unique M element into the shared memory because each thread has a unique combination of tx and ty. Together, these threads will load a dark square subset of M in Fig. 5.10. In a similar way, in line 20, each thread loads the appropriate N element to shared memory using the linearized index (ph*TILE_WIDTH + ty)*Width + Col. The reader should use the small example in Figs. 5.7 and 5.8 to verify that the address calculation works correctly for individual threads.

The barrier __syncthreads() in line 21 ensures that all threads have finished loading the tiles of M and N into Mds and Nds before any of them can move forward. Recall from Chapter 4, Compute Architecture and Scheduling, that the call to __syncthreads() can be used to make all threads in a block wait for each other to reach the barrier before any of them can proceed. This is important because the M and N elements to be used by a thread can be loaded by other threads. One needs to ensure that all elements are properly loaded into the shared memory before any of the threads start to use the elements. The loop in line 23 then performs one phase of the dot product based on the tile elements. The progression of the loop for thread$_{ty, tx}$ is shown in Fig. 5.10, with the access direction of the M and N elements along the arrow marked with k, the loop variable in line 23. Note that these elements will be accessed from Mds and Nds, the shared memory arrays holding these M and N elements. The barrier __syncthreads() in line 26 ensures that all threads have finished using the M and N elements in the shared memory before any of them move on to the next iteration and load the elements from the next tiles. Thus none of the threads would load the elements too early and corrupt the input values of other threads.

The two __syncthreads() calls in lines 21 and 26 demonstrate two different types of data dependence that parallel programmers often have to reason about when they are coordinating between threads. The first is called a *read-after-write dependence* because threads must wait for data to be written to the proper place by other threads before they try to read it. The second is called a *write-after-read dependence* because a thread must wait for the data to be read by all threads that need it before overwriting it. Other names for read-after-write and write-after-read dependences are true and false dependences, respectively. A read-after-write dependence is a *true dependence* because the reading thread truly needs the data supplied by the writing thread, so it has no choice but to wait for it. A write-after-read dependence is a *false dependence* because the writing thread does not need any data from the reading thread. The dependence is caused by the fact that they are reusing the same memory location and would not exist if they used different locations.

The loop nest from line 16 to line 28 illustrates a technique called *strip-mining*, which takes a long-running loop and break it into phases. Each phase involves an inner loop that executes a few consecutive iterations of the original loop. The original loop becomes an outer loop whose role is to iteratively invoke the inner loop so that all the iterations of the original loop are executed in their original order. By adding barrier synchronizations before and after the inner loop, we force all threads in the same block to focus their work on the same section of input data during each phase. Strip-mining is an important means to creating the phases that are needed by tiling in data parallel programs.[3]

After all phases of the dot product are complete, the execution exits the outer loop. In Line 29, all threads write to their P element using the linearized index calculated from Row and Col.

The benefit of the tiled algorithm is substantial. For matrix multiplication, the global memory accesses are reduced by a factor of TILE_WIDTH. With 16×16 tiles, one can reduce the global memory accesses by a factor of 16. This increases the compute to global memory access ratio from 0.25 OP/B to 4 OP/B. This improvement allows the memory bandwidth of a CUDA device to support a higher computation rate. For example, in the A100 GPU which has a global memory bandwidth of 1555 GB/second, this improvement allows the device to achieve (1555 GB/second)*(4 OP/B)=6220 GFLOPS, which is substantially higher than the 389 GFLOPS achieved by the kernel that did not use tiling.

Although tiling improves throughput substantially, 6220 GFLOPS is still only 32% of the device's peak throughput of 19,500 GFLOPS. One can further optimize the code to reduce the number of global memory accesses and improve throughput. We will see some of these optimizations later in the book, while other advanced optimizations will not be covered. Because of the importance of matrix multiplication in many domains, there are highly optimized libraries, such as cuBLAS and CUTLASS, that already incorporate many of these advanced optimizations. Programmers can use these libraries to immediately achieve close to peak performance in their linear algebra applications.

The effectiveness of tiling at improving the throughput of matrix multiplication in particular and applications in general is not unique to GPUs. There is a long history of applying tiling (or blocking) techniques to improve performance on CPUs by ensuring that the data that is reused by a CPU thread within a particular time window will be found in the cache. One key difference is that tiling techniques on CPUs rely on the CPU cache to keep reused data on-chip implicitly, whereas tiling techniques on GPUs use shared memory explicitly to keep the data on-chip. The reason is that a CPU core typically runs one or two threads at a time, so a thread can rely on the cache keeping recently used data around. In contrast, a GPU SM runs many threads simultaneously to be able to hide latency. These threads may compete for cache slots, which makes the GPU cache less reliable, necessitating the use of shared memory for important data that is to be reused.

---

[3]The reader should note that strip-mining has long been used in programming CPUs. Strip-mining followed by loop interchange is often used to enable tiling for improved locality in sequential programs. Strip-mining is also the main vehicle for vectorizing compilers to generate vector or SIMD instructions for CPU programs.

While the performance improvement of the tiled matrix multiplication kernel is impressive, it does make a few simplifying assumptions. First, the width of the matrices is assumed to be a multiple of the width of thread blocks. This prevents the kernel from correctly processing matrices with arbitrary width. The second assumption is that the matrices are square matrices. This is not always true in practice. In the next section we will present a kernel with boundary checks that removes these assumptions.

5.5 **Boundary checks**

We now extend the tiled matrix multiplication kernel to handle matrices with arbitrary width. The extensions will have to allow the kernel to correctly handle matrices whose width is not a multiple of the tile width. Let's change the small example in Fig. 5.7 to use 3×3 M, N, and P matrices. The revised example is shown in Fig. 5.11. Note that the width of the matrices is 3, which is not a multiple of the tile width (which is 2). Fig. 5.11 shows the memory access pattern during the second phase of block$_{0,0}$. We see that thread$_{0,1}$ and thread$_{1,1}$ will attempt to load M elements that do not exist. Similarly, we see that thread$_{1,0}$ and thread$_{1,1}$ will attempt to access N elements that do not exist.

Accessing nonexisting elements is problematic in two ways. In the case of accessing a nonexisting element that is past the end of a row (M accesses by thread$_{0,1}$ and thread$_{1,1}$ in Fig. 5.11), these accesses will be done to incorrect elements. In our example the threads will attempt to access $M_{0,3}$ and $M_{1,3}$, which do not exist. So what will happen to these memory loads? To answer this question, we need to go back to the linearized layout of two-dimensional matrices.

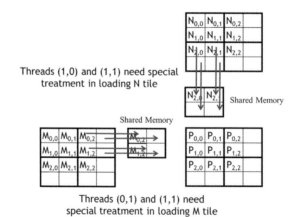

FIGURE 5.11

Loading input matrix elements that are close to the edge: phase 1 of block$_{0,0}$.

The element after $M_{0,2}$ in the linearized layout is $M_{1,0}$. Although thead$_{0,1}$ is attempting to access $M_{0,3}$, it will end up getting $M_{1,0}$. The use of this value in the subsequent inner product calculation will obviously corrupt the output value.

A similar problem arises in accessing an element that is past the end of a column (N accesses by thread$_{1,0}$ and thread$_{1,1}$ in Fig. 5.11). These accesses are to memory locations outside the allocated area for the array. In some systems they will return random values from other data structures. In other systems these accesses will be rejected, causing the program to abort. Either way, the outcome of such accesses is undesirable.

From our discussion so far, it may seem that the problematic accesses arise only in the last phase of execution of the threads. This would suggest that we can deal with it by taking special actions during the last phase of the tiled kernel execution. Unfortunately, this is not true. Problematic accesses can arise in all phases. Fig. 5.12 shows the memory access pattern of block$_{1,1}$ during phase 0. We see that thread$_{1,0}$ and thread$_{1,1}$ attempt to access nonexisting M elements $M_{3,0}$ and $M_{3,1}$, whereas thread$_{0,1}$ and thread$_{1,1}$ attempt to access $N_{0,3}$ and $N_{1,3}$, which do not exist.

Note that these problematic accesses cannot be prevented by simply excluding the threads that do not calculate valid P elements. For example, thread$_{1,0}$ in block$_{1,1}$ does not calculate any valid P element. However, it needs to load $M_{2,1}$ during phase 0 for other threads in block$_{1,1}$ to use. Furthermore, note that some threads that calculate valid P elements will attempt to access M or N elements that do not exist. For example, as we saw in Fig. 5.11, thread$_{0,1}$ of block 0,0 calculates a valid P element $P_{0,1}$. However, it attempts to access a nonexisting $M_{0,3}$ during phase 1. These two facts indicate that we will need to use different boundary condition tests for loading M tiles, loading N tiles, and calculating/

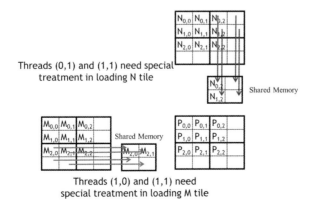

FIGURE 5.12

Loading input elements during phase 0 of block$_{1,1}$.

storing P elements. A rule of thumb to follow is that every memory access needs to have a corresponding check that ensures that the indices used in the access are within the bounds of the array being accessed.

Let's start with the boundary test condition for loading input tiles. When a thread is to load an input tile element, it should test whether the input element it is attempting to load is a valid element. This is easily done by examining the y and x indices. For example, in line 19 in Fig. 5.9, the linearized index is a derived from a y index of Row and an x index of ph*TILE_WIDTH + tx. The boundary condition test would be that both of indices are smaller than Width: Row < Width && (ph*TILE_WIDTH+tx) < Width. If the condition is true, the thread should go ahead and load the M element. The reader should verify that the condition test for loading the N element is (ph*TILE_WIDTH +ty) < Width && Col < Width.

If the condition is false, the thread should not load the element. The question is what should be placed into the shared memory location. The answer is 0.0, a value that will not cause any harm if it is used in the inner product calculation. If any thread uses this 0.0 value in the calculation of its inner product, there will not be any change in the inner product value.

Finally, a thread should store its final inner product value only if it is responsible for calculating a valid P element. The test for this condition is (Row < Width) && (Col < Width). The kernel code with the additional boundary condition checks is shown in Fig. 5.13.

With the boundary condition checks, the tile matrix multiplication kernel is just one step away from being a general matrix multiplication kernel. In general,

```
14    // Loop over the M and N tiles required to compute P element
15    float Pvalue = 0;
16    for (int ph = 0; ph < ceil(Width/(float)TILE_WIDTH); ++ph) {
17
18        // Collaborative loading of M and N tiles into shared memory
..        if ((Row < Width) && (ph*TILE_WIDTH+tx) < Width)
19            Mds[ty][tx] = M[Row*Width + ph*TILE_WIDTH + tx];
..        else Mds[ty][tx] = 0.0f;
..        if ((ph*TILE_WIDTH+ty) < Width && Col < Width)
20            Nds[ty][tx] = N[(ph*TILE_WIDTH + ty)*Width + Col];
..        else Nds[ty][tx] = 0.0f;
21        __syncthreads();
22
23        for (int k = 0; k < TILE_WIDTH; ++k) {
24            Pvalue += Mds[ty][k] * Nds[k][tx];
25        }
26        __syncthreads();
27
28    }
..    if (Row < Width) && (Col < Width)
29        P[Row*Width + Col] = Pvalue;
```

FIGURE 5.13

Tiled matrix multiplication kernel with boundary condition checks.

matrix multiplication is defined for rectangular matrices: a $j \times k$ M matrix multiplied with a $k \times l$ N matrix results in a $j \times l$ P matrix. Our kernel can handle only square matrices so far.

Fortunately, it is quite easy to extend our kernel further into a general matrix multiplication kernel. We need to make a few simple changes. First, the `Width` argument is replaced by three unsigned integer arguments: `j`, `k`, `l`. Where `Width` is used to refer to the height of M or height of P, replace it with `j`. Where `Width` is used to refer to the width of M or height of N, replace it with `k`. Where `Width` is used to refer to the width of N or width of P, replace it with `l`. The revision of the kernel with these changes is left as an exercise.

5.6 Impact of memory usage on occupancy

Recall that in Chapter 4, Compute Architecture and Scheduling, we discussed the importance of maximizing the occupancy of threads on SMs to be able to tolerate long latency operations. The memory usage of a kernel plays an important role in occupancy tuning. While CUDA registers and shared memory can be extremely effective at reducing the number of accesses to global memory, one must be careful to stay within the SM's capacity of these memories. Each CUDA device offers limited resources, which limits the number threads that can simultaneously reside in the SM for a given application. In general, the more resources each thread requires, the fewer the number of threads that can reside in each SM.

We saw in Chapter 4, Compute Architecture and Scheduling, how register usage can be a limiting factor for occupancy. Shared memory usage can also limit the number of threads that can be assigned to each SM. For example, the A100 GPU can be configured to have up to 164 KB of shared memory per SM and supports a maximum of 2048 threads per SM. Thus for all 2048 thread slots to be used, a thread block should not use more than an average of (164 KB)/(2048 threads)=82 B/thread. In the tiled matrix multiplication example, every block has TILE_WIDTH^2 threads, and uses $\text{TILE\_WIDTH}^2\text{*4B}$ of shared memory for `Mds` and $\text{TILE\_WIDTH}^2\text{*4B}$ of shared memory for `Nds`. Thus the thread block uses an average of $(\text{TILE\_WIDTH}^2\text{*4B} + \text{TILE\_WIDTH}^2\text{*4B})/(\text{TILE\_WIDTH}^2$ threads)=8 B/thread of shared memory. Therefore the tiled matrix multiplication kernel's occupancy is not limited by the shared memory.

However, consider a kernel that has thread blocks that use 32 KB of shared memory, each of which has 256 threads. In this case, the kernel uses an average of (32 KB)/(256 threads)=132 B/thread of shared memory. With such shared memory usage, the kernel cannot achieve full occupancy. Each SM can host a maximum of only (164 KB)/(132 B/thread)=1272 threads. Therefore the maximum achievable occupancy of this kernel will be (1272 assigned threads)/(2048 maximum threads)=62%.

Note that the size of shared memory in each SM can also vary from device to device. Each generation or model of devices can have a different amount of shared memory in each SM. It is often desirable for a kernel to be able to use different amounts of shared memory according to the amount available in the hardware. That is, we may want a host code to dynamically determine the size of the shared memory and adjust the amount of shared memory that is used by a kernel. This can be done by calling the cudaGetDeviceProperties function. Assume that variable &devProp is passed to the function. In this case, the field devProp. sharedMemPerBlock gives the amount of shared memory that is available in each SM. The programmer can then determine the amount of shared memory that should be used by each block.

Unfortunately, the kernels in Figs. 5.9 and 5.13 do not support any dynamic adjustment of shared memory usage by the host code. The declarations that are used in Fig. 5.9 hardwire the size of its shared memory usage to a compile-time constant:

```
__shared__ float Mds[TILE_WIDTH][TILE_WIDTH];
__shared__ float Nds[TILE_WIDTH][TILE_WIDTH];
```

That is, the size of Mds and Nds is set to be TILE_WIDTH^2 elements, whatever the value of TILE_WIDTH is set to be at compile time. Since the code contains

```
#define TILE_WIDTH 16
```

both Mds and Nds will have 256 elements. If we want to change the size of Mds and Nds, we need to change the value of TILE_WIDTH and recompile the code. The kernel cannot easily adjust its shared memory usage at runtime without recompilation.

We can enable such adjustment with a different style of declaration in CUDA by adding a C extern keyword in front of the shared memory declaration and omitting the size of the array in the declaration. Based on this style, the declarations for Mds and Nds need to be merged into one dynamically allocated array:

```
extern __shared__ Mds_Nds[];
```

Since there is only one merged array, we will also need to manually define where the Mds section of the array starts and where the Nds section starts. Note that the merged array is one-dimensional. We will need to access it by using a linearized index based on the vertical and horizontal indices.

At runtime, when we call the kernel, we can dynamically configure the amount of shared memory to be used for each block according to the device query result and supply that as a third configuration parameter to the kernel call. For example, the revised kernel could be launched with the following statements:

```
size_t size =
calculate_appropriate_SM_usage(devProp.sharedMemPerBlock,
...);

matrixMulKernel<<<dimGrid,dimBlock,size>>>(Md, Nd, Pd,
Width, size/2, size/2);
```

where `size_t` is a built-in type for declaring a variable to hold the size information for dynamically allocated data structures. The size is expressed in number of bytes. In our matrix multiplication example, for a 16×16 tile, we have a size of $2 \times 16 \times 16 \times 4 = 2048$ bytes to accommodate both `Mds` and `Nds`. We have omitted the details of the calculation for setting the value of size at runtime and leave it as an exercise for the reader.

In Fig. 5.14 we show how one can modify the kernel code in Figs. 5.9 and 5.11 to use dynamically sized shared memory for the `Mds` and `Nds` arrays. It may also be useful to pass the sizes of each section of the array as arguments into the kernel function. In this example we added two arguments: The first argument is the size of the `Mds` section, and the second argument is the size of the `Nds` section, both in terms of bytes. Note that in the host code above, we passed size/2 as the values of these arguments, which is 1024 bytes. With the assignments in lines 06 and 07, the rest of the kernel code can use `Mds` and `Nds` as the base of the array and use a linearized index to access the `Mds` and `Nds` elements. For example, instead of using `Mds[ty][tx]`, one would use `Mds[ty*TILE_WIDTH+tx]`.

```
01    #define TILE_WIDTH 16
02    __global__ void matrixMulKernel(float* M, float* N, float* P, int Width,
                                       unsigned Mdz_sz, unsigned Nds_sz) {
03
04        extern __shared__ char float Mds_Nds[];
05
06        float *Mds = (float *) Mds_Nds;
07        float *Nds = (float *) Mds_Nds + Mds_sz;
```

FIGURE 5.14

Tiled matrix multiplication kernel with dynamically sized shared memory usage.

5.7 Summary

In summary, the execution speed of a program in modern processors can be severely limited by the speed of the memory. To achieve good utilization of the execution throughput of a CUDA devices, one needs to strive for a high compute to global memory access ratio in the kernel code. If the ratio is low, the kernel is memory-bound. That is, its execution speed is limited by the rate at which its operands are accessed from memory.

CUDA provides access to registers, shared memory, and constant memory. These memories are much smaller than the global memory but can be accessed at much higher speed. Using these memories effectively requires redesign of the algorithm. We use matrix multiplication as an example to illustrate tiling, a popular strategy to enhance locality of data access and enable effective use of shared memory. In parallel programming, tiling uses barrier synchronization to force multiple threads to jointly focus on a subset of the input data at each phase of the execution so that the subset data can be placed into these special memory types to enable much higher access speed.

However, it is important for CUDA programmers to be aware of the limited sizes of these special types of memory. Their capacities are implementation dependent. Once their capacities have been exceeded, they limit the number of threads that can be executing simultaneously in each SM and can negatively affect the GPU's computation throughput as well as its ability to tolerate latency. The ability to reason about hardware limitations when developing an application is a key aspect of parallel programming.

Although we introduced tiled algorithms in the context of CUDA C programming, it is an effective strategy for achieving high-performance in virtually all types of parallel computing systems. The reason is that an application must exhibit locality in data access to make effective use of high-speed memories in these systems. For example, in a multicore CPU system, data locality allows an application to effectively use on-chip data caches to reduce memory access latency and achieve high performance. These on-chip data caches are also of limited size and require the computation to exhibit locality. Therefore the reader will also find the tiled algorithm useful when developing a parallel application for other types of parallel computing systems using other programming models.

Our goal for this chapter was to introduce the concept of locality, tiling, and different CUDA memory types. We introduced a tiled matrix multiplication kernel using shared memory. We further studied the need for boundary test conditions to allow for arbitrary data dimensions in applying tiling techniques. We also briefly discussed the use of dynamically sized shared memory allocation so that the kernel can adjust the size of shared memory that is used by each block according to the hardware capability. We did not discuss the use of registers in tiling. We will explain the use of registers in tiled algorithms when we discuss parallel algorithm patterns in Part II of the book.

Exercises

1. Consider matrix addition. Can one use shared memory to reduce the global memory bandwidth consumption? Hint: Analyze the elements that are accessed by each thread and see whether there is any commonality between threads.

2. Draw the equivalent of Fig. 5.7 for a 8×8 matrix multiplication with 2×2 tiling and 4×4 tiling. Verify that the reduction in global memory bandwidth is indeed proportional to the dimension size of the tiles.

3. What type of incorrect execution behavior can happen if one forgot to use one or both __syncthreads() in the kernel of Fig. 5.9?

4. Assuming that capacity is not an issue for registers or shared memory, give one important reason why it would be valuable to use shared memory instead of registers to hold values fetched from global memory? Explain your answer.

5. For our tiled matrix-matrix multiplication kernel, if we use a 32×32 tile, what is the reduction of memory bandwidth usage for input matrices M and N?

6. Assume that a CUDA kernel is launched with 1000 thread blocks, each of which has 512 threads. If a variable is declared as a local variable in the kernel, how many versions of the variable will be created through the lifetime of the execution of the kernel?

7. In the previous question, if a variable is declared as a shared memory variable, how many versions of the variable will be created through the lifetime of the execution of the kernel?

8. Consider performing a matrix multiplication of two input matrices with dimensions $N \times N$. How many times is each element in the input matrices requested from global memory when:
   a. There is no tiling?
   b. Tiles of size $T \times T$ are used?

9. A kernel performs 36 floating-point operations and seven 32-bit global memory accesses per thread. For each of the following device properties, indicate whether this kernel is compute-bound or memory-bound.
   a. Peak FLOPS=200 GFLOPS, peak memory bandwidth=100 GB/second
   b. Peak FLOPS=300 GFLOPS, peak memory bandwidth=250 GB/second

10. To manipulate tiles, a new CUDA programmer has written a device kernel that will transpose each tile in a matrix. The tiles are of size BLOCK_WIDTH by BLOCK_WIDTH, and each of the dimensions of matrix A is known to be a multiple of BLOCK_WIDTH. The kernel invocation and code are shown below. BLOCK_WIDTH is known at compile time and could be set anywhere from 1 to 20.

```
01  dim3 blockDim(BLOCK_WIDTH,BLOCK_WIDTH);
02  dim3 gridDim(A_width/blockDim.x,A_height/blockDim.y);
03  BlockTranspose<<<gridDim, blockDim>>>(A, A_width, A_height);

04  __global__ void
05  BlockTranspose(float* A_elements, int A_width, int A_height)
06  {
07      __shared__ float blockA[BLOCK_WIDTH][BLOCK_WIDTH];

08      int baseIdx = blockIdx.x * BLOCK_SIZE + threadIdx.x;
09      baseIdx += (blockIdx.y * BLOCK_SIZE + threadIdx.y) * A_width;

10      blockA[threadIdx.y][threadIdx.x] = A_elements[baseIdx];

11      A_elements[baseIdx] = blockA[threadIdx.x][threadIdx.y];
12  }
```

    a. Out of the possible range of values for BLOCK_SIZE, for what values of BLOCK_SIZE will this kernel function execute correctly on the device?

    b. If the code does not execute correctly for all BLOCK_SIZE values, what is the root cause of this incorrect execution behavior? Suggest a fix to the code to make it work for all BLOCK_SIZE values.

11. Consider the following CUDA kernel and the corresponding host function that calls it:

```
01  __global__ void foo_kernel(float* a, float* b) {
02      unsigned int i = blockIdx.x*blockDim.x + threadIdx.x;
03      float x[4];
04      __shared__ float y_s;
05      __shared__ float b_s[128];
06      for(unsigned int j = 0; j < 4; ++j) {
07          x[j] = a[j*blockDim.x*gridDim.x + i];
08      }
09      if(threadIdx.x == 0) {
10          y_s = 7.4f;
11      }
12      b_s[threadIdx.x] = b[i];
13      __syncthreads();
14      b[i] = 2.5f*x[0] + 3.7f*x[1] + 6.3f*x[2] + 8.5f*x[3]
15              + y_s*b_s[threadIdx.x] + b_s[(threadIdx.x + 3)%128];
16  }
17  void foo(int* a_d, int* b_d) {
18      unsigned int N = 1024;
19      foo_kernel <<< (N + 128 - 1)/128, 128 >>>(a_d, b_d);
20  }
```

    a. How many versions of the variable i are there?
    b. How many versions of the array x[] are there?
    c. How many versions of the variable y_s are there?
    d. How many versions of the array b_s[] are there?

e. What is the amount of shared memory used per block (in bytes)?

f. What is the floating-point to global memory access ratio of the kernel (in OP/B)?

12. Consider a GPU with the following hardware limits: 2048 threads/SM, 32 blocks/SM, 64K (65,536) registers/SM, and 96 KB of shared memory/SM. For each of the following kernel characteristics, specify whether the kernel can achieve full occupancy. If not, specify the limiting factor.

    a. The kernel uses 64 threads/block, 27 registers/thread, and 4 KB of shared memory/SM.

    b. The kernel uses 256 threads/block, 31 registers/thread, and 8 KB of shared memory/SM.

Performance considerations

Chapter Outline

6.1 Memory coalescing 124
6.2 Hiding memory latency 133
6.3 Thread coarsening 138
6.4 A checklist of optimizations 141
6.5 Knowing your computation's bottleneck 145
6.6 Summary 146
Exercises 146
References 147

The execution speed of a parallel program can vary greatly depending on the interactions between the resource demands of the program and the resource constraints of the hardware. Managing the interaction between parallel code and hardware resource constraints is important for achieving high performance in virtually all parallel programming models. It is a practical skill that requires deep understanding of the hardware architecture and is best learned through hands-on exercises in a parallel programming model that is designed for high performance.

So far, we have learned about various aspects of the GPU architecture and their implications for performance. In Chapter 4, Compute Architecture and Scheduling, we learned about the compute architecture of the GPU and related performance considerations, such as control divergence and occupancy. In Chapter 5, Memory Architecture and Data Locality, we learned about the on-chip memory architecture of the GPU and the use of shared memory tiling to achieve more data reuse. In this chapter we will briefly present the off-chip memory (DRAM) architecture and discuss related performance considerations such as memory coalescing and memory latency hiding. We then discuss an important type of optimization—thread granularity coarsening—that may target any of the different aspects of the architecture, depending on the application. Finally, we wrap up this part of the book with a checklist of common performance optimizations that will serve as a guide for optimizing the performance of the parallel patterns that will be discussed in the second and third parts of the book.

Programming Massively Parallel Processors. DOI: https://doi.org/10.1016/B978-0-323-91231-0.00016-1

In different applications, different architecture constraints may dominate and become the limiting factors of performance, commonly referred to as *bottlenecks*. One can often dramatically improve the performance of an application on a particular CUDA device by trading one resource usage for another. This strategy works well if the resource constraint that is thus alleviated was the dominating constraint before the strategy was applied and the constraint that is thus exacerbated does not have negative effects on parallel execution. Without such an understanding, performance tuning would be guesswork; plausible strategies may or may not lead to performance enhancements.

6.1 Memory coalescing

One of the most important factors of CUDA kernel performance is accessing data in the global memory, the limited bandwidth of which can become the bottleneck. CUDA applications extensively exploit data parallelism. Naturally, CUDA applications tend to process a massive amount of data from the global memory within a short period of time, In Chapter 5, Memory Architecture and Data Locality, we studied tiling techniques that leverage the shared memory to reduce the total amount of data that must be accessed from the global memory by a collection of threads in each thread block. In this chapter we will further discuss memory coalescing techniques for moving data between global memory and shared memories or registers in an efficient manner. Memory coalescing techniques are often used in conjunction with tiling techniques to allow CUDA devices to reach their performance potential by efficiently utilizing the global memory bandwidth.[1]

The global memory of a CUDA device is implemented with DRAM. Data bits are stored in DRAM cells that are small capacitors, in which the presence or absence of a tiny amount of electrical charge distinguishes between a 1 and a 0 value. Reading data from a DRAM cell requires the small capacitor to use its tiny electrical charge to drive a highly capacitive line leading to a sensor and set off the sensor's detection mechanism that determines whether a sufficient amount of charge is present in the capacitor to qualify as a "1." This process takes tens of nanoseconds in modern DRAM chips (see the "Why is DRAM So Slow?" sidebar). This is in sharp contrast to the subnanosecond clock cycle time of modern computing devices. Because this process is very slow relative to the desired data access speed (subnanosecond access per byte), modern DRAM designs use parallelism to increase their rate of data access, commonly referred to as memory access throughput.

---

[1] Recent CUDA devices use on-chip caches for global memory data. Such caches automatically coalesce more of the kernel access patterns and somewhat reduce the need for programmers to manually rearrange their access patterns. However, even with caches, coalescing techniques will continue to have significant effects on kernel execution performance in the foreseeable future.

Why Are DRAMs So Slow?

The following figure shows a DRAM cell and the path for accessing its content. The decoder is an electronic circuit that uses a transistor to drive a line connected to the outlet gates of thousands of cells. It can take a long time for the line to be fully charged or discharged to the desired level.

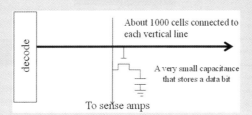

A more formidable challenge is for the cell to drive the vertical line to the sense amplifiers and allow the sense amplifier to detect its content. This is based on electrical charge sharing. The gate lets out the tiny amount of electrical charge that is stored in the cell. If the cell content is "1," the tiny amount of charge must raise the electrical potential of the large capacitance of the long bit line to a sufficiently high level that it can trigger the detection mechanism of the sense amplifier. A good analogy would be for someone to hold a small cup of coffee at one end of a long hallway and a person at the other end of the hallway to use the aroma propagated along the hallway to determine the flavor of the coffee.

One could speed up the process by using a larger, stronger capacitor in each cell. However, the DRAMs have been going in the opposite direction. The capacitors in each cell have been steadily reduced in size and thus reduced in their strength over time so that more bits can be stored in each chip. This is why the access latency of DRAMs has not decreased over time.

Each time a DRAM location is accessed, a range of consecutive locations that include the requested location are accessed. Many sensors are provided in each DRAM chip, and they all work in parallel. Each senses the content of a bit within these consecutive locations. Once detected by the sensors, the data from all these consecutive locations can be transferred at high speed to the processor. These consecutive locations accessed and delivered are referred to as DRAM *bursts*. If an application makes focused use of data from these bursts, the DRAMs can supply the data at a much higher rate than would be the case if a truly random sequence of locations were accessed.

Recognizing the burst organization of modern DRAMs, current CUDA devices employ a technique that allows programmers to achieve high global memory

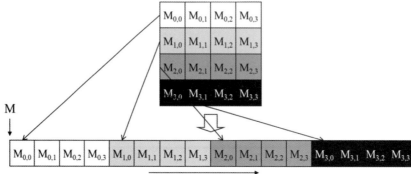

FIGURE 6.1

Placing matrix elements into a linear array based on row-major order.

access efficiency by organizing memory accesses of threads into favorable patterns. This technique takes advantage of the fact that threads in a warp execute the same instruction at any given point in time. When all threads in a warp execute a load instruction, the hardware detects whether they access consecutive global memory locations. In other words, the most favorable access pattern is achieved when all threads in a warp access consecutive global memory locations. In this case, the hardware combines, or *coalesces*, all these accesses into a consolidated access to consecutive DRAM locations. For example, for a given load instruction of a warp, if thread 0 accesses global memory location X, thread 1 accesses location X + 1, thread 2 accesses location X + 2, and so on, all these accesses will be coalesced, or combined into a single request for consecutive locations when accessing the DRAM.[2] Such coalesced access allows the DRAM to deliver data as a burst.[3]

To understand how to effectively use the coalescing hardware, we need to review how the memory addresses are formed in accessing C multidimensional array elements. Recall from Chapter 3, Multidimensional Grids and Data, (Fig. 3.3 is replicated here as Fig. 6.1 for convenience) that multidimensional array elements in C and CUDA are placed into the linearly addressed memory space according to the row-major convention. Recall that the term *row-major*

---

[2] Different CUDA devices may also impose alignment requirements on the global memory address X. For example, in some CUDA devices, X is required to be aligned to 16-word (i.e., 64-byte) boundaries. That is, the lower six bits of X should all be 0 bits. Such alignment requirements have been relaxed in recent CUDA devices, owing to the presence of second-level caches.

[3] Note that modern CPUs also recognize the DRAM burst organization in their cache memory design. A CPU cache line typically maps to one or more DRAM bursts. Applications that make full use of bytes in each cache line they touch tend to achieve much higher performance than those that randomly access memory locations. The techniques that we present in this chapter can be adapted to help CPU programs to achieve high performance.

refers to the fact that the placement of data preserves the structure of rows: All adjacent elements in a row are placed into consecutive locations in the address space. In Fig. 6.1 the four elements of row 0 are first placed in their order of appearance in the row. Elements in row 1 are then placed, followed by elements of row 2, followed by elements of row 3. It should be clear that $M_{0,0}$ and $M_{1,0}$, though they appear to be consecutive in the two-dimensional matrix, are placed four locations apart in the linearly addressed memory.

Let's assume that the multidimensional array in Fig. 6.1 is a matrix that is used as the second input matrix in matrix multiplication. In this case, consecutive threads in a warp that are assigned to consecutive output elements will iterate through consecutive columns of this input matrix. The top left part of Fig. 6.2 shows the code for this computation, and the top right part shows the logical view of the access pattern: consecutive threads iterating through consecutive columns. One can tell by inspecting the code that the accesses to M can be coalesced. The index of the array M is `k*Width+col`. The variables `k` and `Width` have the same value across all threads in the warp. The variable `col` is defined as `blockIdx.x*blockDim.x+threadIdx.x`, which means that consecutive threads (with consecutive `threadIdx.x` values) will have consecutive values of `col` and will therefore access consecutive elements of M.

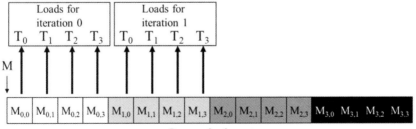

FIGURE 6.2

A coalesced access pattern.

The bottom part of Fig. 6.2 shows the physical view of the access pattern. In iteration 0, consecutive threads will access consecutive elements in row 0 that are adjacent in memory, shown as "Loads for iteration 0" in Fig. 6.2. In iteration 1, consecutive threads will access consecutive elements in row 1 that are also adjacent in memory, shown as "Loads for iteration 1" in Fig. 6.2. This process continues for all rows. As we can see, the memory access pattern that is formed by the threads during this process is a favorable one that can be coalesced. Indeed, in all the kernels that we have implemented so far, our memory accesses have been naturally coalesced.

Now assume that the matrix was stored in column-major order instead of row-major order. There could be various reasons why this might be the case. For example, we might be multiplying by the transpose of a matrix that is stored in row-major order. In linear algebra we often need to use both the original and transposed forms of a matrix. It would be better to avoid creating and storing both forms. A common practice is to create the matrix in one form, say, the original form. When the transposed form is needed, its elements can be accessed by accessing the original form by switching the roles of the row and column indices. In C this is equivalent to viewing the transposed matrix as a column-major layout of the original matrix. Regardless of the reason, let's observe the memory access pattern that is achieved when the second input matrix to our matrix multiplication example is stored in column-major order.

Fig. 6.3 illustrates how consecutive threads iterate through consecutive columns when the matrix is stored in column-major order. The top left part of Fig. 6.3 shows the code, and the top right part shows the logical view of the memory accesses. The program is still trying to have each thread access a column of matrix M. One can tell by inspecting the code that the accesses to M are not favorable for coalescing. The index of the array M is col*Width+k. As before, col is defined as blockIdx.x*blockDim.x+threadIdx.x, which means that consecutive threads (with consecutive threadIdx.x values) will have consecutive values of col. However, in the index to M, col is multiplied by Width, which means that consecutive threads will access elements of M that are Width apart. Therefore the accesses are not favorable for coalescing.

In the bottom portion of Fig. 6.3, we can see that the physical view of the memory accesses is quite different from that in Fig. 6.2. In iteration 0, consecutive threads will logically access consecutive elements in row 0, but this time they are not adjacent in memory because of the column-major layout. These loads are shown as "Loads for iteration 0" in Fig. 6.3. Similarly, in iteration 1, consecutive threads will access consecutive elements in row 1 that are also not adjacent in memory. For a realistic matrix there are typically hundreds or even thousands of elements in each dimension. The M elements that are accessed in each iteration by neighboring threads can be hundreds or even thousands of elements apart. The hardware will determine that accesses to these elements are far away from each other and cannot be coalesced.

There are various strategies for optimizing code to achieve memory coalescing when the computation is not naturally amenable to it. One strategy is to rearrange

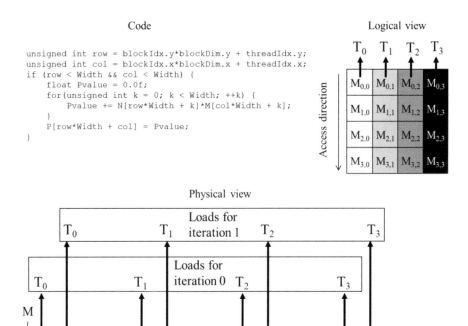

FIGURE 6.3

An uncoalesced access pattern.

how threads are mapped to the data; another strategy is to rearrange the layout of the data itself. We will discuss these strategies in Section 6.4 and see examples throughout this book of how they can be applied. Yet another strategy is to transfer the data between global memory and shared memory in a coalesced manner and carry out the unfavorable access pattern in shared memory, which provides faster access latency. We will also see example optimizations that use this strategy throughout this book, including an optimization that we will apply now to matrix-matrix multiplication in which the second input matrix is in column-major layout. This optimization is called *corner turning*.

Fig. 6.4 illustrates an example of how corner turning can be applied. In this example, A is an input matrix that is stored in row-major layout in global memory, and B is an input matrix that is stored in column-major layout in global memory. They are multiplied to produce an output matrix C that is stored in row-major layout in global memory. The example illustrates how four threads that are responsible for the four consecutive elements at the top edge of the output tile load the input tile elements.

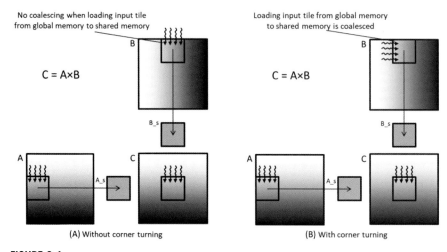

FIGURE 6.4

Applying corner turning to coalesce accesses to matrix B, which is stored in column-major layout.

The access to the input tile in matrix A is similar to that in Chapter 5, Memory Architecture and Data Locality. The four threads load the four elements at the top edge of the input tile. Each thread loads an input element whose local row and column indices within the input tile are the same as those of the thread's output element within the output tile. These accesses are coalesced because consecutive threads access consecutive elements in the same row of A that are adjacent in memory according to the row-major layout.

On the other hand, the access to the input tile in matrix B needs to be different from that in Chapter 5, Memory Architecture and Data Locality. Fig. 6.4(A) shows what the access pattern would be like if we used the same arrangement as in Chapter 5, Memory Architecture and Data Locality. Even though the four threads are logically loading the four consecutive elements at the top edge of the input tile, the elements that are loaded by consecutive threads are far away from each other in the memory because of the column-major layout of the B elements. In other words, consecutive threads that are responsible for consecutive elements in the same row of the output tile load nonconsecutive locations in memory, which results in uncoalesced memory accesses.

This problem can be solved by assigning the four consecutive threads to load the four consecutive elements at the left edge (the same column) in the input tile, as shown in Fig. 6.4(B). Intuitively, we are exchanging the roles of threadIdx.x and threadIdx.y when each thread calculates the linearized index for loading the B input tile. Since B is in column-major layout, consecutive elements in the same column are adjacent in memory. Hence consecutive threads load input elements that are adjacent in memory, which ensures that the memory accesses are coalesced. The code can be written to place the tile of B elements into the shared memory in either column-major layout or row-major layout. Either way, after the input tile has been loaded, each thread can access its inputs with little performance penalty. This is because shared memory is implemented with SRAM technology and does not require coalescing.

The main advantage of memory coalescing is that it reduces global memory traffic by combining multiple memory accesses into a single access. Accesses can be combined when they take place at the same time and access adjacent memory locations. Traffic congestion does not arise only in computing. Most of us have experienced traffic congestion in highway systems, as illustrated in Fig. 6.5. The root cause of highway traffic congestion is that there are too many cars all trying to travel on a road that is designed for a much smaller number of vehicles. When congestion occurs, the travel time for each vehicle is greatly increased. Commute time to work can easily double or triple when there is traffic congestion.

Most solutions for reducing traffic congestion involve the reduction of the number of cars on the road. Assuming that the number of commuters is constant, people need to share rides in order to reduce the number of cars on the road. A common way to share rides is carpooling, in which the members of a group of commuters take turns driving the group to work in one vehicle. Governments usually need to have policies to encourage carpooling. In some countries the government simply disallows certain classes of cars to be on the road on a daily basis. For example, cars with odd license plate numbers may not be allowed on the road on Monday, Wednesday, or Friday. This encourages people whose cars are allowed on different days to form a carpool group. In other countries the government may provide incentives for behavior that reduces the number of cars on the

FIGURE 6.5

Reducing traffic congestion in highway systems.

road. For example, in certain countries, some lanes of congested highways are designated as carpool lanes; only cars with more than two or three people are allowed to use these lanes. There are also countries where the government makes gasoline so expensive that people form carpools to save money. All these measures for encouraging carpooling are designed to overcome the fact that carpooling requires extra effort, as we show in Fig. 6.6.

Carpooling requires workers who wish to carpool to compromise and agree on a common commute schedule. The top half of Fig. 6.6 shows a good schedule pattern for carpooling. Time goes from left to right. Worker A and Worker B have similar schedules for sleep, work, and dinner. This allows these two workers to easily go to work and return home in one car. Their similar schedules allow them to more easily agree on a common departure time and return time. This is not the case for the schedules shown in the bottom half of Fig. 6.6. Worker A and Worker B have very different schedules in this case. Worker A parties until sunrise, sleeps during the day, and goes to work in the evening. Worker B sleeps at night, goes to work in the morning, and returns home for dinner at 6:00 pm. The schedules are so wildly different that these two workers cannot possibly coordinate a common time to drive to work and return home in one car.

Memory coalescing is very similar to carpooling arrangements. We can think of the data as the commuters and the DRAM access requests as the vehicles. When the rate of DRAM requests exceeds the provisioned access bandwidth of the DRAM system, traffic congestion rises, and the arithmetic units become idle. If multiple threads access data from the same DRAM location, they can potentially form a "carpool" and combine their accesses into one DRAM request. However, this requires the threads to have similar execution schedules so that their data accesses can be combined into one. Threads in the same warp are

Good – people have similar schedules

Bad – people have very different schedules

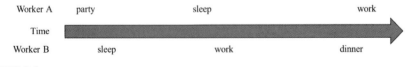

FIGURE 6.6

Carpooling requires synchronization among people.

perfect candidates because they all execute a load instruction simultaneously by virtue of SIMD execution.

6.2 Hiding memory latency

As we explained in Section 6.1, DRAM bursting is a form of parallel organization: Multiple locations are accessed in the DRAM core array in parallel. However, bursting alone is not sufficient to realize the level of DRAM access bandwidth required by modern processors. DRAM systems typically employ two more forms of parallel organization: banks and channels. At the highest level, a processor contains one or more channels. Each channel is a memory controller with a bus that connects a set of DRAM banks to the processor. Fig. 6.7 illustrates a processor that contains four channels, each with a bus that connects four DRAM banks to the processor. In real systems a processor typically has one to eight channels, and a large number of banks is connected to each channel.

The data transfer bandwidth of a bus is defined by its width and clock frequency. Modern *double data rate* (DDR) busses perform two data transfers per clock cycle: one at the rising edge and one at the falling edge of each clock cycle. For example, a 64-bit DDR bus with a clock frequency of 1 GHz has a bandwidth of 8B*2*1 GHz=16GB/s. This seems to be a large number but is often too small for modern CPUs and GPUs. A modern CPU might require a memory bandwidth of at least 32 GB/s, whereas a modern GPU might require 256 GB/s. For this example the CPU would require 2 channels, and the GPU would require 16 channels.

For each channel, the number of banks that is connected to it is determined by the number of banks required to fully utilize the data transfer bandwidth of the bus. This is illustrated in Fig. 6.8. Each bank contains an array of DRAM cells, the sensing amplifiers for accessing these cells, and the interface for delivering bursts of data to the bus (Section 6.1).

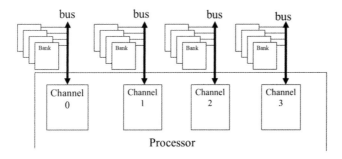

FIGURE 6.7

Channels and banks in DRAM systems.

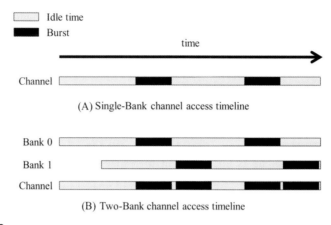

FIGURE 6.8

Banking improves the utilization of data transfer bandwidth of a channel.

Fig. 6.8(A) illustrates the data transfer timing when a single bank is connected to a channel. It shows the timing of two consecutive memory read accesses to the DRAM cells in the bank. Recall from Section 6.1 that each access involves long latency for the decoder to enable the cells and for the cells to share their stored charge with the sensing amplifier. This latency is shown as the gray section at the left end of the time frame. Once the sensing amplifier has completed its work, the burst data is delivered through the bus. The time for transferring the burst data through the bus is shown as the left dark section of the time frame in Fig. 6.8. The second memory read access will incur a similar long access latency (the gray section between the dark sections of the time frame) before its burst data can be transferred (the right dark section).

In reality, the access latency (the gray sections) is much longer than the data transfer time (the dark section). It should be apparent that the access transfer timing of a one-bank organization would grossly underutilize the data transfer bandwidth of the channel bus. For example, if the ratio of DRAM cell array access latency to the data transfer time is 20:1, the maximal utilization of the channel bus would be 1/21=4.8%; that is a 16 GB/s channel would deliver data to the processor at a rate no more than 0.76 GB/s. This would be totally unacceptable. This problem is solved by connecting multiple banks to a channel bus.

When two banks are connected to a channel bus, an access can be initiated in the second bank while the first bank is serving another access. Therefore one can overlap the latency for accessing the DRAM cell arrays. Fig. 6.8(B) shows the timing of a two-bank organization. We assume that bank 0 started at a time earlier than the window shown in Fig. 6.8. Shortly after the first bank starts accessing its cell array, the second bank also starts to access its cell array. When the access in bank 0 is complete, it transfers the burst data (the leftmost dark section of the time frame). Once bank 0 completes its data transfer, bank 1 can transfer its burst data (the second dark section). This pattern repeats for the next accesses.

From Fig. 6.8(B), we can see that by having two banks, we can potentially double the utilization of the data transfer bandwidth of the channel bus. In general, if the ratio of the cell array access latency and data transfer time is R, we need to have at least $R + 1$ banks if we hope to fully utilize the data transfer bandwidth of the channel bus. For example, if the ratio is 20, we will need at least 21 banks connected to each channel bus. In general, the number of banks connected to each channel bus needs to be larger than R for two reasons. One is that having more banks reduces the probability of multiple simultaneous accesses targeting the same bank, a phenomenon called *bank conflict*. Since each bank can serve only one access at a time, the cell array access latency can no longer be overlapped for these conflicting accesses. Having a larger number of banks increases the probability that these accesses will be spread out among multiple banks. The second reason is that the size of each cell array is set to achieve reasonable latency and manufacturability. This limits the number of cells that each bank can provide. One may need many banks just to be able to support the memory size that is required.

There is an important connection between the parallel execution of threads and the parallel organization of the DRAM system. To achieve the memory access bandwidth specified for device, there must be a sufficient number of threads making simultaneous memory accesses. This observation reflects another benefit of maximizing occupancy. Recall that in Chapter 4, Compute Architecture and Scheduling, we saw that maximizing occupancy ensures that there are enough threads resident on the streaming multiprocessors (SMs) to hide core pipeline latency, thereby utilizing the instruction throughput efficiently. As we see now, maximizing occupancy also has the additional benefit of ensuring that enough memory access requests are made to hide DRAM access latency, thereby utilizing the memory bandwidth efficiently. Of course, to achieve the best bandwidth utilization, these memory accesses must be evenly distributed across channels and banks, and each access to a bank must also be a coalesced access.

Fig. 6.9 shows a toy example of distributing the elements of an array M to channels and banks. We assume a small burst size of two elements (8 bytes). The distribution is done by hardware design. The addressing of the channels and backs are such that the first 8 bytes of the array (M[0] and M[1]) are stored in bank 0 of channel 0, the next 8 bytes (M[2] and M[3]) in bank 0 of channel 1, the next 8 bytes (M[4] and M[5]) in bank 0 of channel 2, and the next 8 bytes (M[6] and M[7]) in bank 0 of channel 3.

At this point, the distribution wraps back to channel 0 but will use bank 1 for the next 8 bytes (M[8] and M[9]). Thus elements M[10] and M[11] will be in bank 1 of channel 1, M[12] and M[13] will be in bank 1 of channel 2, and M[14] and M[15] will be in bank 1 of channel 3. Although not shown in the figure, any additional elements will be wrapped around and start with bank 0 of channel 0. For example, if there are more elements, M[16] and M[17] will be stored in bank 0 of channel 0, M[18] and M[19] will be stored in bank 0 of channel 1, and so on.

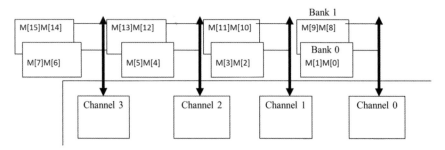

FIGURE 6.9

Distributing array elements into channels and banks.

The distribution scheme illustrated in Fig. 6.9, often referred to as *interleaved data distribution*, spreads the elements across the banks and channels in the system. This scheme ensures that even relatively small arrays are spread out nicely. Thus we assign only enough elements to fully utilize the DRAM burst of bank 0 of channel 0 before moving on to bank 0 of channel 1. In our toy example, as long as we have at least 16 elements, the distribution will involve all the channels and banks for storing the elements.

We now illustrate the interaction between parallel thread execution and the parallel memory organization. We will use the example in Fig. 5.5, replicated as Fig. 6.10. We assume that the multiplication will be performed with 2×2 thread blocks and 2×2 tiles.

During phase 0 of the kernel's execution, all four thread blocks will be loading their first tile. The M elements that are involved in each tile are shown in Fig. 6.11. Row 2 shows the M elements accessed in phase 0, with their 2D indices. Row 3 shows the same M elements with their linearized indices. Assume that all thread blocks are executed in parallel. We see that each block will make two coalesced accesses.

According to the distribution in Fig. 6.9, these coalesced accesses will be made to the two banks in channel 0 as well as the two banks in channel 2. These four accesses will be done in parallel to take advantage of two channels as well as improving the utilization of the data transfer bandwidth of each channel.

We also see that $Block_{0,0}$ and $Block_{0,1}$ will load the same M elements. Most modern devices are equipped with caches that will combine these accesses into one as long as the execution timing of these blocks are sufficiently close to each other. In fact, the cache memories in GPU devices are mainly designed to combine such accesses and reduce the number of accesses to the DRAM system.

Rows 4 and 5 show the M elements loaded during phase 1 of the kernel execution. We see that the accesses are now done to the banks in channel 1 and channel 3. Once again, these accesses will be done in parallel. It should be clear to the reader that there is a symbiotic relationship between the parallel execution of the threads and the parallel structure of the DRAM system. On one hand, good utilization of the potential access bandwidth of the DRAM system requires that many threads

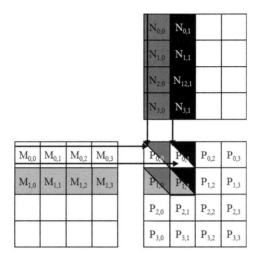

FIGURE 6.10

A small example of matrix multiplication (replicated from Fig. 5.5).

Tiles loaded by	Block 0,0	Block 0,1	Block 1,0	Block 1,1
Phase 0 (2D index)	M[0][0],M[0][1], M[1][0], M[1][1]	M[0][0], M[0][1], M[1][0], M[1][1]	M[2][0], M[2][1], M[3][0], M[3][1]	M[2][0], M[2][1], M[3][0], M[3][1]
Phase 0 (linearized index)	M[0], M[1], M[4], M[5]	M[0], M[1], M[4], M[5]	M[8], M[19], M[12], M[13]	M[8], M[9], M[12], M[13]
Phase 1 (2D index)	M[0][2],M[0][3], M[1][2], M[1][3]	M[0][2],M[0][3], M[1][2], M[1][3]	M[2][2], M[2][3], M[3][2], M[3][3]	M[2][2], M[2][3], M[3][2], M[3][3]
Phase 1 (linearized index)	M[2], M[3], M[6], M[7]	M[2], M[3], M[6], M[7]	M[10], M[11], M[14], M[15]	M[10], M[11], M[14], M[15]

FIGURE 6.11

M elements loaded by thread blocks in each phase.

simultaneously access data in the DRAM. On the other hand, the execution through-put of the device relies on good utilization of the parallel structure of the DRAM system, that is, banks and channels. For example, if the simultaneously executing threads all access data in the same channel, the memory access throughput and the overall device execution speed will be greatly reduced.

The reader is invited to verify that multiplying two larger matrices, such as 8×8 with the same 2×2 thread block configuration, will make use of all the four channels in Fig. 6.9. On the other hand, an increased DRAM burst size would require multiplication of even larger matrices to fully utilize the data transfer bandwidth of all the channels.

6.3 Thread coarsening

So far, in all the kernels that we have seen, work has been parallelized across threads at the finest granularity. That is, each thread was assigned the smallest possible unit of work. For example, in the vector addition kernel, each thread was assigned one output element. In the RGB-to-grayscale conversion and the image blur kernels, each thread was assigned one pixel in the output image. In the matrix multiplication kernels, each thread was assigned one element in the output matrix.

The advantage of parallelizing work across threads at the finest granularity is that it enhances transparent scalability, as discussed in Chapter 4, Compute Architecture and Scheduling. If the hardware has enough resources to perform all the work in parallel, then the application has exposed enough parallelism to fully utilize the hardware. Otherwise, if the hardware does not have enough resources to perform all the work in parallel, the hardware can simply serialize the work by executing the thread blocks one after the other.

The disadvantage of parallelizing work at the finest granularity comes when there is a "price" to be paid for parallelizing that work. This price of parallelism can take many forms, such as redundant loading of data by different thread blocks, redundant work, synchronization overhead, and others. When the threads are executed in parallel by the hardware, this price of parallelism is often worth paying. However, if the hardware ends up serializing the work as a result of insufficient resources, then this price has been paid unnecessarily. In this case, it is better for the programmer to partially serialize the work and reduce the price that is paid for parallelism. This can be done by assigning each thread multiple units of work, which is often referred to as *thread coarsening*.

We demonstrate the thread coarsening optimization using the tiled matrix multiplication example from Chapter 5, Memory Architecture and Data Locality. Fig. 6.12 depicts the memory access pattern of computing two horizontally adjacent output tiles of the output matrix P. For each of these output tiles, we observe that different input tiles of the matrix N need to be loaded. However, the same input tiles of the matrix M are loaded for both the output tiles.

In the tiled implementation in Chapter 5, Memory Architecture and Data Locality, each output tile is processed by a different thread block. Because the shared memory contents cannot be shared across blocks, each block must load its own copy of the input tiles of matrix M. Although having different thread blocks load the same input tile is redundant, it is a price that we pay to be able to process the two output tiles in parallel using different blocks. If these thread blocks run in

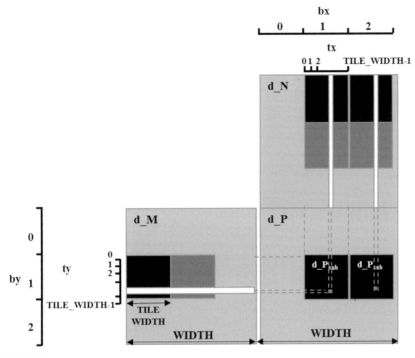

FIGURE 6.12

Thread coarsening for tiled matrix multiplication.

parallel, this price may be worth paying. On the other hand, if these thread blocks are serialized by the hardware, the price is paid in vain. In the latter case, it is better for the programmer to have a single thread block process the two output tiles, whereby each thread in the block processes two output elements. This way, the coarsened thread block would load the input tiles of M once and reuse them for multiple output tiles.

Fig. 6.13 shows how thread coarsening can be applied to the tiled matrix multiplication code from Chapter 5, Memory Architecture and Data Locality. On line 02 a constant COARSE_FACTOR is added to represent the *coarsening factor*, which is the number of original units of work for which each coarsened thread is going to be responsible. On line 13 the initialization of the column index is replaced with an initialization of colStart, which is the index of the first column for which the thread is responsible, since the thread is now responsible for multiple elements with different column indices. In calculating colStart, the block index bx is multiplied by TILE_WIDTH*COARSE_FACTOR instead of just TILE_WIDTH, since each thread block is now responsible for TILE_WIDTH*COARSE_FACTOR columns. On lines 16–19, multiple instances of Pvalue are declared and initialized, one for each element for which the

```
01    #define TILE_WIDTH    32
02    #define COARSE_FACTOR 4
03    __global__ void matrixMulKernel(float* M, float* N, float* P, int width)
{
04
05        __shared__ float Mds[TILE_WIDTH][TILE_WIDTH];
06        __shared__ float Nds[TILE_WIDTH][TILE_WIDTH];
07
08        int bx = blockIdx.x;  int by = blockIdx.y;
09        int tx = threadIdx.x; int ty = threadIdx.y;
10
11        // Identify the row and column of the P element to work on
12        int row = by*TILE_WIDTH + ty;
13        int colStart = bx*TILE_WIDTH*COARSE_FACTOR + tx;
14
15        // Initialize Pvalue for all output elements
16        float Pvalue[COARSE_FACTOR];
17        for(int c = 0; c < COARSE_FACTOR; ++c) {
18            Pvalue[c] = 0.0f;
19        }
20
21        // Loop over the M and N tiles required to compute P element
22        for(int ph = 0; ph < width/TILE_WIDTH; ++ph) {
23
24            // Collaborative loading of M tile into shared memory
25            Mds[ty][tx] = M[row*width + ph*TILE_WIDTH + tx];
26
27            for(int c = 0; c < COARSE_FACTOR; ++c) {
28
29                int col = colStart + c*TILE_WIDTH;
30
31                // Collaborative loading of N tile into shared memory
32                Nds[ty][tx] = N[(ph*TILE_WIDTH + ty)*width + col];
33                __syncthreads();
34
35                for(int k = 0; k < TILE_WIDTH; ++k) {
36                    Pvalue[c] += Mds[ty][k]*Nds[k][tx];
37                }
38                __syncthreads();
39
40            }
41
42        }
43
44        for(int c = 0; c < COARSE_FACTOR; ++c) {
45            int col = colStart + c*TILE_WIDTH;
46            P[row*width + col] = Pvalue[c];
47        }
48
49    }
```

FIGURE 6.13

Code for thread coarsening for tiled matrix multiplication.

coarsened thread is responsible. The loop on line 17 that iterates over the different units of work for which the coarsened thread is responsible is sometimes referred to as a *coarsening loop*. Inside the loop on line 22 that loops over the input tiles, only one tile of M is loaded in each loop iteration, as with the original code. However, for each tile of M that is loaded, multiple tiles of N are loaded and used by the coarsening loop on line 27. This loop first figures out which column of the current tile the coarsened thread is responsible for (line 29), then loads the tile of N (line 32) and uses the tile to compute and update a different Pvalue each iteration (lines 35−37). At the end, on lines 44−47, another coarsening loop is used for each coarsened thread to update the output elements for which it is responsible.

Thread coarsening is a powerful optimization that can result in substantial performance improvement for many applications. It is an optimization that is commonly applied. However, there are several pitfalls to avoid in applying thread coarsening. First, one must be careful not to apply the optimization when it is unnecessary. Recall that thread coarsening is beneficial when there is a price paid for parallelization that can be reduced with coarsening, such as redundant loading of data, redundant work, synchronization overhead, or others. Not all computations have such a price. For example, in the vector addition kernel in Chapter 2, Heterogeneous Data Parallel Computing, no price is paid for processing different vector elements in parallel. Therefore applying thread coarsening to the vector addition kernel would not be expected to make a substantial performance difference. The same applies to the RGB-to-grayscale conversion kernel in Chapter 3, Multidimensional Grids and Data.

The second pitfall to avoid is not to apply so much coarsening that the hardware resources become underutilized. Recall that exposing as much parallelism as possible to the hardware enables transparent scalability. It provides the hardware with the flexibility of parallelizing or serializing work, depending on the amount of execution resources it has. When programmers coarsen threads, they reduce the amount of parallelism that is exposed to the hardware. If the coarsening factor is too high, not enough parallelism will be exposed to the hardware, resulting in some parallel execution resources being unutilized. In practice, different devices have different amounts of execution resources, so the best coarsening factor is usually device-specific and dataset-specific and needs to be retuned for different devices and datasets. Hence when thread coarsening is applied, scalability becomes less transparent.

The third pitfall of applying thread coarsening is to avoid increasing resource consumption to such an extent that it hurts occupancy. Depending on the kernel, thread coarsening may require using more registers per thread or more shared memory per thread block. If this is the case, programmers must be careful not to use too many registers or too much shared memory such that the occupancy is reduced. The performance penalty from reducing occupancy may be more detrimental than the performance benefit that thread coarsening may offer.

6.4 A checklist of optimizations

Throughout this first part of the book, we have covered various common optimizations that CUDA programmers apply to improve the performance of their code. We consolidate these optimizations into a single checklist, shown in Table 6.1. This checklist is not an exhaustive one, but it contains many of the universal

Table 6.1 A checklist of optimizations.

Optimization	Benefit to compute cores	Benefit to memory	Strategies
Maximizing occupancy	More work to hide pipeline latency	More parallel memory accesses to hide DRAM latency	Tuning usage of SM resources such as threads per block, shared memory per block, and registers per thread
Enabling coalesced global memory accesses	Fewer pipeline stalls waiting for global memory accesses	Less global memory traffic and better utilization of bursts/cache lines	Transfer between global memory and shared memory in a coalesced manner and performing uncoalesced accesses in shared memory (e.g., corner turning) Rearranging the mapping of threads to data Rearranging the layout of the data
Minimizing control divergence	High SIMD efficiency (fewer idle cores during SIMD execution)	–	Rearranging the mapping of threads to work and/or data Rearranging the layout of the data
Tiling of reused data	Fewer pipeline stalls waiting for global memory accesses	Less global memory traffic	Placing data that is reused within a block in shared memory or registers so that it is transferred between global memory and the SM only once
Privatization (covered later)	Fewer pipeline stalls waiting for atomic updates	Less contention and serialization of atomic updates	Applying partial updates to a private copy of the data and then updating the universal copy when done
Thread coarsening	Less redundant work, divergence, or synchronization	Less redundant global memory traffic	Assigning multiple units of parallelism to each thread to reduce the price of parallelism when it is incurred unnecessarily

optimizations that are common across different applications and that programmers should first consider. In the second and third parts of the book, we will apply the optimizations in this checklist to various parallel patterns and applications to understand how they operate in different contexts. In this section we will provide a brief review of each optimization and the strategies for applying it.

The first optimization in Table 6.1 is maximizing the occupancy of threads on SMs. This optimization was introduced in Chapter 4, Compute Architecture and Scheduling, where the importance of having many more threads than cores was emphasized as a way to have enough work available to hide long-latency operations in the core pipeline. To maximize occupancy, programmers can tune the resource usage of their kernels to ensure that the maximum number of blocks or registers allowed per SM do not limit the number of threads that can be assigned to the SM simultaneously. In Chapter 5, Memory Architecture and Data Locality, shared memory was introduced as another resource whose usage should be carefully tuned so as not to limit occupancy. In this chapter, the importance of maximizing occupancy was discussed as a means for also hiding memory latency, not just core pipeline latency. Having many threads executing simultaneously ensures that enough memory accesses are generated to fully utilize the memory bandwidth.

The second optimization in Table 6.1 is using coalesced global memory accesses by ensuring that threads in the same warp access adjacent memory locations. This optimization was introduced in this chapter, where the hardware's ability to combine accesses to adjacent memory locations into a single memory request was emphasized as a way for reducing global memory traffic and improving the utilization of DRAM bursts. So far, the kernels that we have looked at in this part of the book have exhibited coalesced accesses naturally. However, we will see many examples in the second and third parts of the book in which memory access patterns are more irregular, thereby requiring more effort to achieve coalescing.

There are multiple strategies that can be employed for achieving coalescing in applications with irregular access patterns. One strategy is to load data from global memory to shared memory in a coalesced manner and then perform the irregular accesses on shared memory. We have already seen an example of this strategy in this chapter, namely, corner turning. We will see another example of this strategy in Chapter 12, Merge, which covers the merge pattern. In this pattern, threads in the same block need to perform a binary search in the same array, so they collaborate to load that array from global memory to shared memory in a coalesced manner, and then each performs the binary search in shared memory. We will also see an example of this strategy in Chapter 13, Sorting, which covers the sort pattern. In this pattern, threads write out results to an array in a scattered manner, so they can collaborate to perform their scattered accesses in the shared memory, then write the result from the shared memory to the global memory with more coalescing enabled for elements with nearby destinations.

Another strategy for achieving coalescing in applications with irregular access patterns is to rearrange how the threads are mapped to the data elements. We will see an example of this strategy in Chapter 10, Reduction and Minimizing Divergence, which covers the reduction pattern. Yet another strategy for achieving coalescing in applications with irregular access patterns is to rearrange how the data itself is laid out. We will see an example of this strategy in Chapter 14,

Sparse Matrix Computation which covers sparse matrix computation and storage formats, particularly in discussing the ELL and JDS formats.

The third optimization in Table 6.1 is minimizing control divergence. Control divergence was introduced in Chapter 4, Compute Architecture and Scheduling, where the importance of threads in the same warp taking the same control path was emphasized as a means for ensuring that all cores are productively utilized during SIMD execution. So far, the kernels that we have looked at in this part of the book have not exhibited control divergence, except for the inevitable divergence at boundary conditions. However, we will see many examples in the second and third parts of the book in which control divergence can be a significant detriment to performance.

There are multiple strategies that can be employed for minimizing control divergence. One strategy is to rearrange how the work and/or data is distributed across the threads to ensure that threads in one warp are all used before threads in other warps are used. We will see an example of this strategy in Chapter 10, Reduction and Minimizing Divergence, which covers the reduction pattern, and Chapter 11, Prefix Sum (Scan), which covers the scan pattern. The strategy of rearranging how work and/or data is distributed across threads can also be used to ensure that threads in the same warp have similar workloads. We will see an example of this in Chapter 15, Graph Traversal, which covers graph traversal, in which we will discuss the tradeoffs between vertex-centric and edge-centric parallelization schemes. Another strategy for minimizing control divergence is to rearrange how the data is laid out to ensure that threads in the same warp that process adjacent data have similar workloads. We will see an example of this strategy in Chapter 14, Sparse Matrix Computation, which covers sparse matrix computation and storage formats, particularly when discussing the JDS format.

The fourth optimization in Table 6.1 is tiling data that is reused within a block by placing it in the shared memory or registers and accessing it repetitively from there, such that it needs to be transferred between global memory and the SM only once. Tiling was introduced in Chapter 5, Memory Architecture and Data Locality, in the context of matrix multiplication, in which threads processing the same output tile collaborate to load the corresponding input tiles to the shared memory and then access these input tiles repetitively from the shared memory. We will see this optimization applied again in most of the parallel patterns in the second and third parts of the book. We will observe the challenges of applying tiling when the input and output tiles have different dimensions. This challenge arises in Chapter 7, Convolution, which covers the convolution pattern, and in Chapter 8, Stencil, which covers the stencil pattern. We will also observe that tiles of data can be stored in registers, not just shared memory. This observation is most pronounced in Chapter 8, Stencil, which covers the stencil pattern. We will additionally observe that tiling is applicable to output data that is accessed repeatedly, not just input data.

The fifth optimization in Table 6.1 is privatization. This optimization has not yet been introduced, but we mention it here for completeness. Privatization relates to the situation in which multiple threads or blocks need to update a universal output. To avoid the overhead of updating the same data concurrently, a private copy of the data can be created and partially updated, and then a final update can be made to the universal copy from the private copy when done. We will see an example of this optimization in Chapter 9, Parallel Histogram, which covers the histogram pattern, in which multiple threads need to update the same histogram counters. We will also see an example of this optimization in Chapter 15, Graph Traversal, which covers graph traversal, in which multiple threads need to add entries to the same queue.

The sixth optimization in Table 6.1 is thread coarsening, in which multiple units of parallelism are assigned to a single thread to reduce the price of parallelism if the hardware was going to serialize the threads anyway. Thread coarsening was introduced in this chapter in the context of tiled matrix multiplication, in which the price of parallelism was loading of the same input tile redundantly by multiple thread blocks that process adjacent output tiles. In this case, assigning one thread block to process multiple adjacent output tiles enables loading an input tile once for all the output tiles. In the second and third parts of the book, we will see thread coarsening applied in different contexts with a different price of parallelism each time. In Chapter 8, Stencil, which covers the stencil pattern, thread coarsening is applied to reduce the redundant loading of input data, as in this chapter. In Chapter 9, Parallel Histogram, which covers the histogram pattern, thread coarsening helps to reduce the number of private copies that need to be committed to the universal copy in the context of the privatization optimization. In Chapter 10, Reduction and Minimizing Divergence, which covers the reduction pattern, and in Chapter 11, Prefix Sum (Scan), which covers the scan pattern, thread coarsening is applied to reduce the overhead from synchronization and control divergence. Also in Chapter 11, Prefix Sum (Scan), which covers the scan pattern, thread coarsening also helps reduce the redundant work that is performed by the parallel algorithm compared to the sequential algorithm. In Chapter 12, Merge, which covers the merge pattern, thread coarsening reduces the number of binary search operations that need to be performed to identify each thread's input segment. In Chapter 13, Sorting, which covers the sort pattern, thread coarsening helps improve memory coalescing.

Again, the checklist in Table 6.1 is not intended to be an exhaustive one, but it contains major types of the optimizations that are common across different computation patterns. These optimizations appear in multiple chapters in the second and third parts of the book. We will also see other optimizations that appear in specific chapters. For example, in Chapter 7, Convolution, which covers the convolution pattern, we will introduce the use of constant memory. In Chapter 10, Reduction and Minimizing Divergence, which covers the scan pattern, we will introduce the double-buffering optimization.

6.5 Knowing your computation's bottleneck

In deciding what optimization to apply to a specific computation, it is important first to understand what resource is limiting the performance of that computation.

The resource that limits the performance of a computation is often referred to as a performance *bottleneck*. Optimizations typically use more of one resource to reduce the burden on another resource. If the optimization that is applied does not target the bottleneck resource, there may be no benefit from the optimization. Worse yet, the optimization attempt may even hurt performance.

For example, shared memory tiling increases the use of shared memory to reduce the pressure on the global memory bandwidth. This optimization is great when the bottleneck resource is the global memory bandwidth and the data being loaded is reused. However, if, for example, the performance is limited by occupancy and occupancy is constrained by the use of too much shared memory already, then applying shared memory tiling is likely to make things worse.

To understand what resource is limiting the performance of a computation, GPU computing platforms typically provide various profiling tools. We refer readers to the CUDA documentation for more information on how to use profiling tools to identify the performance bottlenecks of their computations (NVIDIA, Profiler). Performance bottlenecks may be hardware-specific, meaning that the same computation may encounter different bottlenecks on different devices. For this reason the process of identifying performance bottlenecks and applying performance optimizations requires a good understanding of the GPU architecture and the architectural differences across different GPU devices.

6.6 Summary

In this chapter we covered the off-chip memory (DRAM) architecture of a GPU and discussed related performance considerations, such as global memory access coalescing and hiding memory latency with memory parallelism. We then presented an important optimization: thread granularity coarsening. With the insights that were presented in this chapter and earlier chapters, readers should be able to reason about the performance of any kernel code that they come across. We concluded this part of the book by presenting a checklist of common performance optimizations that are widely used to optimize many computations. We will continue to study practical applications of these optimizations in the parallel computation patterns and application case studies in the next two parts of the book.

Exercises

1. Write a matrix multiplication kernel function that corresponds to the design illustrated in Fig. 6.4.
2. For tiled matrix multiplication, of the possible range of values for BLOCK_SIZE, for what values of BLOCK_SIZE will the kernel completely avoid uncoalesced accesses to global memory? (You need to consider only square blocks.)

3. Consider the following CUDA kernel:

```
01    __global__ void foo_kernel(float* a, float* b, float* c, float* d, float* e) {
02        unsigned int i = blockIdx.x*blockDim.x + threadIdx.x;
03        __shared__ float a_s[256];
04        __shared__ float bc_s[4*256];
05        a_s[threadIdx.x] = a[i];
06        for(unsigned int j = 0; j < 4; ++j) {
07            bc_s[j*256 + threadIdx.x] = b[j*blockDim.x*gridDim.x + i] + c[i*4 + j];
08        }
09        __syncthreads();
10        d[i + 8] = a_s[threadIdx.x];
11        e[i*8] = bc_s[threadIdx.x*4];
12    }
```

For each of the following memory accesses, specify whether they are coalesced or uncoalesced or coalescing is not applicable:

a. The access to array a of line 05
b. The access to array a_s of line 05
c. The access to array b of line 07
d. The access to array c of line 07
e. The access to array bc_s of line 07
f. The access to array a_s of line 10
g. The access to array d of line 10
h. The access to array bc_s of line 11
i. The access to array e of line 11

4. What is the floating point to global memory access ratio (in OP/B) of each of the following matrix-matrix multiplication kernels?

a. The simple kernel described in Chapter 3, Multidimensional Grids and Data, without any optimizations applied.
b. The kernel described in Chapter 5, Memory Architecture and Data Locality, with shared memory tiling applied using a tile size of 32×32.
c. The kernel described in this chapter with shared memory tiling applied using a tile size of 32×32 and thread coarsening applied using a coarsening factor of 4.

References

NVIDIA Profiler User's Guide. https://docs.nvidia.com/cuda/profiler-users-guide.

Parallel Patterns

Convolution
An introduction to constant memory and caching

7

Chapter Outline

7.1 Background 152
7.2 Parallel convolution: a basic algorithm 156
7.3 Constant memory and caching 159
7.4 Tiled convolution with halo cells 163
7.5 Tiled convolution using caches for halo cells 168
7.6 Summary 170
Exercises 171

In the next several chapters we will discuss a set of important patterns of parallel computation. These patterns are the basis of a wide range of parallel algorithms that appear in many parallel applications. We will start with convolution, which is a popular array operation that is used in various forms in signal processing, digital recording, image processing, video processing, and computer vision. In these application areas, convolution is often performed as a filter that transforms signals and pixels into more desirable values. Our image blur kernel is such a filter that smoothes out the signal values so that one can see the big picture trend. For another example, Gaussian filters are convolution filters that can be used to sharpen boundaries and edges of objects in images.

Convolution typically performs a significant number of arithmetic operations to generate each output element. For large datasets such as high-definition images and videos in which there are many output elements (pixels), the amount of computation can be huge. On one hand, each output data element of convolution can be calculated independently of each other, a desirable trait for parallel computing. On the other hand, there is a substantial amount of input data sharing in processing different output data elements with somewhat challenging boundary conditions. This makes convolution an important use case for sophisticated tiling methods and input data staging methods, which are the focus of this chapter.

Programming Massively Parallel Processors. DOI: https://doi.org/10.1016/B978-0-323-91231-0.00008-2

7.1 Background

Convolution is an array operation in which each output data element is a weighted sum of the corresponding input element and a collection of input elements that are centered on it. The weights that are used in the weighted sum calculation are defined by a filter array, commonly referred to as the *convolution kernel*. Since there is an unfortunate name conflict between the CUDA kernel functions and convolution kernels, we will refer to these filter arrays as *convolution filters* to avoid confusion.

Convolution can be performed on input data of different dimensionality: one-dimensional (1D) (e.g., audio), two-dimensional (2D) (e.g., photo), three-dimensional (3D) (e.g., video), and so on. In audio digital signal processing, the input 1D array elements are sampled signal volume over time. That is, the input data element x_i is the ith sample of the audio signal volume. A convolution on 1D data, referred to as 1D convolution, is mathematically defined as a function that takes an input data array of n elements $[x_0, x_1, \ldots, x_{n-1}]$ and a filter array of $2r + 1$ elements $[f_0, f_1, \ldots, f_{2r}]$ and returns an output data array y:

$$y_i = \sum_{j=-r}^{r} f_{i+j} \times x_i$$

Since the size of the filter is an odd number ($2r + 1$), the weighted sum calculation is symmetric around the element that is being calculated. That is, the weighted sum involves r input elements on each side of the position that is being calculated, which is the reason why r is referred to as the *radius* of the filter.

Fig. 7.1 shows a 1D convolution example in which a five-element ($r = 2$) convolution filter f is applied to a seven-element input array x. We will follow the C language convention by which x and y elements are indexed from 0 to 6 and f elements are indexed from 0 to 4. Since the filter radius is 2, each output element is calculated as the weighted sum of the corresponding input element, two elements on the left, and two elements on the right.

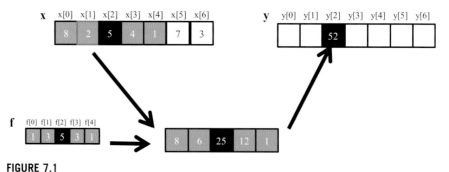

FIGURE 7.1

A 1D convolution example, inside elements.

For example, the value of y[2] is generated as the weighted sum of x[0] (i.e., x[2 − 2]) through x[4] (i.e., x[2 + 2]). In this example we arbitrarily assume that the values of the x elements are [8, 2, 5, 4, 1, 7, 3]. The f elements define the weights, whose values are 1, 3, 5, 3, 1 in this example. Each f element is multiplied to the corresponding x element values before the products are summed together. As shown in Fig. 7.1, the calculation for y[2] is as follows:

$$y[2] = f[0]*x[0] + f[1]*x[1] + f[2]*x[2] + f[3]*x[3] + f[4]*x[4]$$
$$= 1*8 + 3*2 + 5*5 + 3*4 + 1*1$$
$$= 52$$

In Fig. 7.1 the calculation for y[i] can be viewed as an inner product between the subarray of x that starts at x[I − 2] and the f array. Fig. 7.2 shows the calculation for y[3]. The calculation is shifted by one x element from that of Fig. 7.1. That is, the value of y[3] is the weighted sum of x[1] (i.e., x[3 − 2]), through x [5] (i.e., x[3 + 2]). We can think of the calculation for x[3] is as following inner product:

$$y[3] = f[0]*x[1] + f[1]*x[2] + f[2]*x[3] + f[3]*x[4] + f[4]*x[5]y[3]$$
$$= f[0]*x[1] + f[1]*x[2] + f[2]*x[3] + f[3]*x[4] + f[4]*x[5]$$
$$= 1*2 + 3*5 + 5*4 + 3*1 + 1*7$$
$$= 47$$

Because convolution is defined in terms of neighboring elements, boundary conditions naturally arise in computing output elements that are close to the ends of an array. As shown in Fig. 7.3, when we calculate y[1], there is only one x element to the left of x[1]. That is, there are not enough x elements to calculate y[1] according to our definition of convolution. A typical approach to handling such boundary conditions is to assign a default value to these missing x elements. For most applications the default value is 0, which is what we use in Fig. 7.3. For example, in audio signal processing, we can assume that the signal volume is 0

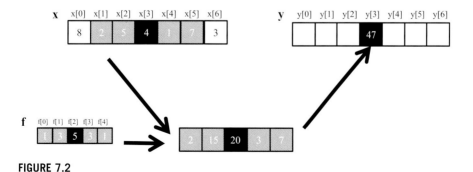

FIGURE 7.2

1D convolution, calculation of y[3].

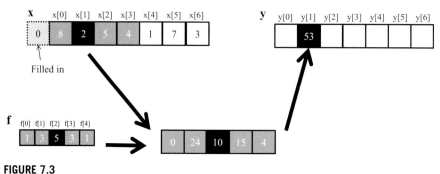

FIGURE 7.3

A 1D convolution boundary condition.

before the recording starts and after it ends. In this case, the calculation of y[1] is as follows:

$$y[1] = f[0]^*0 + f[1]^*x[0] + f[2]^*x[1] + f[3]^*x[2] + f[4]^*x[3]$$
$$= 1^*0 + 3^*8 + 5^*2 + 3^*5 + 1^*4$$
$$= 53$$

The x element that does not exist in this calculation is illustrated as a dashed box in Fig. 7.3. It should be clear that the calculation of y[0] will involve two missing x elements, both of which will be assumed to be 0 for this example. We leave the calculation of y[0] as an exercise. These missing elements are typically referred to as *ghost cells* in the literature. There are also other types of ghost cells due to the use of tiling in parallel computation. These ghost cells can have significant impact on the effectiveness and/or efficiency of tiling. We will come back to this point soon.

Also, not all applications assume that the ghost cells contain 0. For example, some applications might assume that the ghost cells contain the same value as the closest valid data element on the edge.

For image processing and computer vision, input data is typically represented as 2D arrays, with pixels in an $x-y$ space. Image convolutions are therefore 2D convolutions, as illustrated in Fig. 7.4. In a 2D convolution the filter f is also a 2D array. Its x and y dimensions determine the range of neighbors to be included in the weighted sum calculation. If we assume that the dimension of the filter is $(2r_x + 1)$ in the x dimension and $(2r_y + 1)$ in the y dimension, the calculation of each P element can be expressed as follows:

$$P_{y,x} = \sum_{j=-r_y}^{r_y} \sum_{k=-r_x}^{r_x} f_{y+j,x+k} \times N_{y,x}$$

In Fig. 7.4 we use a 5×5 filter for simplicity; that is, $r_y = 2$ and $r_x = 2$. In general, the filter does not have to be but is typically a square array. To generate an output element, we take the subarray whose center is at the corresponding location in the input array N. We then perform pairwise multiplication between

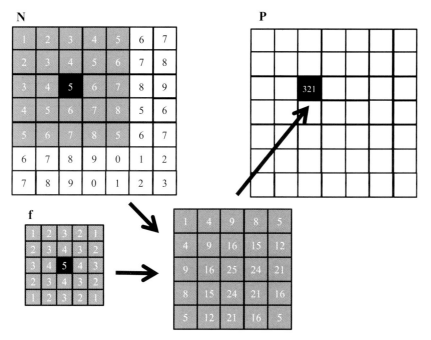

FIGURE 7.4

A 2D convolution example.

elements of the filter array and those of the image array. For our example the result is shown as the 5 $\times$ 5 product array below N and P in Fig. 7.4. The value of the output element is the sum of all elements of the product array.

The example in Fig. 7.4 shows the calculation of P2,2. For brevity, we will use $N_{y,x}$ to denote $N[y][x]$ in addressing a C array. Since N and P are most likely dynamically allocated arrays, we will be using linearized indices in our actual code examples. The calculation is as follows:

```
P2,2 = N0,0*M0,0 + N0,1*M0,1 + N0,2*M0,2 + N0,3*M0,3 + N0,4*M0,4
     + N1,0*M1,0 + N1,1*M1,1 + N1,2*M1,2 + N1,3*M1,3 + N1,4*M1,4
     + N2,0*M2,0 + N2,1*M2,1 + N2,2*M2,2 + N2,3*M2,3 + N2,4*M2,4
     + N3,0*M3,0 + N3,1*M3,1 + N3,2*M3,2 + N3,3*M3,3 + N3,4*M3,4
     + N4,0*M4,0 + N4,1*M4,1 + N4,2*M4,2 + N4,3*M4,3 + N4,4*M4,4
   = 1*1 + 2*2 + 3*3 + 4*2 + 5*1
     + 2*2 + 3*3 + 4*4 + 5*3 + 6*2
     + 3*3 + 4*4 + 5*5 + 6*4 + 7*3
     + 4*2 + 5*3 + 6*4 + 7*3 + 8*2
     + 5*1 + 6*2 + 7*3 + 8*2 + 5*1
   = 1 + 4 + 9 + 8 + 5
     + 4 + 9 + 16 + 15 + 12
     + 9 + 16 + 25 + 24 + 21
     + 8 + 15 + 24 + 21 + 16
     + 5 + 12 + 21 + 16 + 5
   = 321
```

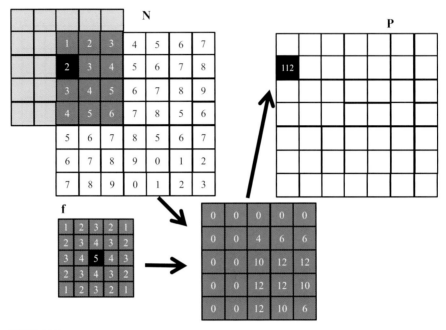

FIGURE 7.5

A 2D convolution boundary condition.

Like 1D convolution, 2D convolution must also deal with boundary conditions. With boundaries in both the x and y dimensions, there are more complex boundary conditions: The calculation of an output element may involve boundary conditions along a horizontal boundary, a vertical boundary, or both. Fig. 7.5 illustrates the calculation of a P element that involves both boundaries. From Fig. 7.5 the calculation of $P_{1,0}$ involves two missing columns and one missing row in the subarray of N. As in 1D convolution, different applications assume different default values for these missing N elements. In our example we assume that the default value is 0. These boundary conditions also affect the efficiency of tiling. We will come back to this point soon.

7.2 Parallel convolution: a basic algorithm

The fact that the calculation of all output elements can be done in parallel in a convolution makes convolution an ideal use case for parallel computing. Based on our experience in matrix multiplication, we can quickly write a simple parallel convolution kernel. We will show code examples for 2D convolution, and the reader is encouraged to adapt these code examples to 1D and 3D as exercises. Also, for simplicity we will assume square filters.

The first step is to define the major input parameters for the kernel. We assume that the 2D convolution kernel receives five arguments: a pointer to the input array, N; a pointer to the filter, F; a pointer to the output array, P; the radius of the square filter, r; the width of the input and output arrays, width; and the height of the input and output arrays, height. Thus we have the following setup:

```
__global__ void
convolution_2D_basic_kernel(float *N, float *F, float *P, int r,
                            int width, int height) {
    // kernel body
}
```

The second step is to determine and implement the mapping of threads to output elements. Since the output array is 2D, a simple and good approach is to organize the threads into a 2D grid and have each thread in the grid calculate one output element. Each block, with up to 1024 threads in a block, can calculate up to 1024 output elements. Fig. 7.6 shows a toy example in which the input and output are 16 × 16 images. We assume in this toy example that each thread block is organized as a 4 × 4 array of threads: four threads in the x dimension and four in the y dimension. The grid in this example is organized as a 4 × 4 array of blocks. The assignment of threads to output elements—output pixels in this example—is simple: Every thread is assigned to calculate an output pixel whose x and y indices are the same as the thread's x and y indices.

The reader should recognize that the parallelization arrangement in Fig. 7.6 is the same as the ColorToGrayScaleConversion example in Chapter 3, Multidimensional

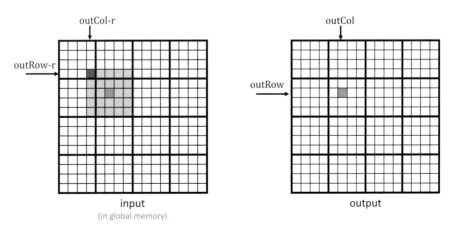

FIGURE 7.6

Parallelization and thread organization for 2D convolution.

Grids and Data. Therefore we can use the statements in lines 02 and 03 of the kernel in Fig. 7.7 to calculate the output element indices from the block index, block dimension, and thread index for each thread. For example, thread$_{1,1}$ of block$_{1,1}$ is mapped to output element P[1*4+1][1*4+1]=P[5][5], which is marked as a green square in Fig. 7.6.

Once we have determined the output element indices for each thread, we can identify the input *N* elements that are needed for calculating the output element. As illustrated in Fig. 7.6, the calculation of P[5][5] (green square) by thread$_{1,\ 1}$ of block$_{1,\ 1}$ will use the input elements whose *x* indices range from outCol - r=3 to outCol + r=7 and whose y indices range from outRow - r=3 to outRow + r=7. For all threads, outCol - r and outRow - r define the upper-left corner (heavily shaded square) of the patch of input elements (lightly shaded area) needed for P[outRow][outCol]. Therefore we can use a doubly nested loop to iterate through all these index values and perform this calculation (lines 05−13 of Fig. 7.7).

The register variable Pvalue will accumulate all intermediate results to save DRAM bandwidth. The if-statement in the inner for-loop tests whether any of the input *N* elements that are used are ghost cells on the left, right, top, or bottom side of the *N* array. Since we assume that 0 values will be used for ghost cells, we can simply skip the multiplication and accumulation of the ghost cell element and its corresponding filter element. After the end of the loop, we release the Pvalue into the output P element (line 14).

We make two observations on the kernel in Fig. 7.7. First, there will be control flow divergence. The threads that calculate the output elements near the four edges of the P array will need to handle ghost cells. As we showed in Section 7.1, each of these threads will encounter a different number of ghost cells. Therefore they will all be somewhat different decisions in the if-statement (line 09). The thread that calculates P[0][0] will skip the multiply-accumulate statement most of the time, whereas the one that calculates P[0][1] will skip fewer times, and so on. The cost of control divergence will depend

```
01  __global__ void convolution_2D_basic_kernel(float *N, float *F, float *P,
       int r, int width, int height) {
02     int outCol = blockIdx.x*blockDim.x + threadIdx.x;
03     int outRow = blockIdx.y*blockDim.y + threadIdx.y;
04     float Pvalue = 0.0f;
05     for (int fRow = 0; fRow < 2*r+1; fRow++) {
06       for (int fCol = 0; fCol < 2*r+1; fCol++) {
07         inRow = outRow - r + fRow;
08         inCol = outCol - r + fCol;
09         if (inRow >= 0 && inRow < height && inCol >= 0 && inCol < width) {
10           Pvalue += F[fRow][fCol]*N[inRow*width + inCol];
11         }
12       }
13     }
14     P[outRow][outCol] = Pvalue;
15  }
```

FIGURE 7.7

A 2D convolution kernel with boundary condition handling.

on the value of width and height of the input array and the radius of the filter. For large input arrays and small filters, control divergence occurs only in computing a small portion of the output elements, which will keep the effect of control divergence small. Since convolution is often applied to large images, we expect the effect of control divergence to range from modest to insignificant.

A more serious problem is memory bandwidth. The ratio of floating-point arithmetic calculation to global memory accesses is only about 0.25 OP/B (2 operations for every 8 bytes loaded on line 10). As we saw in the matrix multiplication example, this simple kernel can be expected to run only at a tiny fraction of the peak performance. We will discuss two key techniques for reducing the number of global memory accesses in the next two sections.

7.3 Constant memory and caching

There are three interesting properties in the way the filter array F is used in convolution. First, the size of F is typically small; the radius of most convolution filters is 7 or smaller. Even in 3D convolution the filter typically contains only less than or equal to $7^3 = 343$ elements. Second, the contents of F do not change throughout the execution of the convolution kernel. Third, all threads access the filter elements. Even better, all threads access the F elements in the same order, starting from F[0][0] and moving by one element at a time through the iterations of the doubly nested for-loop in Fig. 7.7. These three properties make the filter an excellent candidate for constant memory and caching (Fig. 7.8).

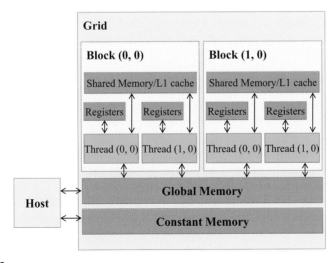

FIGURE 7.8

A review of the CUDA memory model.

As we discussed in Chapter 5, Memory Architecture and Data Locality (Table 5.1), the CUDA C allows programmers to declare variables to reside in the constant memory. Like global memory variables, constant memory variables are visible to all thread blocks. The main difference is that the value of a constant memory variable cannot be modified by threads during kernel execution. Furthermore, the size of the constant memory is quite small, currently at 64 KB.

To use constant memory, the host code needs to allocate and copy constant memory variables in a different way than global memory variables. We assume that the radius of the filter is specified in the compile-time constant FILTER_RADIUS. To declare an F array in constant memory, the host code declares it a global variable as follows:

```
#define FILTER_RADIUS 2
__constant__ float F[2*FILTER_RADIUS+1][2*FILTER_RADIUS+1];
```

Note that this is a global variable declaration and should be outside any function in the source file. The keyword __constant__ (two underscores on each side) tells the compiler that array F should be placed into the device constant memory.

Assume that the host code has already allocated and initialized the mask in a filter F_h array in the host memory with (2*FILTER_RADIUS+1)2 elements. The contents of the F_h can be transferred from the host memory to F in the device constant memory as follows:

```
cudaMemcpyToSymbol(F,F_h,(2*FILTER_RADIUS+1)*(2*FILTER_RADIUS+1)*sizeof(float));
```

Note that this is a special memory copy function that informs the CUDA runtime that the data being copied into the constant memory will not be changed during kernel execution. In general, the use of cudaMemcpyToSymble() function is as follows:

```
cudaMemcpyToSymbol(dest, src, size)
```

where dest is a pointer to the destination location in the constant memory, src is a pointer to the source data in the host memory, and size is the number of bytes to be copied.[1]

Kernel functions access constant memory variables as global variables. Therefore their pointers do not need to be passed to the kernel as arguments. We can revise our kernel to use the constant memory as shown in Fig. 7.9. Note that the kernel looks almost identical to that in Fig. 7.7. The only difference is that F is no longer accessed through a pointer that is passed in as a parameter. It is now

---

[1]The function can take two more arguments, namely, offset and kind, but these are seldom used and are often omitted. The reader is referred to CUDA C Programming Guide for details of these arguments.

```
01  __global__ void convolution_2D_const_mem_kernel(float *N, float *P, int r,
        int width, int height) {
02      int outCol = blockIdx.x*blockDim.x + threadIdx.x;
03      int outRow = blockIdx.y*blockDim.y + threadIdx.y;
04      float Pvalue = 0.0f;
05      for (int fRow = 0; fRow < 2*r+1; fRow++) {
06        for (int fCol = 0; fCol < 2*r+1; fCol++) {
07            inRow = outRow - r + fRow;
08            inCol = outCol - r + fCol;
09            if (inRow >= 0 && inRow < height && inCol >= 0 && inCol < width) {
10                Pvalue += F[fRow][fCol]*N[inRow*width + inCol];
11            }
12        }
13      }
14      P[outRow*width+outCol] = Pvalue;
15  }
```

FIGURE 7.9

A 2D convolution kernel using constant memory for F.

accessed as a global variable. Keep in mind that all the C language scoping rules for global variables apply here. If the host code and kernel code are in different files, the kernel code file must include the relevant external declaration information to ensure that the declaration of F is visible to the kernel.

Like global memory variables, constant memory variables are also located in DRAM. However, because the CUDA runtime knows that constant memory variables are not modified during kernel execution, it directs the hardware to aggressively cache the constant memory variables during kernel execution. To understand the benefit of constant memory usage, we need to first understand more about modern processor memory and cache hierarchies.

As we discussed in Chapter 6, Performance Considerations, the long latency and limited bandwidth of DRAM form a bottleneck in virtually all modern processors. To mitigate the effect of this memory bottleneck, modern processors commonly employ on-chip cache memories, or caches, to reduce the number of variables that need to be accessed from the main memory (DRAM), as shown in Fig. 7.10.

Unlike the CUDA shared memory, or scratchpad memories in general, caches are "transparent" to programs. That is, to use CUDA shared memory to hold the value of a global variable, a program needs to declare variables as __shared__ and explicitly copy the value of the global memory variable into the shared memory variable. On the other hand, in using caches, the program simply accesses the original global memory variables. The processor hardware will automatically retain the most recently or frequently used variables in the cache and remember their original global memory address. When one of the retained variables is used later, the hardware will detect from their addresses that a copy of the variable is available in cache. The value of the variable will then be served from the cache, eliminating the need to access DRAM.

There is a tradeoff between the size of a memory and the speed of a memory. As a result, modern processors often employ multiple levels of caches. The numbering convention for these cache levels reflects the distance to the processor. The lowest

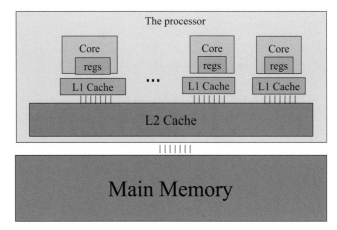

FIGURE 7.10

A simplified view of the cache hierarchy of modern processors.

level, L1 or level 1, is the cache that is directly attached to a processor core, as shown in Fig. 7.10. It runs at a speed close to that of the processor in both latency and bandwidth. However, an L1 cache is small, typically between 16 and 64 KB in capacity. L2 caches are larger, in the range of a few hundred kilobytes to a small number of MBs but can take tens of cycles to access. They are typically shared among multiple processor cores, or streaming multiprocessors (SMs) in a CUDA device, so the access bandwidth is shared among SMs. In some high-end processors today, there are even L3 caches that can be of hundreds of megabytes in size.

Constant memory variables play an interesting role in designing and using memories in massively parallel processors. Since these constant memory variables are not modified during kernel execution, there is no need to support writes by threads when caching them in an SM. Supporting high-throughput writes into a general cache requires sophisticated hardware logic and is costly in terms of chip area and power consumption. Without the need for supporting writes, a specialized cache for constant memory variables can be designed in a highly efficient manner in terms of chip area and power consumption. Furthermore, since the constant memory is quite small (64 KB), a small, specialized cache can be highly effective in capturing the heavily used constant memory variables for each kernel. This specialized cache is called a *constant cache* in modern GPUs. As a result, when all threads in a warp access the same constant memory variable, as is the case of F in Fig. 7.9, where the indices for accessing F are independent of the thread indices, the constant caches can provide a tremendous amount of bandwidth to satisfy the data needs of these threads. Also, since the size of F is typically small, we can assume that all F elements are effectively always accessed from the constant cache. Therefore we can simply assume that no DRAM bandwidth is spent on accesses to the F elements. With the use of constant memory and caching, we have effectively doubled the ratio of floating-point arithmetic to memory access to around 0.5 OP/B (2 operations for every 4 bytes loaded on line 10).

As it turns out, the accesses to the input N array elements can also benefit from caching. We will come back to this point in Section 7.5.

7.4 **Tiled convolution with halo cells**

We can address the memory bandwidth bottleneck of convolution with a tiled convolution algorithm. Recall that in a tiled algorithm, threads collaborate to load input elements into an on-chip memory for subsequent use of these elements. We will first establish the definitions of input and output tiles, since these definitions are important for understanding the design of the algorithm. We will refer to the collection of output elements processed by each block as an *output tile*. Recall that Fig. 7.6 shows a toy example of a 16 × 16 2D convolution using 16 blocks of 16 threads each. In that example there are 16 output tiles. Keep in mind that we use 16 threads per block to keep the example small. In practice, there should be at least 32 threads, or one warp, per block and typically many more to achieve good occupancy and data reuse. From this point on, we will assume that the F elements are in the constant memory.

We define an input tile as the collection of input N elements that are needed to calculate the P elements in an output tile. Fig. 7.11 shows the input tile (the shaded patch on the left side) that corresponds to an output tile (the shaded patch on the right side). Note that the dimensions of the input tile need to be extended by the radius of the filter (2 in this example) in each direction to ensure that it includes all the halo input elements that are needed for calculating the P elements at the edges of the output tile. This extension can make the input tiles significantly larger than output tiles.

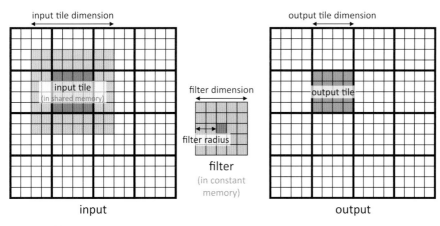

FIGURE 7.11

Input tile versus output tile in a 2D convolution.

In this toy example, each output tile consists of $4^2 = 16$ P-elements, whereas each input tile consists of $(4 + 4)^2 = 8^2 = 64$ elements. In this case, the input tiles are $4 \times$ larger than the output tiles. However, this large ratio is because we assume a tiny output tile dimension for ease of visualization in the toy example. In practice, the output tile dimensions would be much larger, and the ratio between input tile size and output tile size would be closer to 1.0. For example, if the output size is $16 \times 16 = 256$, with the same 5×5 filter, the input tile size would be $(16 + 4)^2 = 400$. The ratio between the input tile size and the output size would be about 1.6. Although this ratio is much less than 4, it shows that the input tile size can still be significantly larger than output tiles even for practical output tile dimensions.

In this section we present a class of tiled convolution algorithms in which all threads in a block first collaboratively load the input tile into the shared memory before they calculate the elements of the output tile by accessing the input elements from the shared memory. This should sound familiar to the reader; the strategy resembles that of the tiled matrix multiplication algorithms that were discussed in Chapter 5, Memory Architecture and Data Locality. The main difference is that the tiled matrix multiplication algorithms in Chapter 5, Memory Architecture and Data Locality, assume that the input tiles are of the same dimension as the output tiles, whereas the convolution input tiles are larger than the output tiles. This difference between input tile size and output tile size complicates the design of tiled convolution kernels.

There are two simple thread organizations for addressing the discrepancy between the input tile size and the output tile size. The first one launches thread blocks whose dimension matches that of the input tiles. This simplifies the loading of the input tiles, as each thread needs to load just one input element. However, since the block dimension is larger than that of the output tile, some of the threads need to be disabled during the calculation of output elements, which can reduce the efficiency of execution resource utilization. The second approach launches blocks whose dimension matches that of the output tiles. On one hand, this second strategy makes the input tile loading more complex, as the threads need to iterate to ensure that all input tile elements are loaded. On the other hand, it simplifies the calculation of the output elements, since the dimension of the block is the same as the output tile, and there is no need to disable any threads during the calculation of output elements. We will present the design of a kernel based on the first thread organization and leave the second organization as an exercise.

Fig. 7.12 shows a kernel that is based on the first thread organization. Each thread first calculates the column index (col) and row index (row) of the input or output element that it is responsible for loading or computing (lines 06–07). The kernel allocates a shared memory array N_s whose size is the same as an input tile (line 09) and loads the input tile to the shared memory array (lines 10–15). The conditions in line 10 are used by each thread to check whether the input tile element that it is attempting to load is a ghost cell. If so, the thread does not perform a memory load. Rather, it places a zero into the shared memory. All threads perform a barrier synchronization (line 15) to ensure that the entire input tile is in

```
01  #define IN_TILE_DIM 32
02  #define OUT_TILE_DIM ((IN_TILE_DIM) - 2*(FILTER_RADIUS))
03  __constant__ float F_c[2*FILTER_RADIUS+1][2*FILTER_RADIUS+1];
04  __global__ void convolution_tiled_2D_const_mem_kernel(float *N, float *P,
05                                                        int width, int height) {
06      int col = blockIdx.x*OUT_TILE_DIM + threadIdx.x - FILTER_RADIUS;
07      int row = blockIdx.y*OUT_TILE_DIM + threadIdx.y - FILTER_RADIUS;
08      //loading input tile
09      __shared__ N_s[IN_TILE_DIM][IN_TILE_DIM];
10      if(row>=0 && row<height && col>=0 && col<width) {
11          N_s[threadIdx.y][threadIdx.x] = N[row*width + col];
12      } else {
13          N_s[threadIdx.y][threadIdx.x] = 0.0;
14      }
15      __syncthreads();
16      // Calculating output elements
17      int tileCol = threadIdx.x - FILTER_RADIUS;
18      int tileRow = threadIdx.y - FILTER_RADIUS;
19      // turning off the threads at the edges of the block
20      if (col >= 0 && col < width && row >=0 && row < height) {
21          if (tileCol>=0 && tileCol<OUT_TILE_DIM && tileRow>=0
22                          && tileRow<OUT_TILE_DIM){
23              float Pvalue = 0.0f;
24              for (int fRow = 0; fRow < 2*FILTER_RADIUS+1; fRow++) {
25                  for (int fCol = 0; fCol < 2*FILTER_RADIUS+1; fCol++) {
26                      Pvalue += F[fRow][fCol]*N_s[tileRow+fRow][tileCol+fCol];
27                  }
28              }
29              P[row*width+col] = Pvalue;
30          }
31      }
32  }
```

FIGURE 7.12

A tiled 2D convolution kernel using constant memory for F.

place in the shared memory before any thread is allowed to proceed with the calculation of output elements.

Now that all the input tile elements are in the N_ds array, each thread can calculate their output P element value using the N_ds elements. Keep in mind that the output tile is smaller than the input tile and that the blocks are of the same size as the input tiles, so only a subset of the threads in each block will be used to calculate the output tile elements. There are multiple ways in which we can select the threads for this calculation. We use a design that deactivates FILTER_RADIUS exterior layers of threads, as illustrated in Fig. 7.13.

Fig. 7.13 shows a small example of convolution using a 3 × 3 filter (FILTER_RADIUS=1), 8 × 8 input tiles, 8 × 8 blocks, and 6 × 6 output tiles. The left side of Fig. 7.13 shows the input tile and the thread block. Since they are of the same size, they are overlaid on top of each other. With our design, we deactivate FILTER_RADIUS=1 exterior layer of threads. The heavy-line box at the center of the left side of Fig. 7.13 encloses the active threads for calculating the output tile elements. In this example the threadIdx.x and threadIdx.y values of the active threads both range from 1 to 6.

Fig. 7.13 also shows the mapping of the active threads to the output tile elements: Active thread (tx, ty) will calculate output element (tx - FILTER_RADIUS, ty

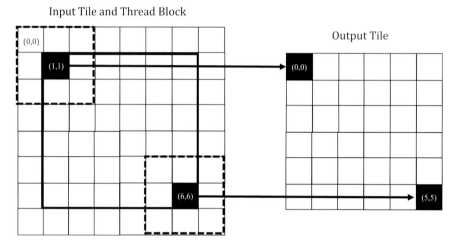

FIGURE 7.13

A small example that illustrates the thread organization for using the input tile elements in the shared memory to calculate the output tile elements.

- FILTER_RADIUS) using a patch of input tile elements whose upper-left corner is element (tx - FILTER_RADIUS, ty - FILTER_RADIUS) of the input tile. This is reflected in lines 17−18 of Fig. 7.12, where the column index (tileCol) and row index (tileRow) are assigned threadIdx.x-FILTER_RADIUS and threadId.y-FILTER_RADIUS, respectively.

In our small example in Fig. 7.13, tileCol and tileRow of thread (1,1) receive 0 and 0, respectively. Thus thread (1, 1) calculates element (0,0) of the output tile using the 3 × 3 patch of input tile elements highlighted with the dashed box at the upper-left corner of the input tile. The fRow-fCol loop nest on lines 24−28 of Fig. 7.12 iterates through the patch and generates the output element. Thread (1,1) in the block will iterate through the patch whose upper-left corner is N_s[0][0], whereas thread (5,5) will iterate through the patch whose upper-left corner is N_s[5][5].

In lines 06−07, blockIdx.x*OUT_TILE_DIM and blockIdx.y*OUT_TILE_DIM are the horizontal and vertical P array indices, respectively, of the beginning of the output tile assigned to the block. As we discussed earlier, threadIdx.x-r and threadIdx.y-r give the offset into the tile. Thus the row and the col variables provide the index of the output element assigned to each active thread. Each thread uses these two indices to write the final value of the output element in line 29.

The tiled 2D convolution kernel in Fig. 7.12 is significantly longer and more complex than the basic kernel in Fig. 7.9. We introduced the additional complexity to reduce the number of DRAM accesses for the N elements. The goal is to improve the arithmetic-to-global memory access ratio so that the achieved performance is not limited or less limited by the DRAM bandwidth. Recall from

Section 7.4 that the arithmetic-to-global memory access ratio of the kernel in Fig. 7.9 is 0.5 OP/B. Let us now derive this ratio for the kernel in Fig. 7.12.

For the blocks that handle tiles at the edges of the data, the threads that handle ghost cells do not perform any memory access for these ghost cells. This reduces the number of memory accesses for these blocks. We can calculate the reduced number of memory accesses by enumerating the number of threads that use each ghost cell. However, it should be clear that for large input arrays, the effect of ghost cells for small mask sizes will be insignificant. Therefore we will ignore the effect of ghost cells when we calculate the arithmetic-to-global memory access ratio in tiled convolution kernels and consider only the internal thread blocks whose halo cells are not ghost cells.

We now calculate the arithmetic-to-global memory access ratio for the tiled kernel in Fig. 7.12. Every thread that is assigned to an output tile element performs one multiplication and one addition for every element of the filter. Therefore the threads in an internal block collectively perform `OUT_TILE_DIM`^{2}`*(2*FILTER_RADIUS + 1)`^{2}`*2` arithmetic operations. As for the global memory accesses, all the global memory accesses have been shifted to the code that loads the N elements into the shared memory. Each thread that is assigned to an input tile element loads one 4-byte input value. Therefore `IN_TILE_DIM`^{2}`*4=(OUT_TILE_DIM+2*FILTER_RADIUS)`^{2}`*4` bytes are loaded by each internal block. Therefore the arithmetic-to-global memory access ratio for the tiled kernel is

$$\frac{\text{OUT\_TILE\_DIM}^2*(2*\text{FILTER\_RADIUS} + 1)^2*2}{(\text{OUT\_TILE\_DIM} + 2*\text{FILTER\_RADIUS})^2*4}$$

For our example with a 5×5 filter and 32×32 input tiles (28×28 output tiles), the ratio is $\frac{28^2 \times 5^2 * 2}{32^2 * 4} = 9.57 OP/B$. An input tile size of 32×32 is the largest that is achievable on current GPUs. However, we can perform an asymptotic analysis on the tile size to get an upper bound on the arithmetic-to-global memory access ratio that is achievable for this computation. If `OUT_TILE_DIM` is much larger than `FILTER_RADIUS`, we can consider `OUT_TILE_DIM+2*FILTER_RADIUS` to be approximately `OUT_TILE_DIM`. This simplifies the expression to `(2*FILTER_RADIUS+1)`^{2}`*2/4`. This should be quite an intuitive result. In the original algorithm, each N element is redundantly loaded by approximately `(2*FILTER_RADIUS+1)`^{2} threads, each of which performs two arithmetic operations with it. Thus if the tile size is infinitely large and each 4-byte element is loaded only into the shared memory once, the ratio should be `(2*FILTER_RADIUS+1)`^{2}`*2/4`.

Fig. 7.14 shows how the arithmetic-to-global memory access ratio of the tiled convolution kernel for different filter sizes varies with tile dimension, including an asymptotic bound. The bound on the ratio with a 5×5 filter is 12.5 OP/B. However, the ratio that is actually achievable with the 32×32 limit on thread block size is 9.57 OP/B. For a larger filter, such as 9×9 in the bottom row of Fig. 7.14, the bound on the ratio is 40.5 OP/B. However, the ratio that is actually achievable with the 32×32 limit on thread block size is 22.78 OP/B. Therefore we observe that a larger filter size has a higher ratio because each input element

IN_TILE_DIM		8	16	32	Bound
5x5 filter (FILTER_RADIUS = 2)	**OUT_TILE_DIM**	4	12	28	-
	Ratio	3.13	7.03	9.57	12.5
9x9 filter (FILTER_RADIUS = 4)	**OUT_TILE_DIM**	-	8	24	-
	Ratio	-	10.13	22.78	40.5

FIGURE 7.14

Arithmetic-to-global memory access ratio as a function of tile size and filter size for a 2D tiled convolution.

is used by more threads. However, the larger filter size also has a higher disparity between the bound and the ratio that is actually achieved because of the larger number of halo elements that force a smaller output tile.

The reader should always be careful when using small block and tile sizes. They may result in significantly less reduction in memory accesses than expected. For example, in Figs. 7.14, 7.8 × 8 blocks (input tiles) result in only a ratio of 3.13 OP/B for 5 × 5 filters. In practice, smaller tile sizes are often used because of an insufficient amount of on-chip memory, especially in 3D convolution, in which the amount of on-chip memory that is needed grows quickly with the dimension of the tile.

7.5 Tiled convolution using caches for halo cells

In Fig. 7.12, much of the complexity of the code has to do with the fact that the input tiles and blocks are larger than the output tiles because of the loading of halo cells. Recall that the halo cells of an input tile of a block are also the internal elements of neighboring tiles. For example, in Fig. 7.11 the lightly shaded halo cells of an input tile are also internal elements of the input tiles of neighboring blocks. There is a significant probability that by the time a block needs its halo cells, they are already in L2 cache because of the accesses by its neighboring blocks. As a result, the memory accesses to these halo cells may be naturally served from L2 cache without causing additional DRAM traffic. That is, we can leave the accesses to these halo cells in the original N elements rather than loading them into the N_ds. We now present a tiled convolution algorithm that uses the same dimension for input and output tiles and loads only the internal elements of each tile into the shared memory.

Fig. 7.15 shows a 2D convolution kernel using caching for halo cells. In this tiled kernel, the shared memory N_ds array needs to hold only the internal elements of the tile. Thus the input tiles and output tiles are of the same dimension, which is defined as constant TILE_DIM (line 1). With this simplification, N_s is declared to have TILE_DIM elements in both x and y dimensions (line 6).

```
01  #define TILE_DIM 32
02  __constant__ float F_c[2*FILTER_RADIUS+1][2*FILTER_RADIUS+1];
03  __global__ void convolution_cached_tiled_2D_const_mem_kernel(float *N,
                                    float *P, int width, int height) {
04      int col = blockIdx.x*TILE_DIM + threadIdx.x;
05      int row = blockIdx.y*TILE_DIM + threadIdx.y;
        //loading input tile
06      __shared__ N_s[TILE_DIM][TILE_DIM];
07      if(row<height && col<width) {
08        N_s[threadIdx.y][threadIdx.x] = N[row*width + col];
09      } else {
10        N_s[threadIdx.y][threadIdx.x] = 0.0;
11      }
12      __syncthreads();
        // Calculating output elements
        // turning off the threads at the edges of the block
13      if (col < width && row < height) {
14        float Pvalue = 0.0f;
15        for (int fRow = 0; fRow < 2*FILTER_RADIUS+1; fRow++) {
16          for (int fCol = 0; fCol < 2*FILTER_RADIUS+1; fCol++) {
17            if (threadIdx.x-FILTER_RADIUS+fCol >= 0 &&
18                threadIdx.x-FILTER_RADIUS+fCol < TILE_DIM &&
19                threadIdx.y-FILTER_RADIUS+fRow >= 0 &&
20                threadIdx.y-FILTER_RADIUS+fRow < TILE_DIM){
21              Pvalue += F[fRow][fCol]*N_s[threadIdx.y+fRow][threadIdx.x+fCol];
22            }
23            else {
24              if (row-FILTER_RADIUS+fRow >= 0 &&
25                  row-FILTER_RADIUS+fRow < height &&
26                  col-FILTER_RADIUS+fCol >=0 &&
27                  col-FILTER_RADIUS+fCol < width) {
24                Pvalue += F[fRow][fCol]*
25                                      N[(row-FILTER_RADIUS+fRow)*width+col-
FILTER_RADIUS+fCol];
26              }
27            }
28          }
29          P[row*width+col] = Pvalue;
30        }
31      }
32  }
```

FIGURE 7.15

A tiled 2D convolution kernel using caching for halos and constant memory for F.

Because the input tiles and output tiles are of the same size, the thread blocks can be launched with the same size of the input/output tiles. Loading of the N_s elements becomes simpler, since each thread can simply load the input element that has the same x and y coordinates as its assigned output element (lines 4−5 and 7−11). The condition for loading an input element is also simplified in line 7: Because the kernel no longer loads halo cells into shared memory, there is no danger of loading ghost cells. Thus the condition needs to check only for the usual boundary condition that a tile may extend beyond the valid range of the input data.

However, the body of the loop that calculates P elements becomes more complex. It needs to add conditions to check for use of both halo cells and ghost cells. The handling of halo cells is done with the conditions in lines 17−20, which tests whether the input element falls within the interior of the input tile. If so, the element is accessed from the shared memory. If not, the conditions in lines 24−27 check whether the halo cells are ghost cells. If so, no action is taken for the element, since we assume that the ghost values are 0. Otherwise, the element is accessed from the global memory. The reader should verify that the conditions for handling the ghost cells are similar to those used in Fig. 7.7.

A subtle advantage of the kernel in Fig. 7.15 compared to the kernel in Fig. 7.12 is that its block size, input tile size, and output tile size can be the same and can be a power of 2. Because the input tile size and output tile size are different for the kernel in Fig. 7.12, there is likely more memory divergence and control divergence during the execution of that kernel.

7.6 Summary

In this chapter we have studied convolution as an important parallel computation pattern. While convolution is used in many applications, such as computer vision and video processing, it also represents a general pattern that forms the basis of many parallel algorithms. For example, one can view the stencil algorithms in partial differential equation solvers as a special case of convolution; this will be the subject of Chapter 8, Stencil. For another example, one can also view the calculation of grid point force or potential value as a special case of convolution, which will be presented in Chapter 17, Iterative Magnetic Resonance Imaging Reconstruction. We will also apply much of what we learned in this chapter on convolutional neural networks in Chapter 16, Deep Learning.

We presented a basic parallel convolution algorithm whose implementation will be limited by DRAM bandwidth for accessing both the input and filter elements. We then introduced constant memory and a simple modification to the kernel and host code to take advantage of constant caching and eliminate practically all DRAM accesses for the filter elements. We further introduced a tiled parallel convolution algorithm that reduces DRAM bandwidth consumption by leveraging the shared memory while introducing more control flow divergence and programming complexity. Finally, we presented a tiled parallel convolution algorithm that takes advantage of the L1 and L2 caches for handling halo cells.

We presented an analysis of the benefit of tiling in terms of elevated arithmetic-to-global memory access ratio. The analysis is an important skill and will be useful in understanding the benefit of tiling for other patterns. Through the analysis we can learn about the limitation of small tile sizes, which is especially pronounced for large filters and 3D convolutions.

Although we have shown kernel examples for only 1D and 2D convolutions, the techniques are directly applicable to 3D convolutions as well. In general, the index calculation for the input and output arrays are more complex, owing to higher dimensionality. Also, one will have more loop nesting for each thread, since multiple dimensions need to be traversed in loading tiles and/or calculating output values. We encourage the reader to complete these higher-dimension kernels as homework exercises.

Exercises

1. Calculate the P[0] value in Fig. 7.3.
2. Consider performing a 1D convolution on array $N = \{4,1,3,2,3\}$ with filter F $= \{2,1,4\}$. What is the resulting output array?
3. What do you think the following 1D convolution filters are doing?
   a. [0 1 0]
   b. [0 0 1]
   c. [1 0 0]
   d. $[-1/2\ 0\ 1/2]$
   e. [1/3 1/3 1/3]
4. Consider performing a 1D convolution on an array of size N with a filter of size M:
   a. How many ghost cells are there in total?
   b. How many multiplications are performed if ghost cells are treated as multiplications (by 0)?
   c. How many multiplications are performed if ghost cells are not treated as multiplications?
5. Consider performing a 2D convolution on a square matrix of size $N \times N$ with a square filter of size $M \times M$:
   a. How many ghost cells are there in total?
   b. How many multiplications are performed if ghost cells are treated as multiplications (by 0)?
   c. How many multiplications are performed if ghost cells are not treated as multiplications?
6. Consider performing a 2D convolution on a rectangular matrix of size $N_1 \times N_2$ with a rectangular mask of size $M_1 \times M_2$:
   a. How many ghost cells are there in total?
   b. How many multiplications are performed if ghost cells are treated as multiplications (by 0)?
   c. How many multiplications are performed if ghost cells are not treated as multiplications?
7. Consider performing a 2D tiled convolution with the kernel shown in Fig. 7.12 on an array of size $N \times N$ with a filter of size $M \times M$ using an output tile of size $T \times T$.
   a. How many thread blocks are needed?
   b. How many threads are needed per block?
   c. How much shared memory is needed per block?
   d. Repeat the same questions if you were using the kernel in Fig. 7.15.
8. Revise the 2D kernel in Fig. 7.7 to perform 3D convolution.
9. Revise the 2D kernel in Fig. 7.9 to perform 3D convolution.
10. Revise the tiled 2D kernel in Fig. 7.12 to perform 3D convolution.

Stencil

8

Chapter Outline

8.1 Background 174
8.2 Parallel stencil: a basic algorithm 178
8.3 Shared memory tiling for stencil sweep 179
8.4 Thread coarsening 183
8.5 Register tiling 186
8.6 Summary 188
Exercises 188

Stencils are foundational to numerical methods for solving partial differential equations in application domains such as fluid dynamics, heat conductance, combustion, weather forecasting, climate simulation, and electromagnetics. The data that is processed by stencil-based algorithms consists of discretized quantities of physical significance, such as mass, velocity, force, acceleration, temperature, electrical field, and energy, whose relationships with each other are governed by differential equations. A common use of stencils is to approximate the derivative values of a function based on the function values within a range of input variable values. Stencils bear strong resemblance to convolution in that both stencils and convolution calculate the new value of an element of a multidimensional array based on the current value of the element at the same position and those in the neighborhood in another multidimensional array. Therefore stencils also need to deal with halo cells and ghost cells. Unlike convolution, a stencil computation is used to iteratively solve the values of continuous, differentiable functions within the domain of interest. The data elements and the weight coefficients that are used for the elements in the stencil neighborhood are governed by the differential equations that are being solved. Some stencil patterns are amenable to optimizations that are not applicable to convolution. In the solvers in which initial conditions are iteratively propagated through the domain, the calculations of output values may have dependences and need to be performed according to some ordering constraints. Furthermore, because of the numerical accuracy requirements in solving differential questions, the data that is processed by stencils tends to be high-precision floating data that consumes more on-chip memory for tiling techniques. Because of these differences, stencils tend to motivate different optimizations than convolution does.

Programming Massively Parallel Processors. DOI: https://doi.org/10.1016/B978-0-323-91231-0.00017-3

8.1 Background

The first step in using computers to numerically evaluate and solve functions, models, variables, and equations is to convert them into a discrete representation. For example, Fig. 8.1A shows the sine function $y = \sin(x)$ for $0 \le x \le \pi$. Fig. 8.1B shows the design of a one-dimensional (1D) regular (structured) grid whose seven grid points correspond to x values that are of constant spacing ($\frac{\pi}{6}$) apart. In general, structured grids cover an n-dimensional Euclidean space with identical parallelotopes (e.g., segments in one dimension, rectangles in two dimension, bricks in three dimensions). As we will see later, with structured grids, derivatives of variables can be conveniently expressed as finite differences. Therefore structured grids are used mainly in finite-difference methods. Unstructured grids are more complex and are used in finite-element and finite-volume methods. For simplicity we will use only regular grids and thus finite-difference methods in this book.

Fig. 8.1C shows the resulting discrete representation in which the sine function is represented with its values at the seven grid points. In this case, the representation is stored in a 1D array F. Note that the x values are implicitly assumed to be $i\frac{\pi}{6}$, where i is the index of the array element. For example, the x value that corresponds to element F[2] is 0.87, which is the sine value of $2\frac{\pi}{6}$.

In a discrete representation, one needs to use an interpolation technique such as linear or splines to derive the approximate value of the function for x values that do not correspond to any of the grid points. The fidelity of the representation or how accurate the function values from these approximate interpolation techniques are depends on the spacing between grid points: The smaller the spacing, the more accurate the approximations. By decreasing the spacing, one can improve the accuracy of the representation at the cost of more storage and, as we will see, more computation when we solve a partial differential equation.

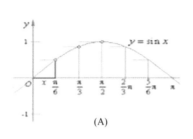

(A)

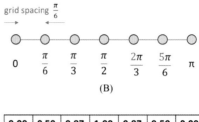

(B)

| 0.00 | 0.50 | 0.87 | 1.00 | 0.87 | 0.50 | 0.00 |

(C)

FIGURE 8.1

(A) Sine as a continuous, differentiable function for $0 \le x \le \pi$. (B) Design of a regular grid with constant spacing ($\frac{\pi}{6}$) between grid point for discretization. (C) Resulting discrete representation of the sine function for $0 \le x \le \pi$.

The fidelity of a discrete representation also depends on the precision of the numbers used. Since we are approximating continuous functions, floating-point numbers are typically used for the grid point values. Mainstream CPUs and GPUs support double-precision (64-bit), single-precisions (32-bit), and half-precision (16-bit) representations today. Among the three, double-precision numbers offer the best precision and the most fidelity in discrete representations. However, modern CPUs and GPUs typically have much higher arithmetic computation throughput for single-precision and half-precision arithmetic. Also, since double-precision numbers consist of more bits, reading and writing double-precision numbers consumes more memory bandwidth. Storing these double-precision numbers also requires memory capacity. This can pose a significant challenge for tiling techniques that require a significant number of grid point values to be stored in on-chip memory and registers.

Let us discuss the definition of stencils with a little more formalism. In mathematics a stencil is a geometric pattern of weights applied at each point of a structured grid. The pattern specifies how the values of the grid point of interest can be derived from the values at neighboring points using a numerical approximation routine. For example, a stencil may specify how the derivative value of a function at a point of interest is approximated by using finite differences between the values of the function at the point and its neighbors. Since partial differential equations express the relationships between functions, variables, and their derivatives, stencils offer a convenient basis for specifying how finite difference methods numerically compute the solutions to partial differential equations.

For example, assume that we have $f(x)$ discretized into a 1D grid array F and we would like to calculate the discretized derivative of $f(x)$, $f'(x)$. We can use the classic finite difference approximation for the first derivative:

$$f'(x) = \frac{f(x+h) - f(x-h)}{2h} + O(h^2)$$

That is, the derivative of a function at point x can be approximated by the difference of the function values at two neighboring points divided by the difference of the x values of these neighboring points. The value h is the spacing between neighboring points in the grid. The error is expressed by the term $O(h^2)$, meaning that the error is proportional to the square of h. Obviously, the smaller the h value, the better the approximation. In our example in Fig. 8.1 the h value is $\frac{\pi}{6}$ or 0.52. The value is not small enough to make the approximation error negligible but should be able to result in a reasonably close approximation.

Since the grid spacing is h, the current estimated $f(x-h)$, $f(x)$, and $f(x+h)$ values are in F[i − 1], F[i], and F[i + 1], respectively, where $x = i{*}h$. Therefore we can calculate the derivative values of $f(x)$ at each grid point into an output array FD:

$$FD[i] = \frac{F[i+1] - F[i-1]}{2{*}h}$$

for all the grid points. This expression can be rewritten as

$$FD[i] = \frac{-1}{2*h} * F[i-1] + \frac{1}{2*h} * F[i+1]$$

That is, the calculation of the estimated function derivative value at grid point involves the current estimated function values at grid points [i − 1, i, i + 1] with coefficients $\left[\frac{-1}{2h}, 0, \frac{1}{2h}\right]$, which defines a 1D three-point stencil, as shown in Fig. 8.2A. If we are approximating higher derivative values at grid points, we would need to use higher-order finite differences. For example, if the differential equation includes up to the second derivative of $f(x)$, we will use a stencil involving [i − 2, i − 1, i, i + 1, i + 2], which is a 1D five-point stencil, as shown in Fig. 8.2B. In general, if the equation involves up to the nth derivative, the stencil will involve n grid points on each side of the center grid point. Fig. 8.2C shows a 1D seven-point stencil. The number of grid points on each side of the center point is called the *order* of the stencil, as it reflects the order of the derivative being approximated. According to this definition, the stencils in Fig. 8.3 are of order 1, 2, and 3, respectively.

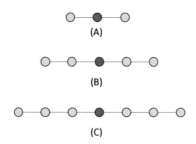

FIGURE 8.2

One-dimensional stencil examples. (A) Three-point (order 1) stencil. (B) Five-point (order 2) stencil. (C) Seven-point (order 3) stencil.

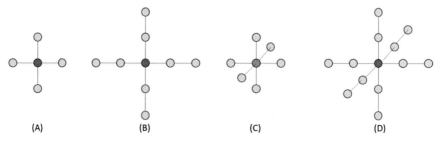

FIGURE 8.3

(A) Two-dimensional five-point stencil (order 1). (B) Two-dimensional nine-point stencil (order 2). (C) Three-dimensional seven-point stencil (order 1). (D) Three-dimensional 13-point stencil (order 2).

It should be obvious that solving a partial differential equation of two variables would require the function values to be discretized into a two-dimensional (2D) grid, and we will use a 2D stencil to calculate the approximate partial derivatives. If the partial differential equation involves exclusively the partial derivatives by only one of the variables, for example, $\frac{\partial f(x,y)}{\partial x}$, $\frac{\partial f(x,y)}{\partial y}$, but not $\frac{\partial f(x,y)}{\partial x \partial y}$, we can use 2D stencils whose selected grid points are all along the x axis and y axis. For example, for a partial differential equation involving only first derives by x and first derivatives by y, we can use a 2D stencil that involves two grid points on each side of the center point along the x axis and the y axis, which results in the 2D five-point stencil in Fig. 8.3A. If the equation involves up to second-order derivatives only by x or by y, we will use a 2D nine-point stencil, as shown in Fig. 8.3B.

Fig. 8.4 summarizes the concepts of discretization, numerical grids, and application of stencils on the grid points. Functions are discretized into their grid point values which are stored in multi-dimensional arrays. In Fig. 8.4 a function of two variables is discretized as a 2D grid which is stored as a 2D array. The stencil that is used in Fig. 8.4 is 2D and is used to calculate an approximate derivative value (output) at each grid point from function values at the neighboring grid points and the grid point itself. In this chapter we will focus on the computation pattern in which a stencil is applied to all the relevant input grid points to generate the output values at all grid points, which will be referred to as a *stencil sweep*.

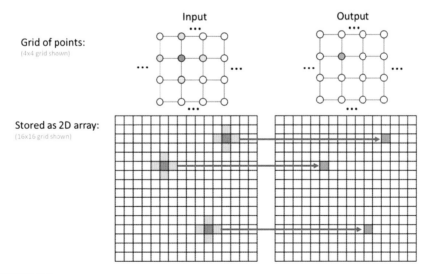

FIGURE 8.4

A 2D grid example and a five-point (order 1) stencil used to calculate the approximate derivative values at grid points.

8.2 Parallel stencil: a basic algorithm

We will first present a basic kernel for stencil sweep. For simplicity we assume that there is no dependence between output grid points when generating the output grid point values within a stencil sweep. We further assume that the grid point values on the boundaries store boundary conditions and will not change from input to output, as illustrated in Fig. 8.5. That is, the shaded inside area in the output grid will be calculated, whereas the unshaded boundary cells will remain the same as the input values. This is a reasonable assumption, since stencils are used mainly to solve differential equations with boundary conditions.

Fig. 8.6 shows a basic kernel that performs a stencil sweep. This kernel assumes that each thread block is responsible for calculating a tile of output grid values and that each thread is assigned to one of the output grid points. A 2D tiling example of the output grid in which each thread block is responsible for a

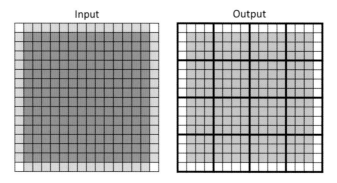

FIGURE 8.5

Simplifying boundary condition. The boundary cells contain boundary conditions that will not be updated from one iteration to the next. Thus only the inner output grid points need to be calculated during each stencil sweep.

```
01  __global__ void stencil_kernel(float* in, float* out, unsigned int N) {
02      unsigned int i = blockIdx.z*blockDim.z + threadIdx.z;
03      unsigned int j = blockIdx.y*blockDim.y + threadIdx.y;
04      unsigned int k = blockIdx.x*blockDim.x + threadIdx.x;
05      if(i >= 1 && i < N - 1 && j >= 1 && j < N - 1&& k >= 1 && k < N - 1) {
06          out[i*N*N + j*N + k] = c0*in[i*N*N + j*N + k]
07                              + c1*in[i*N*N + j*N + (k - 1)]
08                              + c2*in[i*N*N + j*N + (k + 1)]
09                              + c3*in[i*N*N + (j - 1)*N + k]
10                              + c4*in[i*N*N + (j + 1)*N + k]
11                              + c5*in[(i - 1)*N*N + j*N + k]
12                              + c6*in[(i + 1)*N*N + j*N + k];
13      }
14  }
```

FIGURE 8.6

A basic stencil sweep kernel.

4×4 output tile is shown in Fig. 8.5. However, since most real-world applications solve three-dimensional (3D) differential equations, the kernel in Fig. 8.6 assumes a 3D grid and a 3D seven-point stencil like the one in Fig. 8.3C. The assignment of threads to grid points is done with the familiar linear expressions involving the x, y, and z fields of `blockIdx`, `blockDim`, and `threadIdx` (lines 02−04). Once each thread has been assigned to a 3D grid point, the input values at that grid point and all neighboring grid points are multiplied by different coefficients (c0 to c6 on lines 06−12) and added. The values of these coefficients depend on the differential equation that is being solved, as we explained in the background section.

Let us now calculate the floating-point to global memory access ratio for the kernel in Fig. 8.6. Each thread performs 13 floating-point operations (seven multiplications and six additions) and loads seven input values that are 4 bytes each. Therefore the floating-point to global memory access ratio for this kernel is $13/(7*4) = 0.46$ OP/B (operations per byte). As we discussed in Chapter 5, Memory Architecture and Data Locality, this ratio needs to be much larger for the performance of the kernel to be reasonably close to the level that is supported by the arithmetic compute resources. We will need to use a tiling technique like that discussed in Chapter 7, Convolution, to elevate the floating-point to global memory access ratio.

8.3 **Shared memory tiling for stencil sweep**

As we saw in Chapter 5, Memory Architecture and Data Locality, the ratio of floating-point operations to global memory accessing operations can be significantly elevated with shared memory tiling. As the reader probably suspected, the design of shared memory tiling for stencils is almost identical to that of convolution. However, there are a few subtle but important differences.

Fig. 8.7 shows the input and output tiles for a 2D five-point stencil applied to a small grid example. A quick comparison with Figure 7.11 shows a small difference between convolution and stencil sweep: The input tiles of the five-point stencil do not include the corner grid points. This property will become important when we explore register tiling later in this chapter. For the purpose of shared memory tiling, we can expect the input data reuse in a 2D five-point stencil to be significantly lower than that in a 3×3 convolution. As we discussed in Chapter 7, Convolution, the upper bound of the arithmetic to global memory access ratio of a 2D 3×3 convolution is 4.5 OP/B. However, for a 2D five-point stencil, the upper bound on the ratio is only 2.5 OP/B. This is because each output grid point value uses only five input grid values, compared to the nine input pixel values in 3×3 convolution.

The difference is even more pronounced when the number of dimensions and the order of the stencil increases. For example, if we increase the order of the 2D

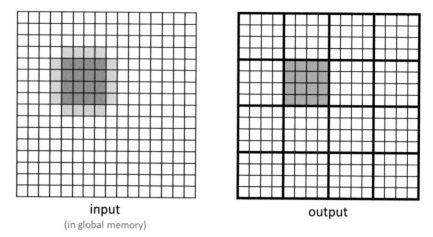

input
(in global memory)

output

FIGURE 8.7

Input and output tiles for a 2D five-point stencil.

stencil from 1 (one grid point on each side, five-point stencil) to 2 (two grid points on each side, nine-point stencil), the upper bound on the ratio is 4.5 OP/B, compared to 12.5 OP/B for its counterpart 2D 5×5 convolution. This discrepancy is further pronounced when the order of the 2D stencil is increased to 3 (three grid points on each side, 13-point stencil). The upper bound on the ratio is 6.5 OP/B, compared to 24.5 OP/B for its counterpart 2D 7×7 convolution.

When we move into 3D, the discrepancy between the upper bound on the arithmetic to global memory access ratio of stencil sweep and convolution is even more pronounced. For example, a 3D third-order stencil (3 points on each side, 19-point stencil) has an upper bound of 9.5 OP/B, compared to 171.5 OP/B for its counterpart 3D $7 \times 7 \times 7$ convolution. That is, the benefit of loading of an input grid point value into the shared memory for a stencil sweep can be significantly lower than that for convolution, especially for 3D, which is the prominent use case for stencils. As we will see later in the chapter, this small but significant difference motivates the use of thread coarsening and register tiling in the third dimension.

Since all the strategies for loading input tiles for convolution apply directly to stencil sweep, we present in Fig. 8.8 a kernel like the convolution kernel in Figure 7.12 in which blocks are of the same size as input tiles and some of the threads are turned off in calculating output grid point values. The kernel is adapted from the basic stencil sweep kernel in Fig. 8.6, so we will focus only on the changes that are made during the adaptation. Like the tiled convolution kernel, the tiled stencil sweep kernel first calculates the beginning x, y, and z coordinates of the input patch that is used for each thread. The value 1 that is subtracted in each expression is because the kernel assumes a 3D seven-point stencil with

```
01   __global__ void stencil_kernel(float* in, float* out, unsigned int N) {
02     int i = blockIdx.z*OUT_TILE_DIM + threadIdx.z - 1;
03     int j = blockIdx.y*OUT_TILE_DIM + threadIdx.y - 1;
04     int k = blockIdx.x*OUT_TILE_DIM + threadIdx.x - 1;
05     __shared__ float in_s[IN_TILE_DIM][IN_TILE_DIM][IN_TILE_DIM];
06     if(i >= 0 && i < N && j >= 0 && j < N && k >= 0 && k < N) {
07       in_s[threadIdx.z][threadIdx.y][threadIdx.x] = in[i*N*N + j*N + k];
08     }
09     __syncthreads();
10     if(i >= 1 && i < N-1 && j >= 1 && j < N-1 && k >= 1 && k < N-1) {
11       if(threadIdx.z >= 1 && threadIdx.z < IN_TILE_DIM-1 && threadIdx.y >= 1
12         && threadIdx.y<IN_TILE_DIM-1 && threadIdx.x>=1 && threadIdx.x<IN_TILE_DIM-1){
13         out[i*N*N + j*N + k] = c0*in_s[threadIdx.z][threadIdx.y][threadIdx.x]
14                         + c1*in_s[threadIdx.z][threadIdx.y][threadIdx.x-1]
15                         + c2*in_s[threadIdx.z][threadIdx.y][threadIdx.x+1]
16                         + c3*in_s[threadIdx.z][threadIdx.y-1][threadIdx.x]
17                         + c4*in_s[threadIdx.z][threadIdx.y+1][threadIdx.x]
18                         + c5*in_s[threadIdx.z-1][threadIdx.y][threadIdx.x]
19                         + c6*in_s[threadIdx.z+1][threadIdx.y][threadIdx.x];
20       }
21     }
22   }
```

FIGURE 8.8

A 3D seven-point stencil sweep kernel with shared memory tiling.

one grid point on each side (lines 02−04). In general, the value that is subtracted should be the order of the stencil.

The kernel allocates an in_s array in shared memory to hold the input tile for each block (line 05). Every thread loads one input element. Like the tiled convolution kernel, each thread loads the beginning element of the cubic input patch that contains the stencil grid point pattern. Because of the subtraction in lines 02−04, it is possible that some of the threads may attempt to load ghost cells of the grid. The conditions $i >= 0$, $j >= 0$, and $k >= 0$ (line 06) guard against these out-of-bound accesses. Because the blocks are larger than the output tiles, it is also possible that some of the threads at the end of the x, y, and z dimensions of a block attempt to access the ghost cells outside the upper bound of each dimension of the grid array. The conditions $I < N$, $j < N$, and $k < N$ (line 6) guard against these out-of-bound accesses. All threads in the thread block collaboratively load the input tile into the shared memory (line 07) and use the barrier synchronization to wait until all input tile grid points are in the shared memory (line 09).

Each block calculates its output tile in lines 10−21. The conditions in line 10 reflect the simplifying assumption that the boundary points of both the input grid and the output hold initial condition values and do not need to be calculated from iteration to iteration by the kernel. Therefore threads whose output grid points fall on these boundary positions are turned off. Note that the boundary grid points form a layer at the surface of the grid.

The conditions in lines 12−13 turn off the extra threads that were launched just to load the input tile grid points. The conditions allow those threads whose i, j, and k index values fall within the output tile to calculate the output grid points selected by these indices. Finally, each active thread calculates its output grid point value using the input grid points specified by the seven-point stencil.

We can evaluate the effectiveness of shared memory tiling by calculating the arithmetic to global memory access ratio that this kernel achieves. Recall that the original stencil sweep kernel achieved a ratio of 0.46 OP/B. With the shared memory tiling kernel, let us assume that each input tile is a cube with T grid points in each dimension and that each output tile has $T - 2$ grid points in each dimension. Therefore each block has $(T - 2)^3$ active threads calculating output grid point values, and each active thread performs 13 floating-point multiplication or addition operations, which is a total of $13*(T - 2)^3$ floating-point arithmetic operations. Moreover, each block loads an input tile by performing T^3 loads that are 4 bytes each. Therefore the floating point to global memory access ratio of the tiled kernel can be calculated as follows:

$$\frac{13*(T-2)^3}{4*T^3} = \frac{13}{4} * \left(1 - \frac{2}{T}\right)^3 \quad OP/B$$

That is, the larger the T value, the more the input grid point values are reused. The upper bound on the ratio as T increases asymptotically is $13/4 = 3.25$ OP/B.

Unfortunately, the 1024 limit of the block size on current hardware makes it difficult to have large T values. The practical limit on T is 8 because an $8 \times 8 \times 8$ thread block has a total of 512 threads. Furthermore, the amount of shared memory that is used for the input tile is proportional to T^3. Thus a larger T dramatically increases the consumption of the shared memory. These hardware constraints force us to use small tile sizes for the tiled stencil kernel. In contrast, convolution is often used to process 2D images in which larger tile dimensions (T value) such as 32×32 can be used.

There are two major disadvantages to the small limit on the T value that is imposed by the hardware. The first disadvantage is that it limits the reuse ratio and thus the compute to memory access ratio. For $T = 8$ the ratio for a seven-point stencil is only 1.37 OP/B, which is much less than the upper bound of 3.25 OP/B. The reuse ratio decreases as the T value decreases because of the halo overhead. As we discussed in Chapter 7, Convolution, halo elements are less reused than the nonhalo elements are. As the portion of halo elements in the input tile increases, both the data reuse ratio and the floating-point to global memory access ratio decrease. For example, for a convolution filter with radius 1, a 32×32 2D input tile has 1024 input elements. The corresponding output tile has $30 \times 30 = 900$ elements, which means that $1024 - 900 = 124$ of the input elements are halo elements. The portion of halo elements in the input tile is about 12%. In contrast, for a 3D stencil of order 1, an $8 \times 8 \times 8$ 3D input tile has 512 elements. The corresponding output tile has $6 \times 6 \times 6 = 216$ elements, which means that $512 - 216 = 296$ of the input elements are halo elements. The portion of halo elements in the input tile is about 58%!

The second disadvantage of a small tile size is that it has an adverse impact on memory coalescing. For an $8 \times 8 \times 8$ tile, every warp that consists of 32 threads will be responsible for loading four different rows of the tile that have eight input values each. Hence on the same load instruction the threads of the warp will access at least four distant locations in global memory. These accesses cannot be coalesced and will underutilize the DRAM bandwidth. Therefore T needs to be a much larger value for the reuse level to be closer to 3.25 OP/B and to enable full use of the DRAM bandwidth. The need for a larger T motivates the approach that we will cover in the following section.

8.4 Thread coarsening

As we mentioned in the previous section, the fact that stencils are typically applied to 3D grids and the sparse nature of the stencil patterns can make stencil sweep a less profitable target of shared memory tiling than convolution. This section presents the use of thread coarsening to overcome the block size limitation by coarsening the work that is done by each thread from calculating one grid point value to a column of grid point values, as illustrated in Fig. 8.9. Recall from Section 6.3 that with thread coarsening, the programmer partially serializes parallel units of work into each thread and reduces the price paid for parallelism. In this case, the price that is paid for parallelism is the low data reuse due to the loading of halo elements by each block.

In Fig. 8.9 we assume that each input tile consists of $T^3 = 6^3 = 216$ grid points. Note that to make the inside of the input tile visible, we have peeled away the front, left, and top layers of the tile. We also assume that each output tile consists of $(T-2)^3 = 4^3 = 64$ grid points. The x, y, and z directions in the illustration are shown with the coordinate system for the input and the output. Each x-y plane

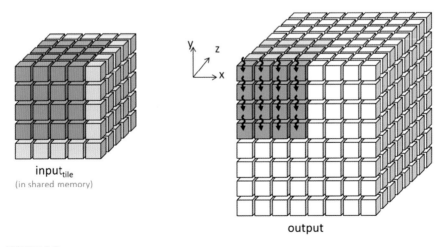

input_tile
(in shared memory)

output

FIGURE 8.9

Thread coarsening in the z direction for a 3D seven-point stencil sweep.

of the input tile consists of $6^2 = 36$ grid points, and each x-y plane of the output tile consists of $4^2 = 16$ grid points. The thread block that is assigned to process this tile consists of the same number of threads as one x-y plane of the input tile (i.e., 6×6). In the illustration we show only the internal threads of the thread block that are active in computing output tile values (i.e., 4×4).

Fig. 8.10 shows a kernel with thread coarsening in the z direction for a 3D seven-point stencil sweep. The idea is for the thread block to iterate in the z direction (into the figure), calculating the values of grid points in one x-y plane of the output tile during each iteration. The kernel first assigns each thread to a grid point in an x-y plane of the output (lines 03−04). Note that i is the z index of the output tile grid point calculated by each thread. During each iteration, all threads in a block will be processing an x-y plane of an output tile; thus they will all be calculating output grid points whose z indices are identical.

```
01  __global__ void stencil_kernel(float* in, float* out, unsigned int N) {
02      int iStart = blockIdx.z*OUT_TILE_DIM;
03      int j = blockIdx.y*OUT_TILE_DIM + threadIdx.y - 1;
04      int k = blockIdx.x*OUT_TILE_DIM + threadIdx.x - 1;
05      __shared__ float inPrev_s[IN_TILE_DIM][IN_TILE_DIM];
06      __shared__ float inCurr_s[IN_TILE_DIM][IN_TILE_DIM];
07      __shared__ float inNext_s[IN_TILE_DIM][IN_TILE_DIM];
08      if(iStart-1 >= 0 && iStart-1 < N && j >= 0 && j < N && k >= 0 && k < N) {
09          inPrev_s[threadIdx.y][threadIdx.x] = in[(iStart - 1)*N*N + j*N + k];
10      }
11      if(iStart >= 0 && iStart < N && j >= 0 && j < N && k >= 0 && k < N) {
12          inCurr_s[threadIdx.y][threadIdx.x] = in[iStart*N*N + j*N + k];
13      }
14      for(int i = iStart; i < iStart + OUT_TILE_DIM; ++i) {
15          if(i + 1 >= 0 && i + 1 < N && j >= 0 && j < N && k >= 0 && k < N) {
16              inNext_s[threadIdx.y][threadIdx.x] = in[(i + 1)*N*N + j*N + k];
17          }
18          __syncthreads();
19          if(i >= 1 && i < N - 1 && j >= 1 && j < N - 1 && k >= 1 && k < N - 1) {
20              if(threadIdx.y >= 1 && threadIdx.y < IN_TILE_DIM - 1
21                  && threadIdx.x >= 1 && threadIdx.x < IN_TILE_DIM - 1) {
22                  out[i*N*N + j*N + k] = c0*inCurr_s[threadIdx.y][threadIdx.x]
23                      + c1*inCurr_s[threadIdx.y][threadIdx.x-1]
24                      + c2*inCurr_s[threadIdx.y][threadIdx.x+1]
25                      + c3*inCurr_s[threadIdx.y+1][threadIdx.x]
26                      + c4*inCurr_s[threadIdx.y-1][threadIdx.x]
27                      + c5*inPrev_s[threadIdx.y][threadIdx.x]
28                      + c6*inNext_s[threadIdx.y][threadIdx.x];
29              }
30          }
31          __syncthreads();
32          inPrev_s[threadIdx.y][threadIdx.x] = inCurr_s[threadIdx.y][threadIdx.x];
33          inCurr_s[threadIdx.y][threadIdx.x] = inNext_s[threadIdx.y][threadIdx.x];
34      }
35  }
```

FIGURE 8.10

Kernel with thread coarsening in the z direction for a 3D seven-point stencil sweep.

Initially, each block needs to load into the shared memory the three input tile planes that contain all the points that are needed to calculate the values of the output tile plane that is the closest to the reader (marked with threads) in Fig. 8.9. This is done by having all the threads in the block load the first layer (lines 08−10) into the shared memory array inPrev_s and the second layer (lines 11−13) into the shared memory array inCurr_s. For the first layer, inPrev_s is loaded from the front layer of the input tile that has been peeled off for visibility into the internal layers.

During the first iteration, all threads in a block collaborate to load the third layer needed for the current output tile layer into the shared memory array inNext_s (lines 15−17). All threads then wait on a barrier (line 18) until all have completed loading the input tile layers. The conditions in lines 19−21 serve the same purpose as their counterparts in the shared memory kernel in Fig. 8.8.

Each thread then calculates its output grid point value in the current output tile plane using the four x-y neighbors stored in inCurr_s, the z neighbor in inPrev_s, and the z neighbor in inNext_s. All threads in the block then wait at the barrier to ensure that everyone completes its calculation before they move on to the next output tile plane. Once off the barrier, all threads collaborate to move the contents of inCurr_s to inPrev_s and the contents of inNext_s to inCurr_s. This is because the roles that are played by the input tile planes change when the threads move by one output plane in the z direction. Thus by the end of each iteration, the block has two of the three input tile planes needed for calculating the output tile plane of the next iteration. All threads then move into the next iteration and load the third plane of the input tile needed for the output plane of the iteration. The updated mappings of inPrev_s, inCurr_s, and inNext_s in preparation for the calculation of the second output tile plane are illustrated in Fig. 8.11.

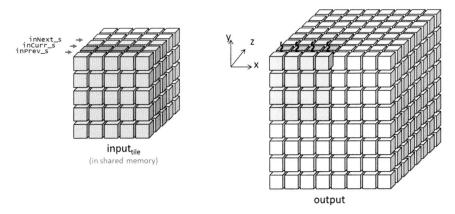

FIGURE 8.11

The mapping of the shared memory arrays to the input tile after the first iteration.

The advantages of the thread coarsening kernel are that it increases the tile size without increasing the number of threads and that it does not require all planes of the input tile to be present in the shared memory. The thread block size is now only T^2 instead of T^3, so we can use a much larger T value, such as 32, which would result in a block size of 1024 threads. With this T value we can expect that the floating-point arithmetic to global memory access ratio will be $\frac{13}{4} * \left(1 - \frac{2}{32}\right)^3 = 2.68OP/B$, which is a significant improvement over the 1.37 OP/B ratio of the original shared memory tiling kernel and closer to the 3.25 OP/B upper bound. Moreover, at any point in time, only three layers of the input tile need to be in the shared memory. The shared memory capacity requirement is now $3T^2$ elements instead of T^3 elements. For T = 32 the shared memory consumption is now at a reasonable level of $3*32^2*4B = 12KB$ per block.

8.5 Register tiling

The special characteristics of some stencil patterns can give rise to new optimization opportunities. Here, we present an optimization that can be especially effective for stencil patterns that involve only neighbors along the x, y, and z directions of the center point. All stencils in Fig. 8.3 fall into this description. The 3D seven-point stencil sweep kernel in Fig. 8.10 reflects this property. Each inPrev_s and inNext_s element is used by only one thread in the calculation of the output tile grid point with the same x-y indices. Only the inCurr_s elements are accessed by multiple threads and truly need to be in the shared memory. The z neighbors in inPrev_s and inNext_s can instead stay in the registers of the single user thread.

We take advantage of this property with the register tiling kernel in Fig. 8.12. The kernel is built on the thread coarsening kernel in Fig. 8.10 with some simple but important modifications. We will focus on these modifications. First, we create the three register variables inPrev, inCurr, and inNext (lines 05, 07, 08). The register variables inPrev and inNext replace the shared memory arrays inPrev_s and inNext, respectively. In comparison, we keep inCurr_s to allow the x-y neighbor grid point values to be shared among threads. Therefore the amount of shared memory that is used by this kernel is reduced to one-third of that by the kernel in Fig. 8.12.

The initial loading of the previous and current input tile planes (lines 09−15) and the loading of the next plane of the input tile before each new iteration (lines 17−19) are all performed with register variables as destination. Thus the three planes of the "active part" of the input tile are held in the registers across the threads of the same block. In addition, the kernel always maintains a copy of the current plane of the input tile in the shared memory (lines 14 and 34). That is, the x-y neighbors of the active input tile plane are always available to all threads that need to access these neighbors.

```
01 __global__ void stencil_kernel(float* in, float* out, unsigned int N) {
02    int iStart = blockIdx.z*OUT_TILE_DIM;
03    int j = blockIdx.y*OUT_TILE_DIM + threadIdx.y - 1;
04    int k = blockIdx.x*OUT_TILE_DIM + threadIdx.x - 1;
05    float inPrev;
06    __shared__ float inCurr_s[IN_TILE_DIM][IN_TILE_DIM];
07    float inCurr;
08    float inNext;
09    if(iStart-1 >= 0 && iStart-1 < N && j >= 0 && j < N && k >= 0 && k < N) {
10        inPrev = in[(iStart - 1)*N*N + j*N + k];
11    }
12    if(iStart >= 0 && iStart < N && j >= 0 && j < N && k >= 0 && k < N) {
13        inCurr = in[iStart*N*N + j*N + k];
14        inCurr_s[threadIdx.y][threadIdx.x] = inCurr;
15    }
16    for(int i = iStart; i < iStart + OUT_TILE_DIM; ++i) {
17        if(i + 1 >= 0 && i + 1 < N && j >= 0 && j < N && k >= 0 && k < N) {
18            inNext = in[(i + 1)*N*N + j*N + k];
19        }
20        __syncthreads();
21        if(i >= 1 && i < N - 1 && j >= 1 && j < N - 1 && k >= 1 && k < N - 1) {
22            if(threadIdx.y >= 1 && threadIdx.y < IN_TILE_DIM - 1
23                && threadIdx.x >= 1 && threadIdx.x < IN_TILE_DIM - 1) {
24                out[i*N*N + j*N + k] = c0*inCurr
25                                    + c1*inCurr_s[threadIdx.y][threadIdx.x-1]
26                                    + c2*inCurr_s[threadIdx.y][threadIdx.x+1]
27                                    + c3*inCurr_s[threadIdx.y+1][threadIdx.x]
28                                    + c4*inCurr_s[threadIdx.y-1][threadIdx.x]
29                                    + c5*inPrev
30                                    + c6*inNext;
31            }
32        }
33        __syncthreads();
34        inPrev = inCurr;
35        inCurr = inNext;
34        inCurr_s[threadIdx.y][threadIdx.x] = inNext_s;
35    }
35 }
```

FIGURE 8.12

Kernel with thread coarsening and register tiling in the z direction for a 3D seven-point stencil sweep.

The kernels in Figs. 8.10 and 8.12 both keep only the active part of the input tile in the on-chip memory. The number of planes in the active part depends on the order of the stencil and is 3 for the 3D seven-point stencil. The coarsening and register tiling kernel in Fig. 8.12 has two advantages over the coarsening kernel in Fig. 8.10. First, many reads from and writes to the shared memory are now shifted into registers. Since registers have significantly lower latency and higher bandwidth than the shared memory, we expect the code to run faster. Second, each block consumes only one-third of the shared memory. This is, of course, achieved at the cost of three more registers used by each thread, or 3072 more registers per block, assuming 32×32 blocks. The reader should keep in mind that register use will become even higher for higher-order stencils. If the register usage becomes a problem, one can go back to storing some of the planes in shared memory. This scenario represents a common tradeoff that often needs to be made between shared memory and register usage.

Overall, the data reuse is now spread across registers and the shared memory. The number of global memory accesses has not changed. The overall data reuse if we consider both registers and the shared memory remains the same as the thread coarsening kernel that uses only the shared memory for the input tile. Thus there is no impact on the consumption of the global memory bandwidth when we add register tiling to thread coarsening.

Note that the idea of storing a tile of data collectively in the registers of a block's threads is one that we have seen before. In the matrix multiplication kernels in Chapters 3, Multidimensional Grids and Data, and 5, Memory Architecture and Data Locality, and in the convolution kernel in Chapter 7, Convolution, we stored the output value computed by each thread in a register of that thread. Hence the output tile that is computed by a block was stored collectively in the registers of that block's threads. Therefore register tiling is not a new optimization but one that we have applied before. It just became more apparent in this chapter because we are now using registers to store part of the input tile: the same tile was sometimes stored in registers and other times stored in shared memory throughout the course of the computation.

8.6 Summary

In this chapter we dived into stencil sweep computation, which seems to be just convolution with special filter patterns. However, because the stencils come from discretization and numerical approximation of derivatives in solving differential equations, they have two characteristics that motivate and enable new optimizations. First stencil sweeps are typically done on 3D grids, whereas convolution is typically done on 2D images or a small number of time slices of 2D images. This makes the tiling considerations different between the two and motivates thread coarsening for 3D stencils to enable larger input tiles and more data reuse. Second, the stencil patterns can sometimes enable register tiling of input data to further improve data access throughput and alleviate shared memory pressure.

Exercises

1. Consider a 3D stencil computation on a grid of size $120 \times 120 \times 120$, including boundary cells.
   a. What is the number of output grid points that is computed during each stencil sweep?
   b. For the basic kernel in Fig. 8.6, what is the number of thread blocks that are needed, assuming a block size of $8 \times 8 \times 8$?

    c. For the kernel with shared memory tiling in Fig. 8.8, what is the number of thread blocks that are needed, assuming a block size of $8 \times 8 \times 8$?

    d. For the kernel with shared memory tiling and thread coarsening in Fig. 8.10, what is the number of thread blocks that are needed, assuming a block size of 32×32?

2. Consider an implementation of a seven-point (3D) stencil with shared memory tiling and thread coarsening applied. The implementation is similar to those in Figs. 8.10 and 8.12, except that the tiles are not perfect cubes. Instead, a thread block size of 32×32 is used as well as a coarsening factor of 16 (i.e., each thread block processes 16 consecutive output planes in the z dimension).

    a. What is the size of the input tile (in number of elements) that the thread block loads throughout its lifetime?

    b. What is the size of the output tile (in number of elements) that the thread block processes throughout its lifetime?

    c. What is the floating point to global memory access ratio (in OP/B) of the kernel?

    d. How much shared memory (in bytes) is needed by each thread block if register tiling is not used, as in Fig. 8.10?

    e. How much shared memory (in bytes) is needed by each thread block if register tiling is used, as in Fig. 8.12?

Parallel histogram

An introduction to atomic operations and privatization

9

Chapter Outline

9.1 Background 192
9.2 Atomic operations and a basic histogram kernel 194
9.3 Latency and throughput of atomic operations 198
9.4 Privatization 200
9.5 Coarsening 203
9.6 Aggregation 206
9.7 Summary 208
Exercises 209
References 210

The parallel computation patterns that we have presented so far all allow the task of computing each output element to be exclusively assigned to, or owned by, a thread. Therefore these patterns are amenable to the owner-computes rule, in which every thread can write into its designated output element(s) without any concern about interference from other threads. This chapter introduces the parallel histogram computation pattern, in which each output element can potentially be updated by any thread. Therefore one must take care to coordinate among threads as they update output elements and avoid any interference that could corrupt the final result. In practice, there are many other important parallel computation patterns in which output interference cannot be easily avoided. Therefore parallel histogram algorithms provide an example of output interference that occurs in these patterns. We will first examine a baseline approach that uses *atomic operations* to serialize the updates to each element. This baseline approach is simple but inefficient, often resulting in disappointing execution speed. We will then present some widely used optimization techniques, most notably privatization, to significantly enhance execution speed while preserving correctness. The cost and benefit of these techniques depend on the underlying hardware as well as the characteristics of the input data. It is therefore important for a developer to understand the key ideas of these techniques and to be able to reason about their applicability in different circumstances.

Programming Massively Parallel Processors. DOI: https://doi.org/10.1016/B978-0-323-91231-0.00015-X

9.1 Background

A histogram is a display of the number count or percentage of occurrences of data values in a dataset. In the most common form of histogram, the value intervals are plotted along the horizontal axis, and the count of data values in each interval is represented as the height of a rectangle, or bar, rising from the horizontal axis. For example, a histogram can be used to show the frequency of letters of the alphabet in the phrase "programming massively parallel processors." For simplicity we assume that the input phrase is in all lowercase. By inspection we see that there are four instances of the letter "a," zero of the letter "b," one of the letter "c," and so on. We define each value interval as a continuous range of four letters of the alphabet. Thus the first value interval is "a" through "d," the second value interval is "e" through "h," and so on. Fig. 9.1 shows a histogram that displays the frequency of letters in the phrase "programming massively parallel processors" according to our definition of value intervals.

Histograms provide useful summaries of datasets. In our example we can see that the phrase being represented consists of letters that are heavily concentrated in the middle intervals of the alphabet and is noticeably sparse in the later intervals. The shape of the histogram is sometimes referred to as a *feature* of the dataset and provides a quick way to determine whether there are significant phenomena in the dataset. For example, the shape of a histogram of the purchase categories and locations of a credit card account can be used to detect fraudulent usage. When the shape of the histogram deviates significantly from the norm, the system raises a flag of potential concern.

Many application domains rely on histograms to summarize datasets for data analysis. One such area is computer vision. Histograms of different types of object images, such as faces versus cars, tend to exhibit different shapes. For example, one can plot the histogram of pixel luminous values in an image or an

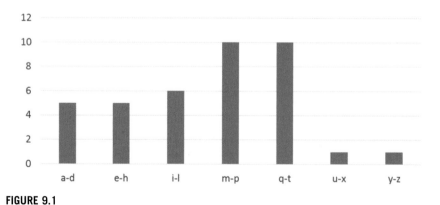

FIGURE 9.1

A histogram representation of the phrase "programming massively parallel processors."

area of an image. Such a histogram of the sky on a sunny day might have only a small number of very tall bars in the high-value intervals of the luminous spectrum. By dividing an image into subareas and analyzing the histograms for these subareas, one can quickly identify the interesting subareas of an image that potentially contain the objects of interest. The process of computing histograms of image subareas is an important approach to *feature extraction* in computer vision, in which the features refer to patterns of interest in images. In practice, whenever there is a large volume of data that needs to be analyzed to distill interesting events, histograms are likely used as a foundational computation. Credit card fraudulence detection and computer vision obviously meet this description. Other application domains with such needs include speech recognition, website purchase recommendations, and scientific data analysis, such as correlating heavenly object movements in astrophysics.

Histograms can be easily computed in a sequential manner. Fig. 9.2 shows a sequential function that calculates the histogram defined in Fig. 9.1. For simplicity the histogram function is required to recognize only lowercase letters. The C code assumes that the input dataset comes in a `char` array `data` and the histogram will be generated into the `int` array `histo` (line 01). The number of input data items is specified in function parameter `length`. The for-loop (lines 02–07) sequentially traverses the array, identifies the alphabet index of the character in the visited position `data[i]`, saves the alphabet index into the alphabet_position variable, and increments the `histo[alphabet_position/4]` element associated with that interval. The calculation of the alphabet index relies on the fact that the input string is based on the standard ASCII code representation in which the alphabet letters "a" through "z" are encoded into consecutive values according to their order in the alphabet.

Although one might not know the exact encoded value of each letter, one can assume that the encoded value of a letter is the encoded value of "a" plus the alphabet position difference between that letter and "a." In the input, each character is stored in its encoded value. Thus the expression data[i] − "a" (line 03) derives the alphabet position of the letter with the alphabet position of "a" being 0. If the position value is greater than or equal to 0 and less than 26, the data character is indeed a lowercase alphabet letter (line 04). Keep in mind that we defined the intervals

```
01  void histogram_sequential(char *data, unsigned int length,
                              unsigned int *histo) {
02      for(unsigned int i = 0; i < length; ++i) {
03          int alphabet_position = data[i] - 'a';
04          if(alphabet_position >= 0 && alphabet_position < 26)
05              histo[alphabet_position/4]++;
06      }
07  }
08  }
```

FIGURE 9.2

A simple C function for calculating histogram for an input text string.

such that each interval contains four alphabet letters. Therefore the interval index for the letter is its alphabet position value divided by 4. We use the interval index to increment the appropriate `histo` array element (line 05).

The C code in Fig. 9.2 is quite simple and efficient. The computational complexity of the algorithm is O(N), where N is the number of input data elements. The data array elements are accessed sequentially in the for-loop, so the CPU cache lines are well used whenever they are fetched from the system DRAM. The `histo` array is so small that it fits well in the level-one (L1) data cache of the CPU, which ensures fast updates to the `histo` elements. For most modern CPUs, one can expect the execution speed of this code to be memory bound, that is, limited by the rate at which the `data` elements can be brought from DRAM into the CPU cache.

9.2 Atomic operations and a basic histogram kernel

The most straightforward approach to parallelizing histogram computation is to launch as many threads as there are data elements and have each thread process one input element. Each thread reads its assigned input element and increments the appropriate interval counter for the character. Fig. 9.3 illustrates an example of this parallelization strategy. Note that multiple threads need to update the same counter (m-p), which is a conflict that is referred to as *output interference*. Programmers must understand the concepts of race conditions and atomic operations in order to confidently handle such output interferences in their parallel code.

An increment to an interval counter in the histo array is an update, or read-modify-write, operation on a memory location. The operation involves reading the memory location (read), adding one to the original value (modify), and writing the new value back to the memory location (write). Read-modify-write is a frequently used operation for coordinating collaborative activities.

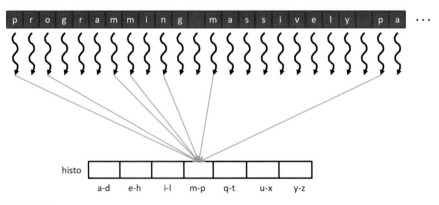

FIGURE 9.3

Basic parallelization of a histogram.

Time	Thread 1	Thread 2
1	(0) Old ← histo[x]	
2	(1) New ← Old + 1	
3	(1) histo[x] ← New	
4		(1) Old ← histo[x]
5		(2) New ← Old + 1
6		(2) histo[x] ← New

(A)

Time	Thread 1	Thread 2
1	(0) Old ← histo[x]	
2	(1) New ← Old + 1	
3		(0) Old ← histo[x]
4	(1) histo[x] ← New	
5		(1) New ← Old + 1
6		(1) histo[x] ← New

(B)

FIGURE 9.4

Race condition in updating a `histo` array element: (A) One possible interleaving of instructions; (B) Another possible interleaving of instructions.

For example, when we make a flight reservation with an airline, we bring up the seat map and look for available seats (read), we pick a seat to reserve (modify), and that changes the seat status to unavailable in the seat map (write). A bad potential scenario can happen as follows:

- Two customers simultaneously bring up seat map of the same flight.
- Both customers pick the same seat, say, 9C.
- Both customers change the status of seat 9C to unavailable.

After the sequence, both customers think that they have seat 9C. We can imagine that they will have an unpleasant situation when they board the flight and find out that one of them cannot take the reserved seat! Believe it or not, such unpleasant situations happen in real life because of flaws in airline reservation software.

For another example, some stores allow customers to wait for service without standing in line. They ask each customer to take a number from one of the kiosks. There is a display that shows the number that will be served next. When a service agent becomes available, the agent asks the customer to present the ticket that matches the number, verifies the ticket, and updates the display number to the next higher number. Ideally, all customers will be served in the order in which they enter the store. An undesirable outcome would be that two customers simultaneously sign in at two kiosks and both receive tickets with the same number. When a service agent calls for that number, both customers expect to be the one who should receive service.

In both examples, undesirable outcomes are caused by a phenomenon called read-modify-write *race condition*, in which the outcome of two or more simultaneous update operations varies depending on the relative timing of the operations that are involved.[1] Some outcomes are correct, and some are incorrect. Fig. 9.4 illustrates a race condition when two threads attempt to update the same histo element in our text histogram example. Each row in Fig. 9.4 shows the activity during a time period, with time progressing from top to bottom.

---

[1] Note that this is similar but not the same as the write-after-read race condition in Chapter 10, Reduction and Minimizing Divergence, when we discussed the need for a barrier synchronization between the reads from and writes to the XY array in each iteration of the Kogge-Stone scan kernel.

Fig. 9.4A depicts a scenario in which thread 1 completes all three parts of its read-modify-write sequence during time periods 1 through 3 before thread 2 starts its sequence at time period 4. The value in the parenthesis in front of each operation shows the value being written into the destination, assuming that the value of histo[x] was initially 0. In this scenario the value of histo[x] afterwards is 2, exactly what one would expect. That is, both threads successfully incremented histo[x]. The element value starts with 0 and becomes 2 after the operations complete.

In Fig. 9.4B the read-modify-write sequences of the two threads overlap. Note that thread 1 writes the new value into histo[x] at time period 4. When thread 2 reads histo[x] at time period 3, it still has the value 0. As a result, the new value that it calculates and eventually writes to histo[x] is 1 rather than 2. The problem is that thread 2 read histo[x] too early, before thread 1 had completed its update. The net outcome is that the value of histo[x] afterwards is 1, which is incorrect. The update by thread 1 is lost.

During parallel execution, threads can run in any order relative to each other. In our example, thread 2 can easily start its update sequence ahead of thread 1. Fig. 9.5 shows two such scenarios. In Fig. 9.5A, thread 2 completes its update before thread 1 starts its. In Fig. 9.5B, thread 1 starts its update before thread 2 has completed its. It should be obvious that the sequences in Fig. 9.5A result in a correct outcome for histo[x], but those in Fig. 9.5B produce an incorrect outcome.

The fact that the final value of histo[x] varies depending on the relative timing of the operations that are involved indicates that there is a race condition. We can eliminate such variation by eliminating the possible interleaving of operation sequences of thread 1 and thread 2. That is, we would like to allow the timings shown in Figs. 9.4A and 9.5A while eliminating the possibilities shown in Figs. 9.4B and 9.5B. This can be accomplished by using *atomic operations*.

An atomic operation on a memory location is an operation that performs a read-modify-write sequence on the memory location in such a way that no other read-modify-write sequence to the location can overlap with it. That is, the read, modify, and write parts of the operation form an undividable unit, hence the name atomic operation. In practice, atomic operations are realized with hardware support to lock out other operations to the same location until the current

Time	Thread 1	Thread 2
1		(0) Old ← histo[x]
2		(1) New ← Old + 1
3		(1) histo[x] ← New
4	(1) Old ← histo[x]	
5	(2) New ← Old + 1	
6	(2) histo[x] ← New	

(A)

Time	Thread 1	Thread 2
1		(0) Old ← histo[x]
2		(1) New ← Old + 1
3	(0) Old ← histo[x]	
4		(1) histo[x] ← New
5	(1) New ← Old + 1	
6	(1) histo[x] ← New	

(B)

FIGURE 9.5

Race condition scenarios in which thread 2 runs ahead of thread 1: (A) One possible interleaving of instructions; (B) Another possible interleaving of instructions.

operation is complete. In our example, such support eliminates the possibility depicted in Figs. 9.4B and 9.5B, since the trailing thread cannot start its update sequence until the leading thread has completed its.

It is important to remember that atomic operations do not enforce any particular execution order between threads. In our example, both orders shown in Figs. 9.4A and 9.5A are allowed by atomic operations. Thread 1 can run either ahead of or behind thread 2. The rule that is being enforced is that if both threads perform atomic operations on the same memory location, the atomic operation that is performed by the trailing thread cannot be started until the atomic operation of the leading thread completes. This effectively serializes the atomic operations that are being performed on a memory location.

Atomic operations are usually named according to the modification that is performed on the memory location. In our text histogram example we are adding a value to the memory location, so the atomic operation is called atomic add. Other types of atomic operations include subtraction, increment, decrement, minimum, maximum, logical and, and logical or. A CUDA kernel can perform an atomic add operation on a memory location through a function call:

```
int atomicAdd(int* address, int val);
```

The atomicAdd function is an intrinsic function (see the sidebar "Intrinsic Functions") that is compiled into a hardware atomic operation instruction. This instruction reads the 32-bit word pointed to by the address argument in global or shared memory, adds val to the old content, and stores the result back to memory at the same address. The function returns the old value at the address.

Intrinsic Functions

Modern processors often offer special instructions that either perform critical functionality (such as the atomic operations) or substantial performance enhancement (such as vector instructions). These instructions are typically exposed to the programmers as intrinsic functions, or simply instrinsics. From the programmer's perspective, these are library functions. However, they are treated in a special way by compilers; each such call is translated into the corresponding special instruction. There is typically no function call in the final code, just the special instructions in line with the user code. All major modern compilers, such as the GNU Compiler Collection (gcc), Intel C Compiler, and Clang/LLVM C Compiler support intrinsics.

Fig. 9.6 shows a CUDA kernel that performs parallel histogram computation. The code is similar to the sequential code in Fig. 9.2 with two key distinctions. The first distinction is that the loop over input elements is replaced with a thread index

```
01   __global__ void histo_kernel(char *data, unsigned int length,
                                   unsigned int *histo)  {
02      unsigned int i = blockIdx.x*blockDim.x + threadIdx.x;
03      if (i < length) {
04          int alphabet_position = data[i] - 'a';
05          if (alphabet_position >= 0 && alpha_position < 26) {
06              atomicAdd(&(histo[alphabet_position/4]), 1);
07          }
08      }
09   }
```

FIGURE 9.6

A CUDA kernel for calculation histogram.

calculation (line 02) and a boundary check (line 03) to assign a thread to each input element. The second distinction is that the increment expression in Fig. 9.2:

$$histo[alphabet\_position/4]++$$

becomes an `atomicAdd()` function call in Fig. 9.6 (line 06). The address of the location to be updated, `&(histo[alphabet_position/4])`, is the first argument. The value to be added to the location, 1, is the second argument. This ensures that any simultaneous updates to any `histo` array element by different threads are properly serialized.

9.3 Latency and throughput of atomic operations

The atomic operation that is used in the kernel of Fig. 9.6 ensures the correctness of updates by serializing any simultaneous updates to a location. As we know, serializing any portion of a massively parallel program can drastically increase the execution time and reduce the execution speed of the program. Therefore it is important that such serialized operations account for as little execution time as possible.

As we learned in Chapter 5, Memory Architecture and Data Locality, the access latency to data in DRAMs can take hundreds of clock cycles. In Chapter 4, Compute Architecture and Scheduling, we learned that GPUs use zero-cycle context switching to tolerate such latency. In Chapter 6, Performance Considerations, we learned that as long as we have many threads whose memory access latencies can overlap with each other, the execution speed is limited by the throughput of the memory system. Therefore it is important that GPUs make full use DRAM bursts, banks, and channels to achieve high memory access throughput.

It should be clear to the reader at this point that the key to high memory access throughput is to have many DRAM accesses that are simultaneously in progress. Unfortunately, this strategy breaks down when many atomic operations update the same memory location. In this case, the read-modify-write sequence of a trailing thread cannot start until the read-modify-write sequence of a leading thread is

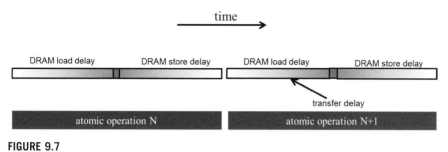

FIGURE 9.7

The throughput of an atomic operation is determined by the memory access latency.

complete. As is shown in Fig. 9.7, the execution of atomic operations at the same memory location is such that there can be only one in progress. The duration of each atomic operation is approximately the latency of a memory load (left section of the atomic operation time) plus the latency of a memory store (right section of the atomic operation time). The length of these time sections of each read-modify-write operation, usually hundreds of clock cycles, defines the minimum amount of time that must be dedicated to servicing each atomic operation and limits the throughput, or the rate at which atomic operations can be performed.

For example, assume a memory system with a 64-bit (8-byte) double data rate DRAM interface per channel, eight channels, 1 GHz clock frequency, and typical access latency of 200 cycles. The peak access throughput of the memory system is 8 (bytes/transfer) * 2 (transfers per clock per channel) * 1 G (clocks per second) * 8 (channels) = 128 GB/s. Assuming that each data accessed is 4 bytes, the system has a peak access throughput of 32 G data elements per second.

However, in performing atomic operations on a particular memory location, the highest throughput that one can achieve is one atomic operation every 400 cycles (200 cycles for the read and 200 cycles for the write). This translates into a time-based throughput of 1/400 atomics/clock * 1 G (clocks/second) = 2.5 M atomics/second. This is dramatically lower than most users expect from a GPU memory system. Furthermore, the long latency of the sequence of atomic operations will likely dominate the kernel execution time and can dramatically lower the execution speed of the kernel.

In practice, not all atomic operations will be performed on a single memory location. In our text histogram example, the histogram has seven intervals. If the input characters were uniformly distributed in the alphabet, the atomic operations would be evenly distributed among the histo elements. This would boost the throughput to 7*2.5 M = 17.5 M atomic operations per second. In reality, the boost factor tends to be much lower than the number of intervals in the histogram because the characters tend to have a biased distribution in the alphabet. For example, in Fig. 9.1 we see that the characters in the example phrase are heavily biased toward the m-p and q-t intervals. The heavy contention traffic to update these intervals will likely reduce the achievable throughput to only around (28/10)*2.5 M = 7 M.

One approach to improving the throughput of atomic operations is to reduce the access latency to the heavily contended locations. Cache memories are the primary tool for reducing memory access latency. For this reason, modern GPUs allow atomic operations to be performed in the last-level cache, which is shared among all streaming multiprocessors (SMs). During an atomic operation, if the updated variable is found in the last-level cache, it is updated in the cache. If it cannot be found in the last-level cache, it triggers a cache miss and is brought into the cache, where it is updated. Since the variables that are updated by atomic operations tend to be heavily accessed by many threads, these variables tend to remain in the cache once they have been brought in from DRAM. Because the access time to the last-level cache is in tens of cycles rather than hundreds of cycles, the throughput of atomic operations is improved by at least an order of magnitude compared to early generations of GPU. This is an important reason why most modern GPUs support atomic operations in the last-level cache.

9.4 Privatization

Another approach to improving the throughput of atomic operations is to alleviate the contention by directing the traffic away from the heavily contended locations. This can be achieved with a technique referred to as *privatization* that is commonly used to address the heavy output interference problems in parallel computing. The idea is to replicate highly contended output data structures into private copies so that each subset of threads can update its private copy. The benefit is that the private copies can be accessed with much less contention and often at much lower latency. These private copies can dramatically increase the throughput for updating the data structures. The downside is that the private copies need to be merged into the original data structure after the computation completes. One must carefully balance between the level of contention and the merging cost. Therefore in massively parallel systems, privatization is typically done for subsets of threads rather than individual threads.

In our text histogram example we can create multiple private histograms and designate a subset of threads to update each of them. For example, we can create two private copies and have even-index blocks to update one of them and odd-index blocks to update the other. For another example, we can create four private copies and have blocks whose indices are of the form $4n+i$ to update the ith private version for $I = 0, \ldots, 3$. A common approach is to create a private copy for each thread block. This approach has multiple advantages that we will see later.

Fig. 9.8 shows an example of how privatization is applied to the text histogram example from Fig. 9.3. In this example the threads are organized into thread blocks, each of which consists of eight threads (in practice, thread blocks are much larger). Each thread block receives a private copy of the histogram that it updates. As shown in Fig. 9.8, rather than having contention across all the threads that update the same histogram bin, contention will be experienced only between threads in the same block and when the private copies are being merged at the end.

Fig. 9.9 presents a simple kernel that creates and associates a private copy of the histogram to every block. In this scheme, up to 1024 threads would work on a copy of the histogram. In this kernel the private histograms are in the global memory. These private copies will likely be cached in the L2 cache for reduced latency and improved throughput.

The first part of the kernel in Fig. 9.9 (lines 02−08) is similar to the kernel in Fig. 9.6 with one key distinction. The kernel in Fig. 9.9 assumes that the host code will allocate enough device memory for the histo array to hold all the

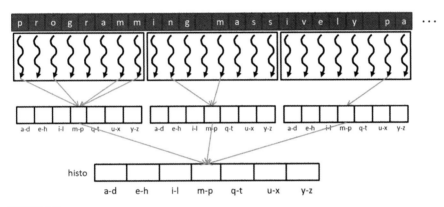

FIGURE 9.8

Private copies of histogram reduce contention of atomic operations.

```
01   __global__ void histo_private_kernel(char *data, unsigned int length,
                                      unsigned int *histo) {
02       unsigned int i = blockIdx.x*blockDim.x + threadIdx.x;
03       if(i < length) {
04           int alphabet_position = data[i] - 'a';
05           if (alphabet_position >= 0 && alphabet_position < 26) {
06               atomicAdd(&(histo[blockIdx.x*NUM_BINS + alphabet_position/4]), 1);
07           }
08       }
09       if(blockIdx.x > 0) {
10           __syncthreads();
11           for(unsigned int bin=threadIdx.x; bin<NUM_BINS; bin += blockDim.x){
12               unsigned int binValue = histo[blockIdx.x*NUM_BINS + bin];
13               if(binValue > 0) {
14                   atomicAdd(&(histo[bin]), binValue);
15               }
16           }
17       }
18   }
```

FIGURE 9.9

Histogram kernel with private versions in global memory for thread blocks.

private copies of the histogram, which amounts to gridDim.x*NUM_BINS*4 bytes. This is reflected in line 06, where each thread adds an offset of blockIdx.x*NUM_BINS to the index when performing atomic add on `histo` elements (bins of the histogram). This offset shifts the position to the private copy for the block to which the thread belongs. In this case, the level of contention is reduced by a factor that is approximately the number of active blocks across all SMs. The effect of reduced contention can result in orders of magnitude of improvement in the update throughput for the kernel.

At the end of the execution, each thread block will commit the values in private copy into the version produced by block 0 (lines 09−17). That is, we promote the private copy of block 0 into a public copy that will hold the total results from all block. The threads in the block first wait for each other to finish updating the private copy (line 10). Next, the threads iterate over the private histogram bins (line 11), each thread being responsible for committing one or more of the private bins. A loop is used to accommodate an arbitrary number of bins. Each thread reads the value of the private bin for which it is responsible (line 13) and checks whether the bin is nonzero (line 13). If it is, the thread commits the value by atomically adding it to the copy of block 0 (line 14). Note that the addition needs to be performed atomically because threads from multiple blocks can be simultaneously performing the addition on the same location. Therefore at the end of the kernel execution, the final histogram will be in the first NUM_BINS elements of the histo array. Since only one thread from each block will be updating any given histo array element during this phase of the kernel execution, the level of contention for each location is very modest.

One benefit of creating a private copy of the histogram on a per-thread-block basis is that the threads can use __syncthreads() to wait for each other before committing. If the private copy were accessed by multiple blocks, we would have needed to call another kernel to merge the private copies or used other sophisticated techniques. Another benefit of creating a private copy of the histogram on a per-thread-block basis is that if the number of bins in the histogram is small enough, the private copy of the histogram can be declared in shared memory. Using shared memory would not be possible if the private copy were accessed by multiple blocks because blocks do not have visibility of each other's shared memory.

Recall that any reduction in latency directly translates into improved throughput of atomic operations on the same memory location. The latency for accessing memory can be dramatically reduced by placing data in the shared memory. Shared memory is private to each SM and has very short access latency (a few cycles). This reduced latency directly translates into increased throughput of atomic operations.

Fig. 9.10 shows a privatized histogram kernel that stores the private copies in the shared memory instead of global memory. The key difference from the kernel code in Fig. 9.9 is that the private copy of the histogram is allocated in shared memory in the `histo_s` array and is initialized to 0 in parallel by the threads of

```
01  __global__ void histo_private_kernel(char* data, unsigned int length,
                                          unsigned int* histo) {
02        // Initialize privatized bins
03      __shared__ unsigned int histo_s[NUM_BINS];
04      for(unsigned int bin = threadIdx.x; bin< NUM_BINS; bin += blockDim.x) {
05        histo_s[bin] = 0u;
06      }
07      __syncthreads();
08        // Histogram
09      unsigned int i = blockIdx.x*blockDim.x + threadIdx.x;
10      if(i < length) {
11        int alphabet_position = data[i] - 'a';
12        if(alphabet_position >= 0 && alphabet_position < 26) {
13          atomicAdd(&(histo_s[alphabet_position/4]), 1);
14        }
15      }
16      __syncthreads();
17        // Commit to global memory
18      for(unsigned int bin=threadIdx.x; bin<NUM_BINS; bin += blockDim.x) {
19          unsigned int binValue = histo_s[bin];
20          if(binValue > 0) {
21            atomicAdd(&(histo[bin]), binValue);
22          }
23      }
24  }
```

FIGURE 9.10

A privatized text histogram kernel using the shared memory.

the block (line 02−06). The barrier synchronization (line 07) ensures that all bins of the private histogram have been properly initialized before any thread starts to update them. The remaining code is identical to that in Fig. 9.9 except that the first atomic operation is performed on the elements of the shared memory array histo_s (line 13) and the private bin value is later read from there (line 19).

9.5 Coarsening

We have seen that privatization is effective in reducing the contention of atomic operations and that storing the privatized histogram in the shared memory reduces the latency of each atomic operation. However, the overhead of privatization is the need to commit the private copies to the public copy. This commit operation is done once per thread block. Hence the more thread blocks we use, the larger this overhead is. The overhead is usually worth paying when the thread blocks are executed in parallel. However, if the number of thread blocks that are launched exceeds the number that can be executed simultaneously by the hardware, the hardware schedule will serialize these thread blocks. In this case, the privatization overhead is incurred unnecessarily.

We can reduce the overhead of privatization via thread coarsening. In other words, we can reduce the number of private copies that are committed to the public copy by reducing the number of blocks and having each thread process multiple input elements. In this section we look at two strategies for assigning multiple input elements to a thread: contiguous partitioning and interleaved partitioning.

Fig. 9.11 shows an example of the contiguous partitioning strategy. The input is partitioned into contiguous segments, and each segment is assigned to a thread. Fig. 9.12 shows the histogram kernel with coarsening applied using the contiguous partitioning strategy. The difference from Fig. 9.10 is on lines 09−10. In Fig. 9.10 the input element index i corresponded to the global thread index, so

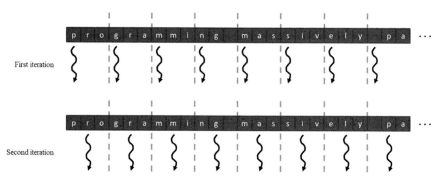

FIGURE 9.11

Contiguous partitioning of input elements.

```
01  __global__ void histo_private_kernel(char* data, unsigned int length,
                                          unsigned int* histo) {
02      // Initialize privatized bins
03      __shared__ unsigned int histo_s[NUM_BINS];
04      for(unsigned int bin = threadIdx.x; bin<NUM_BINS; bin += blockDim.x) {
05          histo_s[binIdx] = 0u;
06      }
07      __syncthreads();
08      // Histogram
09      unsigned int tid = blockIdx.x*blockDim.x + threadIdx.x;
10      for(unsigned int i=tid*CFACTOR; i<min((tid+1)*CFACTOR, length); ++i) {
11          int alphabet_position = data[i] - 'a';
12          if(alphabet_position >= 0 && alphabet_position < 26) {
13              atomicAdd(&(histo_s[alphabet_position/4]), 1);
14          }
15      }
16      __syncthreads();
17      // Commit to global memory
18      for(unsigned int bin = threadIdx.x; bin<NUM_BINS; bin += blockDim.x) {
19          unsigned int binValue = histo_s[binIdx];
20          if(binValue > 0) {
21              atomicAdd(&(histo[binIdx]), binValue);
22          }
23      }
24  }
```

FIGURE 9.12

Histogram kernel with coarsening using contiguous partitioning.

each thread received one input element. In Fig. 9.11 the input elements index `i` is the index of a loop that iterates from `tid*CFACTOR` to `(tid + 1)*CFACTOR` where `CFACTOR` is the coarsening factor. Therefore each thread takes a contiguous segment of `CFACTOR` elements. The `min` operation in the loop bound ensures that the threads at the end do not read out of bounds.

Partitioning data into contiguous segments is conceptually simple and intuitive. On a CPU, where parallel execution typically involves a small number of threads, contiguous partitioning is often the best-performing strategy, since the sequential access pattern by each thread makes good use of cache lines. Since each CPU cache typically supports only a small number of threads, there is little interference in cache usage by different threads. The data in cache lines, once brought in for a thread, can be expected to remain for the subsequent accesses.

In contrast, contiguous partitioning on GPUs results in a suboptimal memory access pattern. As we learned in Chapter 5, Memory Architecture and Data Locality, the large number of simultaneously active threads in an SM typically causes so much interference in the cache that one cannot expect data to remain in the cache for all the sequential accesses by a single thread. Instead, we need to make sure that threads in a warp access consecutive locations to enable memory coalescing. This observation motivates interleaved partitioning.

Fig. 9.13 shows an example of the interleaved partitioning strategy. During the first iteration, the eight threads access characters 0 through 7 ("programm"). With memory coalescing, all the elements will be fetched with only one DRAM access. During the second iteration the four threads access the characters "ing mass" in one coalesced memory access. It should be clear why this is called interleaved partitioning: The partitions to be processed by different threads are interleaved with each other. Obviously, this is a toy example, and in reality, there will be many more threads. There are also more subtle performance considerations. For example, each thread should process four characters (a 32-bit word) in each iteration to fully utilize the interconnect bandwidth between the caches and the SMs.

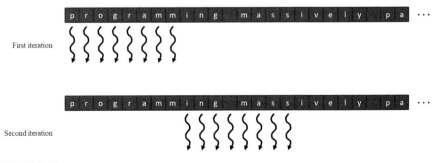

FIGURE 9.13

Interleaved partitioning of input elements.

```
01   __global__ void histo_private_kernel(char* data, unsigned int length,
                                          unsigned int* histo){
02      // Initialize privatized bins
03      __shared__ unsigned int histo_s[NUM_BINS];
04      for(unsigned int bin=threadIdx.x; bin<NUM_BINS; bin += blockDim.x) {
05          histo_s[binIdx] = 0u;
06      }
07      __syncthreads();
08      // Histogram
09      unsigned int tid = blockIdx.x*blockDim.x + threadIdx.x;
10      for(unsigned int i = tid; i < length; i += blockDim.x*gridDim.x) {
11          int alphabet_position = data[i] - 'a';
12          if(alphabet_position >= 0 && alphabet_position < 26) {
13              atomicAdd(&(histo_s[alphabet_position/4]), 1);
14          }
15      }
16      __syncthreads();
17      // Commit to global memory
18      for(unsigned int bin = threadIdx.x; bin<NUM_BINS; bin += blockDim.x) {
19          unsigned int binValue = histo_s[binIdx];
20          if(binValue > 0) {
21              atomicAdd(&(histo[binIdx]), binValue);
22          }
23      }
24  }
```

FIGURE 9.14

Histogram kernel with coarsening using interleaved partitioning.

Fig. 9.14 shows the histogram kernel with coarsening applied by using the interleaved partitioning strategy. The difference from Figs. 9.10 and 9.12 is again on lines 09–10. In the first iteration of the loop, each thread accesses the data array using its global thread index: Thread 0 accesses element 0, thread 1 accesses element 1, thread 2 accesses element 2, and so on. Thus all threads jointly process the first blockDim.x*gridDim.x elements of the input. In the second iteration, all threads add blockDim.x*gridDim.x to their indices and jointly process the next section of blockDim.x*gridDim.x elements.

When the index of a thread exceeds the valid range of the input buffer (its private i variable value is greater than or equal to length), the thread has completed processing its partition and will exit the loop. Since the size of the buffer might not be a multiple of the total number of threads, some of the threads might not participate in the processing of the last section. Therefore some threads will execute one fewer loop iteration than others.

9.6 Aggregation

Some datasets have a large concentration of identical data values in localized areas. For example, in pictures of the sky, there can be large patches of pixels of identical value. Such a high concentration of identical values causes heavy contention and reduced throughput of parallel histogram computation.

For such datasets a simple and yet effective optimization is for each thread to aggregate consecutive updates into a single update if they are updating the same element of the histogram (Merrill, 2015). Such aggregation reduces the number of atomic operations to the highly contended histogram elements, thus improving the effective throughput of the computation.

Fig. 9.15 shows an aggregated text histogram kernel. The key changes compared to the kernel in Fig. 9.14 are as follows: Each thread declares an additional accumulator variable (line 09) that keeps track of the number of updates aggregated thus far and a prevBinIdx variable (line 10) that tracks the index of the histogram bin that was last encountered and is being aggregated. Each thread initializes the accumulator variable to zero, indicating that no updates has been initially aggregated, and the prevBinIdx to −1 so that no alphabet input will match it.

```
01   __global__ void histo_private_kernel(char* data, unsigned int length,
                                     unsigned int* histo){
02      // Initialize privatized bins
03      __shared__ unsigned int histo_s[NUM_BINS];
04      for(unsigned int bin = threadIdx.x; bin < NUM_BINS; bin += blockDim.x){
05         histo_s[bin] = 0u;
06      }
07      __syncthreads();
08      // Histogram
09      unsigned int accumulator = 0;
10      int prevBinIdx = -1;
11      unsigned int tid = blockIdx.x*blockDim.x + threadIdx.x;
12      for(unsigned int i = tid; i < length; i += blockDim.x*gridDim.x) {
13         int alphabet_position = data[i] - 'a';
14         if(alphabet_position >= 0 && alphabet_position < 26) {
15            int bin = alphabet_position/4;
16            if(bin == prevBinIdx) {
17               ++accumulator;
18            } else {
19               if(accumulator > 0) {
20                  atomicAdd(&(histo_s[prevBinIdx]), accumulator);
21               }
22               accumulator = 1;
23               prevBinIdx = bin;
24            }
25         }
26      }
27      if(accumulator > 0) {
28         atomicAdd(&(histo_s[prevBinIdx]), accumulator);
29      }
30      __syncthreads();
31      // Commit to global memory
32      for(unsigned int bin = threadIdx.x; bin<NUM_BINS; bin += blockDim.x) {
33         unsigned int binValue = histo_s[bin];
34         if(binValue > 0) {
35            atomicAdd(&(histo[bin]), binValue);
36         }
37      }
38   }
```

FIGURE 9.15

An aggregated text histogram kernel.

When an alphabet data is found, the thread compares the index of the histogram element to be updated with that being aggregated (line 16). If the index is the same, the thread simply increments the accumulator (line 17), extending the streak of aggregated updates by one. If the index is different, the streak of aggregated updates to the histogram element has ended. The thread uses atomic operation to add the `accumulator` value to the histogram element whose index is tracked by `prevBinIdx` (lines 19−21). This effectively flushes out the total contribution of the previous streak of aggregated updates.

With this scheme, the update is always at least one element behind. In the extreme case in which there is no streak, all the updates will simply always be one element behind. This is the reason why after a thread has completed scanning all input elements and exited the loop, the threads need to check whether there is a need to flush out the `accumulator` value (line 27). If so, the accumulator value is flushed to the right `histo_s` element (line 28).

One important observation is that the aggregated kernel requires more statements and variables. Thus if the contention rate is low, an aggregated kernel may execute at lower speed than the simple kernel. However, if the data distribution leads to heavy contention in atomic operation execution, aggregation may result in significantly higher speed. The added if-statement can potentially exhibit control divergence. However, if there is either no contention or heavy contention, there will be little control divergence, since the threads would either all be flushing the accumulator value or all be in a streak. In the case in which some threads will be in a streak and some will be flushing out their accumulator values, the control divergence is likely to be compensated by the reduced contention.

9.7 Summary

Computing histograms is important for analyzing large datasets. It also represents an important class of parallel computation patterns in which the output location of each thread is data-dependent, which makes it infeasible to apply the owner-computes rule. It is therefore a natural vehicle for introducing the concept of read-modify-write race conditions and the practical use of atomic operations that ensure the integrity of concurrent read-modify-write operations to the same memory location.

Unfortunately, as we explained in this chapter, atomic operations have much lower throughput than simpler memory read or write operations because their throughput is approximately the inverse of two times the memory latency. Thus in the presence of heavy contention, histogram computation can have surprisingly low computation throughput. Privatization is introduced as an important optimization technique that systematically reduces contention and can further enable the use of shared memory, which supports low latency and thus high throughput. In fact, supporting fast atomic operations among threads in a block is an important use case of the shared memory. Coarsening was also applied to reduce the number of private copies that need to be merged, and different coarsening strategies that use contiguous partitioning and interleaved partitioning were compared. Finally, for datasets that cause heavy contention, aggregation can also lead to significantly higher execution speed.

Exercises

1. Assume that each atomic operation in a DRAM system has a total latency of 100 ns. What is the maximum throughput that we can get for atomic operations on the same global memory variable?

2. For a processor that supports atomic operations in L2 cache, assume that each atomic operation takes 4 ns to complete in L2 cache and 100 ns to complete in DRAM. Assume that 90% of the atomic operations hit in L2 cache. What is the approximate throughput for atomic operations on the same global memory variable?

3. In Exercise 1, assume that a kernel performs five floating-point operations per atomic operation. What is the maximum floating-point throughput of the kernel execution as limited by the throughput of the atomic operations?

4. In Exercise 1, assume that we privatize the global memory variable into shared memory variables in the kernel and that the shared memory access latency is 1 ns. All original global memory atomic operations are converted into shared memory atomic operation. For simplicity, assume that the additional global memory atomic operations for accumulating privatized variable into the global variable adds 10% to the total execution time. Assume that a kernel performs five floating-point operations per atomic operation. What is the maximum floating-point throughput of the kernel execution as limited by the throughput of the atomic operations?

5. To perform an atomic add operation to add the value of an integer variable Partial to a global memory integer variable Total, which one of the following statements should be used?
   a. atomicAdd(Total, 1);
   b. atomicAdd(&Total, &Partial);
   c. atomicAdd(Total, &Partial);
   d. atomicAdd(&Total, Partial);

6. Consider a histogram kernel that processes an input with 524,288 elements to produce a histogram with 128 bins. The kernel is configured with 1024 threads per block.
   a. What is the total number of atomic operations that are performed on global memory by the kernel in Fig. 9.6 where no privatization, shared memory, and thread coarsening are used?

b. What is the maximum number of atomic operations that may be performed on global memory by the kernel in Fig. 9.10 where privatization and shared memory are used but not thread coarsening?

c. What is the maximum number of atomic operations that may be performed on global memory by the kernel in Fig. 9.14 where privatization, shared memory, and thread coarsening are used with a coarsening factor of 4?

References

Merrill, D., 2015. Using compression to improve the performance response of parallel histogram computation, NVIDIA Research Technical Report.

Reduction

And minimizing divergence

Chapter Outline

10.1 Background 211
10.2 Reduction trees 213
10.3 A simple reduction kernel 217
10.4 Minimizing control divergence 219
10.5 Minimizing memory divergence 223
10.6 Minimizing global memory accesses 225
10.7 Hierarchical reduction for arbitrary input length 226
10.8 Thread coarsening for reduced overhead 228
10.9 Summary 231
Exercises 232

A reduction derives a single value from an array of values. The single value could be the sum, the maximum value, the minimal value, and so on among all elements. The value can also be of various types: integer, single-precision floating-point, double-precision floating-point, half-precision floating-point, characters, and so on. All these types of reductions have the same computation structure. Like a histogram, reduction is an important computation pattern, as it generates a summary from a large amount of data. Parallel reduction is an important parallel pattern that requires parallel threads to coordinate with each other to get correct results. Such coordination must be done carefully to avoid performance bottlenecks, which are commonly found in parallel computing systems. Parallel reduction is therefore a good vehicle for illustrating these performance bottlenecks and introducing techniques for mitigating them.

10.1 Background

Mathematically, a reduction can be defined for a set of items based on a binary operator if the operator has a well-defined identity value. For example, a floating-point addition operator has an identity value of 0.0; that is, an addition of any floating-point value v and value 0.0 results in the value v itself. Thus a reduction

Programming Massively Parallel Processors. DOI: https://doi.org/10.1016/B978-0-323-91231-0.00023-9

can be defined for a set of floating-point numbers based on the addition operator that produces the sum of all the floating-point numbers in the set. For example, for the set {7.0, 2.1, 5.3, 9.0, 11.2}, the sum reduction would produce 7.0+2.1 +5.3+9.0+11.2 = 34.6.

A reduction can be performed by sequentially going through every element of the array. Fig. 10.1 shows a sequential sum reduction code in C. The code initializes the result variable sum to the identity value 0.0. It then uses a for-loop to iterate through the input array that holds the set of values. During the ith iteration, the code performs an addition operation on the current value of sum and the ith element of the input array. In our example, after iteration 0, the sum variable contains 0.0+7.0 = 7.0. After iteration 1, the sum variable contains 7.0+2.1 = 9.1. Thus after each iteration, another value of the input array would be added (accumulated) to the sum variable. After iteration 5, the sum variable contains 34.6, which is the reduction result.

Reduction can be defined for many other operators. A product reduction can be defined for a floating-point multiplication operator whose identity value is 1.0. A product reduction of a set of floating-point numbers is the product of all these numbers. A minimum (min) reduction can be defined for a minimum comparison operator that returns the smaller value of the two inputs. For real numbers, the identity value for the minimum operator is $+\infty$. A maximum (max) reduction can be defined for a maximum (max) comparison operator that returns the larger value of the two input. For real numbers, the identity value for the maximum operator is $-\infty$.

Fig. 10.2 shows a general form of reduction for an operator, which is defined as a function that takes two inputs and returns a value. When an element is visited during an iteration of the for-loop, the action to take depends on the type of reduction being performed. For example, for a max reduction the Operator function performs a comparison between the two inputs and returns the larger value of the two. For a min reduction the values of the two inputs are compared by the operator function, and the

```
01    sum = 0.0f;
02    for(i = 0; i < N; ++i) {
03        sum += input[i];
04    }
```

FIGURE 10.1

A simple sum reduction sequential code.

```
01    acc = IDENTITY;
02    for(i = 0; i < N; ++i) {
03        acc = Operator(acc, input[i]);
04    }
```

FIGURE 10.2

The general form of a reduction sequential code.

smaller value is returned. The sequential algorithm ends when all the elements have been visited by the for-loop. For a set of N elements the for-loop iterates N iterations and produces the reduction result at the exit of the loop.

10.2 **Reduction trees**

Parallel reduction algorithms have been studied extensively in the literature. The basic concept of parallel reduction is illustrated in Fig. 10.3, where time progresses downwards in the vertical direction and the activities that threads perform in parallel in each time step are shown in the horizontal direction.

During the first round (time step), four max operations are performed in parallel on the four pairs of the original elements. These four operations produce partial reduction results: the four larger values from the four pairs of original elements. During the second time step, two max operations are performed in parallel on the two pairs of partial reduction results and produce two partial results that are even closer to the final reduction result. These two partial results are the largest value of the first four elements and the largest value of the second four elements in the original input. During the third and final time step, one max operation is performed to generate the final result, the largest value 7 from the original input.

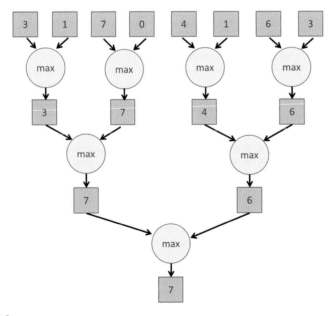

FIGURE 10.3

A parallel max reduction tree.

Note that the order of performing the operations will be changed from a sequential reduction algorithm to a parallel reduction algorithm. For example, for the input at the top of Fig. 10.3, a sequential max reduction like the one in Fig. 10.2 would start first by comparing the identity value $(-\infty)$ in acc with the input value 3 and update acc with the winner, which is 3. It will then compare the value of acc (3) with the input value 1 and update acc with the winner, which is 3. This will be followed by comparing the value of acc (3) with the input value 7 and updating acc with the winner, which is 7. However, in the parallel reduction of Fig. 10.3 the input value 7 is first compared with the input value 0 before it is compared against the maximum of 3 and 1.

As we have seen, parallel reduction assumes that the order of applying the operator to the input values does not matter. In a max reduction, no matter what the order is for applying the operator to the input values, the outcome will be the same. This property is guaranteed mathematically if the operator is associative. An operator Θ is associative if $(a \Theta b) \Theta c = a \Theta (b \Theta c)$. For example, integer addition is associative $((1+2)+3 = 1+(2+3) = 6)$, whereas integer subtraction is not associative $((1-2)-3 \neq 1-(2-3))$. That is, if an operator is associative, one can insert parentheses at arbitrary positions of an expression involving the operator and the results are all the same. With this equivalence relation, one can convert any order of operator application to any other order while preserving the equivalence of results. Strictly speaking, floating-point additions are not associative, owing to potentially rounding results for different ways of introducing parentheses. However, most applications accept floating-point operation results to be the same if they are within a tolerable difference from each other. Such definition allows developers and compiler writers to treat floating-point addition as an associative operator. Interested readers are referred to Appendix A for a detailed treatment.

The conversion from the sequential reduction in Fig. 10.2 to the reduction tree in Fig. 10.3 requires that the operator be associative. We can think of a reduction as a list of operations. The difference of ordering between Fig. 10.2 and Fig. 10.3 is just inserting parenthesis at different positions of the same list. For Fig. 10.2, the parentheses are:

((((((3 max 1) max 7) max 0) max 4) max 1) max 6) max 3

Whereas the parentheses for Fig. 10.3 are:

((3 max 1) max (7 max 0)) max ((4 max 1) max (6 max 3))

We will apply an optimization in Section 10.4 that not only rearranges the order of applying the operator but also rearranges the order of the operands. To rearrange the order of the operands, this optimization further requires the operator to be commutative. An operator is commutative if $a \Theta b = b \Theta a$. That is, the position of the operands can be rearranged in an expression and the results are the same. Note that the max operator is also commutative, as are many other operators such as min, sum, and product. Obviously, not all operators are commutative. For example, addition is commutative $(1+2 = 2+1)$, whereas integer subtraction is not $(1 - 2 \neq 2 - 1)$.

The parallel reduction pattern in Fig. 10.3 is called a reduction tree because it looks like a tree whose leaves are the original input elements and whose root is the final result. The term *reduction tree* is not to be confused with tree data structures, in which the nodes are linked either explicitly with pointers or implicitly with assigned positions. In reduction trees the edges are conceptual, reflecting information flow from operations performed in one time step to those in the next time step.

The parallel operations result in significant improvement over the sequential code in the number of time steps needed to produce the final result. In the example in Fig. 10.3 the for-loop in the sequential code iterates eight times, or takes eight time steps, to visit all of the input elements and produce the final result. On the other hand, with the parallel operations in Fig. 10.3 the parallel reduction tree approach takes only three time steps: four max operations during the first time step, two during the second, and one during the third. This is a decrease of $5/8 = 62.5\%$ in terms of number of time steps, or a speedup of $8/3 = 2.67$. There is, of course, a cost to the parallel approach: One must have enough hardware comparators to perform up to four max operations in the same time step. For N input values, a reduction tree performs $\frac{1}{2}$ N operations during the first round, $\frac{1}{4}$ N operations in the second round, and so on. Therefore the total number of operations that are performed is defined by the geometric series $\frac{1}{2}$ N$+\frac{1}{4}$ N$+\frac{1}{8}$ N$+\dots \frac{1}{N}$ N $= N - 1$ operations, which is similar to the sequential algorithm.

In terms of time steps, a reduction tree takes $\log_2 N$ steps to complete the reduction process for N input values. Thus it can reduce $N = 1024$ input values in just ten steps, assuming that there are enough execution resources. During the first step, we need $\frac{1}{2}$ N $= 512$ execution resources! Note that the number of resources that are needed diminishes quickly as we progress in time steps. During the final time step, we need to have only one execution resource. The level of parallelism at each time step is the same as the number of execution units that are required. It is interesting to calculate the average level of parallelism across all time steps. The average parallelism is the total number of operations that are performed divided by the number of time steps, which is $(N - 1)/\log_2 N$. For $N = 1024$ the average parallelism across the ten time steps is 102.3, whereas the peak parallelism is 512 (during the first time step). Such variation in the level of parallelism and resource consumption across time steps makes reduction trees a challenging parallel pattern for parallel computing systems.

Fig. 10.5 shows a sum reduction tree example for eight input values. Everything we presented so far about the number of time steps and resources consumed for max reduction trees is also applicable to sum reduction trees. It takes $\log_2 8 = 3$ time steps to complete the reduction using a maximum of four adders. We will use this example to illustrate the design of sum reduction kernels.

Parallel Reduction in Sports and Competitions

Parallel reduction has been used in sports and competitions long before the dawn of computing. Fig. 10.4 shows the schedule of the 2010 World Cup quarterfinals, semifinals, and the final game in South Africa. It should be clear that this is just a rearranged reduction tree. The elimination process of the World Cup is a maximum reduction in which the maximum operator returns the team that "beats" the other team. The tournament "reduction" is done in multiple rounds. The teams are divided into pairs. During the first round, all pairs play in parallel. Winners of the first round advance to the second round, whose winners advance to the third round, and so on. With eight teams entering a tournament, four winners will emerge from the first round (quarterfinals in Fig. 10.4), two from the second round (semifinals in Fig. 10.4), and one final winner (champion) from the third round (final in Fig. 10.4). Each round is a time step of the reduction process.

FIGURE 10.4

The 2010 World Cup Finals as a reduction tree.

It should be easy to see that even with 1024 teams, it takes only 10 rounds to determine the final winner. The trick is to have enough resources to hold the 512 games in parallel during the first round, 256 games in the second round, 128 games in the third round, and so on. With enough resources, even with 60,000 teams, we can determine the final winner in just 16 rounds. It is interesting to note that while reduction trees can greatly speed up the reduction process, they also consume quite a bit of resources. In the World Cup example, a game requires a large soccer stadium, officials, and staff as well as hotels and restaurants to accommodate the massive number of fans in the audience. The four quarterfinals in Fig. 10.4 were played in three cities (Nelson Mandela Bay/Port Elizabeth, Cape Town, and Johannesburg) that all together provided enough resources to host the four games. Note that the two games in Johannesburg were played on two different days. Thus sharing resources between two games made the reduction process take more time. We will see similar tradeoffs in computation reduction trees.

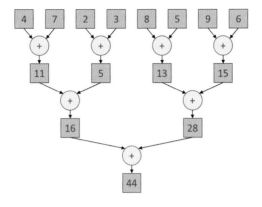

FIGURE 10.5

A parallel sum reduction tree.

10.3 A simple reduction kernel

We are now ready to develop a simple kernel to perform the parallel sum reduction tree shown in Fig. 10.5. Since the reduction tree requires collaboration across all threads, which is not possible across an entire grid, we will start by implementing a kernel that performs a sum reduction tree within a single block. That is, for an input array of N elements we will call this simple kernel and launch a grid with one block of ½N threads. Since a block can have up to 1024 threads, we can process up to 2048 input elements. We will eliminate this limitation in Section 10.8. During the first time step, all ½N threads will participate, and each thread adds two elements to produce ½N partial sums. During the next time step, half of the threads will drop off, and only ¼N threads will continue to participate to produce ¼N partial sums. This process will continue until the last time step, in which only one thread will remain and produce the total sum.

Fig. 10.6 shows the code of the simple sum kernel function, and Fig. 10.7 illustrates the execution of the reduction tree that is implemented by this code. Note that in Fig. 10.7 the time progresses from top to bottom. We assume that the input array is in the global memory and that a pointer to the array is passed as an argument when the kernel function is called. Each thread is assigned to a data location that is `2*threadIdx.x` (line 02). That is, the threads are assigned to the even locations in the input array: thread 0 to `input[0]`, thread 1 to `input[2]`, thread 2 to `input[4]`, and so on, as shown in the top row of Fig. 10.7. Each thread will be the "owner" of the location to which it is assigned and will be the only thread that writes into that location. The design of the kernel follows the "owner computes" approach, in which every data location is owned by a unique thread and can be updated only by that owner thread.

```
01     __global__ void SimpleSumReductionKernel(float* input, float* output) {
02         unsigned int i = 2*threadIdx.x;
03         for (unsigned int stride = 1; stride <= blockDim.x; stride *= 2) {
04             if (threadIdx.x % stride == 0) {
05                 input[i] += input[i + stride];
06             }
07             __syncthreads();
08         }
09         if(threadIdx.x == 0) {
10             *output = input[0];
11         }
12     }
```

FIGURE 10.6

A simple sum reduction kernel.

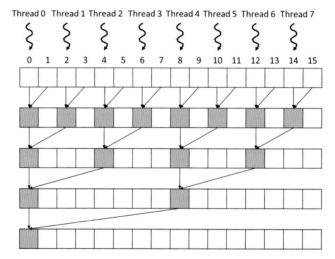

FIGURE 10.7

The assignment of threads ("owners") to the `input` array locations and progress of execution over time for the `SimpleSumReudctionKernel` in Fig. 10.6. The time progresses from top to bottom, and each level corresponds to one iteration of the for-loop.

The top row of Fig. 10.7 shows the assignment of threads to the locations of the input array, and each of the subsequent rows shows the writes to the input array locations at each time step, that is, iteration of the for-loop in Fig. 10.6 (line 03). The locations that the kernel overwrites in each iteration of the for-loop are marked as filled positions of the input array in Fig. 10.7. For example, at the end of the first iteration, locations with even indices are overwritten with the partial sums of pairs of the original elements (0–1, 2–3, 4–5, etc.) in the input array. At the end of the second iteration, the locations whose indices are multiples of 4 are overwritten with the partial sum of four adjacent original elements (0–3, 4–7, etc.) in the input array.

In Fig. 10.6 a stride variable is used for the threads to reach for the appropriate partial sums for accumulation into their owner locations. The stride variable is initialized to 1 (line 03). The value of the stride variable is doubled in each iteration so the stride variable value will be 1, 2, 4, 8, etc., until it becomes greater than `blockIdx.x`, the total number of threads in the block. As shown in Fig. 10.7, each active thread in an iteration uses the stride variable to add into its owned location the input array element that is of distance stride away. For example, in iteration 1, Thread 0 uses stride value 1 to add input[1] into its owned position input[0]. This updates input[0] to the partial sum of the first pair of original values of input[0] and input[1]. In the second iteration, Thread 0 uses stride value 2 to add input[2] to input[0]. At this time, input[2] contains the sum of the original values of input[2] and input[3] and input[0] contains the sum of the original values of input[0] and input[1]. So, after the second iteration, input[0] contains the sum of the original values of the first four elements of the input array. After the last iteration, input[0] contains the sum of all original elements of the input array and thus the result of the sum reduction. This value is written by Thread 0 as the final output (line 10).

We now turn to the if-statement in Fig. 10.6 (line 04). The condition of the if-statement is set up to select the active threads in each iteration. As shown in Fig. 10.7, during iteration n, the threads whose thread index (`threadIdx.x`) values are multiples of 2^n are to perform addition. The condition is `threadIdx.x % stride == 0`, which tests whether the thread index value is a multiple of the value of the stride variable. Recall that the value of stride is 1, 2, 4, 8, ... through the iterations, or 2^n for iteration n. Thus the condition indeed tests whether the thread index values are multiples of 2^n. Recall that all threads execute the same kernel code. The threads whose thread index value satisfies the if-condition are the active threads that perform the addition statement (line 05). The threads whose thread index values fail to satisfy the condition are the inactive threads that skip the addition statement. As the iterations progress, fewer and fewer threads remain active. At the last iteration, only thread 0 remains active and produces the sum reduction result.

The `__syncthreads()` statement (line 07 of Fig. 10.6) in the for-loop ensures that all partial sums that were calculated by the iteration have been written into their destination locations in the input array before any one of threads is allowed to begin the next iteration. This way, all threads that enter an iteration will be able to correctly use the partial sums that were produced in the previous iteration. For example, after the first iteration the even elements will be replaced by the pairwise partial sums. The `__syncthreads()` statement ensures that all these partial sums from the first iteration have indeed been written to the even locations of the input array and are ready to be used by the active threads in the second iteration.

10.4 Minimizing control divergence

The kernel code in Fig. 10.6 implements the parallel reduction tree in Fig. 10.7 and produces the expected sum reduction result. Unfortunately, its management of active and inactive threads in each iteration results in a high degree of control divergence. For example, as shown in Fig. 10.7, only those threads whose `threadIdx.x` values are even will execute the addition statement during the second iteration. As we explained in Chapter 4, Compute Architecture and Scheduling, control divergence can significantly reduce the execution resource utilization efficiency, or the percentage of resources that are used in generating useful results. In this example, all 32 threads in a warp consume execution resources, but only half of them are active, wasting half of the execution resources. The waste of execution resources due to divergence increases over time. During the third iteration, only one-fourth of the threads in a warp are active, wasting three-quarters of the execution resources. During iteration 5, only one out of the 32 threads in a warp are active, wasting $^{31}/_{32}$ of the execution resources.

If the size of the input array is greater than 32, entire warps will become inactive after the fifth iteration. For example, for an input size of 256, 128 threads or four warps would be launched. All four warps would have the same divergence pattern, as we explained in the previous paragraph for iterations 1 through 5. During the sixth iteration, warp 1 and warp 3 would become completely inactive and thus exhibit no control divergence. On the other hand, warp 0 and warp 2 would have only one active thread, exhibiting control divergence and wasting $^{31}/_{32}$ of the execution resource. During the seventh iteration, only warp 0 would be active, exhibiting control divergence and wasting $^{31}/_{32}$ of the execution resource.

In general, the execution resource utilization efficiency for an input array of size N can be calculated as the ratio between the total number of active threads to the total number of execution resources that are consumed. The total number of execution resources that are consumed is proportional to the total number of active warps across all iterations, since every active warp, no matter how few of its threads are active, consumes full execution resources. This number can be calculated as follows:

$$\left(N/64^*5 + N/64^*{}^{1\!/_2} + N/64^*{}^{1\!/_4} + \ldots + 1\right)^*32$$

Here, N/64 is the total number of warps that are launched, since N/2 threads will be launched and every 32 threads form a warp. The N/64 term is multiplied by 5 because all launched warps are active for five iterations. After the fifth iteration the number of warps is reduced by half in each successive iteration. The expression in parentheses gives the total number of active warps across all the iterations. The second term reflects that each active warp consumes full execution resources for all 32 threads regardless of the number of active threads in these warps. For an input array size of 256, the consumed execution resource is $(4^*5+2+1)^*32 = 736$.

The number of execution results committed by the active threads is the total number of active threads across all iterations:

$$N/64^*(32 + 16 + 8 + 4 + 2 + 1) + N/64^*{}^{1\!/_2}{}^*1 + N/64^*{}^{1\!/_4}{}^*1 + \ldots + 1$$

The terms in the parenthesis give the active threads in the first five iterations for all N/64 warps. Starting at the sixth iteration, the number of active warps is reduced by half in each iteration, and there is only one active thread in each active warp. For an input array size of 256, the total number of committed results is $4*(32+16+8+4+2+1)+2+1 = 255$. This result should be intuitive because the total number of operations that are needed to reduce 256 values is 255.

Putting the previous two results together, we find that the execution resource utilization efficiency for an input array size of 256 is $255/736 = 0.35$. This ratio states that the parallel execution resources did not achieve their full potential in speeding up this computation. On average, only about 35% of the resources consumed contributed to the sum reduction result. That is, we used only about 35% of the hardware's potential to speed up the computation.

Based on this analysis, we see that there is widespread control divergence across warps and over time. As the reader might have wondered, there may be a better way to assign threads to the input array locations to reduce control divergence and improve resource utilization efficiency. The problem with the assignment illustrated in Fig. 10.7 is that the partial sum locations become increasingly distant from each other, and thus the active threads that own these locations are also increasingly distant from each other as time progresses. This increasing distance between active threads contributes to the increasing level of control divergence.

There is indeed a better assignment strategy that significantly reduces control divergence. The idea is that we should arrange the threads and their owned positions so that they can remain close to each other as time progresses. That is, we would like to have the stride value decrease, rather than increase, over time. The revised assignment strategy is shown in Fig. 10.8 for an input array of 16 elements. Here, we assign the threads to the first half of the locations. During the first iteration, each thread reaches halfway across the input array and adds an input element

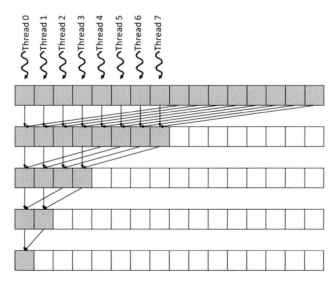

FIGURE 10.8

A better assignment of threads to input array locations for reduced control divergence.

to its owner location. In our example, thread 0 adds input[8] to its owned position input[0], thread 1 adds input[9] to its owned position input[1], and so on. During each subsequent iteration, half of the active threads drop off, and all remaining active threads add an input element whose position is the number of active threads away from its owner position. In our example, during the third iteration there are two remaining active threads: Thread 0 adds input[2] into its owned position input [0], and thread 1 adds input[3] into its owned position input[1]. Note that if we compare the operation and operand orders of Fig. 10.8 to Fig. 10.7, there is effectively a reordering of the operands in the list rather than just inserting parentheses in different ways. For the result to always remain the same with such reordering, the operation must be commutative as well as being associative.

Fig. 10.9 shows a kernel with some subtle but critical changes to the simple kernel in Fig. 10.6. The owner position variable i is set to `threadIdx.x` rather than `2*threadIdx.x` (line 02). Thus the owner positions of all threads are now adjacent to each other, as illustrated in Fig. 10.8. The stride value is initialized as `blockDim.x` and is reduced by half until it reaches 1 (line 03). In each iteration, only the threads whose indices are smaller than the stride value remain active (line 04). Thus all active threads are of consecutive thread indices, as shown in Fig. 10.8. Instead of adding neighbor elements in the first round, it adds elements that are half a section away from each other, and the section size is always twice the number of remaining active threads. All pairs that are added during the first round are `blockDim.x` away from each other. After the first iteration, all the pairwise sums are stored in the first half of the input array, as shown in Fig. 10.8. The loop divides the stride by 2 before entering the next iteration. Thus for the second iteration the stride variable value is half of the `blockDim.x` value. That is, the remaining active threads add elements that are a quarter of a section away from each other during the second iteration.

The kernel in Fig. 10.9 still has an if-statement (line 04) in the loop. The number of threads that execute an addition operation (line 06) in each iteration is the same as in Fig. 10.6. Then why should there be a difference in control divergence between the two kernels? The answer lies in the positions of threads that perform the addition operation relative to those that do not. Let us consider the example

```
01    __global__ void ConvergentSumReductionKernel(float* input, float* output) {
02        unsigned int i = threadIdx.x;
03        for (unsigned int stride = blockDim.x; stride >= 1; stride /= 2) {
04            if (threadIdx.x < stride) {
05                input[i] += input[i + stride];
06            }
07            __syncthreads();
08        }
09        if(threadIdx.x == 0) {
10            *output = input[0];
11        }
12    }
```

FIGURE 10.9

A kernel with less control divergence and improved execution resource utilization efficiency.

of an input array of 256 elements. During the first iteration, all threads are active, so there is no control divergence. During the second iteration, threads 0 through 63 execute the add statement (active), while threads 64 through 127 do not (inactive). The pairwise sums are stored in elements 0 through 63 during the second iteration. Since the warps consist of 32 threads with consecutive threadIdx.x values, all threads in warp 0 through warp 1 execute the add statement, whereas all threads in warp 2 through warp 3 become inactive. Since all threads in each warp take the same path of execution, there is no control divergence!

However, the kernel in Fig. 10.9 does not completely eliminate the divergence caused by the if-statement. The reader should verify that for the 256-element example, starting with the fourth iteration, the number of threads that execute the addition operation will fall below 32. That is, the final five iterations will have only 16, 8, 4, 2, and 1 thread(s) performing the addition. This means that the kernel execution will still have divergence in these iterations. However, the number of iterations of the loop that has divergence is reduced from ten to five. We can calculate the total number of execution resources consumed as follows:

$$\left(\mathrm{N}/64^*1 + \mathrm{N}/64^*{}^1\!/_2 + \ldots + 1 + 5^*1\right)^*32$$

The part in parentheses reflects the fact that in each subsequent iteration, half of the warps become entirely inactive and no longer consume execution resources. This series continues until there is only one full warp of active threads. The last term (5^*1) reflects the fact that for the final five iterations, there is only one active warp, and all its 32 threads consume execution resources even though only a fraction of the threads are active. Thus the sum in the parentheses gives the total number of warp executions through all iterations, which, when multiplied by 32, gives the total amount of execution resources that are consumed.

For our 256-element example the execution resources that are consumed are $(4+2+1+5^*1)^*32 = 384$, which is almost half of 736, the resources that were consumed by the kernel in Fig. 10.6. Since the number of active threads in each iteration did not change from Fig. 10.7 to Fig. 10.8, the efficiency of the new kernel in Fig. 10.9 is $255/384 = 66\%$, which is almost double the efficiency of the kernel in Fig. 10.6. Note also that since the warps are scheduled to take turns executing in a streaming multiprocessor of limited execution resources, the total execution time will also improve with the reduced resource consumption.

The difference between the kernels in Fig. 10.6 and Fig. 10.9 is small but can have a significant performance impact. It requires someone with clear understanding of the execution of threads on the single-instruction, multiple-data hardware of the device to be able to confidently make such adjustments.

10.5 Minimizing memory divergence

The simple kernel in Fig. 10.6 has another performance issue: memory divergence. As we explained in Chapter 5, Memory Architecture and Data Locality, it is important to achieve memory coalescing within each warp. That is, adjacent threads in a warp should access adjacent locations when they access global memory. Unfortunately, in Fig. 10.7, adjacent threads do not access adjacent locations. In each iteration, each thread performs two global memory reads and one global memory write. The first read is from its owned location, the second read is from the location that is of stride distance away from its owned location, and the write is to its owned location. Since the locations owned by adjacent thread are not adjacent locations, the accesses that are made by adjacent threads will not be fully coalesced. During each iteration the memory locations that are collectively accessed by a warp are of stride distance away from each other.

For example, as shown in Fig. 10.7, when all threads in a warp perform their first read during the first iteration, the locations are two elements away from each other. As a result, two global memory requests are triggered, and half the data returned will not be used by the threads. The same behavior occurs for the second read and the write. During the second iteration, every other thread drops out, and the locations that are collectively accessed by the warp are four elements away from each other. Two global memory requests are again performed, and only one-fourth of the data returned will be used by the threads. This will continue until there is only one active thread for each warp that remains active. Only when there is one active thread in the warp will the warp perform one global memory request. Thus the total number of global memory requests is as follows:

$$(N/64 * 5 * 2 + N/64 * 1 + N/64 * \frac{1}{2} + N/64 * \frac{1}{4} + \ldots + 1) * 3$$

The first term $(N/64 * 5 * 2)$ corresponds to the first five iterations, in which all $N/64$ warps have two or more active threads, so each warp performs two global memory requests. The remaining terms account for the final iterations, in which each warp has only one active thread and performs one global memory request and half of the warps drop out in each subsequent iteration. The multiplication by 3 accounts for the two reads and one write by each active thread during each iteration. In the 256-element example the total number of global memory requests performed by the kernel is $(4 * 5 * 2 + 4 + 2 + 1) * 3 = 141$.

For the kernel in Fig. 10.9 the adjacent threads in each warp always access adjacent locations in the global memory, so the accesses are always coalesced. As a result, each warp triggers only one global memory request on any read or write. As the iterations progress, entire warps drop out, so no global memory access will be performed by any thread in these inactive warps. Half of the warps drop out in each iteration until there is only one warp for the final five iterations. Therefore the total number of global memory requests performed by the kernel is as follows:

$$((N/64 + N/64 * \frac{1}{2} + N/64 * \frac{1}{4} + \ldots + 1) + 5) * 3$$

For the 256-element example the total number of global memory requests performed is $((4 + 2 + 1) + 5) * 3 = 36$. The improved kernel results in $141/36 = 3.9 \times$ fewer global memory requests. Since DRAM bandwidth is a limited resource, the execution time is likely to be significantly longer for the simple kernel in Fig. 10.6.

For a 2048-element example the total number of global memory requests that are performed by the kernel in Fig. 10.6 is $(32*5*2+32+16+8+4+2+1)*3 = 1149$, whereas the number of global memory requests that are performed by the kernel in Fig. 10.9 is $(32+16+8+4+2+1+5)*3 = 204$. The ratio is 5.6, even more than in the 256-element example. This is because of the inefficient execution pattern of the kernel in Fig. 10.6, in which there are more active warps during the initial five iterations of the execution and each active warp triggers twice the number of global memory requests as the convergent kernel in Fig. 10.9.

In conclusion, the convergent kernel offers more efficiency in using both execution resources and DRAM bandwidth. The advantage comes from both reduced control divergence and improved memory coalescing.

10.6 Minimizing global memory accesses

The convergent kernel in Fig. 10.9 can be further improved by using shared memory. Note that in each iteration, threads write their partial sum result values out to the global memory, and these values are reread by the same threads and other threads in the next iteration. Since the shared memory has much shorter latency and higher bandwidth than the global memory, we can further improve the execution speed by keeping the partial sum results in the shared memory. This idea is illustrated in Fig. 10.10.

The strategy for using the shared memory is implemented in the kernel shown in Fig. 10.11. The idea is to use each thread to load and add two of the original

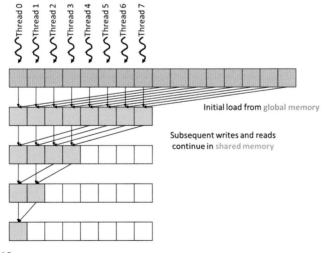

FIGURE 10.10

Using shared memory to reduce accesses to the global memory.

```
01    __global__ void SharedMemorySumReductionKernel(float* input) {
02        __shared__ float input_s[BLOCK_DIM];
03        unsigned int t = threadIdx.x;
04        input_s[t] = input[t] + input[t + BLOCK_DIM];
05        for (unsigned int stride = blockDim.x/2; stride >= 1; stride /= 2) {
06            __syncthreads();
07            if (threadIdx.x < stride) {
08                input_s[t] += input_s[t + stride];
09            }
10        }
11        if (threadIdx.x == 0) {
12            *output = input_s[0];
13        }
14    }
```

FIGURE 10.11

A kernel that uses shared memory to reduce global memory accesses.

elements before writing the partial sum into the shared memory (line 04). Since the first iteration is already done when accessing the global memory locations outside the loop, the for-loop starts with blockDim.x/2 (line 04) instead of blockDim.x. The __syncthreads() is moved to the beginning of the loop to ensure that we synchronize between the shared memory accesses and the first iteration of the loop. The threads proceed with the remaining iterations by reading and writing the shared memory (line 08). Finally, at the end of the kernel, thread 0 writes the sum into output, maintaining the same behavior as in the previous kernels (lines 11–13).

Using the kernel in Fig. 10.11, the number of global memory accesses are reduced to the initial loading of the original contents of the input array and the final write to input[0]. Thus for an N-element reduction the number of global memory accesses is just N+1. Note also that both global memory reads in Fig. 10.11 (line 04) are coalesced. So with coalescing, there will be only (N/32) +1 global memory requests. For the 256-element example the total number of global memory requests that are triggered will be reduced from 36 for the kernel in Fig. 10.9 to 8+1 = 9 for the shared memory kernel in Fig. 10.10, a 4× improvement. Another benefit of using shared memory, besides reducing the number of global memory accesses, is that the input array is not modified. This property is useful if the original values of the array are needed for some other computation in another part of the program.

10.7 Hierarchical reduction for arbitrary input length

All the kernels that we have studied so far assume that they will be launched with one thread block. The main reason for this assumption is that __syncthreads() is used as a barrier synchronization among all the active threads. Recall that __syncthreads() can be used only among threads in the same block. This limits the level of parallelism to 1024 threads on current hardware. For large input arrays that contain millions or even billions of elements, we can benefit from launching more threads to further accelerate the reduction process. Since we do not have a good way to perform barrier synchronization among threads in different blocks, we will need to allow threads in different blocks to execute independently.

Fig. 10.12 illustrates the concept of hierarchical, segmented multiblock reduction using atomic operations, and Fig. 10.13 shows the corresponding kernel implementation. The idea is to partition the input array into segments so that each segment is of appropriate size for a block. All blocks then independently execute a reduction tree and accumulate their results to the final output using an atomic add operation.

The partitioning is done by assigning a different value to the `segment` variable according to the thread's block index (line 03). The size of each segment is

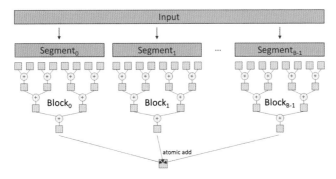

FIGURE 10.12

Segmented multiblock reduction using atomic operations.

```
01    __global__ SegmentedSumReductionKernel(float* input, float* output) {
02        __shared__ float input_s[BLOCK_DIM];
03        unsigned int segment = 2*blockDim.x*blockIdx.x;
04        unsigned int i = segment + threadIdx.x;
05        unsigned int t = threadIdx.x;
06        input_s[t] = input[i] + input[i + BLOCK_DIM];
07        for (unsigned int stride = blockDim.x/2; stride >= 1; stride /= 2){
08            __syncthreads();
09            if (t < stride) {
10                input_s[t] += input_s[t + stride];
11            }
12        }
13        if (t == 0) {
14            atomicAdd(output, input_s[0]);
15        }
16    }
```

FIGURE 10.13

A segmented multiblock sum reduction kernel using atomic operations.

2*blockDim.x. That is, each block processes 2*blockDim.x elements. Thus when we multiply the size of each segment by blockIdx.x of a block, we have the starting location of the segment to be processed by the block. For example, if we have 1024 threads in a block, the segment size would be 2*1024 = 2048. The starting locations of segments would be 0 for block 0, 2048 (2048*1) for block 1, 4096 (2048*2) for block 2, and so on.

Once we know the starting location for each block, all threads in a block can simply work on the assigned segment as if it is the entire input data. Within a block, we assign the owned location to each thread by adding the threadIdx.x to the segment starting location for the block to which the thread belongs (line 04). The local variable i holds the owned location of the thread in the global input array, whereas t holds the owned location of the thread in the shared input_s array. Line 06 is adapted to use i instead of t when accessing the global input array. The for-loop from Fig. 10.11 is used without change. This is because each block has its own private input_s in the shared memory, so it can be accessed with t = threadIdx.x as if the segment is the entire input.

Once the reduction tree for-loop is complete, the partial sum for the segment is in input_s[0]. The if-statement in line 16 of Fig. 10.13 selects thread 0 to contribute the value in input_s[0] to output, as illustrated in the bottom part of Fig. 10.12. This is done with an atomic add, as shown in line 14 of Fig. 10.13. Once all blocks of the grid have completed execution, the kernel will return, and the total sum is in the memory location pointed to by output.

10.8 Thread coarsening for reduced overhead

The reduction kernels that we have worked with so far all try to maximize parallelism by using as many threads as possible. That is, for a reduction of N elements, N/2 threads are launched. With a thread block size of 1024 threads, the resulting number of thread blocks is N/2048. However, in processors with limited execution resources the hardware may have only enough resources to execute a portion of the thread blocks in parallel. In this case, the hardware will serialize the surplus thread blocks, executing a new thread block whenever an old one has completed.

To parallelize reduction, we have actually paid a heavy price to distribute the work across multiple thread blocks. As we saw in earlier sections, hardware underutilization increases with each successive stage of the reduction tree because of more warps becoming idle and the final warp experiencing more control divergence. The phase in which the hardware is underutilized occurs for every thread block that we launch. It is an inevitable price to pay if the thread blocks are to actually run in parallel. However, if the hardware is to serialize these thread blocks, we are better off serializing them ourselves in a more efficient manner. As we discussed in Chapter 6, Performance Considerations, thread granularity coarsening, or *thread coarsening* for brevity, is a category of optimizations that serialize some of the work into fewer threads to reduce parallelization overhead. We start by showing an implementation of parallel reduction with thread coarsening applied by assigning more elements to each thread block. We then further elaborate on how this implementation reduces hardware underutilization.

Fig. 10.14 illustrates how thread coarsening can be applied to the example in Fig. 10.10. In Fig. 10.10, each thread block received 16 elements, which is two elements per thread. Each thread independently adds the two elements for which it is responsible; then the threads collaborate to execute a reduction tree. In Fig. 10.14 we coarsen the thread block by a factor of 2. Hence each thread block receives twice the number of elements, that is, 32 elements, which is four elements per thread. In this case, each thread independently adds four elements before the threads collaborate to execute a reduction tree. The three steps to add the four elements are illustrated by the first three rows of arrows in Fig. 10.14. Note that all threads are active during these three steps. Moreover, since the threads independently add the four elements for which they are responsible, they do not need to synchronize, and they do not need to store their partial sums to shared memory until after all four elements have been added. The remaining steps in performing the reduction tree are the same as those in Fig. 10.10.

Fig. 10.15 shows the kernel code for implementing reduction with thread coarsening for the multiblock segmented kernel. Compared to Fig. 10.13, the kernel has two main differences. The first difference is that when the beginning of the block's segment is identified, we multiply by COARSE_FACTOR to reflect the fact that the size of the block's segment is COARSE_FACTOR times larger (line 03). The second difference is that when adding the elements for which the thread is responsible, rather than just adding two elements (line 06 in Fig. 10.13), we use a coarsening loop to iterate over the elements and add them based on

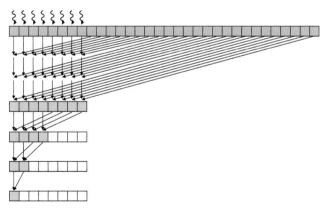

FIGURE 10.14

Thread coarsening in reduction.

```
01    __global__ CoarsenedSumReductionKernel(float* input, float* output) {
02        __shared__ float input_s[BLOCK_DIM];
03        unsigned int segment = COARSE_FACTOR*2*blockDim.x*blockIdx.x;
04        unsigned int i = segment + threadIdx.x;
05        unsigned int t = threadIdx.x;
06        float sum = input[i];
07        for(unsigned int tile = 1; tile < COARSE_FACTOR*2; ++tile) {
08            sum += input[i + tile*BLOCK_DIM];
09        }
10        input_s[t] = sum;
11        for (unsigned int stride = blockDim.x/2; stride >= 1; stride /= 2){
12            __syncthreads();
13            if (t < stride) {
14                input_s[t] += input_s[t + stride];
15            }
16        }
17        if (t == 0) {
18            atomicAdd(output, input_s[0]);
19        }
20    }
```

FIGURE 10.15

Sum reduction kernel with thread coarsening.

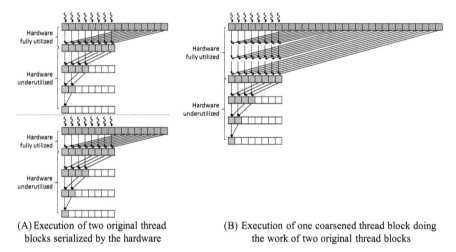

(A) Execution of two original thread   (B) Execution of one coarsened thread block doing
blocks serialized by the hardware   the work of two original thread blocks

FIGURE 10.16

Comparing parallel reduction with and without thread coarsening.

COARSE_FACTOR (lines 06−09 in Fig. 10.15). Note that all threads are active throughout this coarsening loop, the partial sum is accumulated to the local variable sum, and no calls to __syncthreads() are made in the loop because the threads act independently.

Fig. 10.16 compares the execution of two original thread blocks without coarsening serialized by the hardware, shown in Fig. 10.16A with one coarsened thread block performing the work of two thread blocks, shown in Fig. 10.16B. In

Fig. 10.16A the first thread block performs one step in which each thread adds the two elements for which it is responsible. All threads are active during this step, so the hardware is fully utilized. The remaining three steps execute the reduction tree in which half the threads drop out each step, underutilizing the hardware. Moreover, each step requires a barrier synchronization as well as accesses to shared memory. When the first thread block is done, the hardware then schedules the second thread block, which follows the same steps but on a different segment of the data. Overall, the two blocks collectively take a total of eight steps, of which two steps fully utilize the hardware and six steps underutilize the hardware and require barrier synchronization and shared memory access.

By contrast, in Fig. 10.16B the same amount of data is processed by only a single thread block that is coarsened by a factor of 2. This thread block initially takes three steps in which each thread adds the four elements for which it is responsible. All threads are active during all three steps, so the hardware is fully utilized, and no barrier synchronizations or accesses to shared memory are performed. The remaining three steps execute the reduction tree in which half the threads drop out each step, underutilizing the hardware, and barrier synchronization and accesses to shared memory are needed. Overall, only six steps are needed (instead of eight), of which three steps (instead of two) fully utilize the hardware and three steps (instead of six) underutilize the hardware and require barrier synchronization and shared memory access. Therefore thread coarsening effectively reduces the overhead from hardware underutilization, synchronization, and access to shared memory.

Theoretically, we can increase the coarsening factor well beyond two. However, one must keep in mind that as we coarsen threads, less work will be done in parallel. Therefore increasing the coarsening factor will reduce the amount of data parallelism that is being exploited by the hardware. If we increase the coarsening factor too much, such that we launch fewer thread blocks than the hardware is capable of executing, we will no longer be able to take full advantage of the parallel hardware execution resources. The best coarsening factor ensures that there are enough thread blocks to fully utilize the hardware, which usually depends on the total size of the input as well as the characteristics of the specific device.

10.9 Summary

The parallel reduction pattern is important, as it plays a key row in many data-processing applications. Although the sequential code is simple, it should be clear to the reader that several techniques, such as thread index assignment for reduced divergence, using shared memory for reduced global memory accesses, segmented reduction with atomic operations, and thread coarsening, are needed to achieve high performance for large inputs. The reduction computation is also an important foundation for the prefix-sum pattern that is an important algorithm component for parallelizing many applications and will be the topic of Chapter 11, Prefix Sum (Scan).

Exercises

1. For the simple reduction kernel in Fig. 10.6, if the number of elements is 1024 and the warp size is 32, how many warps in the block will have divergence during the fifth iteration?
2. For the improved reduction kernel in Fig. 10.9, if the number of elements is 1024 and the warp size is 32, how many warps will have divergence during the fifth iteration?
3. Modify the kernel in Fig. 10.9 to use the access pattern illustrated below.

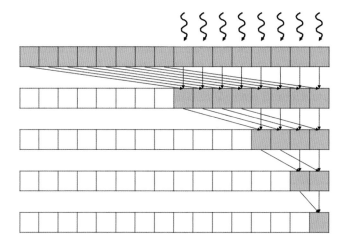

4. Modify the kernel in Fig. 10.15 to perform a max reduction instead of a sum reduction.
5. Modify the kernel in Fig. 10.15 to work for an arbitrary length input that is not necessarily a multiple of COARSE_FACTOR*2*blockDim.x. Add an extra parameter N to the kernel that represents the length of the input.
6. Assume that parallel reduction is to be applied on the following input array:

6	2	7	4	5	8	3	1

Show how the contents of the array change after each iteration if:

a. The unoptimized kernel in Fig. 10.6 is used.

Initial array: | 6 | 2 | 7 | 4 | 5 | 8 | 3 | 1 |

b. The kernel optimized for coalescing and divergence in Fig. 10.9 is used.

Initial array: | 6 | 2 | 7 | 4 | 5 | 8 | 3 | 1 |

Prefix sum (scan)

An introduction to work efficiency in parallel algorithms

11

With special contributions from Li-Wen Chang, Juan Gómez-Luna and John Owens

Chapter Outline

11.1 Background 236
11.2 Parallel scan with the Kogge-Stone algorithm 238
11.3 Speed and work efficiency consideration 244
11.4 Parallel scan with the Brent-Kung algorithm 246
11.5 Coarsening for even more work efficiency 251
11.6 Segmented parallel scan for arbitrary-length inputs 253
11.7 Single-pass scan for memory access efficiency 256
11.8 Summary 259
Exercises 260
References 261

Our next parallel pattern is prefix sum, which is also commonly known as scan. Parallel scan is frequently used to parallelize seemingly sequential operations, such as resource allocation, work assignment, and polynomial evaluation. In general, if a computation is naturally described as a mathematical recursion in which each item in a series is defined in terms of the previous item, it can likely be parallelized as a parallel scan operation. Parallel scan plays a key role in massively parallel computing for a simple reason: Any sequential section of an application can drastically limit the overall performance of the application. Many such sequential sections can be converted into parallel computation with parallel scan. For this reason, parallel scan is often used as a primitive operation in parallel algorithms that perform radix sort, quick sort, string comparison, polynomial evaluation, solving recurrences, tree operations, and stream compaction. The radix sort example will be presented in Chapter 13, Sorting.

Another reason why parallel scan is an important parallel pattern is that it is a typical example of where the work performed by some parallel algorithms can have higher complexity than the work performed by a sequential algorithm, leading to a tradeoff that needs to be carefully made between algorithm complexity and parallelization. As we will show, a slight increase in algorithm complexity can make parallel

Programming Massively Parallel Processors. DOI: https://doi.org/10.1016/B978-0-323-91231-0.00022-7

scan run more slowly than sequential scan for large datasets. Such consideration is becoming even more important in the age of "big data," in which massive datasets challenge tradition algorithms that have high computational complexity.

11.1 Background

Mathematically, an *inclusive scan* operation takes a binary associative operator $\oplus$ and an input array of n elements $[x_0, x_1, \ldots, x_{n-1}]$, and returns the following output array:

$$[x_0, \ (x_0 \oplus x_1), \ldots, (x_0 \oplus x_1 \oplus \ldots \oplus x_{n-1})]$$

For example, if $\oplus$ is addition, an inclusive scan operation on the input array [3 1 7 0 4 1 6 3] would return [2, 3+1, 3+1+7, 3+1+7+0, $\ldots$, 3+1+7+0+4+1+6+3] =[3 4 11 11 15 16 22 25]. The name "inclusive" scan comes from the fact that each output element *includes* the effect of the corresponding input element.

We can illustrate the applications for inclusive scan operations using an example of cutting sausage for a group of people. Assume that we have a 40-inch sausage to be served to eight people. Each person has ordered a different amount in terms of inches: 3, 1, 7, 0, 4, 1, 6, and 3. That is, Person 0 wants 3 inches of sausage, Person 1 wants 1 inch, and so on. We can cut the sausage either sequentially or in parallel. The sequential way is very straightforward. We first cut a 3-inch section for Person 0. The sausage is now 37 inches long. We then cut a one-inch section for Person 1. The sausage becomes 36 inches long. We can continue to cut more sections until we serve the 3-inch section to Person 7. At that point, we have served a total of 25 inches of sausage, with 15 inches remaining.

With an inclusive scan operation, we can calculate the locations of all the cutting points based on the amount ordered by each person. That is, given an addition operation and an order input array [3 1 7 0 4 1 6 3], the inclusive scan operation returns [3 4 11 11 15 16 22 25]. The numbers in the return array are the cutting locations. With this information, one can simultaneously make all the eight cuts that will generate the sections that each person ordered. The first cut point is at the 3-inch location, so the first section will be 3 inches, as ordered by Person 0. The second cut point is at the 4-inch location; therefore the second section will be 1-inch long, as ordered by Person 1. The final cut point will be at the 25-inch location, which will produce a 3-inch-long section, since the previous cut point is at the 22-inch point. This gives Person 7 what she ordered. Note that since all the cut points are known from the scan operation, all cuts can be done in parallel or in any arbitrary sequence.

In summary, an intuitive way of thinking about inclusive scan is that the operation takes a request from a group of people and identifies all the cut points that allow the orders to be served all at once. The order could be for sausage, bread, campground space, or a contiguous chunk of memory in a computer. As long as we can quickly calculate all the cut points, all orders can be served in parallel.

An *exclusive scan* operation is similar to an inclusive scan operation with a slightly different arrangement of the output array:

$$[i, x_0, (x_0 \oplus x_1), \ldots, (x_0 \oplus x_1 \oplus \ldots \oplus x_{n-2})]$$

That is, each output element *excludes* the effect of the corresponding input element. The first output element is i, the identity value for operator $\oplus$, while the last output element only reflects the contribution of up to x_{n-2}. An identity value for a binary operator is defined as a value that, when used as an input operand, causes the operation to generate an output value that is the same as the other input operand's value. In the case of the addition operator, the identity value is 0, as any number added with zero will result in itself.

The applications of an exclusive scan operation are pretty much the same as those for inclusive scan. The inclusive scan provides slightly different information. In the sausage example, an exclusive scan would return [0 3 4 11 11 15 16 22], which are the beginning points of the cut sections. For example, the section for Person 0 starts at the 0-inch point. For another example, the section for Person 7 starts at the 22-inch point. The beginning point information is important in applications such as memory allocation, in which the allocated memory is returned to the requester via a pointer to its beginning point.

Note that it is easy to convert between the inclusive scan output and the exclusive scan output. One simply needs to shift all elements and fill in an element. When converting from inclusive to exclusive, one can simply shift all elements to the right and fill in identity value for the 0th element. When converting from exclusive to inclusive, one needs to shift all elements to the left and fill in the last element with the previous last element $\oplus$ the last input element. It is just a matter of convenience that we can directly generate an inclusive or exclusive scan depending on whether we care about the cut points or the beginning points for the sections. Therefore we will present parallel algorithms and implementations only for inclusive scan.

Before we present parallel scan algorithms and their implementations, we would like to show a sequential inclusive scan algorithm and its implementation. We will assume that the operator involved is addition. The code in Fig. 11.1 assumes that the input elements are in the x array and the output elements are to be written into the y array.

The code initializes the output element y[0] with the value of input element x[0] (line 02). In each iteration of the loop (lines 03−05), the loop body adds one more input element to the previous output element (which stores the accumulation of all the previous input elements) to generate one more output element.

It should be clear that the work done by the sequential implementation of inclusive scan in Fig. 11.1 is linearly proportional to the number of input elements; that is, the computational complexity of the sequential algorithm is $O(N)$.

In Sections 11.2−11.5, we will present alternative algorithms for performing parallel *segmented scan*, in which every thread block will perform a scan on a segment, that is, a section, of elements in the input array in parallel. We will then present in Sections 11.6 and 11.7 methods that combine the segmented scan results into the scan output for the entire input array.

```
01    void sequential_scan(float *x, float *y, unsigned int N) {
02        y[0] = x[0];
03        for(unsigned int i = 1; i < N; ++i) {
04            y[i] = y[i - 1] + x[i];
05        }
06    }
```

FIGURE 11.1

A simple sequential implementation of inclusive scan based on addition.

11.2 Parallel scan with the Kogge-Stone algorithm

We start with a simple parallel inclusive scan algorithm by performing a reduction operation for each output element. One might be tempted to use each thread to perform sequential reduction as shown in Fig. 10.2 for one output element. After all, this allows the calculations for all output elements to be performed in parallel. Unfortunately, this approach will be unlikely to improve the execution time over the sequential scan code in Fig. 11.1. This is because the calculation of y_{n-1} will take n steps, the same number of steps taken by the sequential scan code, and each step (iteration) in the reduction involves the same amount of work as each iteration of the sequential scan. Since the completion time of a parallel program is limited by the thread that takes the longest time, this approach is unlikely be any faster than sequential scan. In fact, with limited computing resources, the execution time of this naïve parallel scan algorithm can be much longer than that of the sequential algorithm. The computation cost, or the total number of operations performed, would unfortunately be much higher for the proposed approach. Since the number of reduction steps for output element i would be i, the total number of steps performed by all threads would be

$$\sum_{i=0}^{n-1} i = \frac{n \cdot (n-1)}{2}$$

That is, the proposed approach has a computation complexity of $O(N^2)$, which is higher than the complexity of the sequential scan, which is $O(N)$, while offering no speedup. The higher computational complexity means that considerably more execution resources need to be provisioned. This is obviously a bad idea.

A better approach is to adapt the parallel reduction tree in Chapter 10, Reduction and Minimizing Divergence, to calculate each output element with a reduction tree of the relevant input elements. There are multiple ways to design the reduction tree for each output element. Since the reduction tree for element i involves i add operations, this approach would still increase the computational complexity to $O(N^2)$ unless we find a way to share the partial sums across the reduction trees of different output elements. We present such a sharing approach that is based on the Kogge-Stone algorithm, which was originally invented for designing fast adder circuits in the 1970s (Kogge & Stone, 1973). This algorithm is still being used in the design of high-speed computer arithmetic hardware.

The algorithm, illustrated in Fig. 11.2, is an in-place scan algorithm that operates on an array XY that originally contains input elements. It iteratively evolves the contents of the array into output elements. Before the algorithm begins, we assume that XY[i] contains input element x_i. After k iterations, XY[i] will contain the sum of up to 2^k input elements at and before the location. For example, after one iteration, XY[i] will contain $x_{i-1}+x_i$ and at the end of iteration 2, XY[i] will contain $x_{i-3}+x_{i-2}+x_{i-1}+x_i$, and so on.

Fig. 11.2 illustrates the algorithm with a 16-element input example. Each vertical line represents an element of the XY array, with XY[0] in the leftmost position. The vertical direction shows the progress of iterations, starting from the top of the figure. For inclusive scan, by definition, y_0 is x_0, so XY[0] contains its final answer. In the first iteration, each position other than XY[0] receives the sum of its current content and that of its left neighbor. This is illustrated by the first row of addition operators in Fig. 11.2. As a result, XY[i] contains $x_{i-1}+x_i$. This is reflected in the labeling boxes under the first row of addition operators in Fig. 11.2. For example, after the first iteration, XY[3] contains x_2+x_3, shown as

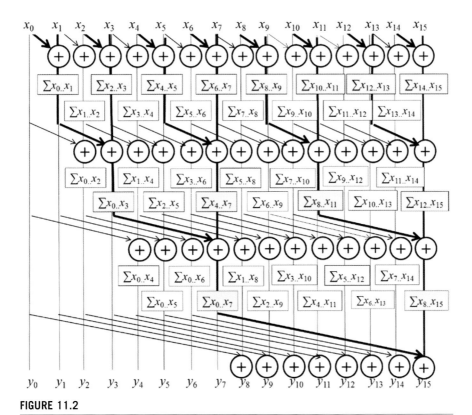

FIGURE 11.2

A parallel inclusive scan algorithm based on Kogge-Stone adder design.

$\sum x_2 \ldots x_3$. Note that after the first iteration, XY[1] is equal to x_0+x_1, which is the final answer for this position. So, there should be no further changes to XY[1] in subsequent iterations.

In the second iteration, each position other than XY[0] and XY[1] receives the sum of its current content and that of the position that is two elements away. This is illustrated in the labeled boxes below the second row of addition operators. As a result, XY[i] becomes $x_{i-3}+x_{i-2}+x_{i-1}+x_i$. For example, after the second iteration, XY[3] becomes $x_0+x_1+x_2+x_3$, shown as $\sum x_0 \ldots x_3$. Note that after the second iteration, XY[2] and XY[3] have reached their final answers and will not need to be changed in subsequent iterations. The reader is encouraged to work through the rest of the iterations.

Fig. 11.3 shows the parallel implementation of the algorithm illustrated in Fig. 11.2. We implement a kernel that performs local scans on different segments (sections) of the input that are each small enough for a single block to handle. Later, we will make final adjustments to consolidate these sectional scan results for large input arrays. The size of a section is defined as a compile-time constant SECTION_SIZE. We assume that the kernel function will be called using SECTION_SIZE as the block size, so there will be the same number of threads and section elements. We assign each thread to evolve the contents of one XY element.

The implementation shown in Fig. 11.3 assumes that input values were originally in a global memory array X, whose address is passed into the kernel as an argument (line 01). We will have all the threads in the block collaboratively load the X array elements into a shared memory array XY (line 02). This is done by having each thread calculate its global data index i=blockIdx.x*blockDim.x+threadIdx.x (line 03) for the output vector element position it is responsible for. Each thread loads the input element at

```
01    __global__ void Kogge_Stone_scan_kernel(float *X, float *Y, unsigned int N){
02        __shared__ float XY[SECTION_SIZE];
03        unsigned int i = blockIdx.x*blockDim.x + threadIdx.x;
04        if(i < N) {
05            XY[threadIdx.x] = X[i];
06        } else {
07            XY[threadIdx.x] = 0.0f;
08        }
09        for(unsigned int stride = 1; stride < blockDim.x; stride *= 2) {
10            __syncthreads();
11            float temp;
12            if(threadIdx.x >= stride)
13                temp = XY[threadIdx.x] + XY[threadIdx.x-stride];
14            __syncthreads();
15            if(threadIdx.x >= stride)
16                XY[threadIdx.x] = temp;
17        }
18        if(i < N) {
19            Y[i] = XY[threadIdx.x];
20        }
21    }
```

FIGURE 11.3

A Kogge-Stone kernel for inclusive (segmented) scan.

that position into the shared memory at the beginning of the kernel (lines 04−08). At the end of the kernel, each thread will write its result into the assigned output array Y (lines 18−20).

We now focus on the implementation of the iterative calculations for each XY element in Fig. 11.3 as a for-loop (lines 09−17). The loop iterates through the reduction tree for the XY array position that is assigned to a thread. When the stride value becomes greater than a thread's threadIdx.x value, it means that the thread's assigned XY position has already accumulated all the required input values and the thread no longer needs to be active (lines 12 and 15). Note that we use a barrier synchronization (line 10) to make sure that all threads have finished their previous iteration before any of them starts the next iteration. This is the same use of __syncthreads() as in the reduction discussion in Chapter 10, Reduction and Minimizing Divergence.

There is, however, a very important difference compared to reduction in updating of the XY elements (lines 12−16) in each iteration of the for-loop. Note that each active thread first stores the partial sum for its position into a temp variable (in a register). After all threads have completed a second barrier synchronization (line 14), all of them store their partial sum values to their XY positions (line 16). The need for the extra temp and __syncthreads() has to do with a write-after-read data dependence hazard in these updates. Each active thread adds the XY value at its own position (XY[threadIdx.x]) and that at a position of another thread (XY[threadIdx.x-stride]). If a thread i writes to its output position before another thread $i+stride$ has had the chance to read the old value at that position, the new value can corrupt the addition performed by the other thread. The corruption may or may not occur, depending on the execution timing of the threads involved, which is referred to as a race condition. Note that this race condition is different from the one we saw in Chapter 9, Parallel Histogram, with the histogram pattern. The race condition in Chapter 9, Parallel Histogram, was a read-modify-write race condition that can be solved with atomic operations. For the write-after-read race condition that we see here, a different solution is required.

The race condition can be easily observed in Fig. 11.2. Let us examine the activities of thread 4 (x_4) and thread 6 (x_6) during iteration 2, which is represented as the addition operations in the second row from the top. Note that thread 6 needs to add the old value of XY[4] (x_3+x_4) to the old value XY[6] (x_5+x_6) to generate the new value of XY[6] ($x_3+x_4+x_5+x_6$). However, if thread 4 stores its addition result for the iteration ($x_1+x_2+x_3+x_4$) into XY[4] too early, thread 6 could end up using the new value as its input and store ($x_1+x_2+x_3+x_4+x_5+x_6$) into XY[6]. Since x_1+x_2 will be added again to XY[6] by thread 6 in the third iteration, the final answer in XY[6] will become ($2x_1+2x_2+x_3+x_4+x_5+x_6$), which is obviously incorrect. On the other hand, if thread 6 happens to read the old value in XY[4] before thread 4 overwrites it during iteration 2, the results will be correct. That is, the execution result of the code may or may not be correct, depending on the timing of thread execution, and the execution results can vary from run to run. Such lack of reproducibility can make debugging a nightmare.

The race condition is overcome with the temporary variable used in line 13 and the __syncthreads( ) barrier in line 14. In line 13, all active threads first perform addition and write into their private temp variables. Therefore none of the old values in XY locations will be overwritten. The barrier __syncthread( ) in line 14 ensures that all active threads have completed their read of the old XY values before any of them can move forward and perform a write. Thus it is safe for the statement in line 16 to overwrite the XY locations.

The reason why an updated XY position may be used by another active thread is that the Kogge-Stone approach reuses the partial sums across reduction trees to reduce the computational complexity. We will study this point further in Section 11.3. The reader might wonder why the reduction tree kernels in Chapter 10, Reduction and Minimizing Divergence, did not need to use temporary variables and an extra __syncthreads(). The answer is that there is no race condition caused by a write-after-read hazard in these reduction kernels. This is because the elements written to by the active threads in an iteration are not read by any of the other active threads during the same iteration. This should be apparent by inspecting Fig. 10.7 and 10.8. For example, in Fig. 10.8, each active thread takes its inputs from its own position (input[threadIdx.x]) and a position that is of stride distance to the right (input[threadIdx.x+stride]). None of the stride distance positions are updated by any active threads during any given iteration. Therefore all active threads will always be able to read the old value of their respective input[threadIdx.x]. Since the execution within a thread is always sequential, each thread will always be able to read the old value in input[threadIdx.x] before writing the new value into the position. The reader should verify that the same property holds in Fig. 10.7.

If we want to avoid having a second barrier synchronization on every iteration, another way to overcome the race condition is to use separate arrays for input and output. If separate arrays are used, the location that is being written to is different from the location that is being read from, so there is no longer any potential write-after-read race condition. This approach would require having two shared memory buffers instead of one. In the beginning, we load from the global memory to the first buffer. In the first iteration we read from the first buffer and write to the second buffer. After the iteration is over, the second buffer has the most up-to-date results, and the results in the first buffer are no longer needed. Hence in the second iteration we read from the second buffer and write to the first buffer. Following the same reasoning, in the third iteration we read from the first buffer and write to the second buffer. We continue alternating input/output buffers until the iterations complete. This optimization is called *double-buffering*. Double-buffering is commonly used in parallel programming as a way to overcome write-after-read race conditions. We leave the implementation of this optimization as an exercise for the reader.

Furthermore, as is shown in Fig. 11.2, the actions on the smaller positions of XY end earlier than those on the larger positions (see the if-statement condition). This will cause some level of control divergence in the first warp when stride values are small. Note that adjacent threads will tend to execute the same number of iterations. The effect of divergence should be quite modest for large block sizes, since divergence will arise only in the first warp. The detailed analysis is left as an exercise for the reader.

Although we have shown only an inclusive scan kernel, we can easily convert an inclusive scan kernel to an exclusive scan kernel. Recall that an exclusive scan is equivalent to an inclusive scan with all elements shifted to the right by one position and element 0 filled with the identity value. This is illustrated in Fig. 11.4. Note that the only real difference is the alignment of elements on top of the picture. All labeling boxes are updated to reflect the new alignment. All iterative operations remain the same.

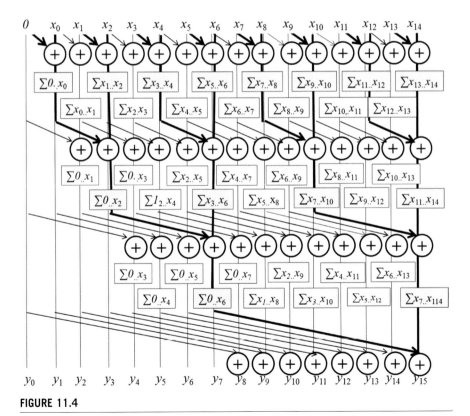

FIGURE 11.4

A parallel exclusive scan algorithm based on Kogge-Stone adder design.

We can now easily convert the kernel in Fig. 11.3 into an exclusive scan kernel. The only modification we need to make is to load 0 into XY[0] and `X[i-1]` into `XY[threadIdx.x]`, as shown in the following code:

```
if (i < N && threadIdx.x != 0) {
    XY[threadIdx.x] = X[i-1];
} else {
    XY[threadIdx.x] = 0.0f;
}
```

By substituting these four lines of code for lines 04−08 of Fig. 11.3, we convert the inclusive scan kernel into an exclusive scan kernel. We leave the work to finish the exclusive scan kernel as an exercise for the reader.

11.3 Speed and work efficiency consideration

One important consideration in analyzing parallel algorithms is *work efficiency*. The work efficiency of an algorithm refers to the extent to which the work that is performed by the algorithm is close to the minimum amount of work needed for the computation. For example, the minimum number of additions required by the scan operation is $N - 1$ additions, or $O(N)$, which is the number of additions that the sequential algorithm performs. However, as we saw in the beginning of Section 11.2, the naïve parallel algorithm performs $N*(N - 1)/2$ additions, or $O(N^2)$, which is substantially larger than the sequential algorithm. For this reason, the naïve parallel algorithm is not work efficient.

We now analyze the work efficiency of the Kogge-Stone kernel in Fig. 11.3, focusing on the work of a single thread block. All threads iterate up to $\log_2 N$ steps, where N is the SECTION_SIZE. In each iteration the number of inactive threads is equal to the stride size. Therefore we can calculate the amount of work done (one iteration of the for-loop, represented by the add operation in Fig. 8.1) for the algorithm as

$$\sum_{stride} (N - stride), \text{ for strides } 1, 2, 4, \ldots N/2 \left(\log_2 N \text{ terms}\right)$$

The first part of each term is independent of stride, and its summation adds up to $N*\log_2 (N)$. The second part is a familiar geometric series and sums up to $(N - 1)$. So, the total amount of work done is

$$N*\log_2(N) - (N - 1)$$

The good news is that the computational complexity of the Kogge-Stone approach is $O(N*\log_2(N))$, better than the $O(N^2)$ complexity of a naïve approach that performs complete reduction trees for all output elements. The bad news is that the Kogge-Stone algorithm is still not as work efficient as the sequential algorithm. Even for modest-sized sections, the kernel in Fig. 11.3 does much more work than the sequential algorithm. In the case of 512 elements, the kernel does approximately eight times more work than the sequential code. The ratio will increase as N becomes larger.

Although the Kogge-Stone algorithm performs more computations than the sequential algorithm, it does so in fewer steps because of parallel execution. The for-loop of the sequential code executes N iterations. As for the kernel code, the for-loop of each thread executes up to $\log_2 N$ iterations, which defines the minimal number of steps needed for executing the kernel. With unlimited execution resources, the reduction in the number of steps of the kernel code over the sequential code would be approximately $N/\log_2(N)$. For $N=512$, the reduction in the number of steps would be about $512/9=56.9\times$.

In a real CUDA GPU device, the amount of work done by the Kogge-Stone kernel is more than the theoretical $N*\log2(N) - (N-1)$. This is because we are using N threads. While many of the threads stop participating in the execution of the for-loop, some of them still consume execution resources until the entire warp completes execution. Realistically, the amount of execution resources consumed by the Kogge-Stone is closer to $N*\log2(N)$.

We will use the concept of computation steps as an approximate indicator for comparing between scan algorithms. The sequential scan should take approximately N steps to process N input elements. For example, the sequential scan should take approximately 1024 steps to process 1024 input elements. With P execution units in the CUDA device, we can expect the Kogge-Stone kernel to execute for $(N*\log2(N))/P$ steps. If P is equal to N, that is, if we have enough execution units to process all input element in parallel, then we need $\log2(N)$ steps, as we saw earlier. However, P could be smaller than N. For example, if we use 1024 threads and 32 execution units to process 1024 input elements, the kernel will likely take $(1024*10)/32=320$ steps. In this case, we expect to achieve a $1024/320=3.2\times$ reduction in the number of steps.

The additional work done by the Kogge-Stone kernel over the sequential code is problematic in two ways. First, the use of hardware for executing the parallel kernel is much less efficient. If the hardware does not have enough resources (i.e., if P is small), the parallel algorithm could end up needing more steps than the sequential algorithm. Hence the parallel algorithm will be slower. Second, all the extra work consumes additional energy. This makes the kernel less appropriate for power-constrained environments such as mobile applications.

The strength of the Kogge-Stone kernel is that it can achieve very good execution speed when there is enough hardware resources. It is typically used to calculate the scan result for a section with a modest number of elements, such as 512 or 1024. This, of course, assumes that GPUs can provide sufficient hardware resources and use the additional parallelism to tolerate latencies. As we have seen, its execution has a very limited amount of control divergence. In newer GPU architecture generations its computation can be efficiently performed with shuffle instructions within warps. We will see later in this chapter that it is an important component of the modern high-speed parallel scan algorithms.

11.4 Parallel scan with the Brent-Kung algorithm

While the Kogge-Stone kernel in Fig. 11.3 is conceptually simple, its work efficiency is quite low for some practical applications. Just by inspecting Figs. 11.2 and 11.4, we can see that there are potential opportunities for further sharing of some intermediate results. However, to allow more sharing across multiple threads, we need to strategically calculate the intermediate results and distribute them to different threads, which may require additional computation steps.

As we know, the fastest parallel way to produce sum values for a set of values is a reduction tree. With sufficient execution units, a reduction tree can generate the sum for N values in $\log_2(N)$ time units. The tree can also generate several sub-sums that can be used in the calculation of some of the scan output values. This observation was used as a basis for the Kogge-Stone adder design and also forms the basis of the Brent-Kung adder design (Brent & Kung, 1979). The Brent-Kung adder design can also be used to implement a parallel scan algorithm with better work efficiency.

Fig. 11.5 illustrates the steps for a parallel inclusive scan algorithm based on the Brent-Kung adder design. In the top half of Fig. 11.5, we produce the sum of all 16 elements in four steps. We use the minimal number of operations needed to generate the sum. During the first step, only the odd element of XY[i] will be updated to XY[i-1]+XY[i]. During the second step, only the XY elements whose indices are of the form of $4*n - 1$, which are 3, 7, 11, and 15 in Fig. 11.5, will be updated. During the third step, only the XY elements whose indices are of the form $8*n - 1$, which are 7 and 15, will be updated. Finally, during the fourth step, only XY[15] is updated. The total number of operations performed is 8+4+2+1=15. In general, for a scan section of N elements, we would do $(N/2)+(N/4)+\ldots+2+1=N - 1$ operations for this reduction phase.

The second part of the algorithm is to use a reverse tree to distribute the partial sums to the positions that can use them to complete the result of those positions. The

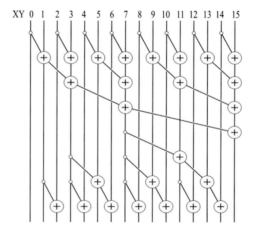

FIGURE 11.5

A parallel inclusive scan algorithm based on Brent-Kung adder design.

distribution of partial sums is illustrated in the bottom half of Fig. 11.5. To understand the design of the reverse tree, we should first analyze the needs for additional values to complete the scan output at each position of XY. It should be apparent from an inspection of Fig. 11.5 that the additions in the reduction tree always accumulate input elements in a continuous range. Therefore we know that the values that have been accumulated into each position of XY can always be expressed as a range of input elements $x_i \ldots x_j$, where x_i is the starting position and x_j is the ending position (inclusive).

Fig. 11.6 shows the state of each position (column), including both the values already accumulated into the position and the need for additional input element values at each level (row) of the reverse tree. The state of each position initially and after each level of additions in the reverse tree is expressed as the input elements, in the form $x_i \ldots x_j$, that have already been accounted for in the position. For example, $x_8 \ldots x_{11}$ in row Initial and column 11 indicates that the values of x_8, x_9, x_{10}, and x_{11} have been accumulated into XY[11] before the reverse tree begins (right after the reduction phase shown in the bottom portion of Fig. 11.5). At the end of the reduction tree phase, we have quite a few positions that are complete with the final scan values. In our example, XY[0], XY[1], XY[3], XY[7], and XY[15] are all complete with their final answers.

The need for additional input element values is indicated by the shade of each cell in Fig. 11.6: White means that the position needs to accumulate partial sums from three other positions, light gray means 2, dark gray means 1, and black means 0. For example, initially, XY[14] is marked white because it has only the value of x_{14} at the end of the reduction tree phase and needs to accumulate the partial sums from XY[7] ($x_0 \ldots x_7$), XY[11] ($x_8 \ldots x_{11}$), and XY[13] ($x_{12} \ldots x_{13}$) to complete its final scan value ($x_0 \ldots x_{14}$). The reader should verify that because of the structure of the reduction tree, the XY positions for an input of size N elements will never need the accumulation from more than $\log_2(N) - 1$ partial sums from other XY positions. Furthermore, these partial sum positions will always be 1, 2, 4, ... (powers of 2) away from each other. In our example, XY[14] needs $\log_2(16) - 1 = 3$ partial sums from positions that are 1 (between XY[14] and XY[13]), 2 (between XY[13] and XY[11]), and 4 (between XY[11] and XY[7]).

To organize our second half of the addition operations, we will first show all the operations that need partial sums from four positions away, then two positions

	0	1	2	3	4	5	6	7	8	9	10	11	12	13	14	15
Initial	x_0	$x_0\text{-}x_1$	x_2	$x_0\text{-}x_3$	x_4	$x_4..x_5$	x_6	$x_0..x_7$	x_8	$x_8..x_9$	x_{10}	$x_8.x_{11}$	x_{12}	$x_{12}.x_{13}$	x_{14}	$x_0\text{-}x_{15}$
Level 1												$x_0.x_{11}$				
Level 2						$x_0.x_5$				$x_0.x_9$				$x_0.x_{13}$		
Level 3			$x_0.x_2$		$x_0.x_4$		$x_0.x_6$		$x_0.x_8$		$x_0.x_{10}$		$x_0.x_{12}$		$x_0.x_{14}$	

FIGURE 11.6

Progression of values in XY after each level of additions in the reverse tree.

away, then one position away. During the first level of the reverse tree, we add XY[7] to XY[11], which brings XY[11] to the final answer. In Fig. 11.6, position 11 is the only one that advances to its final answer. During the second level, we complete XY[5], XY[9], and XY[13], which can be completed with the partial sums that are two positions away: XY[3], XY[7], and XY[11], respectively. Finally, during the third level, we complete all even positions XY[2], XY[4], XY [6], XY[8], XY[10], and XY[12] by accumulating the partial sums that are one position away (immediate left neighbor of each position).

We are now ready to implement the Brent-Kung approach to scan. We could implement the reduction tree phase of the parallel scan using the following loop:

```
for(unsigned int stride = 1; stride <= blockDim.x; stride *= 2) {
    __syncthreads();
    if ((threadIdx.x + 1)%(2*stride) == 0) {
        XY[threadIdx.x] += XY[threadIdx.x - stride];
    }
}
```

Note that this loop is similar to the reduction in Fig. 10.6. There are only two differences. The first difference is that we accumulate the sum value toward the highest position, which is XY[blockDim.x-1], rather than XY[0]. This is because the final result of the highest position is the total sum. For this reason, each active thread reaches for a partial sum to its left by subtracting the stride value from its index. The second difference is that we want the active threads to have a thread index of the form $2^n - 1$ rather than 2^n. This is why we add 1 to the threadIdx.x before the modulo (%) operation when we select the threads for performing addition in each iteration.

One drawback of this style of reduction is that it has significant control divergence problems. As we saw in Chapter 10, Reduction and Minimizing Divergence, a better way is to use a decreasing number of contiguous threads to perform the additions as the loop advances. Unfortunately, the technique we used to reduce divergence in Fig. 10.8 cannot be used in the scan reduction tree phase, since it does not generate the needed partial sum values in the intermediate XY positions. Therefore we resort to a more sophisticated thread index to data index mapping that maps a continuous section of threads to a series of data positions that are of stride distance apart. The following code does so by mapping a continuous section of threads to the XY positions whose indices are of the form $k*2^n - 1$:

```
for(unsigned int stride = 1; stride <= blockDim.x; stride *= 2) {
    __syncthreads();
    int index = (threadIdx.x + 1)*2*stride - 1;
    if(index < SECTION_SIZE) {
        XY[index] += XY[index - stride];
    }
}
```

By using such a complex index calculation in each iteration of the for-loop, a contiguous set of threads starting from thread 0 will be used in every iteration to avoid control divergence within warps. In our small example in Fig. 11.5, there are 16 threads in the block. In the first iteration, stride is equal to 1. The first eight consecutive threads in the block will satisfy the if-condition. The XY index values calculated for these threads will be 1, 3, 5, 7, 9, 11, 13, and 15. These threads will perform the first row of additions in Fig. 11.5. In the second iteration, stride is equal to 2. Only the first four threads in the block will satisfy the if-condition. The index values calculated for these threads will be 3, 7, 11, and 15. These threads will perform the second row of additions in Fig. 11.5. Note that since each iteration will always be using consecutive threads, the control divergence problem does not arise until the number of active threads drops below the warp size.

The reverse tree is a little more complex to implement. We see that the stride value decreases from SECTION_SIZE/4 to 1. In each iteration we need to "push" the value of XY elements from positions that are multiples of twice the stride value minus 1 to the right by stride positions. For example, in Fig. 11.5 the stride value decreases from 4 (2^2) down to 1. In the first iteration we would like to push (add) the value of XY[7] into XY[11], where 7 is $2*2^2 - 1$ and distance (stride) is 2^2. Note that only thread 0 will be used for this iteration, since the index calculated for other threads will be too large to satisfy the if-condition. In the second iteration we push the values of XY[3], XY[7], and XY[11] to XY[5], XY[9], and XY[13], respectively. The indices 3, 7, and 11 are $1*2*2^1 - 1$, $2*2*2^1 - 1$, and $3*2*2^1 - 1$, respectively. The destination positions are 2^1 positions away from the source positions. Finally, in the third iteration we push the values at all the odd positions to their even position right-hand neighbor (stride=2^0).

On the basis of the discussions above, the reverse tree can be implemented with the following loop:

```
for (int stride = SECTION_SIZE/4; stride > 0; stride /= 2) {
    __syncthreads();
    int index = (threadIdx.x + 1)*stride*2 - 1;
    if(index + stride < SECTION_SIZE) {
        XY[index + stride] += XY[index];
    }
}
```

The calculation of index is similar to that in the reduction tree phase. The XY [index+stride] +=XY[index] statement reflects the push from the threads' mapped location into a higher position that is stride away.

The final kernel code for a Brent-Kung parallel scan is shown in Fig. 11.7. The reader should notice that we never need to have more than SECTION_SIZE/2 threads for either the reduction phase or the distribution phase. Therefore we could simply launch a kernel with SECTION_SIZE/2 threads in a block. Since we

```
01    __global__ void Brent_Kung_scan_kernel(float *X, float *Y, unsigned int N) {
02        __shared__ float XY[SECTION_SIZE];
03        unsigned int i = 2*blockIdx.x*blockDim.x + threadIdx.x;
04        if(i < N) XY[threadIdx.x] = X[i];
05        if(i + blockDim.x < N) XY[threadIdx.x + blockDim.x] = X[i + blockDim.x];
06        for(unsigned int stride = 1; stride <= blockDim.x; stride *= 2) {
07            __syncthreads();
08            unsigned int index = (threadIdx.x + 1)*2*stride - 1;
09            if(index < SECTION_SIZE) {
10                XY[index] += XY[index - stride];
11            }
12        }
13        for (int stride = SECTION_SIZE/4; stride > 0; stride /= 2) {
14            __syncthreads();
15            unsigned int index = (threadIdx.x + 1)*stride*2 - 1;
16            if(index + stride < SECTION_SIZE) {
17                XY[index + stride] += XY[index];
18            }
19        }
20        __syncthreads();
21        if (i < N) Y[i] = XY[threadIdx.x];
22        if (i + blockDim.x < N) Y[i + blockDim.x] = XY[threadIdx.x + blockDim.x];
23    }
```

FIGURE 11.7

A Brent-Kung kernel for inclusive (segmented) scan.

can have up to 1024 threads in a block, each scan section can have up to 2048 elements. However, we will need to have each thread load two X elements at the beginning and store two Y elements at the end.

As was in the case of the Kogge-Stone scan kernel, one can easily adapt the Brent-Kung inclusive parallel scan kernel into an exclusive scan kernel with a minor adjustment to the statement that loads X elements into XY. Interested readers should also read Harris et al., 2007, for an interesting natively exclusive scan kernel that is based on a different way of designing the reverse tree phase of the scan kernel.

We now turn our attention to the analysis of the number of operations in the reverse tree stage. The number of operations is $(16/8) - 1 + (16/4) - 1 + (16/2) - 1$. In general, for N input elements the total number of operations would be $(2 - 1) + (4 - 1) + \ldots + (N/4 - 1) + (N/2 - 1)$, which is $N - 1 - \log_2(N)$. Therefore the total number of operations in the parallel scan, including both the reduction tree ($N - 1$ operations) and the reverse tree ($N - 1 - \log_2(N)$ operations) phases, is $2^*N - 2 - \log_2(N)$. Note that the total number of operations is now $O(N)$, as opposed to $O(N^*\log_2 N)$ for the Kogge-Stone algorithm.

The advantage of the Brent-Kung algorithm over the Kogge-Stone algorithm is quite clear. As the input section becomes bigger, the Brent-Kung algorithm never performs more than 2 times the number of operations performed by the sequential algorithm. In an energy-constrained execution environment the Brent-Kung algorithm strikes a good balance between parallelism and efficiency.

While the Brent-Kung algorithm has a much higher level of theoretical work efficiency than the Kogge-Stone algorithm, its advantage in a CUDA kernel implementation is more limited. Recall that the Brent-Kung algorithm is using $N/2$ threads. The major difference is that the number of active threads drops much faster through the reduction tree than the Kogge-Stone algorithm. However, some of the inactive threads may still consume execution resources in a CUDA device because they are bound to other active threads by SIMD. This makes the advantage in work efficiency of Brent-Kung over Kogge-Stone less drastic in a CUDA device.

The main disadvantage of Brent-Kung over Kogge-Stone is its potentially longer execution time despite its higher work efficiency. With infinite execution resources, Brent-Kung should take about twice as long as Kogge-Stone, owing to the need for additional steps to perform the reverse tree phase. However, the speed comparison can be quite different when we have limited execution resources. Using the example in Section 11.3, if we process 1024 input elements with 32 execution units, the Brent-Kung kernel is expected to take approximately $(2*1024 - 2 - 10)/32=63.6$ steps. The reader should verify that with control divergence there will be about five more steps when the total number of active threads drops below 32 in each phase. This results in a speedup of $1024/73.6=14$ over sequential execution. This is in comparison with the 320 time units and speedup of 3.2 for Kogge-Stone. The comparison would be to Kogge-Stone's advantage, of course, when there are many more execution resources and/or when the latencies are much longer.

11.5 Coarsening for even more work efficiency

The overhead of parallelizing scan across multiple threads is like reduction in that it includes the hardware underutilization and synchronization overhead of the tree execution pattern. However, scan has an additional parallelization overhead, and that is reduced work efficiency. As we have seen, parallel scan is less work efficient than sequential scan. This lower work efficiency is an acceptable price to pay to parallelize if the threads were actually to run in parallel. However, if the hardware were to serialize them, we would be better off serializing them ourselves via thread coarsening to improve work efficiency.

We can design a parallel segmented scan algorithm that achieves even better work efficiency by adding a phase of fully independent sequential scans on subsections of the input. Each thread block receives a section of the input that is larger than the original section by the coarsening factor. At the beginning of the algorithm we partition the block's section of the input into multiple contiguous subsections: one for each thread. The number of subsections is the same as the number of threads in the thread block.

The coarsened scan is divided into three phases as shown in Fig. 11.8. During the first phase, we have each thread perform a sequential scan on its contiguous subsection. For example, in Fig. 11.8 we assume that there are four threads in a block. We partition the 16-element input section into four subsections with four elements each. Thread 0 will perform scan on its section (2, 1, 3, 1) and generate (2, 3, 6, 7). Thread 1 will perform scan on its section (0, 4, 1, 2) and generate (0, 4, 5, 7), and so on.

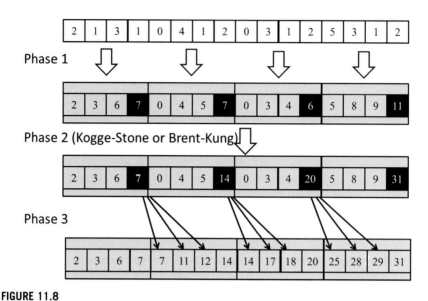

FIGURE 11.8

A three-phase parallel scan for higher work efficiency.

Note that if each thread directly performs scan by accessing the input from global memory, their accesses would not be coalesced. For example, during the first iteration, thread 0 would be accessing input element 0, thread 1 would be accessing input element 4, and so on. Therefore we improve memory coalescing by using shared memory to absorb the memory accesses that cannot be coalesced, as was mentioned in Chapter 6, Performance Considerations. That is, we transfer data between shared memory and global memory in a coalesced manner and perform the memory accesses with the unfavorable access pattern in shared memory. At the beginning of the first phase, all threads collaborate to load the input into the shared memory in an iterative manner. In each iteration, adjacent threads load adjacent elements to enable memory coalescing. For example, in Fig. 11.8 we have all threads collaborate and load four elements in a coalesced manner: Thread 0 loads element 0, thread 1 loads element 1, and so on. All threads then move to load the next four elements: Thread 0 loads element 4, thread 1 loads element 5, and so on.

Once all input elements are in the shared memory, the threads access their own subsection from the shared memory and perform a sequential scan on it. This is shown as Phase 1 in Fig. 11.8. Note that at the end of Phase 1 the last element of each section (highlighted as black in the second row) contains the sum of all input elements in the section. For example, the last element of section 0 contains value 7, the sum of the input elements (2, 1, 3, 1) in the section.

During the second phase, all threads in each block collaborate and perform a scan operation on a logical array that consists of the last element of each section.

This can be done with a Kogge-Stone or Brent-Kung algorithm, since there are only a modest number of elements (number of threads in a block). Note that the thread-to-element mappings need to be slightly modified from those in Figs. 11.3 and 11.7, since the elements that need to be scanned are of stride (four elements in Fig. 11.8) distance away from each other.

In the third phase, each thread adds the new value of the last element of its predecessor's section to its elements. The last elements of each subsection do not need to be updated during this phase. For example, in Fig. 11.8, thread 1 adds the value 7 to elements (0, 4, 5) in its section to produce (7, 11, 12). The last element of the section is already the correct value 14 and does not need to be updated.

With this three-phase approach, we can use a much smaller number of threads than the number of elements in a section. The maximal size of the section is no longer limited by the number of threads one can have in a block but rather by the size of the shared memory; all elements of the section need to fit into the shared memory.

The major advantage of thread coarsening for scan is its efficient use of execution resources. Assume that we use Kogge-Stone for phase 2. For an input list of N elements, if we use T threads, the amount of work done by each phase is $N - T$ for phase 1, $T^*\log_2 T$ for phase 2, and $N - T$ for phase 3. If we use P execution units, we can expect that the execution will take $(N - T + T^*\log_2 T + N - T)/P$ steps. For example, if we use 64 threads and 32 execution units to process 1024 elements, the algorithm should take approximately $(1024 - 64 + 64^*6 + 1024 - 64)/32 = 72$ steps. We leave the implementation of the coarsened scan kernel as an exercise for the reader.

11.6 Segmented parallel scan for arbitrary-length inputs

For many applications the number of elements to be processed by a scan operation can be in the millions or even billions. The kernels that we have presented so far perform local block-wide scans on sections of the input, but we still need a way to consolidate the results from different sections. To do so, we can use a hierarchical scan approach, as illustrated in Fig. 11.9.

For a large dataset we first partition the input into sections so that each of them can fit into the shared memory of a streaming multiprocessor and be processed by a single block. Assume that we call one of the kernels in Figs. 11.3 and 11.7 on a large input dataset. At the end of the grid execution, the Y array will contain the scan results for individual sections, called *scan blocks* in Fig. 11.9. Each element in a scan block only contains the accumulated values of all preceding elements in the same scan block. These scan blocks need to be combined into the final result; that is, we need to call another kernel that adds the sum of all elements in preceding scan blocks to each element of a scan block.

Fig. 11.10 shows a small example of the hierarchical scan approach of Fig. 11.9. In this example there are 16 input elements that are divided into four

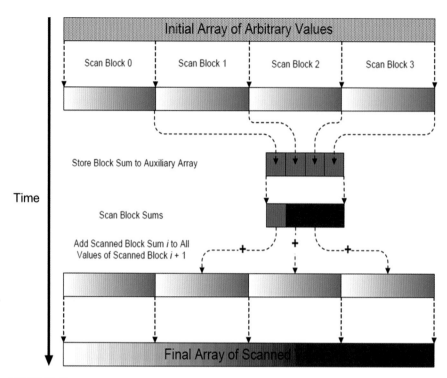

FIGURE 11.9

A hierarchical scan for arbitrary length inputs.

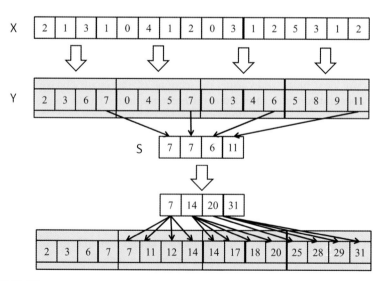

FIGURE 11.10

An example of hierarchical scan.

scan blocks. We can use the Kogge-Stone kernel, the Brent-Kung kernel, or a coarsened kernel to process the individual scan blocks. The kernel treats the four scan blocks as independent input datasets. After the scan kernel terminates, each Y element contains the scan result within its scan block. For example, scan block 1 has inputs 0, 4, 1, 2. The scan kernel produces the scan result for this section, which is 0, 4, 5, 7. Note that these results do not contain the contributions from any of the elements in scan block 0. To produce the final result for this scan block, the sum of all elements in scan block 0, that is, 2+1+3+1=7, should be added to every result element of scan block 1. For another example the inputs in scan block 2 are 0, 3, 1, 2. The kernel produces the scan result for this scan block, which is 0, 3, 4, 6. To produce the final results for this scan block, the sum of all elements in both scan block 0 and scan block 1, that is, 2+1+3+1+0+4+1+2=14, should be added to every result element of scan block 2.

It is important to note that the last output element of each scan block gives the sum of all input elements of the scan block. These values are 7, 7, 6, and 11 in Fig. 11.10. This brings us to the second step of the segmented scan algorithm in Fig. 11.9, which gathers the last result elements from each scan block into an array and performs a scan on these output elements. This step is also illustrated in Fig. 11.10, where the last scan output elements of all scan blocks are collected into a new array S. While the second step of Fig. 11.10 is logically the same as the second step of Fig. 11.8, the main difference is that Fig. 11.10 involves threads from different thread blocks. As a result, the last element of each section needs to be collected (written) into a global memory array so that they can be visible across thread blocks.

Gathering the last result of each scan block can be done by changing the code at the end of the scan kernel so that the last thread of each block writes its result into an S array using its blockIdx.x as the array index. A scan operation is then performed on S to produce output values 7, 14, 20, 31. Note that each of these second-level scan output values are the accumulated sum from the beginning location X[0] to the end location of each scan block. That is, the value in S[0]=7 is the accumulated sum from X[0] to the end of scan block 0, which is X[3]. The value in S[1]=14 is the accumulated sum from X[0] to the end of scan block 1, which is X[7]. Therefore the output values in the S array give the scan results at "strategic" locations of the original scan problem. In other words, in Fig. 11.10 the output values in S[0], S[1], S[2], and S[3] give the final scan results for the original problem at positions X[3], X[7], X[11], and X[15], respectively. These results can be used to bring the partial results in each scan block to their final values.

This brings us to the last step of the segmented scan algorithm in Fig. 11.10. The second-level scan output values are added to the values of their corresponding scan blocks. For example, in Fig. 11.10, the value of S[0] (value 7) will be added to Y[0], Y[1], Y[2], Y[3] of thread block 1, which completes the results in these positions. The final results in these positions are 7, 11, 12, 14. This is because S[0] contains the sum of the values of the original input X[0] through

X[3]. These final results are 14, 17, 18, and 20. The value of S[1] (14) will be added to Y[8], Y[9], Y[10], Y[11], which completes the results in these positions. The value of S[2] (20) will be added to Y[12], Y[13], Y[14], Y[15]. Finally, the value of S[3] is the sum of all elements of the original input, which is also the final result in Y[15].

Readers who are familiar with computer arithmetic algorithms should recognize that the principle behind the segmented scan algorithm is quite similar to the principle behind carry look-ahead in hardware adders of modern processors. This should be no surprise, considering that the two parallel scan algorithms that we have studied so far are also based on innovative hardware adder designs.

We can implement the segmented scan with three kernels. The first kernel is largely the same as the three-phase kernel. (We could just as easily use the Kogge-Stone kernel or the Brent-Kung kernel.) We need to add one more parameter S, which has the dimension of N/SECTION_SIZE. At the end of the kernel, we add a conditional statement for the last thread in the block to write the output value of the last XY element in the scan block to the blockIdx.x position of S:

```
__syncthreads();
if (threadIdx.x == blockDim.x - 1) {
    S[blockIdx.x] = XY[SECTION_SIZE - 1];
}
```

The second kernel is simply one of the three parallel scan kernels configured with a single thread block, which takes S as input and writes S as output without producing any partial sums.

The third kernel takes the S array and Y array as inputs and writes its output back into Y. Assuming that we launch the kernel with SECTION_SIZE threads in each block, each thread adds one of the S elements (selected by the blockIdx.x-1) to one Y element:

```
unsigned int i = blockIdx.x*blockDim.x + threadIdx.x;
Y[i] += S[blockIdx.x - 1];
```

In other words, the threads in a block add the sum of all previous scan blocks to the elements of their scan block. We leave it as an exercise for the reader to complete the details of each kernel and complete the host code.

11.7 Single-pass scan for memory access efficiency

In the segmented scan mentioned in Section 11.6, the partially scanned results (scan blocks) are stored into global memory before launching the global scan kernel, and then reloaded back from the global memory by the third kernel. The time for performing these extra memory stores and loads is not overlapped with the computation in the subsequent kernels and can significantly affect the speed of the segmented scan algorithms. To avoid such a negative impact, multiple techniques have been proposed (Dotsenko et al., 2008; Merrill & Garland, 2016; Yan et al., 2013). In this chapter a stream-based scan algorithm is discussed. The reader is encouraged to read the references to understand the other techniques.

In the context of CUDA C programming, a stream-based scan algorithm (not to be confused with CUDA streams to be introduced in Chapter 20, Programming a Heterogeneous Computing Cluster), or domino-style scan algorithm, refers to a segmented scan algorithm in which partial sum data is passed in one direction through the global memory between adjacent thread blocks in the same grid. Stream-based scan builds on a key observation that the global scan step (the middle part of Fig. 11.9) can be performed in a domino fashion and does not truly require a grid-wide synchronization. For example, in Fig. 11.10, scan block 0 can pass its partial sum value 7 to scan block 1 and complete its job. scan block 1 receives the partial sum value 7 from scan block 0, sums up with its local partial sum value 7 to get 14, passes its partial sum value 14 to scan block 2, and then completes its final step by adding 7 to all partial scan values in its scan block. This process continues for all thread blocks.

To implement a domino-style scan algorithm, one can write a single kernel to perform all three steps of the segmented scan algorithm in Fig. 11.9. Thread block i first performs a scan on its scan block, using one of the three parallel algorithms we presented in Sections 11.2 through 11.5. It then waits for its left neighbor block, $i - 1$, to pass the sum value. Once it receives the sum from block $i - 1$, it adds the value to its local sum and passes the cumulative sum value to its right neighbor block, $i+1$. It then moves on to add the sum value received from block $i - 1$ to all partial scan values to produce all the output values of the scan block.

During the first phase of the kernel, all blocks can execute in parallel. They will be serialized during the data-passing phase. However, as soon as each block receives the sum value from its predecessor, it can perform its final phase in parallel with all other blocks that have received the sum values from their predecessors. As long as the sum values can be passed through the blocks quickly, there can be ample parallelism among blocks during the third phase.

To make this domino-style scan work, adjacent (block) synchronization is needed (Yan et al., 2013). Adjacent synchronization is a customized synchronization to allow the adjacent thread blocks to synchronize and/or exchange data. Particularly, in scan, the data are passed from scan block $i - 1$ to scan block i, as in a producer-consumer chain. On the producer side (scan block $i - 1$), a flag is set to a particular value after the partial sum has been stored to memory, while on the consumer side (scan block i), the flag is checked to see whether it is that particular value before the passed partial sum is loaded. As has been mentioned, the loaded value is further added with the local sum and then is passed to the next block (scan block $i+1$). Adjacent synchronization can be implemented by using atomic operations. The following code segment illustrates the use of atomic operations to implement adjacent synchronization:

```
__shared__ float previous_sum;
if (threadIdx.x == 0){
    // Wait for previous flag
    while(atomicAdd(&flags[bid], 0) == 0) { }
    // Read previous partial sum
    previous_sum = scan_value[bid];
    // Propagate partial sum
    scan_value[bid + 1] = previous_sum + local_sum;
    // Memory fence
    __threadfence();
    // Set flag
    atomicAdd(&flags[bid + 1], 1);
}
__syncthreads();
```

This code section is executed by only one leader thread in each block (e.g., thread with index 0). The rest of threads will wait at __syncthreads() in the last line. In block bid, the leader thread checks flags[bid], a global memory array, repeatedly until it is set. Then it loads the partial sum from its predecessor by accessing the global memory array scan_value[bid] and stores the value into its local shared memory variable previous_sum. It adds the previous_sum with its local partial sum local_sum and stores the result into the global memory array scan_value[bid+1]. The memory fence function __threadfence() is required to ensure that the scan_value[bid+1] value arrives to the global memory before the flag is set with atomicAdd().

Although it may appear that the atomic operations on the flags array and the accesses to the scan_value array incur global memory traffic, these operations are mostly performed in the second-level caches of recent GPU architectures (Chapter 9, Parallel Histogram). Any such stores and loads to the global memory will likely be overlapped with the phase 1 and phase 3 computational activities of other blocks. On the other hand, when executing the three-kernel segmented scan algorithm in Section 11.5, the stores to and loads from the S array in the global memory are in a separate kernel and cannot be overlapped with phase 1 or phase 3.

There is one subtle issue with domino-style algorithms. In GPUs, thread blocks may not always be scheduled linearly according to their blockIdx values, which means that scan block i may be scheduled and performed after scan block i +1. In this situation the execution order arranged by the scheduler might contradict the execution order assumed by the adjacent synchronization code and cause performance degradation or even a deadlock. For example, the scheduler may schedule scan block i through scan block $i+N$ before it schedules scan block $i - 1$. If scan block i through scan block $i+N$ occupy all the streaming multiprocessors, scan block $i - 1$ would not be able to start execution until at least one of them finishes execution. However, all of them are waiting for the sum value from scan block $i - 1$. This causes the system to deadlock.

There are multiple techniques to resolve this issue (Gupta et al., 2012; Yan et al., 2013). Here, we discuss only one particular method, dynamic block index assignment, and leave the rest as a reference for readers. Dynamic block index assignment decouples the assignment of the thread block index from the built-in blockIdx.x. In the single-pass scan, the value of the bid variable of each block is no longer tied to the value of blockIdx.x. Instead, it is determined by using the following code at the beginning of the kernel:

```
__shared__ unsigned int bid_s;
if (threadIdx.x == 0) {
    bid_s = atomicAdd(blockCounter, 1);
}
__syncthreads();
unsigned int bid = bid_s;
```

The leader thread atomically increments a global counter variable pointed to by blockCounter. The global counter stores the dynamic block index of the next block that is scheduled. The leader thread then stores the acquired dynamic block index value into a shared memory variable bid_s so that it is accessible by all threads of the block after __syncthreads(). This guarantees that all scan blocks are scheduled linearly and prevents a potential deadlock. In other words, if a block obtains a bid value of i, then it is guaranteed that a block with value $i - 1$ has been scheduled because it has executed the atomic operation.

11.8 Summary

In this chapter we studied parallel scan, also known as prefix sum, as an important parallel computation pattern. Scan is used to enable parallel allocation of resources to parties whose needs are not uniform. It converts seemingly sequential computation based on mathematical recurrence into parallel computation, which helps to reduce sequential bottlenecks in many applications. We show that a simple sequential scan algorithm performs only $N - 1$, or $O(N)$, additions for an input of N elements.

We first introduced a parallel Kogge-Stone segmented scan algorithm that is fast and conceptually simple but not work-efficient. The algorithm performs $O(N^*\log_2 N)$ operations, which is more than its sequential counterpart. As the size of the dataset increases, the number of execution units that are needed for a parallel algorithm to break even with the simple sequential algorithm also increases. Therefore Kogge-Stone scan algorithms are typically used to process modest-sized scan blocks in processors with abundant execution resources.

We then presented a parallel Brent-Kung segmented scan algorithm that is conceptually more complicated. Using a reduction tree phase and a reverse tree phase, the algorithm performs only $2*N - 3$, or $O(N)$, additions no matter how large the input datasets are. Such a work-efficient algorithm whose number of operations grows linearly with the size of the input set is often also referred to as a data-scalable algorithm. Although the Brent-Kung algorithm has better work efficiency than the Kogge-Stone algorithm, it requires more steps to complete. Therefore in a system with enough execution resources, the Kogge-Stone algorithm is expected to have better performance despite being less work efficient.

We also applied thread coarsening to mitigate the hardware underutilization and synchronization overhead of parallel scan and to improve its work efficiency. Thread coarsening was applied by having each thread in the block perform a work-efficient sequential scan on its own subsection of input elements before the threads collaborate to perform the less work-efficient block-wide parallel scan to produce the entire block's section.

We presented a hierarchical scan approach to extend the parallel scan algorithms to handle input sets of arbitrary sizes. Unfortunately, a straightforward, three-kernel implementation of the segmented scan algorithm incurs redundant global memory accesses whose latencies are not overlapped with computation. For this reason we also presented a domino-style hierarchical scan algorithm to enable a single-pass, single-kernel implementation and improve the global memory access efficiency of the hierarchical scan algorithm. However, this approach requires a carefully designed adjacent block synchronization mechanism using atomic operations, thread memory fence, and barrier synchronization. Special care also must be taken to prevent deadlocks by using dynamic block index assignment.

There are further optimization opportunities for even higher performance implementations using, for example, warp-level shuffle operations. In general, implementing and optimizing parallel scan algorithms on GPUs are complex processes, and the average user is more likely to use a parallel scan library for GPUs such as Thrust (Bell and Hoberock, 2012) than to implement their own scan kernels from scratch. Nevertheless, parallel scan is an important parallel pattern, and it offers an interesting and relevant case study of the tradeoffs that go into optimizing parallel patterns.

Exercises

1. Consider the following array: [4 6 7 1 2 8 5 2]. Perform a parallel inclusive prefix scan on the array, using the Kogge-Stone algorithm. Report the intermediate states of the array after each step.
2. Modify the Kogge-Stone parallel scan kernel in Fig. 11.3 to use double-buffering instead of a second call to __syncthreads() to overcome the write-after-read race condition.

3. Analyze the Kogge-Stone parallel scan kernel in Fig. 11.3. Show that control divergence occurs only in the first warp of each block for stride values up to half of the warp size. That is, for warp size 32, control divergence will occur to iterations for stride values 1, 2, 4, 8, and 16.

4. For the Kogge-Stone scan kernel based on reduction trees, assume that we have 2048 elements. Which of the following gives the closest approximation of how many add operations will be performed?

5. Consider the following array: [4 6 7 1 2 8 5 2]. Perform a parallel inclusive prefix scan on the array, using the Brent-Kung algorithm. Report the intermediate states of the array after each step.

6. For the Brent-Kung scan kernel, assume that we have 2048 elements. How many add operations will be performed in both the reduction tree phase and the inverse reduction tree phase?

7. Use the algorithm in Fig. 11.4 to complete an exclusive scan kernel.

8. Complete the host code and all three kernels for the segmented parallel scan algorithm in Fig. 11.9.

References

Bell, N., Hoberock, J., 2012. "Thrust: A productivity-oriented library for CUDA." GPU computing gems Jade edition. Morgan Kaufmann, 359–371.

Brent, R. P., & Kung, H. T., 1979. A regular layout for parallel adders, Technical Report, Computer Science Department, Carnegie-Mellon University.

Dotsenko, Y., Govindaraju, N.K., Sloan, P.P., Boyd, C., Manferdelli, J., 2008. Fast scan algorithms on graphics processors. Proc. 22nd Annu. Int. Conf. Supercomputing, 205–213.

Gupta, K., Stuart, J.A., Owens, J.D., 2012. A study of persistent threads style GPU programming for GPGPU workloads. Innovative Parallel Comput. (InPar) 1–14. IEEE.

Harris, M., Sengupta, S., & Owens, J. D. (2007). Parallel prefix sum with CUDA. GPU Gems 3. http://developer.download.nvidia.com/compute/cuda/1_1/Website/projects/scan/doc/scan.pdf.

Kogge, P., Stone, H., 1973. A parallel algorithm for the efficient solution of a general class of recurrence equations. IEEE Trans. Computers C-22, 783–791.

Merrill, D., & Garland, M. (2016, March). Single-pass parallel prefix scan with decoupled look-back. Technical Report NVR2016-001, NVIDIA Research.

Yan, S., Long, G., Zhang, Y., 2013. StreamScan: Fast scan algorithms for GPUs without global barrier synchronization, PPoPP. ACM SIGPLAN Not. 48 (8), 229–238.

Merge

An introduction to dynamic input data identification

12

With special contributions from Li-Wen Chang and Jie Lv

Chapter Outline

12.1 Background 263
12.2 A sequential merge algorithm 265
12.3 A parallelization approach 266
12.4 Co-rank function implementation 268
12.5 A basic parallel merge kernel 273
12.6 A tiled merge kernel to improve coalescing 275
12.7 A circular buffer merge kernel 282
12.8 Thread coarsening for merge 288
12.9 Summary 288
Exercises 289
References 289

Our next parallel pattern is an ordered merge operation, which takes two sorted lists and generates a combined sorted list. Ordered merge operations can be used as a building block of sorting algorithms, as we will see in Chapter 13, Sorting. Ordered merge operations also form the basis of modern map-reduce frameworks. This chapter presents a parallel ordered merge algorithm in which the input data for each thread is dynamically determined. The dynamic nature of the data access makes it challenging to exploit locality and tiling techniques for improved memory access efficiency and performance. The principles behind dynamic input data identification are also relevant to many other important computations, such as set intersection and set union. We present increasingly sophisticated buffer management schemes for achieving increasing levels of memory access efficiency for order merged and other operations that determine their input data dynamically.

12.1 Background

An ordered merge function takes two sorted lists A and B and merges them into a single sorted list C. For this chapter we assume that the sorted lists are stored in arrays. We further assume that each element in such an array has a key. An order relation denoted by $\leq$ is defined on the keys. For example, the keys may be simply integer values, and $\leq$ may be defined as the conventional *less than or equal to* relation between these integer values. In the simplest case, the elements consist of just keys.

Suppose that we have two elements e_1 and e_2 whose keys are k_1 and k_2, respectively. In a sorted list based on the relation $\leq$, if e_1 appears before e_2, then $k_1 \leq k_2$. A merge function based on an ordering relation R takes two sorted input arrays A and B having m and n elements, respectively, where m and n do not have be to equal. Both array A and array B are sorted on the basis of the ordering relation R. The function produces an output sorted array C having m + n elements. Array C consists of all the input elements from arrays A and B and is sorted by the ordering relation R.

Fig. 12.1 shows the operation of a simple merge function based on the conventional numerical ordering relation. Array A has five elements (m=5), and array B has four elements (n=4). The merge function generates array C with all its 9 elements (m + n) from A and B. These elements must be sorted. The arrows in Fig. 12.1 show how elements of A and B should be placed into C to complete the merge operation. Whenever the numerical values are equal between an element of A and an element of B, the element of A should appear first in the output list C. This requirement ensures the stability of the ordered merge operation.

In general, an ordering operation is stable if elements with equal key values are placed in the same order in the output as the order in which they appear in the input. The example in Fig. 12.1 demonstrates stability both with and across the input lists of the merge operation. For example, the two elements whose values are 10 are copied from B into C while maintaining their original order. This illustrates stability within an input list of the merge operation. For another example the A element whose value is 7 goes into C before the B element of the same value. This illustrates stability across input lists of the merge operation. The stability property allows the ordering operation to preserve previous orderings that are not captured by the key that is used in the current ordering operation. For example, the lists A and B might have been previously sorted according to a different key before being sorted by the current key to be used for merging.

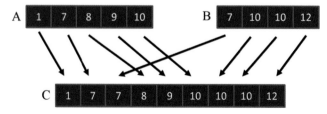

FIGURE 12.1

Example of a merge operation.

Maintaining stability in the merge operation allows the merge operation to preserve the work that was done in the previous steps.

The merge operation is the core of merge sort, an important parallelizable sort algorithm. As we will see in Chapter 13, Sorting, a parallel merge sort function divides the input list into multiple sections and distributes them to parallel threads. The threads sort the individual section(s) and then cooperatively merge the sorted sections. Such a divide-and-concur approach allows efficient parallelization of sorting.

In modern map-reduce distributed computing frameworks, such as Hadoop, the computation is distributed to a massive number of compute nodes. The reduce process assembles the result of these compute nodes into the final result. Many applications require that the results be sorted according to an ordering relation. These results are typically assembled by using the merge operation in a reduction tree pattern. As a result, efficient merge operations are critical to the efficiency of these frameworks.

12.2 A sequential merge algorithm

The merge operation can be implemented with a straightforward sequential algorithm. Fig. 12.2 shows a sequential merge function.

The sequential function in Fig. 12.2 consists of two main parts. The first part consists of a while-loop (line 05) that visits the A and B list elements in order. The loop starts with the first elements: A[0] and B[0]. Every iteration fills one

```
01    void merge_sequential(int *A, int m, int *B, int n, int *C) {
02        int i = 0; // Index into A
03        int j = 0; // Index into B
04        int k = 0; // Index into C
05        while ((i < m) && (j < n)) { // Handle start of A[] and B[]
06            if (A[i] <= B[j]) {
07                C[k++] = A[i++];
08            } else {
09                C[k++] = B[j++];
10            }
11        }
12        if (i == m) { // Done with A[], handle remaining B[]
13            while(j < n) {
14                C[k++] = B[j++];
15            }
16        } else { // Done with B[], handle remaining A[]
17            while(i < m) {
18                C[k++] = A[i++];
19            }
20        }
21    }
```

FIGURE 12.2

A sequential merge function.

position in the output array C; either one element of A or one element of B will be selected for the position (lines 06–10). The loop uses i and j to identify the A and B elements that are currently under consideration; i and j are both 0 when the execution first enters the loop. The loop further uses k to identify the current position to be filled in the output list array C. In each iteration, if element A[i] is less than or equal to B[j], the value of A[i] is assigned to C[k]. In this case, the execution increments both i and k before going to the next iteration. Otherwise, the value of B[j] is assigned to C[k]. In this case, the execution increments both j and k before going to the next iteration.

The execution exits the while-loop when it reaches either the end of array A or the end of array B. The execution moves on to the second part, which is on the right Fig. 12.2. If array A is the one that has been completely visited, as indicated by the fact that i is equal to m, then the code copies the remaining elements of array B to the remaining positions of array C (lines 13–15). Otherwise, array B is the one that was completely visited, so the code copies the remaining elements of A to the remaining positions of C (lines 17–19). Note that the if-else construct is unnecessary for correctness. We can simply have the two while-loops (lines 13–15 and 17–19) follow the first while-loop. Only one of the two while-loops will be entered, depending on whether A or B was exhausted by the first while-loop. However, we include the if-else construct to make the code more intuitive for the reader.

We can illustrate the operation of the sequential merge function using the simple example from Fig. 12.1. During the first three (0–2) iterations of the while-loop, A[0], A[1], and B[0] are assigned to C[0], C[1], and C[2], respectively. The execution continues until the end of iteration 5. At this point, list A is completely visited, and the execution exits the while loop. A total of six C positions have been filled by A[0] through A[4] and B[0]. The loop in the true branch of the if-construct is used to copy the remaining B elements, that is, B[1] through B[3], into the remaining C positions.

The sequential merge function visits every input element from both A and B once and writes into each C position once. Its algorithm complexity is $O(m + n)$, and its execution time is linearly proportional to the total number of elements to be merged.

12.3 A parallelization approach

Siebert and Traff (2012) proposed an approach to parallelizing the merge operation. In their approach, each thread first determines the range of output positions (output range) that it is going to produce and uses that output range as the input to a *co-rank function* to identify the corresponding input ranges that will be merged to produce the output range. Once the input and output ranges have been determined, each thread can independently access its two input subarrays and one output subarray. Such independence allows each thread to perform the sequential merge function on their subarrays to do the merge in parallel. It should be clear that the key to the proposed parallelization approach is the co-rank function. We will now formulate the co-rank function.

Let A and B be two input arrays with m and n elements, respectively. We assume that both input arrays are sorted according to an ordering relation. The index of each array starts from 0. Let C be the sorted output array that is generated by merging A and B. Obviously, C has m + n elements. We can make the following observation:

Observation 1: For any k such that $0 \leq k < m + n$, there is either (case 1) an i such that $0 \leq i < m$ and C[k] receives its value from A[i] or (case 2) a j such that $0 \leq j < n$ and C[k] receives its value from B[j] in the merge process.

Fig. 12.3 shows the two cases of observation 1. In the first case, the C element in question comes from array A. For example, in Fig. 12.3A, C[4] (value 9) receives its values from A[3]. In this case, k=4 and i=3. We can see that the prefix subarray C[0]−C[3] of C[4] (the subarray of four elements that precedes C [4]) is the result of merging the prefix subarray A[0]−A[2] of A[3] (the subarray of three elements that precedes A[3]) and the prefix subarray B[0] of B[1] (the

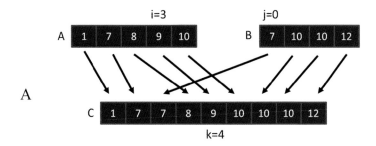

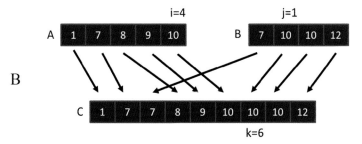

FIGURE 12.3

Examples of observation 1.

subarray of 4 − 3=1 element that precedes B[1]). The general formula is that sub-array C[0]−C[k − 1] (k elements) is the result of merging A[0]−A[i − 1] (i elements) and B[0]−B[k − i − 1] (k − i elements).

In the second case, the C element in question comes from array B. For example, in Fig. 12.3B, C[6] receives its value from B[1]. In this case, k=6 and j=1. The prefix subarray C[0]−C[5] of C[6] (the subarray of six elements that precedes C[6]) is the result of merging the prefix subarray A[0]−A[4] (the subarray of five elements that precedes A[5]) and B[0] (the subarray of 1 element that precedes B[1]). The general formula for this case is that subarray C[0]−C[k − 1] (k elements) is the result of merging A[0]−A[k − j − 1] (k − j elements) and B[0]−B[j − 1] (j elements).

In the first case, we find i and derive j as k − i. In the second case, we find j and derive i as k - j. We can take advantage of the symmetry and summarize the two cases into one observation:

Observation 2: For any k such that $0 \leq k < m + n$, we can find i and j such that k=i + j, $0 \leq i < m$ and $0 \leq j < n$ and the subarray C[0]−C[k − 1] is the result of merging subarray A[0]−A[i − 1] and subarray B[0]−B[j − 1].

Siebert and Traff (2012) also proved that i and j, which define the prefix sub-arrays of A and B that are needed to produce the prefix subarray of C of length k, are unique. For an element C[k] the index k is referred to as its rank. The unique indices i and j are referred to as its co-ranks. For example, in Fig. 12.3A, the rank and co-rank of C[4] are 4, 3, and 1. For another example the rank and co-rank of C[6] are 6, 5, and 1.

The concept of co-rank gives us a path to parallelizing the merge function. We can divide the work among threads by dividing the output array into subar-rays and assigning the generation of one subarray to each thread. Once the assignment has been done, the rank of output elements to be generated by each thread is known. Each thread then uses the co-rank function to determine the two input subarrays that it needs to merge into its output subarray.

Note that the main difference between the parallelization of the merge function and the parallelization of all our previous patterns is that the range of input data to be used by each thread cannot be determined with a simple index calculation. The range of input elements to be used by each thread depends on the actual input values. This makes the parallelized merge operation an interesting and challenging parallel computation pattern.

12.4 Co-rank function implementation

We define the co-rank function as a function that takes the rank (k) of an element in an output array C and information about the two input arrays A and B and returns the co-rank value (i) for the corresponding element in the input array A. The co-rank function has the following signature:

```
int co_rank(int k, int * A, int m, int * B, int n)
```

where k is the rank of the C element in question, A is a pointer to the input A array, m is the size of the A array, B is a pointer to the input B array, n is the size of the input B array, and the return value is i, the co-rank of k in A. The caller can then derive the j, the co-rank value of k in B, as k − i.

Before we study the implementation details of the co-rank function, it is beneficial to first learn about the ways in which a parallel merge function will use it. Such use of the co-rank function is illustrated in Fig. 12.4, where we use two threads to perform the merge operation. We assume that thread 0 generates C [0]−C[3] and thread 1 generates C[4]−C[8].

Intuitively, each thread calls the co-rank function to derive the beginning positions of the subarrays of A and B that will be merged into the C subarray that is assigned to the thread. For example, thread 1 calls the co-rank function with parameters (4, A, 5, B, 4). The goal of the co-rank function for thread 1 is to identify for its rank value k1=4 the co-rank values i1=3 and j1=1. That is, the subarray starting at C[4] is to be generated by merging the subarrays starting at A [3] and B[1]. Intuitively, we are looking for a total of four elements from A and B that will fill the first four elements of the output array prior to where thread 1 will merge its elements. By visual inspection we see that the choice of i1=3 and j1=1 meets our need. Thread 0 will take A[0]−A[2] and B[0], leaving out A[3] (value 9) and B[1] (value 10), which is where thread 1 will start merging.

If we changed the value of i1 to 2, we need to set the j1 value to 2 so that we can still have a total of four elements prior to thread 1. However, this means that we would include B[1] whose value is 10 in thread 0's elements. This value is larger than A[2] (value 8) that would be included in thread 1's elements. Such a change would make the resulting C array not properly sorted. On the other hand,

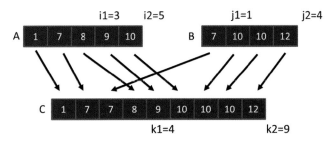

FIGURE 12.4

Example of co-rank function execution.

if we changed the value of i1 to 4, we need to set the j1 value to 0 to keep the total number of elements at 4. However, this would mean that we include A[3] (value 9) in thread 0's elements, which is larger than B[0] (value 7), which would be incorrectly included in thread 1's elements. These two examples point to a search algorithm can quickly identify the value.

In addition to identifying where its input segments start, thread 1 also needs to identify where they end. For this reason, thread 1 also calls the co-rank function with parameters (9, A, 5, B, 4). From Fig. 12.4 we see that the co-rank function should produce co-rank values i2=5 and j2=4. That is, since C[9] is beyond the last element of the C array, all elements of the A and B arrays should have been exhausted if one were trying to generate a C subarray starting at C[9]. In general, the input subarrays to be used by thread t are defined by the co-rank values for thread t and thread t + 1: $A[i_t]-A[i_{t+1}]$ and $B[j_t]-B[j_{t+1}]$.

The co-rank function is essentially a search operation. Since both input arrays are sorted, we can use a binary search or even a higher radix search to achieve a computational complexity of O(log N) for the search. Fig. 12.5 shows a co-rank function based on binary search. The co-rank function uses two pairs of marker variables to delineate the range of A array indices and the range of B array indices being considered for the co-rank values. Variables i and j are the candidate co-rank return values that are being considered in the current binary search iteration. Variables i_low and j_low are the smallest possible co-rank values that could be generated by the function. Line 02 initializes i to its largest possible

```
01    int co_rank(int k, int* A, int m, int* B, int n) {
02        int i = k < m ? k : m; // i = min(k,m)
03        int j = k - i;
04        int i_low = 0 > (k-n) ? 0 : k-n; // i_low = max(0,k-n)
05        int j_low = 0 > (k-m) ? 0 : k-m; // i_low = max(0,k-m)
06        int delta;
07        bool active = true;
08        while(active) {
09            if (i > 0 && j < n && A[i-1] > B[j]) {
10                delta = ((i - i_low +1) >> 1) ; // ceil(i-i_low)/2)
11                j_low = j;
12                j = j + delta;
13                i = i - delta;
14            } else if (j > 0 && i < m && B[j-1] >= A[i]) {
15                delta = ((j - j_low +1) >> 1) ;
16                i_low = i;
17                i = i + delta;
18                j = j - delta;
19            } else {
20                active = false;
21            }
22        }
23        return i;
24    }
```

FIGURE 12.5

A co-rank function based on binary search.

value. If the k value is greater than m, line 02 initializes i to m, since the co-rank i value cannot be larger than the size of the A array. Otherwise, line 02 initializes i to k, since i cannot be larger than k. The co-rank j value is initialized as k − i (line 03). Throughout the execution the co-rank function maintains this important invariant relation. The sum of the i and j variables is always equal to the value of the input variable k (the rank value).

The initialization of the i_low and j_low variables (lines 4 and 5) requires a little more explanation. These variables allow us to limit the scope of the search and make it faster. Functionally, we could set both values to zero and let the rest of the execution elevate them to more accurate values. This makes sense when the k value is smaller than m and n. However, when k is larger than n, we know that the i value cannot be less than k − n. The reason is that the greatest number of C[k] prefix subarray elements that can come from the B array is n. Therefore a minimum of k − n elements must come from A. Therefore the i value can never be smaller than k − n; we may as well set i_low to k − n. Following the same argument, the j_low value cannot be less than k − m, which is the least number of elements of B that must be used in the merge process and thus the lower bound of the final co-rank j value.

We will use the example in Fig. 12.6 to illustrate the operation of the co-rank function in Fig. 12.5. The example assumes that three threads are used to merge arrays A and B into C. Each thread is responsible for generating an output subarray of three elements. We will first trace through the binary search steps of the co-rank function for thread 1, which is responsible for generating C[3]−C[5]. The reader should be able to determine that thread 1 calls the co-rank function with parameters (3, A, 5, B, 4).

As is shown in Fig. 12.5, line 2 of the co-rank function initializes i to 3, which is the k value, since k is smaller than m (value 5) in this example. Also, i_low is set 0. The i and i_low values define the section of A array that is currently being searched to determine the final co-rank i value. Thus only 0, 1, 2, and 3 are being considered for the co-rank i value. Similarly, the j and j_low values are set to 0 and 0.

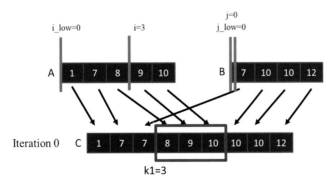

FIGURE 12.6

Iteration 0 of the co-rank function operation example for thread 1.

The main body of the co-rank function is a while-loop (line 08) that iteratively zooms into the final co-rank i and j values. The goal is to find a pair of i and j values that result in A[i-1] ≤ B[j] and B[j-1] < A[i]. The intuition is that we choose the i and j values so none of the values in the A subarray used for generating the previous output subarray (referred to as the previous A subarray) should be greater than any elements in the B subarray used for generating the current output subarray (referred to as the current B subarray). Note that the largest A element in the previous subarray could be equal to the smallest element in the current B subarray, since the A elements take precedence in placement into the output array whenever a tie occurs between an A element and a B element because of the stability requirement.

In Fig. 12.5 the first if-construct in the while-loop (line 09) tests whether the current i value is too high. If so, it will adjust the marker values so that it reduces the search range for i by about half toward the smaller end. This is done by reducing the i value by about half the difference between i and i_low. In Fig. 12.7, for iteration 0 of the while-loop, the if-construct finds that the i value (3) is too high, since A[i − 1], whose value is 8, is greater than B[j], whose value is 7. The next few statements proceed to reduce the search range for i by reducing its value by delta=(3 − 0 + 1) ≫ 1=2 (lines 10 and 13) while keeping the i_low value unchanged. Therefore the i_low and i values for the next iteration will be 0 and 1.

The code also makes the search range for j to be comparable to that of i by shifting it to above the current j location. This adjustment maintains the property that the sum of i and j should be equal to k. The adjustment is done by assigning the current j value to j_low (line 11) and adding the delta value to j (line 12). In our example the j_low and j values for the next iteration will be 0 and 2.

During iteration 1 of the while-loop, illustrated in Fig. 12.7, the i and j values are 1 and 2. The if-construct (line 9) finds the i value to be acceptable since A[i − 1] is A[0] whose value is 1, while B[j] is B[2] whose value is 10, so A[i − 1] is less than B[j]. Thus the condition of the first if-construct fails, and the body of the if-construct is skipped. However, the j value is found to be too high during this iteration, since B[j − 1] is B[1] (line 14), whose value is 10, while A[i] is A

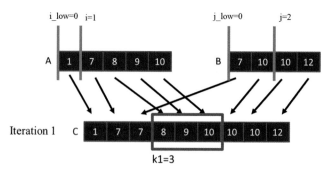

FIGURE 12.7

Iteration 1 of the co-rank function operation example for thread 1.

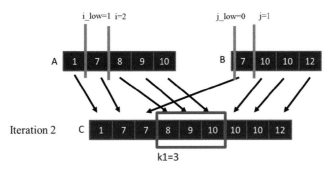

FIGURE 12.8

Iteration 2 of the co-rank function operation example for thread 0.

[1], whose value is 7. Therefore the second if-construct will adjust the markers for the next iteration so that the search range for j will be reduced by about half toward the lower values. This is done by subtracting delta=(j − j_low + 1) ≫ 1=1 from j (lines 15 and 18). As a result, the j_low and j values for the next iteration will be 0 and 1. It also makes the next search range for i the same size as that for j but shifts it up by delta locations. This is done by assigning the current i value to i_low (line 16) and adding the delta value to i (line 17). Therefore the i_low and i values for the next iteration will be 1 and 2, respectively.

During iteration 2, illustrated in Fig. 12.8, the i and j values are 2 and 1. Both if-constructs (lines 9 and 14) will find both i and j values acceptable. For the first if-construct, A[i − 1] is A[1] (value 7) and B[j] is B[1] (value 10), so the condition A[i − 1] ≤ B[j] is satisfied. For the second if-construct, B[j − 1] is B[0] (value 7) and A [i] is A[2] (value 8), so the condition B[j − 1] < A[i] is also satisfied. The co-rank function sets a flag to exit the while-loop (lines 20 and 08) and returns the final i value 2 as the co-rank i value (line 23). The caller thread can derive the final co-rank j value as k − i=3 − 2=1. An inspection of Fig. 12.8 confirms that co-rank values 2 and 1 indeed identify the correct A and B input subarrays for thread 1.

The reader should repeat the same process for thread 2 as an exercise. Also, note that if the input streams are much longer, the delta values will be reduced by half in each step, so the algorithm is of $\log_2(N)$ complexity, where N is the maximum of the two input array sizes.

12.5 A basic parallel merge kernel

For the rest of this chapter we assume that the input A and B arrays reside in the global memory. We further assume that a kernel is launched to merge the two input arrays to produce an output array C that is also in the global memory. Fig. 12.9 shows a basic kernel that is a straightforward implementation of the parallel merge function described in Section 12.3.

```
01  __global__ void merge_basic_kernel(int* A, int m, int* B, int n, int* C) {
02      int tid = blockIdx.x*blockDim.x + threadIdx.x;
03      int elementsPerThread = ceil((m+n)/(blockDim.x*gridDim.x));
04      int k_curr = tid*elementsPerThread; // start output index
05      int k_next = min((tid+1)*elementsPerThread, m+n); // end output index
06      int i_curr = co_rank(k_curr, A, m, B, n);
07      int i_next = co_rank(k_next, A, m, B, n);
08      int j_curr = k_curr - i_curr;
09      int j_next = k_next - i_next;
10      merge_sequential(&A[i_curr], i_next-i_curr, &B[j_curr], j_next-j_curr, &C[k_curr]);
11  }
```

FIGURE 12.9

A basic merge kernel.

As we can see, the kernel is simple. It first divides the work among threads by calculating the starting point of the output subarray to be produced by the current thread (k_curr) and that of the next thread (k_next). Keep in mind that the total number of output elements may not be a multiple of the number of threads. Each thread then makes two calls to the co-rank function. The first call uses k_curr as the rank parameter, which is the first (lowest-indexed) element of the output subarray that the current thread is to generate. The returned co-rank value, i_curr, gives the lowest-indexed input A array element that belongs to the input subarray to be used by the thread. This co-rank value can also be used to get j_curr for the B input subarray. The i_curr and j_curr values mark the beginning of the input subarrays for the thread. Therefore &A[i_curr] and &B[j_curr] are the pointers to the beginning of the input subarrays to be used by the current thread.

The second call uses k_next as the rank parameter to get the co-rank values for the next thread. These co-rank values mark the positions of the lowest-indexed input array elements to be used by the next thread. Therefore i_next − i_curr and j_next − j_curr give the sizes of the subarrays of A and B to be used by the current thread. The pointer to the beginning of the output subarray to be produced by the current thread is &C[k_curr]. The final step of the kernel is to call the merge_sequential function (from Fig. 12.2) with these parameters.

The execution of the basic merge kernel can be illustrated with the example in Fig. 12.8. The k_curr values for the three threads (threads 0, 1, and 2) will be 0, 3, and 6. We will focus on the execution of thread 1 whose k_curr value will be 3. The i_curr and j_curr values determined from the first co-rank function call are 2 and 1. The k_next value for thread 1 will be 6. The second call to the co-rank function helps determine the i_next and j_next values of 5 and 1. Thread 1 then calls the merge function with parameters (&A[2], 3, &B[1], 0, &C[3]). Note that the 0 value for parameter n indicates that none of the three elements of the output subarray for thread 1 should come from array B. This is indeed the case in Fig. 12.8: output elements C[3] − C[5] all come from A[2] − A[4].

While the basic merge kernel is quite simple and elegant, it falls short in memory access efficiency. First, it is clear that when executing the merge_sequential function, adjacent threads in a warp are not accessing adjacent memory locations when they read and write the input and output subarray elements. For the example in Fig. 12.8, during the first iteration of the merge_sequential function execution, the three adjacent threads would read A[0], A[2], and B[0]. They will then write to C[0], C[3], and C[6]. Thus their memory accesses are not coalesced, resulting in poor utilization of memory bandwidth.

Second, the threads also need to access A and B elements from the global memory when they execute the co-rank function. Since the co-rank function does a binary search, the access patterns are somewhat irregular and will be unlikely to be coalesced. As a result, these accesses can further reduce the efficiency of utilizing the memory bandwidth. It would be helpful if we can avoid these uncoalesced accesses to the global memory by the co-rank function.

12.6 A tiled merge kernel to improve coalescing

In Chapter 6, Performance Considerations, we mentioned three main strategies for improving memory coalescing in kernels: (1) rearranging the mapping of threads to data, (2) rearranging the data itself, and (3) transferring the data between the global memory and the shared memory in a coalesced manner and performing the irregular accesses in the shared memory. For the merge pattern we will use the third strategy, which leverages shared memory to improve coalescing. Using shared memory also has the advantage of capturing the small amount of data reuse across the co-rank functions and the sequential merge phase.

The key observation is that the input A and B subarrays to be used by the adjacent threads are adjacent to each other in memory. Essentially, all threads in a block will collectively use larger, block-level subarrays of A and B to generate a larger, block-level subarray of C. We can call the co-rank function for the entire block to get the starting and ending locations for the block-level A and B subarrays. Using these block-level co-rank values, all threads in the block can cooperatively load the elements of the block-level A and B subarrays into the shared memory in a coalesced pattern.

Fig. 12.10 shows the block-level design of a tiled merge kernel. In this example, we assume that three blocks will be used for the merge operation. At the bottom of the figure, we show that C is partitioned into three block-level subarrays. We delineate these partitions with gray vertical bars. On the basis of the partition, each block calls the co-rank functions to partition the input array into subarrays to be used for each block. We also delineate the input partitions with gray vertical bars. Note that the input partitions can vary significantly in size according to the actual data element values in the input arrays. For example, in Fig. 12.8 the input A subarray is significantly larger than the input B subarray for thread 0. On the

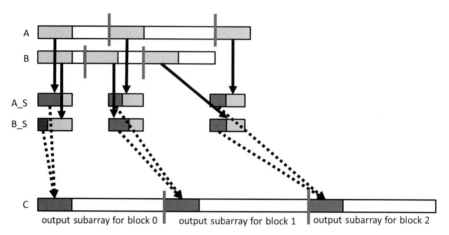

FIGURE 12.10

Design of a tiled merge kernel.

other hand, the input A subarray is significantly smaller than the input B subarray for thread 1. Obviously, the combined size of the two input subarrays must always be equal to the size of the output subarray for each thread.

We will declare two shared memory arrays A_S and B_S for each block. Owing to the limited shared memory size, A_S and B_S may not be able to cover the entire input subarrays for the block. Therefore we will take an iterative approach. Assume that the A_S and B_S arrays can each hold x elements, while each output subarray contains y elements. Each thread block will perform its operation in y/x iterations. During each iteration, all threads in a block will cooperatively load x elements from the block's input A subarray and x elements from its input B subarray.

The first iteration of each thread is illustrated in Fig. 12.10. We show that for each block, a light gray section of the input A subarray is loaded into A_S, and a light gray section of the input B subarray is loaded into B_S. With x A elements and x B elements in the shared memory, the thread block has enough input elements to generate at least x output array elements. All threads are guaranteed to have all the input subarray elements they need for the iteration. One might ask why loading a total of 2x input elements can guarantee the generation of only x output elements. The reason is that in the worst case, all elements of the current output section may all come from one of the input sections. This uncertainty of input usage makes the tiling design for the merge kernel much more challenging than the previous patterns. One can be more accurate in loading the input tiles by first calling the co-rank function for the current and next output sections. In this case, we pay an additional binary search operation to save on redundant data loading. We leave this alternative implementation as an exercise. We will also increase the efficiency of memory bandwidth utilization with a circular buffer design in Section 12.7.

Fig. 12.10 also shows that threads in each block will use a portion of the A_S and a portion of the B_S in each iteration, shown as dark gray sections, to generate a section of x elements in their output C subarray. This process is illustrated with the dotted arrows going from the A_S and B_S dark gray sections to the C dark gray sections. Note that each thread block may well use a different portion of its A_S versus B_S sections. Some blocks may use more elements from A_S, and others may use more from B_S. The actual portions that are used by each block depend on the input data element values.

Fig. 12.11 shows the first part of a tiled merge kernel. A comparison against Fig. 12.9 shows remarkable similarity. This part is essentially the block-level version of the setup code for the thread-level basic merge kernel. Only one thread in the block needs to calculate the co-rank values for the rank values of the beginning output index of the current block and that of the beginning output index of the next block. The values are placed into the shared memory so that they can be visible to all threads in the block. Having only one thread to call the co-rank functions reduces the number of global memory accesses by the co-rank functions and should improve the efficiency of the global memory accesses. A barrier synchronization is used to ensure that all threads wait until the block-level co-rank values are available in the shared memory A_S[0] and A_S[1] locations before they proceed to use the values.

Recall that since the input subarrays may be too large to fit into the shared memory, the kernel takes an iterative approach. The kernel receives a tile_size argument that specifies the number of A elements and B elements to be accommodated in the shared memory. For example, a tile_size value of 1024 means that 1024 A array elements and 1024 B array elements are to be accommodated in the

```
01  __global__ void merge_tiled_kernel(int* A,int m, int* B, int n, int* C, int tile_size) {
    /* shared memory allocation */
02    extern __shared__ int shareAB[];
03    int * A_S = &shareAB[0];                    // shareA is first half of shareAB
04    int * B_S = &shareAB[tile_size];            // shareB is second half of shareAB
05    int C_curr = blockIdx.x * ceil((m+n)/gridDim.x); // start point of block's C subarray
06    int C_next = min((blockIdx.x+1) * ceil((m+n)/gridDim.x), (m+n)); // ending point

07    if (threadIdx.x ==0){
08      A_S[0] = co_rank(C_curr, A, m, B, n); // Make block-level co-rank values visible
09      A_S[1] = co_rank(C_next, A, m, B, n); // to other threads in the block
10    }
11    __syncthreads();
12    int A_curr  = A_S[0];
13    int A_next  = A_S[1];
14    int B_curr = C_curr - A_curr;
15    int B_next  = C_next - A_next;
16    __syncthreads();
```

FIGURE 12.11

Part 1: Identifying block-level output and input subarrays.

shared memory. This means that each block will dedicate (1024 + 1024) × 4=8192 bytes of shared memory to hold the A and B array elements.

As a simple example, assume that we would like to merge an A array of 33,000 elements (m=33,000) with a B array of 31,000 elements (n=31,000). The total number of output C elements is 64,000. Further assume that we will use 16 blocks (gridDim.x=16) and 128 threads in each block (blockDim.x=128). Each block will generate 64,000/16=4000 output C array elements.

If we assume that the tile_size value is 1024, the while-loop in Fig. 12.12 will need to take four iterations for each block to complete the generation of its 4000 output elements. During iteration 0 of the while-loop, the threads in each block will cooperatively load 1024 elements of A and 1024 elements of B into the shared memory. Since there are 128 threads in a block, they can collectively load 128 elements in each iteration of the for-loop (line 26). So the first for-loop in Fig. 12.12 will iterate 8 times for all threads in a block to complete the loading of the 1024 A elements. The second for-loop will also iterate 8 times to complete the loading the 1024 B elements. Note that threads use their threadIdx.x values to select the element to load, so consecutive threads load consecutive elements. The memory accesses are coalesced. We will come back later and explain the if-conditions and how the index expressions for loading the A and B elements are formulated.

Once the input tiles are in the shared memory, individual threads can divide up the input tiles and merge their portions in parallel. This is done by assigning a section of the output to each thread and running the co-rank function to determine the sections of shared memory data that should be used for generating that output section. The code in Fig. 12.13 completes this step. Keep in mind that this is a continuation of the while-loop that started in Fig. 12.12. During each iteration of the while-loop, threads in a block will generate a total of tile_size C elements, using the data that we loaded into shared memory. (The exception is the last

```
17    int counter = 0;                                        //iteration counter
18    int C_length = C_next - C_curr;
19    int A_length = A_next - A_curr;
20    int B_length = B_next - B_curr;
21    int total_iteration = ceil((C_length)/tile_size);        //total iteration
22    int C_completed = 0;
23    int A_consumed = 0;
24    int B_consumed = 0;
25    while(counter < total_iteration){
         /* loading tile-size A and B elements into shared memory */
26       for(int i=0; i<tile_size; i+=blockDim.x){
27           if( i + threadIdx.x < A_length - A_consumed) {
28               A_S[i + threadIdx.x] = A[A_curr + A_consumed + i + threadIdx.x ];
29           }
30       }
31       for(int i=0; i<tile_size; i+=blockDim.x) {
32           if(i + threadIdx.x  < B_length - B_consumed) {
33               B_S[i + threadIdx.x] = B[B_curr + B_consumed + i + threadIdx.x];
34           }
35       }
36       __syncthreads();
```

FIGURE 12.12

Part 2: Loading A and B elements into the shared memory.

```
37        int c_curr  = threadIdx.x   *  (tile_size/blockDim.x);
38        int c_next = (threadIdx.x+1) * (tile_size/blockDim.x);
39        c_curr  = (c_curr <= C_length - C_completed) ? c_curr : C_length - C_completed;
40        c_next = (c_next <= C_length - C_completed) ? c_next : C_length - C_completed;
          /* find co-rank for c_curr and c_next */
41        int a_curr = co_rank(c_curr, A_S, min(tile_size, A_length-A_consumed),
                                       B_S, min(tile_size, B_length-B_consumed));
42        int b_curr = c_curr - a_curr;
43        int a_next = co_rank(c_next, A_S, min(tile_size, A_length-A_consumed),
                                       B_S, min(tile_size, B_length-B_consumed));
44        int b_next = c_next - a_next;

          /* All threads call the sequential merge function */
45        merge_sequential (A_S+a_curr, a_next-a_curr, B_S+b_curr, b_next-b_curr,
              C+C_curr+C_completed+c_curr);
          /* Update the number of A and B elements that have been consumed thus far */
46        counter ++;
47        C_completed += tile_size;
48        A_consumed += co_rank(tile_size,  A_S, tile_size, B_S, tile_size);
49        B_consumed = C_completed - A_consumed;
50        __syncthreads();
51    }
52 }
```

FIGURE 12.13

Part 3: All threads merge their individual subarrays in parallel.

iteration, which will be addressed later.) The co-rank function is run on the data in shared memory for individual threads. Each thread first calculates the starting position of its output range and that of the next thread and then uses these starting positions as the inputs to the co-rank function to identify its input ranges. Each thread will then call the sequential merge function to merge its portions of A and B elements (identified by the co-rank values) from the shared memory into its designated range of C elements.

Let us resume our running example. In each iteration of the while-loop, all threads in a block will be collectively generating 1024 output elements, using the two input tiles of A and B elements in the shared memory. (Once again, we will deal with the last iteration of the while-loop later.) The work is divided among 128 threads, so each thread will be generating eight output elements. While we know that each thread will consume a total of eight input elements in the shared memory, we need to call the co-rank function to find out the exact number of A elements versus B elements that each thread will consume and their start and end locations. For example, one thread may use three A elements and five B elements, while another may use six A elements and two B elements, and so on.

Collectively, the total number of A elements and B elements that are used by all threads in a block for the iteration will add up to 1024 in our example. For example, if all threads in a block use 476 A elements, we know that they also used $1024 - 476 = 548$ B elements. It may even be possible that all threads end up using 1024 A elements and 0 B elements. Keep in mind that a total of 2048 elements are loaded in the shared memory. Therefore in each iteration of the while-loop, only half of the A and B elements that were loaded into the shared memory will be used by all the threads in the block.

We are now ready to examine more details of the kernel function. Recall that we skipped the explanation of the index expressions for loading the A and B elements from the global memory into the shared memory. For each iteration of the while-loop, the starting point for loading the current tile in the A and B array depends on the total number of A and B elements that have been consumed by all threads of the block during the previous iterations of the while-loop. Assume that we keep track of the total number of A elements that were consumed by all the previous iterations of the while-loop in variable A_consumed. We initialize A_consumed to 0 before entering the while-loop. During iteration 0 of the while-loop, all blocks start their tiles from A[A_curr] since A_consumed is 0 at the beginning of iteration 0. During each subsequent iteration of the while-loop, the tile of A elements will start at A[A_curr + A_consumed].

Fig. 12.14 illustrates the index calculation for iteration 1 of the while-loop. In our running example in Fig. 12.10 we show the A_S elements that are consumed by the block of threads during iteration 0 as the dark gray portion of the tile in A_S. During iteration 1 the tile to be loaded from the global memory for block 0 should start at the location right after the section that contains the A elements consumed in iteration 0. In Fig. 12.14, for each block, the section of A elements that is consumed in iteration 0 is shown as the small white section at the beginning of the A subarray (marked by the vertical bars) assigned to the block. Since the length of the small section is given by the value of A_consumed, the tile to be loaded for iteration 1 of the while-loop starts at A[A_curr + A_consumed]. Similarly, the tile to be loaded for iteration 1 of the while-loop starts at B[B_curr + B_consumed].

Note that in Fig. 12.13, A_consumed (line 48) and C_completed are accumulated through the while-loop iterations. Also, B_consumed is derived from the accumulated A_consumed and C_completed values, so it is also accumulated through the while-loop iterations. Therefore they always reflect the number of A

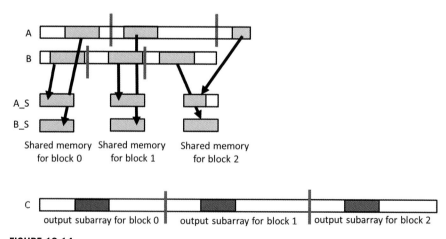

FIGURE 12.14

Iteration 1 of the while-loop in the running example.

and B elements that are consumed by all the iterations so far. At the beginning of each iteration the tiles to be loaded for the iteration always start with A[A_curr + A_consumed] and B[B_curr + B_consumed].

During the last iterations of the while-loop, there may not be enough input A or B elements to fill the input tiles in the shared memory for some of the thread blocks. For example, in Fig. 12.14, for thread block 2, the number of remaining A elements for iteration 1 is less than the tile size. An if-statement should be used to prevent the threads from attempting to load elements that are outside the input subarrays for the block. The first if-statement in Fig. 12.12 (line 27) detects such attempts by checking whether the index of the A_S element that a thread is trying to load exceeds the number of remaining A elements given by the value of the expression A_length − A_consumed. The if-statement ensures that the threads load only the elements that are within the remaining section of the A subarray. The same is done for the B elements (line 32).

With the if-statements and the index expressions, the tile loading process should work well as long as A_consumed and B_consumed give the total number of A and B elements consumed by the thread block in previous iterations of the while-loop. This brings us to the code at the end of the while-loop in Fig. 12.13. These statements update the total number of C elements generated by the while-loop iterations thus far. For all but the last iteration, each iteration generates additional tile_size C elements.

The next two statements update the total number of A and B elements consumed by the threads in the block. For all but the last iteration the number of additional A elements consumed by the thread block is the returned value of

```
co_rank(tile_size, A_S, tile_size, B_S, tile_size)
```

As we mentioned before, the calculation of the number of elements consumed may not be correct at the end of the last iteration of the while-loop. There may not be a full tile of elements left for the final iteration. However, since the while-loop will not iterate any further, the A_consumed, B_consumed, and C_completed values will not be used so the incorrect results will not cause any harm. However, one should remember that if for any reason these values are needed after exiting the while-loop, the three variables will not have the correct values. The values of A_length, B_length, and C_length should be used instead, since all the elements in the designated subarrays to the thread block will have been consumed at the exit of the while-loop.

The tiled kernel achieves substantial reduction in global memory accesses by the co-rank function and makes the global memory accesses coalesce. However, as is, the kernel has a significant deficiency. It makes use of only half of the data that is loaded into the shared memory in each iteration. The unused data in the shared memory is simply reloaded in the next iteration. This wastes half of the memory bandwidth. In the next section we will present a circular buffer scheme for managing the tiles of data elements in the shared memory, which allows the kernel to fully utilize all the A and B elements that have been loaded into the shared memory. As we will see, this increased efficiency comes with a substantial increase in code complexity.

12.7 A circular buffer merge kernel

The design of the circular buffer merge kernel, which will be referred to as merge_circular_buffer_kernel, is largely the same as that of the merge_tiled_kernel kernel in the previous section. The main difference lies in the management of the A and B elements in the shared memory to enable full utilization of all the elements loaded from the global memory. The overall structure of the merge_tiled_kernel is shown in Figs. 12.12 through 12.14; it assumes that the tiles of the A and B elements always start at A_S[0] and B_S[0], respectively. After each while-loop iteration the kernel loads the next tile, starting from A_S[0] and B_S[0]. The inefficiency of the merge_tiled_kernel comes from the fact that part of the next tiles of elements are in the shared memory, but we reload the entire tile from the global memory and write over these remaining elements from the previous iteration.

Fig. 12.15 shows the main idea of merge_circular_buffer_kernel. We will continue to use the example from Figs. 12.10 and 12.14. Two additional variables, A_S_start and B_S_start, are added to allow each iteration of the while-loop in

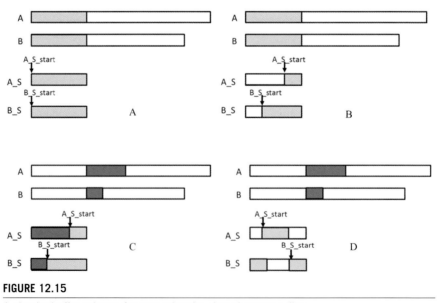

FIGURE 12.15

A circular buffer scheme for managing the shared memory tiles.

Fig. 12.12 to start its A and B tiles at dynamically determined positions inside A_S[0] and B_S[0], respectively. This added tracking allows each iteration of the while-loop to start the tiles with the remaining A and B elements from the previous iteration. Since there is no previous iteration when we first enter the while-loop, these two variables are initialized to 0 before entering the while-loop.

During iteration 0, since the values of A_S_start and B_S_start are both 0, the tiles will start with A_S[0] and B_S[0]. This is illustrated in Fig. 12.15A, where we show the tiles that will be loaded from the global memory (A and B) into the shared memory (A_S and B_S) as light gray sections. Once these tiles have been loaded into the shared memory, merge_circular_buffer_kernel will proceed with the merge operation in the same way as the merge_tile_kernel.

We also need to update the A_S_start and B_S_start variables for use in the next iteration by advancing the value of these variables by the number of A and B elements consumed from the shared memory during the current iteration. Keep in mind that the size of each buffer is limited to tile_size. At some point, we will need to reuse the buffer locations at the beginning part of the A_S and B_S arrays. This is done by checking whether the new A_S_start and B_S_start values exceed the tile_size. If so, we subtract tile_size from them as shown in the following if-statement:

```
A_S_start = (A_S_start + A_S_consumed)%tile_size;
B_S_start = (B_S_start + B_S_consumed)%tile_size;
```

Fig. 12.15B illustrates the update of the A_S_start and B_S_start variables. At the end of iteration 0 a portion of the A tile and a portion of the B tile have been consumed. The consumed portions are shown as white sections in A_S and B_S in Fig. 12.15B. We update the A_S_start and B_S_start values to the position immediately after the consumed sections in the shared memory.

Fig. 12.15C illustrates the operations for filling the A and B tiles at the beginning of iteration 1 of the while-loop. A_S_consumed is a variable that is added to track the number of A elements used in the current iteration. The variable is useful for filling the tile in the next iteration. At the beginning of each iteration we need to load a section of up to A_S_consumed elements to fill up the A tile in the shared memory. Similarly, we need to load a section of up to B_S_consumed elements to fill up the B tile in the shared memory. The two sections that are loaded are shown as dark gray sections in Fig. 12.15C. Note that the tiles effectively "wrap around" in the A_S and B_S arrays, since we are reusing the space of the A and B elements that were consumed during iteration 0.

Fig. 12.15D illustrates the updates to A_S_start and B_S_start at the end of iteration 1. The sections of elements that were consumed during iteration 1 are shown as the white sections. Note that in A_S, the consumed section wraps around to the beginning part of A_S. The value of the A_S_start variable is also wrapped around by the % modulo operator. It should be clear that we will need to adjust the code for loading and using the tiled elements to support this circular usage of the A_S and B_S arrays.

Part 1 of merge_circular_buffer_kernel is identical to that of merge_tiled_kernel in Fig. 12.11, so we will not present it. Fig. 12.16 shows part 2 of the circular buffer kernel. Refer to Fig. 12.12 for variable declarations that remain the same. New variables A_S_start, B_S_start, A_S_consumed, and B_S_consumed are initialized to 0 before we enter the while-loop.

Note that the exit conditions of the two for-loops have been adjusted. Instead of always loading a full tile, as was the case in the merge kernel in Fig. 12.12, each for-loop in Fig. 12.16 is set up to load only the number of elements that are needed to refill the tiles, given by A_S_consumed. The section of the A elements to be loaded by a thread block in the ith for-loop iteration starts at global memory location A[A_curr + A_consumed + i]. Note that i is incremented by blockDim.x after each iteration. Thus the A element to be loaded by a thread in the ith for-loop iteration is A[A_curr + A_consumed + i + threadIdx.x]. The index for each thread to place its A element into the A_S array is A_S_start + (tile_size − A_S_consumed) + I + threadIdx, since the tile starts at A_S[A_S_start] and there are (tile_size − A_S_consumed) elements remaining in the buffer from the previous iteration of the while-loop. The modulo (%) operation checks whether the index value is greater than or equal to tile_size. If it is, it is wrapped back into the beginning part of the array by subtracting tile_size from the index value. The same analysis applies to the for-loop for loading the B tile and is left as an exercise for the reader.

Using the A_S and B_S arrays as circular buffers also incurs additional complexity in the implementation of the co-rank and merge functions. Part of the additional complexity could be reflected in the thread-level code that calls these functions. However, in general, it is better if one can efficiently handle the complexities inside the library functions to minimize the increased level of complexity in the user code. We show such an approach in Fig. 12.17. Fig. 12.17A shows

```
25   int A_S_start = 0;
26   int B_S_start = 0;
27   int A_S_consumed = tile_size;   //in the first iteration, fill the tile_size
28   int B_S_consumed = tile_size;   //in the first iteration, fill the tile_size
29   while(counter < total_iteration) {
         /* loading A_S_consumed elements into A_S */
30       for(int i=0; i<A_S_consumed; i+=blockDim.x) {
31         if(i+threadIdx.x < A_length-A_consumed && (i+threadIdx.x) < A_S_consumed) {
32             A_S[(A_S_start + (tile_size - A_S_consumed)+ i + threadIdx.x)%tile_size] =
                   A[A_curr + A_consumed + i + threadIdx.x ];
33         }
34       }
         /* loading B_S_consumed elements into B_S */
35       for(int i=0; i<B_S_consumed; i+=blockDim.x) {
36         if(i+threadIdx.x < B_length-B_consumed && (i+threadIdx.x) < B_S_consumed) {
37             B_S[(B_S_start + (tile_size - A_S_consumed) +i + threadIdx.x)%tile_size] =
                   B[B_curr + B_consumed + i + threadIdx.x];
38         }
39   }
```

FIGURE 12.16

Part 2 of a circular buffer merge kernel.

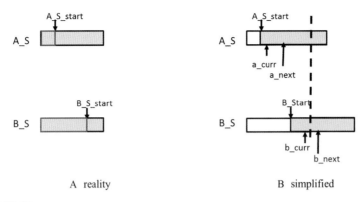

A reality   B simplified

FIGURE 12.17

A simplified model for the co-rank values when using a circular buffer.

the implementation of the circular buffer. A_S_start and B_S_start mark the beginning of the tile in the circular buffer. The tiles wrap around in the A_S and B_S arrays, shown as the light gray section to the left of A_S_start and B_S_start.

Keep in mind that the co-rank values are used for threads to identify the starting position, ending position, and length of the input subarrays that they are to use. When we employ circular buffers, we could provide the co-rank values as the actual indices in the circular buffer. However, this would incur quite a bit of complexity in the merge_circular_buffer_kernel code. For example, the a_next value could be smaller than the a_curr value, since the tile is wrapped around in the A_S array. Thus one would need to test for the case and calculate the length of the section as a_next-a_curr + tile_size. However, in other cases when a_next is larger than a_curr, the length of the section is simply a_next − a_curr.

Fig. 12.17B shows a simplified model for defining, deriving, and using the co-rank values with the circular buffer. In this model, each tile appears to be in a continuous section starting at A_S_start and B_S_start. In the case of the B_S tile in Fig. 12.17A, b_next is wrapped around and would be smaller than b_curr in the circular buffer. However, as is shown in Fig. 12.17B, the simplified model provides the illusion that all elements are in a continuous section of up to tile_size elements; thus a_next is always larger than or equal to a_curr, and b_next is always larger than or equal to b_curr. It is up to the implementation of the co_rank_circular and merge_sequential_circular functions to map this simplified view of the co-rank values into the actual circular buffer indices so that they can carry out their functionalities correctly and efficiently.

The co_rank_circular and merge_sequential_circular functions have the same set of parameters as the original co_rank and merge functions plus three additional parameters: A_S_start, B_S_start, and tile_size. These three additional parameters inform the functions where the current starting point of the buffers are and how big the buffers are. Fig. 12.18 shows the revised thread-level code based

```
40      int c_curr  = threadIdx.x   *  (tile_size/blockDim.x);
41      int c_next = (threadIdx.x+1) *  (tile_size/blockDim.x);

42      c_curr  = (c_curr <= C_length-C_completed) ? c_curr : C_length-C_completed;
43      c_next = (c_next <= C_length-C_completed) ? c_next : C_length-C_completed;
        /* find co-rank for c_curr and c_next */
44      int a_curr = co_rank_circular(c_curr,
                     A_S, min(tile_size, A_length-A_consumed),
                     B_S, min(tile_size, B_length-B_consumed),
                     A_S_start, B_S_start, tile_size);
45      int b_curr = c_curr - a_curr;
46      int a_next = co_rank_circular(c_next,
                     A_S, min(tile_size, A_length-A_consumed),
                     B_S, min(tile_size, B_length-B_consumed),
                     A_S_start, B_S_start, tile_size);

47      int b_next = c_next - a_next;
        /* All threads call the circular-buffer version of the sequential merge function */
48      merge_sequetial_circular( A_S, a_next-a_curr,
                     B_S, b_next-b_curr,   C+C_curr+C_completed+c_curr,
                     A_S_start+a_curr, B_S_start+b_curr, tile_size);

        /* Figure out the work has been done */
49      counter ++;
50      A_S_consumed = co_rank_circular(min(tile_size,C_length-C_completed),
                     A_S, min(tile_size, A_length-A_consumed),
                     B_S, min(tile_size, B_length-B_consumed),
                     A_S_start, B_S_start, tile_size);
51      B_S_consumed = min(tile_size, C_length-C_completed) - A_S_consumed;
52      A_consumed += A_S_consumed;
53      C_completed += min(tile_size, C_length-C_completed);
54      B_consumed = C_completed - A_consumed;

55      A_S_start = (A_S_start + A_S_consumed) % tile_size;
56      B_S_start = (B_S_start + B_S_consumed) % tile_size;
57      __syncthreads();
58    }
59  }
```

FIGURE 12.18

Part 3 of a circular buffer merge kernel.

on the simplified model for the co-rank value using circular buffers. The only change to the code is that the co_rank_circular and merge_sequential_circular functions are called instead of the co_rank and merge functions. This demonstrates that a well-designed library interface can reduce the impact on the user code when employing sophisticated data structures.

Fig. 12.19 shows an implementation of the co-rank function that provides the simplified model for the co-rank values while correctly operating on circular buffers. It treats i, j, i_low, and j_low values in exactly the same way as the co-rank function in Fig. 12.5. The only change is that i, i − 1, j, and j − 1 are no longer used directly as indices in accessing the A_S and B_S arrays. They are used as offsets that are to be added to the values of A_S_start and B_S_start to form the index values i_cir, i_m_1_cir, j_cir, and j_m_1_cir. In each case, we need to test whether the actual index values need to be wrapped around to the beginning part of the buffer. Note that we cannot simply use i_cir − 1 to replace i − 1. We need to form the final index value and check for the need to wrap it around. It should be clear that the simplified model also helps to keep the co-rank function code simple: All the manipulations of the i, j, i_low, and j_low values remain the same; they do not need to deal with the circular nature of the buffers.

```
int co_rank_circular(int k, int* A, int m, int* B, int n, int A_S_start, int
B_S_start, int tile_size) {
    int i= k < m ? k : m;   // i = min(k,m)
    int j = k- i;
    int i_low = 0 > (k-n) ? 0 : k-n; // i_low = max(0, k-n)
    int j_low = 0 > (k-m) ? 0 : k-m; // i_low = max(0,k-m)
    int delta;
    bool active = true;
    while(active) {
        int i_cir = (A_S_start+i) % tile_size;
        int i_m_1_cir = (A_S_start+i-1) % tile_size);
        int j_cir = (B_S_start+j) % tile_size);
        int j_m_1_cir = (B_S_start+i-1) % tile_size);
        if (i > 0 && j < n && A[i_m_1_cir] > B[j_cir]) {
            delta = ((i - i_low +1) >> 1) ; // ceil(i-i_low)/2)
            j_low = j;
            i = i - delta;
            j = j + delta;
        } else if (j > 0 && i < m && B[j_m_1_cir] >= A[i_cir]) {
            delta = ((j - j_low +1) >> 1) ;
            i_low = i;
            i = i + delta;
            j = j - delta;
        } else {
            active = false;
        }
    }
    return i;
}
```

FIGURE 12.19

A co_rank_circular function that operates on circular buffers.

Fig. 12.20 shows an implementation of the merge_sequential_circular function. Similarly to the co_rank_circular function, the logic of the code remains essentially unchanged from the original merge function. The only change is in the way in which i and j are used to access the A and B elements. Since the merge_sequential_circular function will be called only by the thread-level code of merge_circular_buffer_kernel, the A and B elements that are accessed will be in the A_S and B_S arrays. In all four places where i or j is used to access the A or B elements, we need to form the i_cir or j_cir and test whether the index value needs to be wrapped around to the beginning part of the array. Otherwise, the code is the same as that of the merge function in Fig. 12.2.

Although we did not list all parts of merge_circular_buffer_kernel, the reader should be able to put it all together on the basis of the parts that we discussed. The use of tiling and circular buffers adds quite a bit of complexity. In particular, each thread uses quite a few more registers to keep track of the starting point and the remaining number of elements in the buffers. All these additional usages can potentially reduce the occupancy, or the number of thread-blocks that can be assigned to each of the streaming multiprocessors when the kernel is executed. However, since the merge operation is memory bandwidth bound, the computational and register resources are likely underutilized. Thus increasing the number of registers that are used and address calculations to conserve memory bandwidth is a reasonable tradeoff.

```
void merge_sequential_circular(int *A, int m, int *B, int n, int *C, int
A_S_start, int B_S_start, int tile_size) {
    int i = 0;   //virtual index into A
    int j = 0;   //virtual index into B
    int k = 0;  //virtual index into C
    while ((i < m) && (j < n)) {
        int i_cir = (A_S_start + i) % tile_size;
        int j_cir = (B_S_start + j) % tile_size;
        if (A[i_cir] <= B[j_cir]) {
            C[k++] = A[i_cir]; i++;
        } else {
            C[k++] = B[j_cir]; j++;
        }
    }
    if (i == m) { //done with A[] handle remaining B[]
        for (; j < n; j++) {
            int j_cir = (B_S_start + j) % tile_size;
            C[k++] = B[j_cir];
        }
    } else { //done with B[], handle remaining A[]
        for (; i <m; i++) {
            int i_cir = (A_S_start + i) % tile_size);
            C[k++] = A[i_cir];
        }
    }
}
```

FIGURE 12.20

Implementation of the merge_sequential_circular function.

12.8 Thread coarsening for merge

The price of parallelizing merge across many threads is primarily the fact that each thread has to perform its own binary search operations to identify the co-ranks of its output indices. The number of binary search operations that are performed can be reduced by reducing the number of threads that are launched, which can be done by assigning more output elements per thread. All the kernels that are presented in this chapter already have thread coarsening applied because they are all written to process multiple elements per thread. In a completely uncoarsened kernel, each thread would be responsible for a single output element. However, this would require a binary search operation to be performed for every single element, which would be prohibitively expensive. Hence coarsening is essential for amortizing the cost of the binary search operation across a substantial number of elements.

12.9 Summary

In this chapter we introduced the ordered merge pattern whose parallelization requires each thread to dynamically identify its input position ranges. Because the input ranges are data dependent, we resort to a fast search implementation of the co-rank function to identify the input range for each thread. The fact that the input ranges are data dependent also creates extra challenges when we use a tiling technique to conserve memory bandwidth and enable memory coalescing. As a result, we introduced the use of circular buffers to allow us to make full use of the data loaded from global memory. We showed that introducing a more complex data structure, such as a circular buffer, can significantly increase the complexity of the code that uses the data structure. Thus we introduce a simplified buffer access model for the code that manipulates and uses the indices to remain largely unchanged. The actual circular nature of the buffers is exposed only when these indices are used to access the elements in the buffer.

Exercises

1. Assume that we need to merge two lists A=(1, 7, 8, 9, 10) and B=(7, 10, 10, 12). What are the co-rank values for C[8]?
2. Complete the calculation of co-rank functions for thread 2 in Fig. 12.6.
3. For the for-loops that load A and B tiles in Fig. 12.12, add a call to the co-rank function so that we can load only the A and B elements that will be consumed in the current generation of the while-loop.
4. Consider a parallel merge of two arrays of size 1,030,400 and 608,000. Assume that each thread merges eight elements and that a thread block size of 1024 is used.
   a. In the basic merge kernel in Fig. 12.9, how many threads perform a binary search on the data in the global memory?
   b. In the tiled merge kernel in Figs. 12.11−12.13, how many threads perform a binary search on the data in the global memory?
   c. In the tiled merge kernel in Figs. 12.11−12.13, how many threads perform a binary search on the data in the shared memory?

References

Siebert, C., Traff, J.L., 2012. Efficient MPI implementation of a parallel, stable merge algorithm. Proceedings of the 19th European conference on recent advances in the message passing interface (EuroMPI'12). Springer-Verlag Berlin, Heidelberg, pp. 204–213.

Advanced Patterns and Applications

Sorting

13

With special contributions from Michael Garland

Chapter Outline

13.1 Background 294
13.2 Radix sort 295
13.3 Parallel radix sort 296
13.4 Optimizing for memory coalescing 300
13.5 Choice of radix value 302
13.6 Thread coarsening to improve coalescing 305
13.7 Parallel merge sort 306
13.8 Other parallel sort methods 308
13.9 Summary 309
Exercises 310
References 310

Sorting algorithms place the data elements of a list into a certain order. Sorting is foundational to modern data and information services, since the computational complexity of retrieving information from datasets can be significantly reduced if the dataset is in proper order. For example, sorting is often used to canonicalize the data for fast comparison and reconciliation between data lists. Also, the efficiency of many data-processing algorithms can be improved if the data is in certain order. Because of their importance, efficient sorting algorithms have been the subject of many computer science research efforts. Even with these efficient algorithms, sorting large data lists is still time consuming and can benefit from parallel execution. Parallelizing efficient sorting algorithms is challenging and requires elaborate designs. This chapter presents the parallel designs for two important types of efficient sorting algorithms: radix sort and merge sort. Most of the chapter is dedicated to radix sort; merge sort is discussed briefly on the basis of the parallel merge pattern that was covered in Chapter 12, Merge. Other popular parallel sorting algorithms, such as transposition sort and sampling sort, are also briefly discussed.

Programming Massively Parallel Processors. DOI: https://doi.org/10.1016/B978-0-323-91231-0.00019-7

13.1 **Background**

Sorting is one of the earliest applications for computers. A sorting algorithm arranges the elements of a list into a certain order. The order to be enforced by a sorting algorithm depends on the nature of these elements. Examples of popular orders are numerical order for numbers and lexicographical order for text strings. More formally, any sorting algorithm must satisfy the following two conditions:

1. The output is in either nondecreasing or nonincreasing order. For nondecreasing order, each element is no smaller than the previous element according to the desired order. For nonincreasing order, each element is no larger than the previous element according to the desired order.
2. The output is a permutation of the input. That is, the algorithm must retain all of the original input elements while reordering them into the output.

In its simplest form, the elements of a list can be sorted according to the values of each element. For example, the list [5, 2, 7, 1, 3, 2, 8] can be sorted into a nondecreasing order output [1, 2, 2, 3, 5, 7, 8].

A more complex and common use case is that each element consists of a key field and a value field and the list should be sorted on the basis of the key field. For example, assume that each element is a tuple (age, income in thousands of dollars). The list [(30,150), (32,80), (22,45), (29,80)] can be sorted by using the income as the key field into a nonincreasing order [(30,150), (32,80), (29,80), (22,45)].

Sorting algorithms can be classified into stable and unstable algorithms. A stable sort algorithm preserves the original order of appearance when two elements have equal key value. For example, when sorting the list [(30,150), (32,80), (22,45), (29,80)] into a nonincreasing order using income as the key field, a stable sorting algorithm must guarantee that (32, 80) appears before (29,80) because the former appear before the latter in the original input. An unstable sorting algorithm does not offer such a guarantee. Stable algorithms are required if one wishes to use multiple keys to sort a list in a cascaded manner. For example, if each element has a primary key and a secondary key, with stable sorting algorithms, one can first sort the list according to the secondary key and then sort one more time with the primary key. The second sort will preserve the order produced by the first sort.

Sorting algorithms can also be classified into comparison-based and noncomparison-based algorithms. Comparison-based sorting algorithms cannot achieve better than $O(N \cdot logN)$ complexity when sorting a list of N elements because they must perform a minimal number of comparisons among the elements. In contrast, some of the noncomparison-based algorithms can achieve better than $O(N \cdot logN)$ complexity, but they may not generalize to arbitrary types of keys. Both comparison-based and noncomparison-based sorting algorithms can be parallelized. In this chapter we present a parallel noncomparison-based sorting algorithm (radix sort) as well as a parallel comparison-based sorting algorithm (merge sort).

Because of the importance of sorting, the computer science research community has produced a great spectrum of sorting algorithms based on a rich variety of data structures and algorithmic strategies. As a result, introductory computer science classes often use sorting algorithms to illustrate a variety of core algorithm concepts, such as big O notation; divide-and-conquer algorithms; data structures such as heaps and binary trees; randomized algorithms; best-, worst-, and average-case analysis; time-space tradeoffs; and upper and lower bounds. In this chapter we continue this tradition and use two sorting algorithms to illustrate several important parallelization and performance optimization techniques (Satish et al., 2009).

13.2 **Radix sort**

One of the sorting algorithms that is highly amenable to parallelization is radix sort. Radix sort is a noncomparison-based sorting algorithm that works by distributing the keys that are being sorted into buckets on the basis of a radix value (or base in a positional numeral system). If the keys consist of multiple digits, the distribution of the keys is repeated for each digit until all digits are covered. Each iteration is stable, preserving the order of the keys within each bucket from the previous iteration. In processing keys that are represented as binary numbers, choosing a radix value that is a power of 2 is convenient because it makes iterating over the digits and extracting them easy. Each iteration essentially handles a fixed-size slice of the bits from the key. We will start by using a radix of 2 (i.e., a 1-bit radix) and then extend to larger radix values later in the chapter.

Fig. 13.1 shows an example of how a list of 4-bit integers can be sorted with radix sort using a 1-bit radix. Since the keys are 4 bits long and each iteration processes 1 bit, four iterations are required in total. In the first iteration the least significant bit (LSB) is considered. All the keys in the iteration's input list whose LSB is 0 are placed on the left side of the iteration's output list, forming a bucket for the 0 bits. Similarly, all the keys in the iteration's input list whose LSB is 1 are placed on the right side of the iteration's output list forming a bucket for the 1 bits. Note that within each bucket in the output list, the order of the keys is preserved from that in the input list. In other words, keys that are placed in the same bucket (i.e., that have the same LSB) must appear in the same order in the output list as they did in the input list. We will see why this stability requirement is important when we discuss the next iteration.

In the second iteration in Fig. 13.1, the output list from the first iteration becomes the new input list, and the second LSB of each key is considered. As in the first iteration, the keys are separated into two buckets: a bucket for the keys whose second LSB is 0 and another bucket for the keys whose second LSB is 1.

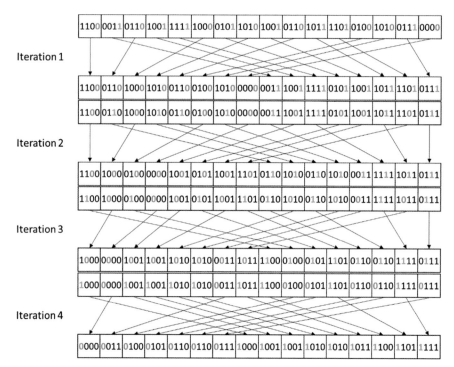

FIGURE 13.1

A radix sort example.

Since the order from the previous iterations is preserved, we observe that the keys in the second iteration's output list are now sorted by the lower two bits. In other words, all the keys whose lower two bits are 00 come first, followed by those whose lower two bits are 01, followed by those whose lower two bits are 10, followed by those whose lower two bits are 11.

In the third iteration in Fig. 13.1 the same process is repeated while considering the third bit in the keys. Again, since the order from previous iterations is preserved, the keys in the output list of the third iteration are sorted by the lower three bits. Finally, in the fourth and last iteration the same process is repeated while considering the fourth or most significant bit. At the end of this iteration the keys in the final output list are sorted by all four bits.

13.3 Parallel radix sort

Each iteration in radix sort depends on the entire result of the previous iteration. Hence the iterations are performed sequentially with respect to each other. The opportunity for parallelizing radix sort arises within each iteration. For the rest of this chapter we will focus on the parallelization of a single radix sort iteration, with the understanding that the iterations will be executed one after the other. In other words, we will focus on the implementation of a kernel that performs a single radix sort iteration and will assume that the host code calls this kernel once for each iteration.

One straightforward approach to parallelize a radix sort iteration on GPUs is to make each thread responsible for one key in the input list. The thread must identify the position of the key in the output list and then store the key to that position. Fig. 13.2 illustrates this parallelization approach that is applied to the first iteration from Fig. 13.1. Threads in Fig. 13.2 are illustrated as curvy arrows, and thread blocks are illustrated as boxes around the arrows. Each thread is responsible for the key below it in the input list. In this example the 16 keys are processed by a grid with four thread blocks having four threads each. In practice, each thread block may have up to 1024 threads, and the input is much larger, resulting in many more thread blocks. However, we have used a small number of threads per block to simplify the illustration.

With every thread assigned to a key in the input list, the challenge remains for each thread to identify the destination index of its key in the output list. Identifying the destination index of the key depends on whether the key maps to the 0 bucket or the 1 bucket. For keys mapping to the 0 bucket, the destination index can be found as follows:

$$
\begin{aligned}
\text{destination of a \textbf{zero}} \ &= \# \ \textbf{zeros} \ \text{before} \\
&= \# \ \textbf{keys} \ \text{before} - \# \ \text{ones before} \\
&= \text{key index} - \# \ \text{ones before}
\end{aligned}
$$

The destination index of a key that maps to the 0 bucket (i.e., destination of a 0) is equivalent to the number of keys before the key that also map to the 0 bucket (i.e., # zeros before). Since all keys map to either the 0 bucket or the

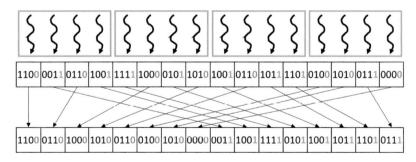

FIGURE 13.2

Parallelizing a radix sort iteration by assigning one input key to each thread.

1 bucket, the number of keys before the key mapping to the 0 bucket is equivalent to the total number of keys before the key (i.e., # keys before) minus the number of keys before the key mapping to the 1 bucket (i.e., # ones before). The total number of keys before the key is just the index of the key in the input list (i.e., the key index), which is trivially available. Hence the only nontrivial part of finding the destination index of a key that maps to the 0 bucket is counting the number of keys before it that map to the 1 bucket. This operation can be done by using an exclusive scan, as we will see shortly.

For keys mapping to the 0 bucket, the destination index can be found as follows:

$$
\begin{aligned}
\text{destination of a one} \;&= \text{\# zeros in total} + \text{\# ones before} \\
&= (\text{\# keys in total} - \text{\# ones in total}) + \text{\# ones before} \\
&= \text{input size} - \text{\# ones in total} + \text{\# ones before}
\end{aligned}
$$

All keys mapping to the 0 bucket must come before the keys mapping to the 1 bucket in the output array. For this reason, the destination index of a key that maps to the 1 bucket (i.e., destination of a 1) is equivalent to the total number of keys mapping to the 0 bucket (i.e., # zeros in total) plus the number of keys before the key that map to the 1 bucket (i.e., # ones before). Since all keys map to either the 0 bucket or the 1 bucket, the total number of keys mapping to the 0 bucket is equivalent to the total number of keys in the input list (i.e., # keys in total) minus the total number of keys mapping to the 1 bucket (i.e., # ones in total). The total number of keys in the input list is just the input size, which is trivially available. Hence the nontrivial part of finding the destination index of a key that maps to the 1 bucket is counting the number of keys before it that map to the 1 bucket, which is the same information that is needed for the 0 bucket case. Again, this operation can be done by using an exclusive scan, as we will see shortly. The total number of keys mapping to the 1 bucket can be found as a byproduct of the exclusive scan.

Fig. 13.3 shows the operations that each thread performs to find its key's destination index in the example in Fig. 13.2. The corresponding kernel code to perform these operations is shown in Fig. 13.4. First, each thread identifies the index of the key for which it is responsible (line 03), performs a boundary check (line 04), and loads the key from the input list (line 06). Next, each thread extracts from the key the bit for the current iteration to identify whether it is a 0 or a 1 (line 07).

Here, the iteration number `iter` tells us the position of the bit in which we are interested. By shifting the key to the right by this amount, we move the bit to the rightmost position. By applying a bitwise-and operation (&) between the shifted key and a 1, we zero out all the bits in the shifted key except the rightmost bit. Hence the value of `bit` will be the value of the bit in which we are interested. In the example in Fig. 13.3, since the example is for iteration 0, the LSB is extracted, as shown in the row labeled bits.

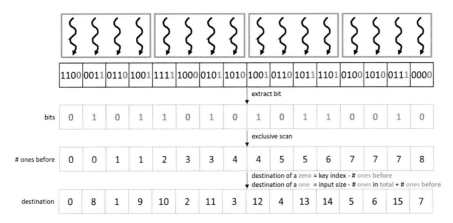

FIGURE 13.3

Finding the destination of each input key.

```
01    __global__ void radix_sort_iter(unsigned int* input, unsigned int* output,
02                    unsigned int* bits, unsigned int N, unsigned int iter) {
03        unsigned int i = blockIdx.x*blockDim.x + threadIdx.x;
04        unsigned int key, bit;
05        if(i < N) {
06            key = input[i];
07            bit = (key >> iter) & 1;
08            bits[i] = bit;
09        }
10        exclusiveScan(bits, N);
11        if(i < N) {
12            unsigned int numOnesBefore = bits[i];
13            unsigned int numOnesTotal = bits[N];
14            unsigned int dst = (bit == 0)?(i - numOnesBefore)
15                                :(N - numOnesTotal - numOnesBefore);
16            output[dst] = key;
17        }
18    }
```

FIGURE 13.4

Radix sort iteration kernel code.

Once each thread has extracted the bit in which it is interested from the key, it stores the bit to memory (line 08), and the threads collaborate to perform an exclusive scan on the bits (line 10). We discussed how to perform an exclusive scan in Chapter 11, Prefix Sum (Scan). The call to exclusive scan is performed outside the boundary check because threads may need to perform a barrier synchronization in the process, so we need to ensure that all threads are active. To synchronize across all threads in the grid, we assume that we can use sophisticated techniques similar to those used in the single-pass scan discussed in Chapter 11, Prefix Sum (Scan). Alternatively, we could terminate the kernel, call another kernel from the host to perform the scan, and then call a third kernel to perform the operations after the scan. In this case, each iteration would require three grid launches instead of one.

The array resulting from the exclusive scan operation contains, at each position, the sum of the bits before that position. Since these bits are either 0 or 1, the sum of the bits before the position is equivalent to the number of the 1's before the position (i.e., the number of keys that map to the 1 bucket). In the example in Fig. 13.3 the result of the exclusive scan is shown in the row labeled # ones before. Each thread accesses this array to obtain the number of 1's before its position (line 12) and the total number of 1's in the input list (line 13). Each thread can then identify the destination of its key, using the expressions that we derived previously (lines 14−15). Having identified its destination index, the thread can proceed to store the key for which it is responsible at the corresponding location in the output list (line 16). In the example in Fig. 13.3 the destination indices are shown in the row labeled destination. The reader can refer to Fig. 13.2 to verify that the values that are obtained are indeed the right destination indices of each element.

13.4 Optimizing for memory coalescing

The approach we just described is effective at parallelizing a radix sort iteration. However, one major source of inefficiency in this approach is that the writes to the output list exhibit an access pattern that cannot be adequately coalesced. Consider how each thread in Fig. 13.2 writes its key to the output list. In the first thread block, the first thread writes to the 0 bucket, the second thread writes to the 1 bucket, the third thread writes to the 0 bucket, and the fourth thread writes to the 1 bucket. Hence threads with consecutive index values are not necessarily writing to consecutive memory locations, resulting in poor coalescing and requiring multiple memory requests to be issued per warp.

Recall from Chapter 6, Performance Considerations, that there are various approaches to enable better memory coalescing in kernels: (1) rearranging the threads, (2) rearranging the data that the threads access, or (3) performing the uncoalesceable accesses on shared memory and transferring data between shared memory and global memory in a coalesced way. To optimize for coalescing in this chapter, we will use the third approach. Instead of having all threads write their keys to global memory buckets in an uncoalesced manner, we will have each thread block maintain its own local buckets in the shared memory. That is, we will no longer perform a global sort as shown in Fig. 13.4. Rather, the threads in each block will first perform a block-level local sort to separate the keys mapping to the 0 bucket and the keys mapping to the 1 bucket in shared memory. After that, the buckets will be written from shared memory to global memory in a coalesced manner.

Fig. 13.5 shows an example of how memory coalescing can be enhanced for the example in Fig. 13.2. In this example, each thread block first performs a local radix sort on the keys that it owns and stores the output list into the shared

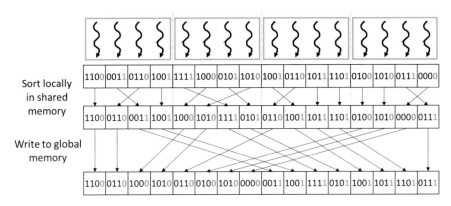

FIGURE 13.5

Optimizing for memory coalescing by sorting locally in shared memory before sorting into the global memory.

memory. The local sort can be done in the same way as the global sort was done previously and requires each thread block to perform only a local exclusive scan instead of requiring a global one. After the local sort, each thread block writes its local buckets to the global buckets in a more coalesced way. For example, in Fig. 13.5, consider how the first thread block writes out its buckets to global memory. The first two threads both write to adjacent locations in global memory when writing the 0 bucket, while the last two threads also write to adjacent locations in global memory when writing the 1 bucket. Hence the majority of writes to global memory will be coalesced.

The main challenge in this optimization is for each thread block to identify the beginning position of each of its local buckets in the corresponding global bucket. The beginning position of a thread block's local buckets depends on the sizes of the local buckets in the other thread blocks. In particular, the position of a thread block's local 0 bucket is after all the local 0 buckets of the preceding thread blocks. On the other hand, the position of a thread block's local 1 bucket is after all the local 0 buckets of all the thread blocks and all the local 1 buckets of the preceding thread blocks. These positions can be obtained by performing an exclusive scan on the thread blocks' local bucket sizes.

Fig. 13.6 shows an example of how an exclusive scan can be used to find the position of each thread block's local buckets. After completing the local radix sort, each thread block identifies the number of keys in each of its local buckets. Next, each thread block stores these values in a table as shown in Fig. 13.6. The table is stored in row-major order, meaning that it places the sizes of the local 0 buckets for all thread blocks consecutively, followed by the sizes of the local 1 buckets. After the table has been constructed, an exclusive scan is executed on the linearized table. The resulting table consists of the beginning positions of each thread block's local buckets, which are the values we are looking for.

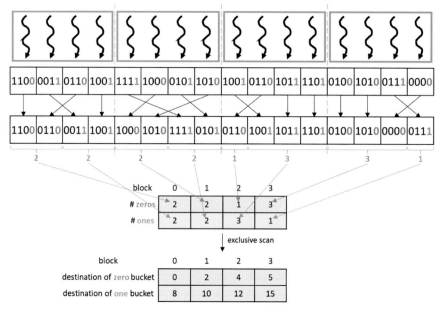

FIGURE 13.6

Finding the destination of each thread block's local buckets.

Once a thread block has identified the beginning position of its local buckets in global memory, the threads in the block can proceed to store their keys from the local buckets to the global buckets. To do so, each thread needs to keep track of the number of keys in the 0 bucket versus the 1 bucket. During the write phase, threads in each block will be writing a key in either of the buckets depending on its thread index values. For example, for block 2 in Fig. 13.6, thread 0 writes the single key in the 0 bucket, and threads 1−3 write the three keys in the 1 bucket. In comparison, for block 3 in Fig. 13.6, threads 0−2 write the three keys in the 0 bucket, and thread 3 writes the 1 key in the one bucket. Hence each thread needs to test whether it is responsible for writing a key in the local 0 bucket or the 1 bucket. Each block tracks the number of keys in each of its two local buckets so that the threads can determine where their threadIdx values fall and participate in the writing of the 0 bucket keys or 1 bucket keys. We leave the implementation of this optimization as an exercise for the reader.

13.5 Choice of radix value

So far, we have seen how radix sort can be parallelized by using a 1-bit radix as an example. For the 4-bit keys in the example, four iterations (one for each bit) are needed for the keys to be fully sorted. In general, for N-bit keys, N iterations are needed to fully sort the keys. To reduce the number of iterations that are needed, a larger radix value can be used.

Fig. 13.7 shows an example of how radix sort can be performed using a 2-bit radix. Each iteration uses two bits to distribute the keys to buckets. Hence the 4-bit keys can be fully sorted by using only two iterations. In the first iteration the lower two bits are considered. The keys are distributed across four buckets corresponding to the keys where the lower two bits are 00, 01, 10, and 11. In the second iteration the upper two bits are considered. The keys are then distributed across four buckets based on the upper two bits. Similar to the 1-bit example, the order of the keys within each bucket is preserved from the previous iteration. Preserving the order of the keys within each bucket ensures that after the second iteration the keys are fully sorted by all four bits.

Similar to the 1-bit example, each iteration can be parallelized by assigning a thread to each key in the input list to find the key's destination index and store it in the output list. To optimize for memory coalescing, each thread block can sort its keys locally in the shared memory and then write the local buckets to global memory in a coalesced manner. An example of how to parallelize a radix sort iteration and optimize it for memory coalescing using the shared memory is shown in Fig. 13.8.

The key distinction between the 1-bit example and the 2-bit example is how to separate the keys into four buckets instead of two. For the local sort inside of each thread block, a 2-bit radix sort is performed by applying two consecutive 1-bit radix sort iterations. Each of these 1-bit iterations requires its own exclusive scan operation. However, these operations are local to the thread block, so there is no coordination across thread blocks in between the two 1-bit iterations. In general, for an r-bit radix, r local 1-bit iterations are needed to sort the keys into 2^r local buckets.

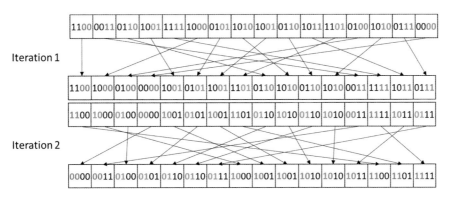

FIGURE 13.7

Radix sort example with 2-bit radix.

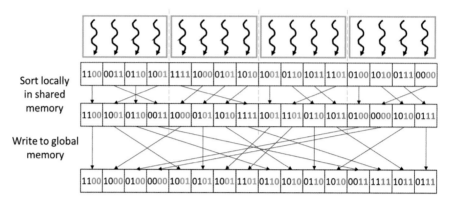

Sort locally
in shared
memory

Write to global
memory

FIGURE 13.8

Parallelizing a radix sort iteration and optimizing it for memory coalescing using the shared memory for a 2-bit radix.

After the local sort is complete, each thread block must find the position of each of its local buckets in the global output list. Fig. 13.9 shows an example of how the destination of each local bucket can be found for the 2-bit radix example. The procedure is similar to the 1-bit example in Fig. 13.6. Each thread block stores the number of keys in each local bucket to a table, which is then scanned to obtain the global position of each of the local buckets. The main distinction from the 1-bit radix example is that each thread block has four local buckets instead of two, so the exclusive scan operation is performed on a table with four rows instead of two. In general, for an r-bit radix the exclusive scan operation is performed on a table with 2^r rows.

We have seen that the advantage of using a larger radix is that it reduces the number of iterations that are needed to fully sort the keys. Fewer iterations means fewer grid launches, global memory accesses, and global exclusive scan operations. However, using a larger radix also has disadvantages. The first disadvantage is that each thread block has more local buckets where each bucket has fewer keys. As a result, each thread block has more distinct global memory bucket sections that it needs to write to and less data that it needs to write to each section. For this reason, the opportunities for memory coalescing decrease as the radix gets larger. The second disadvantage is that the table on which the global exclusive scan is applied gets larger with a larger radix. For this reason, the overhead of the global exclusive scan increases as the radix increases. Therefore the radix cannot be made arbitrarily large. The choice of radix value must strike a balance between the number of iterations on one hand and the memory coalescing behavior as well as the overhead of the global exclusive scan on the other hand. We leave the implementation of radix sort with a multibit radix as an exercise for the reader.

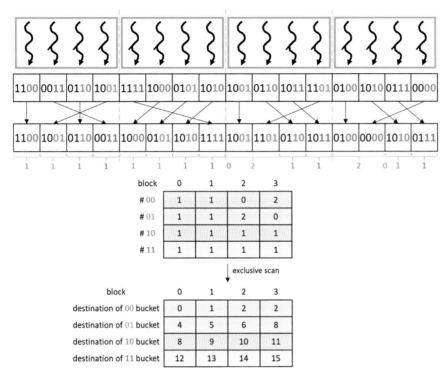

FIGURE 13.9

Finding the destination of each block's local buckets for a 2-bit radix.

13.6 **Thread coarsening to improve coalescing**

The price of parallelizing radix sort across many thread blocks is poor coalescing of writes to global memory. Each thread block has its own local buckets that it writes to global memory. Having more thread blocks means having fewer keys per thread block, which means that the local buckets are going to be smaller, exposing fewer opportunities for coalescing when they are written to global memory. If these thread blocks were to be executed in parallel, the price of poor coalescing might be worth paying. However, if these thread blocks were to be serialized by the hardware, the price would be paid unnecessarily.

To address this issue, thread coarsening can be applied whereby each thread is assigned to multiple keys in the input list instead of just one. Fig. 13.10 illustrates how thread coarsening can be applied to a radix sort iteration for the 2-bit radix example. In this case, each thread block is responsible for more keys than was the case in the example in Fig. 13.8. Consequently, the local buckets of each thread block are larger, exposing more opportunities for coalescing. When we compare

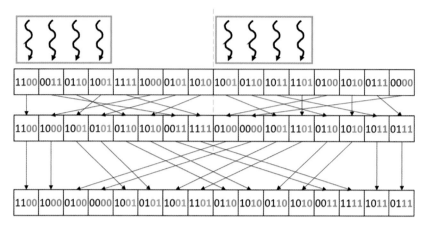

FIGURE 13.10

Radix sort for a 2-bit radix with thread coarsening to improve memory coalescing.

Fig. 13.8 and Fig. 13.10, it is clear that in Fig. 13.10 it is more likely the case that consecutive threads write to consecutive memory locations.

Another price for parallelizing radix sort across many thread blocks is the overhead of performing the global exclusive scan to identify the destination of each thread block's local buckets. Recall from Fig. 13.9 that the size of the table on which the exclusive scan is performed is proportional to the number of buckets as well as the number of blocks. By applying thread coarsening, the number of blocks is reduced, thereby reducing the size of the table and the overhead of the exclusive scan operation. We leave the application of thread coarsening to radix sort as an exercise for the reader.

13.7 Parallel merge sort

Radix sort is suitable when keys are to be sorted in lexicographic order. However, if keys are to be sorted on the basis of a complex order defined by a complex comparison operator, then radix sort is not suitable, and a comparison-based sorting algorithm is necessary. Moreover, an implementation of a comparison-based sorting algorithm can be more easily adapted to different types of keys by simply changing the comparison operator. In contrast, adapting an implementation of a noncomparison-based sorting algorithm such as radix sort to different types of keys may involve creating different versions of the implementation. These considerations may make comparison-based sorting more favorable in some cases, despite their higher complexity.

One comparison-based sort that is amenable to parallelization is merge sort. Merge sort works by dividing the input list into segments, sorting each segment (using merge sort or another sorting algorithm), and then performing an ordered merge of the sorted segments.

Fig. 13.11 shows an example of how merge sort can be parallelized. Initially, the input list is divided into many segments, each of which are sorted independently, using some efficient sorting algorithm. After that, every pair of segments is merged into a single segment. This process is repeated until all the keys become part of the same segment.

At each stage, the computation can be parallelized by performing different merge operations in parallel as well as parallelizing within merge operations. In the earlier stages, there are more independent merge operations that can be performed in parallel. In the later stages, there are fewer independent merge operations, but each merge operation merges more keys, exposing more parallelism within the merge operation. For example, in Fig. 13.11 the first merge stage consists of four independent merge operations. Hence our grid of eight thread blocks may assign two thread blocks to process each merge operation in parallel. In the next stage, there are only two merge operations, but each operation merges twice the number of keys. Hence our grid of eight thread blocks may assign four thread blocks to process each merge operation in parallel. We saw how to parallelize a merge operation in Chapter 12, Merge. We leave the implementation of merge sort based on parallel merge as an exercise for the reader.

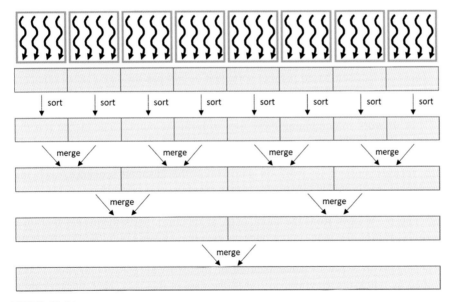

FIGURE 13.11

Parallelizing merge sort.

13.8 Other parallel sort methods

The algorithms outlined above are only two of the many possible ways to sort data in parallel. In this section, we briefly outline some of the other methods that may be of interest to readers.

Among the simplest of parallel sorting methods is the odd-even transposition sort. It begins by comparing, in parallel, every even/odd pair of keys, namely, those with indices k and k + 1 starting at the first *even* index. The position of the keys is swapped if the key at position k + 1 is less than the key at position k. This step is then repeated for every odd/even pair of keys, namely, those with indices k and k + 1 starting at the first *odd* index. These alternating phases are repeated until both are completed with no keys needing to be swapped. The odd-even transposition sort is quite similar to sequential bubble sort algorithms, and like bubble sort, it is inefficient on large sequences, since it may perform $O(N^2)$ work of a sequence of N elements.

Transposition sort uses a fixed pattern of comparisons and swaps elements when they are out of order. It is easily parallelized because each step compares pairs of keys that do not overlap. There is an entire category of sorting methods that use fixed patterns of comparison to sort sequences, often in parallel. These methods are usually referred to as *sorting networks*, and the best-known parallel sorting networks are Batcher's bitonic sort and odd-even merge sort (Batcher, 1968). Batcher's algorithms operate on sequences of fixed length and are more efficient than odd-even transposition sort, requiring only $O(N \cdot \log^2 N)$ comparisons for a sequence of N elements. Even though the cost of these algorithms is asymptotically worse than the $O(N \cdot \log N)$ cost of methods such as merge sort, in practice, they are often the most efficient methods on small sequences because of their simplicity.

Most comparison-based parallel sorts that do not use the fixed set of comparisons that are typical of sorting networks can be divided into two broad categories. The first partitions the unsorted input into tiles, sorts each tile, and then performs most of its work in combining these tiles to form the output. The merge sort that we described in this chapter is an example of such an algorithm; most of the work is performed in the merge tree that combines sorted tiles. The second category focuses most of its work on partitioning the unsorted sequence, such that combining partitions is relatively trivial. Sample sort algorithms (Frazer and McKellar, 1970) are the typical example of this category. Sample sort begins by selecting p − 1 keys from the input (e.g., at random), sorts them, and then uses them to partition the input into p buckets such that all keys in bucket k are greater than all keys in any bucket j < k and less than all in any bucket j > k. This step is analogous to a p-way generalization of the two-way partitioning that is performed by quicksort. Having partitioned the data in this way, each bucket can be sorted independently, and the sorted output is formed by merely concatenating the buckets in order. Sample sort algorithms are often the most efficient choice for extremely large sequences in which data must be distributed across multiple physical memories, including across the memories of multiple GPUs in a single node. In practice, oversampling the keys is common, since modest oversampling will result in balanced partitions with high probability (Blelloch et al., 1991).

Just as merge sort and sample sort typify bottom-up and top-down strategies for comparison-based sorting, radix sorting algorithms can be designed to follow a bottom-up or top-down strategy. The radix sort that we described in this chapter is more completely described as an LSB or, more generally, least significant digit (LSD), radix sort. The successive steps of the algorithm start with the LSD of the key and work toward the most significant digit (MSD). A MSD radix sort adopts the opposite strategy. It begins by using the MSD to partition the input into buckets that correspond to the possible values of that digit. This same partitioning is then applied independently in each bucket, using the next MSD. Upon reaching the LSD, the entire sequence will have been sorted. Like sample sort, MSD radix sort is often a better choice for very large sequences. Whereas the LSD radix sort requires global shuffling of data in each step, each step of MSD radix sort operates on progressively more localized regions of the data.

13.9 **Summary**

In this chapter we have seen how to sort keys (and their associated values) on GPUs in parallel. In most of the chapter we focused on radix sort, which sorts keys by distributing them across buckets. The distribution process is repeated for each digit in the key while preserving the order from the previous digit's iteration to ensure that the keys are sorted according to all the digits at the end. Each iteration is parallelized by assigning a thread to each key in the input list and having that thread find the destination of the key in the output list, which involves collaborating with other threads to perform an exclusive scan operation.

One of the key challenges in optimizing radix sort is achieving coalesced memory accesses in writing the keys to the output list. An important optimization to enhance coalescing is to have each thread block perform a local sort to local buckets in shared memory and then write each local bucket to global memory in a coalesced manner. Another optimization is to increase the size of the radix to reduce the number of iterations that are needed and thus the number of grids that are launched. However, the radix size should not be increased too much because it would result in poorer coalescing and more overhead from the global exclusive scan operation. Finally, applying thread coarsening is effective at improving memory coalescing as well as reducing the overhead of the global exclusive scan.

Radix sort has the advantage of having computation complexity that is lower than $O(N log(N))$. However, radix sort only works for limited types of keys such as integers. Therefore we also look at the parallelization of comparison-based sorting that is applicable to general types of keys. A class of comparison-based sorting algorithms that is amenable to parallelization is merge sort. Merge sort can be parallelized by performing independent merge operations of different input segments in parallel as well as parallelizing within each merge operation, as we saw in Chapter 12, Merge.

The process of implementing and optimizing parallel sorting algorithms on GPUs is complex, and the average user is more likely to use a parallel sorting library for GPUs, such as Thrust (Bell and Hoberock, 2012), than to implement one's own sorting kernels from scratch. Nevertheless, parallel sorting remains an interesting case study of the tradeoffs that go into optimizing parallel patterns.

Exercises

1. Extend the kernel in Fig. 13.4 by using shared memory to improve memory coalescing.
2. Extend the kernel in Fig. 13.4 to work for a multibit radix.
3. Extend the kernel in Fig. 13.4 by applying thread coarsening to improve memory coalescing.
4. Implement parallel merge sort using the parallel merge implementation from Chapter 12, Merge.

References

Batcher, K.E., 1968. Sorting networks and their applications. In: Proceedings of the AFIPS Spring Joint Computer Conference.

Bell, N., Hoberock, J., 2012. Thrust: a productivity-oriented library for CUDA. GPU Computing Gems Jade Edition. Morgan Kaufmann, pp. 359–371.

Blelloch, G.E., Leiserson, C.E., Maggs, B.M., Plaxton, C.G., Smith, S.J., Zagha, M., 1991, A comparison of sorting algorithms for the Connection Machine CM-2. In: Proceedings of the Third ACM Symposium on Parallel Algorithms and Architectures.

Frazer, W.D., McKellar, A.C., 1970. Samplesort: a sampling approach to minimal storage tree sorting. Journal of ACM 17 (3).

Satish, N., Harris M., Garland, M., 2009. Designing efficient sorting algorithms for many-core GPUs. In: Proceedings of the IEEE International Symposium on Parallel and Distributed Processing.

Sparse matrix computation 14

Chapter Outline

14.1 Background 312
14.2 A simple SpMV kernel with the COO format 314
14.3 Grouping row nonzeros with the CSR format 317
14.4 Improving memory coalescing with the ELL format 320
14.5 Regulating padding with the hybrid ELL-COO format 324
14.6 Reducing control divergence with the JDS format 325
14.7 Summary 328
Exercises 329
References 329

Our next parallel pattern is sparse matrix computation. In a sparse matrix the majority of the elements are zeros. Storing and processing these zero elements are wasteful in terms of memory capacity, memory bandwidth, time, and energy. Many important real-world problems involve sparse matrix computation. Because of the importance of these problems, several sparse matrix storage formats and their corresponding processing methods have been proposed and widely used in the field. All these methods employ some type of compaction techniques to avoid storing or processing zero elements at the cost of introducing some level of irregularity into the data representation. Unfortunately, such irregularity can lead to underutilization of memory bandwidth, control flow divergence, and load imbalance in parallel computing. It is therefore important to strike a good balance between compaction and regularization. Some storage formats achieve a higher level of compaction at a high level of irregularity. Others achieve a more modest level of compaction while keeping the representation more regular. The relative performance of a parallel computation using each storage format is known to be heavily dependent on the distribution of nonzero elements in the sparse matrices. Understanding the wealth of work in sparse matrix storage formats and their corresponding parallel algorithms gives a parallel programmer important background for addressing compaction and regularization challenges in solving related problems.

Programming Massively Parallel Processors. DOI: https://doi.org/10.1016/B978-0-323-91231-0.00010-0

14.1 Background

A sparse matrix is a matrix in which most of the elements are zeros. Sparse matrices arise in many scientific, engineering, and financial modeling problems. For example, matrices can be used to represent the coefficients in a linear system of equations. Each row of the matrix represents one equation of the linear system. In many science and engineering problems the large number of variables and equations that are involved are sparsely coupled. That is, each equation involves only a small number of variables. This is illustrated in Fig. 14.1, in which each column of the matrix corresponds to the coefficients for a variable: column 0 for x_0, column 1 for x_1, and so on. For example, the fact that row 0 has nonzero elements in columns 0 and 1 indicates that only variables x_0 and x_1 are involved in equation 0. It should be clear that variables x_0, x_2, and x_3 are present in equation 1, variables x_1 and x_2 are present in equation 2, and only variable x_3 is present in equation 3. Sparse matrices are typically stored in a format, or representation, that avoids storing zero elements.

Matrices are often used in solving linear systems of N equations of N variables in the form of $A*X + Y = 0$, where A is an N $\times$ N matrix, X is a vector of N variables, and Y is a vector of N constant values. The objective is to solve for the X variable values that will satisfy all the equations. An intuitive approach is to invert the matrix so that $X = A^{-1} * (-Y)$. This can be done for matrices of moderate size through methods such as Gaussian elimination. While it is theoretically possible to use these methods to solve the equations that are represented by sparse matrices, the sheer size of many sparse matrices can overwhelm this intuitive approach. Furthermore, an inverse sparse matrix is often much larger than the original because the inversion process tends to generate many additional nonzero elements, which are called "fill-ins." As a result, it is often impractical to compute and store the inverse matrix in solving real-world problems.

Linear systems of equations represented in sparse matrices can be better solved with an iterative approach. When the sparse matrix A is positive-definite (i.e., $x^T A x > 0$ for all nonzero vectors x in R^n), one can use conjugate gradient methods to iteratively solve the corresponding linear system with guaranteed convergence to a solution (Hestenes and Stiefel, 1952). Conjugate gradient methods guess a solution for X, and perform $A*X + Y$, and see whether the result is close

	Col 0	Col 1	Col 2	Col 3
Row 0	1	7		
Row 1	5		3	9
Row 2		2	8	
Row 3				6

FIGURE 14.1

A simple sparse matrix example.

to a 0 vector. If not, we can use a gradient vector formula to refine the guessed X and perform another iteration of A*X + Y. These iterative solution methods for linear systems are closely related to the iterative solution methods for differential equations that we introduced in Chapter 8, Stencil.

The most time-consuming part of iterative approaches to solving linear systems of equations is in the evaluation of A*X + Y, which is a sparse matrix-vector multiplication and accumulation. Fig. 14.2 shows a small example of matrix-vector multiplication and accumulation in which A is a sparse matrix. The dark squares in A represent nonzero elements. In contrast, both X and Y are typically dense vectors. That is, most of the elements of X and Y hold nonzero values. Owing to its importance, standardized library function interfaces have been created to perform this operation under the name SpMV (sparse matrix vector multiplication and accumulation). We will use SpMV to illustrate the important tradeoffs between different storage formats in parallel sparse matrix computation.

The main objective of the different sparse matrix storage formats is to remove all the zero elements from the matrix representation. Removing all the zero elements not only saves storage but also eliminates the need to fetch these zero elements from memory and perform useless multiplication or addition operations with them. This can significantly reduce the consumption of memory bandwidth and computation resources.

There are various design considerations that go into the structure of a sparse matrix storage formats. The following is a list of some of the key considerations:

• Space efficiency (or compaction): the amount of memory capacity that is required to represent the matrix using the storage format
• Flexibility: the extent to which the storage format makes it easy to modify the matrix by adding or removing nonzeros
• Accessibility: the kinds of data that the storage format makes it easy to access
• Memory access efficiency: the extent to which the storage format enables an efficient memory access pattern for a particular computation (one facet of regularization)
• Load balance: the extent to which the storage format balances the load across different threads for a particular computation (another facet of regularization)

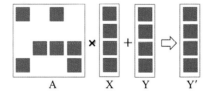

FIGURE 14.2

A small example of matrix-vector multiplication and accumulation.

Throughout this chapter we will introduce different storage formats and examine how these storage formats compare in each of these design considerations.

14.2 A simple SpMV kernel with the COO format

The first sparse matrix storage format that we will discuss is the coordinate list (COO) format. The COO format is illustrated in Fig. 14.3. COO stores the nonzero values in a one-dimensional array, which is shown as the `value` array. Each nonzero element is stored with both its column index and its row index. We have both `colIdx` and `rowIdx` arrays to accompany the `value` array. For example, A [0,0] of our small example is stored at the entry with index 0 in the `value` array (1 in `value[0]`) with both its column index (0 in `colIdx[0]`) and its row index (0 in `rowIdx[0]`) stored at the same position in the other arrays.

COO completely removes all zero elements from the storage. It does incur storage overhead by introducing the `colIdx` and `rowIdx` arrays. In our small example, in which the number of zero elements is not much larger than the number of nonzero elements, the storage overhead is actually more than the space that is saved by not storing the zero elements. However, it should be clear that for sparse matrices in which the vast majority of elements are zeros, the overhead that is introduced is far less than the space that is saved by not storing zeros. For example, in a sparse matrix in which only 1% of the elements are nonzero values, the total storage for the COO representation, including all the overhead, would be around 3% of the space required to store both zero and nonzero elements.

One approach to performing SpMV in parallel using a sparse matrix represented in the COO format is to assign a thread to each nonzero element in the matrix. An example of this parallelization approach is illustrated in Fig. 14.4, and the corresponding code is shown in Fig. 14.5. In this approach, each thread identifies the index of the nonzero element for which it is responsible (line 02) and ensures that it is within bounds (line 03). Next, the thread identifies the row index (line 04), column index (line 05), and value (line 06) of the nonzero element for which it is responsible from the `rowIdx`, `colIdx`, and `value` arrays, respectively. It then looks up the input vector value at the location corresponding to the column index, multiplies it by the nonzero value, then accumulates the result to the output

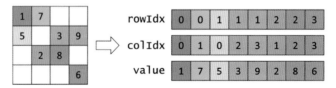

FIGURE 14.3

Example of the coordinate list (COO) format.

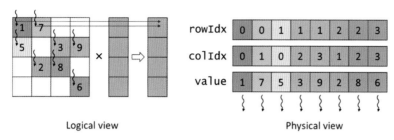

rowIdx 0 0 1 1 1 2 2 3

colIdx 0 1 0 2 3 1 2 3

value   1 7 5 3 9 2 8 6

Logical view   Physical view

FIGURE 14.4

Example of parallelizing SpMV with the COO format.

```
01    __global__ void spmv_coo_kernel(COOMatrix cooMatrix, float* x, float* y) {
02        unsigned int i = blockIdx.x*blockDim.x + threadIdx.x;
03        if(i < cooMatrix.numNonzeros) {
04            unsigned int row = cooMatrix.rowIdx[i];
05            unsigned int col = cooMatrix.colIdx[i];
06            float value = cooMatrix.value[i];
07            atomicAdd(&y[row], x[col]*value);
08        }
09    }
```

FIGURE 14.5

A parallel SpMV/COO kernel.

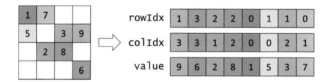

rowIdx 1 3 2 2 0 1 1 0

colIdx 3 3 1 2 0 0 2 1

value   9 6 2 8 1 5 3 7

FIGURE 14.6

Reordering coordinate list (COO) format.

value at the corresponding row index (line 07). An atomic operation is used for the accumulation because multiple threads may update the same output element, as is the case with the first two threads mapped to row 0 of the matrix in Fig. 14.4. It should be obvious that any SpMV computation code will reflect the storage format assumed. Therefore we add the storage format to the name of the kernel to clarify the combination that was used. We also refer to the SpMV code in Fig. 14.5 as SpMV/COO.

Now we examine the COO format under the design considerations listed in Section 14.1: space efficiency, flexibility, accessibility, memory access efficiency, and load balance. For space efficiency we defer the discussion for later, when we have introduced other formats. For flexibility we observe that we can arbitrarily reorder the elements in a COO format without losing any information as long as we reorder the `rowIdx`, `colIdx`, and `value` arrays in the same way. This is illustrated by using our small example in Fig. 14.6, where we have reordered the elements of `rowIdx`, `colIdx`, and `value`. Now `value[0]` actually contains an element from row 1 and column 3 of the original sparse matrix. Because we have also shifted the row index and column index values along with the data value, we can correctly identify this element's location in the original sparse matrix.

In the COO format, we can process the elements in any order we want. The correct `y` element that is identified by `rowIdx[i]` will receive the correct contribution from the product of `value[i]` and `x[colIdx[i]]`. If we make sure that we somehow perform this operation for all elements of `value`, we will calculate the correct final answer regardless of the order in which we process these elements.

The reader may ask why we would want to reorder these elements. One reason is that the data may be read from a file that does not provide the nonzeros in a particular order, and we still need a consistent way of representing the data. For this reason, COO is a popular choice of storage format when the matrix is initially being constructed. Another reason is that not having to provide any ordering enables nonzeros to be added to the matrix by simply appending entries at the end of each of the three arrays. For this reason, COO is a popular choice of storage format when the matrix is modified throughout the computation. We will see another benefit of the flexibility of the COO format in Section 14.5.

The next design consideration that we look at is accessibility. COO makes it easy to access, for a given nonzero, its corresponding row index and column index. This feature of COO enables parallelization across nonzero elements in SpMV/COO. On the other hand, COO does not make it easy to access, for a given row or column, all the nonzeros in that row or column. For this reason, COO would not be a good choice of format if the computation required a row-wise or column-wise traversal of the matrix.

For memory access efficiency we refer to the physical view in Fig. 14.4 for how the threads access the matrix data from memory. The access pattern is such that consecutive threads access consecutive elements in each of the three arrays that form the COO format. Therefore accesses to the matrix by SpMV/COO are coalesced.

For load balance we recall that each thread is responsible for a single nonzero value. Hence all threads are responsible for the same amount of work, which means that we do not expect any control divergence to take place in SpMV/COO except for the threads at the boundary.

The main drawback of SpMV/COO is the need to use atomic operations. The reason for using atomic operations is that multiple threads are assigned to nonzeros in the same row and therefore need to update the same output value. The atomic operations can be avoided if all the nonzeros in the same row are assigned to the same thread such that the thread will be the only one updating the corresponding output value. However, recall that the COO format does not give this accessibility. In the COO format, it is not easy to access, for a given row, all the nonzeros in that row. In the next section we will see another storage format that provides this accessibility.

14.3 **Grouping row nonzeros with the CSR format**

In the previous section we saw that parallelizing SpMV with the COO format suffers from the use of atomic operations because the same output value is updated by multiple threads. These atomic operations can be avoided if the same thread is responsible for all the nonzeros of a row, which requires the storage format to give us the ability to access, for a given row, all the nonzeros in that row. This kind of accessibility is provided by the compressed sparse row (CSR) storage format.

Fig. 14.7 illustrates how the matrix in Fig. 14.1 can be stored by using the CSR format. Like the COO format, CSR stores the nonzero values in a one-dimensional array shown as the value array in Fig. 14.2. However, these nonzero values are grouped by row. For example, we store the nonzero elements of row 0 (1 and 7) first, followed by the nonzero elements of row 1 (5, 3, and 9), followed by the nonzero elements of row 2 (2 and 8), and finally the nonzero elements of row 3 (6).

Also similar to the COO format, CSR stores for each nonzero element in the value array its column index at the same position in the colIdx array. Naturally, these column indices are grouped by row as the values are. In Fig. 14.7 the non-zeros of each row are sorted by their column indices in increasing order. Sorting the nonzeros in this way results in favorable memory access patterns, but it is not necessary. The nonzeros within each row may not necessarily be sorted by their column index, and the kernel that is presented in this section will still work correctly. When the nonzeros within each row are sorted by their column index, the layout of the value array (and the colIdx array) for CSR can be viewed as the row-major layout of the matrix after eliminating all the zero elements.

The key distinction between the COO format and the CSR format is that the CSR format replaces the rowIdx array with a rowPtrs array that stores the starting offset of each row's nonzeros in the colIdx and value arrays. In Fig. 14.7 we show a rowPtrs array whose elements are the indices for the beginning locations of each row. That is, rowPtrs[0] indicates that row 0 starts at location 0 of the value array, rowPtrs[1] indicates that row 1 starts at location 2, and so on. Note that rowPtrs[4] stores the starting location of a nonexistent "row 4." This is for convenience, as some algorithms need to use the starting location of the next row

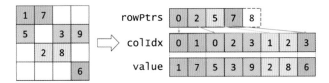

FIGURE 14.7

Example of compressed sparse row (CSR) format.

to delineate the end of the current row. This extra marker gives a convenient way to locate the ending location of row 3.

To perform SpMV in parallel using a sparse matrix represented in the CSR format, one can assign a thread to each row of the matrix. An example of this parallelization approach is illustrated in Fig. 14.8, and the corresponding code is shown in Fig. 14.9. In this approach, each thread identifies the row that it is responsible for (line 02) and ensures that it is within bounds (line 03). Next, the thread loops through the nonzero elements of its row to perform the dot product (lines 05–06). To find the row's nonzero elements, the thread looks up their starting index in the `rowPtrs` array (`rowPtrs[row]`). It also finds where they end by looking up the starting index of the next row's nonzeros (`rowPtrs[row + 1]`). For each nonzero element the thread identifies its column index (line 07) and value (line 08). It then looks up the input value at the location corresponding to the column index, multiplies it by the nonzero value, and accumulates the result to a local variable `sum` (line 09). The `sum` variable is initialized to 0 before the dot product loop begins (line 04) and is accumulated to the output vector after the loop is over (line 11). Notice that the accumulation of the `sum` to the output vector does not require atomic operations. The reason is that each row is traversed by a single thread, so each thread will write to a distinct output value, as illustrated in Fig. 14.8.

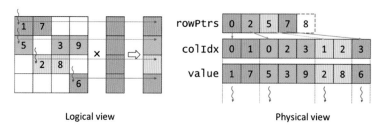

FIGURE 14.8

Example of parallelizing SpMV with the CSR format.

```
01  __global__ void spmv_csr_kernel(CSRMatrix csrMatrix, float* x, float* y) {
02      unsigned int row = blockIdx.x*blockDim.x + threadIdx.x;
03      if(row < csrMatrix.numRows) {
04          float sum = 0.0f;
05          for(unsigned int i=csrMatrix.rowPtrs[row]; i<csrMatrix.rowPtrs[row+1];
06                                                                        ++i) {
07              unsigned int col = csrMatrix.colIdx[i];
08              float value = csrMatrix.value[i];
09              sum += x[col]*value;
10          }
11          y[row] += sum;
12      }
13  }
```

FIGURE 14.9

A parallel SpMV/CSR kernel.

Now we examine the CSR format under the design considerations listed in Section 14.1: space efficiency, flexibility, accessibility, memory access efficiency, and load balance. For space efficiency we observe that CSR is more space efficient than COO. COO requires three arrays, `rowIdx`, `colIdx`, and `value`, each of which has as many elements as the number of nonzeros. In contrast, CSR requires only two arrays, `colIdx` and `value`, with as many elements as the number of nonzeros. The third array, `rowPtrs`, requires only as many elements as the number of rows plus one, which makes it substantially smaller than the `rowIdx` array in COO. This difference makes CSR more space efficient than COO.

For flexibility we observe that CSR is less flexible than COO when it comes to adding nonzeros to the matrix. In COO a nonzero can be added by simply appending it to the ends of the arrays. In CSR a nonzero to be added must be added to the specific row to which it belongs. This means that the nonzero elements of the later rows would all need to be shifted, and the row pointers of the later rows would all need to be incremented accordingly. For this reason, adding nonzeros to a CSR matrix is substantially more expensive than adding them to a COO matrix.

For accessibility, CSR makes it easy to access, for a given row, the nonzeros in that row. This feature of CSR enables parallelization across rows in SpMV/ CSR, which is what allows it to avoid atomic operations in comparison with SpMV/COO. In a real-world sparse matrix application there are usually thousands to millions of rows, each of which contains tens to hundreds of nonzero elements. This makes parallelization across rows seem very appropriate: There are many threads, and each thread has a substantial amount of work. On the other hand, for some applications the sparse matrix may not have enough rows to fully utilize all the GPU threads. In these kinds of applications the COO format can extract more parallelism, since there are more nonzeros than rows. Moreover, CSR does not make it easy to access, for a given column, all the nonzeros in that column. Thus an application may need to maintain an additional, more column-oriented layout of the matrix if easy access to all elements of a column is needed.

For memory access efficiency we refer to the physical view in Fig. 14.8 for how the threads access the matrix data from memory during the first iteration of the dot product loop. The access pattern is such that consecutive threads access data elements that are far apart. In particular, threads 0, 1, 2, and 3 will access `value[0]`, `value[2]`, `value[5]`, and `value[7]`, respectively, in the first iteration of their dot product loop. They will then access `value[1]`, `value[3]`, `value[6]`, and no data, respectively, in the second iteration, and so on. As a result, the accesses to the matrix by the parallel SpMV/CSR kernel in Fig. 14.9 are not coalesced. The kernel does not make efficient use of memory bandwidth.

For load balance we observe that the SpMV/CSR kernel can potentially have significant control flow divergence in all warps. The number of iterations that are taken by a thread in the dot product loop depends on the number of nonzero elements in the row that is assigned to the thread. Since the distribution of nonzero elements among rows can be random, adjacent rows can have very different number of nonzero elements. As a result, there can be widespread control flow divergence in most or even all warps.

In summary, we have seen that the advantages of CSR over COO are that it has better space efficiency and that it gives us access to all the nonzeros of a row, allowing us to avoid atomic operations by parallelizing the computation across rows in SpMV/CSR. On the other hand, the disadvantages of CSR over COO are that it provides less flexibility with adding nonzero elements to the sparse matrix, it exhibits a memory access pattern that is not amenable to coalescing, and it causes high control divergence. In the following sections we discuss additional storage formats that sacrifice some space efficiency as compared to CSR in order to improve memory coalescing and reduce control divergence. Note that converting from COO to CSR on the GPU is an excellent exercise for the reader, using multiple fundamental parallel computing primitives, including histogram and prefix sum.

14.4 Improving memory coalescing with the ELL format

The problem of noncoalesced memory accesses can be addressed by applying data padding and transposition on the sparse matrix data. These ideas were used in the ELL storage format, whose name came from the sparse matrix package in ELLPACK, a package for solving elliptic boundary value problems (Rice and Boisvert, 1984).

A simple way to understand the ELL format is to start with the CSR format, as is illustrated in Fig. 14.10. From a CSR representation that groups nonzeros by row, we determine the rows with the maximal number of nonzero elements. We

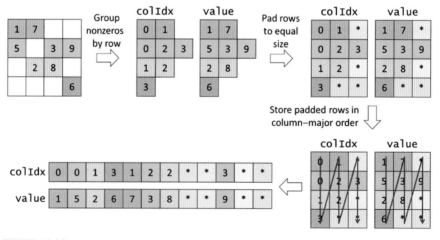

FIGURE 14.10

Example of ELL storage format.

then add padding elements to all other rows after the nonzero elements to make them the same length as the maximal rows. This makes the matrix a rectangular matrix. For our small sparse matrix example we determine that row 1 has the maximal number of elements. We then add one padding element to row 0, one padding element to row 2, and two padding elements to row 3 to make all them the same length. These additional padding elements are shown as squares with an * in Fig. 14.11. Now the matrix has become a rectangular matrix. Note that the `colIdx` array also needs to be padded the same way to preserve its correspondence to the `values` array.

We can now lay the padded matrix out in column-major order. That is, we will place all elements of column 0 in consecutive memory locations, followed by all elements of column 1, and so on. This is equivalent to transposing the rectangular matrix in the row-major order used by the C language. In terms of our small example, after the transposition, `value[0]` through `value[3]` now contain 1, 5, 2, 6, which are the 0th elements of all rows. This is illustrated in the bottom left portion of Fig. 14.10. Similarly, `colIdx[0]` through `colIdx[3]` contain the column positions of 0th elements of all rows. Note that we no longer need the `rowPtrs`, since the beginning of row r is now simply `value[r]`. With the padded elements it is also very easy to move from the current element of row r to the next element by simply adding the number of rows in the original matrix to the index. For example, the 0th element of row 2 is in `value[2]`, and the next element is in `value[2+4]`, which is equivalent to `value[6]`, where 4 is the number of rows in the original matrix in our small example.

We illustrate how to parallelize SpMV using the ELL format in Fig. 14.11, along with a parallel SpMV/ELL kernel in Fig. 14.12. Like CSR, each thread is assigned to a different row of the matrix (line 02), and a boundary check ensures that the row is within bounds (line 03). Next, a dot product loop goes through the nonzero elements of each row (line 05). Note that the SpMV/ELL kernel assumes that the input matrix has a vector `ellMatrix.nnzPerRow` that records the number of nonzeros in each row and allows each thread to iterate only through the nonzeros in its assigned row. If the input matrix does not have this vector, the kernel can simply iterate through all elements, including the padding elements, and still

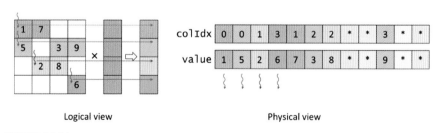

Logical view   Physical view

FIGURE 14.11

Example of parallelizing SpMV with the ELL format.

```
01    __global__ void spmv_ell_kernel(ELLMatrix ellMatrix, float* x, float* y) {
02        unsigned int row = blockIdx.x*blockDim.x + threadIdx.x;
03        if(row < ellMatrix.numRows) {
04            float sum = 0.0f;
05            for(unsigned int t = 0; t < ellMatrix.nnzPerRow[row]; ++t) {
06                unsigned int i = t*ellMatrix.numRows + row;
07                unsigned int col = ellMatrix.colIdx[i];
08                float value = ellMatrix.value[i];
09                sum += x[col]*value;
10            }
11            y[row] = sum;
12        }
13    }
```

FIGURE 14.12

A parallel SpMV/ELL kernel.

execute correctly, since the padding elements have value zero and will not affect the output values. Next, since the compressed matrix is stored in column-major order, the index i of the nonzero element in the one-dimensional array can be found by multiplying the iteration number t by the number of rows and adding the row index (line 06). Next, the thread loads the column index (line 07) and nonzero value (line 08) from the ELL matrix arrays. Note that the accesses to these arrays are coalesced because the index i is expressed in terms of row, which itself is expressed in terms of threadIdx.x, meaning that consecutive threads have consecutive array indices. Next, the thread looks up the input value, multiplies it by the nonzero value, and accumulates the result to a local variable sum (line 09). The sum variable is initialized to 0 before the dot product loop begins (line 04) and is accumulated to the output vector after the loop is over (line 11).

Now we examine the ELL format under the design considerations listed in Section 14.1: space efficiency, flexibility, accessibility, memory access efficiency, and load balance. For space efficiency we observe that the ELL format is less space efficient than the CSR format, owing to the space overhead of the padding elements. The overhead of the padding elements highly depends on the distribution of nonzeros in the matrix. In situations in which one or a small number of rows have an exceedingly large number of nonzero elements, the ELL format will result in an excessive number of padded elements. Consider our sample matrix; in the ELL format we have replaced a 4×4 matrix with a 4×3 matrix, and with the overhead from the column indices we are storing more data than was contained in the original 4×4 matrix. For a more realistic example, if a 1000×1000 sparse matrix has 1% of its elements of nonzero value, then on average, each row has ten nonzero elements. With the overhead, the size of a CSR representation would be about 2% of the uncompressed total size. Assume that one of the rows has 200 nonzero values while all other rows have less than 10. Using the ELL format, we will pad all other rows to 200 elements. This makes the ELL representation about 40% of the uncompressed total size and 20 times larger than the CSR representation. This calls for a method to control the number of padded elements when we convert from the CSR format to the ELL format, which we will introduce in the next section.

For flexibility we observe that ELL is more flexible than CSR when it comes to adding nonzeros to the matrix. In CSR, adding a nonzero to a row would require shifting all the nonzeros of the subsequent rows and incrementing their row pointers. However, in ELL, as long as a row does not have the maximum number of nonzeros in the matrix, a nonzero can be added to the row by simply replacing a padding element with an actual value.

For accessibility, ELL gives us the accessibility of both CSR and COO. We saw in Fig. 14.12 how ELL allows us to access, given a row index, the nonzeros of that row. However, ELL also allows us to access, given the index of a nonzero element, the row and column index of that element. The column index is trivial to find, as it can be accessed from the `colIdx` array at the same location `i`. However, the row index can also be accessed, owing to the regular nature of the padded matrix. Recall that the index `i` of the nonzero element was calculated in Fig. 14.9 as follows:

```
i = t*ellMatrix.numRows + row
```

Therefore if instead `i` is given and we would like to find `row`, it can be found as follows:

```
row = i%ellMatrix.numRows
```

because `row` is always less than `ellMatrix.numRows`, so `row%ellMatrix.numRows` is simply `row` itself. This accessibility of ELL allows parallelization across both rows as well as nonzero elements.

For memory access efficiency we refer to the physical view in Fig. 14.11 for how the threads access the matrix data from memory during the first iteration of the dot product loop. The access pattern is such that consecutive threads access consecutive data elements. With the elements arranged in column-major order, all adjacent threads are now accessing adjacent memory locations, enabling memory coalescing and thus making more efficient use of memory bandwidth. Some GPU architectures, especially in the older generations, have more strict address alignment rules for memory coalescing. One can force each iteration of the SpMV/ELL kernel to be fully aligned to architecturally specified alignment units such as 64 bytes by adding a few rows to the end of the matrix before transposition.

For load balance we observe that SpMV/ELL still exhibits the same load imbalance as SpMV/CSR because each thread still loops over the number of nonzeros in the row for which it is responsible. Therefore ELL does not address the problem of control divergence.

In summary, the ELL format improves on the CSR format by allowing more flexibility to add nonzeros by replacing padding elements, better accessibility, and, most important, more opportunities for memory coalescing in SpMV/ELL. However, ELL has worse space efficiency than CSR, and the control divergence of SpMV/ELL is as bad as that of SpMV/CSR. In the next section we will see how we can improve on the ELL format to address the problems of space efficiency and control divergence.

14.5 Regulating padding with the hybrid ELL-COO format

The problems of low space efficiency and control divergence in the ELL format are most pronounced when one or a small number of rows have exceedingly large number of nonzero elements. If we have a mechanism to "take away" some elements from these rows, we can reduce the number of padded elements in ELL and also reduce the control divergence. The answer lies in an important use case for the COO format.

The COO format can be used to curb the length of rows in the ELL format. Before we convert a sparse matrix to ELL, we can take away some of the elements from the rows with exceedingly large numbers of nonzero elements and place the elements into a separate COO storage. We can use SpMV/ELL on the remaining elements. With the excess elements removed from the extra-long rows, the number of padded elements for other rows can be significantly reduced. We can then use a SpMV/COO to finish the job. This approach of employing two formats to collaboratively complete a computation is often referred to as a hybrid method.

Fig. 14.13 illustrates how an example matrix can be represented using the hybrid ELL-COO format. We see that in the ELL format alone, rows 1 and 6 have the largest number of nonzero elements, causing the other rows to have excessive padding. To address this issue, we remove the last three nonzero elements of row 2 and the last two nonzero elements of row 6 from the ELL representation and move them into a separate COO representation. By removing these elements, we reduce the maximal number of nonzero elements among all rows in the small sparse matrix from 5 to 2. As shown in Fig. 14.13, we reduced the number of padded elements from 22 to 3. More important, all threads now need to take only two iterations.

The reader may wonder whether the additional work done to separate COO elements from an ELL format could incur too much overhead. The answer is that it depends. In situations in which a sparse matrix is used in only one SpMV calculation, this extra work can indeed incur significant overhead. However, in many real-work applications, the SpMV is performed on the same sparse kernel

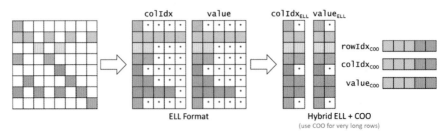

FIGURE 14.13

Hybrid ELL-COO example.

repeatedly in an iterative solver. In each iteration of the solver the x and y vectors vary, but the sparse matrix remains the same, since its elements correspond to the coefficients of the linear system of equations being solved, and these coefficients do not change from iteration to iteration. Therefore the work done to produce both the hybrid ELL and COO representation can be amortized across many iterations. We will come back to this point in the next section.

Now we examine the hybrid ELL-COO format under the design considerations listed in Section 14.1: space efficiency, flexibility, accessibility, memory access efficiency, and load balance. For space efficiency we observe that the hybrid ELL-COO format has better space efficiency than the ELL format alone because it reduces the amount of padding used.

For flexibility we observe that the hybrid ELL-COO format is more flexible than just ELL when it comes to adding nonzeros to the matrix. With ELL we can add nonzero elements by replacing padding elements for rows that have them. With hybrid COO-ELL we can also add nonzeros by replacing padding elements. However, we can also append nonzeros to the COO part of the format if the row does not have any padding elements that can be replaced in the ELL part.

For accessibility we observe that the hybrid ELL-COO format sacrifices accessibility compared to the ELL format alone. In particular, it is not always possible to access, given a row index, all the nonzeros in that row. Such an access can be done only for the rows that fit in the ELL part of the format. If the row overflows to the COO part, then finding all the nonzeros of the row would require searching the COO part, which is expensive.

For memory access efficiency, both SpMV/ELL and SpMV/COO exhibit coalesced memory accesses to the sparse matrix. Hence their combination will also result in a coalesced access pattern.

For load balance, removing nonzeros from the long rows in the ELL part of the format reduces control divergence of the SpMV/ELL kernel. These nonzeros are placed in the COO part of the format, which does not affect control divergence, since SpMV/COO does not exhibit control divergence, as we have seen.

In summary, the hybrid ELL-COO format, in comparison with the ELL format alone, improves space efficiency by reducing padding, provides more flexibility for adding nonzeros to the matrix, retains the coalesced memory access pattern, and reduces control divergence. The price that is paid is a small limitation in accessibility, in which it becomes more difficult to access all the nonzeros of a given row if that row overflows to the COO part of the format.

14.6 Reducing control divergence with the JDS format

We have seen that the ELL format can be used to achieve coalesced memory access patterns when accessing the sparse matrix in SpMV and that the hybrid ELL-COO format can further improve space efficiency by reducing padding and can also reduce control divergence. In this section we will look at another format that can achieve coalesced memory access patterns in SpMV and also reduce control divergence without the need to perform any padding. The idea is to sort the rows according to their length, say, from the longest to the shortest. Since the sorted matrix looks largely like a triangular matrix, the format is often referred to as the jagged diagonal storage (JDS) format.

Fig. 14.14 illustrates how a matrix can be stored using the JDS format. First, the nonzeros are grouped by row, as in the CSR and ELL formats. Next, the rows are sorted by the number of nonzeros in each row in increasing order. As we sort the rows, we typically maintain an additional `row` array that preserves the index of the original row. Whenever we exchange two rows in the sorting process, we also exchange the corresponding elements of the `row` array. Thus we can always keep track the original position of all rows. After the rows have been sorted, the nonzeros in the `value` array and their corresponding column indices in the `colIdx` array are stored in column-major order. A `iterPtr` array is added to track the beginning of the nonzero elements for each iteration.

Fig. 14.15 illustrates how SpMV can be parallelized by using the JDS format. Each thread is assigned to a row of the matrix and iterates through the nonzeros of that row, performing the dot product along the way. The threads use the `iterPtr` array to identify where the nonzeros of each iteration begin. It should be clear from the physical view on the right side of Fig. 14.15, which depicts the first iteration for each thread, that the threads access the nonzeros and column indices in the JDS arrays in a coalesced manner. The code for implementing SpMV/JDS is left as an exercise.

In another variation of the JDS format, the rows, after being sorted, can be partitioned into sections of rows. Since the rows have been sorted, all rows in a

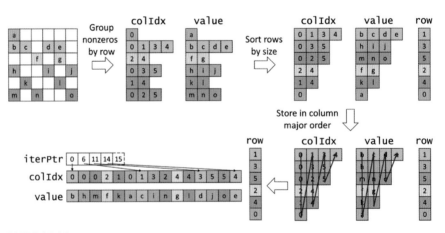

FIGURE 14.14

Example of JDS storage format.

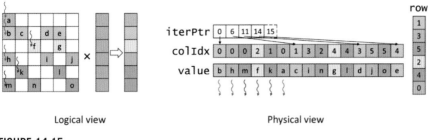

FIGURE 14.15

Example of parallelizing SpMV with the JDS format.

section will likely have more or less uniform numbers of nonzero elements. We can then generate the ELL representation for each section. Within each section we need to pad the rows only to match the row with the maximum number of elements in that section. This would reduce the number of padding elements substantially in comparison to one ELL representation of the entire matrix. In this variation of JDS, the iterPtr array would not be needed. Instead, one would need a section pointer array that points to the beginning of each ELL section only (as opposed to each iteration).

The reader should ask whether sorting rows will result in incorrect solutions to the linear system of equations. Recall that we can freely reorder equations of a linear system without changing the solution. As long as we reorder the y elements along with the rows, we are effectively reordering the equations. Therefore we will end up with the correct solution. The only extra step is to reorder the final solution back to the original order using the row array. The other question is whether sorting will incur significant overhead. The answer is similar to what we saw in the hybrid ELL-COO method. As long as the SpMV/JDS kernel is used in an iterative solver, one can afford to perform such sorting as well as the reordering of the final solution x elements and amortize the cost among many iterations of the solver.

Now we examine the ELL format under the design considerations listed in Section 14.1: space efficiency, flexibility, accessibility, memory access efficiency, and load balance. For space efficiency the JDS format is more space efficient than the ELL format because it avoids padding. The variant of JDS that uses ELL for each section has padding, but the amount of padding is less than that with the ELL format.

For flexibility the JDS format does not make it easy to add nonzeros to a row of the matrix. It is even less flexible than the CSR format because adding nonzeros changes the sizes of the rows, which may require rows to be resorted.

For accessibility the JDS format is similar to the CSR format in that it allows us to access, given a row index, the nonzero elements of that row. On the other hand, it does not make it easy to access, given a nonzero, the row index and column index of that nonzero, as the COO and ELL formats do.

For memory access efficiency the JDS format is like the ELL format in that it stores the nonzeros in column-major order. Accordingly, the JDS format enables accesses to the sparse matrix to happen in a coalesced manner. Because JDS does not require padding, the starting location of memory accesses in each iteration, as shown in the physical view of Fig. 14.15, can vary in arbitrary ways. As a result, there is no simple, inexpensive way to force all iterations of the SpMV/JDS kernel to start at architecturally specified alignment boundaries. This lack of option to force alignment can make memory accesses for JDS less efficient than those in ELL.

For load balance, the unique feature of JDS is that it sorts the rows of the matrix such that threads in the same warp are likely to iterate over rows of similar length. Therefore JDS is effective at reducing control divergence.

14.7 Summary

In this chapter we presented sparse matrix computation as an important parallel pattern. Sparse matrices are important in many real-world applications that involve modeling complex phenomenon. Furthermore, sparse matrix computation is a simple example of data-dependent performance behavior of many large real-world applications. Due to the large amount of zero elements, compaction techniques are used to reduce the amount of storage, memory accesses, and computation performed on these zero elements. Using this pattern, we introduce the concept of regularization using hybrid methods and sorting/partitioning. These regularization methods are used in many real-world applications. Interestingly, some of the regularization techniques reintroduce zero elements into the compacted representations. We use hybrid methods to mitigate the pathological cases in which we could introduce too many zero elements. Readers are referred to Bell and Garland (2009) and encouraged to experiment with different sparse datasets to gain more insight into the data-dependent performance behavior of the various SpMV kernels presented in this chapter.

It should be clear that both the execution efficiency and memory bandwidth efficiency of the parallel SpMV kernels depend on the distribution of the input data matrix. This is quite different from most of the kernels we have studied so far. However, such data-dependent performance behavior is quite common in real-world applications. This is one of the reasons why parallel SpMV is such an important parallel pattern. It is simple, yet it illustrates an important behavior in many complex parallel applications.

We would like to make an additional remark on the performance of sparse matrix computation as compared to dense matrix computation. In general, the FLOPS ratings that are achieved by either CPUs or GPUs are much lower for sparse matrix computation than for dense matrix computation. This is especially true for SpMV, in which there is no data reuse in the sparse matrix. The OP/B is essentially 0.25, limiting the achievable FLOPS rate to a small fraction of the peak performance. The various formats are important for both CPUs and GPUs, since both are limited by memory bandwidth when performing SpMV. People are often surprised by the low FLOPS rating of this type of computation on both CPUs and GPUs in the past. After reading this chapter, you should be no longer be surprised.

Exercises

1. Consider the following sparse matrix:

$$
\begin{matrix}
1 & 0 & 7 & 0 \\
0 & 0 & 8 & 0 \\
0 & 4 & 3 & 0 \\
2 & 0 & 0 & 1
\end{matrix}
$$

   Represent it in each of the following formats: (1) COO, (2) CSR, (3) ELL, and (4) JDS.

2. Given a sparse matrix of integers with m rows, n columns, and z nonzeros, how many integers are needed to represent the matrix in (1) COO, (2) CSR, (3) ELL, and (4) JDS? If the information that is provided is not enough to allow an answer, indicate what information is missing.

3. Implement the code to convert from COO to CSR using fundamental parallel computing primitives, including histogram and prefix sum.

4. Implement the host code for producing the hybrid ELL-COO format and using it to perform SpMV. Launch the ELL kernel to execute on the device, and compute the contributions of the COO elements on the host.

5. Implement a kernel that performs parallel SpMV using a matrix stored in the JDS format.

References

Bell, N., Garland, M., 2009. Implementing sparse matrix-vector multiplication on throughput-oriented processors. In: Proceedings of the ACM Conference on High-Performance Computing Networking Storage and Analysis (SC'09).

Hestenes, M.R., Stiefel, E., 1952. Methods of Conjugate Gradients for Solving Linear Systems (PDF). J. Res. Nat. Bureau Stand. 49 (6).

Rice, J.R., Boisvert, R.F., 1984. Solving Elliptic Problems Using ELLPACK. Springer, Verlag, p. 497.

Graph traversal

15

With special contributions from John Owens and Juan Gómez-Luna

Chapter Outline

15.1 Background 332
15.2 Breadth-first search 335
15.3 Vertex-centric parallelization of breadth-first search 338
15.4 Edge-centric parallelization of breadth-first search 343
15.5 Improving efficiency with frontiers 345
15.6 Reducing contention with privatization 348
15.7 Other optimizations 350
15.8 Summary 352
Exercises 353
References 354

A graph is a data structure that represents the relationships between entities. The entities involved are represented as vertices, and the relations are represented as edges. Many important real-world problems are naturally formulated as large-scale graph problems and can benefit from massively parallel computation. Prominent examples include social networks and driving direction map services. There are multiple strategies for parallelizing graph computations, some of which are centered on processing vertices in parallel, while others are centered on processing edges in parallel. Graphs are intrinsically related to sparse matrices. Thus graph computation can also be formulated in terms of sparse matrix operations. However, one can often improve the efficiency of graph computation by exploiting properties that are specific to the type of graph computation being performed. In this chapter we will focus on graph search, a graph computation that underlies many real-world applications.

15.1 Background

A graph data structure represents the relations between entities. For example, in social media, the entities are users, and the relations are connections between users. For another example, in driving direction map services, the entities are locations, and the relations are the roadways between the locations. Some relations are bidirectional, such as friend connections in a social network. Other relations are directional, such as one-way streets in a road network. In this chapter we will focus on directional relations. Bidirectional relations can be represented with two directional relations, one for each direction.

Fig. 15.1 shows an example of a simple graph with directional edges. A directional relation is represented as an arrowed edge going from a source vertex to a destination vertex. We assign a unique number to each vertex, also called the vertex *id*. There is one edge going from vertex 0 to vertex 1, one edge going from vertex 0 to vertex 2, and so on.

An intuitive representation of a graph is an *adjacency matrix*. If there is an edge going from a source vertex *i* to a destination vertex *j*, the value of element $A[i][j]$ of the adjacency matrix is 1. Otherwise, it is 0. Fig. 15.2 shows the adjacency matrix for the simple graph in Fig. 15.1. We see that $A[1][3]$ and $A[4][5]$ are 1, since there are edges going from vertex 1 to vertex 3. For clarity we leave the 0 values out of the adjacency matrix. That is, if an element is empty, its value is understood to be 0.

If a graph with N vertices is *fully connected*, that is, every vertex is connected with all other vertices, each vertex should have $(N - 1)$ outgoing edges. There should be a total of $N(N - 1)$ edges, since there is no edge going from a vertex to itself. For example, if our nine-vertex graph were fully connected, there should be eight edges going out of each vertex. There should be a total of 72 edges. Obviously, our graph is much less connected; each vertex has three or fewer outgoing edges. Such a graph is referred to as being *sparsely connected*. That is, the average number of outgoing edges from each vertex is much smaller than $N - 1$.

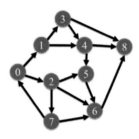

FIGURE 15.1

A simple graph example with 9 vertices and 15 directional edges.

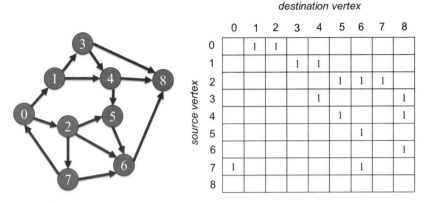

destination vertex

source vertex	0	1	2	3	4	5	6	7	8
0		1	1						
1				1	1				
2						1	1	1	
3					1				1
4						1			1
5							1		
6									1
7	1						1		
8									

FIGURE 15.2

Adjacency matrix representation of the simple graph example.

At this point, the reader has most likely made the correct observation that sparsely connected graphs can probably benefit from a sparse matrix representation. As we have seen in Chapter 14, Sparse Matrix Computation, using a compressed representation of the matrix can drastically reduce the amount of storage required and the number of wasted operations on the zero elements. Indeed, many real-world graphs are sparsely connected. For example, in a social network such as Facebook, Twitter, or LinkedIn, the average number of connections for each user is much smaller than the total number of users. This makes the number of nonzero elements in the adjacency matrix much smaller than the total number of elements.

Fig. 15.3 shows three representations of our simple graph example using three different storage formats: compressed sparse row (CSR), compressed sparse column (CSC), and coordinate (COO). We will refer to the row indices and pointers arrays as the `src` and `srcPtrs` arrays, respectively, and the column indices and pointers arrays as the `dst` and `dstPtrs` arrays, respectively. If we take CSR as an example, recall that in a CSR representation of a sparse matrix each row pointer gives the starting location for the nonzero elements in a row. Similarly, in a CSR representation of a graph, each source vertex pointer (`srcPtrs`) gives the starting location of the outgoing edges of the vertex. For example, `srcPtrs[3]=7` gives the starting location of the nonzero elements in row 3 of the original adjacency matrix. Also, `srcPtrs[4]=9` gives the starting location of the nonzero elements in row 4 of the original matrix. Thus we expect to find the nonzero data for row 3 in `data[7]` and `data[8]` and the column indices (destination vertices) for these elements in `dst[7]` and `dst[8]`. These are the data and column indices for the two edges leaving vertex 3. The reason we call the column index array `dst` is that the column index of an element in the adjacency matrix gives the destination vertex of the represented edge. In our example, we see that the destination of the two edges for source vertex 3 are `dst[7]=4` and `dst[8]=8`. We leave it as an exercise to the reader to draw similar analogies for the CSC and COO representations.

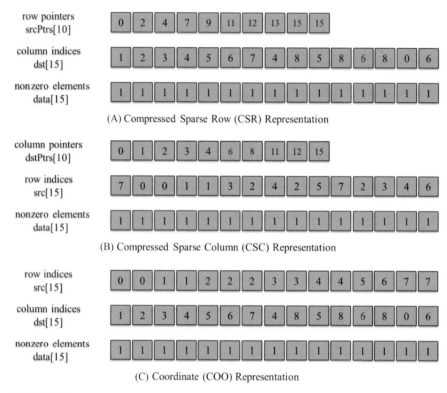

row pointers
srcPtrs[10]

column indices
dst[15]

nonzero elements
data[15]

(A) Compressed Sparse Row (CSR) Representation

column pointers
dstPtrs[10]

row indices
src[15]

nonzero elements
data[15]

(B) Compressed Sparse Column (CSC) Representation

row indices
src[15]

column indices
dst[15]

nonzero elements
data[15]

(C) Coordinate (COO) Representation

FIGURE 15.3

Three sparse matrix representations of the adjacency matrix: (A) CSR, (B) CSC, (C) COO. *COO*, coordinate; *CSC*, compressed sparse column; *CSR*, compressed sparse row.

Note that the `data` array in this example is unnecessary. Since the value of all its elements is 1, we do not need to store it. We can make the data implicit, that is, whenever a nonzero element exists, we can just assume that it is 1. For example, the existence of each column index in the destination array of a CSR representation implies that an edge exists. However, in some applications the adjacency matrix may store additional information about the relationship, such as the distance between two locations or the date on which two social network users became connected. In those applications the data array will need to be explicitly stored.

Sparse representation can lead to significant savings in storing the adjacency matrix. For our example, assuming that the `data` array can be eliminated, the CSR representation requires storage for 25 locations versus the $9^2=81$ locations if we stored the entire adjacency matrix. For real-life problems in which a very small fraction of the adjacency matrix elements are nonzero, the savings can be tremendous.

Different graphs may have drastically different structures. One way to characterize these structures is to look at the distribution of the number of edges that are connected to each vertex (the *vertex degree*). A road network, expressed as a graph, would have a relatively uniform degree distribution with a low average degree per vertex because each road intersection (vertex) would typically have only a low number of roads connected to it. On the other hand, a graph of Twitter followers, in which each incoming edge represents a "follow," would have a much broader distribution of vertex degrees, with a large-degree vertex representing a popular Twitter user. The structure of the graph may influence the choice of algorithm to implement a particular graph application.

Recall from Chapter 14, Sparse Matrix Computation, that each sparse matrix representation gives different accessibility to the represented data. Hence the choice of which representation to use for the graph has implications for which information about the graph is made easily accessible to the graph traversal algorithm. The CSR representations give easy access to the outgoing edges of a given vertex. The CSC representation gives easy access to the incoming edges of a given vertex. The COO representation gives easy access to the source and destination vertices of a given edge. Therefore the choice of the graph representation goes hand-in-hand with the choice of the graph traversal algorithm. We demonstrate this concept throughout this chapter by examining different parallel implementations of breadth-first search, a widely used graph search computation.

15.2 Breadth-first search

An important graph computation is breadth-first search (BFS). BFS is often used to discover the shortest number of edges that one needs to traverse to go from one vertex to another vertex of the graph. In the graph example in Fig. 15.1 we may need to find all the alternative routes that we could take going from the location represented by vertex 0 to that represented by vertex 5. By visual inspection we see that there are three possible paths: $0 \to 1 \to 3 \to 4 \to 5$, $0 \to 1 \to 4 \to 5$, and $0 \to 2 \to 5$, with $0 \to 2 \to 5$ being the shortest. There are different ways of summarizing the outcome of a BFS traversal. One way is, given a vertex that is referred to as the root, to label each vertex with the smallest number of edges that one needs to traverse to go from the root to that vertex.

Fig. 15.4(A) shows the desired BFS result with vertex 0 as the root. Through one edge, we can get to vertices 1 and 2. Thus we label these vertices as belonging to level 1. By traversing another edge, we can get to vertices 3 (through vertex 1), 4 (through vertex 1), 5 (through vertex 2), 6 (through vertex 2), and 7 (through vertex 2). Thus we label these vertices as belonging to level 2. Finally, by traversing one more edge, we can get to vertex 8 (through any of vertices 3, 4, or 6).

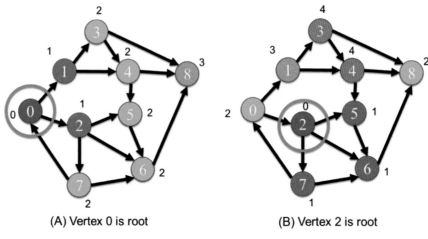

(A) Vertex 0 is root   (B) Vertex 2 is root

FIGURE 15.4

(A and B) Two examples of breadth-first search results for two different root vertices. The labels adjacent to each vertex indicate the number of hops (depth) from the root vertex.

The BFS result would be quite different with another vertex as the root. Fig. 15.4(B) shows the desired result of BFS with vertex 2 as the root. The level 1 vertices are 5, 6, and 7. The level 2 vertices are 8 (through vertex 6) and 0 (through vertex 7). Only vertex 1 is at level 3 (through vertex 0). Finally, the level 4 vertices are 3 and 4 (both through vertex 1). It is interesting to note that the outcome is quite different for each vertex even though we moved the root to a vertex that is only one edge away from the original root.

One can view the labeling actions of BFS as constructing a BFS tree that is rooted in the root node of the search. The tree consists of all the labeled vertices and only the edges traversed during the search that go from a vertex at one level to vertices at the next level.

Once we have all the vertices labeled with their level, we can easily find a path from the root vertex to any of the vertices where the number of edges traveled is equivalent to the level. For example, in Fig. 15.4(B), we see that vertex 1 is labeled as level 3, so we know that the smallest number of edges between the root (vertex 2) and vertex 1 is 3. If we need to find the path, we can simply start from the destination vertex and trace back to the root. At each step, we select the predecessor whose level is one less than that of the current vertex. If there are multiple predecessors with the same level, we can randomly pick one. Any vertex thus selected would give a sound solution. The fact that there are multiple predecessors to choose from means that there are multiple equally good solutions to the problem. In our example we can find a shortest path from vertex 2 to vertex 1 by starting from vertex 1, choosing vertex 0, then vertex 7, and then vertex 2. Therefore a solution path is $2{\rightarrow}7{\rightarrow}0{\rightarrow}1$. This of course assumes that each vertex has a list of the source vertices of all the incoming edges so that one can find the predecessors of a given vertex.

Fig. 15.5 shows an important application of BFS in computer-aided design (CAD). In designing an integrated circuit chip, there are many electronic components that need to be connected to complete the design. The connectors of these components are called net terminals. Fig. 15.5(A) shows two such net terminals as round dots; one belongs to a component in the upper left part, and the other belongs to another component in the lower right part of the chip. Assume that the design requires that these two net terminals be connected. This is done by running, or routing, a wire of a given width from the first net terminal to the second net terminal.

The routing software represents the chip as a grid of wiring blocks in which each block can potentially serve as a piece of a wire. A wire can be formed by extending in either the horizontal or the vertical direction. For example, the black J-shape in the lower half of the chip consists of 21 wiring blocks and connects three net terminals. Once a wiring block is used as part of a wire, it can no longer be used as part of any other wires. Furthermore, it forms a blockage for wiring blocks around it. No wires can be extended from a used block's lower neighbor to its upper neighbor or from its left neighbor to its right neighbor, and so on. Once a wire is formed, all other wires must be routed around it. Routing blocks can also be occupied by circuit components, which impose the same blockage constraint as when they are used as part of a wire. This is why the problem is called a maze routing problem. The previously formed circuit components and wires form a maze for the wires that have yet to be formed. The maze routing software finds a route for each additional wire given all the constraints from the previously formed components and wires.

The maze routing application represents the chip as a graph. The routing blocks are vertices. An edge from vertex i to vertex j indicates that one can extend a wire from block i to block j. Once a block is occupied by a wire or a component, it is either marked as a blockage vertex or taken away from the graph, depending on the design of the application. Fig. 15.5 shows that the

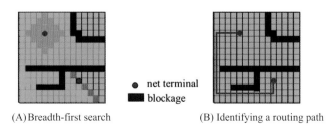

(A) Breadth-first search   ● net terminal   ▇ blockage   (B) Identifying a routing path

FIGURE 15.5

Maze routing in integrated circuits—an application for breadth-first search: (A) breadth-first search, (B) identifying a routing path.

application solves the maze routing problem with a BFS from the root net terminal to the target net terminal. This is done by starting with the root vertex and labeling the vertices into levels. The immediate vertical or horizontal neighbors (a total of four) that are not blockages are marked as level 1. We see that all four neighbors of the root are reachable and will be marked as level 1. The neighbors of level 1 vertices that are neither blockages nor visited by the current search will be marked as level 2. The reader should verify that there are four level 1 vertices, eight level 2 vertices, twelve level 3 vertices, and so on in Fig. 15.5(A). As we can see, the BFS essentially forms a wavefront of vertices for each level. These wavefronts start small for level 1 but can grow very large very quickly in a few levels.

Fig. 15.5(B) shows that once the BFS is complete, we can form a wire by finding a shortest path from the root to the target. As was explained earlier, this can be done by starting with the target vertex and tracing back to the predecessors whose levels are one lower than that of the current vertex. Whenever there are multiple predecessors that have equivalent levels, there are multiple routes that are of the same length. One could design heuristics to choose the predecessor in a way that minimizes the difficulty of constraints for wires that have yet to be formed.

15.3 Vertex-centric parallelization of breadth-first search

A natural way to parallelize graph algorithms is to perform operations on different vertices or edges in parallel. In fact, many parallel implementations of graph algorithms can be classified as vertex-centric or edge-centric. A vertex-centric parallel implementation assigns threads to vertices and has each thread perform an operation on its vertex, which usually involves iterating over the neighbors of that vertex. Depending on the algorithm, the neighbors of interest may be those that are reachable via the outgoing edges, the incoming edges, or both. In contrast, an edge-centric parallel implementation assigns threads to edges and has each thread perform an operation on its edge, which usually involves looking up the source and destination vertices of that edge. In this section we look at two different vertex-centric parallel implementations of BFS: one that iterates over outgoing edges and one that iterates over incoming edges. In the next section we look at an edge-centric parallel implementation of BFS and compare.

The parallel implementations that we will look at follow the same strategy when it comes to iterating over levels. In all implementations we start by labeling the root vertex as belonging to level 0. We then call a kernel to label all the neighbors of the root vertex as belonging to level 1. After that, we call a kernel to label all the unvisited neighbors of the level 1 vertices as belonging to level 2. Then we call a kernel to label all the unvisited neighbors of the level 2 vertices as belonging to level 3. This process continues until no new vertices are visited and labeled.

```
01  __global__ void bfs_kernel(CSRGraph csrGraph, unsigned int* level,
02                  unsigned int* newVertexVisited, unsigned int currLevel) {
03      unsigned int vertex = blockIdx.x*blockDim.x + threadIdx.x;
04      if(vertex < csrGraph.numVertices) {
05          if(level[vertex] == currLevel - 1) {
06              for(unsigned int edge = csrGraph.srcPtrs[vertex];
07                      edge < csrGraph.srcPtrs[vertex + 1]; ++edge) {
08                  unsigned int neighbor = csrGraph.dst[edge];
09                  if(level[neighbor] == UINT_MAX) { // Neighbor not visited
10                      level[neighbor] = currLevel;
11                      *newVertexVisited = 1;
12                  }
13              }
14          }
15      }
16  }
```

FIGURE 15.6

A vertex-centric push (top-down) BFS kernel. *BFS*, breadth-first search.

The reason a separate kernel is called for each level is that we need to wait until all vertices in a previous level have been labeled before proceeding to label vertices in the next level. Otherwise, we risk labeling a vertex incorrectly. In the rest of this section we focus on implementing the kernel that is called for each level. That is, we will implement a BFS kernel that, given a level, labels all the vertices that belong to that level on the basis of the labels of the vertices from previous levels.

The first vertex-centric parallel implementation assigns each thread to a vertex to iterate over the vertex's outgoing edges (Harish and Narayanan, 2007). Each thread first checks whether its vertex belongs to the previous level. If so, the thread will iterate over the outgoing edges to label all the unvisited neighbors as belonging to the current level. This vertex-centric implementation is often referred to as a *top-down* or *push* implementation.[1] Since this implementation requires accessibility to the outgoing edges of a given source vertex (i.e., nonzero elements of a given row of the adjacency matrix), a CSR representation is needed.

Fig. 15.6 shows the kernel code for the vertex-centric push implementation, and Fig. 15.7 shows an example of how this kernel performs a traversal from level 1 (previous level) to level 2 (current level). The kernel starts by assigning a thread to each vertex (line 03), and each thread ensures that its vertex id is within bounds (line 04). Next, each thread checks whether its vertex belongs to the previous level (line 05). In Fig. 15.7, only the threads assigned to vertices 1 and 2 will pass this check. The threads that pass this check will then use the CSR srcPtrs array to locate the outgoing edges of the vertex and iterate over them (lines 06−07). For each outgoing edge, the thread finds the neighbor at the destination of the edge using the CSR dst array (line 08). The thread then checks

---

[1] If we are constructing a BFS tree, this implementation can be seen as assigning threads to parent vertices in the BFS tree in search of their children, hence the name *top-down*. This terminology assumes that the root of the tree is on the top and the leaves of the tree are at the bottom. *Push* refers to each active vertex's action of pushing its depth via its outgoing edges to all its neighbors.

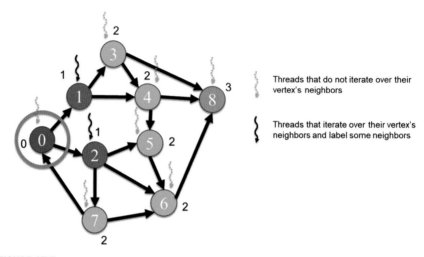

FIGURE 15.7

Example of a vertex-centric push BFS traversal from level 1 to level 2. *BFS*, breadth-first search.

whether the neighbor has not been visited by checking whether the neighbor has been assigned to a level yet (line 09).

Initially, all vertex levels are set to UINT_MAX, which means that the vertex is unreachable. Hence a neighbor has not been visited if its level is still UINT_MAX. If the neighbor has not been visited, the thread will label the neighbor as belonging to the current level (line 10). Finally, the thread will set a flag indicating that a new vertex has been visited (line 11). This flag is used by the launching code to decide whether a new grid needs to be launched to process a new level or we have reached the end. Note that multiple threads can assign 1 to the flag and the code will still execute correctly. This property is termed *idempotence*. In an idempotent operation such as this one, we do not need an atomic operation because the threads are not performing a read-modify-write operation. All threads write the same value, so the outcome is the same regardless of how many threads perform a write operation.

The second vertex-centric parallel implementation assigns each thread to a vertex to iterate over the vertex's incoming edges. Each thread first checks whether its vertex has been visited yet. If not, the thread will iterate over the incoming edges to find whether any of the neighbors belong to the previous level. If the thread finds a neighbor that belongs to the previous level, the thread will label its vertex as belonging to the current level. This vertex-centric implementation is often referred to as a *bottom-up* or *pull* implementation.[2] Since this

---

[2] If we are constructing a BFS tree, this implementation can be seen as assigning threads to potential child vertices in the BFS tree in search of their parents, hence, the name *bottom-up*. *Pull* refers to each vertex's action of reaching back to its predecessors and pulling active status from them.

implementation requires accessibility to the incoming edges of a given destination vertex (i.e., nonzero elements of a given column of the adjacency matrix), a CSC representation is needed.

Fig. 15.8 shows the kernel code for the vertex-centric pull implementation, and Fig. 15.9 shows an example of how this kernel performs a traversal from level 1 to level 2. The kernel starts by assigning a thread to each vertex (line 03), and each thread ensures that its vertex id is within bounds (line 04). Next, each thread checks whether its vertex has not been visited yet (line 05). In Fig. 15.9 the threads that are assigned to vertices 3–8 all pass this check. The threads that

```
01  __global__ void bfs_kernel(CSCGraph cscGraph, unsigned int* level,
02                unsigned int* newVertexVisited, unsigned int currLevel) {
03      unsigned int vertex = blockIdx.x*blockDim.x + threadIdx.x;
04      if(vertex < cscGraph.numVertices) {
05          if(level[vertex] == UINT_MAX) { // Vertex not yet visited
06              for(unsigned int edge = cscGraph.dstPtrs[vertex];
07                      edge < cscGraph.dstPtrs[vertex + 1]; ++edge) {
08                  unsigned int neighbor = cscGraph.src[edge];
09                  if(level[neighbor] == currLevel - 1) {
10                      level[vertex] = currLevel;
11                      *newVertexVisited = 1;
12                      break;
13                  }
14              }
15          }
16      }
17  }
```

FIGURE 15.8

A vertex-centric pull (bottom-up) BFS kernel. *BFS*, breadth-first search.

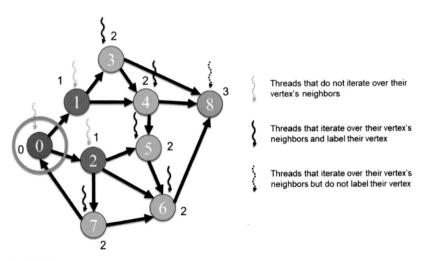

FIGURE 15.9

Example of a vertex-centric pull (bottom-up) traversal from level 1 to level 2.

pass this check will then use the CSC `dstPtrs` array to locate the incoming edges of the vertex and iterate over them (lines 06−07). For each incoming edge, the thread finds the neighbor at the source of the edge, using the CSC `src` array (line 08). The thread then checks whether the neighbor belongs to the previous level (line 09). If so, the thread will label its vertex as belonging to the current level (line 10) and set a flag indicating that a new vertex has been visited (line 11). The thread will also break out of the loop (line 12).

The justification for breaking out of the loop is as follows. For a thread to establish that its vertex is in the current level, it is sufficient for the thread's vertex to have one neighbor in the previous level. Therefore it is unnecessary for the thread to check the rest of the neighbors. Only the threads whose vertices do not have any neighbors in the previous level will end up looping over the entire neighbors list. In Fig. 15.9, only the thread assigned to vertex 8 will loop over the entire neighbor list without breaking.

In comparing the push and pull vertex-centric parallel implementations, there are two key differences to consider that have an important impact on performance. The first difference is that in the push implementation a thread loops over its vertex's entire neighbor list, whereas in the pull implementation a thread may break out of the loop early. For graphs with low degree and low variance, such as road networks or CAD circuit models, this difference may not be important because the neighbor lists are small and similar in size. However, for graphs with high degree and high variance, such as social networks, the neighbor lists are long and may vary substantially in size, resulting in high load imbalance and control divergence across threads. For this reason, breaking out of the loop early can provide substantial performance gains by reducing load imbalance and control divergence.

The second important difference between the two implementations is that in the push implementation, only the threads assigned to vertices in the previous level loop over their neighbor list, whereas in the pull implementation, all the threads assigned to any unvisited vertex loop over their neighbor list. For earlier levels, we expect to have a relatively small number of vertices per level and a large number of unvisited vertices in the graph. For this reason, the push implementation typically performs better for earlier levels because it iterates over fewer neighbor lists. In contrast, for later levels, we expect to have more vertices per level and fewer unvisited vertices in the graph. Moreover, the chances of finding a visited neighbor in the pull approach and exiting the loop early are higher. For this reason the pull implementation typically performs better for later levels.

Based on this observation, a common optimization is to use the push implementation for earlier levels, then switch to the pull implementation for later levels. This approach is often referred to as a *direction-optimized* implementation. The choice of when to switch between implementations usually depends on the type of graph. Low-degree graphs usually have many levels, and it takes a while to reach a point at which the levels have many vertices and a substantial number of vertices have already been visited. On the other hand, high-degree graphs usually have few levels, and the levels grow very quickly. The high-degree graphs in which it takes only a few levels to get from any vertex to any other vertex are usually referred to as *small world graphs*. Because of these properties, switching from the push implementation to the pull implementation usually happens much earlier for high-degree graphs than for low-degree graphs.

Recall that the push implementation uses a CSR representation of the graph, whereas the pull implementation uses a CSC representation of the graph. For this reason, if a direction-optimized implementation is to be used, both a CSR and a CSC representation of the graph need to be stored. In many applications, such as social networks or maze routing, the graph is undirected, which means that the adjacency matrix is symmetric. In this case, the CSR and CSC representations are equivalent, so only one of them needs to be stored and can be used by both implementations.

15.4 Edge-centric parallelization of breadth-first search

In this section we look at an edge-centric parallel implementation of BFS. In this implementation, each thread is assigned to an edge. It checks whether the source vertex of the edge belongs to the previous level and whether the destination vertex of the edge is unvisited. If so, it labels the unvisited destination vertex as belonging to the current level. Since this implementation requires accessibility to the source and destination vertices of a given edge (i.e., row and column indices of a given nonzero), a COO data structure is needed.

Fig. 15.10 shows the kernel code for the edge-centric parallel implementation, while Fig. 15.11 shows an example of how this kernel performs a traversal from level 1 to level 2. The kernel starts by assigning a thread to each edge (line 03), and each thread ensures that its edge id is within bounds (line 04). Next, each thread finds the source vertex of its edge, using the COO `src` array (line 05), and checks whether the vertex belongs to the previous level (line 06). In Fig. 15.11, only the threads assigned to the outgoing edges of vertices 1 and 2 will pass this

```
01  __global__ void bfs_kernel(COOGraph cooGraph, unsigned int* level,
02                  unsigned int* newVertexVisited, unsigned int currLevel) {
03      unsigned int edge = blockIdx.x*blockDim.x + threadIdx.x;
04      if(edge < cooGraph.numEdges) {
05          unsigned int vertex = cooGraph.src[edge];
06          if(level[vertex] == currLevel - 1) {
07              unsigned int neighbor = cooGraph.dst[edge];
08              if(level[neighbor] == UINT_MAX) { // Neighbor not visited
09                  level[neighbor] = currLevel;
10                  *newVertexVisited = 1;
11              }
12          }
13      }
14  }
```

FIGURE 15.10

An edge-centric BFS kernel. *BFS,* breadth-first search.

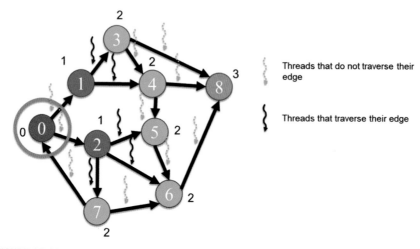

Threads that do not traverse their edge

Threads that traverse their edge

FIGURE 15.11

Example of an edge-centric traversal from level 1 to level 2.

check. The threads that pass this check will locate the neighbor at the destination of the edge, using the COO `dst` array (line 07), and check whether the neighbor has not been visited (line 08). If not, the thread will label the neighbor as belonging to the current level (line 09). Finally, the thread will set a flag indicating that a new vertex has been visited (line 10).

The edge-centric parallel implementation has two main advantages over the vertex-centric parallel implementations. The first advantage is that the edge-centric implementation exposes more parallelism. In the vertex-centric implementations, if the number of vertices is small, we may not launch enough threads to fully occupy the device. Since a graph typically has many more edges than vertices, the edge-centric implementation can launch more threads. Hence the edge-centric implementation is usually more suitable for small graphs.

The second advantage of the edge-centric implementation over the vertex-centric implementations is that it exhibits less load imbalance and control divergence. In the vertex-centric implementations, each thread iterates over a different number of edges, depending on the degree of the vertex to which it is assigned. In contrast, in the edge-centric implementation, each thread traverses only one edge. With respect to the vertex-centric implementation the edge-centric implementation is an example of rearranging the mapping of threads to work or data to reduce control divergence, as was discussed in Chapter 6, Performance Considerations. The edge-centric implementation is usually more suitable for high-degree graphs that have a large variation in the degrees of vertices.

The disadvantage of the edge-centric implementation is that it checks every edge in the graph. In contrast, the vertex-centric implementations can skip an entire edge list if the implementation determines that a vertex is not relevant for the level. For example, consider the case in which some vertex v has n edges and is not relevant for a particular level. In the edge-centric implementation our launch includes n threads, one for each edge, and each of these threads independently inspects v and discovers that the edge is irrelevant. In contrast, in the vertex-centric implementations, our launch includes only one thread for v that skips all n edges after inspecting v once to determine that it is irrelevant. Another disadvantage of the edge-centric implementation is that it uses COO, which requires more storage space to store the edges compared to CSR and CSC, which are used by the vertex-centric implementations.

The reader may have noticed that the code examples in the previous section and this one resemble our implementations of sparse matrix-vector multiplication (SpMV) in Chapter 14, Sparse Matrix Computation. In fact, with a slightly different formulation we can express a BFS level iteration entirely in terms of SpMV and a few other vector operations, in which the SpMV operation is the dominant operation. Beyond BFS, many other graph computations can also be formulated in terms of sparse matrix computations, using the adjacency matrix (Jeremy and Gilbert, 2011). Such a formulation is often referred to as the *linear-algebraic formulation* of graph problems and is the focus of an API specification known as GraphBLAS. The advantage of linear-algebraic formulations is that they can leverage mature and highly optimized parallel libraries for sparse linear algebra to perform graph computations. The disadvantage of linear-algebraic formulations is that they may miss out on optimizations that take advantage of specific properties of the graph algorithm in question.

15.5 Improving efficiency with frontiers

In the approaches that we discussed in the previous two sections, we checked every vertex or edge in every iteration for their relevance to the level in question. The advantage of this strategy is that the kernels are highly parallel and do not require any synchronization across threads. The disadvantage is that many unnecessary threads are launched and a lot of wasted work is performed. For example, in the vertex-centric implementations we launch a thread for every vertex in the graph, many of which simply discover that the vertex is not relevant and do not perform any work. Similarly, in the edge-centric implementation we launch a thread for every edge in the graph; many of the threads simply discover that the edge is not relevant and do not perform any useful work.

In this section we aim to avoid launching unnecessary threads and eliminate the redundant checks that they perform in each iteration. We will focus on the vertex-centric push approach that was presented in Section 15.3. Recall that in the vertex-centric push approach, for each level, a thread is launched for each vertex in the graph. The thread checks whether its vertex is in the previous level, and if so, it labels all the vertex's unvisited neighbors as belonging to the current level.

On the other hand, the threads whose vertices are not in the current level do not do anything. Ideally, these threads should not even be launched. To avoid launching these threads, we can have the threads processing the vertices in the previous level collaborate to construct a *frontier* of the vertices that they visit. Hence for the current level, threads need to be launched only for the vertices in that frontier (Luo et al., 2010).

Fig. 15.12 shows the kernel code for the vertex-centric push implementation that uses frontiers, and Fig. 15.13 shows an example of how this kernel performs a traversal from level 1 to level 2. A key distinction from the previous approach is that the kernel takes additional parameters to represent the frontiers. The additional parameters include the arrays prevFrontier and currFrontier to store the vertices in the previous and current frontiers, respectively. They also include pointers to the counters numPrevFrontier and numCurrFrontier that store the number of vertices in each frontier. Note that the flag for indicating that a new vertex has been visited is no longer needed. Instead, the host can tell that the end has been reached when the number of vertices in the current frontier is 0.

We now look at the body of the kernel in Fig. 15.12. The kernel starts by assigning a thread to each element of the previous frontier (line 05), and each thread ensures that its element id is within bounds (line 06). In Fig. 15.13, only vertices 1 and 2 are in the previous frontier, so only two threads are launched. Each thread loads its element from the previous frontier, which contains the index of the vertex that it is processing (line 07). The thread uses the CSR srcPtrs array to locate the outgoing edges of the vertex and iterate over them (lines 08−09). For each outgoing edge, the thread finds the neighbor at the destination of the edge, using the CSR dst array (line 10). The thread then checks whether the neighbor has not been visited; if not, it labels the neighbor as belonging to the current level (line 11). An important distinction from the previous implementation is that an atomic operation is used to perform the checking and labeling operation. The reason will be explained shortly. If a thread succeeds in labeling the

```
01  __global__ void bfs_kernel(CSRGraph csrGraph, unsigned int* level,
02              unsigned int* prevFrontier, unsigned int* currFrontier,
03              unsigned int numPrevFrontier, unsigned int* numCurrFrontier,
04              unsigned int currLevel) {
05      unsigned int i = blockIdx.x*blockDim.x + threadIdx.x;
06      if(i < numPrevFrontier) {
07          unsigned int vertex = prevFrontier[i];
08          for(unsigned int edge = csrGraph.srcPtrs[vertex];
09                  edge < csrGraph.srcPtrs[vertex + 1]; ++edge) {
10              unsigned int neighbor = csrGraph.dst[edge];
11              if(atomicCAS(&level[neighbor],UINT_MAX,currLevel) == UINT_MAX) {
12                  unsigned int currFrontierIdx = atomicAdd(numCurrFrontier, 1);
13                  currFrontier[currFrontierIdx] = neighbor;
14              }
15          }
16      }
17  }
```

FIGURE 15.12

A vertex-centric push (top-down) BFS kernel with frontiers. *BFS*, breadth-first search.

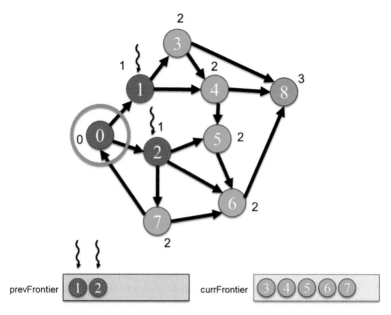

FIGURE 15.13

Example of a vertex-centric push (top-down) BFS traversal from level 1 to level 2 with frontiers. *BFS*, breadth-first search.

neighbor, it must add the neighbor to the current frontier. To do so, the thread increments the size of the current frontier (line 12) and adds the neighbor to the corresponding location (line 13). The size of the current frontier needs to be incremented atomically (line 12) because multiple threads may be incrementing it simultaneously, so we need to ensure that no race condition takes place.

We now turn our attention to the atomic operation on line 11. As a thread iterates through the neighbors of its vertex, it checks whether the neighbor has been visited; if not, it labels the neighbor as belonging to the current level. In the vertex-centric push kernel without frontiers in Fig. 15.12, this checking and labeling operation is performed without atomic operations (09−10). In that implementation, if multiple threads check the old label of the same unvisited neighbor before any of them are able to label it, multiple threads may end up labeling the neighbor. Since all threads are labeling the neighbor with the same label (the operation is idempotent), it is okay to allow the threads to label the neighbor redundantly. In contrast, in the frontier-based implementation in Fig. 15.12, each thread not only labels the unvisited neighbor but also adds it to the frontier. Hence if multiple threads observe the neighbor as unvisited, they will all add the neighbor to the frontier, causing it to be added multiple times. If the neighbor is added multiple times to the frontier, it will be processed multiple times in the next level, which is redundant and wasteful.

To avoid having multiple threads observe the neighbor as unvisited, the checking and updating of the neighbor's label should be performed atomically. In other words, we must check whether the neighbor has not been visited, and if not, label it as part of the current level all in one atomic operation. An atomic operation that can perform all of these steps is *compare-and-swap*, which is provided by the `atomicCAS` intrinsic function. This function takes three parameters: the address of the data in memory, the value to which we want to compare the data, and the value to which we would like to set the data if the comparison succeeds. In our case (line 11), we would like to compare `level[neighbor]` to `UINT_MAX` to check whether the neighbor is unvisited and set `level[neighbor]` to `currLevel` if the comparison succeeds. As with other atomic operations, `atomicCAS` returns the old value of the data that was stored. Therefore we can check whether the compare-and-swap operation succeeded by comparing the return value of `atomicCAS` with the value that `atomicCAS` compared with, which in this case is `UINT_MAX`.

As was mentioned earlier, the advantage of this frontier-based approach over the approach described in the previous section is that it reduces redundant work by only launching threads to process the relevant vertices. The disadvantage of this frontier-based approach is the overhead of the long-latency atomic operations, especially when these operations contend on the same data. For the `atomicCAS` operation (line 11) we expect the contention to be moderate because only some threads, not all, will visit the same unvisited neighbor. However, for the `atomicAdd` operation (line 12) we expect the contention to be high because all threads increment the same counter to add vertices to the same frontier. In the next section we look at how this contention can be reduced.

15.6 Reducing contention with privatization

Recall from Chapter 6, Performance Considerations, that one optimization that can be applied to reduce the contention of atomic operations on the same data is privatization. Privatization reduces contention of atomics by applying partial updates to a private copy of the data, then updating the public copy when done. We saw an example of privatization in the histogram pattern in Chapter 9, Parallel Histogram, where threads in the same block updated a local histogram that was private to the block, then updated the public histogram at the end.

Privatization can also be applied in the context of concurrent frontier updates (increments to `numCurrFrontier`) to reduce the contention on inserting into the frontier. We can have each thread block maintain its own local frontier throughout the computation and update the public frontier when done. Hence threads will contend on the same data only with other threads in the same block. Moreover, the local frontier and its counter can be stored in shared memory, which enables lower-latency atomic operations on the counter and stores to the local frontier. Furthermore, when the local frontier in shared memory is stored to the public frontier in global memory, the accesses can be coalesced.

Fig. 15.14 shows the kernel code for the vertex-centric push implementation that uses privatized frontiers, while Fig. 15.15 illustrates the privatization of the frontiers. The kernel starts by declaring a private frontier for each thread block in shared memory (lines 07−08). One thread in the block initializes the frontier's counter to 0 (lines 09−11), and all threads in the block wait at the __syncthreads barrier for the initialization to complete before they start using the counter (line 12). The next part of the code is similar to the previous version: Each thread loads its vertex from the frontier (line 17), iterates over its outgoing edges (lines 18−19), finds the neighbor at the destination of the edge (line 20), and atomically checks whether the neighbor is unvisited and visits it if it is unvisited (line 21).

```
01  __global__ void bfs_kernel(CSRGraph csrGraph, unsigned int* level,
02                unsigned int* prevFrontier, unsigned int* currFrontier,
03                unsigned int numPrevFrontier, unsigned int* numCurrFrontier,
04                unsigned int currLevel) {
05
06      // Initialize privatized frontier
07      __shared__ unsigned int currFrontier_s[LOCAL_FRONTIER_CAPACITY];
08      __shared__ unsigned int numCurrFrontier_s;
09      if(threadIdx.x == 0) {
10          numCurrFrontier_s = 0;
11      }
12      __syncthreads();
13
14      // Perform BFS
15      unsigned int i = blockIdx.x*blockDim.x + threadIdx.x;
16      if(i < numPrevFrontier) {
17          unsigned int vertex = prevFrontier[i];
18          for(unsigned int edge = csrGraph.srcPtrs[vertex];
19                  edge < csrGraph.srcPtrs[vertex + 1]; ++edge) {
20              unsigned int neighbor = csrGraph.dst[edge];
21              if(atomicCAS(&level[neighbor], UINT_MAX, currLevel) == UINT_MAX) {
22                  unsigned int currFrontierIdx_s = atomicAdd(&numCurrFrontier_s, 1);
23                  if(currFrontierIdx_s < LOCAL_FRONTIER_CAPACITY) {
24                      currFrontier_s[currFrontierIdx_s] = neighbor;
25                  } else {
26                      numCurrFrontier_s = LOCAL_FRONTIER_CAPACITY;
27                      unsigned int currFrontierIdx = atomicAdd(numCurrFrontier, 1);
28                      currFrontier[currFrontierIdx] = neighbor;
29                  }
30              }
31          }
32      }
33      __syncthreads();
34
35      // Allocate in global frontier
36      __shared__ unsigned int currFrontierStartIdx;
37      if(threadIdx.x == 0) {
38          currFrontierStartIdx = atomicAdd(numCurrFrontier, numCurrFrontier_s);
39      }
40      __syncthreads();
41
42      // Commit to global frontier
43      for(unsigned int currFrontierIdx_s = threadIdx.x;
44              currFrontierIdx_s < numCurrFrontier_s; currFrontierIdx_s += blockDim.x) {
45          unsigned int currFrontierIdx = currFrontierStartIdx + currFrontierIdx_s;
46          currFrontier[currFrontierIdx] = currFrontier_s[currFrontierIdx_s];
47      }
48
49  }
```

FIGURE 15.14

A vertex-centric push (top-down) BFS kernel with privatization of frontiers. *BFS*, breadth-first search.

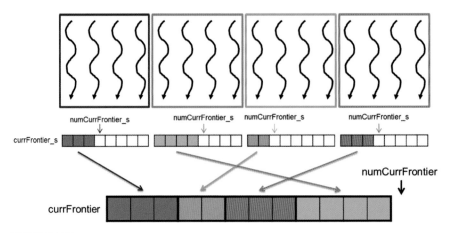

FIGURE 15.15

Privatization of frontiers example.

If the thread succeeds in visiting the neighbor, that is, the neighbor is unvisited, it adds the neighbor to the local frontier. The thread first atomically increments the local frontier counter (line 22). If the local frontier is not full (line 23), the thread adds the neighbor to the local frontier (line 24). Otherwise, if the local frontier has overflowed, the thread restores the value of the local counter (line 26) and adds the neighbor in the global frontier by atomically incrementing the global counter (line 27) and storing the neighbor at the corresponding location (line 28).

After all threads in a block have iterated over their vertices' neighbors, they need to store the privatized local frontier to the global frontier. First, the threads wait for each other to complete to ensure that no more neighbors will be added to the local frontier (line 33). Next, one thread in the block acts on behalf of the others to allocate space in the global frontier for all the elements in the local frontier (lines 36−39) while all the threads wait for it (line 40). Finally, the threads iterate over the vertices in the local frontier (line 43−44) and store them in the public frontier (line 45−46). Notice that the index into the public frontier `currFrontierIdx` is expressed in terms of `currFrontierIdx_s`, which is expressed in terms of `threadIdx.x`. Therefore threads with consecutive thread index values store to consecutive global memory locations, which means that the stores are coalesced.

15.7 Other optimizations

Reducing launch overhead

In most graphs, the frontiers of the initial iterations of a BFS can be quite small. The frontier of the first iteration has only the neighbors of the source. The frontier of the next iteration has all the unvisited neighbors of the current frontier vertices. In some cases, the frontiers of the last few iterations can also be small. For these iterations the overhead of terminating a grid and launching a new one may outweigh the benefit of parallelism. One way to deal with these iterations with small frontiers is to prepare another kernel that uses only one thread block but may perform multiple consecutive iterations. The kernel uses only a local block-level frontier and uses __syncthreads() to synchronize across all threads in between levels.

This optimization is illustrated in Fig. 15.16. In this example, levels 0 and 1 can each be processed by a single thread block. Rather than launching a separate grid for levels 0 and 1, we launch a single-block grid and use __syncthreads() to synchronize between levels. Once the frontier reaches a size that overflows the block-level frontier, the threads in the block copy the block-level frontier contents to the global frontier and return to the host code. The host code will then call the regular kernel in the subsequent level iterations until the frontier is small again. The single-block kernel thus eliminates the launch overhead for the iterations with small frontiers. We leave its implementation as an exercise for the reader.

Improving load balance

Recall that in the vertex-centric implementations the amount of work to be done by each thread depends on the connectivity of the vertex that is

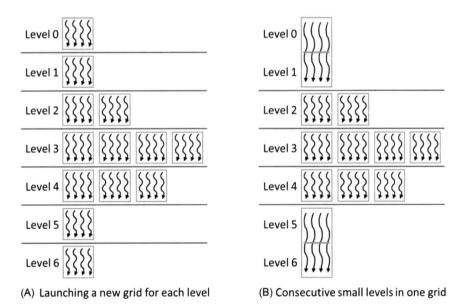

(A) Launching a new grid for each level   (B) Consecutive small levels in one grid

FIGURE 15.16

Executing multiple levels in one grid for levels with small frontiers: (A) launching a new grid for each level, (B) consecutive small levels in one grid.

assigned to it. In some graphs, such as social network graphs, some vertices (celebrities) may have degrees that are several orders of magnitude higher than those of other vertices. When this happens, one or a few of the threads can take excessively long and slow down the execution of the entire grid. We have seen one way to address this issue, which is by using an edge-centric parallel implementation instead. Another way in which we can potentially address this issue is by sorting the vertices of a frontier into *buckets* depending on their degree and processing each bucket in a separate kernel with an appropriately sized group of processors. One notable implementation (Merrill and Garland, 2012) uses three different buckets for vertices with small, medium, and large degrees. The kernel processing the small buckets assigns each vertex to a single thread; the kernel processing the medium buckets assigns each vertex to a single warp; and the kernel processing the large buckets assigns each vertex to an entire thread block. This technique is particularly useful for graphs with a high variation in vertex degrees.

Further challenges

While BFS is among the simplest graph applications, it exhibits the challenges that are characteristic of more complex applications: problem decomposition for extracting parallelism, taking advantage of privatization, implementing fine-grained load balancing, and ensuring proper synchronization. Graph computation is applicable to a wide range of interesting problems, particularly in the areas of making recommendations, detecting communities, finding patterns within a graph, and identifying anomalies. One significant challenge is to handle graphs whose size exceeds the memory capacity of the GPU. Another interesting opportunity is to preprocess the graph into other formats before beginning computation in order to expose more parallelism or locality or to facilitate load balancing.

15.8 Summary

In this chapter we have seen the challenges that are associated with parallelizing graph computations, using breadth-first search as an example. We started with a brief introduction to the representation of graphs. We discussed the differences between vertex-centric and edge-centric parallel implementations and observed the tradeoffs between them. We also saw how to eliminate redundant work by using frontiers and optimized the use of frontiers by using privatization. We also briefly discussed other advanced optimizations to reduce synchronization overhead and improve load balance.

Exercises

1. Consider the following directed unweighted graph:

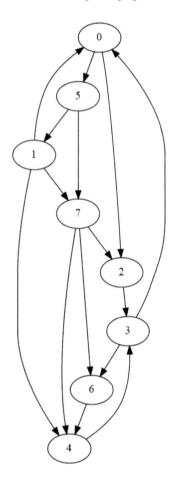

a. Represent the graph using an adjacency matrix.
b. Represent the graph in the CSR format. The neighbor list of each vertex must be sorted.
c. Parallel BFS is executed on this graph starting from vertex 0 (i.e., vertex 0 is in level 0). For each iteration of the BFS traversal:
    i. If a vertex-centric push implementation is used:
        1. How many threads are launched?
        2. How many threads iterate over their vertex's neighbors?
    ii. If a vertex-centric pull implementation is used:
        1. How many threads are launched?

      2. How many threads iterate over their vertex's neighbors?

      3. How many threads label their vertex?

   iii. If an edge-centric implementation is used:

      1. How many threads are launched?

      2. How many threads may label a vertex?

   iv. If a vertex-centric push frontier-based implementation is used:

      1. How many threads are launched?

      2. How many threads iterate over their vertex's neighbors?

2. Implement the host code for the direction-optimized BFS implementation described in Section 15.3.

3. Implement the single-block BFS kernel described in Section 15.7.

References

Harish, P., Narayanan, P.J., 2007. Accelerating large graph algorithms on the GPU using CUDA. In: International Conference on High-Performance Computing (HiPC), India.

Jeremy, K., Gilbert, J. (Eds.), 2011. Graph Algorithms in the Language of Linear Algebra. Society for Industrial and Applied Mathematics.

Luo, L., Wong, M., Hwu, W., 2010. An effective GPU implementation of breadth-first search. In: ACM/IEEE Design Automation Conference (DAC).

Merrill, D., Garland, M., 2012. Scalable GPU graph traversal. In: Proceedings of the 17th ACM SIGPLAN Symposium on Principles and Practice of Parallel Programming (PPoPP).

Deep learning

16

With special contributions from Carl Pearson and Boris Ginsburg

Chapter Outline

16.1 Background 356
16.2 Convolutional neural networks 366
16.3 Convolutional layer: a CUDA inference kernel 376
16.4 Formulating a convolutional layer as GEMM 379
16.5 CUDNN library 385
16.6 Summary 387
Exercises 388
References 388

This chapter presents an application case study on deep learning, a recent branch of machine learning using artificial neural networks. Machine learning has been used in many application domains to train or adapt application logic according to the experience gleaned from datasets. To be effective, one often needs to conduct such training with a massive amount of data. While machine learning has existed as a subject of computer science for a long time, it has recently gained a great deal of practical industry acceptance for two reasons. The first reason is the massive amounts of data available from the pervasive use of the internet. The second reason is the inexpensive, massively parallel GPU computing systems that can effectively train application logic with these massive datasets. We will start with a brief introduction to machine learning and deep learning and then consider in more detail one of the most popular deep learning algorithms: convolutional neural networks (CNN). CNN have a high compute to memory access ratio and high levels of parallelism, which make them a perfect candidate for GPU acceleration. We will first present a basic implementation of a convolutional neural network. Next, we will show how we can improve this basic implementation with shared memory. We will then show how one can formulate the convolutional layers as matrix multiplication, which can be accelerated by using highly optimized hardware and software in modern GPUs.

16.1 Background

Machine learning, a term coined by Arthur Samuel of IBM in 1959 (Samuel, 1959), is a field of computer science that studies methods for learning application logic from data rather than designing explicit algorithms. Machine learning is most successful in computing tasks in which designing explicit algorithms is infeasible, mostly because there is not enough knowledge in the design of such explicit algorithms. That is, one can give examples of what should happen in various situations but not general rules for making such decisions for all possible inputs. For example, machine learning has contributed to the recent improvements in application areas such as automatic speech recognition, computer vision, natural language processing, and recommender systems. In these application areas, one can provide many input examples and what should come out for each input, but there is no algorithm that can correctly process all possible inputs.

The kinds of application logic that are created with machine learning can be organized according to the types of tasks that they perform. There is a wide range of machine learning tasks. Here, we show a few out of a large number:

1. Classification: to determine to which of the k categories an input belongs. An example is object recognition, such as determining which type of food is shown in a photo.
2. Regression: to predict a numerical value given some inputs. An example is to predict the price of a stock at the end of the next trading day.
3. Transcription: to convert unstructured data into textual form. An example is optical character recognition.
4. Translation: to convert a sequence of symbols in one language to a sequence of symbols in another. An example is translating from English to Chinese.
5. Embedding: to convert an input to a vector while preserving relationships between entities. An example is to convert a natural language sentence into a multidimensional vector.

The reader is referred to a large body of literature on the mathematical background and practical solutions to the various tasks of machine learning. The purpose of the chapter is to introduce the computation kernels that are involved in the neural network approach to the classification task. A concrete understanding of these kernels will allow the reader to understand and develop kernels for deep learning approaches to other machine learning tasks. Therefore in this section we will go into details about the classification task to establish the background knowledge that is needed to understand neural networks. Mathematically, a classifier is a function f that maps an input to k categories or labels:

$$f: R^n \rightarrow \{1, 2, \ldots, k\}$$

The function f is parameterized by θ that maps input vector x to numerical code y, that is,

$$y = f(x, \theta)$$

The parameter θ is commonly referred to as the *model*. It encapsulates weights that are learned from data. This definition of θ is best illustrated with a concrete example. Let us consider a linear classifier called a *perceptron* (Rosenblatt, 1957): $y = sign(W \cdot x + b)$, where W is vector of weights of the same length as x and b is a bias constant. The sign function returns value 1 if its input is positive, 0 if its input is 0, and -1 if its input is negative. That is, the sign function as a classifier activates, that is, finalizes, the mapping of the input value into three categories: $\{-1, 0, 1\}$; therefore it is often called the *activation* function. Activation functions introduce nonlinearity into an otherwise linear function of a perceptron. In this case, the model θ is the combination of the vector W and the constant b. The structure of the model is a sign function whose input is a linear expression of input x elements where the coefficients are elements of W, and the constant is b.

Fig. 16.1 shows a perceptron example in which each input is a two-dimensional (2D) vector (x_1, x_2). The linear perceptron's model θ consists of a weight vector (w_1, w_2) and a bias constant b. As shown in Fig. 16.1, the linear expression $w_1 x_1 + w_2 \cdot x_2 + b$ defines a line in the $x_1 - x_2$ space that cuts the space into two parts: the part in which all points make the expression greater than zero and the part in which all points make the expression less than zero. All points on the line make the expression equal to 0.

Visually, given a combination of (w_1, w_2) and b values, we can draw a line in the (x_1, x_2) space, as shown in Fig. 16.1. For example, for a perceptron whose model is $(w_1, w_2) = (2, 3)$ and $b = -6$, we can easily draw a line by connecting the two intersection points with the x_1 axis $((\frac{-b}{w_1}, 0) = (3, 0))$ and the x_2 axis

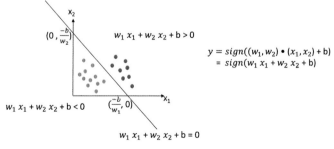

FIGURE 16.1

A perceptron linear classifier example in which the input is a two-dimensional vector.

$((0, \frac{-b}{w_2}) = (0, 2))$. The line thus drawn corresponds to the equation $2x_1 + 3x_2 - 6 = 0$ With this drawing, we can easily visualize the outcome of input points: Any point above the line (shown as blue dots in Fig. 16.1) is classified as class 1, any point on the line is classified as class 0, and any point below the line (shown as orange dots in Fig. 16.1) is classified as class -1.

The process of computing the class for an input is commonly referred to as *inference* for the classifier. In the case of a perceptron we simply plug the input coordinate values into $y = sign\ (W \cdot x + b)$. In our example, if the input point is $(5, -1)$, we can perform inference by plugging its coordinates into the perceptron function:

$$y = sign(2 * 5 + 3 * (-1) + 6) = sign(13) = 1$$

Therefore $(5, -1)$ is classified to class 1, that is, it is among the blue dots.

Multilayer classifiers

Linear classifiers are useful when there is a way to draw hyperplanes (i.e., lines in a 2D space and planes in a three-dimensional [3D] space) that partition the space into regions and thus define each class of data points. Ideally, each class of data points should occupy exactly one such region. For example, in a 2D, 2-class classifier, we need to be able to draw a line that separates points of one class from those of the other. Unfortunately, this is not always feasible.

Consider the classifiers in Fig. 16.2. Assume that all input's coordinates fall in the range of [0, 1]. The classifier should classify all points whose x_1 and x_2 values are both greater than 0.5 (points that fall in the upper right quadrant of the domain) as class 1 and the rest as class -1. This classifier could be approximately implemented with a line like that shown in Fig. 16.2(A). For example, a line $2x_1 + 2x_2 - 3 = 0$ would classify most of the points properly. However, some of the orange points whose x_1 and x_2 are both greater than 0.5 but the sum is less than 1.5, for example, (0.55, 0.65), would be misclassified into class -1 (blue). This is because any line will necessarily either cut away part of the upper right quadrant or include part of the rest of the domain. There is no single line that can properly classify all possible inputs.

A *multilayer perceptron* (MLP) allows the use of multiple lines to implement more complex classification patterns. In a multilayer perceptron, each layer consists of one or more perceptrons. The outputs of perceptrons in one layer are the inputs to those in the next layer. An interesting and useful property is that while the inputs to the first layer have an infinite number of possible values, the output of the first layer and thus the input to the second layer can have only a modest number of possible values. For example, if the perceptron from Fig. 16.1 was used as a first layer, its outputs would be restricted to $\{-1, 0, 1\}$.

Fig. 16.2(B) shows a two-layer perceptron that can precisely implement the desired classification pattern. The first layer consists of two perceptrons. The first one, $y_1 = sign(x_1 - 0.5)$, classifies all points whose x_1 coordinate is greater than

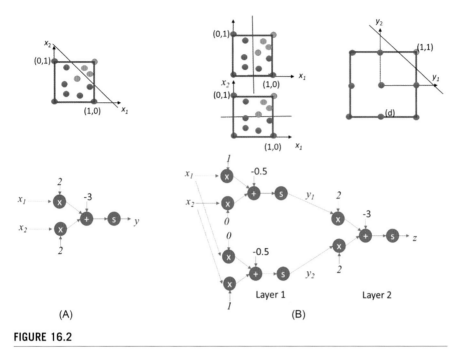

FIGURE 16.2

A multilayer perceptron example.

0.5 as class 1; that is, the output value is 1. The rest of the points are classified as either class -1 or class 0. The second classifier in the first layer, $y_2 = sign(x_2 - 0.5)$, classifies all points whose x_2 coordinate is greater than 0.5 into class 1. The rest of the points are classified as class -1.

Therefore the output of the first layer (y_1, y_2) can only be one of the following nine possibilities: $(-1, -1)$, $(-1, 0)$, $(-1,1)$, $(0, -1)$ $(0, 0)$ $(0, 1)$ $(1, -1)$, $(1, 0)$, $(1,1)$. That is, there are only nine possible input pair values to the second layer. Out of these nine possibilities, $(1, 1)$ is special. All the original input points in the orange category are mapped to $(1, 1)$ by the first layer. Therefore we can use a simple perceptron in the second layer to draw a line between $(1, 1)$ and the eight other possible points in the y_1-y_2 space, shown in Fig. 16.2B. This can be done by a line $2y_1 + 2y_2 - 3 = 0$ or many other lines that are small variations of it.

Let us use the (0.55, 0.65) input that was misclassified by the single-layer perceptron in Fig. 16.2A. When processed by the two-layer perceptron, the upper perceptron of first layer in Fig. 16.2B generates $y_1 = 1$, and the lower perceptron generates $y_2 = 1$. On the basis of these input values, the perceptron in the second layer generates $z = 1$, the correct classification for (0.55, 0.65).

Note that a two-layer perceptron still has significant limitations. For example, assume that we need to build a perceptron to classify the input points shown in Fig. 16.3A. The values of the orange input points can result in input

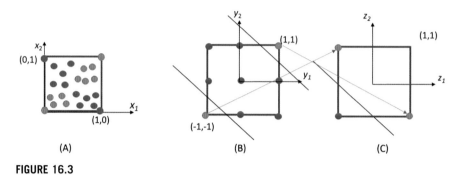

FIGURE 16.3

Need for perceptrons with more than two layers.

values $(-1, -1)$ or $(1, 1)$ to the second layer. We see that there is no way to draw a single line to properly classify the points in the second layer. We show in Fig. 16.2B that we can add another line by adding another perceptron in the second layer. The function would be $z_2 = sign(-2y_1 - 2y_2 - 3)$ or small variations of it. The reader should verify that all blue points in Fig. 16.3B will be mapped to the $(-1, -1)$ in the z_1-z_2 space. Whereas $(1, 1)$ and $(-1, -1)$ in the $y_1 - y_2$ space are mapped to $(1, -1)$ and $(-1, 1)$ in the $z_1 - z_2$ space. Now we can draw a line $z_1 + z_2 + 1 = 0$ or small variations of it to properly classify the points, as shown in Fig. 16.3C. Obviously, if we need to partition the input domain into more regions, we might need even more layers to perform proper classification.

Layer 1 in Fig. 16.2B is a small example of a fully connected layer, in which every output (i.e., y_1, y_2) is a function of every input (i.e., x_1, x_2). In general, in a fully connected layer, every one of the m outputs is a function of all the n inputs. All the weights of a fully connected layer form an m $\times$ n weight matrix W, where each of the m rows is the weight vector (of size n elements) to be applied to the input vector (of size n elements) to produce one of the m outputs. Therefore the process of evaluating all the outputs from the inputs of a fully connected layer is a matrix-vector multiplication. As we will see, fully connected layers are core components of many types of neural networks, and we will further study the GPU implementations.

Fully connected layers become extremely expensive when m and n become large. The main reason is that a fully connected layer requires an m $\times$ n weight matrix. For example, in an image recognition application, n is the number of pixels in the input image, and m is the number of classifications that need to be performed on the input pixels. In this case, n is in the millions for high-resolution images, and m can be in the hundreds or more depending on the variety of objects that need to be recognized. Also, the objects can be of different scales and orientations in the images; many classifiers may need to be in place to deal with these variations. Feeding all these classifiers with all inputs is both expensive and likely wasteful.

Convolutional layers reduce the cost of fully connected layers by reducing the number of inputs each classifier takes and sharing the same weights across classifiers. In a convolutional layer, each classifier takes only a patch of the input image and performs convolution on the pixels in the patch based on the weights. The output is called an output feature map, since each pixel in the output is the activation result of a classifier. Sharing weights across classifiers allows the convolutional layers to have large numbers of classifiers, that is, large m values, without an excessive number of weights. Computationally, this can be implemented as a 2D convolution. However, this approach effectively applies the same classifier to a different part of an image. One can have different sets of weights applicd to the same input and generate multiple output feature maps, as we will see later in this chapter.

Training models

So far, we have assumed that the model parameters used by a classifier are somehow available. Now we turn to training, or the process of using data to determine the values of the model parameters θ, including the weights (w_1, w_2) and the bias b. For simplicity we will assume supervised training, in which input data labeled with desired output values are used to determine the weight and bias values. Other training modalities, such as semisupervised and reinforcement learning, have also been developed to reduce the reliance on labeled data. The reader is referred to the literature to understand how training can be accomplished under such circumstances.

Error function

In general, training treats the model parameters as unknown variables and solves an inverse problem given the labeled input data. In the perceptron example in Fig. 16.1, each data point that is used for training would be labeled with its desired classification result: -1, 0, or 1. The training process typically starts with an initial guess of the (w_1, w_2) and b values and performs inference on the input data and generates classification results. These classification results are compared to the labels. An error function, sometimes referred to as a cost function, is defined to quantify the difference between the classification result and the corresponding label for each data point. For example, assume that y is the classification output class and t is the label. The following is an example error function:

$$E = \frac{(y-t)^2}{2}$$

This error function has the nice property that the error value is always positive as long as there is any difference, positive or negative, between the values of y and t. If we need to sum up the error across many input data points, both positive and negative differences will contribute to the total rather than canceling each other out. One can also define the error as the absolute value of the difference, among many other options. As we will see, the coefficient $\frac{1}{2}$ simplifies the computation involved in solving the model parameters.

Stochastic gradient descent

The training process will attempt to find the model parameter values that minimize the sum of the error function values for all the training data points. This can be done with a *stochastic gradient descent* approach, which repeatedly runs different permutations of the input dataset through the classifier, evolves the parameter values, and checks whether the parameter values have converged in that their values have stabilized and changed less than a threshold since the last iteration. Once the parameter values converge, the training process ends.

Epoch

During each iteration of the training process, called an *epoch*, the training input dataset is first randomly shuffled, that is, permutated, before it is fed to the classifier. This randomization of the input data ordering helps to avoid suboptimal solutions. For each input data element, its classifier output y value is compared with the label data to generate the error function value. In our perceptron example, if a data label is (class) 1 and the classifier output is (class) -1, the error function value using $E = \frac{(y-t)^2}{2}$ would be 2. If the error function value is larger than a threshold, a backpropagation operation is activated to make changes to the parameters so that the inference error can be reduced.

Backpropagation

The idea of backpropagation is to start with the error function and look back into the classifier and identify the way in which each parameter contributes to the error function value (LeCun et al., 1990). If the error function value increases when a parameter's value increases for a data element, we should decrease the parameter value so that the error function value can decrease for this data point. Otherwise, we should increase the parameter value to reduce the error function value for the data point. Mathematically, the rate and direction in which a function's value changes as one of its input variables changes are the partial derivative of the function over the variable. For a perceptron the model parameters and the input data points are considered input variables for the purpose of calculating the partial derivatives of the error function. Therefore the backpropagation operation will need to derive the partial derivative values of the error function over the model parameters for each input data element that triggers the backpropagation operation.

  Let us use the perceptron $y = sign(w_1 x_1 + w_2 x_2 + b)$ to illustrate the backpropagation operation. Assume error function $E = \frac{(y-t)^2}{2}$ and that the backpropagation is triggered by a training input data element (5, 2). The goal is to modify the w_1, w_2, and b values so that the perceptron will more likely classify (5, 2) correctly. That is, we need to derive the values of partial derivatives $\frac{\partial E}{\partial w_1}$, $\frac{\partial E}{\partial w_2}$, and $\frac{\partial E}{\partial b}$ in order to make changes to the w_1, w_2, and b values.

Chain rule

We see that E is a function of y and y is a function of w_1, w_2, and b. Thus we can use the chain rule to derive these partial derivatives. For w_1,

$$\frac{\partial E}{\partial w_1} = \frac{\partial E}{\partial y} \frac{\partial y}{\partial w_1}$$

$\frac{\partial E}{\partial y}$ is straightforward:

$$\frac{\partial E}{\partial y} = \frac{\partial \frac{(y-t)^2}{2}}{\partial y} = y - t$$

However, we face a challenge with $\frac{\partial y}{\partial w_1}$. Note that the sign function is not a differentiable function, as it is not continuous at 0. To solve this problem, the machine learning community commonly use a smoother version of the sign function that is differentiable near zero and close to the sign function value for x values away from 0. A simple example of such a smoother version is the sigmoid function $s = \frac{1 - e^{-x}}{1 + e^{-x}}$. For x values that are negative with large absolute value, the sigmoid expression is dominated by the e^{-x} terms, and the sigmoid function value will be approximately -1. For x values that are positive with large absolute values, the e^{-x} terms diminish, and the function value will be approximately 1. For x values that are close to 0, the function value increases rapidly from near -1 to near 1. Thus the sigmoid function closely approximates the behavior of a sign function and yet is continuous differentiable for all x values. With this change from sign to sigmoid, the perceptron is $y = sigmoid(w_1 x_1 + w_2 x_2 + b)$. We can express $\frac{\partial y}{\partial w_1}$ as $\frac{\partial sigmoid(k)}{\partial k} \frac{\partial k}{\partial w_1}$ using the chain rule with an intermediate variable $k = w_1 x_1 + w_2 x_2 + b$. Based on calculus manipulation, $\frac{\partial k}{\partial w_1}$ is simply x_1 and

$$\frac{\partial sigmoid(k)}{\partial k} = \left(\frac{1 - e^{-k}}{1 + e^{-k}}\right)' = (1 - e^{-k})'\left(\frac{1}{1 + e^{-k}}\right) + (1 - e^{-k})\left(\frac{1}{1 + e^{-k}}\right)'$$

$$= e^{-k}\left(\frac{1}{1 + e^{-k}}\right) + (1 - e^{-k})\left(-1 \times \left(\frac{1}{1 + e^{-k}}\right)^2 (-e^{-k})\right) = \frac{2e^{-k}}{(1 + e^{-k})^2}$$

Putting it all together, we have

$$\frac{\partial E}{\partial w_1} = (y - t)\frac{2e^{-k}}{(1 + e^{-k})^2}x_1$$

Similarly,

$$\frac{\partial E}{\partial w_2} = (y - t)\frac{2e^{-k}}{(1 + e^{-k})^2}x_2$$

$$\frac{\partial E}{\partial b} = (y - t)\frac{2e^{-k}}{(1 + e^{-k})^2}$$

where

$$k = w_1 x_1 + w_2 x_2 + b$$

It should be clear that all the three partial derivative values can be completely determined by the combination of the input data (x_1, x_2 and t) and the current values of the model parameters (w_1, w_2 and b). The final step for the backpropagation is to modify the parameter values. Recall that the partial derivative of a function over a variable gives the direction and rate of change in the function value as the variable changes its value. If the partial derivative of the error function over a parameter has a positive value given the combination of input data and current parameter values, we want to decrease the value of the parameter so that the error function value will decrease. On the other hand, if the partial derivative of the error function of the variable has a negative value, we want to increase the value of the parameter so that the error function value will decrease.

Learning rate

Numerically, we would like to make bigger changes to the parameters to whose change the error function is more sensitive, that is, when the absolute value of the partial derivative of the error function over this parameter is a large value. These considerations lead to us to subtract from each parameter a value that is proportional to the partial derivative of the error function over that parameter. This is accomplished by multiplying the partial derivatives with a constant ε, called the learning rate constant in machine learning, before it is subtracted from the parameter value. The larger ε is, the faster the values of the parameters evolve so the solution can potentially be reached with fewer iterations. However, large ε also increases the chance of instability and prevents the parameter values from converging to a solution. In our perceptron example, the modifications to the parameters are as follows:

$$w_1 \leftarrow w_1 - \varepsilon \frac{\partial E}{\partial w_1}$$

$$w_2 \leftarrow w_2 - \varepsilon \frac{\partial E}{\partial w_2}$$

$$b \leftarrow b - \varepsilon \frac{\partial E}{\partial b}$$

For the rest of this chapter we will use a generic symbol θ to represent the model parameters in formula and expressions. That is, we will represent the three expressions above with one generic expression:

$$\theta \leftarrow \theta - \varepsilon \frac{\partial E}{\partial}$$

The reader should understand that for each of these generic expressions one can replace θ with any of the parameters to apply the expression to the parameter.

Minibatch

In practice, because the backtracking process is quite expensive, it is not triggered by individual data points whose inference result differs from its label. Rather, after the inputs are randomly shuffled in an epoch, they are divided into segments called *minibatches*. The training process runs an entire minibatch through the inference and accumulates their error function values. If the total error in the minibatch is too large, backpropagation is triggered for the minibatch. During backpropagation the inference results of each data point in the minibatch are checked, and if it is not correct, the data is used to derive partial derivative values that are used to modify the model parameter values as described above.

Training multilayer classifiers

For multilayer classifiers the backpropagation starts with the last layer and modifies the parameter values in that layer as we discussed above. The question is how we should modify the parameters of the previous layers. Keep in mind that we can derive $\frac{\partial E}{\partial \theta}$ based on $\frac{\partial E}{\partial y}$, as we have demonstrated for the final layer. Once we have $\frac{\partial E}{\partial y}$ for the previous layer, we have everything we need to calculate the modifications to the parameters in that layer.

A simple and yet important observation is that the output of the previous layer is also the input to the final layer. Therefore $\frac{\partial E}{\partial y}$ of the previous layer is really the $\frac{\partial E}{\partial x}$ of the final layer. Therefore the key is to derive $\frac{\partial E}{\partial x}$ for the final layer after we modify the parameter values of the final layer. As we can see below, $\frac{\partial E}{\partial x}$ is not that different from $\frac{\partial E}{\partial \theta}$, that is, $\frac{\partial E}{\partial x} = \frac{\partial E}{\partial y}\frac{\partial y}{\partial x}$.

$\frac{\partial E}{\partial y}$ can be simply reused from the derivations for the parameters. $\frac{\partial y}{\partial x}$ is also quite straightforward since the inputs play the same role as the parameters as far as y is concerned. We simply need to do a partial derivative of the intermediate function k with respect to the inputs. For our perceptron example, we have

$$\frac{\partial E}{\partial x_1} = (y - t)\frac{2e^{-k}}{(1 + e^{-k})^2}w_1$$

$$\frac{\partial E}{\partial x_2} = (y - t)\frac{2e^{-k}}{(1 + e^{-k})^2}w_2$$

where $k = w_1x_1 + w_2x_2 + b$. In the perceptron example in Fig. 16.2B, x_1 of the final layer (layer 2) is y_1, output of the top perceptron of layer 1 and x_2 is y_2, output of the bottom perceptron of layer 1. Now we are ready to proceed with the calculation of $\frac{\partial E}{\partial \theta}$ for the two perceptrons in the previous layer. Obviously, this process can be repeated if there are more layers.

Feedforward networks

By connecting layers of classifiers and feeding the output of each layer to the next, we form a feedforward network. Fig. 16.2B shows an example of a two-layer feedforward network. All our discussions on inference with and training of multilayer perceptrons (MLP) assume this property. In a feedforward network, all outputs of an earlier layer go to one or more of the later layers. There are no connections from a later layer output to an earlier layer input. Therefore the backpropagation can simply iterate from the final stage backwards with no complications caused by feedback loops.

16.2 Convolutional neural networks

A deep learning procedure (LeCun et al., 2015) uses a hierarchy of feature extractors to learn complex features, which can achieve more accurate pattern recognition results if there is enough training data to allow the system to properly train the parameters of all the layers of feature extractors to automatically discover an adequate number of relevant patterns. There is one category of deep learning procedures that are easier to train and that can be generalized much better than others. These deep learning procedures are based on a particular type of feedforward network called the convolutional neural network (CNN).

The CNN was invented in late 1980s (LeCun et al., 1998). By the early 1990s, CNNs had been applied to automated speech recognition, optical character recognition (OCR), handwriting recognition, and face recognition (LeCun et al., 1990). However, until the late 1990s the mainstream of computer vision and that of automated speech recognition had been based on carefully engineered features. The amount of labeled data was insufficient for a deep learning system to compete with recognition or classification functions crafted by human experts. It was a common belief that it was computationally infeasible to automatically build hierarchical feature extractors that have enough layers to perform better than human-defined application-specific feature extractors.

Interest in deep feedforward networks was revived around 2006 by a group of researchers who introduced unsupervised learning methods that could create multilayer, hierarchical feature detectors without requiring labeled data (Hinton et al., 2006, Raina et al., 2009). The first major application of this approach was in speech recognition. The breakthrough was made possible by GPUs that allowed researchers to train networks ten times faster than traditional CPUs. This advancement, coupled with the massive amount of media data available online, drastically elevated the position of deep learning approaches. Despite their success in speech, CNN were largely ignored in the field of computer vision until 2012.

In 2012 a group of researchers from the University of Toronto trained a large, deep convolutional neural network to classify 1000 different classes in the ILSVRC contest (Krizhevsky et al., 2012). The network was huge by the norms of the time: It had approximately 60 million parameters and 650,000 neurons. It was trained on 1.2 million high-resolution images from the ImageNet database. The network was trained in only one week on two GPUs using a CUDA-based

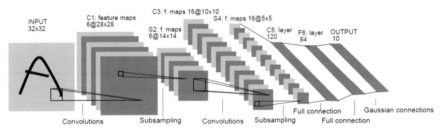

FIGURE 16.4

LeNet-5, a convolutional neural network for handwritten digit recognition. The letter A in the input should be classified as none of the ten classes (digits).

convolutional neural network library written by Alex Krizhevsky (Krizhevsky). The network achieved breakthrough results with a winning test error rate of 15.3%. In comparison, the second-place team that used the traditional computer vision algorithms had an error rate of 26.2%. This success triggered a revolution in computer vision, and CNN became a mainstream tool in computer vision, natural language processing, reinforcement learning, and many other traditional machine learning areas.

This section presents the sequential implementation of CNN inference and training. We will use LeNet-5, the network that was designed in the late 1980s for digit recognition (LeCun et al., 1990). As shown in Fig. 16.4, LeNet-5 is composed of three types of layers: convolutional layers, subsampling layers, and fully connected layers. These three types of layers continue to be the key components of today's neural networks. We will consider the logical design and sequential implementation of each type of layer. The input to the network is shown as a gray image with a handwritten digit represented as a 2D 32 × 32 pixel array. The last layer computes the output, which is the probability that the original image belongs to each one of the ten classes (digits) that the network is set up to recognize.

Convolutional neural network inference

The computation in a convolutional network is organized as a sequence of layers. We will call inputs to and outputs from layers *feature maps* or simply *features*. For example, in Fig. 16.4 the computation of the C1 convolutional layer at the input end of the network is organized to generate six output feature maps from the INPUT pixel array. The output to be produced for input feature maps consists of pixels, each of which is produced by performing a convolution between a small local patch of the feature map pixels produced by the previous layer (INPUT in the case of C1) and a set of weights (i.e., convolution filters as defined in Chapter 7: Convolution) called a *filter bank*. The convolution result is then fed into an activation function such as sigmoid to produce an output pixel in the

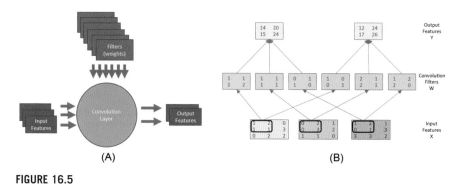

FIGURE 16.5

Forward propagation path of a convolutional layer.

output feature map. One can think of the convolutional layer for each pixel of an output feature map as a perceptron whose inputs are the patch of pixels in the input feature maps. That is, the value of each output pixel is the sum of convolution results from the corresponding patches in all input feature maps.

Fig. 16.5 shows a small convolutional layer example. There are three input feature maps, two output feature maps, and six filter banks. Different pairs of input and output feature map pairs in a layer use different filter banks. Since there are three input feature maps and two output feature maps in Fig. 16.5, we need $3 \times 2 = 6$ filter banks. For the C3 layer of LeNet in Fig. 16.4 there are six input feature maps and 16 output feature maps. Thus a total of $6 \times 16 = 96$ filter banks are used in C3.

Fig. 16.5B illustrates more details of the calculations done by a convolutional layer. We omitted the activation function for the output pixels for simplicity. We show that each output feature map is the sum of convolutions of all input feature maps. For example, the upper left corner element of output feature map 0 (value 14) is calculated as the convolution between the circled patch of input feature maps and the corresponding filter banks:

$$(1, 2, 1, 1) \cdot (1, 1, 2, 2) + (0, 2, 0, 3) \cdot (1, 1, 1, 1) + (1, 2, 0, 1) \cdot (0, 1, 1, 0)$$
$$= 1 + 2 + 2 + 2 + 0 + 2 + 0 + 3 + 0 + 2 + 0 + 0$$
$$= 14$$

One can also think of the three input maps as a 3D input feature map and the three filter banks as a 3D filter bank. Each output feature map is simply the 3D convolution result of the 3D input feature map and the 3D filter bank. In Fig. 16.5B the three 2D filter banks on the left form a 3D filter bank, and the three on the right form a second 3D filter bank. In general, if a convolutional layer has n input feature maps and m output feature maps, $n*m$ different 2D filter banks will be used. One can also think about these filter banks as m 3D filter banks. Although not shown in Fig. 16.4, all 2D filter banks used in LeNet-5 are 5×5 convolution filters.

Recall from Chapter 7, Convolution, that generating a convolution output image from an input image and a convolution filter requires one to make assumptions about the "ghost cells." Instead of making such assumptions, the LeNet-5 design simply uses two elements at the edge of each dimension as ghost cells. This reduces the size of each dimension by four: two at the top, two at the bottom, two at the left, and two at the right. As a result, we see that for layer C1, the 32×32 INPUT image results in an output feature map that is a 28×28 image. Fig. 16.4 illustrates this computation by showing that a pixel in the C1 layer is generated from a square (5×5, although not explicitly shown) patch of INPUT pixels.

We assume that the input feature maps are stored in a 3D array X[C, H, W], where C is the number of input feature maps, H is the height of each input map image, and W is the width of each input map image. That is, the highest-dimension index selects one of the feature maps (often referred to as channels), and the indices of the lower two dimensions select one of the pixels in an input feature map. For example, the input feature maps for the C1 layer are stored in X[1, 32, 32], since there is only one input feature map (INPUT in Fig. 16.4) that consists of 32 pixels in each of the x and y dimensions. This also reflects the fact that one can think of the 2D input feature maps to a layer altogether as forming a 3D input feature map.

The output feature maps of a convolutional layer are also stored in a 3D array Y[M, H − K + 1, W − K + 1], where M is the number of output feature maps and K is the height (and width) of each 2D filter. For example, the output feature maps for the C1 layer are stored in Y[6, 28, 28], since C1 generates six output feature maps using 5×5 filters. The filter banks are stored in a four-dimensional array W[M, C, K, K].[1] There are $M \times C$ filter banks. Filter bank W[m, c,_,_] is used when using input feature map X[c,_,_] to calculate output feature map Y[m, _,_]. Recall that each output feature map is the sum of convolutions of all input feature maps. Therefore we can consider the forward propagation path of a convolutional layer as set of M 3D convolutions in which each 3D convolution is specified by a 3D filter bank that is a $C \times K \times K$ submatrix of W.

Fig. 16.6 shows a sequential C implementation of the forward propagation path of a convolutional layer. Each iteration of the outermost (m) for-loop (lines 04−12) generates an output feature map. Each iteration of the next two levels (h and w) of for-loops (lines 05−12) generates one pixel of the current output feature map. The innermost three loop levels (lines 08−11) perform the 3D convolution between the input feature maps and the 3D filter banks.

The output feature maps of a convolutional layer typically go through a sub-sampling layer (also known as a pooling layer). A subsampling layer reduces the size of image maps by combining pixels. For example, in Fig. 16.4, subsampling layer S2 takes the six input feature maps of size 28×28 and generates six

---

[1] Note that W is used for both the width of images and the name of the filter bank (weight) matrix. In each case the usage should be clear from the context.

```
01   void convLayer_forward(int M, int C, int H, int W, int K, float* X, float* W,
                             float* Y) {
02       int H_out = H - K + 1;
03       int W_out = W - K + 1;

04       for(int m = 0;  m < M;  m++)            // for each output feature map
05         for(int h = 0; h < H_out; h++)        // for each output element
06           for(int w = 0; w < W_out; w++) {
07             Y[m, h, w] = 0;
08             for(int c = 0;  c < C; c++)      // sum over all input feature maps
09               for(int p = 0; p < K; p++) // KxK  filter
10                 for(int q = 0; q < K; q++)
11                   Y[m, h, w] +=  X[c, h + p, w + q] * W[m, c, p, q];
12         }
13   }
```

FIGURE 16.6

A C implementation of the forward propagation path of a convolutional layer.

```
01   void subsamplingLayer_forward(int M, int H, int W, int K, float* Y, float*
     S){
02       for(int m = 0;  m < M;  m++)            // for each output feature map
03         for(int h = 0; h < H/K; h++)          // for each output element,
04           for(int w = 0; w < W/K; w++) {      // this code assumes that H and W
05             S[m, x, y] = 0.;                  // are multiples of K
06             for(int p = 0; p < K; p++) {      // loop over KxK input samples
07               for(int q = 0; q < K; q++)
08                 S[m, h, w] += Y[m, K*h + p, K*w+ q] /(K*K);
09             }
                                                 // add bias and apply non-linear activation
10             S[m, h, w] = sigmoid(S[m, h, w] + b[m]);
11           }
12   }
```

FIGURE 16.7

A sequential C implementation of the forward propagation path of a subsampling layer. The layer also includes an activation function, which is included in a convolutional layer if there is no subsampling layer after the convolutional layer.

feature maps of size 14×14. Each pixel in a subsampling output feature map is generated from a 2×2 neighborhood in the corresponding input feature map. The values of these four pixels are averaged to form one pixel in the output feature map. The output of a subsampling layer has the same number of output feature maps as the previous layer, but each map has half the number of rows and columns. For example, the number of output feature maps (six) of the subsampling layer S2 is the same as the number of its input feature maps, or the output feature maps of the convolutional layer C1.

Fig. 16.7 shows a sequential C implementation of the forward propagation path of a subsampling layer. Each iteration of the outermost (m) for-loop (lines 02−11) generates an output feature map. The next two levels (h and w) of for-loops (lines 03−11) generates individual pixels of the current output map. The two innermost for-loops (lines 06−09) sum up the pixels in the neighborhood. K is equal to 2 in our LeNet-5 subsampling example in Fig. 16.4. A bias value b[m] that is specific to each output feature map is then added to each output feature map, and the sum goes through a sigmoid activation function. The reader should recognize that each output pixel is generated by the equivalent of a perceptron that takes four of the input pixels in each feature map as its input and generates a pixel in the corresponding output feature map. ReLU is another frequently used activation function that is a simple nonlinear filter that passes only nonnegative values: Y = X, if X $\geq$ 0 and 0 otherwise.

To complete our example, convolutional layer C3 has 16 output feature maps, each of which is a 10 $\times$ 10 image. This layer has 6 $\times$ 16 = 96 filter banks, and each filter bank has 5 $\times$ 5 = 25 weights. The output of C3 is passed into the sub-sampling layer S4, which generates 16 5 $\times$ 5 output feature maps. Finally, the last convolutional layer C5 uses 16 $\times$ 120 = 1920 5 $\times$ 5 filter banks to generate 120 one-pixel output features from its 16 input feature maps.

These feature maps are passed through fully connected layer F6, which has 84 output units, in which each output is fully connected to all inputs. The output is computed as a product of a weight matrix W with an input vector X, and then a bias is added and the output is passed through sigmoid. For the F6 example, W is a 120 $\times$ 84 matrix. In summary, the output is an 84-element vector Y6 = sigmoid (W * X + b). The reader should recognize that this is equivalent to 84 percep-trons, and each perceptron takes all 120 one-pixel x values generated by the C5 layer as its input. We leave the detailed implementation of a fully connected layer as an exercise.

The final stage is an output layer that uses Gaussian filters to generate a vector of ten elements, which correspond to the probability that the input image contains one of the ten digits.

Convolutional neural network backpropagation

Training of CNNs is based on the stochastic gradient descent method and the backpropagation procedure that were discussed in Section 16.1 (Rumelhart et al., 1986). The training dataset is labeled with the "correct answer." In the handwrit-ing recognition example the labels give the correct letter in the image. The label information can be used to generate the "correct" output of the last stage: the cor-rect probability values of the ten-element vector, where the probability of the cor-rect digit is 1.0 and those for all other digits are 0.0.

For each training image, the final stage of the network calculates the loss (error) function as the difference between the generated output probability vector element values and the "correct" output vector element values. Given a sequence of training images, we can numerically calculate the gradient of the loss function with respect to the elements of the output vector. Intuitively, it gives the rate at which the loss function value changes when the values of the output vector ele-ments change.

The backpropagation process starts by calculating the gradient of loss function $\frac{\partial E}{\partial y}$ for the last layer. It then propagates the gradient from the last layer toward the first layer through all layers of the network. Each layer receives as its input $\frac{\partial E}{\partial y}$

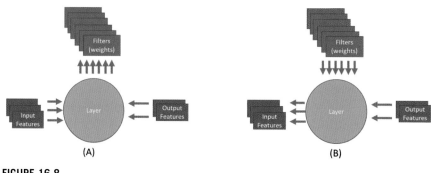

(A)   (B)

FIGURE 16.8

Backpropagation of (A) $\frac{\partial E}{\partial w}$ and (B) $\frac{\partial E}{\partial x}$ for a layer in CNN.

gradient with respect to its output feature maps (which is just the $\frac{\partial E}{\partial x}$ of the later layer) and computes its own $\frac{\partial E}{\partial x}$ gradient with respect to its input feature maps, as shown in Fig. 16.8B. This process repeats until it finishes adjusting the input layer of the network.

If a layer has learned parameters ("weights") w, then the layer also computes its $\frac{\partial E}{\partial w}$ gradient of loss with respect to its weights, as shown in Fig. 16.8A. For example, the fully connected layer is given as $y = w \cdot x$. The backpropagation of the gradient $\frac{\partial E}{\partial y}$ is given by the following equation:

$$\frac{\partial E}{\partial x} = w^T \frac{\partial E}{\partial y} \quad \text{and} \quad \frac{\partial E}{\partial w} = \frac{\partial E}{\partial y} x^T$$

This equation can be derived on an element-by-element basis, as we did for the two-layer perceptron example. Recall that each fully connected layer output pixel is calculated by a perceptron that takes the pixels in the input feature map as input. As we showed for training MLP in Section 16.1, $\frac{\partial E}{\partial x}$ for one of the inputs x is the sum of products between $\frac{\partial E}{\partial y}$ for each output y element to which the input element contributes and the w value via which the x value contributes to the y value. Because each row of the w matrix relates all the x elements (columns) to a y element (one of the rows) for the fully connected layer, each column of w (i.e., row of w^T) relates all y (i.e., $\frac{\partial E}{\partial y}$) elements back to an x (i.e., $\frac{\partial E}{\partial x}$) element, since transposition switches the roles of rows and columns. Thus the matrix-vector multiplication $w^T \frac{\partial E}{\partial y}$ results in a vector that has the $\frac{\partial E}{\partial x}$ values for all input x elements.

Similarly, since each w element is multiplied by one x element to generate a y element, the $\frac{\partial E}{\partial w}$ of each w element can be calculated as the product of an element of $\frac{\partial E}{\partial y}$ with an x element. Thus the matrix multiplication between $\frac{\partial E}{\partial y}$ (a single-column matrix) and x^T (a single-row matrix) results in a matrix of $\frac{\partial E}{\partial w}$ values for all w elements of the fully connected layer. This can also be seen as an outer product between the $\frac{\partial E}{\partial y}$ and x vectors.

Let's turn our attention to the backpropagation for a convolutional layer. We will start from the calculation of $\frac{\partial E}{\partial x}$ from $\frac{\partial E}{\partial y}$, which will ultimately be used to calculate the gradients for the previous layer. The gradient $\frac{\partial E}{\partial x}$ with respect to the channel c of input x is given as the sum of the "backward convolution" with the corresponding $W(m, c)$ over all the m layer outputs:

$$\frac{\partial E}{\partial x}(c, h, w) = \sum_{m=0}^{M-1}\sum_{p=0}^{K-1}\sum_{q=0}^{K-1}\left(\frac{\partial E}{\partial y}(m, h-p, w-q) * w(m, c, k-p, k-q)\right)$$

The backward convolution through the $h - p$ and $w - q$ indexing allows the gradients of all output y elements that received contributions from an x element in the forward convolution to contribute to the gradient of that x element through the same weights. This is because in the forward inference of the convolutional layer, any change in the value of the x element is multiplied by these w elements and contributes to the change in the loss function value through these y elements. Fig. 16.9 shows the indexing pattern using a small example with 3×3 filter banks. The nine shaded y elements in the output feature map are the y elements that receive contributions from $x_{h,w}$ in forward interference. For example, input element $x_{h,w}$ contributes to $y_{h-2,w-2}$ through multiplication with $w_{2,2}$ and to $y_{h,w}$ through multiplication with $w_{0,0}$. Therefore during backpropagation, $\frac{\partial E}{\partial x_{h,w}}$ should receive contribution from the $\frac{\partial E}{\partial y}$ values of these nine elements, and the computation is equivalent to a convolution with a transposed filter bank w^T.

Fig. 16.10 shows the C code for calculating each element of $\frac{\partial E}{\partial x}$ for each input feature map. Note that the code assumes that $\frac{\partial E}{\partial y}$ has been calculated for all the output feature maps of the layer and passed in with a pointer argument dE_dY. This is a reasonable assumption, since $\frac{\partial E}{\partial y}$ for the current layer is the $\frac{\partial E}{\partial x}$ for its immediate next layer, whose gradients should have been calculated in the backpropagation before reaching the current layer. It also assumes that the space of $\frac{\partial E}{\partial x}$ has been allocated in the device memory whose handle is passed in as a pointer argument dE_dX. The function generates all the elements of $\frac{\partial E}{\partial x}$.

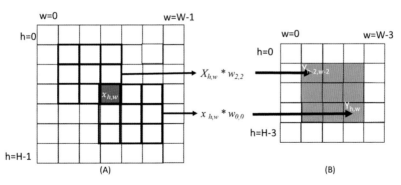

FIGURE 16.9

Convolutional layer. Backpropagation of (A) $\partial E/\partial w$ and (B) $\partial E/\partial x$.

```
01   void convLayer_backward_x_grad(int M, int C, int H_in, int W_in, int K,
                                    float* dE_dY, float* W, float* dE_dX) {
02       int H_out = H_in - K + 1;
03       int W_out = W_in - K + 1;
04       for(int c = 0;  c < C; c++)
05          for(int h = 0; h < H_in; h++)
06             for(int w = 0; w < W_in; w++)
07                dE_dX[c, h, w] = 0;

08       for(int m = 0;  m < M;  m++)
09          for(int h = 0; h < H-1; h++)
10             for(int w = 0; w < W-1; w++)
11                for(int c = 0;  c < C; c++)
12                   for(int p = 0; p < K; p++)
13                      for(int q = 0; q < K; q++)
14                         if(h-p >= 0 && w-p >=0 && h-p < H_out and w-p < W_OUT)
15                            dE_dX[c, h, w] += dE_dY[m, h-p, w-p] * W[m, c, k-p, k-q];
16   }
```

FIGURE 16.10

$\frac{\partial E}{\partial x}$ calculation of the backward path of a convolutional layer.

```
01   void convLayer_backward_w_grad(int M, int C, int H, int W, int K, float*
                                    dE_dY, float* X, float* dE_dW) {
02       int H_out = H - K + 1;
03       int W_out = W - K + 1;
04       for(int m = 0; m < M; m++)
05          for(int c = 0; c < C; c++)
06             for(int p = 0; p < K; p++)
07                for(int q = 0; q < K; q++)
08                   dE_dW[m, c, p, q] = 0.;

09       for(int m = 0;  m < M;  m++)
10          for(int h = 0; h < H_out; h++)
11             for(int w = 0; w < W_out; w++)
12                for(int c = 0;  c < C; c++)
13                   for(int p = 0; p < K; p++)
14                      for(int q = 0; q < K; q++)
15                         dE_dW[m, c, p, q] += X[c, h+p, w+q] * dE_dY[m, c, h, w];
16   }
```

FIGURE 16.11

$\frac{\partial E}{\partial w}$ calculation of the backward path of a convolutional layer.

The sequential code for calculating $\frac{\partial E}{\partial w}$ for a convolutional layer computation is similar to that of $\frac{\partial E}{\partial x}$ and is shown in Fig. 16.11. Since each $W(m, c)$ affects all elements of output $Y(m)$, we should accumulate gradients for each $W(m, c)$ over all pixels in the corresponding output feature map:

$$\frac{\partial E}{\partial W}(m, c, p, q) = \sum_{h=0}^{H_{out}-1} \sum_{w=0}^{W_{out}-1} \left(X(c, h+p, w+q) * \frac{\partial E}{\partial Y}(m, h, w) \right)$$

Note that while the calculation of $\frac{\partial E}{\partial x}$ is important for propagating the gradient to the previous layer, the calculation of the $\frac{\partial E}{\partial w}$ is key to the adjustments to the weight values of the current layer.

```
01   void convLayer_batched(int N, int M, int C, int H, int W, int K, float* X,
                             float* W, float* Y) {
02      int H_out = H - K + 1;
03      int W_out = W - K + 1;
04      for(int n = 0;  n < N;  n++)       // for each sample in the mini-batch
05        for(int m = 0;  m < M;  m++)          // for each output feature map
06          for(int h = 0; h < H_out; h++)       // for each output element
07            for(int w = 0; w < W_out; w++) {
08              Y[n, m, h, w] = 0;
09              for (int c = 0;   c < C; c++ // sum over all input feature maps
10                for (int p = 0; p < K; p++)           // KxK  filter
11                  for (int q = 0; q < K; q++)
12                    Y[n,m,h,w] = Y[n,m,h,w] + X[n, c, h+p, w+q]*W[m,c,p,q];
13            }
14      }
```

FIGURE 16.12

Forward path of a convolutional layer with minibatch training.

After the $\frac{\partial E}{\partial w}$ values at all filter bank element positions have been computed, weights are updated to minimize the expected error using the formula presented in Section 16.1: $w \leftarrow w - \varepsilon * \frac{\partial E}{\partial w}$, where ε is the learning rate constant. The initial value of ε is set empirically and reduced through the epochs according to the rule defined by user. The value of ε is reduced through the epochs to ensure that the weights converge to a minimal error. Recall that the negative sign of the adjustment term causes the change to be opposite to the direction of the gradient so that the change will likely reduce the error. Recall also that the weight values of the layers determine how the input is transformed through the network. The adjustment of these weight values of all the layers adapts the behavior of the network. That is, the network "learns" from a sequence of labeled training data and adapts its behavior by adjusting all weight values at all its layers for inputs whose inference results were incorrect and triggered backpropagation.

As we discussed in Section 16.1, backpropagation is typically triggered after a forward pass has been performed on a minibatch of N images from the training dataset, and the gradients have been computed for this minibatch. The learned weights are updated with the gradients that are calculated for the minibatch, and the process is repeated with another minibatch.[2] This adds one additional dimension to all previously described arrays, indexed with n, the index of the sample in the minibatch. It also adds one additional loop over samples.

Fig. 16.12 shows the revised forward path implementation of a convolutional layer. It generates the output feature maps for all the samples of a minibatch.

---

[2] If we work by the "optimization book," we should return used samples back to the training set and then build a new minibatch by randomly picking the next samples. In practice, we iterate sequentially over the whole training set. In machine learning, a pass through the training set is called an *epoch*. Then we shuffle the whole training set and start the next epoch.

16.3 Convolutional layer: a CUDA inference kernel

The computation pattern in training a convolutional neural network is like matrix multiplication: It is both compute intensive and highly parallel. We can process different samples in a minibatch, different output feature maps for the same sample, and different elements for each output feature map in parallel. In Fig. 16.12 the n-loop (line 04, over samples in a minibatch), the m-loop (line 05, over output feature maps), and the nested h-w-loops (lines 06–07, over pixels of each output feature map) are all parallel loops in that their iterations can be executed in parallel. These four loop levels together offer a massive level of parallelism.

The innermost three loop levels, the c-loop (over the input feature maps or channels) and the nested p-q-loops (over the weights in a filter bank), also offer a significant level of parallelism. However, to parallelize them, one would need to use atomic operations in accumulating into the Y elements, since different iterations of these loop levels can perform read-modify-write on the same Y elements. Therefore we will keep these loops serial unless we really need more parallelism.

Assuming that we exploit the four levels of "easy" parallelism (n, m, h, w) in the convolutional layer, the total number of parallel iterations is the product $N*M*H\_out*W\_out$. This high degree of available parallelism makes the convolutional layer an excellent candidate for GPU acceleration. We can easily design a kernel with thread organizations that are designed to capture the parallelism.

We first need to make some high-level design decisions about the thread organization. Assume that we will have each thread compute one element of one output feature map. We will use 2D thread blocks, in which each thread block computes a tile of TILE_WIDTH $\times$ TILE_WIDTH pixels in one output feature map. For example, if we set TILE_WIDTH = 16, we would have a total of 256 threads per block. This captures part of the nested h-w-loop level parallelism in processing the pixels of each output feature map.

Blocks can be organized into a 3D grid in several different ways. Each option designates the grid dimensions to capture the n, m, and h-w parallelism in different combinations. We will present the details of one of the options and leave it as an exercise for the reader to explore different options and evaluate the potential pros and cons of each option. The option that we present in detail is as follows:

1. The first dimension (X) corresponds to the (M) output features maps covered by each block.
2. The second dimension (Y) reflects the location of a block's output tile inside the output feature map.
3. The third dimension (Z) in the grid corresponds to samples (N) in the minibatch.

Fig. 16.13 shows the host code that launches a kernel based on the thread organization proposed above. The number of blocks in the X and Z dimensions of the grid are straightforward; They are simply M, the number of output feature

```
01   # define TILE_WIDTH 16
02   W_grid = W_out/TILE_WIDTH;   // number of horizontal tiles per output map
03   H_grid = H_out/TILE_WIDTH;   // number of vertical tiles per output map
04   T = H_grid * W_grid;
05   dim3 blockDim(TILE_WIDTH, TILE_WIDTH, 1);
06   dim3 gridDim(M, T, N);
07   ConvLayerForward_Kernel<<< gridDim, blockDim>>>(…);
```

FIGURE 16.13

Host code for launching a convolutional layer kernel.

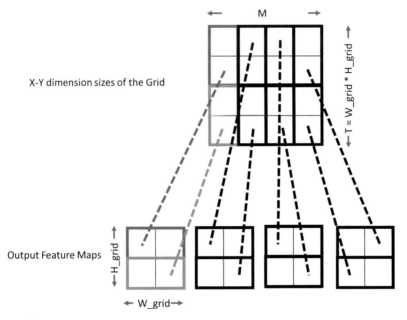

FIGURE 16.14

Mapping output feature map tiles to blocks in the *X-Y* dimension of the grid.

maps, and N, the number of samples in a minibatch. The arrangement in the Y dimension is a little more complex and is illustrated in Fig. 16.14. Ideally, we would like to dedicate two dimensions of the grid indices to the vertical and horizontal tile indices for simplicity. However, we have only one dimension for both, since we are using X for the output feature map index and Z for the sample index in a minibatch. Therefore we linearize the tile indices to encode both the horizontal and vertical tile indices of output feature map tiles.

In the example in Fig. 16.14, each sample has four output feature maps ($M = 4$), and each output feature map consists of 2×2 tiles (H_grid = 2 in line 02 and W_grid = 2 in line 03) of $16 \times 16 = 256$ pixels each. The grid organization assigns each block to calculate one of these tiles.

```
01  __global__ void
02  ConvLayerForward_Kernel(int C, int W_grid, int K, float* X, float* W,
                                float* Y) {
03      int m = blockIdx.x;
04      int h = (blockIdx.y / W_grid)*TILE_WIDTH + threadIdx.y;
05      int w = (blockIdx.y % W_grid)*TILE_WIDTH + threadIdx.x;
06      int n = blockIdx.z;
07      float acc = 0.;
08      for (int c = 0;  c < C; c++) {          // sum over all input channels
09          for (int p = 0; p < K; p++)         // loop over KxK  filter
10              for (int q = 0; q < K; q++)
11                  acc += X[n, c, h + p, w + q] * W[m, c, p, q];
12      }
13      Y[n, m, h, w] = acc;
14  }
```

FIGURE 16.15

Kernel for the forward path of a convolutional layer.

We have already assigned each output feature map to the X dimension, which is reflected as the four blocks in the X dimension, each corresponding to one of the output feature maps. As shown in the bottom of Fig. 16.14, we linearize the four tiles in each output feature map and assign them to the blocks in the Y dimension. Thus tiles (0, 0), (0, 1), (1, 0), and (1, 1) are mapped using row-major order to the blocks with blockIdx.y values 0, 1, 2, and 3, respectively. Thus the total number of bocks in the Y dimension is 4 (T = H_grid*W_grid = 4 in line 04). Thus we will launch a grid with gridDim (4, 4, N) in lines 06−07.

Fig. 16.15 shows a kernel based on the thread organization above. Note that in the code, we use multidimensional indices in array accesses for clarity. We leave it to the reader to translate this pseudo-code into regular C, assuming that X, Y, and W must be accessed via linearized indexing based on row-major layout (Chapter 3, Multidimensional Grids and Data).

Each thread starts by generating the n (batch), m (feature map), h (vertical), and w (horizontal) indices of its assigned output feature map pixel. The n (line 06) and m (line 03) indices are straightforward, given the host code. For the h index calculation in line 04, the blockIdx.y value is first divided by W_grid to recover the tile index in the vertical direction, as illustrated in Fig. 16.13. This tile index is then expanded by the TILE_WIDTH and added to the threadIdx.y to form the actual vertical pixel index into the output feature map (line 04). The derivation of the horizontal pixel index is similar (line 05).

The kernel in Fig. 16.15 has a high degree of parallelism but consumes too much global memory bandwidth. As in the convolution pattern discussions in Chapter 7, Convolution, the execution speed of the kernel will be limited by the global memory bandwidth. As we also saw in Chapter 7, Convolution, we can use constant memory caching and shared memory tiling to dramatically reduce the global memory traffic and improve the execution speed of the kernel. These optimizations to the convolution inference kernel are left as an exercise for the reader.

16.4 **Formulating a convolutional layer as GEMM**

We can build an even faster convolutional layer by representing it as an equivalent matrix multiplication operation and then using a highly efficient GEMM (general matrix multiply) kernel from the CUDA linear algebra library cuBLAS. This method was proposed by Chellapilla et al. (2006). The central idea is unfolding and duplicating input feature map pixels in such a way that all elements that are needed to compute one output feature map pixel will be stored as one sequential column of the matrix that is thus produced. This formulates the forward operation of the convolutional layer to one large matrix multiplication.[3]

Consider a small example convolutional layer that takes as input $C = 3$ feature maps, each of which is of size 3×3, and produces $M = 2$ output features, each of which is of size 2×2, as shown in Fig. 16.5 and again, for convenience, at the top of Fig. 16.16. It uses $M \times C = 6$ filter banks, each of which is 2×2. The matrix version of this layer will be constructed in the following way.

First, we will rearrange all input pixels. Since the results of the convolutions are summed across input features, the input features can be concatenated into one large matrix. Each input feature map becomes a section of rows in the large matrix. As shown in Fig. 16.16, input feature maps 0, 1, and 2 become the top, middle, and bottom sections, respectively, of the "input features X_unrolled" matrix.

The rearrangement is done so that each column of the resulting matrix contains all the input values necessary to compute one element of an output feature. For example, in Fig. 16.16, all the input feature pixels that are needed for calculating the value at (0, 0) of output feature map 0 are circled in the input feature maps:

$$Y_{0,0,0} = (1, 2, 1, 1) \cdot (1, 1, 2, 2) + (0, 2, 0, 3) \cdot (1, 1, 1, 1) + (1, 2, 0, 1) \cdot (0, 1, 1, 0)$$
$$= 1 + 2 + 2 + 2 + 0 + 2 + 0 + 3 + 0 + 2 + 0 + 0$$
$$= 14$$

where the first term of each inner product is a vector formed by linearizing the patch of x pixels circled in Fig. 16.16. The second term is a vector that is formed by linearizing the filter bank that is used for the convolution. In both cases, linearization is done by using the row-major order. It is also clear that we can reformulate the three inner products into one inner product:

$$Y_{0,0,0} = (1, 2, 1, 1, 0, 2, 0, 3, 1, 2, 0, 1) \cdot (1, 1, 2, 2, 1, 1, 1, 1, 0, 1, 1, 0)$$
$$= 1 + 2 + 2 + 2 + 0 + 2 + 0 + 3 + 0 + 2 + 0 + 0$$
$$= 14$$

---

[3] See also https://petewarden.com/2015/04/20/why-gemm-is-at-the-heart-of-deep-learning/ for a very detailed explanation.

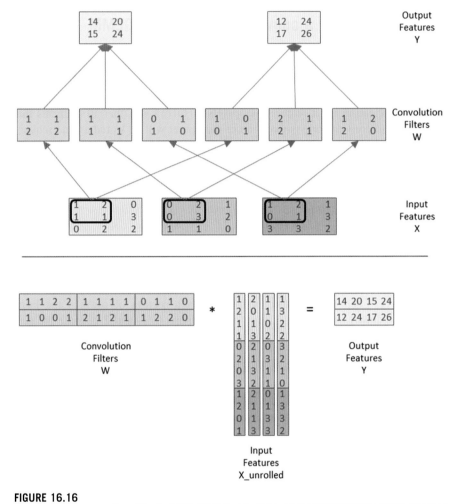

FIGURE 16.16

Formulation of convolutional layer as GEMM.

As shown in the bottom of Fig. 16.16, the concatenated vector from the filter banks becomes row 0 of the filter matrix, and the concatenated vector from the input feature maps becomes column 0 of the input feature map unrolled matrix. During matrix multiplication the row of the filter bank matrix and the column of the input feature matrix will produce one pixel of the output feature map.

Note that matrix multiplication of the 2×12 filter matrix and the 12×8 input feature map matrix produces a 2×8 output feature map matrix. The top section of the output feature map matrix is the linearized form of output feature map 0, and the bottom is output feature map 1. Both are already in row-major order, so they can be used as individual input feature maps for the next layer. As for the filter banks, each row of the filter matrix is simply the row-major order view of the original filter bank. Thus the filter matrix is simply the concatenation of all the original filter banks. There is no physical rearrangement or relocation of filter elements that are involved.

We make an important observation that the patches of input feature map pixels for calculating different pixels of the output feature map overlap with each other, owing to the nature of convolution. This means that each input feature map pixel is replicated multiple times as we produce the expanded input feature matrix. For example, the center pixel of each 3×3 input feature map is used four times to compute the four pixels of an output feature, so it will be duplicated four times. The middle pixel on each edge is used two times, so it will be duplicated two times. The four pixels at corners of each input feature are used only one time and will not need to be duplicated. Therefore the total number of pixels in the expanded input feature matrix section is $4*1 + 2*4 + 1*4 = 16$. Since each original input feature map has only nine pixels, the GEMM formulation incurs an expansion ratio of $16/9 = 1.8$ for representing input feature maps.

In general, the size of the unrolled input feature map matrix can be derived from the number of input feature map elements that are required to generate each output feature map element. The height, or the number of rows, of the expanded matrix is the number of input feature elements contributing to each output feature map element, which is $C*K*K$: each output element is the convolution of $K*K$ elements from each input feature map and there are C input feature maps. In our example, the K is 2 since the filter bank is 2×2 and there are three input feature maps. Thus the height of the expanded matrix should be $3*2*2 = 12$, which is exactly the height of the matrix shown in Fig. 16.16.

The width, or the number columns, of the expanded matrix is the number of elements in each output feature map. If each output feature map is an H_out $\times$ W_out matrix, the number of columns of the expanded matrix is H_out*W_out. In our example, each output feature map is a 2×2 matrix, yielding four columns in the expanded matrix. Note that the number of output feature maps *M* does not play into the duplication. This is because all output feature maps are computed from the same expanded input feature map matrix.

The ratio of expansion for the input feature maps is the size of the expanded matrix over the total size of the original input feature maps. The reader should verify that the expansion ratio is as follows:

$$\frac{C * K * K * H\_out * W\_out}{C * H\_in * W\_in}$$

where H_in and W_in are the height and width, respectively, of each input feature map. In our example the ratio is $(3*2*2*2*2)/(3*3*3) = 16/9$. In general, if the input feature maps and output feature maps are much larger than the filter banks, the ratio of expansion will approach $K*K$.

The filter banks are represented as a filter bank matrix in a fully linearized layout, in which each row contains all weight values that are needed to produce one output feature map. The height of the filter bank matrix is the number of output feature maps (*M*). Computing different output feature maps involves sharing a single expanded input feature map matrix. The width of the filter bank matrix is the number of weight values that are needed for generating each output feature map element, which is C*K*K. Recall that there is no duplication when placing the weight values into the filter bank matrix. For example, the filter bank matrix is simply a concatenated arrangement of the six filter banks in Fig. 16.16.

When we multiply the filter bank matrix *W* by the expanded input matrix X_unrolled, the output feature maps are computed as a matrix *Y* of height *M* and width H_out*W_out. That is, each row of *Y* is a complete output feature map.

Let's discuss now how we can implement this algorithm in CUDA. Let's first discuss the data layout. We can start from the layout of the input and output matrices.

1. We assume that the input feature map samples in a minibatch will be supplied in the same way as those for the basic CUDA kernel. It is organized as an N × C × H × W array, where N is the number of samples in a minibatch, C is the number of input feature maps, H is the height of each input feature map, and W is the width of each input feature map.

2. As we showed in Fig. 16.16, the matrix multiplication will naturally produce an output Y stored as an M × (H_out*W_out) array. This is what the original basic CUDA kernel would produce.

3. Since the filter bank matrix does not involve duplication of weight values, we assume that it will be prepared ahead of time and organized as an M × C × K^2 array as illustrated in Fig. 16.16.

The preparation of the unrolled input feature map matrix X_unroll is more complex. Since each expansion increases the size of input by up to K^2 times, the expansion ratio can be very large for typical K values of 5 or larger. The memory footprint for keeping all sample input feature maps for a minibatch can be prohibitively large. To reduce the memory footprint, we will allocate only one buffer for X_unrolled [C * K * K * H_out * W_out]. We will reuse this buffer by looping over samples in the minibatch. During each iteration we convert the sample input feature map from its original form into the unrolled matrix.

Fig. 16.17 shows a sequential function that produces the X_unroll array by gathering and duplicating the elements of an input feature map X. The function uses five levels of loops. The innermost two levels of for-loop (w and h, lines 08−13) place one input feature map element for each of the output feature map elements. The next two levels (p and q, lines 06−14) repeat the process for each of the K*K filter matrix elements. The outermost loop repeats the process of all

```
01    void unroll(int C, int H, int W, int K, float* X, float* X_unroll) {
02        int H_out = H - K + 1;
03        int W_out = W - K + 1;
04        for(int c = 0; c < C; c++) {
              // Beginning row index of the section for channel C input feature
              // map in the unrolled matrix
05            w_base = c * (K*K);
06            for(int p = 0; p < K; p++) {
07                for(int q = 0; q < K; q++) {
08                    for(int h = 0; h <  H_out; h++) {
09                        int h_unroll = w_base + p*K + q;
10                        for(int w = 0; w < W_out; w ++) {
11                            int w_unroll = h * W_out + w;
12                            X_unroll[h_unroll, w_unroll) = X(c, h + p, w + q);
13                        }
14                    }
15                }
16            }
17        }
18    }
```

FIGURE 16.17

A C function that generates the unrolled X matrix. The array accesses are in multidimensional indexing form for clarity and need to be linearized for the code to be compilable.

input feature maps. This implementation is conceptually straightforward and can be quite easily parallelized since the loops do not impose dependencies among their iterations. Also, successive iterations of the innermost loop (w, lines 10−13) read from a localized tile of one of the input feature maps in X and write into sequential locations (same row in X_unroll) in the expanded matrix X_unroll. This should result in efficient memory bandwidth usage on a CPU.

We are now ready to design a CUDA kernel which implements the input feature map unrolling. Each CUDA thread will be responsible for gathering (K*K) input elements from one input feature map for one element of an output feature map. The total number of threads will be (C * H_out * W_out). We will use one-dimensional thread blocks and extract multidimensional indices from the linearized thread index.

Fig. 16.18 shows an implementation of the unroll kernel. Note that each thread will build a K*K section of a column, shown as a shaded box in the Input Features X_Unrolled array in Fig. 16.16. Each such section contains all elements of a patch of the input feature map X from channel c, required for performing a convolution operation with the corresponding filter to produce one element of output Y.

Comparing the loop structures of Figs. 16.17 and 16.18 shows that the innermost two loop levels in Fig. 16.17 have been changed into outer level loops in Fig. 16.18. This interchange allows the work for collecting the input elements that are needed for calculating output elements to be done in parallel by multiple threads. Furthermore, having each thread collect all input feature map elements from an input feature map that are needed for generating an output generates a coalesced memory write pattern. As illustrated in Fig. 16.16, adjacent threads will

```
01    __global__ void
02    unroll_Kernel(int C, int H, int W, int K, float* X, float* X_unroll) {
03        int t = blockIdx.x * blockDim.x + threadIdx.x;
04        int H_out = H - K + 1;
05        int W_out = W - K + 1;
          // Width of the unrolled input feature matrix
06        int W_unroll = H_out * W_out;
07        if (t < C * W_unroll) {
              // Channel of the input feature map being collected by the thread
08            int c = t / W_unroll;
              // Column index of the unrolled matrix to write a strip of
              // input elements into (also, the linearized index of the output
              // element for which the thread is collecting input elements)
09            int w_unroll = t % W_unroll;
              // Horizontal and vertical indices of the output element
10            int h_out = w_unroll / W_out;
11            int w_out = w_unroll % W_out;
              // Starting row index for the unrolled matrix section for channel c
12            int w_base = c * K * K;
13            for(int p = 0; p < K; p++)
14                for(int q = 0; q < K; q++) {
                      // Row index of the unrolled matrix for the thread to write
                      // the input element into for the current iteration
15                    int h_unroll = w_base + p*K + q;
16                    X_unroll[h_unroll, w_unroll] = X[c, h_out + p, w_out + q];
17                }
18        }
19    }
```

FIGURE 16.18

A CUDA kernel implementation for unrolling input feature maps. The array accesses are in multidimensional indexing form for clarity and need to be linearized for the code to be compilable.

be writing adjacent X_unroll elements in a row as they all move vertically to complete their sections. The read access patterns to X are similar and can be analyzed by an inspection of the w_out values for adjacent threads. We leave the detailed analysis of the read access pattern as an exercise.

An important high-level assumption is that we keep the input feature maps, filter bank weights, and output feature maps in the device memory. The filter bank matrix is prepared once and stored in the device global memory for use by all input feature maps. For each sample in the minibatch, we launch the unroll_Kernel to prepare an expanded matrix and launch a matrix multiplication kernel, as outlined in Fig. 16.16.

Implementing convolutions with matrix multiplication can be very efficient, since matrix multiplication is highly optimized on all hardware platforms. Matrix multiplication is especially fast on GPUs because it has a high ratio of floating-point operations per byte of global memory data access. This ratio increases as the matrices get larger, meaning that matrix multiplication is less efficient on small matrices. Accordingly, this approach to convolution is most effective when it creates large matrices for multiplication.

As we mentioned earlier, the filter bank matrix is an $M \times (C * K * K)$ matrix and the expanded input feature map matrix is a $(C * K * K) \times (H\_out * W\_out)$

matrix. Note that except for the height of the filter bank matrix, the sizes of all dimensions depend on products of the parameters to the convolution, not the parameters themselves. While individual parameters can be small, their products tend to be large. For example, it is often true that in early layers of a convolutional network, C is small, but H_out and W_out are large. On the other hand, at the end of the network, C is large, but H_out and W_out are small. Hence the product C*H_out*W_out is usually large for all layers. This means that the sizes of the matrices tend to be consistently large for all layers, and so the performance using this approach tends to be high.

One disadvantage of forming the expanded input feature map matrix is that it involves duplicating the input data up to K*K times, which can require the allocation of a prohibitively large amount of memory. To work around this limitation, implementations such as the one shown in Fig. 16.16 materialize the X_unroll matrix piece by piece, for example, by forming the expanded input feature map matrix and calling matrix multiplication iteratively for each sample of the minibatch. However, this limits the parallelism in the implementation, and can sometimes lead to cases where the matrix multiplications are too small to effectively utilize the GPU. Another disadvantage of this formulation is that it lowers the computational intensity of the convolutions because X_unroll must be written and read, in addition to reading X itself, requiring significantly more memory traffic than the direct approach. Accordingly, the highest performance implementation has even more complex arrangements in realizing the unrolling algorithm to both maximize GPU utilization while keeping the reading from DRAM minimal. We will come back to this point when we present the CUDNN approach in the next section.

16.5 **CUDNN library**

CUDNN is a library of optimized routines for implementing deep learning primitives. It was designed to make it much easier for deep learning frameworks to take advantage of GPUs. It provides a flexible and easy-to-use C-language deep learning API that integrates neatly into existing deep learning frameworks (e.g., Caffe, Tensorflow, Theano, Torch). The library requires that input and output data be resident in the GPU device memory, as we discussed in the previous section. This requirement is analogous to that of cuBLAS.

The library is thread-safe in that its routines can be called from different host threads. Convolutional routines for the forward and backward paths use a common descriptor that encapsulates the attributes of the layer. Tensors and filters are accessed through opaque descriptors, with the flexibility to specify the tensor layout using arbitrary strides along each dimension. The most important computational primitive in CNN is a special form of batched convolution.

Table 16.1 Convolution parameters for CUDNN. Note that the CUDNN naming convention is slightly different from what we used in previous sections.

Parameter	Meaning
N	Number of images in minibatch
C	Number of input feature maps
H	Height of input image
W	Width of input image
K	Number of output feature maps
R	Height of filter
S	Width of filter
u	Vertical stride
v	Horizontal stride
pad_h	Height of zero padding
pad_w	Width of zero padding

In this section we describe the forward form of this convolution. The CUDNN parameters that govern this convolution are listed Table 16.1.

There are two inputs to the convolution:

1. D is a four-dimensional $N \times C \times H \times W$ tensor, which contains the input data.[4]
2. F is a four-dimensional $K \times C \times R \times S$ tensor, which contains the convolutional filters.

The input data array (tensor) D ranges over N samples in a minibatch, C input feature maps per sample, H rows per input feature map, and W columns per input feature map. The filters range over K output feature maps, C input feature maps, R rows per filter bank, and S columns per filter bank. The output is also a four-dimensional tensor O that ranges over N samples in the minibatch, K output feature maps, P rows per output feature map, and Q columns per output feature map, where $P = f(H; R; u; pad\_h)$ and $Q = f(W; S; v; pad\_w)$, meaning that the height and width of the output feature maps depend on the input feature map and filter bank height and width, along with padding and striding choices. The striding parameters u and v allow the user to reduce the computational load by computing only a subset of the output pixels. The padding parameters allow the user to specify how many rows or columns of 0 entries are appended to each feature map for improved memory alignment and/or vectorized execution.

---

[4] *Tensor* is a mathematical term for arrays that have more than two dimensions. In mathematics, matrices have only two dimensions. Arrays with three or more dimensions are called tensors. For the purpose of this book, a T-dimensional tensor can be treated simply as a T-dimensional array.

CUDNN (Chetlur et al., 2014) supports multiple algorithms for implementing a convolutional layer: matrix multiplication—based GEMM (Tan et al., 2011) and Winograd (Lavin & Scott, 2016), FFT-based (Vasilache et al., 2014), and so on. The GEMM-based algorithm to implement the convolutions with a matrix multiplication is similar to the approach presented in Section 16.4. As we discussed at the end of Section 16.4, materializing the expanded input feature matrix in global memory can be costly in terms of both global memory space and bandwidth consumption. CUDNN avoids this problem by lazily generating and loading the expanded input feature map matrix X_unroll into on-chip memory only, rather than by gathering it in off-chip memory before calling a matrix multiplication routine. NVIDIA provides a matrix multiplication—based routine that achieves a high utilization of the maximal theoretical floating-point throughput on GPUs. The algorithm for this routine is similar to the algorithm described by Tan et al. (2011). Fixed-size submatrices of the input matrices A and B are successively read into on-chip memory and are then used to compute a submatrix of the output matrix C. All indexing complexities that are imposed by the convolution are handled in the management of tiles in this routine. We compute on tiles of A and B while fetching the next tiles of A and B from off-chip memory into on-chip caches and other memories. This technique hides the memory latency that is associated with the data transfer, allowing the matrix multiplication computation to be limited only by the time it takes to perform the arithmetic calculations.

Since the tiling that is required for the matrix multiplication routine is independent of any parameters from the convolution, the mapping between the tile boundaries of X_unroll and the convolution problem is nontrivial. Accordingly, the CUDNN approach entails computing this mapping and using it to load the correct elements of A and B into on-chip memories. This happens dynamically as the computation proceeds, which allows the CUDNN convolution implementation to exploit optimized infrastructure for matrix multiplication. It requires additional indexing arithmetic compared to a matrix multiplication, but it fully leverages the computational engine of matrix multiplication to perform the work. After the computation is complete, CUDNN performs the required tensor transposition to store the result in the user's desired data layout.

16.6 Summary

This chapter started with a brief introduction to machine learning. It then dove more deeply into the classification task and introduced perceptrons, a type of linear classifier that is foundational for understanding modern CNN. We discussed how the forward inference and backward propagation training passes are implemented for both single-layer and MLP. In particular, we discussed the need for differentiable activation functions and how the model parameters can be updated through chain rules in a multilayer perceptron network during the training process.

Based on the conceptual and mathematical understanding of perceptrons, we presented a basic convolutional neural network and the implementation of its major types of layers. These layers can be viewed as special cases and/or simple adaptations of perceptrons. We then built on the convolution pattern in Chapter 7, Convolution, to present a CUDA kernel implementation of the convolutional layer, the most computationally intensive layer of CNN.

We then presented techniques for formulating convolutional layers as matrix multiplications by unrolling the input feature maps into a matrix. The conversion allows the convolutional layers to benefit from highly optimized GEMM libraries for GPUs. We also presented the C and CUDA implementations of the unrolling procedure for the input matrix and discussed the pros and cons of the unrolling approach.

We ended the chapter with an overview of the CUDNN library, which is used by most deep learning frameworks. Users of these frameworks can benefit from the highly optimized layer implementations without writing CUDA kernels themselves.

Exercises

1. Implement the forward pass for the pooling layer described in Section 16.2.
2. We used an [N × C × H × W] layout for input and output features. Can we reduce the memory bandwidth by changing it to an [N × H × W × C] layout? What are potential benefits of using a [C × H × W × N] layout?
3. Implement the backward pass for the convolutional layer described in Section 16.2.
4. Analyze the read access pattern to X in the unroll_Kernel in Fig. 16.18 and show whether the memory reads that are done by adjacent threads can be coalesced.

References

Chellapilla K., Puri S., Simard P., 2006. High Performance Convolutional Neural Networks for Document Processing, https://hal.archives-ouvertes.fr/inria-00112631/document.

Chetlur S., Woolley C., Vandermersch P., Cohen J., Tran J., 2014. cuDNN: Efficient Primitives for Deep Learning NVIDIA.

Hinton, G.E., Osindero, S., Teh, Y.-W., 2006. A fast learning algorithm for deep belief nets. Neural Comp. 18, 1527–1554. Available from: https://www.cs.toronto.edu/~hinton/absps/fastnc.pdf.

Krizhevsky, A., Cuda-convnet, https://code.google.com/p/cuda-convnet/.

Krizhevsky, A., Sutskever, I., Hinton, G., 2012. ImageNet classification with deep convolutional neural networks. In Proc. Adv. NIPS 25 1090–1098, https://papers.nips.cc/paper/4824-imagenet-classification-with-deep-convolutional-neural-networks.pdf.

Lavin, A., Scott G., 2016. Fast algorithms for convolutional neural networks. In: Proceedings of the IEEE Conference on Computer Vision and Pattern Recognition.

LeCun, Y., et al., 1990. Handwritten digit recognition with a back-propagation network. In Proc. Adv. Neural Inf. Process. Syst. 396−404, http://yann.lecun.com/exdb/publis/pdf/lecun-90c.pdf.

LeCun, Y., Bengio, Y., Hinton, G.E., 2015. Deep learning. Nature 521, 436−444 (28 May 2015). Available from: http://www.nature.com/nature/journal/v521/n7553/full/nature14539.html.

LeCun, Y., Bottou, L., Bengio, Y., Haffner, P., 1998. Gradient-based learning applied to document recognition. Proc. IEEE 86 (11), 2278−2324. Available from: http://yann.lecun.com/exdb/publis/pdf/lecun-01a.pdf.

Raina, R., Madhavan, A., Ng, A.Y., 2009. Large-scale deep unsupervised learning using graphics processors. Proc. 26th ICML 873−880. Available from: http://www.andrewng.org/portfolio/large-scale-deep-unsupervised-learning-using-graphics-processors/.

Rosenblatt, F., 1957. The Perceptron—A Perceiving and Recognizing Automaton. Report 85−460-1. Cornell Aeronautical Laboratory.

Rumelhart, D.E., Hinton, G.E., Williams, R.J., 1986. Learning representations by back-propagating errors. Nature 323 (6088), 533−536.

Samuel, A., 1959. Some studies in machine learning using the game of checkers. IBM J. Res. Dev. 3 (3), 210−229. Available from: https://doi.org/10.1147/rd.33.0210. CiteSeerX 10.1.1.368.2254.

Tan, G., Li, L., Treichler, S., Phillips, E., Bao, Y., Sun, N., 2011. Fast implementation of DGEMM on Fermi GPU. Supercomputing 11.

Vasilache N., Johnson J., Mathieu M., Chintala S., Piantino S, LeCun Y., 2014. Fast Convolutional Nets With fbfft: A GPU Performance Evaluation, http://arxiv.org/pdf/1412.7580v3.pdf.

Iterative magnetic resonance imaging reconstruction

17

Chapter Outline

17.1 Background 391
17.2 Iterative reconstruction 394
17.3 Computing F^{H}D 396
17.4 Summary 412
Exercises 413
References 414

In this chapter we start with the background and problem formulation of a relatively simple application that has traditionally been constrained by the limited capabilities of mainstream computing systems. We show that parallel execution not only speeds up the existing approaches but also allows the applications experts to pursue an approach that has been known to provide benefit but was previously ignored because of the excessive computational requirements. This approach represents an increasingly important class of computational methods that derive statistically optimal estimation of unknown values from a very large amount of observational data. We use an example algorithm and its implementation source code from such an approach to illustrate how a developer can systematically determine the kernel parallelism structure, assign variables into different types of memories, steer around limitations of the hardware, validate results, and assess the impact of performance improvements.

17.1 Background

Magnetic resonance imaging (MRI) is commonly used as a medical procedure to safely and noninvasively probe the structure and function of biological tissues in all regions of the body. Images that are generated by using MRI have had a profound impact in both clinical and research settings. MRI consists of two phases: acquisition (scan) and reconstruction. During the acquisition phase, the scanner samples data in the k-space domain (i.e., the spatial frequency domain or Fourier transform domain) along a predefined trajectory. These samples are then

Programming Massively Parallel Processors. DOI: https://doi.org/10.1016/B978-0-323-91231-0.00012-4

transformed into the desired image during the reconstruction phase. Intuitively, the reconstruction phase estimates the shape and texture of the tissues on the basis of the observation k-space data collected from the scanner.

The application of MRI is often limited by high noise levels, significant imaging artifacts, and/or long data acquisition times. In clinical settings, short scan times not only increase scanner throughput but also reduce patient discomfort, and this tends to mitigate motion-related artifacts. High image resolution and fidelity are important because they enable early detection of pathology, leading to improved prognoses for patients. However, the goals of short scan time, high resolution, and high signal-to-noise ratio (SNR) often conflict; improvements in one metric tend to come at the expense of one or both of the others. New technological breakthroughs are needed to enable simultaneous improvement on all of three dimensions. This study presents a case in which massively parallel computing provides such a breakthrough.

The reader is referred to MRI textbooks such as Liang and Lauterbur (1999) for the physics principles behind MRI. For this case study, we will focus on the computational complexity in the reconstruction phase and how the complexity is affected by the k-space sampling trajectory. The k-space sampling trajectory used by the MRI scanner can significantly affect the quality of the reconstructed image, the time complexity of the reconstruction algorithm, and the time required for the scanner to acquire the samples. Eq. (17.1) shows a formulation that relates the k-space samples to the reconstructed image for a class of reconstruction methods:

$$\widehat{m}(\mathbf{r}) = \sum_j W(\mathbf{k}_j) s(\mathbf{k}_j) e i 2\pi \mathbf{k}_j \, \mathbf{r} \qquad (17.1)$$

In Eq. (17.1), $m(\mathbf{r})$ is the reconstructed image, $s(\mathbf{k})$ is the measured k-space data, and $W(\mathbf{k})$ is the weighting function that accounts for nonuniform sampling; that is, $W(\mathbf{k})$ decreases the influence of data from k-space regions where a higher density of samples points are taken. For this class of reconstructions, $W(\mathbf{k})$ can also serve as an *apodization* filtering function that reduces the influence of noise and reduces artifacts due to finite sampling.

If data are acquired at uniformly spaced Cartesian grid points in the k-space under ideal conditions, then the $W(\mathbf{k})$ weighting function is a constant and can thus be factored out of the summation in Eq. (17.1). Furthermore, with the uniformly spaced Cartesian grid samples, the exponential terms in Eq. (17.1) are uniformly spaced in the k-space. As a result, the reconstruction of $m(\mathbf{r})$ becomes an inverse fast Fourier transform (FFT) on $s(\mathbf{k})$, an extremely efficient computation method. A collection of data measured at such uniformed spaced Cartesian grid points is referred to as a *Cartesian scan trajectory*. Fig. 17.1A depicts a Cartesian scan trajectory. In practice, Cartesian scan trajectories allow straightforward implementation on scanners and are widely used in clinical settings today.

Although the inverse FFT reconstruction of Cartesian scan data is computationally efficient, non-Cartesian scan trajectories often have an advantage in reduced sensitivity to patient motion, better ability to provide self-calibrating field

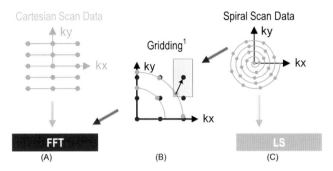

FIGURE 17.1

Scanner k-space trajectories and their associated reconstruction strategies: (A) Cartesian trajectory with FFT reconstruction, (B) spiral (or non-Cartesian trajectory in general) followed by gridding to enable FFT reconstruction, (C) spiral (non-Cartesian) trajectory with a linear solver−based reconstruction.

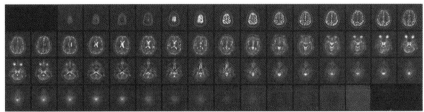

Courtesy of Keith Thulborn and Ian Atkinson, Center for MR Research, University of Illinois at Chicago

FIGURE 17.2

Non-Cartesian k-space sample trajectory and accurate linear solver−based reconstruction enable new capabilities with exciting medical applications.

inhomogeneity information, and reduced requirements for scanner hardware performance. As a result, non-Cartesian scan trajectories such as spirals (shown in Fig. 17.1(C)), radial lines (also known as projection imaging), and rosettes have been proposed to reduce motion-related artifacts and address scanner hardware performance limitations. These improvements have recently allowed the reconstructed image pixel values to be used for measuring subtle phenomenon such as tissue chemical anomalies before they become anatomical pathology.

Fig. 17.2 shows such an MRI reconstruction-based measurement that generates a map of sodium, a heavily regulated substance in normal human tissues. The information can be used to track tissue health in stroke and cancer treatment processes. Because sodium is much less abundant than water molecules in human tissues, measuring sodium levels reliably requires a higher SNR through a higher number of samples and therefore needs to mitigate the extra scan time with non-Cartesian scan trajectories. The improved SNR enables reliable collection of in vivo concentration data on chemical substances, such as sodium, in human tissues. The variation or shifting of the sodium concentration suggests early signs of disease development or tissue death. For example, the sodium map of a human brain shown in Fig. 17.2 can be used to give early indication of brain tumor tissue responsiveness to chemotherapy protocols, enabling individualized medicine.

Image reconstruction from non-Cartesian trajectory data presents both challenges and opportunities. The main challenge arises from the fact that the exponential terms are no longer uniformly spaced; the summation does not have the form of an FFT anymore. Therefore one can no longer perform reconstruction by directly applying an inverse FFT to the k-space samples. In a commonly used approach called gridding, the samples are first interpolated onto a uniform Cartesian grid and then reconstructed by using the FFT (see Fig. 17.1B). For example, a convolution approach to gridding takes a k-space data point, convolves it with a gridding convolution mask, and accumulates the results on a Cartesian grid. As we saw in Chapter 7, Convolution, is quite computationally intensive and is an important pattern for massively parallel computing. The reader already has the skills for accelerating convolution gridding computation with parallel computing and thus facilitating the application of the current FFT approach to non-Cartesian trajectory data.

In this chapter we will cover an iterative, statistically optimal image reconstruction method that can accurately model imaging physics and bound the noise error in the resulting image pixel values. Such statistically optimal methods are gaining importance in the wake of big data analytics. However, such iterative reconstruction methods have been impractical for large-scale three-dimensional (3D) problems, owing their excessive computational requirements compared to gridding. Recently, these reconstructions have become viable in clinical settings because of the wide availability of GPUs. An iterative reconstruction algorithm that used to take hours using high-end sequential CPUs to reconstruct an image of moderate resolution now takes only minutes using both CPUs and GPUs, a delay that is acceptable in clinical settings.

17.2 Iterative reconstruction

Haldar and Liang proposed a linear solver–based iterative reconstruction algorithm (Stone et al., 2008) for non-Cartesian scan data, as shown in Fig. 17.1C. The algorithm allows for explicitly modeling the physics of the scanner data acquisition process and can thus reduce the artifacts in the reconstructed image. However, it is computationally expensive. We use this as an example of innovative methods that have required too much computation time to be considered practical. We will show that massively parallel execution can reduce the reconstruction time to the order of a minute so that the new imaging capabilities, such as sodium imaging, can be deployed in clinical settings.

Fig. 17.3 shows a solution of the quasi-Bayesian estimation problem formulation of the iterative linear solver−based reconstruction approach, where ρ is a vector containing voxel values for the reconstructed image, F is a matrix that models the physics of imaging process, D is a vector of data samples from the scanner, and W is a matrix that can incorporate prior information such as anatomical constraints. F^H and W^H are the Hermitian transpose (or conjugate transpose) of F and W, respectively, by taking the transpose and then taking the complex conjugate of each entry (the complex conjugate of $a + ib$ being $a − ib$). In clinical settings, the anatomical constraints represented in W are derived from one or more high-resolution, high-SNR water molecule scans of the patient. These water molecule scans reveal features such as the location of anatomical structures. The matrix W is derived from these reference images. The problem is to solve for ρ given all the other matrices and vectors.

On the surface, the computational solution to the problem formulation in Fig. 17.3 should be very straightforward. It involves matrix multiplication and addition ($F^HF+\lambda W^HW$), matrix-vector multiplication (F^HD), matrix inversion ($F^HF +\lambda W^HW)^{-1}$, and finally matrix multiplication (($F^HF+\lambda W^HW)^{-1}*F^HD$). However, the sizes of the matrices make this straightforward approach extremely time-consuming. The dimensions of F^H and F matrices are determined by the number of voxels in the 3D reconstructed image and the number of k-space samples used in the reconstruction. Even in a modest resolution 128^3-voxel reconstruction, there are 128^3=2 million columns in F with N elements in each column, where N is the number of k-space samples that are used (size of D). Obviously, F is extremely large. Such massive dimensions are commonly encountered in big data analytics when one tries to use iterative solver methods to estimate the major contributing factors of a massive amount of noisy observational data.

The sizes of the matrices that are involved are so large that the matrix operations that are involved in a direct solution of the equation in Fig. 17.3 using

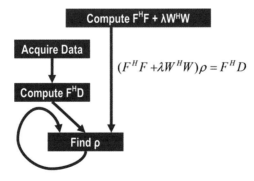

FIGURE 17.3

An iterative linear solver−based approach to reconstructing non-Cartesian k-space sample data.

methods such as Gaussian elimination are practically intractable. An iterative method for matrix inversion, such as the conjugate gradient (CG) algorithm, is therefore preferred. The CG algorithm reconstructs the image by iteratively solving the equation in Fig. 17.3 for ρ. During each iteration the CG algorithm updates the current image estimate ρ to improve the value of the quasi-Bayesian cost function. The computational efficiency of the CG technique is determined largely by the efficiency of matrix-vector multiplication operations involving $F^H F + \lambda W^H W$ and ρ, as these operations are required during each iteration of the CG algorithm.

Fortunately, the matrix W often has a sparse structure that permits efficient implementation of $W^H W$, and the matrix $F^H F$ is Toeplitz, which enables efficient matrix-vector multiplication via the FFT. Stone et al. (2008) present a GPU-accelerated method for calculating Q, a data structure that allows us to quickly calculate matrix-vector multiplication involving $F^H F$ without actually calculating $F^H F$ itself. The calculation of Q can take days on a high-end CPU core. Since F models the physics of the image process, it needs to be done only once for a given scanner and planned trajectory. Thus Q needs to be calculated only once and is used for multiple scans using the same scan trajectory.

The matrix-vector multiply to calculate $F^H D$ takes about one order of magnitude less time than Q but can still take about 3 hours for a 128^3-voxel reconstruction on a high-end sequential CPU. Recall that D is the vector of data samples from the scanner. Thus since $F^H D$ needs to be computed for every image acquisition, it is desirable to reduce the computation time of $F^H D$ to minutes.[1] We will show the details of this process. As it turns out, the core computational structure of Q is identical to that of $F^H D$; Q just involves much more computation because it deals with matrix multiplication rather than just matrix-vector multiplication. Thus it suffices to discuss one of them from the parallelization perspective. We will focus on $F^H D$, since this is the one that will need to be run for each data acquisition.

The "find ρ" step in Fig. 17.3 performs the actual CG based on $F^H D$. As we explain earlier, precalculation of Q makes this step much less computationally intensive than $F^H D$, accounting for less than 1% of the execution of the reconstruction of each image on a sequential CPU. As a result, we will leave the CG solver out of the parallelization scope and focus on $F^H D$ in this chapter. However, we will revisit its status at the end of the chapter.

17.3 Computing $F^H D$

Fig. 17.4 shows a sequential C implementation of the computations for the core step of computing a data structure for computing $F^H D$. The computations

---

[1] Note that the $F^H D$ computation can be approximated with gridding and can run in a few seconds with perhaps reduced quality of the final reconstructed image.

```
01  for (int m = 0; m < M; m++) {
02    rMu[m] = rPhi[m]*rD[m] + iPhi[m]*iD[m];
03    iMu[m] = rPhi[m]*iD[m] - iPhi[m]*rD[m];
04    for (int n = 0; n < N; n++) {
05      float expFhD = 2*PI*(kx[m]*x[n] + ky[m]*y[n] + kz[m]*z[n]);
06      float cArg = cos(expFhD);
07      float sArg = sin(expFhD);
08      rFhD[n] +=  rMu[m]*cArg - iMu[m]*sArg;
09      iFhD[n] +=  iMu[m]*cArg + rMu[m]*sArg;
10    }
11  }
```

FIGURE 17.4

Computation of F^{H}D.

start with an outer loop that iterates through the k-space samples (line 01). A quick glance at Fig. 17.4 shows that the C implementation of F^{H}D is an excellent candidate for acceleration because it exhibits substantial data parallelism. The algorithm first computes the real and imaginary components of Mu (rMu and iMu) at the current sample point in the k-space. It then enters an inner n-loop that computes the contribution of the current k-space sample to the real and imaginary components of F^{H}D at each voxel in the image space. Keep in mind that M is the total number of k-space samples and N is the total number of voxels in the reconstructed image. The value of F^{H}D at any voxel depends on the values of all k-space sample points. However, no voxel elements of F^{H}D depend on any other voxel elements of F^{H}D. Therefore all elements of F^{H}D can be computed in parallel. Specifically, all iterations of the outer loop can be done in parallel, and all iterations of the inner loop can be done in parallel. However, the calculations of the inner loop have a dependence on the calculation done by the preceding statements in the same iteration of the outer loop.

Despite the algorithm's abundant inherent parallelism, potential performance bottlenecks are evident. First, in the loop that computes the elements of F^{H}D, the ratio of floating-point operations to memory accesses is at best 0.75 OP/B and at worst 0.25 OP/B. The best case assumes that the sin and cos trigonometry operations are computed by using five-element Taylor series that require 13 and 12 floating-point operations, respectively. The worst case assumes that each trigonometric operation is computed as a single operation in hardware. As we saw in Chapter 5, Memory Architecture and Data Locality, a substantially higher floating-point arithmetic to global memory access ratio is needed for the kernel not to be limited by memory bandwidth. Thus the memory accesses will clearly limit the performance of the kernel unless the ratio is drastically increased.

Second, the ratio of floating-point arithmetic to floating-point trigonometry functions is only 13:2. Thus a GPU-based implementation must tolerate or avoid stalls due to the long latency and low throughput of the sin and cos operations. Without a good way to reduce the cost of trigonometry functions, the performance will likely be dominated by the time that is spent in these functions.

We are now ready to take the steps in converting F^HD from sequential C code to a CUDA kernel.

Step 1: Determine the kernel parallelism structure

The conversion of the loops in Fig. 17.4 into a CUDA kernel is conceptually straightforward. Since all iterations of the outer loop of Fig. 17.4 can be executed in parallel, we can simply convert the outer loop into a CUDA kernel by mapping its iterations to CUDA threads. Fig. 17.5 shows a kernel from such a straightforward conversion. Each thread implements an iteration of the original outer loop; that is, we use each thread to calculate the contribution of one k-space sample to all F^HD elements. The original outer loop has M iterations, and M can be in the millions. We obviously need to have a large number of thread blocks to generate enough threads to implement all these iterations.

To make performance tuning easy, we declare a constant `FHD_THREADS_PER_BLOCK` that defines the number of threads in each thread block when we invoke the cmpFhD kernel. Thus we will use `M/FHD_THREADS_PER_BLOCK` for the grid size and `FHD_THREADS_PER_BLOCK` for the block size when invoking the kernel. Within the kernel, each thread calculates the original iteration of the outer loop that it is assigned to cover, using the familiar formula `blockIdx.x*FHD_THREADS_PER_BLOCK + threadIdx.x`. For example, assume that there are 1,000,000 k-space samples and we decide to use 1024 threads per block. The grid size at kernel innovation will be 1,000,000/1024=977 blocks. The block size will be 1,024. The calculation of m for each thread will be equivalent to `blockIdx.x*1024+threadIdx`.

While the kernel of Fig. 17.5 exploits ample parallelism, it suffers from a major problem: All threads write into all rFhD and iFhD voxel elements. This means that the kernel must use atomic operations in the global memory in the inner loop in order to keep threads from trashing each other's contributions to the voxel value (lines 10−11). As we saw in Chapter 9, Parallel Histogram, heavy

```
01  #define FHD_THREADS_PER_BLOCK 1024
02  __global__ void cmpFhD(float* rPhi, iPhi, rD, iD,
03       kx, ky, kz, x, y, z, rMu, iMu, rFhD, iFhD, int N) {
04     int m = blockIdx.x * FHD_THREADS_PER_BLOCK + threadIdx.x;
05     rMu[m] = rPhi[m]*rD[m] + iPhi[m]*iD[m];
06     iMu[m] = rPhi[m]*iD[m] - iPhi[m]*rD[m];
07     for (int n = 0; n < N; n++) {
08       float expFhD = 2*PI*(kx[m]*x[n] + ky[m]*y[n] + kz[m]*z[n]);
09       float cArg = cos(expFhD);  float sArg = sin(expFhD);
10       atomicAdd(&rFhD[n],rMu[m]*cArg - iMu[m]*sArg);
11       atomicAdd(&iFhD[n],iMu[m]*cArg + rMu[m]*sArg);
12     }
13  }
```

FIGURE 17.5

First version of the F^HD kernel.

use of atomic operations on global memory data can seriously reduce the performance of parallel execution. Furthermore, the size of the rFhD and iFhD arrays, which is the total number of voxels in the reconstructed image, makes privatization in shared memory infeasible. We need to explore other options.

The arrangement for each thread to take an input element (k-space sample in this application) and update all or many output elements (voxels of the reconstructed image in this application) is referred to as the *scatter approach*. Intuitively, each thread scatters the effect of an input to many output values. Unfortunately, threads in the scatter approach can update the same output elements and potentially trash each other's contributions. Thus atomic operations are needed for a scatter approach in general and tend to negatively impact the performance of parallel execution.

A potentially better alternative to the scatter approach is to use each thread to calculate one output element by collecting the contributions from all input elements, which is referred to as the *gather approach*. The gather approach ensures that the threads update only their designated output elements and never interfere with each other. In our application, parallelization based on the gather approach assigns each thread to calculate one pair of rFhD and iFhD elements from all k-space samples. As a result, there is no interference between threads and no need for atomic operations.

To adopt the gather approach, we need to make the n-loop the outer loop so that we can assign each iteration of the n-loop to a thread. This can be done by swapping the inner loop and the outer loop in Fig. 17.4 so that each of the new outer loop iterations processes one rFhD/iFhD element pair. That is, each of the new outer loop iterations will execute the new inner loop that accumulates the contribution of all k-space samples to the rFhD/iFhD element pair handled by the outer loop iteration. This transformation of the loop structure is called *loop interchange*. It requires a perfectly nested loop, meaning that there is no statement between the outer for-loop statement and the inner for-loop statement. However, this is not true for the FhD code in Fig. 17.4. We need to find a way to move the calculation of rMu and iMu elements out of the way.

From a quick inspection of Fig. 17.4 we see that the F^{H}D calculation can be split into two separate loops, as is shown in Fig. 17.6, using a technique called *loop fission* or loop splitting. This transformation takes the body of a loop and splits it into two loops. In the case of F^{H}D the outer loop consists of two parts: the statements before the inner loop and the inner loop itself. As is shown in Fig. 17.6, we can perform loop fission on the outer loop by placing the statements before the inner loop into a first loop and the inner loop into a second loop.

An important consideration in loop fission is that the transformation changes the relative execution order of the two parts of the original outer loop. In the original outer loop, both parts of the first iteration execute before the second iteration. After fission the first part of all iterations will execute; they are then followed by the second part of all iterations. The reader should be able to verify that this change of execution order does not affect the execution results for F^{H}D. This is

```
01  for (int m = 0; m < M; m++) {
02    rMu[m] = rPhi[m]*rD[m] + iPhi[m]*iD[m];
03    iMu[m] = rPhi[m]*iD[m] - iPhi[m]*rD[m];
04  }
05  for (int m = 0; m < M; m++) {
06    for (int n = 0; n < N; n++) {
07      float expFhD = 2*PI*(kx[m]*x[n] + ky[m]*y[n] + kz[m]*z[n]);
08      float cArg = cos(expFhD);
09      float sArg = sin(expFhD);
10      rFhD[n] +=  rMu[m]*cArg - iMu[m]*sArg;
11      iFhD[n] +=  iMu[m]*cArg + rMu[m]*sArg;
12    }
13  }
```

FIGURE 17.6

Loop fission on the $F^H D$ computation.

```
01  #define MU_THREADS_PER_BLOCK 1024
02  __global__ void cmpMu(float* rPhi, iPhi, rD, iD, rMu, iMu)  {
03    int m = blockIdx.x*MU_THREAEDS_PER_BLOCK + threadIdx.x;
04    rMu[m] = rPhi[m]*rD[m] + iPhi[m]*iD[m];
05    iMu[m] = rPhi[m]*iD[m] - iPhi[m]*rD[m];
06  }
```

FIGURE 17.7

The cmpMu kernel.

because the execution of the first part of each iteration does not depend on the result of the second part of any preceding iterations of the original outer loop. Loop fission is a transformation that is often done by advanced compilers that are capable of analyzing the (lack of) dependence between statements across loop iterations.

With loop fission the $F^H D$ computation is now done in two steps. The first step is a single-level loop that calculates the rMu and iMu elements for use in the second loop. The second step corresponds to the second loop that calculates the $F^H D$ elements based on the rMu and iMu elements calculated in the first step. Each step can now be converted into its own CUDA kernel. The two CUDA kernels will execute sequentially with respect to each other. Since the second loop needs to use the results from the first loop, separating these two loops into two kernels that execute in sequence does not sacrifice any parallelism.

The cmpMu() kernel in Fig. 17.7 implements the first loop. The conversion of the first loop from sequential C code to a CUDA kernel is straightforward: Each thread executes one iteration of the original C code. Since the M value can be very big, reflecting the large number of k-space samples, such a mapping can result in a large number of threads. Since each thread block can have up to 1024 threads in each block, we will need to use multiple blocks to allow the large number of threads. This can be accomplished by having a number of threads in each block, specified by MU_THREADS_PER_BLOCK in Fig. 17.7, and by employing M/MU_THREADS_PER_BLOCK blocks needed to cover all M iterations of the original loop. For example, if there are 1,000,000 k-space samples, the kernel could be invoked with a configuration of 1024 threads per block and 1,000,000/1024 = 977 blocks. This is done by defining `MU_THREADS_PER_BLOCK` as 1024 and using it as the block size and `M/MU_THREADS_PER_BLOCK` as the grid size during kernel innovation.

Within the kernel, each thread can identify the iteration assigned to it by using its `blockIdx` and `threadIdx` values. Since the threading structure is one-dimensional, only `blockIdx.x` and `threadIdx.x` need to be used. Because each block covers a section of the original iterations, the iteration covered by a thread is `blockIdx.x*MU_THREADS_PER_BLOCK + threadIdx`. For example, assume that `MU_THREADS_PER_BLOCK = 1024`. The thread with `blockIdx.x=0` and `threadIdx.x=37` covers the 37th iteration of the original loop, whereas the thread with `blockIdx.x=5` and `threadIdx.x=2` covers the 5122nd (5*1024+2) iteration of the original loop. Using this iteration number to access the Mu, Phi, and D arrays ensures that the arrays are covered by the threads in the same way they were covered by the iterations of the original loop. Because every thread writes into its own Mu element, there is no potential conflict between any of these threads.

Determining the structure of the second kernel requires a little more work. An inspection of the second loop in Fig. 17.6 shows that there are at least three options in designing the second kernel. In the first option, each thread corresponds to one iteration of the inner loop. This option creates the most number of threads and thus exploits the largest amount of parallelism. However, the number of threads would be N*M, with N in the millions and M in hundreds of thousands. Their product would result in too many threads in the grid, more than are needed to fully utilize the device.

A second option is to use each thread to implement an iteration of the outer loop. This option employs fewer threads than the first option. Instead of generating N*M threads, this option generates M threads. Since M corresponds to the number of k-space samples and a large number of samples, on the order of a hundred thousand, are typically used to calculate F^{H}D, this option still exploits a large amount of parallelism. However, this kernel suffers the same problem as the kernel in Fig. 17.5. That is, each thread will write into all rFhD and iFhD elements, thus creating an extremely large number of conflicts between threads. As is the case of Fig. 17.5, the code in Fig. 17.8 requires atomic operations that will significantly slow down the parallel execution. Thus this option does not work well.

A third option is to use each thread to compute one pair of rFhD and iFhD output elements. This option requires us to interchange the inner and outer loops and then use each thread to implement an iteration of the new outer loop. The transformation is shown in Fig. 17.9. Loop interchange is necessary because the loop being implemented by the CUDA threads must be the outer loop. Loop interchange makes each of the new outer loop iterations process a pair of rFhD and iFhD output elements and makes each inner loop collect the contributions of all input elements to this pair of output elements.

```
01  #define FHD_THREADS_PER_BLOCK 1024
02  __global__ void cmpFhD(float* rPhi, iPhi, phiMag,
03          kx, ky, kz, x, y, z, rMu, iMu, int N) {

04    int m = blockIdx.x * FHD_THREADS_PER_BLOCK + threadIdx.x;
05    for (int n = 0; n < N; n++) {
06      float expFhD = 2*PI*(kx[m]*x[n]+ky[m]*y[n]+kz[m]*z[n]);
07      float cArg = cos(expFhD);
08      float sArg = sin(expFhD);
09      atomicAdd(&rFhD[n],rMu[m]*cArg - iMu[m]*sArg);
10      atomicAdd(&iFhD[n],iMu[m]*cArg + rMu[m]*sArg);
11    }
12  }
```

FIGURE 17.8

Second option of the $F^H D$ kernel.

```
01  for (int n = 0; n < N; n++) {
02    for (int m = 0; m < M; m++) {
03      float expFhD = 2*PI*(kx[m]*x[n] + ky[m]*y[n] + kz[m]*z[n]);
04      float cArg = cos(expFhD);
05      float sArg = sin(expFhD);
06      rFhD[n] +=  rMu[m]*cArg - iMu[m]*sArg;
07      iFhD[n] +=  iMu[m]*cArg + rMu[m]*sArg;
08    }
09  }
```

FIGURE 17.9

Loop interchange of the $F^H D$ computation.

Loop interchange is permissible here because all iterations of both levels of loops are independent of each other. They can be executed in any order relative to one another. Loop interchange, which changes the order of the iterations, is allowed when these iterations can be executed in any order. This option allows us to convert the new outer loop into a kernel to be executed by N threads. Since N corresponds to the number of voxels in the reconstructed image, the N value can be very large for higher-resolution images. For a 128^3 image, there are $128^3 = 2,097,152$ threads, resulting in a large amount of parallelism. For higher resolutions, such as 512^3, we may need to either use multidimensional grids, launch multiple grids, or assign multiple voxels to a single thread. The threads in this third option all accumulate into their own rFhD and iFhD elements, since every thread has a unique n value. There is no conflict between threads. This makes this third option the best choice among the three options.

The kernel that is derived from the interchanged loops is shown in Fig. 17.10. The outer loop has been stripped away; each thread covers an iteration of the outer (n) loop, where n is equal to `blockIdx.x*FHD_THREADS_PER_BLOCK + threadIdx.x`. Once this iteration (n) value has been identified, the thread executes the inner (m) loop based on that n value. This kernel can be invoked with a number of threads in each block, specified by a global constant `FHD_THREADS_PER_BLOCK`. Assuming that N is the variable that stores the number of voxels in the reconstructed image,

```
01  #define FHD_THREADS_PER_BLOCK 1024
02  __global__ void cmpFhD(float* rPhi, iPhi, phiMag,
03          kx, ky, kz, x, y, z, rMu, iMu, int M) {

04    int n = blockIdx.x * FHD_THREADS_PER_BLOCK + threadIdx.x;
05    for (int m = 0; m < M; m++) {
06      float expFhD = 2*PI*(kx[m]*x[n]+ky[m]*y[n]+kz[m]*z[n]);
07      float cArg = cos(expFhD);
08      float sArg = sin(expFhD);
09      rFhD[n] +=  rMu[m]*cArg - iMu[m]*sArg;
10      iFhD[n] +=  iMu[m]*cArg + rMu[m]*sArg;
11    }
12  }
```

FIGURE 17.10

Third option of the FHD kernel.

N/FHD_THREADS_PER_BLOCK blocks cover all N iterations of the original loop. For example, if there are 2,097,152 voxels, the kernel could be invoked with a configuration of 1024 threads per block and 2,097,152/1024 = 2048 blocks. In Fig. 17.10 this is done by assigning 1024 to FHD_THREADS_PER_BLOCK and using it as the block size and N/FHD_THREADS_PER_BLOCK as the grid size during kernel innovation.

Step 2: Getting around the memory bandwidth limitation

The simple cmpFhD kernel in Fig. 17.10 will perform significantly better than the kernels in Figs. 17.5 and 17.8 but will still result in limited speedup, owing to memory bandwidth limitations. A quick analysis shows that the execution is limited by the low compute to global memory access ratio of each thread. In the original loop, each iteration performs at least 14 memory accesses: kx[m], ky[m], kz [m], x[n], y[n], z[n], rMu[m] twice, iMu[m] twice, rFhD[n] read and write, and iFhD[n] read and write. Meanwhile, about 13 floating-point multiplication, addition, or trigonometry operations are performed in each iteration. Therefore the compute to global memory access ratio is 13/(14*4)=0.23 OP/B, which is too low according to our analysis in Chapter 5, Memory Architecture and Data Locality. We can immediately improve the compute to global memory access ratio by assigning some of the array elements to automatic variables. As we discussed in Chapter 5, Memory Architecture and Data Locality, the automatic variables will reside in registers, thus converting reads and writes to the global memory into reads and writes to on-chip registers. A quick review of the kernel in Fig. 17.10 shows that for each thread, the same x[n], y[n], and z[n] elements are used across all iterations of the for-loop (lines 05−06). This means that we can load these elements into automatic variables before the execution enters the loop. The kernel can then use the automatic variables inside the loop, thus converting global memory accesses to register accesses. Furthermore, the loop repeatedly reads from and writes into rFhD[n] and iFhD[n]. We can have the iterations read from and write into two automatic variables and write only the contents of these

```
01  #define FHD_THREADS_PER_BLOCK 1024
02  __global__ void cmpFhD(float* rPhi, iPhi, phiMag,
                   kx, ky, kz, x, y, z, rMu, iMu, int M) {

03     int n = blockIdx.x * FHD_THREADS_PER_BLOCK + threadIdx.x;
                   // assign frequently accessed coordinate and output
                   // elements into registers
04     float xn_r = x[n]; float yn_r = y[n]; float zn_r = z[n];
05     float rFhDn_r = rFhD[n]; float iFhDn_r = iFhD[n];
06     for (int m = 0; m < M; m++) {
07        float expFhD = 2*PI*(kx[m]*xn_r+ky[m]*yn_r+kz[m]*zn_r);
08        float cArg = cos(expFhD);
09        float sArg = sin(expFhD);
10        rFhDn_r +=  rMu[m]*cArg - iMu[m]*sArg;
11        iFhDn_r +=  iMu[m]*cArg + rMu[m]*sArg;
12     }
13     rFhD[n] = rFhD_r; iFhD[n] = iFhD_r;
14  }
```

FIGURE 17.11

Using registers to reduce memory accesses in the $F^H D$ kernel.

automatic variables into rFhD[n] and iFhD[n] after the execution exits the loop. The resulting code is shown in Fig. 17.11. By increasing the number of registers used by 5 for each thread, we have reduced the memory access done in each iteration from 14 to 7. Thus we have increased the compute to global memory access ratio from 0.23 OP/B to 0.46 OP/B. This is a good improvement and a good use of the precious register resource.

Recall that the register usage can limit the occupancy, that is, the number of blocks that can run in a streaming multiprocessor (SM). By increasing the register usage by 5 in the kernel code, we increase the register usage of each thread block by 5*FHD_THREADS_PER_BLOCK. Assuming that we have 1024 threads per block, we just increased the block register usage by 5120. Since each SM can accommodate a combined register usage of 65,536 registers among all blocks assigned to it (in SM Version 3.5 or higher), we need to be careful, as any further increase of register usage can begin to limit the number of blocks that can be assigned to an SM. Fortunately, the register usage is not a limiting factor to parallelism for this kernel.

We want to further improve the compute to global memory access ratio by eliminating more global memory accesses in the cmpFhD kernel. The next candidates to consider are the k-space samples kx[m], ky[m], and kz[m]. These array elements are accessed differently than the x[n], y[n], and z[n] elements: Different elements of kx, ky, and kz are accessed in each iteration of the loop in Fig. 17.11. This means that we cannot load a k-space element into a register and expect to access that element off a register through all the iterations. Therefore registers will not help here. However, we should notice that the k-space elements are not modified by the kernel. Also, each k-space element is used across all threads in the grid. This means that we might be able to place the k-space elements into the constant memory. Perhaps the constant cache can eliminate most of the DRAM accesses.

An analysis of the loop in Fig. 17.11 reveals that the k-space elements are indeed excellent candidates for the constant memory. The index used for accessing kx, ky, and kz is m. We know that m is independent of threadIdx, which implies that all threads in a warp will be accessing the same element of kx, ky, and kz. This is an ideal access pattern for cached constant memory: Every time an element is brought into the cache, it will be used at least by all 32 threads in a warp for a current generation device. This means that for every 32 accesses to the constant memory, at least 31 of them will be served by the cache. This allows the cache to effectively eliminate 96% or more of the accesses to the global memory. Better yet, each time when a constant is accessed from the cache, it can be broadcast to all the threads in a warp. This makes constant memory almost as efficient as registers for accessing k-space elements.[2]

However, there is a technical issue involved in placing the k-space elements into the constant memory. Recall that constant memory has a capacity of 64KB. However, the size of the k-space samples can be much larger, on the order of millions. A typical way of working around the limitation of constant memory capacity is to break a large dataset down into chunks of 64KB or smaller. The developer must reorganize the kernel so that the kernel will be invoked multiple times, with each invocation of the kernel consuming only a chunk of the large dataset. This turns out to be quite easy for the cmpFhD kernel.

A careful examination of the loop in Fig. 17.11 reveals that all threads will sequentially march through the k-space sample arrays. That is, all threads in the grid access the same k-space element during each iteration. For large datasets the loop in the kernel simply iterates more times. This means that we can divide the loop into sections, with each section processing a chunk of the k-space elements that fit into the 64KB capacity of the constant memory.[3] The host code now invokes the kernel multiple times. Each time the host invokes the kernel, it places a new chunk into the constant memory before calling the kernel function. This is illustrated in Fig. 17.12. (For more recent devices and CUDA versions, a "const __restrict__" declaration of kernel parameters makes the corresponding input data available in the read-only data cache, which is a simpler way of getting the same effect as using constant memory.)

In Fig. 17.12 the `cmpFhD` kernel is called from a loop. The code assumes that kx, ky, and kz arrays are in the host memory. The dimension of kx, ky, and kz is given by M. At each iteration the host code calls the `cudaMemcpyToSymbol()` function to transfer a chunk of the k-space data into the device constant memory, as was discussed in Chapter 7 Convolution, The kernel is then invoked to process

---

[2] The reason why a constant memory access is not exactly as efficient as a register access is that a memory load instruction is still needed for access to the constant memory.

[3] Note that not all accesses to read-only data are as favorable for constant memory as what we have here. In some applications, threads in different blocks access different input elements in the same iteration. Such more diverged access pattern makes it much harder to fit enough of the data into the constant memory for a kernel launch.

```
__constant__ float kx_c[CHUNK_SIZE], ky_c[CHUNK_SIZE], kz_c[CHUNK_SIZE];
...

void main() {
  for (int i = 0; i < M/CHUNK_SIZE; i++);
    cudaMemcpyToSymbol(kx_c,&kx[i*CHUNK_SIZE],4*CHUNK_SIZE,
            cudaMemCpyHostToDevice);
    cudaMemcpyToSymbol(ky_c,&ky[i*CHUNK_SIZE],4*CHUNK_SIZE,
            cudaMemCpyHostToDevice);
    cudaMemcpyToSymbol(kz_c,&kz[i*CHUNK_SIZE],4*CHUNK_SIZE,
            cudaMemCpyHostToDevice);

    ...
    cmpFhD<<<FHD_THREADS_PER_BLOCK, N/FHD_THREADS_PER_BLOCK>>>(rPhi,
                    iPhi, phiMag, x, y, z, rMu, iMu, CHUNK_SIZE);
  }
  /* Need to call kernel one more time if M is not */
  /* perfect multiple of CHUNK SIZE */
}
```

FIGURE 17.12

Host code sequence for chunking k-space data to fit into constant memory.

```
01  #define FHD_THREADS_PER_BLOCK 1024
02  __global__ void cmpFhD(float* rPhi, iPhi, phiMag,
03                          x, y, z, rMu, iMu, int M) {
04    int n = blockIdx.x * FHD_THREADS_PER_BLOCK + threadIdx.x;
05    float xn_r = x[n]; float yn_r = y[n]; float zn_r = z[n];
06    float rFhDn_r = rFhD[n]; float iFhDn_r = iFhD[n];
07    for (int m = 0; m < M; m++) {
08      float expFhD = 2*PI*(kx_c[m]*xn_r+ky_c[m]*yn_r+kz_c[m]*zn_r);
09      float cArg = cos(expFhD);
10      float sArg = sin(expFhD);
11      rFhDn_r +=  rMu[m]*cArg - iMu[m]*sArg;
12      iFhDn_r +=  iMu[m]*cArg + rMu[m]*sArg;
13    }
14    rFhD[n] = rFhD_r; iFhD[n] = iFhD_r;
15  }
```

FIGURE 17.13

Revised F^HD kernel to use constant memory.

the chunk. Note that when M is not a perfect multiple of CHUNK_SIZE, the host code will need to have an additional round of cudaMemcpyToSymbol() and one more kernel invocation to finish the remaining k-space data.

Fig. 17.13 shows a revised kernel that accesses the k-space data from the constant memory. Note that pointers to kx, ky, and kz are no longer in the parameter list of the kernel function. The kx_c, ky_c, and kz_c arrays are accessed as global variables declared under __constant__ keyword, as shown in Fig. 17.12. By accessing these elements from the constant cache, the kernel now has effectively only four global memory accesses to the rMu and iMu arrays. The compiler will typically recognize that the four array accesses are made to only two locations. It will perform only two global accesses, one to `rMu[m]` and one to `iMu[m]`. The values will be stored in temporary register variables for use in the other two. This makes the final number of memory accesses equal to 2. The compute to memory access ratio is up to 1.63 OP/B. This is still not quite ideal but is sufficiently high that the memory bandwidth limitation is no longer the only factor that limits performance. As we will see, we can perform a few other optimizations that make the computation more efficient and further improve performance.

If we ran the code in Figs. 17.12 and 17.13, we would have found out that the performance enhancement was not as high as we expected for some devices. As it turns out, the code shown in these figures does not result in as much memory bandwidth reduction as we expected. The reason is that the constant cache does not perform very well for the code. This has to do with the design of the constant cache and the memory layout of the k-space data. As is shown in Fig. 17.14A, each constant cache entry is designed to store multiple consecutive words. This design reduces the cost of constant cache hardware. When an element is brought into the cache, several elements around it are also brought into the cache. This is illustrated as shaded sections surrounding kx[i], ky[i], and kz[i], which are shown as dark boxes in Fig. 17.14. Three cache lines in the constant cache are needed to support the efficient execution of each iteration of a warp.

In a typical execution we will have a fairly large number of warps that are concurrently executing on an SM. Since different warps can be at very different iterations, they may require many constant cache entries altogether. For example, if we define each thread block to have 1024 threads and expect to assign two blocks to execute concurrently in each SM, we will have (1024/32) × 2=64 warps executing concurrently in an SM. If each of them requires a minimum of three cache lines in the constant cache to sustain efficient execution, in the worst case, we need a total of 64 × 3=192 cache lines. Even if we assume that, on average, three warps will be executing at the same iteration

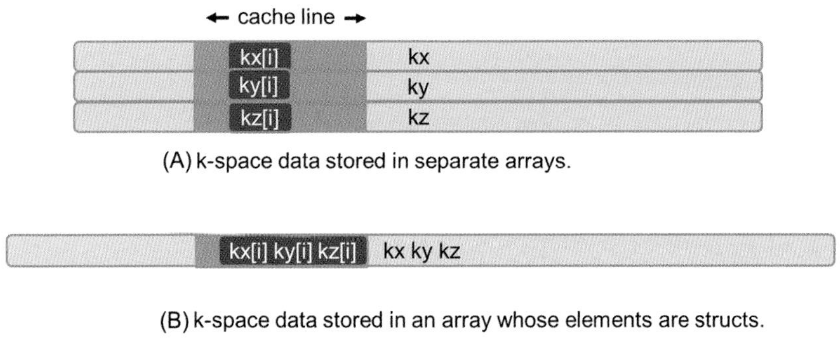

(A) k-space data stored in separate arrays.

(B) k-space data stored in an array whose elements are structs.

FIGURE 17.14

Effect of k-space data layout on constant cache efficiency: (A) k-space data stored in separate arrays, (B) k-space data stored in an array whose elements are structs.

and thus can share cache lines, we still need 64 cache lines. This is referred to as the working set of all the active warps.

Because of cost constraints, the constant caches of some devices have a small number of cache lines, such as 32. When there are not enough cache lines to accommodate the entire working set, the data that are being accessed by different warps begin to compete with each other for the cache lines. By the time a warp moves to its next iteration, the next elements to be accessed have already been purged to make room for the elements that have been accessed by other warps. As it turns out, the constant cache capacity in some devices is indeed insufficient to accommodate the entries for all the warps that are active in an SM. As a result, the constant cache fails to eliminate many of the global memory accesses.

The problem of inefficient use of cache entries has been well studied in the literature and can be solved by adjusting the memory layout of the k-space data. The solution is illustrated in Fig. 17.14B, and the code based on this solution is shown in Figs. 17.15 and 17.16. Rather than having the x, y, and z components of the k-space data stored in three separate arrays, the solution stores these components in an array whose elements make up a struct. In the literature this style of declaration is often referred to as *array of structures*. The declaration of the array is shown in Fig. 17.15 (lines 01−03). We assume that the memory allocation and initialization code (not shown) has placed the x, y, and z components of the k-

```
01   struct kdata {
02       float x, float y, float z;
03   };

04   __constant__ struct kdata k_c[CHUNK_SIZE];
05   …
06   void main() {
07       for (int i = 0; i < M/CHUNK_SIZE; i++){
08           cudaMemcpyToSymbol(k_c,k,12*CHUNK_SIZE,cudaMemCpyHostToDevice);
10           cmpFhD<<<FHD_THREADS_PER_BLOCK, N/FHD_THREADS_PER_BLOCK>>>(…);
11       }
12   }
```

FIGURE 17.15

Adjusting k-space data layout to improve cache efficiency.

```
01   __global__ void cmpFhD(float* rPhi, iPhi, phiMag,
02                          x, y, z, rMu, iMu, int M) {
03       int n = blockIdx.x * FHD_THREADS_PER_BLOCK + threadIdx.x;
04       float xn_r = x[n]; float yn_r = y[n]; float zn_r = z[n];
05       float rFhDn_r = rFhD[n]; float iFhDn_r = iFhD[n];

06       for (int m = 0; m < M; m++) {
07           float expFhD = 2*PI*(k[m].x*xn_r + k[m].y*yn_r + k[m].z*zn_r);
08           float cArg = cos(expFhD);
09           float sArg = sin(expFhD);
10           rFhDn_r +=  rMu[m]*cArg - iMu[m]*sArg;
11           iFhDn_r +=  iMu[m]*cArg + rMu[m]*sArg;
12       }
13       rFhD[n] = rFhD_r; iFhD[n] = iFhD_r;
14   }
```

FIGURE 17.16

Adjusting for the k-space data memory layout in the F^{H}D kernel.

space data into the fields properly. By storing the x, y, and z components in the three fields of an array element, the developer forces these components to be stored in consecutive locations of the constant memory. Therefore all three components that are used by an iteration of a warp can now fit into one cache entry, reducing the number of entries needed to support the execution of all the active warps. Note that since we have only one array to hold all k-space data, we can just use one CUDA Memcpy To Symbol to copy the entire chunk to the device constant memory. Assuming that each k-space sample is a single-precision floating-point number, the size of the transfer is adjusted from `4*CHUNK_SIZE` to `12*CHUNK_SIZE` to reflect the transfer of all the three components in one CUDA Memcpy To Symbol call.

With the new data structure layout, we also need to revise the kernel so that the access is done according to the new layout. The new kernel is shown in Fig. 17.16. Note that kx[m] has become k[m].x, ky[m] has become k[m].y, and so on. This small change to the code can result in significant enhancement of its execution speed on some devices.[4]

Step 3: Using hardware trigonometry functions

CUDA offers hardware implementations of mathematical functions that provide much higher throughput than their software counterparts. A motivation for GPUs to offer such hardware implementations for trigonometry functions such as `sin( )` and `cos( )` is to improve the speed of view angle transformations in graphics applications. These functions are implemented as hardware instructions executed by the SFU (special function units). The procedure for using these functions is quite easy. In the case of the `cmpFhD` kernel, what we need to do is to change the calls to `sin( )` and `cos( )` functions into their hardware versions: `__sin()` and `__cos()` (two "_" characters before the function name). These are intrinsic functions that are recognized by the compiler and translated into SFU instructions. Because these functions are called in a heavily executed loop body, we expect that the change will result in a significant performance improvement. The resulting `cmpFhD` kernel is shown in Fig. 17.17.

However, we need to be careful about the reduced accuracy in switching from software functions to hardware functions. Hardware implementations currently have less accuracy than software libraries (the details are available in the CUDA C Programming Guide). In the case of MRI we need to make sure that the hardware implementation provides enough accuracy, as defined in Fig. 17.18. The testing process involves a "perfect" image (I_0) of a fictitious object, sometimes referred to as a

---

[4] The reader might notice that the adjustment from multiple arrays to an array of structures is the opposite of what is often done to global memory data. When adjacent threads in a warp access consecutive elements of an array of structures in global memory, it is much better to store the fields of the structure into multiple arrays so that the global memory accesses are coalesced. The key difference here is that all threads in a warp are accessing the same elements, not consecutive ones.

```
01  #define FHD_THREADS_PER_BLOCK 1024
02  __global__ void cmpFhD(float* rPhi, iPhi, phiMag,
03          x, y, z, rMu, iMu, int M) {

04      int n = blockIdx.x * FHD_THREADS_PER_BLOCK + threadIdx.x;
05      float xn_r = x[n]; float yn_r = y[n]; float zn_r = z[n];
06      float rFhDn_r = rFhD[n]; float iFhDn_r = iFhD[n];
07      for (int m = 0; m < M; m++) {
08          float expFhD = 2*PI*(k[m].x*xn_r+k[m].y*yn_r+k[m].z*zn_r);
09          float cArg = __cos(expFhD);
10          float sArg = __sin(expFhD);
11          rFhDn_r +=  rMu[m]*cArg - iMu[m]*sArg;
12          iFhDn_r +=  iMu[m]*cArg + rMu[m]*sArg;
13      }
14      rFhD[n] = rFhD_r; iFhD[n] = iFhD_r;
15  }
```

FIGURE 17.17

Using hardware __sin() and __cos() functions.

A.N. Netravali and B.G. Haskell, Digital Pictures: Representation, Compression, and Standards (2nd Ed), Plenum Press, New York, NY (1995).

$$MSE = \frac{1}{mn}\sum_i \sum_j (I(i,j) - I_0(i,j))^2 \qquad PSNR = 20\log_{10}(\frac{\max(I_0(i,j))}{\sqrt{MSE}})$$

FIGURE 17.18

Metrics used to validate the accuracy of hardware functions. I_0 is the perfect image. I is the reconstructed image. PSNR is peak signal-to-noise ratio.

phantom object. We use a reverse process to generate a corresponding "scanned" k-space data that is synthesized. The synthesized scanned data is then processed by the proposed reconstruction system to generate a reconstructed image (I). The values of the voxels in the perfect and reconstructed images are then fed into the peak signal-to-noise ratio (PSNR) formula in Fig. 17.18.

The criteria for passing the test depend on the application for which the image is intended. In our case, we worked with experts in clinical MRI to ensure that the PSNR changes due to hardware functions were well within the accepted limits for their applications. In applications in which the images are used by physicians to form an impression of injury or to evaluate a disease, one also needs to have visual inspection of the image quality. Fig. 17.19 shows the visual comparison of the original "true" image. It then shows that the PSNR that is achieved by CPU double-precision and single-precision implementations are both 27.6 dB, well above the acceptable level for the application. A visual inspection also shows that the reconstructed image indeed corresponds well with the original image.

The advantage of iterative reconstruction compared to a simple bilinear interpolation gridding/iFFT is also obvious in Fig. 17.19. The image reconstructed with the simple gridding/iFFT has a PSNR of only 16.8 dB, substantially lower than the PSNR of 27.6 dB that is achieved by the iterative reconstruction method.

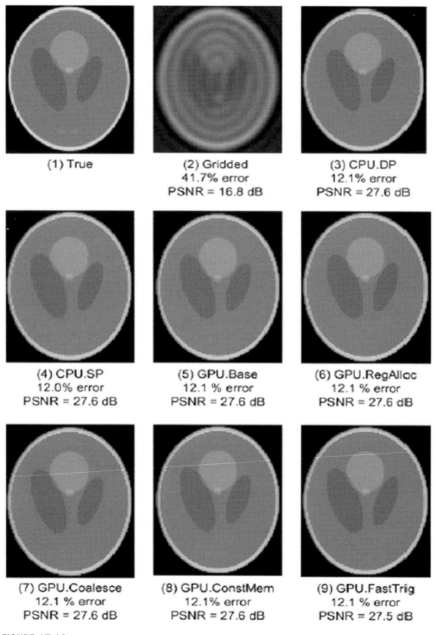

FIGURE 17.19

Validation of floating-point precision and accuracy of the different F^{H}D implementations.

A visual inspection of the gridding/iFFT image in Fig. 17.19 (image 2) shows that there are severe artifacts that can significantly affect the usability of the image for diagnostic purposes. These artifacts do not occur in the images from the iterative reconstruction method.

When we moved from double-precision arithmetic to single-precision arithmetic on the CPU, there was no measurable degradation of PSNR, which remained at 27.6 dB. When we moved the trigonometry function from the software library to the hardware units, we observed a negligible degradation of PSNR, from 27.6 dB to 27.5 dB. The slight loss of PSNR is within an acceptable range for the application. A visual inspection confirms that the reconstructed image does not have significant artifacts compared to the original image.

Step 4: Experimental performance tuning

Up to this point, we have not determined the appropriate values for the configuration parameters of the kernel. One kernel configuration parameter is the number of threads per block. Using an adequate number of threads per block is needed to fully utilize the thread capacity of each SM. Another kernel configuration parameter is the number of times one should unroll the body of the for-loop in Fig. 17.17 (line 07). This can be set by using a "#pragma unroll" followed by the number of unrolls that we want the compiler to perform on a loop. On one hand, unrolling the loop can reduce the number of overhead instructions and potentially reduce the number of clock cycles to process each k-space sample data. On the other hand, too much unrolling can potentially increase the usage of registers and reduce the number of blocks that can fit into an SM.

Note that the effects of these configurations are not isolated from each other. Increasing one parameter value can potentially use the resource that could have been used to increase another parameter value. As a result, one needs to evaluate these parameters jointly in an experimental manner. There can be a large number of combinations to try. In the case of F^HD, the performance improves about 20% by systematically searching all the combinations and choosing the one with the best measured runtime, as compared to a heuristic tuning search effort that explores only some promising trends. Ryoo et al. (2008) present a Pareto optimal curve–based method to screen away most of the inferior combinations.

17.4 Summary

In this chapter we presented the key steps for parallelizing and optimizing a loop-intensive application—iterative reconstruction of MRI images—from its sequential form. We started with the appropriate organization of parallelization: the scatter approach versus the gather approach. We showed that transforming from a scatter approach to a gather approach is key to avoiding atomic operations, which can significantly reduce the performance of parallel execution. We discussed the practical techniques, that is, loop fission and loop interchange, that are needed to enable the gather approach to parallelization.

We further presented the application of optimization techniques, such as promoting array elements into registers, using constant memory/cache for input elements, and using hardware functions to improve the performance of the parallel kernel. There is about a $10\times$ speed improvement going from the basic version to the final optimized version, as was discussed.

Before parallelization and optimization, F^HD used to account for nearly 100% of the execution time. An interesting observation is that in the end, the CG solver (the "find ρ" step in Fig. 17.3) can actually take more time than F^HD. This is because we have accelerated F^HD dramatically. Any further acceleration will now require acceleration of the CG solver. After successful parallelization and optimization, F^HD accounts for only about 50%. The other 50% is largely spent in the CG solver. This is a well-known phenomenon in parallelizing real applications. Because some time-consuming phases of the execution are accelerated by successful parallelization efforts, the execution time becomes dominated by other phases that used to account for insignificant portions of the execution.

Exercises

1. Loop fission splits a loop into two loops. Use the F^HD code in Fig. 17.4 and enumerate the execution order of the two parts of the outer loop body: (1) the statements before the inner loop and (2) the inner loop.
a. List the execution order of these parts from different iterations of the outer loop before fission.
b. List the execution order of these parts from the two loops after fission.
c. Determine whether the execution results in parts (a) and (b) of this exercise will be identical. The execution results are identical if all data required by a part are properly generated and preserved for its consumption before that part executes and the execution result of the part is not overwritten by other parts that should come after the part in the original execution order.
2. Loop interchange swaps the inner loop into the outer loop and vice versa. Use the loops from Fig. 17.9 and enumerate the execution order of the instances of loop body before and after the loop exchange.
a. List the execution order of the loop body from different iterations before loop interchange. Identify these iterations with the values of m and n.
b. List the execution order of the loop body from different iterations after loop interchange. Identify these iterations with the values of m and n.
c. Determine whether the execution results in parts (a) and (b) of this exercise will be identical. The execution results are identical if all data required by a

part are properly generated and preserved for its consumption before that part executes and the execution result of the part is not overwritten by other parts that should come after the part in the original execution order.

3. In Fig. 17.11, identify the difference between the access to x[] and kx[] in the nature of indices used. Use the difference to explain why it does not make sense to try to load kx[n] into a register for the kernel shown in Fig. 17.11.

References

Liang, Z.P., Lauterbur, P., 1999. Principles of Magnetic Resonance Imaging: A Signal Processing Perspective. John Wiley and Sons.

Ryoo, S., Ridrigues, C.I., Stone, S.S., Stratton, J.A., Ueng, Z., Baghsorkhi, S.S., et al., 2008. Program optimization carving for GPU computing. J. Parallel Distrib. Comput. Available from: https://doi.org/10.1016/j.jpdc.2008.050.011.

Stone, S.S., Haldar, J.P., Tsao, S.C., Hwu, W.W., Sutton, B.P., Liang, Z.P., 2008. Accelerating advanced MRI reconstruction on GPUs. J. Parallel Distrib. Comput. 68 (10), 1307−1318. Available from: https://doi.org/10.1016/j.jpdc.2008.050.013.

Electrostatic potential map

18

With special contributions from John Stone

Chapter Outline

18.1 Background 415
18.2 Scatter versus gather in kernel design 417
18.3 Thread coarsening 422
18.4 Memory coalescing 424
18.5 Cutoff binning for data size scalability 425
18.6 Summary 430
Exercises 431
References 431

The previous case study used a statistical estimation application to illustrate the process of selecting an appropriate level of a loop nest for parallel execution, transforming the loops for reduced memory access interference, using constant memory for magnifying the memory bandwidth for read-only data, using registers to reduce the consumption of memory bandwidth, and using special hardware functional units to accelerate trigonometry functions. In this case study, we use a molecular dynamics application based on regular grid data structures to illustrate the use of optimization techniques that achieve global memory access, coalescing and improved computation throughput. As we did in the previous case study, we present a series of implementations of an electrostatic potential map calculation kernel in which each version improves on the previous one. Each version adopts one or more practical techniques from Chapter 6, Performance Considerations. Some of the techniques were used in the previous case study, but some are different: systematic reuse of computational results, thread granularity coarsening, and fast boundary condition checking. This application case study shows that the effective use of these practical techniques can significantly improve the execution throughput of the application.

18.1 Background

This case study is based on visual molecular dynamics (VMD) (Humphrey et al., 1996), a popular software system that was designed for displaying, animating, and analyzing biomolecular systems. VMD has more than 200,000 registered users. It is an important foundation for a modern "computational microscope" with which biologists can observe tiny life forms, such as viruses, that are too small for traditional microscopy techniques. While it has strong built-in support for analyzing biomolecular systems, such as calculating electrostatic potential values at spatial grid points of a molecular system (the focus of this chapter), it has also been a popular tool for displaying other large datasets, such as sequencing data, quantum chemistry simulation data, and volumetric data, owing to its versatility and user extensibility.

While VMD is designed to run on a diverse range of hardware, including laptops, desktops, clusters, and supercomputers, most users use VMD as a desktop science application for interactive three-dimensional (3D) visualization and analysis. For computation that runs too long for interactive use, VMD can also be used in a batch mode to render movies for later use. A motivation for accelerating VMD is to make batch mode jobs fast enough for interactive use. This can drastically improve the productivity of scientific investigations. With CUDA devices widely available in desktop PCs, such acceleration can have broad impact on the VMD user community. To date, multiple aspects of VMD have been accelerated with CUDA, including electrostatic potential map calculation, ion placement, molecular orbital calculation and display, and imaging of gas migration pathways in proteins.

The computation covered in this case study is the calculation of electrostatic potential maps in a grid space. This calculation is often used in the placement of ions into a molecular structure for molecular dynamics simulation. Fig. 18.1

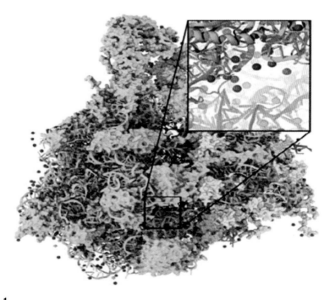

FIGURE 18.1

Electrostatic potential map used in building stable structures for molecular dynamics simulation.

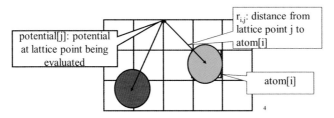

potential[j]: potential at lattice point being evaluated

$r_{i,j}$: distance from lattice point j to atom[i]

atom[i]

FIGURE 18.2

The contribution of atom[i] to the electrostatic potential at lattice point j (potential[j]) is atom[i]. charge/r_{ij}. In the direct coulomb summation method, the total potential at lattice point j is the sum of contributions from all atoms in the system.

shows the placement of ions into a protein structure in preparation for a molecular dynamics simulation. In this application the electrostatic potential map is used to identify spatial locations where ions (red dots) can fit in according to physical laws. The function can also be used to calculate time-averaged electrical field potential maps during molecular dynamics simulation, which is useful for the simulation process as well as the visualization and analysis of simulation results.

There are several methods for calculating electrostatic potential maps. Among them, direct Coulomb summation (DCS) is a highly accurate method that is particularly suitable for GPUs (Stone et al., 2007). The DCS method calculates the electrostatic potential value of each grid point as the sum of contributions from all atoms in the system. This is illustrated in Fig. 18.2. The contribution of atom i to a lattice point j is the charge of atom i divided by the distance from lattice point j to atom i. Since this needs to be done for all grid points and all atoms, the number of calculations is proportional to the product of the total number of atoms in the system and the total number of grid points. For a realistic molecular system this product can be very large. Therefore the calculation of the electrostatic potential map has been traditionally done as a batch job in VMD.

18.2 Scatter versus gather in kernel design

Fig. 18.3 shows the base C code of the DCS code. The function is written to process a two-dimensional (2D) slice of a 3D grid. The function will be called repeatedly for all the slices of the modeled space. The structure of the function is quite simple with three levels of `for` loops. The outer two levels iterate over the y dimension and the x dimension of the grid point space. For each grid point, the innermost for loop iterates over all atoms, calculating the contribution of electrostatic potential energy from all atoms to the grid point. Note that each atom is represented by four consecutive elements of the atoms[] array. The first three elements store the x, y, and z coordinates of the atom and the fourth element the electrical charge of the atom. At the end of the innermost loop, the accumulated

```
01 void cenergy(float *energygrid, dim3 grid, float gridspacing, float z,
02                 const float *atoms, int numatoms) {
03   int atomarrdim = numatoms * 4; //x,y,z, and charge info for each atom
04   for (int j=0; j<grid.y; j++) {
         // calculate y coordinate of the grid point based on j
05     float y = gridspacing * (float) j;
06     for (int i=0; i<grid.x; i++) {
           // calculate x coordinate based on i
07       float x = gridspacing * (float) i;
08       float energy = 0.0f;
09       for (int n=0; n<atomarrdim; n+=4) {
10         float dx = x - atoms[n  ];
11         float dy = y - atoms[n+1];
12         float dz = z - atoms[n+2];
13         energy += atoms[n+3] / sqrtf(dx*dx + dy*dy+ dz*dz);
14       }
15       energygrid[grid.x*grid.y*z + grid.x*j + i] = energy;
16     }
17   }
18 }
```

FIGURE 18.3

An unoptimized direct Coulomb summation C code for a two-dimensional slice.

value of the grid point is written out to the grid data structure. The outer loops then iterate and take the execution to the next grid point.

Note that the DCS function in Fig. 18.3 calculates the x and y coordinates of each grid point on the fly by multiplying the grid point index values by the spacing between grid points. This is a uniform grid method in which all grid points are spaced at the same distance in all three dimensions. The function takes advantage of the fact that all the grid points in the same slice have the same z coordinate. This value is precalculated by the caller of the function and passed in as a function parameter (z). There are, however, several optimizations that can be done to the sequential C code in Fig. 18.3 to significantly improve its execution speed.

Fig. 18.4 shows a C code for DCS with a few optimizations to improve its execution speed and efficiency. First, the innermost loop (n-loop) in Fig. 18.3 has been exchanged into the outermost loop (line 05 in Fig. 18.4). Thus the code iterates over all atoms. For each atom the inner loops (i-loop and j-loop) scatter the contribution of the atom to all the grid points. As we discussed in Chapter 17, Iterative Magnetic Resonance Imaging Reconstruction, the loop interchange is permissible because the three levels of loops in Fig. 18.3 are perfectly nested and all the iterations are independent of each other.

The loop interchange enables two optimizations. First, the z components of the distance between an atom and all grid points in the plane are identical and can be calculated once for the entire slice of the grid point. Therefore the calculation can be done outside the two inner loops (lines 6–7). Similarly, the y components of distance between an atom and all grid points in the same row are identical and can be done outside the innermost loop (lines 11–12). In comparison, the y and z components of the distance were both calculated in the innermost loop in Fig. 18.3. This drastic reduction in the number of calculations makes the

```
01  void cenergy(float *energygrid, dim3 grid, float gridspacing, float z,
02                const float *atoms, int numatoms) {
03    int atomarrdim = numatoms * 4; //x,y,z, and charge info for each atom
      // starting point of the slice in the energy grid
04    int grid_slice_offset = (grid.x*grid.y*z) / gridspacing;
      // calculate potential contribution of each atom
05    for (int n=0; n<atomarrdim; n+=4) {
06      float dz = z - atoms[n+2];   // all grid points in a slice have the same
07      float dz2 = dz*dz;           // z  value, no recalculation in inner loops
08      float charge = atoms[n+3];
09      for (int j=0; j<grid.y; j++) {
10        float y = gridspacing * (float) j;
11        float dy = y - atoms[n+1];  // all grid points in a row have the same
12        float dy2 = dy*dy;          // y value
13        int grid_row_offset =  grid_slice_offset+ grid.x*j;
14        for (int i=0; i<grid.x; i++) {
15          float x = gridspacing * (float) i;
16          float dx = x - atoms[n   ];
17          energygrid[grid_row_offset+i] += charge / sqrtf(dx*dx + dy2+ dz2);
18        }
19      }
20    }
21  }
```

FIGURE 18.4

An optimized direct Coulomb summation C code for a two-dimensional slice.

C code in Fig. 18.4 much faster. These optimizations cannot be done in Fig. 18.3 because the innermost loop iterates over all atoms, so one must recalculate the x, y, and z components of the distance as they change from atom to atom.

For GPU execution we assume that the host program inputs and maintains the atomic charges and their coordinates in the system memory. It also maintains the grid point data structure in the system memory. The DCS kernel is designed to process a 2D slice of the electrostatic potential grid point structure (not to be confused with thread grids). These grid points are like the grid points for discretization that were discussed in Chapter 8, Stencil. For each 2D slice, the CPU transfers its grid data to the device global memory. Similar to the k-space data (Chapter 17, Iterative Magnetic Resonance Imaging Reconstruction), the atom information is divided into chunks to fit into the constant memory. For each chunk of the atom information, the CPU transfers the chunk into the device constant memory, invokes the DCS kernel to calculate the contribution of the current chunk to the current slice, and prepares to transfer the next chunk. After all chunks of the atom information have been processed for the current slice, the slice is transferred back to update the grid point data structure in the CPU system memory. The system then moves on to the next slice.

Let us now focus on the design of DCS kernel. It is natural to parallelize the optimized C code in Fig. 18.4. The resulting kernel is shown in Fig. 18.5. The defined constant CHUNK_SIZE specifies the number of atoms that should be transferred into the GPU constant memory for each kernel call. The value of CHUNK_SIZE*4 should be less than or equal to 64K. The kernel uses each thread to implement an iteration of the outermost loop in Fig. 18.4 and scatters the contribution of its assigned atom to

```
01   __constant__ float atoms[CHUNK_SIZE*4];
02   void __global__ cenergy(float *energygrid, dim3 grid, float gridspacing,
03                           float z) {
04     int n = (blockIdx.x * blockDim .x + threadIdx.x) * 4;
05     float dz = z-atoms[n+2];  // all grid points in a slice have the same
06     float dz2 = dz*dz;        // z value
       // starting position of the slice in the energy grid
07     int grid_slice_offset = (grid.x*grid.y*z) / gridspacing;
08     float charge = atoms[n+3];
09     for (int j=0; j<grid.y; j++) {
10       float y = gridspacing * (float) j;
11       float dy = y-atoms[n+1];   // all grid points in a row have the same
12       float dy2 = dy*dy;         // y value
         // starting position of the row in the energy grid
13       int grid_row_offset =  grid_slice_offset+ grid.x*j;
14       for (int i=0; i<grid.x; i++) {
15         float x = gridspacing * (float) i;
16         float dx = x - atoms[n   ];
17         atomicAdd(&energygrid[grid_row_offset+i],
18                   charge / sqrtf(dx*dx+dy2+dz2));
19       }
20     }
21   }
```

FIGURE 18.5

Direct Coulomb summation kernel using the scatter approach.

all grid points. Unfortunately, as we learned in Chapter 17, Iterative Magnetic Resonance Imaging Reconstruction, this scatter approach to parallelization requires atomic operations for updating the energy grid points (lines 17−18), which significantly reduces the speed of parallel execution.

As we learned in Chapter 17, Iterative Magnetic Resonance Imaging Reconstruction, we can instead use a gather approach in which each thread calculates the accumulated contributions of all atoms to one grid point. This is a preferred approach, since each thread will be writing into its own grid point and there is no need to use atomic operations. However, this requires the loops to be arranged in the ordering of the unoptimized C code in Fig. 18.3; that is, we would be parallelizing a slower C implementation. This exemplifies a frequently experienced dilemma in parallelizing applications: The optimized sequential code is not as amenable to parallelization as the unoptimized sequential code is. The downside is that we can end up with drastically slower execution within each thread, which can reduce the speed benefit of parallelization. We will return to this point later in this chapter.

Fig. 18.6 shows a kernel based on the gather approach. The kernel is based on the unoptimized C code in Fig. 18.3. We form a 2D thread grid that matches the 2D potential grid point organization. To do so, we need to modify the two outer loops in lines 04−06 of Fig. 18.3 into perfectly nested loops so that we can use each thread to execute one iteration of the two-level loop. We can either perform a loop fission (as we did in the previous case study) or move the calculation of the y coordinate (line 05 of Fig. 18.3) into the inner loop. The former would require us to create a new array to hold all y values and would result in two kernels communicating data through the

```
01  __constant__ float atoms[CHUNK_SIZE*4];
02  void __global__ cenergy(float *energygrid, dim3 grid, float gridspacing,
03                          float z, int numatoms) {
04    int i = blockIdx.x * blockDim.x + threadIdx.x;
05    int j = blockIdx.y * blockDim.y + threadIdx.y;
06    int atomarrdim = numatoms * 4;
07    int k = z / gridspacing;
08    float y = gridspacing * (float) j;
09    float x = gridspacing * (float) i;
10    float energy = 0.0f;
      // calculate potential contribution from all atoms
11    for (int n=0; n<atomarrdim; n+=4) {
12      float dx = x - atoms[n  ];
13      float dy = y - atoms[n+1];
14      float dz = z - atoms[n+2];
15      energy += atoms[n+3] / sqrtf(dx*dx + dy*dy + dz*dz);
16    }
17    energygrid[grid.x*grid.y*k + grid.x*j + i] += energy;
18  }
```

FIGURE 18.6

Direct Coulomb summation kernel using the gather approach.

global memory. The latter increases the number of times that the y coordinate will be calculated. In this case, we choose to perform the latter, since there is only a small amount of calculation that can be easily accommodated in the inner loop without significantly increasing the execution time of the inner loop. The amount of work to be absorbed into the inner loop is much smaller than that in Chapter 17, Iterative Magnetic Resonance Imaging Reconstruction. The former would have added a kernel launch overhead for a kernel in which threads do little work. The selected transformation allows all i and j iterations to be executed in parallel. This is a tradeoff between the amount of calculation done and the level of parallelism achieved.

Inside the kernel code in Fig. 18.6, the outer two levels of the loop in Fig. 18.3 have been removed and are replaced by the execution configuration parameters in the kernel invocation (lines 04−05 of Fig. 18.6). Within each thread grid, the thread blocks are organized to calculate the electrostatic potential of tiles of the grid structure. In the simplest kernel, each thread calculates the value at one grid point. In more sophisticated kernels, each thread calculates multiple grid points and exploits the redundancy between the calculations of the grid points to improve execution speed. This is an example of the thread coarsening optimization discussed in Chapter 6, Performance Considerations and will be discussed in the next section.

The performance of the kernel in Fig. 18.6 is quite good, since its execution speed is not hampered by atomic operations. Also, a quick glance over the code shows that each thread does nine floating-point operations for every four memory elements accessed. These atoms[] array elements for each atom are cached in a hardware constant cache memory in each streaming multiprocessor (SM) and are broadcast to many threads. The massive reuse of these constant memory elements across threads makes the constant cache extremely effective, eliminating the vast majority of the DRAM accesses. As a result, global memory bandwidth is not a limiting factor for this kernel.

18.3 Thread coarsening

Although the kernel in Fig. 18.6 avoids the global memory bottleneck through constant caching, it still needs to execute four constant memory access instructions for every nine floating-point operations performed. These memory access instructions consume hardware resources that could otherwise be used to increase the execution throughput of floating-point instructions. Furthermore, the execution of these memory access instructions consumes energy, an important limiting factor for many large-scale parallel computing systems. This section shows that we can use the thread coarsening technique to fuse several threads together so that the atoms[] data can be fetched once from the constant memory, stored in registers, and used for multiple grid points.

Furthermore, as shown in Fig. 18.7, all energy grid points along the same row (y dimension) have the same y coordinate. Therefore the difference between the y coordinate of an atom and the y coordinate of any grid point along a row has the same value. In the DCS kernel in Fig. 18.6, this calculation is redundantly done by all threads for all grid points in a row when calculating the distance between the atom and the grid points. We can eliminate this redundancy and improve the execution efficiency.

The idea is to have each thread calculate the electrostatic potential for multiple energy grid points in the same row. The kernel in Fig. 18.8 has each thread calculate four grid points. For each atom the code calculates dy, the difference of the y coordinates, only once (line 21). It then calculates the expression dy*dy + dz*dz and saves it to the automatic variable dysqdzsq, which is assigned to a register (line 23). This value is the same for all four grid points. The electrical charge information is also accessed from constant memory and stored in the automatic variable charge (line 24). Therefore the calculation of energy0 through energy3 can all just use the values stored in the registers.

Similarly, the x coordinate of the atom is also read from constant memory and used to calculate dx0 through dx3 (lines 17−20). Altogether, this kernel eliminates three accesses to constant memory for the y coordinate of its atom, three accesses for the x coordinate of its atom, three accesses for the charge of the atom, three floating-point subtraction operations, five floating-point multiply operations, and nine floating-point add operations in processing an atom for four grid points. A quick inspection of the kernel code in Fig. 18.8 shows that each

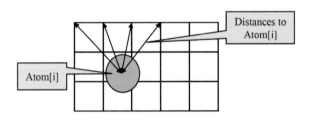

FIGURE 18.7

Reusing computation results among multiple grid points.

```
01   __constant__ float atoms[CHUNK_SIZE*4];
02   #define COARSEN_FACTOR 4
03   void __global__ cenergy(float *energygrid, dim3 grid, float gridspacing,
04                           float z, int numatoms) {
05       int i = blockIdx.x * blockDim.x*COARSEN_FACTOR + threadIdx.x;
06       int j = blockIdx.y * blockDim.y + threadIdx.y;
07       int atomarrdim = numatoms * 4;
08       int k = z / gridspacing;
09       float y = gridspacing * (float) j;
10       float x = gridspacing * (float) i;
11       float energy0 = 0.0f;
12       float energy1 = 0.0f;
13       float energy2 = 0.0f;
14       float energy3 = 0.0f;
15       // calculate potential contribution from all atoms
16       for (int n=0; n<atomarrdim; n+=4) {
17           float dx0 = x - atoms[n ];
18           float dx1 = dx0 +  gridspacing;
19           float dx2 = dx0 + 2*gridspacing;
20           float dx3 = dx0 + 3*gridspacing;
21           float dy = y - atoms[n+1];
22           float dz = z - atoms[n+2];
23           float dysqdzsq = dy*dy + dz*dz;
24           float charge = atoms[n+3];
25           energy0 += charge / sqrtf(dx0*dx0 + dysqdzsq);
26           energy1 += charge / sqrtf(dx1*dx1 + dysqdzsq);
27           energy2 += charge / sqrtf(dx2*dx2 + dysqdzsq);
28           energy3 += charge / sqrtf(dx3*dx3 + dysqdzsq);
29       }
30       energygrid[grid.x*grid.y*k + grid.x*j + i  ] += energy0;
31       energygrid[grid.x*grid.y*k + grid.x*j + i+1] += energy1;
32       energygrid[grid.x*grid.y*k + grid.x*j + i+2] += energy2;
33       energygrid[grid.x*grid.y*k + grid.x*j + i+3] += energy3;
34   }
```

FIGURE 18.8

Direct Coulomb summation kernel with thread coarsening.

iteration of the loop performs four constant memory accesses, three floating-point subtractions, eleven floating-point additions, six floating-point multiplications, and four floating-point divisions for four grid points.

The reader should also verify that the version of DCS kernel in Fig. 18.6 performs 16 constant memory accesses, 12 floating-point subtractions, 12 floating-point additions, 12 floating-point multiplications, and 12 floating-point divisions—a total of 48 floating-point operations for the same four grid points. Going from Fig. 18.6–Fig. 18.8, there is a total reduction from 16 constant memory accesses and 48 operations down to 4 constant memory accesses and 24 floating-point operations, a sizable reduction. One can expect a sizable improvement in both the execution time and the energy consumption of the kernel.

The cost of the optimization is that more registers are used by each thread. This can potentially reduce the number of threads that can be accommodated by each SM. However, since the number of registers stays within the permissible limit, it does not limit the occupancy of GPU execution resources.

18.4 Memory coalescing

While the performance of the DCS kernel in Fig. 18.8 is quite high, a quick profiling run reveals that the threads perform memory writes inefficiently. In lines 30–33, each thread writes four neighboring grid points. Unfortunately, the write pattern of adjacent threads in each warp will result in uncoalesced global memory writes. There are two problems that cause the uncoalesced write pattern in the kernel. First, each thread calculates four adjacent neighboring grid points. Thus for each statement that writes to the energygrid[] array, the threads in a warp are not accessing adjacent locations. Note that two adjacent threads access memory locations that are four elements apart. Thus the 32 locations to be written by all the threads in a warp are spread out, with three elements in between the loaded/written locations. This problem can be solved by assigning adjacent grid points to adjacent threads in each block. We first assign blockDim.x consecutive grid points in the x dimension to the threads. We then assign the next blockDim.x consecutive grid points to the same threads. We repeat the assignment until each thread has the number of grid points desired. This assignment is illustrated in Fig. 18.9.

The kernel code with coarsened thread granularity and coalescing-aware assignment of grid points to threads is shown in Fig. 18.10. Note that the x coordinates that are used to calculate the atom-to-grid-point distances for a thread's assigned grid points are offset by blockDim.x*gridspacing. This reflects the fact that the x coordinates of the four grid points assigned to a thread are blockDim.x grid points away from each other. After the end of the loop, the indices of the memory writes to the energygrid array are blockDim.x away from each other as well. Hence all writes to the energygrid array will be coalesced, and the performance of the kernel will be improved over that of Fig. 18.8.

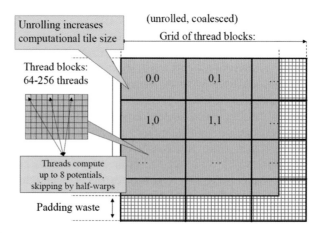

FIGURE 18.9

Organizing threads and memory layout for coalesced writes.

```
01   __constant__ float atoms[CHUNK_SIZE*4];
02   #define COARSEN_FACTOR 4
03   void __global__ cenergy(float *energygrid, dim3 grid, float gridspacing,
04                           float z, int numatoms) {
05       int i = blockIdx.x * blockDim.x*COARSEN_FACTOR + threadIdx.x;
06       int j = blockIdx.y * blockDim.y + threadIdx.y;
07       int atomarrdim = numatoms * 4;
08       int k = z / gridspacing;
09       float y = gridspacing * (float) j;
10       float x = gridspacing * (float) i;
11       float energy0 = 0.0f;
12       float energy1 = 0.0f;
13       float energy2 = 0.0f;
14       float energy3 = 0.0f;
15       // calculate potential contribution from all atoms
16       for (int n=0; n<atomarrdim; n+=4) {
17           float dx0 = x - atoms[n  ];
18           float dx1 = dx0 +   blockDim.x * gridspacing;
19           float dx2 = dx0 + 2*blockDim.x * gridspacing;
20           float dx3 = dx0 + 3*blockDim.x * gridspacing;
21           float dy = y - atoms[n+1];
22           float dz = z - atoms[n+2];
23           float dysqdzsq = dy*dy + dz*dz;
24           float charge = atoms[n+3];
25           energy0 += charge / sqrtf(dx0*dx0 + dysqdzsq);
26           energy1 += charge / sqrtf(dx1*dx1 + dysqdzsq);
27           energy2 += charge / sqrtf(dx2*dx2 + dysqdzsq);
28           energy3 += charge / sqrtf(dx3*dx3 + dysqdzsq);
29       }
30       energygrid[grid.x*grid.y*k + grid.x*j + i                ] += energy0;
31       energygrid[grid.x*grid.y*k + grid.x*j + i +   blockDim.x] += energy1;
32       energygrid[grid.x*grid.y*k + grid.x*j + i + 2*blockDim.x] += energy2;
33       energygrid[grid.x*grid.y*k + grid.x*j + i + 3*blockDim.x] += energy3;
34   }
```

FIGURE 18.10

Direct Coulomb summation kernel with thread coarsening and memory coalescing.

18.5 Cutoff binning for data size scalability

We can typically come up with multiple algorithms to solve a given problem. Some algorithms require fewer steps of computation than others, some expose a higher degree of parallel execution than others, some have better numerical stability than others, and some consume less memory bandwidth than others. Unfortunately, there is often not a single algorithm that is better than others in all the four aspects. Given a problem and a decomposition strategy, a parallel programmer often needs to select an algorithm that achieves the best compromise for a given hardware system.

In general, alternative algorithms for solving the same problem should reach the same solution. Under this requirement, one can optimize the computation for better efficiency and/or more parallelism. In some applications, one can often come up with even more aggressive algorithm strategies if the problem can be solved with slight variation in the final solution. An important algorithm strategy, referred to as *cutoff summation*, can significantly improve the execution efficiency of grid algorithms such as the electrostatic potential calculation by sacrificing a small amount of accuracy. This is based on the observation that many grid calculation problems are based on physical laws in which numerical contributions from particles or samples that are far away from a grid point can be collectively treated with an implicit method at much lower computational complexity.

The cutoff summation strategy is illustrated for the electrostatic potential calculation in Fig. 18.11. Fig. 18.11(A) shows the direct summation algorithms that were discussed in the previous sections of this chapter. Each grid point receives contributions from all atoms. While this is a very parallel approach and achieves excellent speedup, it does not scale well to very large energy grid systems in which the number of atoms increases proportionally to the volume of the system. The amount of computation increases with the square of the volume. For large volume systems, such increase makes the computation excessively long even for massively parallel devices.

We know that each grid point needs to receive accurate contributions from atoms that are close to it. The atoms that are far away from a grid point will have a tiny contribution to the energy value at the grid point because the contribution is inversely proportional to the distance. Fig. 18.11(B) illustrates this observation with a circle drawn around a grid point. The contributions to the grid point energy from atoms outside the circle (dark atoms) are small and can be handled with a separate implicit method. If we can devise an algorithm in which each grid point receives contributions only from atoms within a fixed radius of its coordinate, the computational complexity of the algorithm will be reduced to being linearly proportional to the volume of the system. This would make the computation time of the algorithm linearly proportional to the volume of the system. Such algorithms have been used extensively in sequential computation.

In sequential computing, a simple cutoff algorithm handles one atom at a time. For each atom the algorithm iterates through the grid points that fall within a radius of the atom's coordinate. This is a straightforward procedure, since the

(A) Direct summation
At each grid point, sum the electrostatic potential from all charges

(B) Cutoff summation
Electrostatic potential from nearby charges summed; spatially sort charges first

FIGURE 18.11

(A) Cutoff summation versus (B) direct summation.

grid points are in an array that can be easily indexed as a function of their coordinates. A C implementation of the cutoff algorithm can be derived with minor modifications to the C implementation of DCS in Fig. 18.4 by restricting the range of i and j of the inner loops to the energy grid points that fall into the radius. However, this simple procedure does not carry over easily to parallel execution. The reason is what we discussed in Section 18.2: The atom-centric parallelization does not work well, owing to its scatter memory update behavior.

Therefore we need to find a cutoff binning algorithm based on the grid-centric decomposition: Each thread calculates the energy value at one grid point. Fortunately, there is a well-known approach to adapting a direct summation algorithm, such as the one in Fig. 18.10, into a cutoff binning algorithm. Rodrigues et al. presents such an algorithm for the electrostatic potential problem (Rodrigues et al., 2008).

The key idea of the algorithm is to first sort the input atoms into bins according to their coordinates. Each bin corresponds to a box in the energy grid space, and it contains all atoms whose coordinates fall into the box. These bins are implemented as multidimensional arrays: the x, y, and z dimensions as well as the fourth dimension that is a vector of atoms in the bin.

We define a "neighborhood" of bins for a grid point as the collection of bins that contain all the atoms that can contribute to the energy value of the grid point. Fig. 18.12 shows an example of the neighborhood bins for a grid point. Note that nine bins around the grid point overlap with the circle of cutoff distance. For the correct cutoff summation we need to make sure that all atoms in these nine bins are considered for contribution to the grid point. Note that some of the atoms in the neighborhood bins may not fall into the radius. Therefore in processing an atom from one of the neighborhood bins, all threads need to check whether the atom falls into its radius. This can cause some control divergence among threads in a warp.

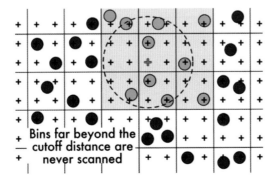

FIGURE 18.12

Neighborhood bins for a grid point.

Although Fig. 18.12 shows only one layer (2D) of bins that immediately surround the bin containing a grid point as its neighborhood, a real algorithm will typically have multiple 3D bins in a grid point's neighborhood. In this approach, all threads iterate through their own neighborhood. They use their block and thread indices to identify the coordinates of their assigned grid point and use these coordinates to identify the appropriate bins to examine. One can think of the neighborhood bins as a stencil in the energy grid space. However, the calculations that are involved in determining the neighborhood bins given a cutoff radius can be a complex geometric problem whose solution can be time consuming. Therefore the neighborhood bins are usually defined for all threads in a block and are prepared before launching the grid.

Fig. 18.13 shows a per-block design of neighborhood bins. Based on the block dimensions and the grid spacing, one can calculate the area (volume in 3D) of energy grid space covered by each block. We show the areas covered by the blocks as squares in Fig. 18.13. For simplicity we assume that each of these areas is also covered by a bin; that is, all atoms that fall into the same square will be collected into the same bin. For example, if the grid spacing is 0.5 Å and the blocks are $8 \times 8 \times 8$, each block would cover a 4 Å $\times$ 4 Å $\times$ 4Å cube in the energy grid space. If we assume a typical cutoff distance of 12 Å for molecular-level force calculation, we need to identify all bins that can potentially be fully or partially covered by any of the 512 circles, each of which is centered at one of the grid points covered by one of the threads in the block. We can also use a conservative approximation by drawing a supercircle that is centered at the center of the bin with a radius that is the cutoff distance plus half of the bin diagonal. The rationale is that this supercircle would cover all the circles that are centered at the corners of the bin. We can simply create a list of the relative positions of the bins that are fully or partially covered by the supercircle.

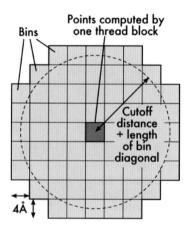

FIGURE 18.13

Identifying the neighborhood bins for all grid points processed by a block.

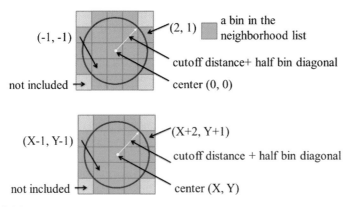

FIGURE 18.14

Neighborhood list using relative offsets.

Fig. 18.14 shows a small example of identifying neighborhood bins. We see that for each bin, there are 9 bins that are fully covered by the supercircle and 12 bins that are partially covered. We can generate a list of 9 + 12=21 neighborhood bins that each thread in a block needs to examine for atoms that are within the cutoff distance of the grid point covered by the thread. These bins are expressed as the relative offset of the bin coordinates. For example, the 9 bins that are fully covered by the supercircle can be expressed as the list $(-1, -1)$, $(0, -1)$, $(1, -1)$, $(-1, 0)$, $(0, 0)$, $(1, 0)$, $(-1, 1)$, $(0, 1)$, and $(1, 1)$, as illustrated in the top portion of Fig. 18.14. The list would be supplied to the kernel, most likely as a constant memory array. During kernel execution, all threads in a block would iterate through the neighborhood list. For each neighborhood bin, the threads apply the offsets to the coordinates of the bin covered by the block and derive the coordinate of the neighbor bin, as illustrated in the bottom portion of Fig. 18.14. They collaborate to load the atoms in the bin into the shared memory and then each thread individually checks whether these atoms fall within the cutoff distance of its assigned grid point. Each thread could make different decisions about including or excluding each atom for contributing to the energy value at its assigned grid point.

The improvement in computational complexity in a cutoff binning algorithm mainly comes from the fact that each thread now examines a much smaller subset of atoms, defined by the neighborhood bins, in a large grid system. However, this makes constant memory much less attractive for holding the atoms. Since thread blocks will be accessing different neighborhoods, the limited-sized constant memory will unlikely be able to hold all the atoms that are needed by all active thread blocks. This motivates the use of global memory to hold a much larger set of atoms. To mitigate the bandwidth consumption, threads in a block collaborate in loading the atom information in each common neighborhood bin into the shared memory. All threads then examine the atoms out of shared memory.

One subtle issue with binning is that bins may end up with different numbers of atoms. Since the atoms are statistically distributed in the grid system, some bins may have lots of atoms, and some bins may end up with no atoms at all. To guarantee memory coalescing, it is important that all bins be of the same size and aligned at appropriate coalescing boundaries. This would require us to fill many bins with dummy atoms whose electrical charge is 0, which causes two negative effects. First, the dummy atoms still occupy global memory and shared memory storage. They also consume data transfer bandwidth to the device. Second, the dummy atoms extend the execution time of the thread blocks whose bins have few real atoms.

A good approach is setting the bin size at a reasonable level that covers the number of atoms in the vast majority of the bins, typically much smaller than the largest possible number of atoms in a bin. The binning process maintains an overflow list. In processing an atom, if the atom's home bin is full, the atom is added to the overflow list instead. After the device completes a kernel, the resulting grid point energy values are transferred back to the host. The host executes a sequential cutoff algorithm on the atoms in the overflow list to complete the missing contributions from these overflow atoms.

As long as the overflow atoms account for only a small percentage (e.g., less than 3%) of the atoms, the additional sequential processing time of the overflow atoms is typically shorter than that of the device execution time. One can also design the kernel so that each kernel invocation calculates the energy values for a subvolume of grid points. After each kernel completes, the host launches the next kernel and processes the overflow atoms for the completed kernel. Thus the host will be processing the overflow atoms while the device executes the next kernel. This approach can hide most, if not all, of the delays in processing overflow atoms, since it is done in parallel with the execution of the next kernel.

18.6 Summary

This chapter presents a series of decisions and tradeoffs in parallelizing the calculation of electrostatic potential energy in a regularly spaced energy grid. We show that parallelizing a highly optimized sequential C implementation of the DCS method leads to a slow scatter kernel that requires heavy use of atomic operations. We then show that one can parallelize a less optimized sequential C code into a gather kernel that has much higher parallel execution speed. We also show that through thread coarsening, we can reclaim much of the efficiency of the optimized sequential execution. We further demonstrate that by carefully choosing the grid points to fold into each thread, the kernel can have completely coalesced memory write patterns.

While DCS is a highly accurate method for calculating the electrostatic potential energy map of a molecular system, it is not a scalable method. The number of operations that are performed by the method grows proportionally with the number of atoms and the number of grid points. When we increase the physical volume of the molecular system to be simulated, we should expect both the number of grid points and the number of atoms to increase proportionally to the physical size. As a result, the number of operations to be performed will be approximately proportional to the square of the physical volume; that is, the number of operations to be performed will grow quadratically with the volume of the system being simulated. This makes the use of DCS method not suitable for simulating realistic biological systems. We show that by slightly reducing the accuracy, a cutoff summation method implemented with the binning technique can dramatically improve the complexity of the computation while retaining a high level of parallelism.

Exercises

1. Complete the host code for configuring the grid and calling the kernel in Fig. 18.6 with all the execution configuration parameters.
2. Compare the number of operations (memory loads, floating-point arithmetic, branches) executed in each iteration of the kernel in Fig. 18.8 with that in Fig. 18.6 for a coarsening factor of 8. Keep in mind that each iteration of the former corresponds to eight iterations of the latter.
3. Give two potential disadvantages associated with increasing the amount of work done in each CUDA thread, as shown in Section 18.3.
4. Use Fig. 18.13 to explain how control divergence can arise when threads in a block process a bin in the neighborhood list.

References

Humphrey, W., Dalke, A., Schulten, K., 1996. VMD – visual molecular dyanmics. J. Mole. Graph. 14, 33−38.

Rodrigues, C.I., Hardy, D.J., Stone, J.E., Schulten, K., Hwu, W.M., 2008. GPU acceleration of cutoff pair potentials for molecular modeling applications. In *Proceedings of the Fifth Conference on Computing Frontiers* (pp. 273−282).

Stone, J.E., Phillips, J.C., Freddolino, P.L., Hardy, D.J., Trabuco, L.G., Schulten, K., 2007. Accelerating molecular modeling applications with graphics processors. J. Comput. Chem. 28, 2618−2640.

Parallel programming and computational thinking

19

Chapter Outline

19.1 Goals of parallel computing 433
19.2 Algorithm selection 436
19.3 Problem decomposition 440
19.4 Computational thinking 444
19.5 Summary 446
References 446

We have so far concentrated on practical knowledge in parallel programming, which consists of CUDA programming interface features, the GPU architecture, performance optimization techniques, parallel patterns, and application case studies. In this chapter we switch our discussions to concepts that are more abstract. We generalize parallel programming into a computational thinking process of designing or selecting parallel algorithms and decomposing a domain problem into well-defined and coordinated work units that can each be efficiently performed by the selected algorithms. A programmer with strong computational thinking skills not only analyzes but also transforms the structure of a domain problem: which parts are inherently serial, which parts are amenable to high-performance parallel execution, and the domain-specific tradeoffs that are involved in moving parts from the former category to the latter. With good algorithm selection and problem decomposition the programmer can achieve an appropriate compromise between parallelism, work efficiency, and resource consumption. A strong combination of domain knowledge and computational thinking skills is often needed for creating successful computational solutions to challenging domain problems. This chapter will give the reader more insight into parallel programming and computational thinking in general.

19.1 Goals of parallel computing

Before we discuss the fundamental concepts of parallel programming, it is important for us to first review the three main reasons why people pursue parallel computing. The first goal is to solve a given problem in less time. For example, an investment firm may need to run a financial portfolio scenario risk analysis package on all its portfolios during after-trading hours. Such an analysis could require 200 hours on a sequential computer. However, the portfolio management process may require that analysis be completed in 4 hours to be in time for major decisions based on the resulting information. Using parallel computing may speed up the analysis and allow it to complete within the required time window.

The second goal of using parallel computing is to solve bigger problems within a given amount of time. In our financial portfolio analysis example the investment firm may be able to run the portfolio scenario risk analysis on its current portfolio within a given time window using sequential computing. However, the firm is planning on expanding the number of holdings in its portfolio. The enlarged problem size would cause the sequential analysis to exceed the allowed time window. Parallel computing that reduces the running time of the bigger problem size can help to accommodate the planned expansion to the portfolio.

The third goal of using parallel computing is to achieve better solutions for a given problem and a given amount of time. The investment firm may have been using an approximate model in its portfolio scenario risk analysis. Using a more accurate model may increase the computational complexity and increase the running time on a sequential computer beyond the allowed window. For example, a more accurate model may require consideration of interactions between more types of risk factors using a more numerically complex formula. Parallel computing that reduces the running time of the more accurate model may complete the analysis within the allowed time window.

In practice, parallel computing may be driven by a combination of these three goals.

It should be clear from our discussion that parallel computing is motivated primarily by increased speed. The first goal is achieved by increased speed in running the existing model on the current problem size. The second goal is achieved by increased speed in running the existing model on a larger problem size. The third goal is achieved by increased speed in running a more complex model on the current problem size. Obviously, the increased speed through parallel computing can be used to achieve a combination of these goals. For example, parallel computing can reduce the runtime of a more complex model on a larger problem size.

It should also be clear from our discussion that applications that are good candidates for parallel computing typically involve large problem sizes and high complexity. That is, these applications process a large amount of data, require much computation in each iteration, and/or perform many iterations on the data. Applications that do not involve large problem sizes or incur high modeling complexity tend to complete within a small amount of time and do not offer much motivation for increased speed.

A real application often consists of multiple modules that work together. Fig. 19.1 shows an overview of the major modules of a molecular dynamics application. For each atom in the system the application needs to calculate the various forms of forces, such as vibrational, rotational, and nonbonded, that are

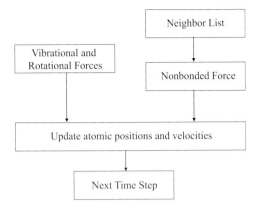

FIGURE 19.1

Major tasks of a molecular dynamics application.

exerted on the atom. Each form of force is calculated with a different method. At the high level, a programmer needs to decide how the work is organized. Note that the amount of work can vary dramatically between these modules. The non-bonded force calculation typically involves interactions among many atoms and incurs many more calculations than the vibrational and rotational forces. Therefore these modules tend to be realized as separate passes over the force data structure.

The programmer needs to decide whether each pass is worth implementing in a CUDA device. For example, the programmer may decide that the vibrational and rotational force calculations do not involve sufficient amount of work to warrant execution on a GPU device. Such a decision would lead to a CUDA program that launches a kernel that calculates nonbonding force fields for all the grid points while continuing to calculate the vibrational and rotational forces for the grid points on the host. The module that updates atom positions and velocities may also run on the host. It first combines the vibrational and rotational forces from the host and the nonbonding forces from the device. It then uses the combined forces to calculate the new atomic positions and velocities.

The portion of work done by the device will ultimately decide the application-level speedup that is achieved by parallelization. For example, assume that the nonbonding force calculation accounts for 95% of the original sequential execution time and it is accelerated by 100$\times$ using a GPU. Further assume that the rest of the application remains on the host and receives no speedup. The application-level speedup is $1/(5\% + 95\%/100) = 1/(5\% + 0.95\%) = 1/(5.95\%) = 17\times$. In the case in which the execution of the host and the CUDA device can be overlapped, the execution time of the parallel section is completely hidden in the host execution time. The application-level speedup would be $1/(5\%) = 20\times$. This is a demonstration of Amdahl's law: The application speedup due to parallel computing is limited by the sequential portion of the application. In this case, even though the sequential portion of the application is quite small (5%), it limits the application-level speedup to 20× despite the nonbonding force calculation having a speedup of 100× and being completely hidden in the shadow of the host execution of the sequential portion. This example illustrates a major challenge in accelerating large applications: The accumulated execution time of small activities that are not worth parallel execution on a CUDA device can become a limiting factor in the speedup that is seen by the end users. We saw this phenomenon in the iterative MRI application study in Chapter 17, Iterative Magnetic Resonance Imaging Reconstruction, in which the CG computation becomes a limiting factor of speedup even though it accounts for only about 1% of the execution time of the original application.

Amdahl's law often motivates task-level parallelization. Although some of these smaller activities do not warrant fine-grained massive parallel execution, it may be desirable to execute some of these activities in parallel with each other when the dataset is large enough. This could be achieved by using a multicore host to execute such tasks in parallel. Alternatively, we could try to simulta-neously execute multiple small kernels, each corresponding to one task. CUDA devices support task parallelism with streams, which will be discussed in Chapter 20, Programming a Heterogeneous Computing Cluster.

An alternative approach to reducing the effect of sequential tasks is to exploit data parallelism in a hierarchical manner. For example, in a Message Passing Interface (MPI, 2009) implementation a molecular dynamics application would typically distrib-ute large chunks of the spatial grids and their associated atoms to nodes of a net-worked computing cluster. By using the host of each node to calculate the vibrational and rotational force for its chunk of atoms, we can take advantage of multiple host CPUs and achieve speedup for these lesser modules. Each node can use a CUDA device to calculate the nonbonding force at a higher level of speedup. The nodes will need to exchange data to accommodate forces that go across chunks and atoms that move across chunk boundaries. We will discuss more details of joint MPI-CUDA pro-gramming in Chapter 20, Programming a Heterogeneous Computing Cluster. The main point here is that MPI and CUDA can be used in a complementary, hierarchical way in applications to jointly achieve a higher level of speed with large datasets.

The process of parallel programming can typically be divided into three steps: algorithm selection, problem decomposition, and performance optimization and tuning. The last step was the focus of previous chapters and received general treatment in Chapter 6, Performance Considerations. In the next two sections of this chapter we will discuss the first two steps with generality as well as depth.

19.2 Algorithm selection

An algorithm is a step-by-step procedure in which each step is precisely stated and can be carried out by a computer. An algorithm must exhibit three essential properties: definiteness, effective computability, and finiteness. Definiteness refers to the notion that each step is precisely stated; there is no room for ambiguity as to what is to be done. Effective computability refers to the fact that each step can be carried out by a computer. Finiteness means that the algorithm must be guaranteed to terminate.

Given a problem, one can typically come up with multiple algorithms to solve the problem. Some require fewer steps of computation than others (i.e., have lower algorithmic complexity), some expose a higher degree of parallel execution than others, some are more generally applicable than others, and some have better accuracy or numerical stability than others. Unfortunately, there is often not a single algorithm that is better than others in all these aspects. A parallel programmer often needs to select an algorithm that achieves the best compromise for a given hardware system.

We have seen examples of assessing the tradeoffs between different algorithms for a computation in several chapters throughout this book. For the prefix sum computation in Chapter 11, Prefix Sum (Scan), we compared two different algorithms for performing parallel prefix sum, namely, the Kogge-Stone algorithm and the Brent-Kung algorithm. Our analysis showed that the Brent-Kung algorithm has lower algorithmic complexity. It requires fewer operations to perform the same computation, which makes it more work efficient. However, we also showed that the Kogge-Stone algorithm exposes more parallelism than the Brent-Kung algorithm, allowing it to complete in fewer iterations. This tradeoff between algorithmic complexity and the amount of parallelism exposed by an algorithm is a classic tradeoff that is encountered by parallel programmers. The best algorithm usually depends on the characteristics of the parallel hardware being targeted as well as the extent to which the higher complexity of an algorithm can be mitigated with hybrid approaches that combine two parallel algorithms or combine a parallel algorithm with a lower-complexity sequential algorithm via thread coarsening.

For the sorting pattern in Chapter 13, Sorting, we compared two different algorithms for performing parallel sorting, namely, radix sort and merge sort. Radix sort can achieve lower algorithmic complexity than merge sort because it is a noncomparison sorting algorithm. It is also highly amenable to parallelization. However, radix sort is not generally applicable because it can be used only with certain types of keys. Merge sort, which is a comparison-based sort, is more generally applicable and can be used with any type of key that has a well-defined comparison operator. The tradeoff between generality and parallel execution efficiency is yet another tradeoff that parallel programmers encounter when selecting a parallel algorithm.

For the electrostatic potential map computation in Chapter 18, Electrostatic Potential Map, we compared two different algorithms for performing the computation, namely, direct Coulomb summation (DCS) and cutoff summation (Rodrigues et al., 2008). These two approaches expose the same amount of parallelism and have the same level of generality; however, they present the classic tradeoff between algorithmic complexity and accuracy. In Chapter 18, Electrostatic Potential Map, we showed that the cutoff summation algorithm can significantly improve the execution efficiency of grid computation by sacrificing a small amount of accuracy. The challenge that is addressed by this technique is that the amount of computation performed by fully accurate methods such as DCS increases with the square of the volume. For large volume systems, such increase makes the computation excessively long even for massively parallel devices. The cutoff summation method is based on the observation that many grid calculation problems are based on physical laws in which numerical contributions from particles or samples that are far away from a grid point are tiny and can be collectively treated with an implicit method at much lower algorithmic complexity. Although this tradeoff between algorithmic complexity and accuracy is not unique to parallel programming and is also encountered with sequential implementations, it may present additional challenges to parallel programmers. We show an example of these additional challenges for the cutoff summation algorithm in the rest of this section.

In sequential computing, a simple cutoff algorithm handles one atom at a time. For each atom the algorithm iterates through the grid points that fall within a radius of the atom's coordinate. This is a straightforward procedure, since the grid points are in an array that can be easily indexed as a function of their coordinates. However, this simple procedure does not carry easily to parallel execution. The reason is that the atom-centric decomposition does not work well, owing to its scatter memory access behavior. Therefore we need to use a cutoff binning algorithm based on the grid-centric decomposition: Each thread calculates the energy value at one grid point. The key idea of the algorithm is to first sort the input atoms into bins according to their coordinates. Each bin corresponds to a box in the grid space and contains all atoms whose coordinate falls into the box. We define a "neighborhood" of bins for a grid point to be the collection of bins that contain all the atoms that can contribute to the energy value of a grid point. We described an efficient way of managing neighborhood bins for all grid points in Chapter 18, Electrostatic Potential Map. In this algorithm, all blocks iterate through their own neighborhood bins, while all threads in a block scan through the atoms in these neighborhood bins together but make individual decisions on whether each atom falls within its cutoff radius.

One subtle issue with binning is that bins may end up with different numbers of atoms. Some bins may have many atoms, and some bins may have no atom at all. A well-known solution is to set the bin size at a reasonable level, typically much smaller than the largest possible number of atoms in a bin. The binning process maintains an overflow list. When atoms are sorted into bins, if an atom's home bin is full, the atom is added to the overflow list instead. After the device has completed executing a cutoff summation kernel for calculating an electrostatic potential map, atoms in the overflow list need to be processed to complete the missing contributions.

Fig. 19.2 shows a comparison of scalability and performance of the various electrostatic potential map algorithms and implementations. Note that the CPU-SSE3 curve is based on a sequential cutoff summation algorithm. For a map with

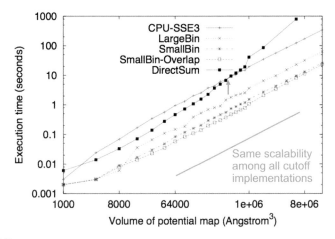

FIGURE 19.2

Scalability and performance of DCS versus cutoff binning.

small volumes, around 1000 $\mathring{A}^3$, the host (CPU with SSE) executes faster than the DCS kernel, as shown in Fig. 19.2. This is because there is not enough work to fully utilize a CUDA device for such a small volume. However, for moderate volumes, between 2000 and 500,000 $\mathring{A}^3$, the direct summation kernel performs significantly better than the host, owing to its massive parallelism. However, as we anticipated, the direct summation kernel scales poorly when the volume size reaches about 1,000,000 $\mathring{A}^3$ and runs longer than the sequential algorithm on the CPU! This is because the algorithmic complexity of the DCS kernel is higher than the sequential cutoff algorithm and thus the amount of work done by kernel grows much faster than that done by the sequential algorithm. For volume sizes larger than 1,000,000 $\mathring{A}^3$ the amount of work is so large that it swamps the hardware execution resources.

Fig. 19.2 also shows the running time of three binning-based implementations of the cutoff summation algorithm. The SmallBin implementation corresponds to the neighborhood bin list approach discussed in Chapter 18, Electrostatic Potential Map, and allows the blocks running the same kernel to process different neighborhoods of atoms. The SmallBin implementation does incur more instruction overhead for loading atoms from global memory into shared memory. For a moderate volume there is a limited number of atoms in the entire system. The ability to examine a smaller number of atoms does not provide sufficient advantage to overcome the additional instruction overhead. The SmallBin-Overlap implementation overlaps the sequential overflow atom processing with the next kernel execution. It provides a slight but noticeable improvement in running time over the SmallBin implementation. The SmallBin-Overlap implementation achieves a 17× speedup over an efficiently implemented sequential CPU-SSE cutoff summation implementation and maintains the same scalability for large volumes.

19.3 Problem decomposition

After an appropriate algorithm has been selected, for a problem to be solved with parallel computing, the problem must be formulated in such a way that it can be decomposed into subproblems that can be safely solved at the same time. Under such formulation and decomposition the programmer writes code and organizes data to solve these subproblems concurrently. Finding parallelism in large computational problems is often conceptually simple but can be challenging in practice. The key is to identify the work to be performed by each unit of parallel execution so that the inherent parallelism of the problem is well utilized.

The two most common strategies for decomposing a problem for parallel execution are the output-centric and input-centric decompositions. As the names imply, an *output-centric* decomposition assigns threads to process different units of the output data in parallel, whereas an *input-centric* decomposition assigns threads to process different units of the input data in parallel. These decomposition strategies are illustrated in Fig. 19.3. While both decomposition strategies lead to the same execution results, they can exhibit very different performance in a given hardware system. The output-centric decomposition usually exhibits the gather memory access behavior, in which each thread gathers or collects the effect of input values into an output value. Fig. 19.3A illustrates the gather access behavior. Gather-based access patterns are usually more desirable in CUDA devices because the threads can accumulate their results in their private registers. Also, multiple threads can share input values and can effectively use constant memory caching or shared memory to conserve global memory bandwidth.

The input-centric decomposition, by contrast, usually exhibits the scatter memory access behavior, in which each thread scatters or distributes the effect of an input value into the output values. The scatter behavior is illustrated in Fig. 19.3B. Scatter-based access patterns are usually undesirable in CUDA devices because multiple threads can update the same grid point at the same time. The grid points must be stored in a memory that can be written by all the threads involved. Atomic operations must be used to prevent race conditions and loss of values during simultaneous writes to an output value by multiple threads. These atomic operations are significantly slower than the register accesses that are used in the output-centric decomposition.

However, aside from the gather versus scatter access patterns, other considerations may go into deciding whether an output-centric or input-centric decomposition (or another decomposition) is more suitable for a particular application. These considerations include the amount of parallelism that is exposed by the decomposition, the ease of identifying which input data contributes to which output data, the load balance induced by the decomposition, and others, depending on the application.

The distinction between input-centric and output-centric decompositions was most evident in Chapters 17, Iterative Magnetic Resonance Imaging Reconstruction, and 18, Electrostatic Potential Map, where the two strategies were both implemented and

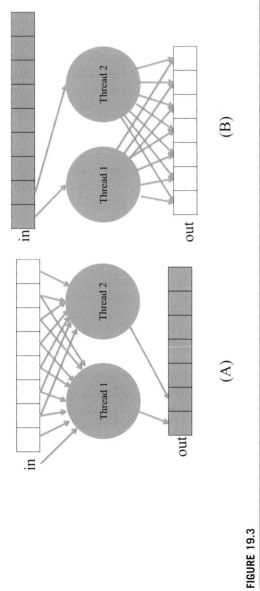

FIGURE 19.3

Problem decomposition strategies. (A) Output-centric. (B) Input-centric.

explicitly compared. However, problem decomposition is an implicit design decision that has been made throughout many computations discussed in this book. We revisit these computations to highlight the problem decomposition that was chosen in each case and why it is advantageous over alternative decompositions.

The image processing (Chapter 3, Multidimensional Grids and Data), matrix multiplication (Chapters 3, 5, and 6), Convolution (Chapter 7), and Stencil (Chapter 8) computations were all parallelized by using an output-centric decomposition. That is, the threads in these computations are assigned to output elements (image pixels, matrix entries, or grid points) and iterate over the input elements that contribute to them. Alternatively, an input-centric decomposition would assign threads to the input elements and have each thread iterate over the output elements to which its input element contributes and make an update using atomic operations. The clear advantage of the output-centric decomposition over the input-centric decomposition in these cases is avoiding atomics by using a gather access pattern instead of a scatter access pattern. On the other hand, none of the other considerations make the input-centric decomposition favorable. There are enough output elements to expose a high degree of parallelism, identifying which input elements are needed by each output element is straightforward, and all output elements require the same amount of work to be computed, so there is no load imbalance.

The histogram computation (Chapter 9, Parallel Histogram) was parallelized by using an input-centric decomposition. That is, each thread is assigned to an input element (or chunk of elements) and updates the output bins on the basis of the input value(s). Since multiple threads may update the same output bin, atomic operations are needed (scatter access pattern). Alternatively, an output-centric decomposition would assign threads to output bins and have each thread search for the inputs that map to the bin and update the bin accordingly. This decomposition would eliminate the atomic operations because each bin would be updated by a single thread (gather access pattern). However, the output-centric decomposition would create many other problems. First, the number of output bins is typically much smaller than the number of input values, so parallelism is substantially reduced. Second, a thread cannot know which input values map to its output bin without inspecting those input values, so each thread will need to iterate over every input value, which is not work efficient. Third, even if threads had some way of quickly identifying which input values mapped to their output bins, each bin would have a different number of input values mapping to it, which would create load imbalance across threads. All these considerations make the input-centric decomposition more favorable for the histogram computation.

The merge operation (Chapter 12, Merge) was parallelized by using an output-centric decomposition; that is, each thread is assigned to an element (or chunk of elements) in the output array and performs a binary search to find the corresponding input element(s) and merge them. While many other computations that favor the output-centric decomposition do so because of the benefit of gathering over scattering, this consideration is not relevant for the merge operation. Every output element in the merge operation is contributed to by only one input element, so an input-centric merge operation would not need to use atomics. However, an input-centric merge operation either would make it more expensive to find the mapping between the input element(s) for which a thread is responsible and the corresponding output element(s) or would incur high load imbalance by having each input thread be responsible for a different number of input elements. For this reason, the output-centric decomposition is preferred.

For sparse matrix computations (Chapter 14, Sparse Matrix Computation) the SpMV/COO kernel used input-centric decomposition, in which threads were assigned to nonzeros in the input matrix and atomically updated the corresponding element in the output vector (scatter access pattern). The remaining kernels used output-centric decomposition, in which threads were assigned to output vector elements and iterated over input nonzeros (gather access pattern). Although the input-centric SpMV/COO kernel performed atomics, it had other advantages over the output-centric kernels, such as extracting more parallelism and having better load balance. Ultimately, the best decomposition for this computation depends on the input dataset. Moreover, the hybrid ELL-COO format showcases an example in which a hybrid output-centric and input-centric decomposition may be beneficial.

For graph traversal (Chapter 15, Graph Traversal) the vertex-centric push implementation and the edge-centric implementation used input-centric decomposition. That is, threads were assigned to vertices or edges and updated the levels of neighboring vertices. In contrast, the vertex-centric pull implementation used output-centric decomposition in which each thread updated only the level of the vertex to which it was assigned. The tradeoff between scatter and gather access patterns is not a concern in selecting between different decompositions because the updates to the level values are idempotent and do not require atomics. However, the amount of parallelism that is extracted and the load balance that is achieved play an important role in deciding which decomposition is more favorable, and the best decomposition ultimately depends on the input dataset. The reader is encouraged to review Chapter 15, Graph Traversal, for a more detailed handling of this topic.

The iterative MRI reconstruction problem (Chapter 17, Iterative Magnetic Resonance Imaging Reconstruction) and the electrostatic potential calculation problem (Chapter 18, Electrostatic Potential Map) both favor the output-centric decomposition because of the benefit over the gather pattern of the scatter pattern in avoiding atomic operations. These chapters already handle the distinction between the two decomposition strategies in depth. The iterative MRI reconstruction problem (Chapter 17, Iterative Magnetic Resonance Imaging Reconstruction) processes a large amount of k-space sample data. Each k-space sample data is also used many times for calculating its contributions to the reconstructed voxel data. For high-resolution reconstruction, each sample data is used a large number of times. We showed that a good decomposition of the FhD problem in MRI reconstruction is an output-centric decomposition that forms subproblems, each of which calculates the value of an FhD element using the gather strategy.

Similarly, the electrostatic potential calculation problem (Chapter 18, Electrostatic Potential Map) involves the calculation of the contribution of many input atoms to the potential energy at a large number of output grid points. A realistic molecular system model typically involves at least hundreds of thousands of atoms and millions of energy grid points. The electrostatic charge information of each atom is used many times in calculating its contributions to the energy grid points. We showed that the decomposition of the electrostatic potential map calculation problem can be atom-centric (i.e., input-centric) or grid-centric (i.e., output-centric). In an atom-centric decomposition, each thread is responsible for calculating the effect of one atom on all grid points. In contrast, a grid-centric decomposition uses each thread to calculate the effect of all atoms on a grid point. The grid-centric (i.e., output-centric) decomposition proved to be better because it uses the more favorable gather access pattern. The amount of parallelism that is exposed by both decompositions is sufficient. For the cutoff summation algorithm the difficulty of mapping input data to output data in the grid-centric decomposition is overcome with the use of binning, and the load imbalance caused by binning is overcome with the SmallBin-Overlap implementation that was discussed in the previous section.

19.4 **Computational thinking**

Computational thinking is arguably the most important aspect of parallel application development (Wing, 2006). We define computational thinking as the thought processes of formulating domain problems in terms of computation steps and algorithms. Like any other thought processes and problem-solving skills, computational thinking is an art. As we mentioned in Chapter 1, Introduction, we believe that computational thinking is best taught with an iterative approach in which students bounce back and forth between practical experience and abstract concepts.

There is a very large volume of literature on a wide range of algorithms, problem decompositions, and optimization strategies that can be hard to understand. It is beyond the scope of this book to provide comprehensive coverage of all the available techniques. We discuss a substantial set of techniques in each of the algorithm, problem decomposition, and optimization steps that have broad applicability. While these techniques are demonstrated using CUDA C implementations, they help the readers build up the foundation for computational thinking in general. We believe that humans understand best when we learn from the bottom up. That is, we first learn the concepts in the context of a particular programming model, which provides us with solid footing before we generalize our knowledge to other programming models. An in-depth experience with the CUDA C implementations also enables us to gain maturity, which will help us learn parallel programming and computational thinking concepts that may not even be pertinent to the GPUs.

There is a myriad of skills that are needed for a parallel programmer to be an effective computational thinker. We summarize these foundational skills as follows:

- Computer architecture: memory organization, caching and locality, memory bandwidth, SIMT versus SPMD versus SIMD execution, and floating-point precision versus accuracy. These concepts are critical in understanding the tradeoffs between algorithms, problem decompositions, and optimizations.
- Programming interfaces and compilers: parallel execution models, types of available memories, types of synchronization support, array data layout, and thread granularity transformation. These concepts are needed for thinking through the arrangements of data structures and loop structures to achieve better performance.
- Domain knowledge: problem formulation, hard versus soft constraints, numerical methods, precision, accuracy, and numerical stability. Understanding these ground rules allows a developer to be much more creative in applying algorithm techniques.

Our goal for this book is to provide a solid foundation for all these areas. Readers should continue to broaden their knowledge in these areas after finishing this book. Most important, the best way of building up more computational thinking skills is to keep solving challenging problems with excellent computational solutions.

A good goal for effective use of computing is making science better, not just faster. This requires reexamining prior assumptions and really thinking about how to apply the big hammer of massively parallel processing. Put another way, there will probably be no Nobel Prizes or Turing Awards awarded for "just recompile" or using more threads with the same computational approach. Truly important scientific discoveries will more likely come from fresh computational thinking. Consider this an exhortation to use this bonanza of computing power to solve new problems in new ways.

There are three approaches for attacking computation-hungry applications with increasing order of difficulty, complexity, and, not surprisingly, potential for payoff. Let us call these "good," "better," and "best."

The "good" approach is simply to "accelerate" legacy program codes. The most basic effort is simply to recompile and run on a new platform or architecture without adding any domain insight or expertise in parallelism. This can be enhanced by using optimized libraries, tools, or directives, such as CuBLAS, CuFFT, Thrust, Matlab, or OpenACC. This approach does not require any algorithm selection, problem decomposition, or optimization and tuning efforts. It can be immediately rewarding for domain scientists, since minimal computer science knowledge or programming skills are required to obtain decent speedups. However, it does not realize the full potential of parallel computing.

The "better" approach involves rewriting existing codes using parallel programming skills to take advantage of new architectures or creating new codes from scratch. This approach is an opportunity for clever thinking about problem decomposition and optimization selection and is good work for nondomain computer scientists, as minimal domain knowledge is required. However, it also does not realize the full potential of parallel computing because of the absence of domain-specific knowledge, which is needed for effective algorithm selection.

The "best" approach involves a holistic attempt at application parallelization involving all three key steps: algorithm selection, problem decomposition, and optimization and tuning. We wish not only to map a known algorithm to a parallel program and optimize it, but also to rethink the numerical methods and algorithms that are used in the solution. The cutoff binning approach in Chapter 18, Electrostatic Potential Map, is a good example. The approach requires domain expertise to trade accuracy for dramatically reduced algorithmic complexity and requires problem decomposition and optimization skills to use the grid-centric decomposition with the binning techniques designed by computer scientists. In this approach, there is the potential for the biggest performance advantage and fundamental new discoveries and capabilities. For example, one may be able to perform high-fidelity simulation of a biochemical system whose size is considered beyond reach with traditional methods. This approach is interdisciplinary and requires both computer science *and* domain insight, but the payoff is worth the effort. It is truly an exciting time to be a computational scientist!

19.5 Summary

In summary, we have discussed the main steps of parallel programming and computational thinking, namely, algorithm selection, problem decomposition, and optimization and tuning. Given a computational problem, the programmer will typically have to select from a variety of algorithms. Some of these algorithms achieve different tradeoffs while maintaining the same numerical accuracy. Others involve sacrificing some level of accuracy to achieve much more scalable running times. For the selected algorithm, different choices of problem decomposition can result in different levels of interference between threads, parallelism exposed, load imbalance, and other performance considerations during parallel execution. Computational thinking skills allow an algorithm designer to work around the roadblocks and reach a good solution.

References

Message Passing Interface Forum, MPI—A Message Passing Interface Standard Version 2.2, http://www.mpi-forum.org/docs/mpi-2.2/mpi22-report.pdf, September 4, 2009.
Rodrigues, C.I., Stone, J., Hardy, D., Hwu, W.W. 2008. GPU acceleration of cutoff-based potential summation. In: ACM Computing Frontier Conference 2008, Italy, May 2008.
Wing, J., 2006. Computational thinking. Commun. ACM 49, 3.

Advanced Practices

Programming a heterogeneous computing cluster

20

An introduction to CUDA streams

With special contributions from Isaac Gelado and Javier Cabezas

Chapter Outline

20.1 Background 449
20.2 A running example 450
20.3 Message passing interface basics 452
20.4 Message passing interface point-to-point communication 455
20.5 Overlapping computation and communication 462
20.6 Message passing interface collective communication 470
20.7 CUDA aware message passing interface 471
20.8 Summary 472
Exercises 472
References 473

So far, we have focused on programming a heterogeneous computing system with one host and one device. In high-performance computing (HPC), applications require the aggregate computing power of a cluster of computing nodes. Many of the HPC clusters today have one or more hosts and one or more devices in each node. Historically, these clusters have been programmed predominately with Message Passing Interface (MPI). In this chapter we will present an introduction to joint MPI/CUDA programming. We will present only the MPI concepts that programmers need to understand to scale their heterogeneous applications to multiple nodes in a cluster environment. In particular, we will focus on domain partitioning, point-to-point communication, and collective communication in the context of scaling a CUDA kernel into multiple nodes.

20.1 Background

Although practically no top supercomputers used GPUs before 2009, the need for better energy efficiency has led to fast adoption of GPUs in recent years. Many of

Programming Massively Parallel Processors. DOI: https://doi.org/10.1016/B978-0-323-91231-0.00007-0

the top supercomputers in the world today use both CPUs and GPUs in each node. The effectiveness of this approach is validated by their high rankings in the Green500 list, which reflects their high energy efficiency.

The dominating programming interface for computing clusters today is MPI (Gropp et al., 1999), which is a set of API functions for communication between processes running in a computing cluster. MPI assumes a distributed memory model in which processes exchange information by sending messages to each other. When an application uses API communication functions, it does not need to deal with the details of the interconnect network. The MPI implementation allows the processes to address each other using logical numbers, in much the same way as using phone numbers in a telephone system: Telephone users can dial each other using phone numbers without knowing exactly where the called person is and how the call is routed.

In a typical MPI application, data and work are partitioned among processes. As is shown in Fig. 20.1, each node can contain one or more processes, shown as clouds within nodes. As these processes progress, they may need data from each other. This need is satisfied by sending and receiving messages. In some cases, the processes also need to synchronize with each other and generate collective results when collaborating on a large task. This is done with collective communication API functions.

20.2 A running example

As a running example we will use a three-dimensional (3D) stencil computation that was introduced in Chapter 8, Stencil. We assume that the computation calculates heat transfer based on a finite difference method for solving a partial differential equation that describes the physical laws of heat transfer. In particular, we will use the Jacobi iterative method, in which in each iteration or time step, the value of a grid point is calculated as a weighted sum of neighbors (north, east, south, west, up, down) and its own value from the previous time step. To achieve high numerical stability, multiple indirect neighbors in each direction are also used in the computation of a grid point. This is a *higher-order stencil*

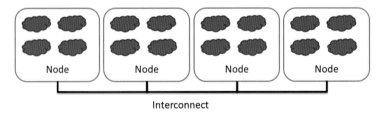

FIGURE 20.1

Programmer's view of MPI processes. *MPI*, Message Passing Interface.

computation, as we discussed in Chapter 8, Stencil. For the purpose of this chapter we assume that four points in each direction will be used.

As is shown in Fig. 20.2, there are a total of 24 neighbor points for calculating the next step value of a grid point. Each point in the grid has x, y, and z coordinates. For a grid point where the coordinate value is $x = i$, $y = j$, and $z = k$, or (i, j, k), its 24 neighbors are ($i - 4, j, k$), ($i - 3, j, k$), ($i - 2, j, k$), ($i - 1, j, k$), ($i + 1, j, k$), ($i + 2, j, k$), ($i + 3, j, k$), ($i + 4, j, k$), ($i, j - 4, k$), ($i, j - 3, k$), ($i, j - 2, k$), ($i, j - 1, k$), ($i, j + 1, k$), ($i, j + 2, k$), ($i, j + 3, k$), ($i, j + 4, k$), ($i, j, k - 4$), ($i, j, k - 3$), ($i, j, k - 2$), ($i, j, k - 1$), ($i, j, k + 1$), ($i, j, k + 2$), ($i, j, k + 3$) and ($i, j, k + 4$). Since the data value of each grid point for the next time step is calculated on the basis of the current data values of 25 points (24 neighbors and itself), this is a 25-point stencil computation.

We assume that the system is modeled as a structured grid in which spacing between grid points is constant within each direction. This allows us to use a 3D array in which each element stores the state of a grid point, as we discussed in Chapter 8, Stencil. The physical distance between adjacent elements in each dimension can be represented by a grid spacing variable. Note that this grid data structure is similar to that used in the electrostatic potential calculation in Chapter 18, Electrostatic Potential Map. Fig. 20.3 illustrates a 3D array that represents a rectangular ventilation duct, with x and y dimensions as the cross sections of the duct and the z dimension the direction of the heat flow along the duct.

We assume that the data is placed in the memory space in the row-major layout, where x is the lowest dimension, y is the next, and z is the highest. That is, all elements with $y = 0$ and $z = 0$ will be placed in consecutive memory locations according to their x coordinate. Fig. 20.4 shows a small example of the

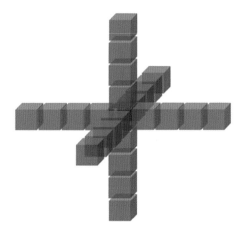

FIGURE 20.2

A 25-point stencil computation example, with four neighbors in each of the x, y, and z directions.

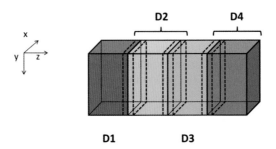

FIGURE 20.3

3D Grid array for the modeling heat transfer in a duct.

D	z=0	z=0	z=1	z=1	z=2	z=2	z=3	z=3
↓	y=0	y=1	y=0	y=1	y=0	y=1	y=0	y=1

x=0	x=1	x=0	x=1	x=0	x=1	x=0	x=1	x=0	x=1	x=0	x=1	x=0	x=1	x=0	x=1

FIGURE 20.4

A small example of memory layout for the 3D grid.

grid data layout. This small example has only 16 data elements in the grid: two elements in the x dimension, two in the y dimension, and four in the z dimension. Both x elements with $y = 0$ and $z = 0$ are placed in memory first. They are followed by all elements with $y = 1$ and $z = 0$. The next group will be elements with $y = 0$ and $z = 1$.

When one uses a computing cluster, it is common to divide the input data into several partitions, called domain partitions, and assign each partition to a node in the cluster. In Fig. 20.3 we show that the 3D array is divided into four domain partitions: D0, D1, D2, and D3. Each of the partitions will be assigned to an MPI compute process.

The domain partitions can be further illustrated with Fig. 20.4. The first section, or slice, of four elements ($z = 0$) is in the first partition; the second section ($z = 1$) is in the second partition; the third section ($z = 2$) is in the third partition; and the fourth section ($z = 3$) is in the fourth partition. This is obviously a toy example. In a real application there are typically hundreds or even thousands of elements in each dimension. For the rest of this chapter it is useful to remember that all elements in a z slice are in consecutive memory locations.

20.3 Message passing interface basics

Like CUDA, MPI programs are based on the SPMD parallel programming model. All MPI processes execute the same program. The MPI system provides a set of

API functions to establish communication systems that allow the processes to communicate with each other. Fig. 20.5 shows five essential MPI functions that set up and tear down the communication system for an MPI application.

We will use a simple MPI program, shown in Fig. 20.6, to illustrate the usage the API functions. To launch an MPI application in a cluster, a user needs to supply the executable file of the program to the *mpirun* command or the *mpiexec* command in the login node of the cluster. Each process starts by initializing the MPI runtime with an `MPI_Init()` call (line 05). This initializes the communication system for all the processes that are running the application. Once the MPI runtime has been initialized, each process calls two functions to prepare for communication. The first function is `MPI_Comm_rank()` (line 06), which returns a unique number to each calling process, which is called the *MPI rank* or process

- `int` **MPI_Init(**`int` ***argc,** `char` *****argv)**
  - Initialize MPI
- `int` **MPI_Comm_rank (**`MPI_Comm` **comm,** `int` ***rank)**
  - Rank of the calling process in group of comm
- `int` **MPI_Comm_size (**`MPI_Comm` **comm,** `int` ***size)**
  - Number of processes in the group of comm
- `int` **MPI_Comm_abort (**`MPI_Comm` **comm)**
  - Terminate MPI comminication connection with an error flag
- `int` **MPI_Finalize ()**
  - Ending an MPI application, close all resources

FIGURE 20.5

Basic MPI functions for establishing and closing a communication system.

```
01  #include "mpi.h"
02  int main(int argc, char *argv[]) {
03      int pad = 0, dimx  = 480+pad, dimy  = 480, dimz  = 400, nreps = 100;
04      int pid=-1, np=-1;
05      MPI_Init(&argc, &argv);
06      MPI_Comm_rank(MPI_COMM_WORLD, &pid);
07      MPI_Comm_size(MPI_COMM_WORLD, &np);
08      if(np < 3) {
09          if(0 == pid) printf("Needed 3 or more processes.\n");
10          MPI_Abort( MPI_COMM_WORLD, 1 ); return 1;
11      }
12      if(pid < np - 1)
13          compute_process(dimx, dimy, dimz / (np - 1), nreps);
14      else
15          data_server( dimx,dimy,dimz );
16      MPI_Finalize();
17      return 0;
18  }
```

FIGURE 20.6

A simple MPI main program.

id for the process. The numbers that are received by the processes vary from 0 to the number of processes minus 1. The MPI rank for a process is analogous to the expression `blockIdx.x*blockDim.x+threadIdx.x` for a CUDA thread. It uniquely identifies the process in a communication, which is also equivalent to the phone number in a telephone system. The main differences are that MPI ranks are one-dimensional.

The `MPI_Comm_rank()` function in line 06 of Fig. 20.6 takes two parameters. The first is an MPI built-in type `MPI_Comm` that specifies the scope of the request, that is, the collection of processes that form the group identified by a `MIP_Comm` variable. Each variable of the `MPI_comm` type is commonly referred to as a communicator. `MPI_Comm` and other MPI built-in types are defined in the "mpi.h" header file (line 01), which should be included in all C program files that use MPI. An MPI application can create one or more *communicators*, each of which is a group of MPI processes for the purpose of communication. `MPI_Comm_rank()` assigns a unique id to each process in a communicator. In Fig. 20.6 the parameter value that is passed is `MPI_COMM_WORLD`, which is used as a default and means that the communicator includes all MPI processes that are running the application.[1]

The second parameter of the `MPI_Comm_rank()` function is a pointer to an integer variable into which the function will deposit the returned rank value. In Fig. 20.6 a variable pid is declared for this purpose. After the `MPI_Comm_rank()` has returned, the pid variable will contain the unique id for the calling process.

The second API function is `MPI_Comm_size()` (line 07), which returns the total number of MPI processes running in the communicator. The `MPI_Comm_size()` function takes two parameters. The first one is of MPI_Comm type that gives the scope of the request. In Fig. 20.6 the parameter value that is passed in is `MPI_COMM_WORLD`, which means that the scope of the `MPI_Comm_size()` is all the processes in the application. Since the scope is all MPI processes, the returned value is the total number of MPI processes that are running the application. This value is configured by the user when the application is executed by using the mpirun command or the mpiexec command. However, the user may not have requested a sufficient number of processes. Also, the system may or may not be able to create all the processes that the user requested. Therefore it is a good practice for an MPI application program to check the actual number of processes that are running.

The second parameter is a pointer to an integer variable into which the `MPI_Comm_size()` function will deposit the return value. In Fig. 20.6 a variable np is declared for this purpose. After the function returns, the variable np contains the number of MPI processes that are running the application. In Fig. 20.6 we assume that the application requires at least 3 MPI processes. Therefore it checks

---

[1] Interested readers should refer to the MPI reference manual (Gropp et al., 1999) for details on creating and using multiple communicators in an application, in particular the definition and use intracommunicators and intercommunicators.

whether the number of processes is at least 3 (line 08). If not, it calls
`MPI_Comm_abort()` function to terminate the communication connections and
return with an error flag value 1 (line 10).

Fig. 20.6 also shows a common pattern for reporting errors or other chores.
There are multiple MPI processes, but we need to report the error only once. The
application code designates the process with `pid = 0` to do the reporting (line 09).
This is similar to the pattern in CUDA kernels in which some tasks need to be
done by only one of the threads in a thread-block.

As is shown in Fig. 20.5, the `MPI_Comm_abort()` function takes two parameters
(line 10). The first sets the scope of the request. In Fig. 20.6 the scope is set as
`MPI_COMM_WORLD`, which means all MPI processes that are running the application.
The second parameter is a code for the type of error that caused the abort. Any
number other than 0 indicates that an error has happened.

If the number of processes satisfies the requirement, the application program
goes on to perform the calculation. In Fig. 20.6, the application uses np − 1 processes (`pid` from 0 to np − 2) to perform the calculation (lines 12−13) and one
process (the last one whose pid is np − 1) to perform I/O service for the other
processes (lines 14−15). We will refer to the process that performs the I/O services as the data server and the processes that perform the calculation as compute
processes. In Fig. 20.6, if the pid of a process is within the range from 0 to np − 2,
it is a compute process and calls the `compute_process()` function (line 13). If the
process pid is np − 1, it is the data server and calls the `data_server()` function
(line 15). This is similar to the pattern in which threads perform different actions
according to their thread ids.

After the application has completed its computation, it notifies the MPI runtime with a call to `MPI_Finalize()`, which frees all MPI communication resources
that are allocated to the application (line 16). The application can then exit with a
return value 0, which indicates that no error has occurred (line 17).

20.4 Message passing interface point-to-point communication

MPI supports two major types of communication. The first is the point-to-point
type, which involves one source process and one destination process. The source
process calls the `MPI_Send()` function, and the destination process calls the
`MPI_Recv()` function. This is analogous to a caller dialing a call and a receiver
answering a call in a telephone system.

Fig. 20.7 shows the syntax for using the `MPI_Send()` function. The first parameter is a pointer to the starting location of the memory area where the data to be
sent can be found. The second parameter is an integer that gives that number of
data elements to be sent. The third parameter is of the MPI built-in type
`MPI_Datatype`. It specifies the type of each data element that is being sent as far

- int **MPI_Send(**void ***buf,** int **count,**
  MPI_Datatype **datatype,** int **dest,** int **tag,**
  MPI_Comm **comm)**
  - − Buf: **starting address of send buffer (pointer)**
  - − Count: **Number of elements in send buffer (nonnegative integer)**
  - − Datatype: **Datatype of each send buffer element (MPI_Datatype)**
  - − Dest: **Rank of destination (integer)**
  - − Tag: **Message tag (integer)**
  - − Comm: **Communicator (handle)**

FIGURE 20.7

Syntax for the MPI_Send() function.

- int **MPI_Recv(**void ***buf,** int **count,**
  MPI_Datatype **datatype,** int **source,** int **tag,**
  MPI_Comm **comm,** MPI_Status ***status)**
  - − buf: **starting address of receive buffer (pointer)**
  - − Count: **Maximum number of elements in receive buffer (integer)**
  - − Datatype: **Datatype of each receive buffer element (MPI_Datatype)**
  - − Source: **Rank of source (integer)**
  - − Tag: **Message tag (integer)**
  - − Comm: **Communicator (handle)**
  - − Status: **Status object (Status)**

FIGURE 20.8

Syntax for the MPI_Recv() function.

as the MPI library implementation is concerned. The values that can be held by a variable or argument of the MPI_Datatype are defined in mpi.h and include MPI_DOUBLE (double-precision floating-point), MPI_FLOAT (single-precision floating-point), MPI_INT (integer), and MPI_CHAR (character). The exact sizes of these types depend on the size of the corresponding C types in the host processor. See the MPI reference manual for more sophisticated use of MPI types (Gropp et al., 1999).

The fourth parameter for MPI_Send() is an integer that gives the MPI rank of the destination process. The fifth parameter gives a tag that can be used to classify the messages that are sent by the same process. The sixth parameter is a communicator that specifies the context in which the destination MPI rank is defined.

Fig. 20.8 shows the syntax for using the MPI_Recv() function. The first parameter is a pointer to the area in memory where the received data should be deposited. The second parameter is an integer that gives the maximum number of elements that the MPI_Recv() function is allowed to receive. The third parameter is an MPI_Datatype that specifies the type of each element to be received. The fourth parameter is an integer that gives the process id of the source of the message. The fifth parameter is an integer that specifies the tag value that is expected by the destination process. If the destination process does not want to be limited to a particular tag value, it can use MPI_ANY_TAG, which means that the receiver is willing to accept messages of any tag value from the source.

We will first use the data server to illustrate the use of point-to-point communication. In a real application the data server process would typically perform data input and output operations for the compute processes. However, input and output have too much system-dependent complexity. Since I/O is not the focus of our discussion, we will avoid the complexity of I/O operations in a cluster environment. That is, instead of reading data from a file system, we will just have the data server initialize the data with random numbers and distribute the data to the compute processes. The first part of the data server code is shown in Fig. 20.9.

The data server function takes four parameters. The first three parameters specify the size of the 3D grid: the number of elements in the *x* dimension, dimx; the number of elements in the *y* dimension, dimy; and the number of elements in

```
01  void data_server(int dimx, int dimy, int dimz, int nreps) {
02      int np;
        /* Set MPI Communication Size */
03      MPI_Comm_size(MPI_COMM_WORLD, &np);
04      unsigned int num_comp_nodes = np - 1, first_node = 0, last_node = np - 2;
05      unsigned int num_points = dimx * dimy * dimz;
06      unsigned int num_bytes  = num_points * sizeof(float);
07      float *input=0, *output=0;
        /* Allocate input data */
08      input = (float *)malloc(num_bytes);
09      output = (float *)malloc(num_bytes);
10      if(input == NULL || output == NULL) {
11          printf("server couldn't allocate memory\n");
12          MPI_Abort( MPI_COMM_WORLD, 1 );
13      }
        /* Initialize input data */
14      random_data(input, dimx, dimy ,dimz , 1, 10);
        /* Calculate number of shared points */
15      int edge_num_points = dimx * dimy * ((dimz / num_comp_nodes) + 4);
16      int int_num_points  = dimx * dimy * ((dimz / num_comp_nodes) + 8);
17      float *send_address = input;
        /* Send data to the first compute node */
18      MPI_Send(send_address, edge_num_points, MPI_FLOAT, first_node,
                    0, MPI_COMM_WORLD );
19      send_address += dimx * dimy * ((dimz / num_comp_nodes) - 4);
        /* Send data to "internal" compute nodes */
20      for(int process = 1; process < last_node; process++) {
21          MPI_Send(send_address, int_num_points, MPI_FLOAT, process,
                        0, MPI_COMM_WORLD);
22          send_address += dimx * dimy * (dimz / num_comp_nodes);
        }
        /* Send data to the last compute node */
23      MPI_Send(send_address, edge_num_points, MPI_FLOAT, last_node,
                    0, MPI_COMM_WORLD);
```

FIGURE 20.9

Data server process code (part 1).

the z dimension, dimz. The fourth parameter specifies the number of iterations that need to be done for all the data points in the grid.

In Fig. 20.9, line 02 declares variable np that will contain the number of processes running the application. Line 03 calls MPI_Comm_size(), which will deposit the number of processes running the application into np. Line 04 declares and initializes several helper variables. The variable num_comp_procs contains the number of compute processes. Since we are reserving one process as the data server, there are np − 1 compute processes. The variable first_proc gives the process id of the first compute process, which is 0. The variable last_proc gives the process id of the last compute process, which is np − 2. That is, line 04 designates the first np − 1 processes, 0 through np − 2, as compute processes. The process with the largest rank serves as the data server. This reflects the design decision, and this decision will also be reflected in the compute process code.

Line 05 declares and initializes the num_points variable that gives the total number of grid data points to be processed, which is simply the product of the number of elements in each dimension, or dimx * dimy * dimz. Line 06 declares and initializes the num_bytes variable, which gives the total number of bytes needed to store all the grid data points. Since each grid data point is a float, this value is num_points * sizeof(float).

Line 07 declares two pointer variables: input and output. These two pointers will point to the input data buffer and the output data buffer. Lines 08 and 09 allocate memory for the input and output buffers and assign their addresses to their respective pointers. Line 10 checks whether the memory allocations were successful. If either of the memory allocation fails, the corresponding pointer will have received a NULL pointer from the malloc() function. In this case, the code aborts the application and reports an error (lines 11−12).

Lines 15 and 16 calculate the number of grid point array elements that should be sent to each compute process. As is shown in Fig. 20.3, there are two types of compute processes: edge processes and internal processes. The first process (process 0, which computes D1) and the last process (process 3, which computes D4) compute an edge partition that has neighbors only on one side. Partition D1, which is assigned to process 0, has a neighbor only on the right side (D2). Partition D4, which is assigned to the last compute process, has a neighbor only on the left side (D3). We call the compute processes that compute edge partitions the *edge processes*. Each of the other processes computes an internal partition that has neighbors on both sizes. For example, process 1 computes partition D2, which has a left neighbor (D1) and a right neighbor (D3). We call the processes that compute internal partitions *internal processes*.

Recall that in the Jacobi iterative method, each calculation step for a grid point needs the values of its immediate neighbors from the previous step. This creates a need for halo cells for grid points at the left and right boundaries of a partition, which are shown as slices defined by dashed lines at the edge of each partition in Fig. 20.3. Note that these halo slices are similar to those in the stencil pattern that was presented in Chapter 8, Stencil. Since we are computing a

25-point stencil with four elements in each direction, each process needs to receive four slices of halo cells that contain all neighbors for each side of the boundary grid points of its partition. For example, in Fig. 20.3, partition D2 needs four halo slices from D1 and four halo slices from D3. Note that a halo slice for D2 is a boundary slice for D1 or D3.

Recall that the total number of grid points is `dimx*dimy*dimz`. Since we are partitioning the grid along the z dimension, the number of grid points in each partition should be `dimx*dimy*(dimz/num_comp_procs)`. Recall that we will need four neighbor slices in each direction in order to calculate values within each partition. Therefore the number of grid points that should be sent to each internal process is `dimx*dimy*((dimz/num_comp_procs) + 8)`. As for an edge process, there is only one neighbor. As in the case of convolution, we assume that zero values will be used for the ghost cells and that no input data needs to be sent for them. For example, partition D1 needs only the four neighbor slices from D2 on the right side. Therefore the number of grid points to be sent to an edge process is `dimx*dimy*((dimz/num_comp_procs) + 4)`. That is, each process receives four slices of halo grid points from the neighbor partition on each side.

Line 17 of Fig. 20.9 sets the `send_address` pointer to point to the beginning of the input grid point array. To send the appropriate partition to each process, we will need to add the appropriate offset to this beginning address for each `MPI_Send()`. We will come back to this point later.

We are now ready to complete the code for the data server. Line 18 sends process 0 its partition. Since this is the first partition, its starting address is also the starting address of the entire grid, which was set up in line 17. Process 0 is an edge process, and it does not have a left neighbor. Therefore the number of grid points to be sent is the value `edge_num_points`, that is, `dimx*dimy*((dimz/num_-comp_procs) + 4)`. The third parameter specifies that the type of each element is an `MPI_FLOAT` which is C float (single-precision, 4 bytes). The fourth parameter specifies that the value of `first_node`, that is, 0, is the MPI rank of the destination process. The fifth parameter specifies 0 for the MPI tag. This is because we are not using tags to distinguish between messages sent from the data server. The sixth parameter specifies that the communicator to be used for interpreting the sender and receiver rank values for the message should be all MPI processes for the current application.

Line 19 of Fig. 20.9 advances the `send_address` pointer to the beginning of the data partition for process 1. From Fig. 20.3 there are `dimx*dimy*(dimz/num_-comp_procs)` elements in partition D1, which means that D2 starts at the location that is `dimx*dimy*(dimz/num_comp_procs)` elements from the starting location of input. Recall that we also need to send the halo cells from D1. Therefore we adjust the starting address for the `MPI_Send()` back by four slices, which results in the expression for advancing the `send_address` pointer in line 19: `dimx*dimy*((dimz/num_comp_procs) - 4)`.

Line 20 is a loop that sends out the MPI messages to the internal processes (process 1 through process np − 3). In our small example for four compute processes, np is 5, so the loop sends the MPI messages to process 1 and process 2. These internal processes need to receive halo grid points for neighbors on both sides. Therefore the second parameter of the `MPI_Send()` in line 21 uses `int_num_nodes`, that is, `dimx*dimy*((dimz/num_comp_procs) + 8)`. The rest of the parameters are similar to that for the `MPI_Send()` in line 18 with the obvious exception that the destination process is specified by the loop variable process, which is incremented from 1 to np − 3 (the `last_node` is np − 2).

Line 22 advances the send address for each internal process by the number of grid points in each partition: `dimx*dimy*dimz/num_comp_nodes`. Note that the starting locations of the halo grid points for internal processes are `dimx*dimy*dimz/num_comp_procs` points apart. Although we need to pull back the starting address by four slices to accommodate halo grid points, we do so for every internal process, so the net distance between the starting locations remains the number of grid points in each partition.

Line 23 sends the data to the process np − 2, the last compute process that has only one neighbor on the left. The reader should be able to reason through all the parameter values that are used. Note that we are not quite done with the data server code. We will come back later for the final part of the data server that collects the output values from all compute processes.

We now turn our attention to the compute processes that receive the input from the data server process. In Fig. 20.10, lines 03−04 establish the process id for the process and the total number of processes for the application. Line 05 establishes that the data server is process np − 1. Lines 06−07 calculate the number of grid points and the number of bytes that should be processed by each internal process. Lines 08−09 calculate the number of grid points and the number of bytes in each halo (4 slices).

Lines 10−12 allocate the host memory and device memory for the input data. Although the edge processes need less halo data, they still allocate the same

```
01  void compute_node_stencil(int dimx, int dimy, int dimz, int nreps ) {
02      int np, pid;
03      MPI_Comm_rank(MPI_COMM_WORLD, &pid);
04      MPI_Comm_size(MPI_COMM_WORLD, &np);
05      int server_process = np - 1;
06      unsigned int num_points      = dimx * dimy * (dimz + 8);
07      unsigned int num_bytes       = num_points * sizeof(float);
08      unsigned int num_halo_points = 4 * dimx * dimy;
09      unsigned int num_halo_bytes  = num_halo_points * sizeof(float);
        /* Allocate host memory */
10      float *h_input  = (float *)malloc(num_bytes);
        /* Allocate device memory for input and output data */
11      float *d_input = NULL;
12      cudaMalloc((void **)&d_input,  num_bytes );
13      float *rcv_address = h_input + ((0 == pid) ? num_halo_points : 0);
14      MPI_Recv(rcv_address, num_points, MPI_FLOAT, server_process,
                 MPI_ANY_TAG, MPI_COMM_WORLD, &status );
15      cudaMemcpy(d_input, h_input, num_bytes, cudaMemcpyHostToDevice);
```

FIGURE 20.10

Compute process code (part 1).

amount of memory for simplicity; part of the allocated memory will not be used by the edge processes. Line 13 sets the starting address of the host memory for receiving the input data from the data server. For all compute processes except process 0, the starting receiving location is simply the starting location of the allocated memory for the input data. However, for process 0, we adjust the receiving location by four slices. This is because for simplicity we assume that the host memory for receiving the input data is arranged in the same way for all compute processes: four slices of halo elements from the left neighbor followed by the partition, followed by four slices of halo elements from the right neighbor. However, as we showed in line 15 of Fig. 20.9, the data server will not send any halo data from the left neighbor to process 0. That is, for process 0, the MPI message from the data server contains only the partition and the halo from the right neighbor. Therefore line 13 adjusts the starting host memory location by four slices so that process 0 will correctly interpret the input data from the data server.

Line 14 receives the MPI message from the data server. Most of the parameters should be familiar. The last parameter reflects any error condition that has occurred when the data are received. The second parameter specifies that all compute processes will receive the full amount of data from the data server. However, the data server will send less data to process 0 and process np − 2. This is not reflected in the code because `MPI_Recv()` allows the second parameter to specify a larger number of data points than are actually received and will place only the actual number of bytes received from the sender into the receiving memory. In the case of process 0, the input data from the data server contains only the partition and the halo from the right neighbor. The received input will be placed by skipping the first four slices of the allocated memory, which correspond to the halo for the (nonexistent) left neighbor. This effect is achieved with the term `((0==pid)? num_halo_points: 0)` on line 13. In the case of process np − 2, the input data contains the halo from the left neighbor and the partition. The received input will be placed from the beginning of the allocated memory, leaving the last four slices of the allocated memory unused.

Line 15 copies the received input data to the device memory. In the case of process 0, the left halo points are not valid. In the case of process np − 2, the right halo points are not valid. However, for simplicity, all compute nodes send the full size to the device memory. The assumption is that the kernels will be launched in such a way that these invalid portions will be correctly ignored. After line 15, all the input data are in the device memory.

Fig. 20.11 shows part 2 of the compute process code. Lines 16−18 allocate host memory and device memory for the output data. The output data buffer in the device memory will be used with the input data buffer in a double-buffering scheme. That is, they will switch roles in each iteration. We will return to this point and cover the rest of the code in Fig. 20.11 later. We are now ready to present the code that performs computation steps on the grid points.

```
16    float *h_output = NULL, *d_output = NULL, *d_vsq = NULL;
17    float *h_output = (float *)malloc(num_bytes);
18    cudaMalloc((void **)&d_output, num_bytes );
19    float *h_left_boundary = NULL, *h_right_boundary = NULL;
20    float *h_left_halo = NULL, *h_right_halo = NULL;
      /* Allocate host memory for halo data */
21    cudaHostAlloc((void **)&h_left_boundary,   num_halo_bytes,
                    cudaHostAllocDefault);
22    cudaHostAlloc((void **)&h_right_boundary, num_halo_bytes,
                    cudaHostAllocDefault);
23    cudaHostAlloc((void **)&h_left_halo,        num_halo_bytes,
                    cudaHostAllocDefault);
24    cudaHostAlloc((void **)&h_right_halo,       num_halo_bytes,
                    cudaHostAllocDefault);
   /* Create streams used for stencil computation */
25    cudaStream_t stream0, stream1;
26    cudaStreamCreate(&stream0);
27    cudaStreamCreate(&stream1);
```

FIGURE 20.11

Compute process code (part 2).

20.5 Overlapping computation and communication

A simple way to perform the computation steps is for each compute process to perform a computation step on its entire partition, exchange halo data with the left and right neighbors, and repeat. While this is a very simple strategy, it is not very effective. The reason is that this strategy forces the system to be in one of the two modes. In the first mode, all compute processes are performing computation steps. During this time, the communication network is not used. In the second mode, all compute processes are exchanging halo data with their left and right neighbors. During this time, the computation hardware is not well utilized. Ideally, we would like to achieve better performance by utilizing both the communication network and the computation hardware all the time. This can be achieved by dividing the computation tasks of each compute process into two stages, as illustrated in Fig. 20.12.

During the first stage (stage 1), each compute process calculates its boundary slices that will be needed as halo cells by its neighbors in the next iteration. Let's continue to assume that we use four slices of halo data. Fig. 20.12 shows the four halo slices as a dashed transparent piece and the four boundary slices as a colored piece. Note that the colored piece of process i will be copied into the dashed piece of process $I + 1$ and the colored piece of process $I + 1$ will be copied into the dashed piece of process i during the next communication. For process 0, the first phase calculates the right four slices of boundary data. For an internal node it calculates the left four slices and the right four slices of its boundary data. For process $n - 2$, it calculates the left four pieces of its boundary data. The rationale is that these boundary slices are needed by their neighbors for the next iteration. If these boundary slices are calculated first, the data can be communicated to the neighbors while the compute processes calculate the rest of their internal grid points.

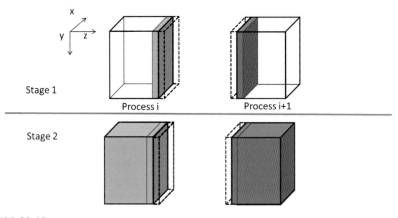

FIGURE 20.12

A two-stage strategy for overlapping computation with communication.

During the second stage (stage 2), each compute process performs two activities in parallel. The first is to communicate its new boundary values to its neighbor processes. This is done by first copying the data from the device memory into the host memory, followed by sending MPI messages to the neighbors. As we will discuss later, we need to be careful that the data that is received from the neighbors is used in the next iteration, not the current iteration. The second activity is to calculate the rest of the data in the partition. If the communication activity takes a shorter amount of time than the calculation activity, we can hide the communication delay and fully utilize the computing hardware all the time. This is usually achieved by having enough slices in the internal part of each partition to allow each compute process to perform enough computation to hide the communication.

To support the parallel activities in stage 2, we need to use two advanced features of the CUDA programming model: *pinned memory allocation* and *streams*. A pinned memory allocation requests that the memory that is allocated not be paged out by the operating system. This is done with the `cudaHostAlloc()` API call. Lines 21−24 in Fig. 20.11 allocate pinned memory buffers for the left and right boundary slices and the left and right halo slices. The left and right boundary slices need to be sent from the device memory to the left and right neighbor processes. The buffers are used as a host memory staging area for the device to copy data into and are then used as the source buffer for `MPI_Send()` to neighbor processes. The left and right halo slices need to be received from neighbor processes. The buffers are used as a host memory staging area for `MPI_Recv()` to use as destination buffers and then to copy data from them to the device memory. These buffers are sometimes referred to as *bounce buffers*, as their main role is to serve as temporary buffers that allow the data to be bounced from the device memory to the remote MPI process and vice versa.

Note that the host memory allocation for the bounce buffers is done with cudaHostAlloc() function rather than the standard malloc() function. The difference is that the cudaHostAlloc() function allocates a *pinned memory* buffer, sometimes also referred to as *page locked memory* buffer. We need to know a little more background on the memory management in operating systems in order to fully understand the concept of pinned memory buffers.

In a modern computer system the operating system manages virtual memory spaces for applications. Each application has access to a large, consecutive address space. In reality the system has a limited amount of physical memory that needs to be shared among all running applications. This sharing is performed by partitioning the virtual memory space into pages and mapping only the actively used pages into physical memory. When there is much demand for memory, the operating system needs to page out some of the pages from the physical memory to mass storage such as disks. Therefore an application may have its data paged out at any time during its execution.

The implementation of cudaMemcpy() uses a type of hardware called a direct memory access (DMA) device. When a cudaMemcpy() function is called to copy between the host and device memories, its implementation uses a DMA operation to complete the task. On the host memory side, the DMA hardware operates on physical addresses; that is, the operating system needs to give a translated physical address to the DMA device. However, there is a chance that the data may be paged out before the DMA operation is complete. The physical memory locations for the data may be reassigned to other data corresponding to a different virtual memory location. In this case, the DMA operation can potentially be corrupted, since its data can be overwritten by the paging activity.

A common solution to this data corruption problem is for the CUDA runtime to perform the copy operation in two steps. For a host-to-device copy, the CUDA runtime first copies the source host memory data into a pinned memory buffer, which means that the memory locations are marked so that the paging mechanism will not page out the data. It then uses the DMA device to copy the data from the pinned memory buffer to the device memory. For a device-to-host copy, the CUDA runtime first uses a DMA device to copy the data from the device memory into a pinned memory buffer. It then copies the data from the pinned memory buffer to the destination host memory location. By using an extra pinned memory buffer, the DMA copy will be safe from any paging activities.

There are two problems with this approach. One is that the extra copy adds delay to the cudaMemcpy() operation. The second is that the extra complexity involved leads to a synchronous implementation of the cudaMemcpy() function. That is, the host program cannot continue to execute until the cudaMemcpy() function has completed its operation and returned. This serializes all copy operations. To support fast copies with more parallelism, CUDA provides a cudaMemcpyAsync() function.

The cudaMemcpyAsync() function requires that the host memory buffer be allocated as a pinned memory buffer. This is done in lines 21−24 in Fig. 20.11 for the host memory buffers of the left boundary, right boundary, left halo, and right halo slices. These buffers are allocated with the `cudaHostAlloc()` function, which ensures that the allocated memory is pinned or page locked from paging activities. Note that the `cudaHostAlloc()` function takes three parameters. The first two are the same as `cudaMalloc()`. The third specifies some options for more advanced usage. For most basic use cases, we can simply use the default value `cudaHostAllocDefault`.

The second advanced CUDA feature that is used for overlapping communication with computation is *streams*, a feature that supports managed concurrent execution of CUDA API functions. A stream is an ordered sequence of operations. When the host code calls a `cudaMemcpyAsync()` function or launches a kernel, it can specify a stream as one of its parameters. By specifying a stream in a `cudaMemcpyAsync()` call, the copy operation is placed into a stream. All operations in the same stream will be done sequentially according to the order in which they are placed into that stream. However, operations in different streams can be executed in parallel without any ordering constraint.

Line 25 of Fig. 20.11 declares two variables that are of CUDA built-in type `cudaStream_t`. These variables are then used in calling the `cudaStreamCreate()` function. Each call to `cudaStreamCreate()` creates a new stream and deposits an identifier of the stream into its parameter. After the calls in lines 26 and 27, the host code can use either stream 0 or stream 1 in subsequent `cudaMemcpyAsync()` calls and kernel calls.

Fig. 20.13 shows part 3 of the compute process. Line 28 declares an MPI status variable that will be used for MPI send and receive. Lines 29−30 calculate the process id of the left and right neighbors of the compute process. The `left_-neighbor` and `right_neighbor` variables will be used by compute processes as

```
28      MPI_Status status;
29      int left_neighbor  = (pid > 0)      ? (pid - 1) : MPI_PROC_NULL;
30      int right_neighbor = (pid < np - 2) ? (pid + 1) : MPI_PROC_NULL;

        /* Upload stencil cofficients */
31      upload_coefficients(coeff, 5);
32      int left_halo_offset   = 0;
33      int right_halo_offset  = dimx * dimy * (4 + dimz);
34      int left_stage1_offset = 0;
35      int right_stage1_offset = dimx * dimy * (dimz - 4);
36      int stage2_offset       = num_halo_points;
37      MPI_Barrier( MPI_COMM_WORLD );
38      for(int i=0; I < nreps; i++) {
            /* Compute boundary values needed by other nodes first */
39          call_stencil_kernel(d_output + left_stage1_offset,
                    d_input + left_stage1_offset, dimx, dimy, 12, stream0);
40          call_stencil_kernel(d_output + right_stage1_offset,
                    d_input + right_stage1_offset, dimx, dimy, 12, stream0);
            /* Compute the remaining points */
41          call_stencil_kernel(d_output + stage2_offset, d_input +
                    stage2_offset, dimx, dimy, dimz, stream1);
```

FIGURE 20.13

Compute process code (part 3).

parameters when they send messages to and receive messages from their neighbors. For process 0, there is no left neighbor, so line 29 assigns an MPI constant `MPI_PROC_NULL` to `left_neighbor` to note this fact. For process np − 2, there is no right neighbor, so line 30 assigns `MPI_PROC_NULL` to right_neighbor. For all the internal processes, lines 29−30 assign pid − 1 to `left_neighbor` and pid + 1 to `right_neighbor`.

Line 31 in Fig. 20.13 calls a function to copy the stencil coefficients to the GPU constant memory. The details will not be shown here because the reader should already be familiar with constant memory. Lines 32−36 set up several offsets that will be used to call kernels and exchange data so that the computation and communication can be overlapped. These offsets define the regions of grid points that will need to be calculated at each stage of Fig. 20.13. They are also visualized in Fig. 20.12.

Note that the total number of slices in each device memory is four slices of left halo points (dashed white) plus four slices of left boundary points plus `dimx*dimy*(dimz − 8)` internal points plus four slices of right boundary points plus four slices of right halo points (dashed white). As illustrated in Fig. 20.14, variable `left_stage1_offset` defines the starting point of the slices that are needed in order to calculate the left boundary slices. This includes 12 slices of data: four slices of left neighbor halo points, four slices of boundary points, and four slices of internal points. These slices are the leftmost in the partition, so the offset value is set to 0 by line 34. Variable `right_stage2_offset` defines the starting point of the slices that are needed for calculating the right boundary slices. This also includes 12 slices: four slices of internal points, four slices of right boundary points, and four slices of right halo cells. The beginning point of these 12 slices can be derived by subtracting 12 from the total number of slices dimz + 8. Therefore the starting offset for these 12 slices is set to `dimx*dimy*(dimz − 4)` by line 35 (Fig. 20.12).

Line 37 in Fig. 20.13 is an MPI barrier synchronization, which is similar to the CUDA `__syncthreads()` across threads in a block. MPI barrier forces all MPI processes that are specified by the input argument to wait for each other. None of the

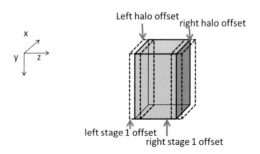

FIGURE 20.14

Device memory offsets used for data exchange with neighbor processes.

processes can continue their execution beyond this point until all have reached this point. The reason why we want the barrier synchronization here is to ensure that all compute nodes have received their input data and are ready to perform the computation steps. Since they will be exchanging data with each other, we would like to make them all start at about the same time. Thus we will not be in a situation in which a few tardy processes delay all other processes during the data exchange. `MPI_Barrier()` is a *collective communication* function. We will discuss collective communication API functions in more detail in the next section.

Line 38 starts a loop that performs the computation steps. For each iteration, each compute process will perform one cycle of the two-stage process shown in Fig. 20.12. Line 39 calls a function that will generate the four slices of the left boundary points in stage 1. We assume that the function will set up the grid configuration and call the stencil kernel that performs one computation step on a region of grid points as described in Chapter 8, Stencil. The `call_stencil_kernel()` function takes several parameters. The first parameter is a pointer to the output data area for the kernel. The second parameter is a pointer to the input data area. In both cases, we add the `left_stage1_offset` to the input and output data in the device memory. The next three parameters specify the dimensions of the portion of the grid to be processed. Note that we need to have four slices on each side in order to correctly perform the computation for all the points in the four left boundary slices. Line 40 does the same for the right boundary points in stage 1. Note that these kernels will be called within stream 0 and will be executed sequentially.

Line 41 calls the `call_stencil_kernel()` function, which will call a stencil kernel function to generate the `dimx*dimy*(dimz − 8)` internal points in stage 2. Note that this also requires four slices of input boundary values on each side, so the total number of input slices is `dimx*dimy*dimz`. The kernel is called in stream 1 and will be executed in parallel with those called by lines 39 and 40.

Fig. 20.15 shows part 4 of the compute process code. Line 42 copies the four slices of left boundary points to the host memory in preparation for data exchange with the left neighbor process. Line 43 copies the four slices of the right boundary points to the host memory in preparation for data exchange with the right neighbor process. Both are asynchronous copies in stream 0 and will wait for the two kernels in stream 0 to complete before they copy data. Line 44 is a synchronization that forces the process to wait for all operations in stream 0 to complete before it can continue. This ensures that the left and right boundary points are in the host memory before the process proceeds with data exchange.

During the data exchange phase, we will have all MPI processes send their boundary slices to their left neighbors. That is, all processes will have their right neighbors sending data to them. It is therefore convenient to have an MPI function that sends data to a destination and receives data from a source. This reduces the number of MPI function calls. The `MPI_Sendrecv()` function in Fig. 20.16 is such a function. It is a combination of `MPI_Send()` and `MPI_Recv()` so we will not elaborate further on the meaning of the parameters.

```
42      /* Copy the data needed by other nodes to the host */
        cudaMemcpyAsync(h_left_boundary, d_output + num_halo_points,
                    num_halo_bytes, cudaMemcpyDeviceToHost, stream0 );
43      cudaMemcpyAsync(h_right_boundary,
                    d_output + right_stage1_offset + num_halo_points,
                    num_halo_bytes, cudaMemcpyDeviceToHost, stream0 );
44      cudaStreamSynchronize(stream0);
        /* Send data to left, get data from right */
45      MPI_Sendrecv(h_left_boundary, num_halo_points, MPI_FLOAT,
                    left_neighbor,  i, h_right_halo,  num_halo_points,
                    MPI_FLOAT, right_neighbor, i, MPI_COMM_WORLD, &status );
        /* Send data to right, get data from left */
46      MPI_Sendrecv(h_right_boundary, num_halo_points, MPI_FLOAT,
                    right_neighbor, i, h_left_halo, num_halo_points,
                    MPI_FLOAT, left_neighbor,  i, MPI_COMM_WORLD, &status );

47      cudaMemcpyAsync(d_output+left_halo_offset,  h_left_halo,
                    num_halo_bytes, cudaMemcpyHostToDevice, stream0);
48      cudaMemcpyAsync(d_output+right_halo_offset, h_right_halo,
                    num_halo_bytes, cudaMemcpyHostToDevice, stream0 );
49      cudaDeviceSynchronize();

50      float *temp = d_output;
51      d_output = d_input; d_input = temp;
52  }
```

FIGURE 20.15

Compute process code (part 4).

- int **MPI_Sendrecv(**void ***sendbuf,** int **sendcount,**
  MPI_Datatype **sendtype,** int **dest,** int **sendtag,** void
  ***recvbuf,** int **recvcount,** MPI_Datatype **recvtype,** int
  source, int **recvtag,** MPI_Comm **comm,** MPI_Status ***status)**
  - Sendbuf: **Initial address of send buffer (choice)**
  - Sendcount: **Number of elements in send buffer (integer)**
  - Sendtype: **Type of elements in send buffer (handle)**
  - Dest: **Rank of destination (integer)**
  - Sendtag: **Send tag (integer)**
  - Recvcount: **Number of elements in receive buffer (integer)**
  - Recvtype: **Type of elements in receive buffer (handle)**
  - Source: **Rank of source (integer)**
  - Recvtag: **Receive tag (integer)**
  - Comm: **Communicator (handle)**
  - Recvbuf: **Initial address of receive buffer (choice)**
  - Status: **Status object (Status). This refers to the receive
    operation.**

FIGURE 20.16

Syntax for the MPI_Sendrecv() function.

Line 45 sends four slices of left boundary points to the left neighbor and receives four slices of right halo points from the right neighbors. Line 46 sends four slices of right boundary points to the right neighbor and receives four slices of left halo points from the left neighbor. In the case of process 0, its left_neighbor has been set to MPI_PROC_NULL in line 27, so the MPI runtime will not send out the message in line 45 or receive the message in line 46 for process 0. Likewise, the MPI runtime will not receive the message in line 45 or send out the message in line 46 for process np − 2. Therefore the conditional assignments in lines 29 and 30 of Fig. 20.13 eliminate the need for special if-then-else statements in lines 45 and 46.

After the MPI messages have been sent and received, lines 47 and 48 transfer the newly received halo points to the d_output buffer of device memory. These copies are done in stream 0, so they will execute in parallel with the kernel launched in stream 1 on line 38.

Line 49 is a synchronization operation for all device activities. This call forces the process to wait for all device activities, including kernels and data copies, to complete. When the cudaDeviceSynchronize() function returns, all d_output data from the current computation step are in place: left halo data from the left neighbor process, boundary data from the kernel launched in line 36, internal data from the kernel launched in line 38, right boundary data from the kernel launched in line 37, and right halo data from the right neighbor.

Lines 50 and 51 swap the d_input and d_output pointers. This changes the output of the d_ouput data of the current computation step into the d_input data of the next computation step. The execution then proceeds to the next computation step by going to the next iteration of the loop of line 35. This will continue until all compute processes have completed the number of computations specified by the parameter nreps.

Fig. 20.17 shows part 5, the final part of the compute process code. Line 53 is a barrier synchronization that forces all processes to wait for each other to finish their computation steps. Lines 54−56 swap d_output with d_input. This is because lines 50 and 51 swapped d_output with d_input in preparation for the

```
     /* Wait for previous communications */
53   MPI_Barrier(MPI_COMM_WORLD);

54   float *temp = d_output;
55   d_output = d_input;
56   d_input = temp;

     /* Send the output, skipping halo points */
57   cudaMemcpy(h_output, d_output, num_bytes, cudaMemcpyDeviceToHost);
     float *send_address = h_output + num_ghost_points;
58   MPI_Send(send_address, dimx * dimy * dimz, MPI_REAL,
                  server_process, DATA_COLLECT, MPI_COMM_WORLD);
59   MPI_Barrier(MPI_COMM_WORLD);

     /* Release resources */
60   free(h_input); free(h_output);
61   cudaFreeHost(h_left_ghost_own); cudaFreeHost(h_right_ghost_own);
62   cudaFreeHost(h_left_ghost); cudaFreeHost(h_right_ghost);
63   cudaFree( d_input ); cudaFree( d_output );
64   }
```

FIGURE 20.17

Compute process code (part 5).

next computation step. However, this is unnecessary for the last computation step, so we use lines 54–56 to undo the swap. Line 57 copies the final output to the host memory. Line 58 sends the output to the data server. Line 59 waits for all processes to complete. Lines 60–63 free all the resources before returning to the main program.

Fig. 20.18 shows part 2, the final part of the data server code, which continues from Fig. 20.9. Line 24 is a barrier synchronization that waits for all compute nodes to complete their computation steps and send their outputs. This barrier corresponds to the barrier at line 59 of the compute process. Lines 26 and 27 receive the output data from all the compute processes. Line 28 stores the output into an external storage. Finally, lines 29 and 30 free resources before returning to the main program.

20.6 Message passing interface collective communication

We saw an example of the MPI collective communication API in the previous section: MPI_Barrier. The other commonly used group collective communication types are broadcast, reduce, gather, and scatter (Gropp et al., 1999). Barrier synchronization MPI_Barrier() is perhaps the most commonly used collective communication function. As we saw in the stencil example, barriers are used to ensure that all MPI processes are ready before they begin to interact with each other. We will not elaborate on the other types of MPI collective communication functions, but we encourage the reader to read the details of these functions. In general, collective communication functions are highly optimized by the MPI runtime developers and system vendors. Using them usually leads to better performance as well as readability and productivity than trying to achieve the same functionality with combinations of send and receive calls.

```
      /* Wait for nodes to compute */
24    MPI_Barrier(MPI_COMM_WORLD);
      /* Collect output data */
25    MPI_Status status;
26    for(int process = 0; process < num_comp_nodes; process++)
27        MPI_Recv(output + process * num_points / num_comp_nodes,
                num_points / num_comp_nodes, MPI_REAL, process,
                DATA_COLLECT, MPI_COMM_WORLD, &status );

      /* Store output data */
28    store_output(output, dimx, dimy, dimz);
      /* Release resources */
29    free(input);
30    free(output);
}
```

FIGURE 20.18

Data server code (part 2).

20.7 **CUDA aware message passing interface**

Modern MPI implementations are aware of the CUDA programming model and are designed to minimize the communication latency between GPUs. Currently, direct interaction between CUDA and MPI is supported by MVAPICH2, IBM Platform MPI, and OpenMPI.

CUDA-aware MPI implementations are capable of sending messages from the GPU memory in one node to the GPU memory in a different node. This effectively removes the need for device-to-host data transfers before sending MPI messages and host-to-device data transfers after receiving an MPI message. This has the potential to simplify the host code and memory data layout. In our stencil example, if we used a CUDA-aware MPI implementation, we will no longer need host-pinned memory allocations and asynchronous memory copies.

The first simplification is that we no longer need to allocate host-pinned memory buffers to transfer the halo points to the host memory to prepare for MPI_Send(). This means that we can safely remove lines 21−24 in Fig. 20.11. However, we still need to use CUDA streams and two separate GPU kernels to start communicating across nodes as soon as the halo elements have been computed.

The second simplification is that we no longer need to asynchronously copy the halo data from the host to the device memory after MPI_Recv(). As a result, we can also remove lines 42 and 43 in Fig. 20.15. Since the MPI calls now accept device memory addresses, we need to modify the calls to MPI_SendRecv to use them. Note that these memory addresses actually correspond to the device addresses of the asynchronous memory copies in the previous versions. Since the CUDA-aware MPI implementations will directly update the contents of the GPU memory, we also remove lines 47 and 48 in Fig. 20.15. Fig. 20.19 shows the modifications to he MPI_SendRecv statements in lines 45 and 46 in Fig. 20.15, so that they directly read from and write to the device memory.

Besides removing the data transfers during the halo exchange using MPI_SendRecv(), it would also be possible to remove the initial and final memory copies by receiving/sending the input/output directly from the GPU memory.

```
MPI_SendRecv(d_output + num_halo_points, num_halo_points, MPI_FLOAT,
        left_neighbor, i, d_output + left_halo_offset, num_halo_points,
        MPI_FLOAT, right_neighbor, i, MPI_COMM_WORLD, &status);
MPI_SendRecv(d_output + right_stage1_offset, num_halo_points,
        num_halo_points, MPI_FLOAT, right_neighbor, i,
        d_output + right_halo_offset, num_halo_points,
        MPI_FLOAT, left_neighbor, i, MPI_COMM_WORLD, &status);
```

FIGURE 20.19

Revised MPI SendRec calls in using CUDA-aware MPI.

20.8 Summary

In this chapter we covered basic patterns of joint CUDA/MPI programming for HPC clusters with heterogeneous computing nodes. All processes in an MPI application run the same program. However, each process can follow different control flow and function call paths to specialize their roles, as illustrated by the data server and the compute processes in our example. We also used the stencil pattern to show how compute processes exchange data. We presented the use of CUDA streams and asynchronous data transfers to enable the overlap of computation and communication. We also showed how to use the MPI barrier to ensure that all processes are ready to exchange data with each other. Finally, we briefly outlined the use of CUDA-aware MPI to simplify the exchange of data in the device memory. We would like to point out that while MPI is a very different programming system, all major MPI concepts that we covered in this chapter, namely, SPMD, MPI ranks, and barriers, have counterparts in the CUDA programming model. This confirms our belief that by teaching parallel programming well with one model, our students can quickly and easily pick up other programming models. We would like to encourage the reader to build on the foundation provided by this chapter and study more advanced MPI features and other important patterns.

Exercises

1. Assume that the 25-point stencil computation in this chapter is applied to a grid whose size is 64 grid points in the x dimension, 64 in the y dimension, and 2048 in the z dimension. The computation is divided across 17 MPI ranks, of which 16 ranks are compute processes and 1 rank is the data server process.
   a. How many output grid point values are computed by each compute process?
   b. How many halo grid points are needed:
      i. By each internal compute process?
      ii. By each edge compute process?
   c. How many boundary grid points are computed in stage 1 of Fig. 20.12:
      i. By each internal compute process?
      ii. By each edge compute process?
   d. How many internal grid points are computed in stage 2 of Fig. 20.12:
      i. By each internal compute process?
      ii. By each edge compute process?
   e. How many bytes are sent in stage 2 of Fig. 20.12:
      i. By each internal compute process?
      ii. By each edge compute process?

2. If the MPI call `MPI_Send`(ptr_a, 1000, `MPI_FLOAT`, 2000, 4, `MPI_COMM_WORLD`) results in a data transfer of 4000 bytes, what is the size of each data element being sent?
   a. 1 byte
   b. 2 bytes
   c. 4 bytes
   d. 8 bytes
3. Which of the following statements is true?
   a. `MPI_Send()` is blocking by default.
   b. `MPI_Recv()` is blocking by default.
   c. MPI messages must be at least 128 bytes.
   d. MPI processes can access the same variable through shared memory.
4. Modify the example code to remove the calls to `cudaMemcpyAsync()` from the compute processes' code by using GPU memory addresses on `MPI_Send` and `MPI_Recv`.

References

Gropp, W., Lusk, E., Skjellum, A., 1999. Using MPI, Portable Parallel Programming with the Message Passing Interface, 2nd Ed. MIT Press, Cambridge, MA, Scientific and Engineering Computation Series. ISBN 978-0-262−57132-6.

CUDA dynamic parallelism

21

With special contributions from Juan Gómez-Luna

Chapter Outline

21.1 Background 476
21.2 Dynamic parallelism overview 478
21.3 An example: Bezier curves 481
21.4 A recursive example: quadtrees 484
21.5 Important considerations 490
21.6 Summary 492
Exercises 493
A21.1 Support code for quadtree example 495
References 497

CUDA dynamic parallelism is an extension to the CUDA programming model that enables a kernel to call other kernels, thereby allowing threads executing on the device to launch new grids of threads. In early versions of CUDA, grids could be launched only from the host code. Algorithms that involved recursion, irregular loop structures, time-space variation, or other constructs that do not fit a flat and single level of parallelism needed to be implemented with multiple kernel calls from the host, which increases the burden on the host, the amount of host-device communication, and the total execution time. In some cases, programmers resort to loop serialization and other awkward techniques to support these algorithmic needs at the cost of software maintainability. The support for dynamic parallelism allows algorithms that dynamically discover new work to prepare and launch new grids without burdening the host or impacting the software maintainability. This chapter describes the extended capabilities of CUDA that enable dynamic parallelism, including the modifications and additions to the CUDA programming interface, as well as guidelines and best practices for exploiting this added capacity.

Programming Massively Parallel Processors. DOI: https://doi.org/10.1016/B978-0-323-91231-0.00001-X

21.1 **Background**

Many real-world applications employ algorithms that have either a variation of work across space or a dynamically varying amount of work performed over time. For example, Fig. 21.1 shows a turbulence simulation example in which the level of required modeling details varies across both space and time. As the combustion flow moves from left to right, the range of activities and intensity increases. The level of details required to model the right side of the model is much higher than that for the left side of the model. On one hand, using a fixed fine grid would incur too much work for no gain for the left side of the model. On the other hand, using a fixed coarse grid would sacrifice too much accuracy for the right side of the model. Ideally, one should use fine grids for the parts of the model that require more details and coarse grids for the parts that do not.

Thus far, we have assumed that all kernels are called from the host code. The amount of work done by a thread grid is predetermined in calling the kernel function. With the single-program, multiple-data programming style for the kernel code, it is tedious if not extremely difficult to have thread blocks use different grid spacing. As a result, this limitation favors the use of a fixed and uniform (regular) grid system. To achieve the desired accuracy, such a fixed grid

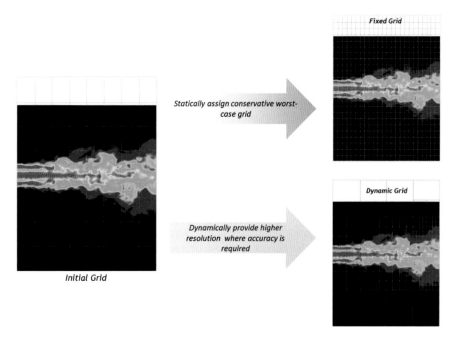

FIGURE 21.1

Fixed versus dynamic grids for a turbulence simulation model.

approach, as illustrated in the upper right portion of Fig. 21.1, typically needs to accommodate the most demanding parts of the model and maintain unnecessary extra data as well as perform unnecessary extra work in parts that do not require as much detail.

A more desirable approach is shown as the dynamic grid in the lower right portion of Fig. 21.1. As the simulation algorithm detects fast-changing simulation quantities in some areas of the model, it refines the grid in those areas to achieve the desired level of accuracy. Such refinement does not need to be done for the areas that do not exhibit such intensive activity. Thus the algorithm can dynamically direct more computational resources to the areas of the model that benefit from additional work.

Fig. 21.2 shows a conceptual comparison of behavior between a system without dynamic parallelism and another one with dynamic parallelism with respect to the simulation model in Fig. 21.1. Without dynamic parallelism the host thread must launch all grids. If new work is discovered, such as refining an area in the model during the execution of a grid, the grid needs to terminate, report back to the host, and have the host launch new grids. This is illustrated in Fig. 21.2A, in which the host launches a grid, receives information from this grid after its termination, and launches subsequent grids for any new work that is discovered by the completed grid. The figure depicts the subsequent grids as being launched one after the other; however, sophisticated optimizations may be applied, such as

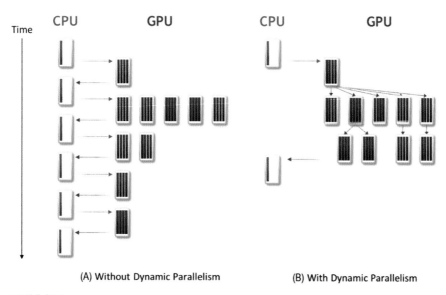

(A) Without Dynamic Parallelism   (B) With Dynamic Parallelism

FIGURE 21.2

Grid launch patterns for algorithms with dynamic work variation, (A) without and (B) with dynamic parallelism.

launching independent grids in different streams or combining them so that they can run in parallel.

Fig. 21.2B shows that with dynamic parallelism the threads that discover new work can just go ahead and launch grids to do the work. In our example, when a thread discovers that an area in the model needs to be refined, it can launch a new grid to perform the computation on the refined area without the overhead of terminating the grid, reporting back to the host, and having the host launch the new grid.

21.2 Dynamic parallelism overview

From the perspective of programmers, dynamic parallelism means that they can write a statement within a kernel that calls another kernel function. In Fig. 21.3 the main function (host code) launches three kernels: A, B, and C. These are kernel calls in the host code, as we have been assuming throughout this book. What is new in Fig. 21.3 is that one of the kernels, B, calls three kernels X, Y, and Z. This would have been illegal in early CUDA systems that do not support dynamic parallelism.

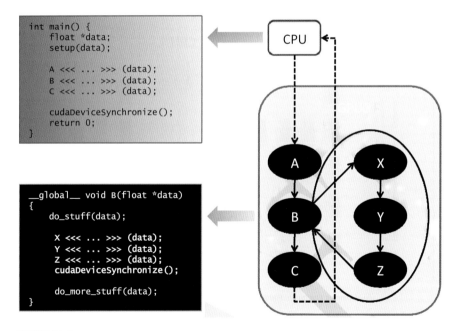

FIGURE 21.3

A simple example of a kernel (B) launching three kernels (X, Y, and Z).

The syntax for calling a kernel from inside of a kernel is the same as that for calling a kernel from the host code:

```
kernel_name<<< Dg, Db, Ns, S >>>([kernel arguments])
```

- Dg is of type dim3 and specifies the dimensions and size of the grid.
- Db is of type dim3 and specifies the dimensions and size of each thread block.
- Ns is of type size_t and specifies the number of bytes of shared memory that are dynamically allocated per-thread block for this call, which is in addition to the statically allocated shared memory. Ns is an optional argument that defaults to 0.
- S is of type cudaStream_t and specifies the stream associated with this call. The stream must have been allocated in the same thread block in which the call is being made. S is an optional argument that defaults to 0. Streams were discussed in Chapter 20, Programming a Heterogeneous Computing Cluster.

To demonstrate how dynamic parallelism can be used, we provide simple examples of kernels without and with dynamic parallelism. The examples are based on a hypothetical parallel algorithm that does not compute useful results but provides a conceptually simple computational pattern that recurs in many applications. It serves to illustrate the difference between the two approaches and how one can use the dynamic parallelism to extract more parallelism while reducing control flow divergence when the amount of work done by each thread in an algorithm can vary dynamically.

Fig. 21.4 shows a simple example kernel coded without dynamic parallelism. In this example, each thread of the kernel performs some computation (line 05), then loops over a list of data elements for which it is responsible (line 07), and performs another computation for each data element (line 08).

This computation pattern recurs frequently in many applications. For example, in graph search, each thread could visit a vertex and then loop over a list of

```
01    __global__ void kernel(unsigned int* start, unsigned int* end,
02        float* someData, float* moreData) {
03
04        unsigned int i = blockIdx.x*blockDim.x + threadIdx.x;
05        doSomeWork_findMoreWork(someData[i]);
06
07        for(unsigned int j = start[i]; j < end[i]; ++j) {
08            doMoreWork(moreData[j]);
09        }
10
11    }
```

FIGURE 21.4

A simple example of a hypothetical parallel algorithm coded in CUDA without dynamic parallelism.

neighboring vertices. The reader should find this kernel structure similar to that of the vertex-centric BFS kernel in Figure 15.14. For another example, in sparse matrix computations, each thread could first identify the starting location of a row of nonzero elements and loop over the nonzero values. In simulations such as the example at the beginning of this chapter, each thread could first process a coarse grid element and then loop over finer grid elements if there is a need for refining the grid.

There are two main problems with writing applications in the style shown in Fig. 21.4. First, if the work in the loop (lines 07−09) can be profitably performed in parallel, then we have missed out on an opportunity to extract more parallelism from the application. Second, if the number of iterations in the loop varies significantly between threads in the same warp, then the resulting control divergence can degrade the performance of the program.

Fig. 21.5 shows a version of the same program that uses dynamic parallelism. In this version the original kernel is separated into two: a parent kernel and a child kernel. The parent kernel starts off the same as the original kernel, executed by a grid of threads that are referred to as the parent grid. Instead of looping, the parent kernel calls a child kernel to continue the work (lines 07−08). The child kernel is executed by grids of threads called the child grids, which perform the work (line 18, Fig. 21.5) that was originally performed inside the loop body (lines 07−09, Fig. 21.4).

Writing the program in this way addresses both problems that were mentioned about the original code. First, the loop iterations are now executed in parallel by the child kernel threads instead of serially by the original kernel thread. Thus we have extracted more parallelism from the program. Second, each thread now executes a single loop iteration, which results in better load balance and eliminates

```
01    __global__ void kernel_parent(unsigned int* start, unsigned int* end,
02          float* someData, float* moreData) {
03
04        unsigned int i = blockIdx.x*blockDim.x + threadIdx.x;
05        doSomeWork(someData[i]);
06
07        kernel_child <<< ceil((end[i]-start[i])/256.0), 256 >>>
08            (start[i], end[i], moreData);
09
10    }
11
12    __global__ void kernel_child(unsigned int start, unsigned int end,
13          float* moreData) {
14
15        unsigned int j = start + blockIdx.x*blockDim.x + threadIdx.x;
16
17        if(j < end) {
18            doMoreWork(moreData[j]);
19        }
20
21    }
```

FIGURE 21.5

A revised example using CUDA dynamic parallelism.

control divergence. Although these two goals could have been achieved by the programmer rewriting the kernels differently, for example, by using an edge-centric breadth-first implementation, such transformations for some applications can be awkward, complicated, and error prone. Dynamic parallelism provides an easy way to express such computational patterns.

21.3 An example: Bezier curves

We now show an example that is a more interesting and useful case: the adaptive subdivision of spline curves. This example illustrates the case of having a variable amount of child grid launches, according to the workload. The example is to calculate Bezier curves (Bezier Curves), which are frequently used in computer graphics to draw smooth, intuitive curves that are defined by a set of *control points*, which are typically defined by a user.

Mathematically, a Bezier curve is defined by a set of control points $\mathbf{P}_0$ through $\mathbf{P}_n$, where n is called the control point's *order* ($n=1$ for linear, 2 for quadratic, 3 for cubic, etc.). The first and last control points are always the end points of the curve; however, the intermediate control points (if any) generally do not lie on the curve.

Linear Bezier curves

Given two control points $\mathbf{P}_0$ and $\mathbf{P}_1$, a linear Bezier curve is simply a straight line connecting these two points. The coordinates of the points on the curve are given by the following linear interpolation formula:

$$\mathbf{B}(t) = \mathbf{P}_0 + t(\mathbf{P}_1 - \mathbf{P}_0) = (1-t)\mathbf{P}_0 + t\mathbf{P}_1, \quad t \in [0, \quad 1]$$

Quadratic Bezier curves

A quadratic Bezier curve is defined by three control points $\mathbf{P}_0$, $\mathbf{P}_1$, and $\mathbf{P}_2$. The points on a quadratic curve are defined as a linear interpolation of corresponding points on the linear Bezier curves from $\mathbf{P}_0$ to $\mathbf{P}_1$ and from $\mathbf{P}_1$ to $\mathbf{P}_2$. The calculation of the coordinates of points on the curve is expressed by the following formula:

$$\mathbf{B}(t) = (1-t)[(1-t)\mathbf{P}_0 + t\mathbf{P}_1] + t[(1-t)\mathbf{P}_0 + t\mathbf{P}_2], \quad t \in [0, \quad 1],$$

which can be simplified into the following formula:

$$\mathbf{B}(t) = (1-t)^2 \mathbf{P}_0 + 2(1-t)t\mathbf{P}_1 + t^2\mathbf{P}_2, \quad t \in [0, \quad 1].$$

Bezier curve calculation (without dynamic parallelism)

Fig. 21.6 shows part of a CUDA C program that calculates the coordinates of points on a Bezier curve. The computeBezierLines kernel starting at line 13 is

```
01    #include <stdio.h>
02    #include <cuda.h>
03
04    #define MAX_TESS_POINTS 32
05
06    // A structure containing all parameters needed to tessellate a Bezier line
07    struct BezierLine {
08        float2 CP[3];                          //Control points for the line
09        float2 vertexPos[MAX_TESS_POINTS]; //Vertex position array to tessellate into
10        int nVertices;                         //Number of tessellated vertices
11    };
12
13    __global__ void computeBezierLines(BezierLine *bLines, int nLines) {
14        int bidx = blockIdx.x;
15        if(bidx < nLines){
16            //Compute the curvature of the line
17            float curvature = computeCurvature(bLines);
18
19            //From the curvature, compute the number of tessellation points
20            int nTessPoints = min(max((int)(curvature*16.0f),4),32);
21            bLines[bidx].nVertices = nTessPoints;
22
23            //Loop through vertices to be tessellated, incrementing by blockDim.x
24            for(int inc = 0; inc < nTessPoints; inc += blockDim.x){
25                int idx = inc + threadIdx.x;  //Compute a unique index for this point
26                if(idx < nTessPoints){
27                    float u = (float)idx/(float)(nTessPoints-1);  //Compute u from idx
28                    float omu = 1.0f - u;   //pre-compute one minus u
29                    float B3u[3]; //Compute quadratic Bezier coefficients
30                    B3u[0] = omu*omu;
31                    B3u[1] = 2.0f*u*omu;
32                    B3u[2] = u*u;
33                    float2 position = {0,0};  //Set position to zero
34                    for(int i = 0; i < 3; i++){
35                        //Add the contribution of the i'th control point to position
36                        position = position + B3u[i] * bLines[bidx].CP[i];
37                    }
38                    //Assign value of vertex position to the correct array element
39                    bLines[bidx].vertexPos[idx] = position;
40                }
41            }
42        }
43    }
```

FIGURE 21.6

Bezier curve calculation without dynamic parallelism.

designed to use a block to calculate the curve points for a set of three control points (of the quadratic Bezier formula). Each thread block first computes a measure of the curvature of the curve defined by the three control points. Intuitively, the larger the curvature, the more points it takes to draw a smooth quadratic Bezier curve for the three control points. This defines the amount of work to be done by each block. This is reflected in lines 20 and 21, in which the total number of points to be calculated by the current thread block is proportional to the curvature value.

In the for-loop in line 24, all threads calculate a consecutive set of Bezier curve points in each iteration. The detailed calculation in the loop body is based on the formula that we presented earlier. The key point is that the number of iterations taken by threads in a block can be very different from the number taken by threads in another block. Depending on the scheduling policy, such variation of the amount of work done by each thread block can result in decreased utilization of streaming multiprocessors (SMs) and thus reduced performance.

Bezier curve calculation (with dynamic parallelism)

Fig. 21.7 shows a Bezier curve calculation code using dynamic parallelism. It breaks the `computeBezierLines` kernel in Fig. 21.6 into two kernels. The first part, `computeBezierLines_parent`, discovers the amount of work to be done for each control point. The second part, `computeBezierLines_child`, performs the calculation.

With the new organization the amount of work that is done for each set of control points by the `computeBezierLines_parent` kernel is much smaller than that for the original `computeBezierLines` kernel. Therefore we use one thread to do this work in `computeBezierLines_parent` rather than using one block in `computeBezierLines`. In line 58, we need to launch only one thread per set of control points. This is reflected by dividing the `N_LINES` by `BLOCK_DIM` to form the number of blocks in the kernel launch configuration.

```
01    struct BezierLine {
02        float2 CP[3];       //Control points for the line
03        float2 *vertexPos;  //Vertex position array to tessellate into
04        int nVertices;      //Number of tessellated vertices
05    };
06    __global__ void computeBezierLines_parent(BezierLine *bLines, int nLines) {
07        //Compute a unique index for each Bezier line
08        int lidx = threadIdx.x + blockDim.x*blockIdx.x;
09        if(lidx < nLines){
10            //Compute the curvature of the line
11            float curvature = computeCurvature(bLines);
12
13            //From the curvature, compute the number of tessellation points
14            bLines[lidx].nVertices = min(max((int)(curvature*16.0f),4),MAX_TESS_POINTS);
15            cudaMalloc((void**)&bLines[lidx].vertexPos,
16                bLines[lidx].nVertices*sizeof(float2));
17
18            //Call the child kernel to compute the tessellated points for each line
19            computeBezierLine_child<<<ceil((float)bLines[lidx].nVertices/32.0f), 32>>>
20                (lidx, bLines, bLines[lidx].nVertices);
21        }
22    }
23    __global__ void computeBezierLine_child(int lidx, BezierLine* bLines,
24        int nTessPoints) {
25        int idx = threadIdx.x + blockDim.x*blockIdx.x;//Compute idx unique to this vertex
26        if(idx < nTessPoints){
27            float u = (float)idx/(float)(nTessPoints-1);  //Compute u from idx
28            float omu = 1.0f - u;   //Pre-compute one minus u
29            float B3u[3];   //Compute quadratic Bezier coefficients
30            B3u[0] = omu*omu;
31            B3u[1] = 2.0f*u*omu;
32            B3u[2] = u*u;
33            float2 position = {0,0};  //Set position to zero
34            for(int i = 0; i < 3; i++) {
35                //Add the contribution of the i'th control point to position
36                position = position + B3u[i] * bLines[lidx].CP[i];
37            }
38            //Assign the value of the vertex position to the correct array element
39            bLines[lidx].vertexPos[idx] = position;
40        }
41    }
42    __global__ void freeVertexMem(BezierLine *bLines, int nLines) {
43        //Compute a unique index for each Bezier line
44        int lidx = threadIdx.x + blockDim.x*blockIdx.x;
45        if(lidx < nLines)
46            cudaFree(bLines[lidx].vertexPos);  //Free the vertex memory for this line
47    }
```

FIGURE 21.7

Bezier calculation with dynamic parallelism.

There are two key differences between the `computeBezierLines_parent` kernel and the `computeBezierLines` kernel. First, the index that is used to access the control points is formed on a thread basis (line 08 in Fig. 21.7) rather than a block basis (line 14 in Fig. 21.6). This is because the work for each control point is done by a thread rather than a block, as we mentioned earlier in the chapter. Second, the memory for storing the calculated Bezier curve points is dynamically determined and allocated in line 15 in Fig. 21.7. This allows the code to assign just enough memory to each set of control points to be placed in the `bLines` variable. Note that in Fig. 21.6, each `BezierLine` element is declared with the maximum possible number of points (line 09). On the other hand, the declaration in Fig. 21.7 has only a pointer to a dynamically allocated storage. Allowing a kernel to call the `cudaMalloc()` function can lead to substantial reduction of memory usage for situations in which the curvature of control points varies significantly.

Once a thread of the `computeBezierLines_parent` kernel has determined the amount of work needed by its set of control points, it calls the `computeBezierLines_child` kernel and launches a child grid to do the work (line 19 in Fig. 21.7). In our example, every thread from the parent grid creates a new grid for its assigned set of control points. This way, the work that is done by each thread block is balanced. The amount of work that is done by each child grid varies.

Dynamic parallelism kernel calls have the same asynchronous semantics as kernel calls from the host. That is, once the child kernel has been called, the parent thread that called it may proceed to execute the subsequent code without waiting for the child grid to complete. If the parent thread wishes to wait for its child grid to complete, it must perform an explicit synchronization similar to what a host thread would do. If no explicit synchronization is made, then the thread can finish executing, but there is an implicit synchronization at the end. The implicit synchronization ensures that all child grids have terminated before the parent grid terminates. We refer the reader to the CUDA C++ Programming Guide for more details about the semantics of parent-child grid synchronization (NVIDIA Corporation, 2021).

After `computeBezierLines_parent` terminates, the memory allocated inside the kernel using `cudaMalloc` still needs to be freed. For this reason, an additional kernel `freeVertexMem` is implemented (lines 42−47) to be called by the host. This kernel frees all storage allocated to the vertices in the `bLines_d` data structure in parallel (line 61). This kernel is necessary because vertex storage allocated on the device by a device kernel has to be freed by a device kernel. We refer the reader to the CUDA C++ Programming Guide for more details about the use of `cudaMalloc` and `cudaFree` on the device (NVIDIA Corporation, 2021).

21.4 A recursive example: quadtrees

Dynamic parallelism also allows programmers to implement recursive algorithms. In this section we illustrate the use of dynamic parallelism for implementing recursion with a *quadtree* (Finkel and Bentley, 1974). Quadtrees partition a two-dimensional space by recursively subdividing it into four equally sized *quadrants*. Each quadrant is considered to be a *node* of the quadtree and contains a number of points. If the number of points in a quadrant is greater than a fixed minimum, the quadrant will be recursively subdivided into four more quadrants, that is, four child nodes.

Fig. 21.8 illustrates the construction of a quadtree with dynamic parallelism. In this implementation, one node (quadrant) is assigned to one block. Initially (depth=0), one block (block 0) is assigned the entire two-dimensional space (root node of the

Fourth Edition   Preproduction Draft

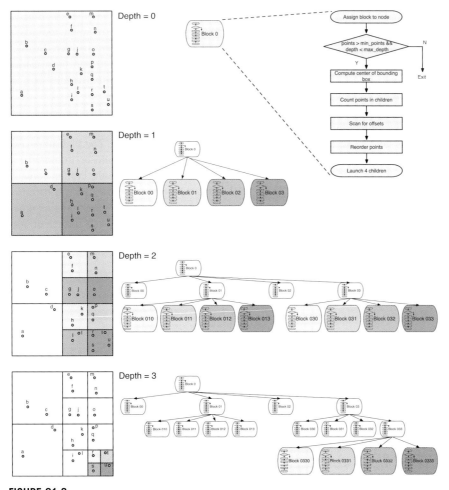

FIGURE 21.8

Quadtree example. Each block is assigned to one quadrant. If the number of points in a quadrant is more than two, the block launches four child blocks. Shadowed blocks are active blocks in each level of depth.

quadtree), which contains all points. It divides the space into four quadrants and launches one block for each quadrant (depth=1). These child blocks (blocks 00 through 03) will again subdivide their quadrants if they contain more points than a fixed minimum. In this example we assume that the minimum is two; thus blocks 00 and 02 do not launch children. Blocks 01 and 03 launch a grid with four blocks each.

As the flow graph in the right-hand side of Fig. 21.8 shows, a block first checks whether the number of points in its quadrant is greater than the minimum required for further division and whether the maximum depth has not been reached. If either of the conditions fails, the work for the quadrant is complete, and the block returns. Otherwise, the block computes the center of the bounding box that surrounds its quadrant. The center is in the middle of four new quadrants. The number of points in each of them is counted. A four-element scan operation is used to compute the offsets to the locations where the points will be stored. Then the points are reordered so that those points in the same quadrant are grouped together and placed into their section of the point storage. Finally, the block launches a child grid with four blocks, one for each of the four new quadrants.

Fig. 21.9 continues the small example in Fig. 21.8 and illustrates in detail how the points are reordered at each level of depth. For the example we assume that each quadrant must have more than two points to be further divided. The algorithm uses two buffers to store the points and reorder them. The points should be in buffer 0 at the end of the algorithm. Thus it might be necessary to swap the buffer contents before leaving if the points are in buffer 1 when the terminating condition is met.

In the initial kernel call from the host code (for depth=0), block 0 is assigned all the points that reside in buffer 0, shown in Fig. 21.9A. Block 0 further divides

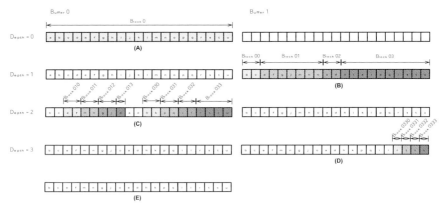

FIGURE 21.9

Quadtree example. At each level of depth, a block groups all points in the same quadrant together. (A) shows the initial input list in Buffer 0, (B) The list after being rearranged into four sublists that correspond to the four quadrants, (C) shows the list after being rearranged to reflect the second-level quadrants, (D) shows the list after being rearranged to reflect the third-level quadrant, (E) the final list is copied into Buffer 0 for return to the caller.

the quadrant into four child quadrants, groups together all points in the same child quadrant, and stores the points according to the quadrants into buffer 1, as shown in Fig. 21.9B. Its four children, block 00 to block 03, are assigned each of the four new quadrants, shown as marked ranges in Fig. 21.9B. Blocks 00 and 02 will not launch children, since the number of points in their respective assigned quadrant is only 2. Blocks 01 and 03 reorder their points to group those in the same quadrant and launch four child blocks each, as shown in Fig. 21.9C. Blocks 010, 011, 012, 013, 030, 031, and 032 do not launch children (they have two or fewer points) and do not need to swap points (they are already in buffer 0). Only block 033 reorders its points and launches four blocks, as shown in Fig. 21.9D. Blocks 0330 to 0333 will exit after swapping their points to buffer 0, which can be seen in Fig. 21.9E.

The kernel code in Fig. 21.10 implements the flow graph from Fig. 21.8. The quadtree is implemented with a node array, in which each element contains all the

```
01   __global__ void build_quadtree_kernel
02              (Quadtree_node *nodes, Points *points, Parameters params) {
03     __shared__ int smem[8]; // To store the number of points in each quadrant
04
05     // The current node in the quadtree
06     Quadtree_node &node = nodes[blockIdx.x];
07     node.set_id(node.id() + blockIdx.x);
08     int num_points = node.num_points(); // The number of points in the node
09
10     // Check the number of points and its depth
11     bool exit = check_num_points_and_depth(node, points, num_points, params);
12     if(exit) return;
13
14     // Compute the center of the bounding box of the points
15     const Bounding_box &bbox = node.bounding_box();
16     float2 center;
17     bbox.compute_center(center);
18
19     // Range of points
20     int range_begin = node.points_begin();
21     int range_end   = node.points_end();
22     const Points &in_points = points[params.point_selector]; // Input points
23     Points &out_points = points[(params.point_selector+1) % 2]; // Output points
24
25     // Count the number of points in each child
26     count_points_in_children(in_points, smem, range_begin, range_end, center);
27
28     // Scan the quadrants' results to know the reordering offset
29     scan_for_offsets(node.points_begin(), smem);
30
31     // Move points
32     reorder_points(out_points, in_points, smem, range_begin, range_end, center);
33
34     // Launch new blocks
35     if (threadIdx.x == blockDim.x-1) {
36         // The children
37         Quadtree_node *children = &nodes[params.num_nodes_at_this_level];
38
39         // Prepare children launch
40         prepare_children(children, node, bbox, smem);
41
42         // Launch 4 children.
43         build_quadtree_kernel<<<4, blockDim.x, 8 *sizeof(int)>>>
44                     (children, points, Parameters(params, true));
45     }
46  }
```

FIGURE 21.10

Quadtree with dynamic parallelism: recursive kernel (support code in Appendix A210.1).

pertinent information for one node of the quadtree (definition given in Appendix A21.1). As the quadtree is constructed, new nodes will be created and placed into the array during the execution of the kernels. The kernel code assumes that the node parameter points to the next available location in the node array.

Every block starts by checking the number of points in its node (quadrant). A point is a pair of floats representing x and y coordinates (definition in Appendix A21.1). If the number of points is less than or equal to the minimum or if the maximum depth is reached (line 11), the block will exit. The maximum depth may be specified on the basis of application requirements or hardware constraints (see Section 12.5). Before exiting, the block may need to write its points from buffer 1

```
001   // Check the number of points and its depth
002   __device__ bool check_num_points_and_depth(Quadtree_node &node, Points *points,
003                                 int num_points, Parameters params){
004     if(params.depth >= params.max_depth || num_points <= params.min_points_per_node) {
005       // Stop the recursion here. Make sure points[0] contains all the points
006       if(params.point_selector == 1) {
007         int it = node.points_begin(), end = node.points_end();
008         for (it += threadIdx.x ; it < end ; it += blockDim.x)
009           if(it < end)
010             points[0].set_point(it, points[1].get_point(it));
011       }
012       return true;
013     }
014     return false;
015   }
016
017   // Count the number of points in each quadrant
018   __device__ void count_points_in_children(const Points &in_points, int* smem,
019     int range_begin, int range_end, float2 center) {
020     // Initizalize shared memory
021     if(threadIdx.x < 4) smem[threadIdx.x] = 0;
022     __syncthreads();
023     // Compute the number of points
024     for(int iter=range_begin+threadIdx.x; iter<range_end; iter+=blockDim.x){
025       float2 p = in_points.get_point(iter); // Load the coordinates of the point
026       if(p.x < center.x && p.y >= center.y)
027         atomicAdd(&smem[0], 1); // Top-left point?
028       if(p.x >= center.x && p.y >= center.y)
029         atomicAdd(&smem[1], 1); // Top-right point?
030       if(p.x < center.x && p.y < center.y)
031         atomicAdd(&smem[2], 1); // Bottom-left point?
032       if(p.x >= center.x && p.y < center.y)
033         atomicAdd(&smem[3], 1); // Bottom-right point?
034     }
035     __syncthreads();
036   }
037
038   // Scan quadrants' results to obtain reordering offset
039   __device__ void scan_for_offsets(int node_points_begin, int* smem){
040     int* smem2 = &smem[4];
041     if(threadIdx.x == 0){
042       for(int i = 0; i < 4; i++)
043         smem2[i] = i==0 ? 0 : smem2[i-1] + smem[i-1]; // Sequential scan
044       for(int i = 0; i < 4; i++)
045         smem2[i] += node_points_begin;  // Global offset
046     }
047     __syncthreads();
048   }
049
050   // Reorder points in order to group the points in each quadrant
051   __device__ void reorder_points(
```

FIGURE 21.11

Quadtree with dynamic parallelism: device functions (support code in Appendix A21.1).

```
052                 Points& out_points, const Points &in_points, int* smem,
053                 int range_begin, int range_end, float2 center){
054     int* smem2 = &smem[4];
055     // Reorder points
056     for(int iter=range_begin+threadIdx.x; iter<range_end; iter+=blockDim.x){
057         int dest;
058         float2 p = in_points.get_point(iter); // Load the coordinates of the point
059         if(p.x<center.x && p.y>=center.y)
060             dest=atomicAdd(&smem2[0],1); // Top-left point?
061         if(p.x>=center.x && p.y>=center.y)
062             dest=atomicAdd(&smem2[1],1); // Top-right point?
063         if(p.x<center.x && p.y<center.y)
064             dest=atomicAdd(&smem2[2],1); // Bottom-left point?
065         if(p.x>=center.x && p.y<center.y)
066             dest=atomicAdd(&smem2[3],1); // Bottom-right point?
067         // Move point
068         out_points.set_point(dest, p);
069     }
070     __syncthreads();
071 }
072
073 // Prepare children launch
074 __device__ void prepare_children(Quadtree_node *children, Quadtree_node &node,
075                             const Bounding_box &bbox, int *smem){
076     int child_offset = 4*node.id(); // The offsets of the children at their level
077
078     // Set IDs
079     children[child_offset+0].set_id(4*node.id()+ 0);
080     children[child_offset+1].set_id(4*node.id()+ 4);
081     children[child_offset+2].set_id(4*node.id()+ 8);
082     children[child_offset+3].set_id(4*node.id()+12);
083
084     // Points of the bounding-box
085     const float2 &p_min = bbox.get_min();
086     const float2 &p_max = bbox.get_max();
087
088     // Set the bounding boxes of the children
089     children[child_offset+0].set_bounding_box(
090         p_min.x , center.y, center.x, p_max.y);     // Top-left
091     children[child_offset+1].set_bounding_box(
092         center.x, center.y, p_max.x , p_max.y);     // Top-right
093     children[child_offset+2].set_bounding_box(
094         p_min.x , p_min.y , center.x, center.y);    // Bottom-left
095     children[child_offset+3].set_bounding_box(
096         center.x, p_min.y , p_max.x , center.y);    // Bottom-right
097
098     // Set the ranges of the children.
099     children[child_offset+0].set_range(node.points_begin(),    smem[4 + 0]);
100     children[child_offset+1].set_range(smem[4 + 0], smem[4 + 1]);
101     children[child_offset+2].set_range(smem[4 + 1], smem[4 + 2]);
102     children[child_offset+3].set_range(smem[4 + 2], smem[4 + 3]);
103 }
```

FIGURE 21.11

(Continued)

to buffer 0 if necessary. This is because the output is expected in buffer 0 after the quadtree is complete. The transfer of points from buffer 1 to buffer 0 is done in the device function check_num_points_and_depth() shown in Fig. 21.11.

Next, the center of the bounding box is computed (line 17). A bounding box is defined by its top-left and bottom-right corners. The coordinates of the top-left and the bottom-right corner points of the bounding box for the current node are given as part of the node data by the caller. The coordinates of the center are computed as the coordinates of the middle point between these two corner points. The definition of a bounding box (including function compute_center()) is given in Appendix A21.1.

As the center separates the four quadrants, one can determine which quadrant each point in the current node belongs to by comparing it with the center point. The number of points in each quadrant are counted (line 26). The device function `count_points_in_children()` can be found in Fig. 21.11. These are simplified for clarity reasons. The threads of the block collaboratively go through the range of points and use atomic operations to update the counters in shared memory for each quadrant.

The device function `scan_for_offsets()` is called then (line 29). As can be seen in Fig. 21.11, it performs a scan on the four counters in shared memory. Then it adds the global offset of the parent quadrant to these values to derive the starting offset for each quadrant's group in the buffer.

Using the quadrants' offsets, the points are reordered with `reorder_points()` (line 32). For simplicity this device function (Fig. 21.11) uses an atomic operation on one of the four quadrant counters to derive the location for placing each point.

Finally, the last thread of the block (line 35) determines the next available location in the node array for children nodes (line 37), prepares the new node contents for the child quadrants (line 40), and launches one child kernel with four thread blocks (line 43). The device function `prepare_children()` prepares the new node contents for the children by setting the limits of the children's bounding boxes and the range of points in each quadrant. The `prepare_children()` function can be found in Figure 13.14 (line 75).

The rest of the definitions can be found in Appendix A21.1.

21.5 Important considerations

In this section we will briefly explain some important considerations for the execution behavior of programs that use dynamic parallelism. It is important for a programmer to understand these considerations well in order to use dynamic parallelism confidently.

Memory and data visibility

When a parent thread passes a memory pointer to a child grid, it must ensure that the memory being pointed to is accessible to the child grid so that the child grid does not attempt to access invalid memory. The memory that can be accessed by both parent threads and their child grids includes global memory, constant memory, and texture memory. A parent thread should not pass pointers to local memory or shared memory to their child grids because local memory and shared memory are private to the thread and the thread block, respectively.

Besides ensuring that the memory that is passed by the parent thread to the child grid is accessible to the child grid, programmers must also be aware of when the data written to that memory by a parent thread will be visible to the child grid and vice versa. There are two points in the execution at which the parent thread and the child grid have the same view of memory: when the parent thread launches the child grid and when the child grid completes as signaled by the completion of a synchronization API call by the parent thread. In other words, when a parent thread launches a child grid, any updates to memory prior to that launch will be seen by the child grid, but there is no such guarantee for updates after that launch. Also, there is no guarantee that any updates to memory made by the child grid will be visible to the parent thread until after the parent thread has synchronized on the completion of the child grid.

We refer the reader to the CUDA C++ Programming Guide for more details about memory and data visibility between parent threads and child grids (NVIDIA Corporation, 2021).

Pending launch pool configuration

The pending launch pool is a buffer that tracks the kernels that are executing or waiting to be executed. This pool is allocated a fixed amount of space, thereby supporting a fixed number of pending kernel calls (2048 by default). If this number is exceeded, a virtualized pool is used, leading to a significant slowdown, which can be an order of magnitude or more. To avoid this slowdown, the programmer can increase the size of the fixed pool by executing the cudaDeviceSetLimit() API call from the host function to set the cudaLimitDevRuntimePendingLaunchCount configuration.

For example, in the Bezier curve calculation in Section 21.3, if N_LINES is set to 4096, then 4096 child grids will be launched, so half of the launches will use the virtualized pool. This will incur a significant performance penalty. However, if the fixed-size pool is set to 4096, the execution time will be reduced substantially.

As a general recommendation, the size of the fixed-size pool should be set to the expected number of launched grids (if it exceeds the default size). In the Bezier curves example we would call cudaDeviceSetLimit (cudaLimitDevRuntimePendingLaunchCount, N_LINES) before calling the computeBezierLines_parent() kernel.

Streams

Just as host code can use streams to execute kernels concurrently, device threads can use streams in launching grids with dynamic parallelism. The scope of a stream is private to the block in which the stream was created. When a stream is not specified in a kernel call, the default NULL stream in the block is used by all threads. This means that all grids that are launched in the same block will be serialized even if they were launched by different threads. However, it is often the case that grids launched by different threads in a block are independent and can be executed concurrently. Therefore programmers must be careful to explicitly use different streams in each thread if they wish to avoid the performance penalty from serialization.

```
// Create non-blocking stream
cudaStream_t stream;
cudaStreamCreateWithFlags(&stream, cudaStreamNonBlocking);

//Call the child kernel to compute the tessellated points for each line
computeBezierLine_child<<<ceil((float)bLines[lidx].nVertices/32.0f), 32, 0, stream>>>
    (lidx, bLines, bLines[lidx].nVertices);

// Destroy stream
cudaStreamDestroy(stream);
```

FIGURE 21.12

Child kernel launch with named streams.

The Bezier curves example in Section 21.3 launches as many child grids as there are parent threads in the computeBezierLines_parent() kernel (line 19 in Fig. 21.7). If the default NULL stream is used, all the grids that are launched by the same parent block will be serialized. Thus using the default NULL stream in launching the computeBezierLines_child() kernel can result in a drastic reduction in parallelism compared to the original kernel without dynamic parallelism.

If more concurrency is desired, named streams must be created and used in each thread. Fig. 21.12 shows the code that should replace line 19 in Fig. 21.7. With this code, kernels that are launched from the same thread block will be placed in different streams and can run concurrently. This would better utilize all SMs, leading to a considerable reduction in the execution time.

Nesting depth

Kernels that are launched with dynamic parallelism may themselves call other kernels, which may in turn call other kernels, and so on. We saw an example of such a kernel in the quadtree application in Section 12.4. Each subordinate launch is considered a new *nesting level*, and the total number of levels that are reached is called the *nesting depth*. The maximum nesting depth supported by current hardware is 24 levels. For this reason, kernels such as the one in the quadtree example should check this limit before deciding whether to make a dynamic launch.

In the presence of parent-child synchronization there are additional constraints on the nesting depth due to the amount of memory required by the system to store the state of the parent grid. This constraint is referred to as the *synchronization depth*. We refer the reader to the CUDA C++ Programming Guide for more details about the nesting depth and synchronization depth (NVIDIA Corporation, 2021).

21.6 Summary

CUDA dynamic parallelism extends the CUDA programming model to allow kernels to call other kernels. This allows each thread to dynamically discover work and launch new grids according to the amount of work that is newly discovered.

It also supports dynamic allocation of device memory by threads. As we showed in the Bezier curve calculation example, these extensions can lead to better work balance across threads and blocks as well as more efficient memory usage. CUDA Dynamic Parallelism also helps programmers to implement recursive algorithms, as the quadtree example shows.

Besides ensuring better work balance, dynamic parallelism offers many advantages in terms of programmability. However, it is important to keep in mind that launching grids with a small number of threads could lead to severe underutilization of the GPU resources. A general recommendation is launching child grids with many blocks, or at least blocks with many threads if the number of blocks is small.

Similarly, nested parallelism, which can be seen as a form of tree processing, provides higher performance when tree nodes are thick (that is, each node deploys many threads) and/or when the branch degree is large (i.e., each parent node has many children). As the nesting depth is limited in hardware, only relatively shallow trees can be implemented efficiently.

To use dynamic parallelism effectively, programmers need to understand details such as visibility of memory contents, pending launch count, and streams. Careful use of memory and streams between parents and children in dynamic parallelism is critical for the correct execution and achieving the expected level of parallelism in launching child grids.

Exercises

1. Which of the following statements are true for the Bezier curves example?
   a. If N_LINES=1024 and BLOCK_DIM=64, the number of child kernels that are launched will be 16.
   b. If N_LINES=1024, the fixed-size pool should be reduced from 2048 (the default) to 1024 to get the best performance.
   c. If N_LINES=1024 and BLOCK_DIM=64 and per-thread streams are used, a total of 16 streams will be deployed.
2. Consider a two-dimensional organization of 64 equidistant points. It is classified with a quadtree. What will be the maximum depth of the quadtree (including the root node)?
   a. 21
   b. 4
   c. 64
   d. 16
3. For the same quadtree, what will be the total number of child kernel launches?
   a. 21
   b. 4

   c. 64

   d. 16

4. **True or False:** Parent kernels can define new __constant__ variables that will be inherited by child kernels.

5. **True or False:** Child kernels can access their parents' shared and local memories.

6. Six blocks of 256 threads run the following parent kernel:

```
__global__ void parent_kernel(int *output, int *input, int *size) {
    // Thread index
    int idx = threadIdx.x + blockDim.x*blockIdx.x;

    // Number of child blocks
    int numBlocks = size[idx] / blockDim.x;

    // Launch child
    child_kernel<<< numBlocks, blockDim.x >>>(output, input, size);

}
```

How many child kernels could run concurrently?

   a. 1536

   b. 256

   c. 6

   d. 1

A21.1 Support code for quadtree example

```
001    // A structure of 2D points
002    class Points {
003        float *m_x;
004        float *m_y;
005
006        public:
007        // Constructor
008        __host__ __device__ Points() : m_x(NULL), m_y(NULL) {}
009
010        // Constructor
011        __host__ __device__ Points(float *x, float *y) : m_x(x), m_y(y) {}
012
013        // Get a point
014        __host__ __device__ __forceinline__ float2 get_point(int idx) const {
015            return make_float2(m_x[idx], m_y[idx]);
016        }
017
018        // Set a point
019        __host__ __device__ __forceinline__ void set_point(int idx, const float2 &p) {
020            m_x[idx] = p.x;
021            m_y[idx] = p.y;
022        }
023
024        // Set the pointers
025        __host__ __device__ __forceinline__ void set(float *x, float *y) {
026            m_x = x;
027            m_y = y;
028        }
029    };
030
031    // A 2D bounding box
032    class Bounding_box {
033        // Extreme points of the bounding box
034        float2 m_p_min;
035        float2 m_p_max;
036
037        public:
038        // Constructor. Create a unit box
039        __host__ __device__ Bounding_box(){
040            m_p_min = make_float2(0.0f, 0.0f);
041            m_p_max = make_float2(1.0f, 1.0f);
042        }
043
044        // Compute the center of the bounding-box
045        __host__ __device__ void compute_center(float2 &center) const {
046            center.x = 0.5f * (m_p_min.x + m_p_max.x);
047            center.y = 0.5f * (m_p_min.y + m_p_max.y);
048        }
049
050        // The points of the box
051        __host__ __device__ __forceinline__ const float2 &get_max() const {
052            return m_p_max;
053        }
054
055        __host__ __device__ __forceinline__ const float2 &get_min() const {
056            return m_p_min;
057        }
058
059        // Does a box contain a point
060        __host__ __device__ bool contains(const float2 &p) const {
061            return p.x>=m_p_min.x && p.x<m_p_max.x && p.y>=m_p_min.y && p.y<m_p_max.y;
062        }
063
```

```
064         // Define the bounding box
065         __host__ __device__ void set(float min_x, float min_y, float max_x, float
max_y){
066             m_p_min.x = min_x;
067             m_p_min.y = min_y;
068             m_p_max.x = max_x;
069             m_p_max.y = max_y;
070         }
071     };
072
073     // A node of a quadree
074     class Quadtree_node {
075         // The identifier of the node
076         int m_id;
077         // The bounding box of the tree
078         Bounding_box m_bounding_box;
079         // The range of points
080         int m_begin, m_end;
081
082     public:
083         // Constructor
084         __host__ __device__ Quadtree_node() : m_id(0), m_begin(0), m_end(0) {}
085
086         // The ID of a node at its level
087         __host__ __device__ int id() const {
088             return m_id;
089         }
090
091         // The ID of a node at its level
092         __host__ __device__ void set_id(int new_id) {
093             m_id = new_id;
094         }
095
096         // The bounding box
097         __host__ __device__ __forceinline__ const Bounding_box &bounding_box() const {
098             return m_bounding_box;
099         }
100
101         // Set the bounding box
102         __host__ __device__ __forceinline__ void set_bounding_box(float min_x,
103             float min_y, float max_x, float max_y) {
104             m_bounding_box.set(min_x, min_y, max_x, max_y);
105         }
106
107         // The number of points in the tree
108         __host__ __device__ __forceinline__ int num_points() const {
109             return m_end - m_begin;
110         }
111
112         // The range of points in the tree
113         __host__ __device__ __forceinline__ int points_begin() const {
114             return m_begin;
115         }
116
117         __host__ __device__ __forceinline__ int points_end() const {
118             return m_end;
119         }
120
121         // Define the range for that node
122         __host__ __device__ __forceinline__ void set_range(int begin, int end) {
123             m_begin = begin;
124             m_end = end;
125         }
126     };
127
128     // Algorithm parameters
129     struct Parameters {
```

```
130        // Choose the right set of points to use as in/out
131        int point_selector;
132        // The number of nodes at a given level (2^k for level k)
133        int num_nodes_at_this_level;
134        // The recursion depth
135        int depth;
136        // The max value for depth
137        const int max_depth;
138        // The minimum number of points in a node to stop recursion
139        const int min_points_per_node;
140
141        // Constructor set to default values.
142        __host__ __device__ Parameters(int max_depth, int min_points_per_node) :
143            point_selector(0),
144            num_nodes_at_this_level(1),
145            depth(0),
146            max_depth(max_depth),
147            min_points_per_node(min_points_per_node) {}
148
149        // Copy constructor. Changes the values for next iteration
150        __host__ __device__ Parameters(const Parameters &params, bool) :
151            point_selector((params.point_selector+1) % 2),
152            num_nodes_at_this_level(4*params.num_nodes_at_this_level),
153            depth(params.depth+1),
154            max_depth(params.max_depth),
155            min_points_per_node(params.min_points_per_node) {}
156    };
```

References

Bezier Curves, http://en.wikipedia.org/wiki/B%C3%A9zier_curve.

Finkel, R.A., Bentley, J.L., 1974. Quad trees: a data structure for retrieval on composite keys. Acta Inform. 4 (1), 1–9.

NVIDIA Corporation, 2021. CUDA C++ programming guide, March.

Advanced practices and future evolution

22

With special contributions from Isaac Gelado and Mark Harris

Chapter Outline

22.1 Model of host/device interaction 500
22.2 Kernel execution control 505
22.3 Memory bandwidth and compute throughput 508
22.4 Programming environment 510
22.5 Future outlook 513
References 513

Our focus throughout this book has been on scalable parallel programming. CUDA C and the GPU hardware have mostly played the role of the programming platform for our examples and exercises. However, the parallel programming concepts and skills that are learned on the basis of CUDA C can be easily adapted for other parallel programming platforms. For example, as we saw in Chapter 20, Programming a Heterogeneous Computing Cluster, Programming a Heterogeneous Computing Cluster: An Introduction to CUDA Streams, most key concepts of Message Passing Interface (MPI), such as processes, rank, and barriers, have counterparts in CUDA C. Furthermore, as we also discussed in Chapter 20, Programming a Heterogeneous Computing Cluster, CUDA-enabled GPUs have become widely available in high-performance computing (HPC) systems. For many readers, CUDA C will likely be an important application development and deployment platform rather than just a learning vehicle. For this reason, it is important for the reader to understand the advanced CUDA C features and practices that are designed to support high-performance programming at the application level. For example, as we saw in Chapter 20, Programming a Heterogeneous Computing Cluster, CUDA streams enable an MPI HPC application to overlap communication with the computation. Such capability is especially important for achieving whole-application performance goals. With this in mind, this chapter will provide the reader with an overview of the advanced features of CUDA C and GPU computing hardware that will be important in achieving high performance and maintainability in your applications. For each feature we will present the basic concepts as well as a brief history of its

Programming Massively Parallel Processors. DOI: https://doi.org/10.1016/B978-0-323-91231-0.00013-6

evolution through different generations of GPU computing. A good understanding of the concepts and the evolution history will help to clear up some common confusion about these features. The goal is to help the reader to establish a conceptual framework for more detailed studies of these features.

22.1 Model of host/device interaction

So far, we have assumed a fairly simple model of interaction between host and device in a heterogeneous computing system. In this simple model, as presented in Chapter 2, Heterogeneous Data Parallel Computing, Heterogeneous Data Parallel Computing, each device has a device memory (CUDA global memory) that is separate from the host memory, or the system memory. The data to be processed by a kernel running on a device needs to be transferred from the host memory to the device memory by calling the `cudaMemcpy()` function. The data that is produced by the device also needs to be transferred from the device memory to the host by calling the `cudaMemcpy()` function before it can be utilized by the host. While the model is simple and easy to understand, it results in several problems at the application level.

First, I/O devices such as disk controllers and network interface cards are designed to operate efficiently on the host memory. Since the device memory is separate from the host memory, input data need to be transferred from the host memory to the device memory, and output data need to be transferred from the device memory to the host memory to be used in I/O operations. Such additional transfers increase the I/O latency and reduce the achievable I/O throughput. For many applications the ability of I/O devices to operate directly on the device memory would improve overall application performance and simplify the application code.

Second, the host memory is where the traditional programming systems place their application data structures. Some of the data structures are large. The device memory in early generations of CUDA-enabled GPUs were small in comparison to the host memory, which forces application developers to partition their large data structures into chunks that fit into the device memory. For example, in Chapter 18, Electrostatic Potential Map, the three-dimensional (3D) electrostatic energy grid array was partitioned into two-dimensional slices that are transferred between the host memory and the device memory. For many applications it would be much better if the entire data structures could reside in the device memory. For some applications there may not even be a good way to partition the data structure into smaller chunks. For these applications it would be best if the GPU could directly access the data in the host memory or have the CUDA runtime system software migrate the data that is used during kernel execution.

These limitations of the host/device interaction model were rooted in the limitations of the memory architecture of early generations of CUDA-enabled

GPUs. In these early devices, the only viable host/device interaction model for applications was the simple model that we assumed in the previous chapters. As more applications adopted GPU computing, their needs motivated CUDA system software developers and GPU hardware designers to provide a better solution. Researchers have been aware of these needs and have proposed solutions since the early days of CUDA (Gelado et al., 2010). The rest of this section will go over a brief history of advancements that address these limitations.

Zero-copy memory and unified virtual address space

In 2009, CUDA 2.2 introduced zero-copy access to system memory. This enables the host code to supply a special device data pointer to host memory to a kernel. The code that is running on the device can use this pointer to directly access the host memory through the system interconnect, such as the PCIe bus, without calling to `cudaMemcpy()`. Zero-copy memory is pinned host memory (Chapter 20, Programming a Heterogeneous Computing Cluster,) and is allocated by calling `cudaHostAlloc()` with `cudaHostAllocMapped` as the value of the flag argument. We mentioned that the other values of the flag argument are for more advanced usage. The data pointer that is returned by `cudaHostAlloc()` cannot be directly passed to the kernel; the host code has to obtain a valid device data pointer, using `cudaHostGetDevicePointer()` first, and pass the device data pointer that is returned by this function to the kernel. This means that different data pointers for host and device codes are used to access the same physical memory.

As we explained in Chapter 20, Programming a Heterogeneous Computing Cluster, the host memory pages must be pinned to prevent the operating system from accidentally paging out the data while the GPU is accessing them. Obviously, the access will suffer from the long latency and limited bandwidth of the system interconnect. The bandwidth of the system interconnect is typically less than 10% of the global memory bandwidth. As we learned in Chapter 5, Memory Architecture and Data Locality, a kernel's performance is typically limited by the global memory bandwidth unless we use tiling techniques to drastically reduce the number of global memory accesses per floating-point operation performed. If most of the memory accesses of a kernel are to zero-copy memory, the kernel's execution speed can be even more severely limited by the bandwidth of the system interconnect. Therefore one should use zero-copy memory only for application data structures that are occasionally and sparsely accessed by a kernel running on a GPU.

In 2011, CUDA 4 introduced the Unified Virtual Addressing. Until this CUDA release, the host and the device had their own virtual address spaces, each of them mapping host or device data pointers to physical host or device memory locations. These disjoint virtual address spaces imply that the same physical memory location could be accessed by different virtual addresses in the host and the device, which effectively happens in using zero-copy memory. The Unified Virtual Address Space (UVAS), first introduced by the GMAC library (Gelado et al., 2010) and adopted in

CUDA 4, uses a single virtual address space that is shared by the host and the device. The UVAS guarantees that each physical memory address is mapped to only one virtual memory location. This enables the CUDA runtime to determine whether a data pointer is referencing host or device memory by just inspecting its virtual memory address. This feature removes the need to specify the data copy direction on `cudaMemcpy()` calls.

It is important to note that the UVAS in CUDA 4 does not guarantee the accessibility of the data that is referenced by a pointer. For example, the host code cannot use a device pointer that is returned by `cudaMalloc()` to directly access the device memory and vice versa. Zero-copy memory is the exception: The host code can directly pass a pointer to zero-copy memory as a kernel launch parameter to the device. When the kernel code dereferences this zero-copy pointer, the pointer value is translated to a physical system memory location and is accessed directly through the PCIe bus. Note that this approach does not necessarily allow the kernel code to dereference a pointer value that is read from a memory location, such as following a chain of pointers while traversing a linked data structure, unless all memory has been allocated by using `cudaHostAlloc()`.

The limitations in both the types of data structures that can be supported and the bandwidth of data accesses of zero-copy memory motivate further improvements in the memory model of GPU architectures beyond UVAS.

Large virtual and physical address spaces

One fundamental limitation of early CUDA-enabled GPUs is the size of their virtual and physical addresses. These early devices support 32-bit virtual addresses and up to 32-bit physical addresses. For these devices the size of the device memory is limited to 4 gigabytes, the maximum amount of memory that can be addressed with 32 physical address bits. Furthermore, CUDA kernels can operate only on datasets whose sizes are less than 4 gigabytes, the maximum number of virtual memory locations that can be accessed through 32-bit pointers, regardless of whether the dataset resides in the host memory or the device memory. Furthermore, modern CPUs are based on 64-bit virtual addresses with 48 bits actually utilized. These host virtual addresses cannot be accommodated by the 32-bit virtual addresses that are used by GPUs, which contributed to the limitation of the types of data structures supported by zero-copy memory.

To remove this limitation, GPU generations starting with the Kepler GPU architecture introduced in 2013 have adopted modern virtual memory architecture with 64-bit virtual addresses and physical addresses of at least 40 bits. The obvious benefits are that these GPUs can incorporate more than 4 gigabytes of DRAM and that CUDA kernels can now operate on large datasets. While the enlarged virtual and physical address spaces obviously enable the use of large device memories, they also open the door for much better host/device interaction models. For example, the host and the device can now use exactly the same pointer value to access a piece of data, regardless of whether it is in the host memory or the device memory.

The large GPU physical address space also allows the CUDA system software to place device memory of different GPUs in the system into a unified physical address space. The benefit is that one GPU can directly access the memory of any other GPU that is attached to the same PCIe bus by simply dereferencing a data pointer that is mapped to the physical address of such a GPU. Prior to the Kepler GPU architecture, communication among different GPUs (e.g., halo exchange in the stencil example in Chapter 20, Programming a Heterogeneous Computing Cluster) was possible only through device-to-device memory copies triggered by the host code. This resulted in extra memory consumed to store the data being copied from other GPUs and extra performance overheads due to the memory copy operations. Direct access to other device memory in the system enables just passing the device pointer to the other GPU in the kernel call and using it to load and/or store the data that need to be communicated.

Unified memory

In 2013, CUDA 6 introduced unified memory, which creates a pool of managed memory that is shared between the CPU and GPU, bridging the CPU-GPU divide. Managed memory is accessible to both the CPU and GPU using a single pointer. Variables in the managed memory can reside in the CPU physical memory, the GPU physical memory, or even both. The CUDA runtime software and hardware implement data migration and coherence support, such as the GMAC system (Gelado et al., 2010). The net effect is that the managed memory looks like CPU memory to code running on the CPU and like GPU memory to code running on the GPU. Of course, the application must perform appropriate synchronization operations such as barriers or atomic operations to coordinate any concurrent accesses to the managed memory locations. A shared global virtual address space allows all variables in an application to have unique addresses. Such memory architecture, when exposed by programming tools and runtime systems to applications, can result in several major benefits.

One such benefit is the reduced amount of effort that is required for porting CPU code to CUDA. In Fig. 22.1 we show a simple CPU code example on the left side. With unified memory, the code can be ported to CUDA with two simple changes. The first change is to use `cudaMallocManaged()` and `cudaFree()` in place of `malloc()` and `free()`. The second change is to launch a kernel and perform device synchronization rather than calling the `qsort()` function. Obviously, one still needs to write or have access to a parallel `qsort` kernel. What we are showing is that the change to the host code is straightforward and easy to maintain.

The performance of the CUDA 6 unified memory was limited by the hardware capabilities of the Kepler and Maxwell GPU architectures. The contents of all managed memory locations that had been modified by the CPU had to be flushed out to the GPU device memory before any grid launch. The CPU and GPU could not simultaneously

CPU Code

```
void sortfile(FILE *fp, int N) {
  char *data;
  data = (char *)malloc(N);

  fread(data, 1, N, fp);

  qsort(data, N, 1, compare);


  use_data(data);

  free(data);
}
```

CUDA 6 Code with Unified Memory

```
void sortfile(FILE *fp, int N) {
  char *data;
  cudaMallocManaged(&data, N);

  fread(data, 1, N, fp);

  qsort<<<...>>>(data,N,1,compare);
  cudaDeviceSynchronize();

  use_data(data);

  cudaFree(data);
}
```

FIGURE 22.1

Unified memory simplifies porting of CPU code (left) to CUDA code (right).

access a managed memory allocation, and the unified memory address space was limited to the size of the GPU physical memory. These limitations are due to the fact that these GPU architectures lacked the ability to support coherence between the host and device memories and that the data migration was mostly performed by software.

In 2016 the Pascal GPU architecture added features to further simplify programming and sharing of memory between CPU and GPU, and further reduce the effort required to use GPUs for significant speedups. Two main hardware features enable these improvements: support for large address spaces and page fault handling capability.

The Pascal GPU architecture extends GPU addressing capabilities to 49-bit virtual addressing. This extension is large enough to cover the 48-bit virtual address spaces of modern CPUs as well as the GPU's own memory. This allows unified memory programs to access the full address spaces of all CPUs and GPUs in the system as a single virtual address space rather than being limited by the amount of data that can be copied to the device memory. As a result, the CPUs and GPUs can truly share the pointer values, enabling the GPUs to traverse pointer-based data structures in the host memory.

Memory page fault handling support in the Pascal GPU architecture is a crucial new feature that provides more seamless unified memory functionality. Combined with the system-wide virtual address space, the ability to handle page faults eliminates the need for the CUDA system software to synchronize (flush) all managed memory contents to the GPU before each grid launch. The CUDA runtime can implement a coherence mechanism by allowing the host and the device to invalidate each other's copy when they modify a variable in the managed memory. The invalidation can be done by using the page mapping and protection mechanisms. When launching a grid, the CUDA system software no longer has to bring all GPU copies of the managed memory data up to date. If the grid accesses a piece of data whose copy in the device memory has been invalidated by the host, the GPU will handle a page fault to bring the data up to date and resume execution.

If a grid running on the GPU accesses a page that is not resident in its device memory, it also will take a page fault, allowing the page to be automatically migrated to the GPU memory on demand. Alternatively, the page may be mapped into the GPU address space for access over the system interconnects (mapping on access can sometimes be faster than migration) if the data is expected to be accessed only occasionally. Note that unified memory is system-wide: GPUs (and CPUs) can fault and migrate memory pages either from CPU memory or from the memory of other GPUs in the system. If a CPU function dereferences a pointer and accesses a variable that is mapped to the GPU physical memory, the data access would still be serviced but perhaps at a longer latency. Such capability allows the CUDA programs to more easily call legacy libraries that have not been ported to GPUs. In the prior CUDA memory architecture the developer must manually transfer data from the device memory to the host memory in order to use legacy library functions to process them on the CPU.

The unified memory with page fault handling capability enables a much more general CPU/GPU interaction mechanism than zero-copy memory. It allows the GPU to traverse large data structures in the host memory. Starting with the Pascal architecture, a GPU device can traverse a linked data structure even if the data structure does not reside in zero-copy memory. This is because the same pointer value is used in the host code and the device code to refer to the same variable. Thus the embedded pointer values of a linked data structure built by the host can be traversed by the device and vice versa. In some application areas, such as CAD, the host physical memory system may have hundreds of gigabytes of capacity. These physical memory systems are needed because the applications require the entire dataset to be "in core." With the ability to directly access very large CPU physical memories, it becomes feasible for GPUs to accelerate these applications.

Virtual address space control

CUDA 11 introduced a set of low-level APIs to give programmers more flexibility regarding memory allocation. The new API allows reserving a range of the virtual address space using `cuMemAddressReserve()`. Later on, the programmer can allocate physical memory on any device using `cuMemCreate()` and map it to any position in the reserved range using `cuMemMap()`. These APIs enable building custom layouts of data structures across multiple devices. For instance, it would be possible to allocate a 3D volume across multiple devices while using a single pointer to reference it.

22.2 Kernel execution control
Function calls within kernel functions

Early CUDA versions did not allow function calls during kernel execution. Although the source code of kernel functions can appear to have function calls, the compiler must be able to inline all function bodies into the kernel object so that there are no function calls in the kernel function at runtime. Although this model works reasonably well for performance-critical portions of many applications, it does not support the common software engineering practices in more sophisticated applications. In particular, it does not support system calls, dynamically linked library calls, recursive function calls, and virtual functions in object-oriented languages such as C++.

Later device architectures, such as Kepler, supported function calls in kernel functions at runtime. This feature is supported in CUDA 5 and beyond. The compiler is no longer required to inline the function bodies. It can still do so as a performance optimization. This capability is partly enabled by a cached and fast implementation of massively parallel call frame stacks for CUDA threads. It makes CUDA device code much more "composable" by allowing different authors to write different CUDA kernel components and assemble them all together without heavy redesign costs. It also allows software vendors to release device libraries without source code for intellectual property protection. However, some limitations still exist. For example, support for virtual functions is limited to objects constructed by device code, and dynamic libraries for device code are not supported.

Support for function calls at runtime also enables recursion and significantly eases the burden on programmers as they transition from legacy CPU-oriented algorithms toward GPU-tuned code. In some cases, developers will be able to "cut and paste" CPU code into a CUDA kernel and obtain a reasonably performing kernel, although continued performance tuning would still add benefit.

With the function call support, kernels can now call standard library functions such as `printf()` and `malloc()`. In our experience, the ability to call `printf()` in a kernel provides a subtle but important aid in debugging and supporting kernels in production software. Many end users are nontechnical and cannot be easily trained to run debuggers that will provide developers with more details on what happened before a crash. The ability to call `printf()` in the kernel allows developers to add a mode to the application to dump internal state so that the end users can submit meaningful bug reports.

CUDA 8 added support for C++11 and, with it, another form of function calls: lambdas. When coupled with metaprogramming techniques, device lambdas enable the development of high-performance reusable code. CUDA also supports passing lambda functions as parameters to CUDA kernels. This feature can be used to write generic kernels (e.g., a sorting kernel), in which the comparison function is just an input parameter to the kernel. CUDA also added experimental support for "extended lambdas," which are enabled with the `−extended-lambda` compiler flag. This feature allows programmers to annotate C++ lambdas with the `__host__` `__device__` modifiers, further simplifying the task of writing reusable code.

Exception handling in kernel functions

Early CUDA systems did not support exception handling in kernel code. While not a significant limitation for performance-critical portions of many high-performance applications, it often incurs software engineering cost in production quality applications that rely on exceptions to detect and handle rare conditions without executing code to explicitly test for such conditions.

With the availability of limited exception handling support, CUDA debuggers allow a user to perform step-by-step execution, to set breakpoints, and or to run a kernel until an invalid memory access happens. In each case, the user can inspect the values of the kernel's local and global variables when the execution is suspended. In our experience, the CUDA debugger is a very helpful tool to detect out-of-bounds memory accesses and potential race conditions.

Simultaneous execution of multiple grids

The earliest CUDA systems allowed only one grid to execute on each GPU device at any point in time. Multiple grids could be submitted for execution using CUDA streams, but they were buffered in a queue that released the next grid after the current one had completed execution. The Fermi GPU architecture and its successors allowed multiple grids from the same application to be executed simultaneously, which reduces the pressure for the application developer to "batch" multiple kernels into a larger kernel in order to more fully utilize a device. Also, it is sometimes beneficial to partition work into chunks that can execute with different levels of priority.

A typical example of the benefit of executing multiple grids simultaneously is for parallel cluster applications that segment work into "local" and "remote" partitions, in which remote work is involved in interactions with other nodes and resides on the critical path of global progress (Chapter 20, Programming a Heterogeneous Computing Cluster). In previous CUDA systems, grids needed to perform a lot of work to utilize the device efficiently, and one had to be careful not to launch local work such that global work could be blocked. This meant choosing between underutilizing the device while waiting for remote work to arrive or eagerly starting on local work to keep the device productive at the cost of increased latency for completing remote work units (Phillips and Stone, 2009). With multiple grid execution the application can use much smaller grid sizes for launching work, and as a result, when high-priority remote work arrives, it can start running with low latency instead of being stuck behind a large grid of local computation.

Hardware queues and dynamic parallelism

In the Kepler architecture and CUDA 5, the multiple grid launch facility was extended by the addition of multiple hardware queues, which allow much more efficient scheduling of thread blocks from multiple grids from multiple streams. In addition, CUDA dynamic parallelism, which was covered in Chapter 21, CUDA Dynamic Parallelism, allows GPU work creation: GPU grids can launch child grids asynchronously, dynamically, and in a data-dependent or compute load−dependent fashion. This reduces CPU-GPU interaction and synchronization, since the GPU can now manage more complex workloads independently. The CPU is in turn free to perform other useful computation.

Interruptable grids

The Fermi GPU architecture allowed a running grid to be "canceled," enabling the creation of CUDA-accelerated apps that allow the user to abort a long-running calculation at any time without requiring significant design effort on the part of the programmer. This enables implementation of user-level task scheduling systems that can better perform load balance between GPU nodes of a computing system and allows more graceful handling of cases in which one GPU is heavily loaded and may be running more slowly than its peers (Stone & Hwu, 2009).

Cooperative kernels

GPU kernels working on irregular data often suffer from load imbalance. CUDA 11 introduced the cooperative kernels to alleviate this problem. A cooperative kernel can execute up to a maximum number of thread blocks that would completely fill the GPU, and the CUDA runtime guarantees that all the thread blocks will execute concurrently. This concurrency guarantee enables thread blocks to safely cooperate without deadlock over shared mutual exclusion mechanisms (e.g., a mutex) that can be used to protect shared data structures (e.g., work queues). Cooperative kernels require a special API, `cudaLaunchCooperativeKernel()`, and provide a device API to identify and partition groups of threads. Cooperative kernels are not limited to a single device but can be called to run in multiple devices using `cudaLaunchCooperativeKernelMultiDevice()`.

22.3 Memory bandwidth and compute throughput

Double-precision speed

Early devices performed double-precision floating-point arithmetic with significant speed reduction (around eight times slower) compared to single-precision. The floating-point arithmetic units of Fermi and its successors were significantly strengthened to perform double-precision arithmetic at about half the speed of single-precision. Applications that are intensive in double-precision floating-point arithmetic benefited tremendously.

In practice, the most significant benefit was obtained by developers who were porting CPU-based numerical applications to GPUs. With the improved double-precision speed, they had little incentive to spend the effort to evaluate whether their applications or portions of their applications could fit into single-precision. This significantly reduced the development cost for porting CPU applications to GPUs and addressed a major criticism of GPUs in their earliest days by the HPC community.

Some applications that were operating on smaller input data types (8-bit, 16-bit, or single-precision floating-point) continued to benefit from using single-precision arithmetic, owing to the reduced bandwidth of using 32-bit versus

64-bit data. Applications such as medical imaging, remote sensing, radio astronomy, seismic analysis, and other natural data frequently fit into this category. The Pascal GPU architecture introduced new hardware support for computing with 16-bit half-precision numbers to further improve the performance and energy efficiency of applications whose data can fit into the half-precision representation. For example, in A100 based on the Ampere architecture, the 16-bit half-precision arithmetic throughput using tensor cores is 156 TFLOPS, a dramatic improvement compared to its 19.5 TFLOPS single-precision throughput.

Better control flow efficiency

Starting with the Fermi GPU architecture, CUDA systems adopted a general compiler-driven predication technique (Mahlke et al., 1995) that can more effectively handle control flow than previous CUDA systems. While this technique was moderately successful in VLIW systems, it provided even more dramatic speed improvements in GPU warp-style SIMD execution systems. This capability broadens the range of applications that can take advantage of GPUs. In particular, major performance benefits can potentially be realized for applications that are very data-driven, such as ray tracing, quantum chemistry visualization, and cellular automata simulation.

Configurable caching and scratchpad

The shared memory in early CUDA systems served as a programmer-managed scratchpad memory and increased the speed of applications in which key data structures have localized and predictable access patterns. Starting with the Fermi GPU architecture, the shared memory was enhanced to a larger on-chip memory that can be configured to be partially cache memory and partially shared memory, which allows coverage of both predictable and less predictable access patterns to benefit from on-chip memory. This configurability allows programmers to apportion the resources according to the best fit for their application.

Applications in an early design stage that are ported directly from CPU code will benefit greatly from caching as the dominant part of the on-chip memory. This further smoothes the performance-tuning process by increasing the level of "easy performance" when a developer ports a CPU application to GPU.

Existing CUDA applications and those that have predictable access patterns have the ability to increase their use of fast shared memory while retaining the same device "occupancy" they had on previous-generation devices. For CUDA applications whose performance or capabilities are limited by the size of the shared memory, the increase in size will be a welcome improvement. For example, in stencil computation (Chapter 8, Stencil, and Chapter 20, Programming a Heterogeneous Computing Cluster), such as finite difference methods for computational fluid dynamics, the increased shared memory capacity improves the memory bandwidth efficiency and the performance of the application.

Enhanced atomic operations

The atomic operations in the Fermi GPU architecture were much faster than those in previous CUDA systems, and the atomic operations in Kepler were even faster. In addition, the Kepler atomic operations were more general. The atomic operations over shared memory variables in the Maxwell GPU architecture were further enhanced in their throughput. Atomic operations are frequently used in random scatter computation patterns, such as histograms (Chapter 9, Parallel Histogram: An Introduction to Atomic Operations and Privatization). Faster atomic operations reduce the need for algorithm transformations such as prefix sum (Chapter 11, Prefix Sum (Scan): An Introduction to Work Efficiency in Parallel Algorithms) (Sengupta et al., 2007) and sorting (Chapter 13, Sorting) (Satish et al., 2009) for implementing such random scattering computations. These transformations tend to increase the number of kernel invocations as well as the total number of operations that are needed to perform the target computation. Faster atomic operations can also reduce the need for involving the host CPU in algorithms that do collective operations or where multiple thread blocks update shared data structures, thus reducing the data transfer pressure between CPU and GPU.

Enhanced global memory access

The speed of random memory access is much faster in Fermi and Kepler than in earlier GPU architectures. Programmers can be less concerned about memory coalescing. This allows more CPU algorithms to be directly used in the GPU as an acceptable base, further smoothing the path of porting applications that access a diversity of data structures, such as ray tracing, and other applications that are heavily object-oriented and may be difficult to convert into perfectly tiled arrays.

The Pascal GPU architecture incorporated HBM2 (High-Bandwidth Memory version 2) 3D-stacked DRAM memory, which provided up to $3 \times$ the memory bandwidth of previous-generation NVIDIA Maxwell architecture GPUs. Pascal was also the first architecture to support the NVLink processor interconnect, which gave Tesla P100 up to $5 \times$ the GPU-GPU and GPU-CPU communication performance of PCI Express 3.0. This interconnect greatly improved the scalability of multi-GPU computation within a node as well as the efficiency of data sharing between GPUs and NVLink-capable CPUs.

22.4 Programming environment

Unified device memory space

In early CUDA devices, shared memory, local memory, and global memory formed their own separate address spaces. The developer could use pointers into the global memory but not others. Starting with the Fermi architecture that was introduced in 2009, these memories became parts of a unified address space. This unified address space enabled a single set of load/store instructions and pointer addresses to access any of the GPU memory spaces (global, local, or shared memory) rather than different instructions and pointers for each. This made it easier to abstract away which memory contains a particular operand, allowing the programmer to deal with this only during allocation and making it simpler to pass CUDA data objects into other procedures and functions, irrespective of which memory area they come from.

This made CUDA code modules much more "composable." That is, a CUDA device function can accept a pointer that may point to any of these memories. For example, without unified GPU address space, a device function needs to have one implementation for each type of memory in which one of its arguments can reside. Unified GPU address space allows variables in all main types of GPU memories to be accessed in the same way, thus allowing one device function to accept arguments that can reside in different types of GPU memory. The code will run faster if a function argument pointer points to a shared memory location and more slowly if it points to a global memory location. The programmer can still perform manual data placement and transfers as a performance optimization. This capability has significantly reduced the cost of building production-quality CUDA libraries. This also enabled full C and C++ pointer support, which was a significant advancement at the time.

Future CUDA compilers will include enhanced support for C++ templates and virtual function calls in kernel functions. Although the hardware enhancements, such as runtime function calling capability, are in place, enhanced C++ language support in the compiler has been taking more time. With these enhancements, future CUDA compilers will support most mainstream C++ features. For example, using C++ features such as new, delete, constructors, and destructors in kernel functions is already supported.

New and evolved programming interfaces continue to improve the productivity of heterogeneous parallel programmers. OpenACC allows developers to annotate their sequential loops with compiler directives to enable a compiler to generate CUDA kernels. One can use the Thrust library of parallel type-generic functions, classes, and iterators to describe their computation and have the underlying mechanism generate and configure the kernels that implement the computation. CUDA FORTRAN allows FORTRAN programmers to develop CUDA kernels in their familiar language. In particular, CUDA FORTRAN offers strong support for indexing into multidimensional arrays. C++AMP allows developers to describe their kernels as parallel loops that operate on logical data structures, such as multidimensional arrays in a C++ application. We fully expect that new innovations will continue to arise to further boost the productivity of developers in this exciting area.

Profiling with critical path analysis

In heterogeneous applications that do significant computation on both CPUs and GPUs, it can be a challenge to locate the best place to spend optimization effort. Ideally, when optimizing code, one would like to target the locations in the application that will provide the highest speedup for the least effort. To this end, CUDA 7.5

introduced PC sampling, providing instruction-level profiling so that the user could pinpoint specific lines of code that are taking the most time in his or her application.

However, a challenge facing the users of such profilers is that the longest-running kernel in an application is not always the most critical optimization target. As Fig. 22.2 shows, Kernel X is the longer-running kernel. However, its execution time is fully overlapped with the CPU execution activity A. Any further improvement in the execution time of Kernel X without simultaneous improvement in the execution time of A is unlikely to improve the application performance. While the execution time of Kernel Y is not as long as that of kernel X, it is on the critical path of the application execution. The CPU is idling while waiting for the completion of Kernel Y. Speeding up Kernel Y will reduce the time the CPU spends waiting, so it is the best optimization target.

In 2016 the Visual Profiler in CUDA 8 provided a critical path analysis between GPU kernels and CPU CUDA API calls, enabling more precise targeting of optimization efforts. Fig. 22.3 shows critical path analysis in the CUDA 8

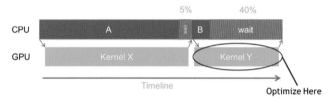

FIGURE 22.2

Importance of critical path analysis for identifying the key kernels to optimize.

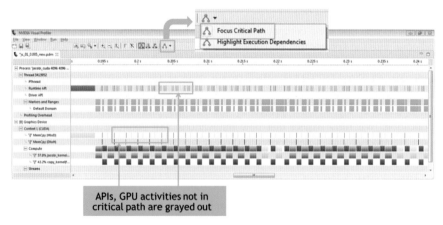

FIGURE 22.3

Application critical path analysis in CUDA 8 Visual Profiler.

Visual Profiler. GPU kernels, copies, and API calls that are not on the critical path are grayed out. Only the activities that are on the critical path of the application execution are highlighted in color. This allows the user to easily identify the kernels and other activities to target the user's optimization efforts.

22.5 Future outlook

The evolution of CUDA continues to increase its support for developer productivity and modern software engineering practices. With the new capabilities and programming language support, the range of applications that will be able to get reasonable performance at minimal development cost will expand significantly. Developers have experienced the reduction in application development, porting, and maintenance cost compared to previous CUDA systems. The existing applications that have been developed with Thrust and similar high-level tools that automatically generate CUDA code will also likely get an immediate boost in their performance. While the benefit of hardware enhancements in memory architecture, kernel execution control, and compute core performance will be visible in the associated SDK releases, the true potential of these enhancements may take years to be fully exploited in the SDKs and runtimes. We predict an exciting time for innovations from both industry and academia in programming tools and runtime environments for GPU computing in the next few years.

References

Gelado, I., Stone, J.E., Cabezas, J., Patel, S., Navarro, N., Hwu, W.W., 2010. An asymmetric distributed shared memory model for heterogeneous parallel systems. In: The ACM/IEEE 15th International Conference on Architectural Support for Programming Languages and Operating Systems (ASPLOS'10), March 2010. Pittsburgh, PA.

Mahlke, S.A., Hank, R.E., Mcormick, J.E., August, D.I., Hwu, W.W., 1995. A comparison of full and partial predicated execution support for ILP processors. In: Proceedings of the 22nd Annual International Symposium on Computer Architecture, Santa Margherita Ligure, Italy, June 1995, pp. 138–150.

Phillips, J., Stone, J., 2009. Probing biomolecular machines using graphics processors. Commun. ACM 52 (10).

Satish, N., Harris, M., Garland, M., 2009. Designing efficient sorting algorithms for many-core GPUs. In: Proceedings of 23rd IEEE International Parallel & Distributed Processing Symposium, May 2009.

Sengupta, S., Harris, M., Zhang, Y., Owens, J.D., 2007. Scan primitives for GPU Computing. In: Proceedings of Graphics Hardware, August 2007, pp. 97–106.

Stone, J.E., Hwu, W.W., 2009. WorkForce: A Lightweight Framework for Managing Multi-GPU Computations, Technical Report, IMPACT Group, University of Illinois at Urbana-Champaign.

Conclusion and outlook

23

Chapter Outline

23.1 Goals revisited 515
23.2 Future outlook 516

You made it! We have arrived at the finishing line. In this final chapter we will briefly review the learning goals that you have achieved through this book. Instead of drawing a conclusion, we will offer our vision for the future of massively parallel computing and how its advancements will affect the future course of science and technology.

23.1 Goals revisited

As we stated in the Introduction, our primary goal is to teach you, the reader, how to program massively parallel processors. We promised that it would become easy once you develop the right intuition and go about it the right way. In particular, we promised to focus on computational thinking skills that would enable you to think about problems in ways that are amenable to parallel computing. We also promised to focus on the factors that limit the performance of parallel applications and provide a systematic approach for optimizing code to overcome these factors.

We delivered on these promises through four steps. In step one, Chapters 2 through 6 introduce the essential concepts of parallel computing and CUDA C and the key performance considerations in developing massively parallel code in CUDA. They also introduce the pertinent computer architecture concepts needed to understand the hardware limitations that must be addressed in high-performance parallel programming. With this knowledge, a developer can be confident in writing their parallel code and reasoning about the relative merit of alternative threading arrangements, loop structures, and coding styles. We conclude this part with a checklist of common optimization techniques that we apply throughout the rest of the book to optimize the performance of various parallel patterns and applications.

In the second step, we introduce six major parallel patterns (Chapters 7 through 12) that have been proven useful in introducing parallelism into

Programming Massively Parallel Processors. DOI: https://doi.org/10.1016/B978-0-323-91231-0.00020-3

many applications. These chapters cover the concepts behind the most useful patterns of parallel computation. Each pattern is illustrated with concrete code examples. Each pattern is also used to introduce important techniques for overcoming frequently encountered parallelization and performance obstacles in parallel programming. We also use these patterns to showcase how the optimizations introduced in the first step can be applied in a wide variety of scenarios.

In the third step, we introduce additional advanced patterns and applications (Chapters 13−19) to reinforce the knowledge and skills gained in the previous step. While in this step, we continue to apply the optimizations that we practiced in the previous step, we put more emphasis on exploring alternative forms of problem decomposition to enable parallelization and analyze the tradeoffs between different decompositions and their associated data structures. The final chapter in this step is dedicated to recap the computational thinking skills (Chapter 19, Parallel Programming and Computational Thinking) that help the reader to generalize the concepts learnt in the previous chapters into the high-level thinking required to tackle a new problem. With these insights, high-performance parallel programming becomes a thought process, rather than a black art.

The fourth step is to expose the reader to related advanced practices in parallel programming. Chapter 20, Programming a Heterogeneous Computing Cluster, presents the basic skills required to program an HPC cluster using MPI and CUDA C. Chapter 21, CUDA Dynamic Parallelism, presents an introduction to dynamic parallelism that helps parallel programmers to address more complex parallel algorithms with dynamically varying workload in many real-world applications. Chapter 22, Advanced Practices and Future Evolution, summarizes other advanced practices as well as expectations for the future evolution of massively parallel processors.

We hope that you have enjoyed the book and agree with us that you are now well equipped for programming massively parallel computing systems.

23.2 Future outlook

Since the introduction of the first CUDA-enabled GPU, the G80, in 2007, the capability of GPUs as massively computing devices has improved at an amazing $452 \times$ in computing throughput and $18 \times$ in memory bandwidth, as shown in Fig. 23.1. These advancements have stimulated tremendous progress in HPC, AI, and data analytics for both science and engineering, with significant impact on many vertical areas such as finance, manufacturing, and medicine. For example, as we have seen in Chapter 16, Deep Learning, GPUs have ignited a revolution in deep learning from very large datasets, with applications in image recognition, speech recognition, and video analytics.

	G80 (2007)	A100 (2020)	A100/G80 Ratio
Compute Throughput	0.345 F32 TFLOPS	156 TFLOPS	452x
Memory Bandwidth	86.4 GB/s	1,555 GB/s	18x
Memory Capacity	1.5GB	40 GB	27x
PCIe Bandwidth	8 GB/s (Gen2 x16, each way)	32 GB/s (Gen4 x16, each way)	4x

FIGURE 23.1

From G80 to A100, a 13-year comparison.

Since the first edition of this book in 2010, the field of parallel computing has also advanced at an amazing pace. The spectrum of problems that can be solved with scalable algorithms has broadened significantly. While the use of GPUs was initially concentrated on regular, dense matrix computation and Monte Carlo methods, their use has quickly expanded into sparse methods, graph computation, and adaptive refinement methods. In many areas, there has also been fast advancement in algorithms. Some of the algorithms presented in the parallel pattern, advanced patterns, and applications chapters represent significant recent advancements.

It is only natural for some of us to wonder if we have reached the end of the fast advancement in parallel computing. From all indications, the answer is definitely no. We are only at the beginning of the parallel computing revolution. The amazing advancement in computing in the past three decades has triggered a paradigm shift in industry. The major innovations used to be driven by physical instruments assisted by computing devices. They are now driven by computing assisted by physical instruments.

For example, two decades ago, GPS revolutionized the way we drive. GPS is primarily based on satellite signal sensing assisted by computing methods that determine the shortest path between two locations. More recently, peer reporting and computing through the map apps in the phones and data services in the cloud have further enabled drivers to change their routes based on the traffic condition. Today, the most exciting revolution in the automobile industry is self-driving cars, which is primarily based on machine-learning computing methods assisted by physical sensors.

For another example, MRI and PET revolutionized medicine in the past two decades. These technologies are primarily based on electromagnetic and light sensors assisted by computational image reconstruction methods. They allowed doctors to see the pathology inside human bodies without surgery. Today, the field of medicine is going through the revolution of individualized medicine, which is primarily driven by computational genomics methods assisted by sequencing sensors.

For yet another example, the semiconductor industry used to rely on advancement in physical light sources assisted by computing methods that enforce design rules in their push to reduce the device feature size in the manufacturing process. Today, the advancement in physical light sources has practically stopped. The advancement in feature size reduction is primarily driven by lithography masks that are computationally designed to orchestrate the interference of light waves to result in extremely precise etching patterns on the chips.

The same kind of paradigm shift has been taking place in many other areas. Computing has become the primary driving force for virtually all exciting innovations in our society. This has created an insatiable demand for faster computing systems. As we discussed in Chapter 1, Introduction, parallel computing is the only viable approach to the growth of computing performance. This powerful demand will continue to motivate the industry to innovate and create more powerful parallel computing devices. One of the highest potential areas for improvement is the level of parallelism in accessing storage data, which has been done with a very low level of parallelism in the past. Radical improvements in accessing massive storage data will likely inspire a whole generation of applications that we currently cannot even imagine.

In conclusion, we are at the dawn of a golden age of computing. The industry will continue to recruit and reward highly skilled parallel programmers. Your work will make a real difference in the field of your choice.

Enjoy the ride!

Numerical considerations

In the early days of computing, floating-point arithmetic capability was found only in mainframes and supercomputers. Although many microprocessors that were designed in the 1980s started to have floating-point coprocessors, their floating-point arithmetic speed was extremely slow, about three orders of magnitude slower than that of mainframes and supercomputers. With advances in microprocessor technology, many microprocessors that were designed in the 1990s, such as Intel Pentium III and AMD Athlon, started to have high-performance floating-point capabilities that rivaled those of supercomputers. High-speed floating-point arithmetic is a standard feature of microprocessors and GPUs today. Floating-point representation allows for a larger dynamic range of representable data values and more precise representation of tiny data values. These desirable properties make floating-point arithmetic the preferred data representative for modeling physical and artificial phenomena, such as combustion, aerodynamics, light illumination, and financial risks. Large-scale evaluation of these models has been driving the need for parallel computing. As a result, it is important for application programmers to understand the nature of floating-point arithmetic in developing their parallel applications. In particular, we will focus on the accuracy of floating-point arithmetic operations, the precision of floating-point number representation, the stability of numerical algorithms, and how they should be taken into consideration in parallel programming.

A.1 Floating-point data representation

The IEEE-754 Floating-Point Standard is an effort to ensure that computer manufacturers conform to a common representation and arithmetic behavior for floating-point data (IEEE Microprocessor Standards Committee, 2008). Most, if not all, computer manufacturers in the world have accepted this standard. In particular, virtually all microprocessors that are designed in the future will either fully conform to or almost fully conform to the IEEE-754 Floating-Point Standard and its more recent IEEE-754 2008 revision. Therefore it is important for application developers to understand the concepts and practical considerations of this standard.

A floating-point number system starts with the representation of a numerical value as bit patterns. In the IEEE Floating-Point Standard, a numerical value is represented in three groups of bits: sign (S), exponent (E), and mantissa (M). With some exceptions that will be detailed later in this appendix, each (S, E, M) pattern uniquely identifies a numerical value according to the following formula:

$$\text{value} = (-1)^S * 1.M * \left\{2^{E-\text{bias}}\right\} \tag{A.1}$$

The interpretation of S is simple: $S = 0$ means a positive number, and $S = 1$ a negative number. Mathematically, any number, including -1, when raised to the power of 0, results in 1. Thus the value is positive. On the other hand, when -1 is raised to the power of 1, it is -1 itself. With a multiplication by -1, the value becomes negative. However, the interpretation of M and E bits is much more complex. We will use the following example to help explain the interpretation of M and E bits.

Assume for the sake of simplicity that each floating-point number consists of a 1-bit sign, a 3-bit exponent, and a 2-bit mantissa. We will use this hypothetical 6-bit format to illustrate the challenges that are involved in encoding E and M. As we discuss numerical values, we will sometimes need to express a number either in decimal place value or in binary place value. Numbers that are expressed in decimal place value will have a subscript $_D$, and those that are expressed in binary place value will have a subscript $_B$. For example, 0.5_D ($5 * 10^{-1}$, since the place to the right of the decimal point carries a weight of 10^{-1}) is the same as 0.1_B ($1 * 2^{-1}$, since the place to the right of the decimal point carries a weight of 2^{-1}).

A.1.1 Normalized representation of M

Eq. (A.1) requires that all values be derived by treating the mantissa value as 1.M, which makes the mantissa bit pattern for each floating-point number unique. For example, in this interpretation of the M bits, the only mantissa bit pattern that is allowed for 0.5_D is the one in which all bits that represent M are 0s:

$$0.5_D = 1.0_B * 2^{-1}$$

Other potential candidates would be $0.1_B * 2^0$ and $10.0_B * 2^{-2}$, but neither fits the form of 1.M. The numbers that satisfy this restriction will be referred to as normalized numbers. Because all mantissa values that satisfy the restriction are of the form 1.XX, we can omit the "1." part from the representation. Therefore the mantissa value of 0.5 in a 2-bit mantissa representation is 00, which is derived by omitting "1." from 1.00. This makes a 2-bit mantissa effectively a 3-bit mantissa. In general, in IEEE format, an m-bit mantissa is effectively an (m + 1)-bit mantissa.

A.1.2 Excess encoding of E

The number of bits that are used to represent E determines the range of numbers that can be represented. Large positive E values result in very large floating-point absolute values. For example, if the value of E is 64, the floating-point number that is being represented is between 2^{64} ($> 10^{18}$) and 2^{65}. You would be extremely happy if this was the balance of your savings account! Large negative E values result in very small floating-point values. For example, if the E value is -64, the number that is being represented is between 2^{-64} ($< 10^{-18}$) and 2^{-63}. This is a very tiny fractional number. The E field allows a floating-point number format to represent a wider range of numbers than integer number formats can. We will come back to this point when we look at the representable numbers of a format.

The IEEE standard adopts an excess or biased encoding convention for E. If E bits are used to represent the exponent E, ($2^{e-1} - 1$) is added to the two's complement representation for the exponent to form its excess representation. A two's complement representation is a system in which the negative value of a number can be derived by first complementing every bit of the value and adding 1 to the result. In our 3-bit exponent representation, there are three bits in the exponent (e = 3). Therefore the value $2^{3-1} - 1 = 011$ will be added to the two's complement representation of the exponent value.

The advantage of excess representation is that an unsigned comparator can be used to compare signed numbers. As shown in Fig. A.1, in our 3-bit exponent representation, the excess-3 bit patterns increase monotonically from -3 to 3 when they are viewed as unsigned numbers. We will refer to each of these bit patterns as the code for the corresponding value. For example, the code for -3 is 000 and that for 3 is 110. Thus if one uses an unsigned number comparator to compare excess-3 code for any number from -3 to 3, the comparator gives the correct comparison result in terms of which number is larger, smaller, and so on. For another example, if one compares excess-3 codes 001 and 100 with an unsigned comparator, 001 is smaller than 100. This is the right conclusion, since the values that they represent, -2 and 1, have exactly the same relation. This is a desirable property for hardware implementation, since unsigned comparators are smaller and faster than signed comparators.

Fig. A.1 also shows that the pattern of all 1's in the excess representation is a reserved pattern. Note that a 0 value and an equal number of positive and

2's complement	Decimal value	Excess-3
101	-3	000
110	-2	001
111	-1	010
000	0	011
001	1	100
010	2	101
011	3	110
100	Reserved pattern	111

FIGURE A.1

Excess-3 encoding, sorted by excess-3 ordering.

negative values result in an odd number of patterns. Having the pattern 111 as either an even number or an odd number would result in an unbalanced number of positive and negative numbers. The IEEE standard uses this special bit pattern in special ways that will be discussed later in this appendix.

Now we are ready to represent 0.5_D with our 6-bit format:

$$0.5_D = 0\ 01000, \text{where } S = 0,\ E = 010, \text{and } M = (1.)\ 00$$

That is, the 6-bit representation for 0.5_D is 001000.

In general, with a normalized mantissa and an excess-coded exponent, the value of a number with an n-bit exponent is

$$\text{value} = (-1)^S * 1.M * 2^{(E - (2^{(n-1)} - 1))} \tag{A.2}$$

A.2 Representable numbers

The representable numbers of a representation format are the numbers that can be exactly represented in the format. For example, if one uses a 3-bit unsigned integer format, the representable numbers are shown in Fig. A.2.

Neither -1 nor 9 can be represented in the format given above. We can draw a number line to identify all the representable numbers, as shown in Fig. A.3, in which all representable numbers of the 3-bit unsigned integer format are marked with stars.

000	0
001	1
010	2
011	3
100	4
101	5
110	6
111	7

FIGURE A.2

Representable numbers of a 3-bit unsigned integer format.

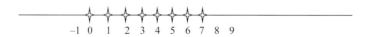

$$-1\quad 0\quad 1\quad 2\quad 3\quad 4\quad 5\quad 6\quad 7\quad 8\quad 9$$

FIGURE A.3

Representable numbers of a 3-bit unsigned integer format.

The representable numbers of a floating-point format can be visualized in a similar manner. In Fig. A.4 we show all the representable numbers of what we have so far and two variations. We use a 5-bit format to keep the size of the table manageable. The format consists of 1-bit S, 2-bit E (excess-1 coded), and 2-bit M (with "1." part omitted). The no-zero column gives the representable numbers of the format we discussed thus far. The reader is encouraged to generate at least part of the no-zero column using Eq. (A.2). Note that with this format, 0 is not one of the representable numbers.

A quick look at how these representable numbers populate the number line, as shown in Fig. A.5, provides further insights into these representable numbers. In Fig. A.5 we show only the positive representable numbers. The negative numbers are symmetric to their positive counterparts on the other side of 0.

We can make five observations. First, the exponent bits define the major intervals of representable numbers. In Fig. A.5 there are three major intervals on each side of 0 because there are two exponent bits. Basically, the major intervals are between powers of 2. With two bits of exponents and one reserved bit pattern (11), there are three powers of 2 ($2^{-1} = 0.5_D$, $2^0 = 1.0_D$, $2^1 = 2.0_D$), each of which starts an interval of representable numbers. Keep in mind that there are also three powers of 2 ($-2^{-1} = -0.5_D$, $-2^0 = -1.0_D$, $-2^1 = -2.0_D$) on the left of zero that are not shown in Fig. A.5.

The second observation is that the mantissa bits define the number of representable numbers in each interval. With two mantissa bits we have four

E	M	No-zero		Abrupt underflow		Denormalized	
		S=0	S=1	S=0	S=1	S=0	S=1
00	00	2^{-1}	$-(2^{-1})$	0	0	0	0
	01	$2^{-1}+1*2^{-3}$	$-(2^{-1}+1*2^{-3})$	0	0	$1*2^{-2}$	$-1*2^{-2}$
	10	$2^{-1}+2*2^{-3}$	$-(2^{-1}+2*2^{-3})$	0	0	$2*2^{-2}$	$-2*2^{-2}$
	11	$2^{-1}+3*2^{-3}$	$-(2^{-1}+3*2^{-3})$	0	0	$3*2^{-2}$	$-3*2^{-2}$
01	00	2^0	$-(2^0)$	2^0	$-(2^0)$	2^0	$-(2^0)$
	01	2^0+1*2^{-2}	$-(2^0+1*2^{-2})$	2^0+1*2^{-2}	$-(2^0+1*2^{-2})$	2^0+1*2^{-2}	$-(2^0+1*2^{-2})$
	10	2^0+2*2^{-2}	$-(2^0+2*2^{-2})$	2^0+2*2^{-2}	$-(2^0+2*2^{-2})$	2^0+2*2^{-2}	$-(2^0+2*2^{-2})$
	11	2^0+3*2^{-2}	$-(2^0+3*2^{-2})$	2^0+3*2^{-2}	$-(2^0+3*2^{-2})$	2^0+3*2^{-2}	$-(2^0+3*2^{-2})$
10	00	2^1	$-(2^1)$	2^1	$-(2^1)$	2^1	$-(2^1)$
	01	2^1+1*2^{-1}	$-(2^1+1*2^{-1})$	2^1+1*2^{-1}	$-(2^1+1*2^{-1})$	2^1+1*2^{-1}	$-(2^1+1*2^{-1})$
	10	2^1+2*2^{-1}	$-(2^1+2*2^{-1})$	2^1+2*2^{-1}	$-(2^1+2*2^{-1})$	2^1+2*2^{-1}	$-(2^1+2*2^{-1})$
	11	2^1+3*2^{-1}	$-(2^1+3*2^{-1})$	2^1+3*2^{-1}	$-(2^1+3*2^{-1})$	2^1+3*2^{-1}	$-(2^1+3*2^{-1})$
11		Reserved pattern					

FIGURE A.4

Representable numbers of no-zero, abrupt underflow, and denormalized formats.

FIGURE A.5

Representable numbers of the no-zero representation.

representable numbers in each interval. In general, with N mantissa bits, we have 2^N representable numbers in each interval. If a value to be represented falls within one of the intervals, it will be rounded to one of these representable numbers. Obviously, the larger the number of representable numbers in each interval, the more precisely we can represent a value in the region. Therefore the number of mantissa bits determines the *precision* of the representation.

The third observation is that 0 is not representable in this format. It is missing from the representable numbers in the no-zero columns of Fig. A.5. Because 0 is one of the most important numbers, not being able to represent 0 in a number representation system is a serious deficiency. We will address this deficiency soon.

The fourth observation is that the representable numbers become closer to each other toward the neighborhood of 0. Each interval is half the size of the previous interval as we move toward zero. In Fig. A.5 the rightmost interval is of width 2, the next interval is of width 1, and the next interval is of width 0.5. Although not shown in Fig. A.5, there are three intervals on the left of zero. They contain the representable negative numbers. The leftmost interval is of width 2, the next interval is of width 1, and the next interval is width 0.5. Since every interval has the same representable numbers, four in Fig. A.5, the representable numbers becomes closer to each other as we move toward zero. In other words, the representative numbers become closer as their absolute values become smaller. This is a desirable trend because as the absolute values of these numbers become smaller, it is more important to represent them more precisely. The distance between representable numbers determines the maximal rounding error for a value that falls into the interval. For example, if you have one billion dollars in your bank account, you might not even notice that there is a $1 rounding error in calculating your balance. However, if the total balance is $10, having a $1 rounding error would be much more noticeable!

The fifth observation is that, unfortunately, the trend of increasing density of representable numbers and thus the increasing precision of representing numbers in the intervals as we move toward 0 does not hold near 0. That is, there is a gap of representable numbers in the immediate vicinity of 0. This is because the range of normalized mantissa precludes 0. This is another serious deficiency. The representation introduces significantly larger ($4\times$) errors in representing numbers between 0 and 0.5 compared to the errors for the larger numbers between 0.5 and 1.0. In general, with m bits in the mantissa, this style of representation would introduce 2^m times more error in the interval closest to zero than in the next interval. For numerical methods that rely on accurate detection of convergence conditions based on very small data values, such deficiency can cause instability in execution time and inaccuracy of results. Furthermore, some algorithms generate small numbers and eventually use them as denominators. The errors in representing these small numbers can be greatly magnified in the division process and cause numerical instability in these algorithms.

One method that can accommodate 0 into a normalized floating-point number system is the *abrupt underflow* convention, which is illustrated in the second set of columns in Fig. A.4. Whenever E is 0, the number is interpreted as 0. In our 5-bit format, this method takes away eight representable numbers (four positive and four negative) in the vicinity of 0 (between -1.0 and $+1.0$) and makes them all 0. Because of its simplicity, some minicomputers in the 1980s used the abrupt underflow convention. Even to this day, some arithmetic units that need to operate at high speed still use the abrupt underflow convention. Although this method makes 0 a representable number, it creates an even larger gap between representable numbers in the vicinity of 0, as shown in Fig. A.6. It is obvious, when compared with Fig. A.5, that the gap of representable numbers has been enlarged significantly (by $2\times$) from 0.5 to 1.0. As we explained earlier, this is very problematic for many numerical algorithms whose correctness reply on accurate representation of small numbers near zero.

The actual method that was adopted by the IEEE standard is called denormalization. The method relaxes the normalization requirement for numbers very close to 0. As is shown in Fig. A.6, whenever $E = 0$, the mantissa is no longer assumed to be of the form 1.XX. Rather, it is assumed to be 0.XX. The value of the exponent is assumed to be the same as in the previous interval. For example, in Fig. A.4 the denormalized representation 00001 has exponent value 00 and mantissa value 01. The mantissa is assumed to be 0.01, and the exponent value is assumed to be the same as that of the previous interval: 0 rather than -1. That is, the value that 00001 represents is now $0.01 * 2^0 = 2^{-2}$. Fig. A.7 shows the representable numbers for the denormalized format. The representation now has uniformly spaced representable numbers in the close vicinity of 0. Intuitively, the denormalized convention takes the four numbers in the last interval of representable numbers of a no-zero representation and spreads them out to cover the gap area. This eliminates the undesirable gap in the previous two methods. Note that the distances between representable numbers in the last two intervals are actually identical. In general, if the n-bit exponent is 0, the value is

$$0.M * 2^{-2^{(n-1)}+2}$$

As we can see, the denormalization formula is quite complex. The hardware also needs to be able to detect whether a number falls into the denormalized

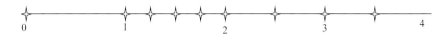

FIGURE A.6

Representable numbers of the abrupt underflow format.

FIGURE A.7

Representable numbers of a denormalization format.

interval and choose the appropriate representation for that number. The amount of hardware required to implement denormalization at high speed is quite significant. Implementations that use a moderate amount of hardware often introduce thousands of clock cycles of delay whenever a denormalized number needs to be generated or used. This was the reason why early generations of CUDA devices did not support denormalization. However, virtually all recent generations of CUDA devices do support denormalization, thanks to the increasing number of available transistors of more recent fabrication processes. More specifically, all CUDA devices of compute capability 1.3 and up support denormalized double-precision operands, and all devices of compute capability 2.0 and up support denormalized single-precision operands.

In summary, the precision of a floating-point representation is measured by the maximal error that we can introduce to a floating-point number by representing that number as one of the representable numbers. The smaller the error, the higher is the precision. The precision of a floating-point representation can be improved by adding more bits to the mantissa. Adding one bit to the representation of the mantissa improves the precision by reducing the maximal error by half. Thus a number system has higher precision when it uses more bits for the mantissa. This is reflected in double-precision versus single-precision numbers in the IEEE standard.

A.3 Special bit patterns and precision in IEEE format

We now turn to more specific details of the actual IEEE format. When all exponent bits are 1s, the number that is represented is an infinity value if the mantissa is 0. It is not a number (NaN) if the mantissa is not 0. All special bit patterns of the IEEE floating-point format are described in Fig. A.8.

All other numbers are normalized floating-point numbers. Single-precision numbers have 1-bit S, 8-bit E, and 23-bit M. Double-precision numbers have 1-bit S, 11-bit E, and 52-bit M. Since a double-precision number has 29 more bits for the mantissa, the largest error for representing a number is reduced to $1/2^{29}$ of that of the single-precision format! With the additional 3 bits of exponent, the double-precision format also extends the number of intervals of representable numbers. This extends the range of representable numbers to very large as well as very small values.

All representable numbers fall between $-\infty$ (negative infinity) and $+\infty$ (positive infinity). An ∞ can be created by overflow, for example, a large number divided by a very small number. Any representable number divided by $+\infty$ or $-\infty$ results in 0.

NaN is generated by operations whose input values do not make sense, such as $0/0$, $0*\infty$, ∞/∞, $\infty-\infty$. NaN is also used for data that has not been properly initialized in a program. There are two types of NaN in the IEEE

exponent	mantissa	meaning
11…1	≠0	NaN
11…1	=0	$(-1)^S * \infty$
00…0	≠0	denormalized
00…0	=0	0

FIGURE A.8

Special bit patterns in the IEEE standard format.

standard: signaling and quiet. Signaling NaNs should be represented with the most significant mantissa bit cleared, whereas quiet NaNs are represented with the most significant mantissa bit set.

Signaling NaNs cause an exception when used as input to arithmetic operations. For example, the operation (1.0 + signaling NaN) raises an exception signal to the operating system. Signaling NaNs are used in situations in which the programmer would like to make sure that the program execution is interrupted whenever any NaN values are used in floating-point computations. These situations usually mean that there is something wrong with the execution of the program. In mission critical applications the execution cannot continue until the validity of the execution can be verified by a separate means. For example, software engineers often mark all the uninitialized data as signaling NaN. This practice ensures the detection of using uninitialized data during program execution. The current generation of GPU hardware does not support signaling NaN, owing to the difficulty of supporting accurate signaling during massively parallel execution.

A quiet NaN generates another quiet NaN without causing an exception when it is used as input to an arithmetic operation. For example, the operation (1.0 + quiet NaN) generates a quiet NaN. Quiet NaNs are typically used in applications in which the user can review the output and decide whether the application should be rerun with a different input for more valid results. When the results are printed, quiet NaNs are printed as "NaN" so that the user can spot them in the output file easily.

A.4 Arithmetic accuracy and rounding

Now that we have a good understanding of the IEEE floating-point format, we are ready to discuss the concept of arithmetic accuracy. While the precision is determined by the number of mantissa bits that are used in a floating-point number format, the accuracy is determined by the operations that are performed on a floating-point number. The accuracy of a floating-point arithmetic operation is measured by the maximal error that is introduced by the operation. The smaller the error, the higher is the accuracy. The most common source of error in floating-point arithmetic is when the operation generates a result that cannot be exactly represented and thus requires rounding. Rounding occurs if the mantissa of the result value needs too many bits to be represented exactly. For example, a multiplication might generate a product value that consists of twice the number of bits as either of the input values. For another example, adding two floating-point numbers can be done by adding their mantissa values together if the two floating-point values have identical exponents. When two input operands to a floating-point addition have different exponents, the mantissa of the one with the smaller exponent is repeatedly divided by 2 or right-shifted (that is, all the mantissa bits are shifted to the right by one bit position) until the exponents are equal. As a result, the final result can have more bits than the format can accommodate.

Alignment shifting of operands can be illustrated with a simple example based on the 5-bit representation in Fig. A.4. Assume that we need to add $1.00_B * 2^{-2}$(0, 00, 01) to $1.00 * 2^1{}_D$ (0, 10, 00), that is, we need to perform the operation $1.00_B * 2^1 + 1.00_B * 2^{-2}$. Owing to the difference in exponent values, the mantissa value of the second number needs to be right-shifted by 3 bit positions before it is added to the first mantissa value. That is, the addition becomes $1.00_B * 2^1 + 0.001_B * 2^1$. The addition can now be performed by adding the mantissa values together. The ideal result would be $1.001_B * 2^1$. However, we can see that this ideal result is not a representable number in a 5-bit representation. It would have required three bits of mantissa, and there are only two mantissa bits in the format. Therefore the best one can do is to generate one of the closest representable numbers, which is either $1.01_B * 2^1$ or $1.00_B * 2^1$. By doing so, we introduce an error, $0.001_B * 2^1$, which is half the place value of the least significant place. We refer to this as 0.5_D ULP (units in the last place). If the hardware is designed to perform arithmetic and rounding operations perfectly, the most error that one should introduce should be no more than 0.5_D ULP. To the best of our knowledge, this is the accuracy that is achieved by addition and subtraction operations in all CUDA devices today.

In practice, some of the more complex arithmetic hardware units, such as division and transcendental functions, are typically implemented with polynomial approximation algorithms. If the hardware does not use a sufficient number of terms in the approximation, the result may have an error that is larger than 0.5_D ULP. For example, if the ideal result of an inversion operation is $1.00_B * 2^1$ but the hardware generates a $1.10_B * 2^1$, owing to the use of an approximation algorithm, the error is 2_D ULP, since the error $(1.10_B - 1.00_B = 0.10_B)$ is two times bigger than the units in the last place (0.01_B). In practice, the hardware inversion operations in some early devices introduce an error that is twice the place value of the least place of the mantissa, or 2 ULP. Thanks to the more abundant transistors in more recent generations of CUDA devices, their hardware arithmetic operations are much more accurate.

A.5 Algorithm considerations

Numerical algorithms often need to sum up a large number of values. For example, the dot product in matrix multiplication needs to sum up pairwise products of input matrix elements. Ideally, the order of summing these values should not affect the final total, since addition is an associative operation. However, with finite precision the order of summing these values can affect the accuracy of the final result. For example, suppose we need to perform a sum reduction on four numbers in our 5-bit representation: $1.00_B * 2^0 + 1.00_B * 2^0 + 1.00_B * 2^{-2} + 1.00_B * 2^{-2}$. If we add up the numbers in strict sequential order, we have the following sequence of operations:

$$1.00_B * 2^0 + 1.00_B * 2^0 + 1.00_B * 2^{-2} + 1.00_B * 2^{-2}$$
$$= 1.00_B * 2^1 + 1.00_B * 2^{-2} + 1.00_B * 2^{-2}$$
$$= 1.00_B * 2^1 + 1.00_B * 2^{-2} = 1.00_B * 2^1$$

Note that in the second and third steps, the smaller operand simply disappears because it is too small in comparison to the larger operand.

Now let's consider a parallel algorithm in which the first two values are added and the second two operands are added in parallel. The algorithm then adds up the pairwise sum:

$$\left(1.00_B * 2^0 + 1.00_B * 2^0\right) + \left(1.00_B * 2^{-2} + 1.00_B * 2^{-2}\right) = 1.00_B * 2^1 + 1.00_B * 2^{-1} = 1.01_B * 2^1$$

The reader should recognize that this algorithm was is the reduction tree of Chapter 10, Reduction and Minimizing Divergence, and it assumes the associativity of the add operation. Note that the results are different from the sequential result. This is because the sum of the third and fourth values is large enough that it now affects the addition result. This discrepancy between sequential algorithms and parallel algorithms often surprises application developers who are not familiar with floating-point precision and accuracy considerations. Although we showed a scenario in which a parallel algorithm produced a more accurate result than a sequential algorithm, the reader should be able to come up with a slightly different scenario in which the parallel algorithm produces a less accurate result than a sequential algorithm would. That is, the associativity of the add operation is not strictly true for floating-point numbers. Experienced application developers either make sure that the variation in the final result can be tolerated or ensure that the data is sorted or grouped in such a way that the parallel algorithm results in the most accurate results.

A common technique to maximize floating-point arithmetic accuracy is to presort data before a reduction computation. In our sum reduction example, if we presort the data according to ascending numerical order, we will have the following:

$$1.00_B * 2^{-2} + 1.00_B * 2^{-2} + 1.00_B * 2^0 + 1.00_B * 2^0$$

When we divide up the numbers into groups in a parallel algorithm, say, the first pair in one group and the second pair in another group, numbers with numerical values that are close to each other are in the same group. Obviously, the sign of the numbers needs to be taken into account during the presorting process. Therefore when we perform addition in these groups, we will likely have accurate results. Furthermore, some parallel algorithms use each thread to sequentially reduce values within each group. Having the numbers sorted in ascending order allows a sequential addition to get higher accuracy. This is a reason why sorting is frequently used in massively parallel numerical algorithms. Interested readers should study more advanced techniques, such as compensated summation algorithm, also known as the Kahan summation algorithm, for getting an even more robust approach to accurate summation of floating-point values (Kahan, 1965).

A.6 Linear solvers and numerical stability

While the order of operations may cause variation in the numerical outcome of reduction operations, it may have even more serious implications for some types of computation, such as solvers for linear systems of equations. In these solvers, different numerical values of input may require different ordering of operations in order to find a solution. If an algorithm fails to follow a desired order of operations for an input, it may fail to find a solution even though the solution exists. Algorithms that can always find an appropriate operation order and thus finding a solution to the problem as long as it exists for any given input values are called *numerically stable*. Algorithms that fall short are referred to as *numerically unstable*.

In some cases, numerical stability considerations can make it more difficult to find efficient parallel algorithms for a computational problem. We can illustrate this phenomenon with a solver that is based on Gaussian elimination. Consider the following system of linear equations:

$$3X + 5Y + 2Z = 19 \tag{A.3}$$

$$2X + 3Y + Z = 11 \tag{A.4}$$

$$X + 2Y + 2Z = 11 \tag{A.5}$$

As long as the three planes represented by these equations have an intersection point, we can use Gaussian elimination to derive the solution that gives the coordinate of the intersection point. We show the process of applying Gaussian elimination to this system in Fig. A.9, in which variables are systematically eliminated from lower positioned equations.

In the first step, all equations are divided by their coefficient for the X variable: 3 for Eq. (A.3), 2 for Eq. (A.4), and 1 for Eq. (A.5). This makes the coefficients for X in all equations the same. In step 2, Eq. (A.3) is subtracted from Eqs. (A.4) and (A.5). These subtractions eliminate variable X from Eqs. (A.4) and (A.5), as shown in Fig. A.9.

We can now treat Eqs. (A.4) and (A.5) as a smaller system of equations with one fewer variable than the original equation. Since they do not have variable X, they can be solved independently from Eq. (A.3). We can make more progress by eliminating variable Y from Eq. (A.5). This is done in step 3 by dividing Eqs. (A.4) and (A.5) by the coefficients for their Y variables: $-1/6$ for Eq. (A.4)

$$
\begin{array}{llll}
3X & + 5Y & + 2Z & = 19 \\
2X & + 3Y & + Z & = 11 \\
X & + 2Y & + 2Z & = 11
\end{array}
\quad\Longrightarrow\quad
\begin{array}{llll}
X & + 5/3Y & + 2/3Z & = 19/3 \\
X & + 3/2Y & + 1/2Z & = 11/2 \\
X & + 2Y & + 2Z & = 11
\end{array}
$$

Original   Step 1: divide equation 1 by 3, equation 2 by 2

$$
\Longrightarrow\quad
\begin{array}{llll}
X & + 5/3Y & +2/3Z & = 19/3 \\
 & -1/6Y & -1/6Z & = -5/6 \\
 & 1/3Y & + 4/3Z & = 14/3
\end{array}
\quad\Longrightarrow\quad
\begin{array}{llll}
X & + 5/3Y & + 2/3Z & = 19/3 \\
 & Y & + Z & = 5 \\
 & Y & + 4Z & = 14
\end{array}
$$

Step 2: subtract equation 1 from equation 2 and equation 3   Step 3: divide equation 2 by –1/6 and equation 3 by 1/3

$$
\Longrightarrow\quad
\begin{array}{llll}
X & + 5/3Y & + 2/3Z & = 19/3 \\
 & Y & + Z & = 5 \\
 & & + 3Z & = 9
\end{array}
\quad\Longrightarrow\quad
\begin{array}{llll}
X & + 5/3Y & + 2/3Z & = 19/3 \\
 & Y & + Z & = 5 \\
 & & Z & = 3
\end{array}
$$

Step 4: subtract equation 2 from equation 3   Step 5: divide equation 3 by 3 Solution for Z!

$$
\Longrightarrow\quad
\begin{array}{llll}
X & + 5/3Y & + 2/3Z & = 19/3 \\
 & Y & & = 2 \\
 & & Z & = 3
\end{array}
\quad\Longrightarrow\quad
\begin{array}{lll}
X & & = 1 \\
 & Y & = 2 \\
 & Z & = 3
\end{array}
$$

Step 6: substitute Z solution into equation 2. Solution for Y!   Step 7: substitute Y and Z into equation 1. Solution for X!

FIGURE A.9

Gaussian elimination and backward substitution for solving systems of linear equations.

and 1/3 for Eq. (A.5). This makes the coefficients for Y in both Eqs. (A.4) and (A.5) the same. In step 4, Eq. (A.4) is subtracted from Eq. (A.5), which eliminates variable Y from Eq. (A.5).

For systems with larger number of equations the process would be repeated more. However, since we have only three variables in this example, the third equation has only the Z variable. We simply need to divide Eq. (A.5) by the coefficient for variable Z. This conveniently gives us the solution Z = 3.

With the solution for the Z variable in hand, we can substitute the Z value into Eq. (A.4) to get the solution Y = 2. We can then substitute both Z = 3 and Y = 2 into Eq. (A.3) to get the solution X = 1. We now have the complete solution for the original system. It should be obvious why step 6 and step 7 form the second phase of the method called backward substitution. We go backwards from the last equation to the first equation to get solutions for more and more variables.

In general, the equations are stored in matrix forms in computers. Since all calculations involve only the coefficients and the right-hand-side values, we can just store these coefficients and right-hand-side values in a matrix. Fig. A.10 shows the matrix view of the Gaussian elimination and backward substitution process. Each row of the matrix corresponds to an original equation. Operations on equations become operations on matrix rows.

After Gaussian elimination the matrix becomes a triangular matrix. This is a very popular type of matrix for various physics and mathematics reasons. We see that the end goal is to make the coefficient part of the matrix into a diagonal form, in which each row has only a value 1 on the diagonal line. This is called an identity matrix because the result of multiplying any matrix multiplied by an identity matrix is itself. This is also the reason why performing Gaussian elimination on a matrix is equivalent to multiplying the matrix by its inverse matrix.

In general, it is straightforward to design a parallel algorithm for the Gaussian elimination procedure that we illustrated in Fig. A.10. For example, we can write

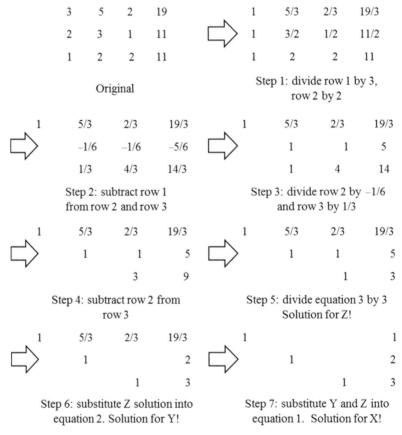

FIGURE A.10

Gaussian elimination and backward substitution in matrix view.

a CUDA kernel and designate each thread to perform all calculations to be done on a row of the matrix. For systems that can fit into shared memory, we can use a thread block to perform Gaussian elimination. All threads iterate through the steps. After each division step, all threads participate in barrier synchronization. They all then perform a subtraction step, after which one thread will stop its participation, since its designated row has no more work to do until the backward substitution phase. After the subtraction step, all threads need to perform barrier synchronization again to ensure that the next step will be done with the updated information. When we have systems of equations with many variables, we can expect a reasonable amount of speedup from the parallel execution.

Unfortunately, the simple Gaussian elimination algorithm that we have been using can suffer from numerical instability. This can be illustrated with the following example:

$$5Y + 2Z = 16 \tag{A.6}$$

$$2X + 3Y + Z = 11 \tag{A.7}$$

$$X + 2Y + 2Z = 11 \tag{A.8}$$

We will encounter a problem when we perform step 1 of the algorithm. The coefficient for the X variable in Eq. (A.6) is zero. We will not be able to divide Eq. (A.6) by the coefficient for variable X and eliminate the X variable from Eqs. (A.7) and (A.8) by subtracting Eq. (A.6) from Eqs. (A.7) and (A.8). The reader should verify that this system of equation is solvable and has the same solution: $X = 1$, $Y = 2$, and $Z = 3$. Therefore the algorithm is numerically unstable. It can fail to generate a solution for certain input values even though the solution exists.

This is a well-known problem with Gaussian elimination algorithms and can be addressed with a method that is commonly referred to as *pivoting*. The idea is to find one of the remaining equations whose coefficient for the lead variable is not zero. By swapping the current top equation with the identified equation, the algorithm can successfully eliminate the lead variable from the rest of the equations. If we apply pivoting to the three equations, we end up with the following set of equations:

$$2X + 3Y + Z = 11 \tag{A.9}$$

$$5Y + 2Z = 16 \tag{A.10}$$

$$X + 2Y + 2Z = 11 \tag{A.11}$$

Note that the coefficient for X in Eq. (A.9) is no longer zero. We can proceed with Gaussian elimination, as illustrated in Fig. A.11.

The reader should follow the steps in Fig. A.11. The most important additional insight is that some equations might not have the variable that the algorithm is eliminating at the current step (see row 2 of step 1 in Fig. A.11). The designated thread does not need to do the division on the equation.

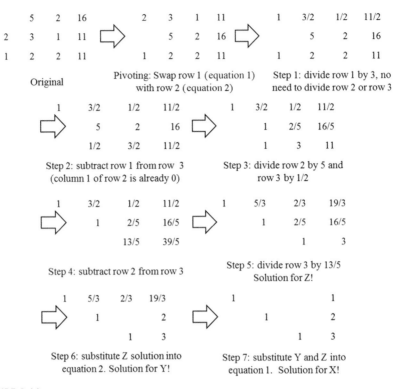

FIGURE A.11

Gaussian elimination with pivoting.

In general, the pivoting step should choose the equation with the largest absolute coefficient value among all the lead variables and swap its equation (row) with the current top equation as well as swap the variable (column) with the current variable. While pivoting is conceptually simple, it can incur significant implementation complexity and performance overhead. In the case of our simple CUDA kernel implementation, recall that each thread is assigned a row. Pivoting requires an inspection and perhaps swapping of coefficient data spread across these threads. This is not a big problem if all coefficients are in the shared memory. We can run a parallel max reduction using threads in the block as long as we control the level of control flow divergence within warps.

However, if the system of linear equations is being solved by multiple thread blocks or even multiple nodes of a compute cluster, the idea of inspecting data that is spread across multiple thread blocks or multiple compute cluster nodes can be an extremely expensive proposition. This is the main motivation for *communication-avoiding algorithms* that avoid a global inspection of data such as pivoting (Ballard et al., 2011). In general, there are two approaches to this problem. Partial pivoting restricts the candidates of the swap operation to come from a localized set of equations so that the cost of global inspection is limited. However, this can slightly reduce the numerical accuracy of the solution. Researchers have also demonstrated that randomization tends to maintain a high level of numerical accuracy for the solution.

A.7 Summary

In this appendix we introduced the concepts of floating-point format and representable numbers, which are foundational to the understanding of precision. On the basis of these concepts, we explained the denormalized numbers and why they are important in many numerical applications. In early CUDA devices, denormalized numbers were not supported. However, more recent hardware generations support denormalized numbers. We also explained the concept of arithmetic accuracy of floating-point operations. It is important for CUDA programmers to understand the potential lower accuracy of fast arithmetic operations implemented in the special function units. More important, the reader should now have a good understanding of why parallel algorithms can often affect the accuracy of calculation results and how sorting and other techniques can be used to improve the accuracy of computation.

Exercises

1. Draw the equivalent of Fig. A.5 for a 6-bit format (1-bit sign, 3-bit mantissa, 2-bit exponent). Use your result to explain what each additional mantissa bit does to the set of representable numbers on the number line.
2. Draw the equivalent of Fig. A.5 for another 6-bit format (1-bit sign, 2-bit mantissa, 3-bit exponent). Use your result to explain what each additional exponent bit does to the set of representable numbers on the number line.
3. Assume that in a new processor design, owing to technical difficulty, the floating-point arithmetic unit that performs addition can only do "round to zero" (rounding by truncating the value toward 0). The hardware maintains a sufficient number of bits that the only error that is introduced is due to rounding. What is the maximal ULP error value for add operations on this machine?
4. A graduate student wrote a CUDA kernel to reduce a large floating-point array to the sum of all its elements. The array will always be sorted from the smallest values to the largest values. To avoid branch divergence, the student decided to implement the algorithm of Fig. A.4. Explain why this can reduce the accuracy of the results.
5. Assume that in an arithmetic unit design, the hardware implements an iterative approximation algorithm that generates two additional accurate

mantissa bits of the result for the sin() function in each clock cycle. The architect decided to allow the arithmetic function to iterate nine clock cycles. Assume that the hardware fills in all remaining mantissa bits as 0's. What would be the maximal ULP error of the hardware implementation of the sin() function in this design for IEEE single-precision numbers? Assume that the omitted "1." mantissa bit must also be generated by the arithmetic unit.

References

IEEE Microprocessor Standards Committee, 2008. Draft Standard for Floating-Point Arithmetic P754, Most recent revision January 2008.

Kahan, W., 1965. Further remarks on reducing truncation errors. Commun. ACM 8 (1), 40. Available from: https://doi.org/10.1145/363707.363723.

Ballard, G., Demmel, J., Holtz, O., Schwartz, O., 2011. Minimizing communication in numerical linear algebra. SIAM J. Matrix Anal. Appl. 32 (3), 866−901.

Index

A

Abrupt underflow convention, 524−525
Abstraction, 13
Accelerator, 7
  computing devices, 7
Accessibility, 313
Acquisition phase, MRI, 391−392
Activation functions, 357
Adjacency matrix, 332
  representation, 333*f*
  sparse representation, 334
Adjacent synchronization, 257−258
Algorithm, 475
  considerations, 528−530
  selection, 436−439
  transformations, 510
Algorithmic complexity, 437
Allocated arrays, 155−156
AMD, 1, 14
AMD Athlon, 519
Amdahl's law, 9−10, 435−436
Anatomical constraints, 395
ANSI C code, 42−43
ANSI C programming language, 27
ANSI C standard, 52−53
Apodization filtering function, 392
Application programming interface (API), 7
  functions, 31
    CUDA, 32*f*, 33*f*
Application software, 1−3, 5−6
Arithmetic accuracy and rounding, 527−528
Arithmetic and logic unit (ALU), 99
Arithmetic hardware units, 528
Arithmetic instructions, 99
Arithmetic intensity, 94
Arithmetic units, 4
Arithmetic-to-global memory ratio, 167
Array data layout, 445
Array of structures, 408−409
Associative operator, 214
Asynchronous
  copies, 467
  memory allocations, 471
Atomic operations, 191, 194−198, 347, 419−420
  intrinsic functions, 197
  latency and throughput of, 198−200, 199*f*
  race condition
    scenarios, 196*f*

atomicAdd function, 197
atomicCAS intrinsic function, 348
Audio digital signal processing, 152
Automated speech recognition, 366
Automatic array variables, 101−102
Automatic speech recognition, 356

B

Backpropagation, 362, 371−372
Backtracking process, 365
Backward convolution, 372−373
Backward substitution, 531
Bank conflict, 135
Banks, 134−135
Barrier synchronization, 71−73, 226−227,
    230−231, 299, 470
  __syncthreads() statement, 73
  example execution of, 72*f*
Barrier__syncthreads (), 110
Basic Linear Algebra Subprograms
    (BLAS), 62
Batcher's algorithms, 308
Batcher's bitonic sort, 308
Bezier curves, 481−484
  calculation, 481−484
  linear, 481
  quadratic, 481
"Big data,", 235−236
Big O notation, 295
Binary search, 270−271
Binary trees, 295
Binning process, 430, 438
Biomolecular systems, 415−416
1-bit radix, 295
Block's segment, 229−230
BlockDim variable, 38−40, 49−52
BlockDim. x variable, 39−40, 49
BlockIdx variable, 38−40, 47−49, 51−52
BlockIdx. x variable, 39−40, 49
Blocks, 76
Bottlenecks, 123−124
Bottom-up strategy, 309
  implementation, 340−341
Bounce buffers, 463
Boundary checks, 112−115
  loading input matrix elements, 112*f*, 113*f*
  tiled matrix multiplication kernel with, 114*f*
Boundary condition problems, 178

537

Brain, sodium map of, 393–394, 393*f*

Breadth-first search (BFS), 335–338, 336*f*
  maze routing in integrated circuits, 337*f*

Brent-Kung adder design, 246

Brent-Kung algorithm, 246–251, 437

Built-in type cudaDeviceProp, 89

Built-in variable, 36–38, 43–44

C

C language
  2D array, 52–53
  ANSI C code, 42–43
  ANSI C programming language, 27
  ANSI C standard, 52–53
  convention, 152
  CUDA, 23
  CUDA C extending, 38–39
  malloc() function, 458
  multidimensional array, 53
  pointers in, 30
  runtime library, 31–32
  scoping rules, 160–161
  traditional C compiler, 42–43
  traditional C program, 27–30

C++ AMP, 511

C++ templates, 511

Cache
  coherence mechanism, 504
  constant, 159–163, 404
  hierarchy of modern processors, 162*f*
  L1 cache, 161–162
  L2 cache, 161–162
  large last-level on-chip caches, 4
  tiled convolution using, 168–170

Caching, 159–163
  configurable, 509
  for halo cells, 168, 169*f*
  hierarchy of modern processors, 162*f*
  in modern GPUs, 17

Calling kernel functions, 40–42

Carpooling, 132

Cartesian grid, 394

Cartesian scan data, 392–393

Cartesian scan trajectory, 392

Cellular automata simulation, 509

Central processing unit (CPU), 1–2, 27, 175
  algorithms, 510
  CPU/GPU interaction mechanism, 505
  design philosophy of, 4
  serial code, 27–28

Chain rule, 363–364

Child grids, 480
  launches, 481

Circular buffer merge kernel, 282–287. *See also*
    Tiled merge kernel
  circular buffer scheme for managing shared
      memory tiles, 282*f*
  co_rank_circular function that operates on
      circular buffers, 287*f*
  merge_sequential_circular function
      implementation, 288*f*
  simplified model for co-rank values using
      circular buffer, 285*f*

Co-rank function, 266–268
  execution, 269*f*
  function based on binary search, 270*f*
  implementation, 268–273
  operation example, 271*f*, 272*f*, 273*f*

Coalesce, 125–126. *See also* Memory coalescing
  coalesce accesses to matrix B, 130*f*
  coalesced access pattern, 127*f*
  uncoalesced access pattern, 129*f*

Coalescing, 275–282. *See also* Memory
    coalescing

Coarsening factor, 139–141

Coarsening loop, 139–141

colIdx array, 314

Collective communication function, 466–467, 470

ColorToGrayscaleConversion function, 58

Column-major layout, 54–55, 128

Communication
  avoiding algorithms, 534–535
  connections, 454–455
  system, 452–453

Communicators, 454

Commutative operator, 214

Compaction, 311

Compare-and-swap, 348

Comparison-based parallel sorts, 308–309

Comparison-based sorting algorithms,
    294–295

Compensated summation algorithm, 529–530

Compile-time constant, 116

Complement representation system, 521

Compressed sparse column (CSC), 333

Compressed sparse row (CSR), 333
  grouping row nonzeros with CSR format,
      317–320
    example of, 317*f*
    example of parallelizing SpMV with, 318*f*
    parallel SpMV/CSR kernel, 318*f*
  parallel SpMV using, 329
  storage format, 317, 333, 334*f*

Computational intensity, 94

Computational methods, 391

"Computational microscope,", 415–416

Computational patterns, 480–481

Computational thinking, 444–446, 515
  algorithm selection, 436–439
  goals of parallel computing, 433–436
  problem decomposition, 440–444
  skills needed for parallel programmer, 444–445
  techniques, 14, 433
Compute architecture, 69–70
  architecture of modern GPU, 70
  block scheduling, 70–71
    thread block assignment to SMs, 71*f*
  control divergence, 79–82
  CUDA-capable GPU, 70*f*
  querying device properties, 87–89
  resource partitioning and occupancy, 85–87
  synchronization and transparent scalability,
    71–74
  warp scheduling and latency tolerance, 83–85
  warps and SIMD hardware, 74–79
Compute capability, 88
Compute process, 455, 458, 460
Compute process code, 458, 460*f*, 461, 462*f*, 465*f*,
  467, 468*f*, 469*f*
Compute to global memory access ratio, 94
Compute Unified Device Architecture (CUDA)/
  CUDA C, 23, 31–32, 38–39, 47–48,
  52–53, 73, 499–500
  __syncthreads() statement, 73
  compilers, 511
  cores, 70
  debugger, 507
  device, 124–125, 416, 435, 525–526
  execution of CUDA program, 27*f*
  GPUs, 75
  grids and blocks, 66–67
  kernel, 37–38, 400
    execution control, 505–508
    function, 93
    performance, 124
  keyword__global__, 38–39
  keywords for function declaration, 39*f*
  model of host/device interaction, 500–505
    unified memory, 503–505
    virtual address space control, 505
    zero-copy memory and unified virtual address
      space, 501–502
  program, 42–43, 257, 481–482
  program structure, 27–28
  programmers, 69–70
  programming environment, 510–513
    profiling with critical path analysis,
      511–513
    unified device memory space, 510–511
  Programming Guide, 89
  programming model, 463, 475

registers, 97, 115
  runtime system launches, 70
  shared memory, 161
  streams, 471, 499–500
  system software, 504
  threads, 28
  throughput computation, 508–510
Computer architecture, 445
Computer vision, 356
Computer-aided design (CAD), 337, 505
  circuit models, 342
Computer-generated graphics, 1
Computing devices, 7
Configurable caching, 509
Conjugate gradient algorithm (CG algorithm),
  395–396
Conjugate gradient method, 312–313
Constant cache, 159–163, 404
Constant memory, 159–163, 404
  2D convolution kernel, 161*f*
  cache hierarchy of modern processors, 162*f*
  CUDA memory model, 159*f*
Constant variables, 102
__constant__ keyword, 102, 160
Contiguous partitioning, 204–205
Control
  divergence, 79–82, 219–223
  flow, 79–80
  points, 481
Control flow efficiency, better, 509
Convolution, 152–156
  1D convolution example, inside elements, 152*f*
  2D convolution
    boundary condition, 156*f*
    example, 155*f*
  blurring approaches, 58–59
  boundary condition, 154*f*
  constant memory and caching, 159–163
  filters, 152
  image convolutions, 154
  kernel, 152
  parallel convolution, 156–159
  pattern, 58–59
  tiled convolution
    with halo cells, 163–168
    using caches for halo cells, 168–170
Convolutional layer, 361, 376–378
  backpropagation for, 372–373, 373*f*
  backward path of, 374*f*
  C implementation of forward propagation path,
    370*f*
  CUDA inference kernel, 376–378
  formulating convolutional layer as GEMM,
    379–385

Convolutional layer (*Continued*)
forward path of convolutional layer with minibatch training, 375*f*
forward propagation path of, 368*f*
host code for launching, 377*f*
kernel for forward path, 378*f*
output feature maps of, 369–370
Convolutional neural network (CNN), 366–375
Cooperative kernels, 508
Coordinate list format (COO format), 314
Corner turning, 128–129
Critical path analysis, 511–513
CuBLAS, 111, 379, 445
CUDA aware message passing interface, 471
revised MPI SendRec calls in using, 471*f*
CUDA dynamic parallelism, 490–492
background, 476–478
Bezier curves, 481–484
dynamic parallelism, 478–481
fixed *vs.* dynamic grids, 476*f*
memory and data visibility, 490–491
nesting depth, 492
pending launch pool configuration, 491
recursive example, 484–490
streams, 491–492
synchronization, 492
synchronization depth, 492
CUDA FORTRAN, 511
CUDA memory types, 96–103
__constant__ keyword, 102
__device__ keyword, 102
__shared__ keyword, 102
CUDA device memory model, 98*f*
CUDA variable declaration type, 101*t*
global memory in CUDA device, 97–99
memory *vs.* registers, 98*f*
pointers, 103
shared memory *vs.* registers in CUDA device SM, 100*f*
CUDA Occupancy Calculator, 87
CUDA thread organization, 37–38
host code, 41–42, 49
multidimensional example of CUDA grid organization, 50*f*
CUDA-enabled GPUs, 499–500
cudaDeviceProp, 89
cudaDeviceSynchronize() function, 469
CudaFree(), 33, 503
cudaGetDeviceProperties function, 88–89
CudaMalloc function, 31–32, 35, 103
CudaMemcpy function, 33, 35, 44
cudaMemcpyAsync() function, 464–465
CudaMemcpyDeviceToHost, 34
CudaMemcpyHostToDevice, 34

cudaMemcpyToSymble() function, 160, 405–406
cudaStreamCreate() function, 465
CUDNN library, 385–387
CuFFT, 445
CUTLASS, 111
Cutoff binning algorithm, 425–430
Cutoff summation, 425–426, 437–438
strategy, 426

D

Data characteristics, 12
Data delivery, 9
Data management techniques, 9
Data padding, 320
Data parallelism, 7, 23
Data reuse, 188
Data sharing, 13–14, 100, 510
Data size scalability, 425–430
Data structures, 295
Data transfer, 31–35
bandwidth, 133
device global memory and, 31–35
timing, 134
Data-dependent performance behavior, 328
Datasets, 415–416
Deadlock, 73
Deep learning
background, 356–366
convolutional layer, 376–378
convolutional neural networks, 366–375
backpropagation, 371–375
inference, 367–371
CUDNN library, 385–387
formulating convolutional layer as GEMM, 379–385
multilayer classifiers, 358–361
training models, 361–366
backpropagation, 362
chain rule, 363–364
epoch, 362
error function, 361–362
feedforward networks, 365–366
learning rate, 364
minibatch, 365
stochastic gradient descent, 362
training multilayer classifiers, 365
Definiteness, 436–437
Denormalization
format, 525
formula, 525–526
Destination vertex, 332
Device code, 27
Device global memory, 31–35

CUDA API functions, 32f, 33f
host code allocation, 32
more complete version of vecAdd(), 34f
threads in grid execute same kernel code, 37f
vecAdd function, 31, 34
Device memory, 500
Device properties, querying, 87−89
__device__ keyword, 102−103
"__device__" function, 39
devProp. maxGridSize(), 89
devProp. maxThreadsPerBlock, 89
devProp. multiProcessorCount, 89
devProp. sharedMemPerBlock, 116
Digital high-definition (HD) TV, 8
Digital twins, 8
Dimensionality, 152
Direct Coulomb summation (DCS), 417, 418f, 419f, 437−438
    code, 417
    kernel, 419
Direct memory access device (DMA device), 464
Direct3D techniques, 7
Direction-optimized implementation, 342−343
Directional relations, 332
Discrete representation, 174
Discretization, 177
Discretized derivative, 175
Disks, 464
Distribution process, 309
Divide-and-concur approach, 265
Divide-and-conquer algorithms, 295
Domain knowledge, 445
Domain partitions, 452
Domains, 173
Domino-style scan algorithm, 257
Dot product, 62−63
Double data rate (DDR), 133
Double-buffering optimization, 242
Double-precision number (64-bit number), 175
Double-precision speed, 508−509
Driving direction map services, 331
dst array, 333
dstPtrs array, 333
Dynamic input data identification, 263
Dynamic parallelism. See CUDA dynamic parallelism
Dynamic random-access memory (DRAM), 5, 10, 161
    bandwidth, 224
    bursting, 133
    bursts, 125
    designs, 124−125
    system, 132−133
Dynamic resources partitioning, 85−86

E
Edge processes, 458
Edge-centric parallel implementation, 343−344
Edges, 331
Electrostatic potential map, 416f
    background, 415−417
    calculation, 415−416, 425−426
    cutoff binning for data size scalability, 425−430
    energy, 417−418
    memory coalescing, 424
    scatter vs. gather in kernel design, 417−421
    thread coarsening, 422−423
ELL format, improving memory coalescing with, 320−323
    example of, 320f
    example of parallelizing SpMV with, 321f
    parallel SpMV/ELL kernel, 322f
Embarrassingly parallel application, 12
Embedding, 356
Energy grid array, 500
Enhanced atomic operations, 510
Enhanced global memory access, 510
Epoch, 362
Error function, 361−362
Exception handling in kernel functions, 506−507
Excess encoding of E, 520−522
    excess-3 encoding, sorted by excess-3 ordering, 521f
Excess representation, 521
Exclusive scan operation, 237
Execution configuration parameters, 40−41
Execution mode
    of CUDA, 16
    parallel, 445
Execution path, 79−80
Execution resource utilization efficiency, 219−220
Execution speed
    CUDA kernels scalability in, 41−42
    of kernel, 378
    of matrix multiplication functions, 96
    of parallel programs, 12, 123
    of sequential programs, 3
Expanded matrix, 381
Exponent, 519−520
Exponent bits, 523
"Extended lambdas,", 506
Extent, 96

F
Face recognition, 366
Facebook, 333
Fadd instruction, 99
False dependence, 110

Fast Fourier transform (FFT), 392
Feature extraction process, 192−193
Feature of dataset, 192
Feedforward networks, 365−366
Fermi GPU architecture, 508
"Fill-ins,", 312
Filter, 157
Filter array, 152
Filter bank, 367−368
   matrix, 382
Financial portfolio analysis, 434
Finite-element method, 174
Finite-volume method, 174
First compute process, 458
Fixed partitioning method, 85
"Flat" memory space, 53−54
Flexibility, 313
Floating-point addition
   instruction, 99
   operator, 211−212, 214
Floating-point arithmetic accuracy, 529
Floating-point arithmetic capability, 519
Floating-point data representation, 519−522
   excess encoding of E, 520−522
   normalized representation of M, 520
Floating-point multiplication, 94
   operator, 212
Floating-point number system, 212, 519−520
Floating-point operations (FLOP), 94
Floating-point representation, 526
Floating-point value, 211−212
FLOPS rating, 328−329
FORTRAN programs, 54−55
Forward propagation path, 369
Fourier transform domain, 391−392
Frontiers, improving efficiency with, 345−348
Fully connected graph, 332
Function calls within kernel functions,
      505−506

G

G80, 7, 516
Gather approach, 399, 420
Gather memory access behavior, 440
Gaussian blur, 58−59
Gaussian elimination, 312, 395−396, 530, 532
General matrix multiply (GEMM), 379
   formulating convolutional layer as, 379−385
   GEMM-based algorithm, 387
Ghost cells, 154, 181, 369
Giga (10^9). *See* Giga floating-point operations per
      second (GFLOPS)

Giga floating-point operations per second
      (GFLOPS), 1, 94−96
Global memory, 70, 273, 300
   access, 94, 225−226, 225*f*, 226*f*
      ratio, 182
   bandwidth, 94−96
      tiled algorithms, 118
      tiled matrix multiplication kernel using shared
         memory, 108*f*
   requests, 224
Global variables, 102−103
"__global__" keyword, 38−39
GMAC system, 503
GPGPU, 7
Gradient backpropagation, 371−372
Graph, 331
   algorithms, 338
   computation, 331, 352
   data structure, 332
Graph search, 331, 335, 479−480
Graph traversal algorithm, 335
   adjacency matrix representation, 333*f*
   background, 332−335
   breadth-first search, 335−338
   edge-centric parallelization of breadth-first
      search, 343−345
   improving efficiency with frontiers, 345−348
   optimizations, 350−352
      improving load balance, 351−352
      reducing launch overhead, 350−351
   reducing contention with privatization, 348−350
   three sparse matrix representations of adjacency
      matrix, 334*f*
   vertex-centric parallelization of breadth-first
      search, 338−343
Graphics API, 7
Graphics chips, 5, 7
Graphics Double Data Rate, 70
Graphics processing unit (GPU), 3, 27, 90, 516
   architecture, 69−70
   complement CPU execution, 10
   computing, 16
   CUDA-enabled GPUs, 499−500
   device, 136
      memory, 385
   hardware, 499−500
Grid, 27−28, 47−48
   algorithms, 425−426
   launch, 43
   points, 177
GridDim variable, 49
GridDim. x variable, 49
Gridding approach, 394

H

Hadoop, 265
Half-precision number (16-bit number), 175
Halo cells, 173
Handwriting recognition, 366
Hardware queues, 507
Hardware trigonometry functions, 409–412
Heaps, 295
Heterogeneous computing cluster, programming
    background, 449–450
    collective communication, 470
    CUDA aware MPI, 471
    MPI, 452–455
    overlapping computation and communication,
        462–470, 463*f*
    point-to-point communication, 455–461
    programmer's view of MPI processes, 450*f*
Heterogeneous parallel computing, 3–7, 449
    CPUs and GPUs, 4*f*
    many-thread trajectory, 3
    multicore trajectory, 3
Hiding memory latency, 133–138
    channels and banks in DRAM systems, 133*f*
    data transfer bandwidth of channel, 134*f*
    matrix multiplication, 137*f*
Hierarchical reduction for arbitrary input length,
    226–228
    segmented multiblock reduction using atomic
        operations, 227*f*
High-bandwidth memory (HBM), 70
High-Bandwidth Memory version 2 (HBM2), 510
High-definition (HD), 8
High-degree graphs, 342–343
High-performance computing (HPC), 2–3, 449
    industry, 27
    systems, 499–500
High-performance parallel programming, 14–15
High-speed floating-point arithmetic, 519
Higher-order stencil computation, 450–451
Histogram, 192–193
    kernel, 194–198
Host code, 27, 32, 476–477
Host memory, 500
"__host__" function, 39
"__host__" keyword, 39
Hybrid ELL-COO format, 324–325
    regulating padding with, 324–325
        example, 324*f*

I

I/O devices, 5, 500
Idempotence, 340
Identity matrix, 532

Identity value, 211–212
IEEE floating-point format, 527–528
IEEE format, special bit patterns and precision in,
    526–527, 527*f*
IEEE standard, 525
IEEE-754 Floating-Point Standard, 519
Image blur, 58–61
    handling boundary conditions for pixels, 61*f*
    image blur kernel, 60*f*
    original image and blurred version, 58*f*
    output pixel, 59*f*
Image-blurring function, 58–59
Inclusive scan operation, 236, 238*f*
Individualized medicine, 517
Inference, 358
Input parameters for kernel, 157
Input tile, 163–164, 180–181, 183–184
Input-centric decomposition, 440
Input-centric SpMV/COO kernel, 443
Installed base of processor, 6
Instruction
    fetch/dispatch unit, 77–79
    pointer, 2
Instruction register (IR), 78
Integer, 309–310
    vector, 48
"Integrated" GPUs, 88
Interested readers, 214
Interleaved data distribution, 136
Interleaved partitioning, 205
Internal processes, 458
Interpolation technique, 174
Intrinsic functions, 197
Intuitive approach, 312
Iterative linear solver–based reconstruction
    approach, 395
Iterative reconstruction, 394–396
iterPtr array, 326

J

Jacobi iterative method, 450–451, 458–459
Jagged diagonal storage format (JDS format),
    325–326
    reducing control divergence with, 325–328
        example of, 326*f*
        parallelizing SpMV example with, 327*f*

K

K-space domain, 391–392
Kahan summation algorithm, 529–530
Kepler GPU architecture, 502–503, 506–507
Kernel call, 43
Kernel execution configuration parameters, 66–67

Kernel execution control, 505–508
    cooperative kernels, 508
    exception handling in kernel functions,
        506–507
    function calls within kernel functions, 505–506
    hardware queues and dynamic parallelism, 507
    interruptable grids, 508
    simultaneous execution of multiple grids, 507
Kernel function, 27–28, 35–40, 47–49, 97,
        160–161, 217, 240
Kernel launch, 43, 420–421
    child kernel launch with named streams, 492*f*
    parameter, 502
Kernel parallelism structure, 398–403
    loop fission, 400*f*
    loop interchange, 402*f*
Kernels, 27, 36, 70, 339, 492
Kogge-Stone algorithm, 238–244, 437
    kernel for inclusive scan, 240*f*
    parallel exclusive scan algorithm, 243*f*
    parallel inclusive scan algorithm, 239*f*

L

Large virtual and physical address spaces,
        502–503
Last-level on-chip caches, 4
Latency
    hiding, 83–84, 123. *See also* Hiding memory
        latency
    tolerance, 83–85
Latency-oriented design, 4
Learning rate, 364
Least significant bit (LSB), 295
Least significant digit (LSD), 309
LeNet-5 design, 369
Lifetime, 101
    of constant variable, 102
    of shared variable, 102
Linear algebra functions, 62*b*
Linear Bezier curves, 481
Linear classifiers, 358
Linear equations system, 530, 534–535
Linear layout, 76
Linear perceptron's model, 357
Linear solver–based iterative reconstruction
        algorithm, 394
Linear solvers, 530–535
Linear system, 312
Linear-algebraic formulation, 345
Linearized index, 114
LinkedIn (social network), 333
Load balance, 313, 351–352
Local sort, 300–301

Locality, 107
Long-latency operation, 83–84
Loop fission technique, 399
Loop interchange, 399
Loop nest, 415
Loop parallelism, 40
Loop splitting technique, 399
Low-degree graphs, 342–343
Luminance value, 24–26

M

Machine learning, 356
    computing methods, 517
    convolutional layer, 376–378
    convolutional neural networks, 366–375
    CUDNN library, 385–387
Magnetic resonance imaging (MRI), 391–392
    Cartesian scan trajectory, 392
    CG algorithm, 395–396
    chunking k-space data, 406*f*
    computing F^HD, 396–412
    experimental performance tuning, 412
    iterative reconstruction, 394–396
    k-space
        elements, 404
        regions, 392
    non-Cartesian k-space sample trajectory, 393*f*
    non-Cartesian scan trajectories, 392–393
    physics principles behind, 392
    quasi-Bayesian estimation problem formulation,
        395
    ratio of floating-point operations, 397
    revolutionized medicine technologies, 517
    scanner k-space trajectories, 393*f*
Mantissa bits, 519–520, 523–524
Many-thread processors, 3
Map matrix, 384–385
Marketplace, 6
Matlab, 445
Matrix, 127
Matrix computation method, 517
Matrix inversion, 395–396
Matrix multiplication, 62–66, 111, 128–129, 376
    matrix multiplication kernel, 64*f*
Matrix-vector multiplication, 395
Max reduction, 214
Maze routing problem, 337, 343
Medical imaging, 508–509
Memory, 70, 96–97
    access efficiency, 94–96, 313
    access throughput, 124–125
    allocation, 237
        function, 32

architecture, 69–70
and data visibility, 490–491
divergence, 223–225
latency, 198–199
throughput, 198–199
Memory architecture and data locality
CUDA memory types, 96–103
importance of memory access efficiency, 94–96
memory usage impact on occupancy, 115–117
tiled matrix multiplication kernel, 107–112
tiling for reduced memory traffic, 103–107
Memory bandwidth, 5, 94–96, 146, 508–510
configurable caching and scratchpad, 509
double-precision speed, 508–509
enhanced atomic operations, 510
enhanced global memory access, 510
Memory bound programs, 94–96, 194
Memory coalescing, 124–133, 205, 223–224,
    300–302, 424
reducing traffic congestion in highway systems,
    131*f*
Memory management, 464
Merge operation, 265
Merge sort, 437
circular buffer merge kernel, 282–287
co-rank function implementation, 268–273
example of merge operation, 264*f*
Hadoop, 265
parallel merge kernel, 273–275
parallelization approach, 266–268
sequential merge algorithm, 265–266
thread coarsening for merge, 288
tiled merge kernel to improve coalescing,
    275–282
Message passing interface (MPI), 13–14, 436,
    449, 499–500
barrier synchronization, 466–467
basics, 452–455
closing communication system, 453*f*
functions for establishing communication
    system, 453*f*
MPI/CUDA programming, 13–14, 436
MPI_Barrier() function, 466–467
MPI_Comm_rank() function, 454
MPI_Comm_size() function, 454
MPI_Recv() function, 455, 456*f*
MPI_Send() function, 455, 456*f*
MPI_Sendrecv() function, 467, 468*f*
overlapping computation and communication,
    462–470
point-to-point communication, 455–461
process, 453–454
programmer's view of MPI processes, 450*f*
rank, 453–454

Microprocessors, 1
Microscopes, 7–8
Minibatch, 365
Mobile applications, 245
Modern computer system, 464
Modern map-reduce frameworks, 263
Molecular dynamics, 415
application, 434–435
simulation, 416–417
Molecular visualization and analysis, 18
Monte Carlo method, 517
Most significant digit (MSD), 309
Multidimensional array, 53–54, 127
Multidimensional data, mapping threads to, 51–58
2D thread grid, 51*f*
memory space, 53*b*
row-major layout for 2D C array, 54*f*
Multidimensional grid organization, 47–51
CUDA grid organization, 50*f*
Multilayer classifiers, 358–361
Multilayer perceptron (MLP), 358, 365–366

N

National Institutes of Health (NIH), 6
Natural language processing, 356
Nesting depth, 492
Net terminals, 337
Neural networks, 9
Non-Cartesian MRI, 18
application of MRI, 392
computing F^HD, 396–412
iterative reconstruction, 394–396
non-Cartesian k-space sample trajectory, 393*f*
non-Cartesian scan trajectories, 392–393
non-Cartesian trajectory data, 394
scanner k-space trajectories, 393*f*
Nonbonded forces, 434–435
Noncomparison-based sorting algorithms,
    294–295
Nonzero element, 314
Normalized representation, 520
Not a number (NaN), 526–527
Number representation system, 524
Numerical algorithms, 528–529
Numerical considerations
algorithm considerations, 528–530
arithmetic accuracy and rounding, 527–528
floating-point data representation, 519–522
linear solvers and numerical stability, 530–535
Gaussian elimination and backward
    substitution, 532*f*
Gaussian elimination with pivoting, 534*f*
solving systems of linear equations, 531*f*

Numerical considerations (*Continued*)
  representable numbers, 522−526
  special bit patterns and precision in IEEE
      format, 526−527, 527*f*
Numerical grids, 177
Numerical methods, 173
Numerical order, 529
Numerical stability, 530−535
Numerically stable values, 530
Numerically unstable values, 530
NVIDIA C compiler (NVCC), 42−43

O

Object images, 192−193
Occupancy, 85−87, 90
  memory usage impact on, 115−117
Odd-even merge sort, 308
Odd-even transposition sort, 308
Off-chip memory, 70, 123
On-chip memory, 93, 163, 509
One destination process, 455
One dimension (1D)
  array, 314
    elements, 152
  convolution, 152, 156
  grids and blocks, 49
  regular grid, 174
  thread organizations, 51−52
One floating-point addition, 94
One source process, 455
Open Compute Language (OpenCL), 14
OpenACC, 445
OpenMP, 13
Operand data delivery logic, 4
Operand value, 99
Operator function, 212−213
Optical character recognition (OCR), 366
Optimal image reconstruction method, 394
Optimizations, 191, 350−352
  checklist of, 141−145, 142*t*
Ordered merge operation, 263
Output interference, 194
Output tile, 163
Output-centric decomposition, 440
Output-centric kernels, 443
Overlapping communication with computation,
    465
"Owner computes" approach, 217

P

Padding
  data padding and transposition, 320
  parallel SpMV/ELL kernel, 322*f*

regulating padding with hybrid ELL-COO
    format, 324−325
Page locked memory buffer, 464
Parallel algorithm, 11−12, 235−236, 529
Parallel computation patterns, 191
Parallel convolution, 156−159
  2D convolution kernel, 158*f*
  kernel with boundary condition handling, 158*f*
  mapping of threads to output elements, 157
  parallelization and thread organization for 2D
      convolution, 157*f*
Parallel execution, 196, 391
Parallel histogram
  algorithms, 191
  computation pattern, 191
Parallel inclusive scan algorithm, 238
Parallel merge kernel, 273−275
  basic merge kernel, 274*f*
Parallel merge sort, 306−307
Parallel ordered merge algorithm, 263
Parallel patterns, 7, 12, 433, 515−516
Parallel programming, 3−4, 11−12, 15, 433−434,
    499−500
Parallel programming interfaces, 13−14
Parallel programming models, 13, 123, 516
Parallel programs, 2−3, 12
Parallel radix sort, 296−300
Parallel reduction algorithm, 211, 213−214
Parallel reduction pattern, 215
  in Sports and Competitions, 216*b*
Parallel scan, 235
  background, 236−237
  with Brent-Kung algorithm, 246−251
  coarsening for even more work efficiency,
      251−253
  implementation of iterative calculations, 241
  with Kogge-Stone algorithm, 238−244
  Kogge-Stone kernel for inclusive scan, 240*f*
  as primitive operation, 235
  segmented parallel scan for arbitrary-length
      inputs, 253−256
  sequential algorithm of computation, 238
  single-pass scan for memory access efficiency,
      256−259
  speed and work efficiency consideration,
      244−245
Parallel sort methods, 308−309
Parallel sorting algorithms, 293
Parallel SpMV/CSR kernel, 319
Parallel stencil, 178−179
  basic stencil sweep kernel, 178*f*
  simplifying boundary condition, 178*f*
Parallelism, 7−9, 138, 183, 215, 350−351
Parallelization approach, 266−268, 446

Parallelize reduction, 228−229
Parallelizing histogram computation, 194
Parent
    grid, 480
    parent-child synchronization, 492
    thread, 484
Partial differential equation, 177, 450−451
Pascal GPU architecture, 504
PCIe bus, 501
Peak signal-to-noise ratio formula (PSNR
        formula), 409−410
Pending launch pool configuration, 491
Perceptron, 357
Performance bottleneck, 145−146
Performance cliff, 86−87
Performance considerations
    checklist of optimizations, 141−145
    hiding memory latency, 133−138
    knowing your computation's bottleneck, 145−146
    memory coalescing, 124−133
    thread coarsening, 138−141
    thread granularity, 123
Performance optimization techniques, 15, 69−70,
        123, 433
Performance portability, 13
PET revolutionized medicine technologies, 517
Phantom object, 409−410
Physical laws, 416−417
Pinned memory
    allocation, 463
    buffer, 464
    streams, 463
Pivoting method, 533
Point-to-point communication, 455−461
Pointer variable, 32
Polynomial evaluation, 235
Prefix sum, 235, 510
Privatization technique, 200−203
    histogram kernel, 201f
    private copies of histogram reduce contention,
        201f
    privatized text histogram kernel, 203f
    reducing contention with, 348−350
Problem decomposition, 440−444
Processor cores, 2
Product reduction, 212
Profilers, 512
Program counter, 2
Programmers, 15
Programming
    environment, 510−513
    interfaces and compilers, 445
    platform, 499−500
PTX files, 42−43

Q
Quadrants, 484−485
Quadratic Bezier curves, 481
Quadtree, 484−485
Quantum chemistry simulation data, 415−416
Quantum chemistry visualization, 509
Quasi-Bayesian estimation problem formulation,
        395
Querying device properties, 87−89
Queues, 507
Quiet NaNs, 527

R
Race condition, 194, 241
Radial lines, 392−393
Radio astronomy, 508−509
Radius, 152
Radix sort, 295−296, 437
Radix value, 302−304
Random-access memory, 31
Randomized algorithms, 295
Rank, 268
Ray tracing, 509
Read-after-write dependence, 110
Read-modify-write, 194
    race condition, 195
Recommender systems, 356
Reduction, 211−213
    general form of reduction sequential code, 212f
    hierarchical reduction for arbitrary input length,
        226−228
    minimizing control divergence, 219−223
        kernel, 222f
        threads to input array locations, 221f
    minimizing global memory accesses, 225−226
    minimizing memory divergence, 223−225
    reduction trees, 213−216
    simple reduction kernel, 217−219
        parallel sum reduction tree, 217f
    simple sum reduction sequential code, 212f
    thread coarsening for reduced overhead,
        228−231
Reduction tree, 213−216, 246
    parallel max reduction tree, 213f
    parallel reduction in sports and competitions,
        216b
    world cup finals as reduction tree, 216f
Redundant work, 348
Register file, 97−99
Registers, 97
    in CUDA, 100
    kernel with thread coarsening and register tiling,
        187f

Registers (*Continued*)
    tiling kernel, 186−188
Regression, 356
Regularization, 311
Remote sensing, 508−509
Representable numbers, 522−526
Representable numbers of floating-point
        format, 523
    3-bit unsigned integer format, 522*f*
    abrupt underflow format, 525*f*
    algorithm considerations, 528−530
    alignment shifting of operands, 528
    arithmetic accuracy and rounding, 527−528
    bit patterns and precision in IEEE format,
        526−527, 527*f*
    denormalization format, 525*f*
    discrepancy between sequential algorithms and
        parallel algorithms, 529
    Gaussian elimination procedure, 532−533, 532*f*,
        534*f*
    major intervals, 523
    mantissa bits, 523−524
    NaN, 526−527
    between negative infinity and positive infinity,
        526
    no-zero, abrupt underflow, and denormalized
        formats, 523*f*
    no-zero representation, 523*f*
    precision of, 523−524
    quiet NaNs, 527
    reduction computation, 529
    signaling NaNs, 527
Resource allocation, 235
Resource and capability queries, 87*b*
Resource assignment, 69−70
Resource partitioning, 85−87
Reverse tree, 249
RGB values, 25−26
Road network graph, 335, 342
Roofline model, 96
Rotational forces, 434−435
Routing blocks, 337
Routing software, 337
Row index, 164−165, 314
Row major layout, 54−55
    for 2D C array, 54*f*
Row-major convention, 126−127
Runtime APIs, 14

S
Sample sort algorithms, 293, 308−309
Scalability, 15
Scalable parallel execution, 23

latency tolerance, 83−85, 83*b*
mapping threads to multidimensional data,
        51−58
    resource assignment, 69−70
    scalable parallel program, 499−500
    synchronization and transparent scalability,
        71−74
    thread scheduling, 80−81
Scalar variables, 101
Scan, 235
Scanner data acquisition process, 394
Scatter approach, 399
Scatter memory access behavior, 438
Scope, 100−101
Scratchpad, 509
Scratchpad memory, 100, 161
Segmented parallel scan, 253−256
Segmented reduction, 231−232
Segmented scan, 237
Seismic analysis, 508−509
Self-driving cars, 517
Semiconductor industry, 518
Sensors, 125
Sequencing data, 415−416
Sequential cutoff algorithm, 430, 438−439
Sequential merge algorithm, 265−266
Sequential merge function, 265*f*, 266
Set intersection, 263
Set union, 263
Shared memory, 71, 115, 300, 509
    variables, 105, 107
__shared__ keyword, 102
Sign, 519−520
Signal-to-noise ratio (SNR), 392
Signaling NaNs, 527
Simulation process, 416−417
Single-CPU microprocessors, 1
Single-instruction, multiple-data (SIMD), 78
    hardware, 74−79
    streaming multiprocessors, 77*f*
    warp diverging at for-loop, 81*f*
    warp diverging at if-else statement, 80*f*
Single-pass scan, 256−259
Single-precisions number (32-bit number), 175
Single-program multiple-data (SPMD),
        35−36
Small cache memories, 5−6
Small world graphs, 342−343
Smartphone, 8
Social network, 331−333, 342−343
    graphs, 351−352
Sodium imaging, 394
Sodium map of Brain, 393−394, 393*f*
Software applications, 2

Sorting, 294−295
  choice of radix value, 302−304
  networks, 308
  optimizing for memory coalescing, 300−302
  parallel merge sort, 306−307
  parallel radix sort, 296−300
  parallel sort methods, 308−309
  radix sort, 295−296
  thread coarsening to improve coalescing,
    305−306
Source vertex, 332
Space efficiency, 313
Sparse matrix computation, 311
  background, 312−314, 312f, 313f
  data padding and transposition, 320
  dot product, 318
  Gaussian elimination, 312
  grouping row nonzeros with CSR format,
    317−320
  improving memory coalescing with ELL format,
    320−323
  iterative approaches, 313
  matrix-vector multiplication and accumulation,
    313f
  parallel SpMV/ELL kernel, 322f
  real-world problems, 311
  reducing control divergence with JDS format,
    325−328, 326f
  regulating padding with hybrid ELL-COO
    format, 324−325
  in science and engineering problems, 312
  simple SpMV kernel with COO format,
    314−316
  solving linear systems of N equations of N
    variables, 312
  sparse matrix, 311−312
  SpMV computation code, 314−315
Sparse matrix representation, 333
Sparse matrix storage formats, 311
Sparse matrix-vector multiplication (SpMV), 313,
    345
  accumulation, 313
  code, 314−315
  SpMV/COO kernel, 443
Sparsely connected graph, 332
Spatial frequency domain, 391−392
Special bit patterns and precision in IEEE format,
    526−527, 527f
Speeding up real applications, 9−11
  sequential and parallel application portions, 11f
Speedup, 9−10, 215
Spirals, 392−393
Stable sort algorithm, 294

Stencil, 174−177
  2D grid, 177f
  differentiable function, 174f
  one-dimensional stencil examples, 176f
  parallel stencil, 178−179
  register tiling, 186−188
  shared memory tiling for stencil sweep,
    179−183
  stencil-based algorithms, 173
  thread coarsening, 183−186
  two-dimensional five-point stencil, 176f
Stencil sweep, 177
  shared memory tiling for, 179−183
Stochastic gradient descent approach, 362
Stream-based scan algorithm, 257
Streaming multiprocessors (SMs), 70, 93, 135,
    161−162, 200, 404, 421, 482
  shared memory *vs.* registers in CUDA device
    SM, 100f
  thread block assignment to, 71f
  unit of thread scheduling in, 75
Streaming processors, 70
Streams, 491−492
Strip-mining technique, 110−111
Stub function, 34
Subarrays, 266−267
Supercomputing, 7−8
Synchronization, 71−74
  depth, 492
  operations, 12
__syncthreads (), 73, 110, 219, 226, 241, 350−351

T
Tensor cores, 94−96
Tera (10^{12}). *See* Tera floating-point operations per
    second (TFLOPS)
Tera floating-point operations per second
    (TFLOPS), 1, 3
Thread(s), 2, 27−28, 47−48
  blocks, 36
  coarsening, 138−141, 183−186, 228−229,
    305−306, 422−423
  code for thread coarsening, 140f
  granularity, 123
  index value, 219
  scheduling, 80−81
ThreadIdx variable, 37−40, 47−48, 50−52
ThreadIdx. x, 37−40, 76, 241
ThreadIdx. y, 76
Threading, 35−40
Three dimension (3D)
  array, 48

Three dimension (3D) (*Continued*)
  block, 77
  convolution, 152
  differential equations, 178–179
  electrostatic energy, 500
  imaging, 8
  space, 358
  stencil computation, 450–451
  third-order stencil, 180
  thread organizations, 51–52
  visualization, 416
Throughput, 94–96
  throughput-oriented design, 5–6
Thrust, 310, 445
Tiled 2D convolution kernel, 166–167
Tiled convolution
  with halo cells, 163–168
    arithmetic-to-global memory access ratio,
      168*f*
    input tile *vs.* output tile, 163*f*
    thread organization for using input tile
      elements, 166*f*
  using caches for halo cells, 168–170
Tiled matrix multiplication, 145
  algorithm, 105
  kernel, 107–112
    calculation of matrix indices in tiled
      multiplication, 109*f*
    occupancy, 115
    using shared memory, 108*f*
Tiled matrix multiplication kernel with boundary
    checks, 114*f*
Tiled merge kernel, 275–282
  design, 276*f*
  identifying block-level output and input
    subarrays, 277*f*
Tiles, 103
Tiling, 175, 179, 263
  efficiency, 154, 156
  for reduced memory traffic, 103–107
    global memory accesses performed by
      threads, 105*f*
    matrix multiplication, 104*f*
    tiled matrix multiplication, 106*f*
Time-space variation, 475
Tissue chemical anomalies, 392–393
Tolerate latency, 118
Top-down strategy, 309
  implementation, 339
Training
  models, 361–366
  multilayer classifiers, 365
  process, 361
Transcription, 356

Translation, 356
Transparent scalability, 71–74
"Transparent" outsourcing model, 31
Transposition, 320
  sort, 293, 308
Trigonometry functions, 409
Twitter (social network), 333
Two-dimension (2D)
  array, 54–55, 154
  convolution, 152, 156
    kernel, 168
  data, 82
  five-point stencil, 179
  grid, 177
  slice, 417–418
  thread organizations, 51–52
  vector, 357

U
Unified device memory space, 510–511
Unified memory, 503–505
Unified Virtual Address Space (UVAS), 501–502
Uniform grid method, 418
Units in last place (ULP), 528
Unstable sort algorithms, 294
Unstructured grids, 174

V
Variable declaration, 102
Vector addition kernel function, 28–31, 38*f*
  simple traditional vector addition C code
    example, 29*f*
Vertex-centric parallel implementation, 339
  vertex-centric pull implementation, 340–343
  vertex-centric push implementation, 339–340,
    342–343, 349
Vertex-centric parallelization, 338–343
Vibrational forces, 434–435
Virtual address spaces, 501–502
Viruses, 415–416
Visual molecular dynamics (VMD), 415–416
Volumetric data, 415–416
von Neumann model, 97–99
  memory *vs.* registers, 98*f*

W
Warp(s)
  analyzing impact of control divergence, 82
  scheduling, 83–85
  and SIMD hardware, 74–79, 78*b*
    blocks are partitioned into warps, 75*f*
    placing 2D threads into linear layout, 76*f*

and SIMD Hardware, 97−99
simple sum reduction kernel, 218*f*
While-loop statement, 272
Wiring block, 337
Work assignment, 235
Work efficiency, 12, 244−245
Work-efficient algorithm, 260
Work-efficient block-wide parallel scan, 260

Work-efficient sequential scan, 260
Write-after-read data dependence, 110, 241

Z

Zero elements, 313
Zero-copy memory, 501−502
Zero-overhead scheduling, 84−85, 84*b*